A SAILOR'S LOG

Frederick T. Wilson as a chief petty officer.
Photo taken after his Asiatic cruise.
Courtesy Muriel Wilson MacFall.

A Sailor's Log

*Water-Tender Frederick T. Wilson, USN,
on Asiatic Station, 1899–1901*

Edited and with an Introduction
by James R. Reckner

The Kent State University Press
KENT & LONDON

To those humble,
unsung toilers of the great white fighting ships,
the "black gang," my shipmates,
this book is dedicated.
—Frederick T. Wilson

© 2004 by The Kent State University Press, Kent, Ohio 44242
ALL RIGHTS RESERVED
Library of Congress Catalog Card Number 2003016212
ISBN 0-87338-782-1
Manufactured in the United States of America
08 07 06 05 04   5 4 3 2 1

Library of Congress Cataloging-in-Publication Data
Wilson, Frederick T., 1868–
A sailor's log : water-tender Frederick T. Wilson, USN,
on Asiatic Station, 1899–1901 / edited and with an
introduction by James R. Reckner.
p. cm.
Includes bibliographical references and index.
ISBN 0-87338-782-1 (alk. paper) ∞
1. Wilson, Frederick T., 1868—Diaries. 2. Sailors—United States—Diaries.
3. United States. Navy—Sea life. I. Reckner, James R., 1940– II. Title.
V63.W554A3   2003
359'.0092—dc22   2003016212

British Library Cataloging-in-Publication data are available.

CONTENTS

Preface vii

Acknowledgments ix

Introduction xi

Prologue: To Asiatic Station 1

ONE Manila 48

TWO Nagasaki 64

THREE Aground in the Yellow Sea 95

FOUR Kure, Japan 126

FIVE Woosung, China 163

SIX Shanghai 188

SEVEN Afloat and Ashore in Shanghai 217

EIGHT Bolo-Men, Routine, and Discipline 250

NINE Hong Kong 276

TEN Amoy, China, and Yokohama 308

ELEVEN Homeward Bound 328

Epilogue 354

Notes 360

Bibliography 381

Index 384

Preface

This is a "Sailor's Log." There are many "Sailor's Logs," and most of them are a line shot from the quarter or half deck, and many of them are vastly interesting from their point of view.[1] This point of view is directly from the fo'castle. Perhaps it will also prove not entirely devoid of interest. It is a faithful record of my last two years in the service of the United States Navy, in many climes and on many ships, and under many conditions, and being my experience, is also the experience of my shipmates, of all that serve the common cause.

I have read with pleasure another "Sailor's Log," doubly interesting from the fact that I once had the extreme honor of serving under its distinguished author, our most picturesque naval officer of today, "Fighting Bob."[2] 'Twas when I was a "Rookie," an[d] a most humble one at that, a "snipe," an[d], it please your honors, officially a "coal-passer," that most humble, but necessary, evil, the lowest in rating in the service, an object that isn't supposed to be human at all, but has to delve wherever dirt and grime is thickest, in back connection, in bilge, in mucky feed tank, in boiler, and in [coal] bunker. Poor coal passer! Cursed and damned by all parts of the ship, whose very foot prints are watched as he crosses spotless deck[s], who is blamed for every spot of dirt on deck and paint work as a matter of course. He is even looked askance by landsman and marine, poor non-combatant that he is. Like many others of humble calling, his necessity and worth goes unrecognized.

This book will, I trust, make you better acquainted with the service as it really is. It presents the point of view of the many, not the few. If it pleases and helps to pass pleasantly an idle hour, it will have fulfilled all that is expected of it. It is the truth. It cannot be as elegant in diction as those written by the habitants of the "half deck." God wot.[3] Look at the difference.

F.T.W.

Acknowledgments

This work would never have seen print without the dogged determination of Frederick T. Wilson's daughter, Muriel Wilson MacFall. She, over several years, worked to develop a typescript of her father's original manuscript and tirelessly called its existence to the attention of naval authorities. Her enthusiasm stirred a good colleague and friend, Dr. Harold D. Langley, to action. It was he who recruited me to this project. As I once again transcribed the original manuscript, Mrs. MacFall, now over ninety years of age, was very patient and supportive, answering my many questions as they arose. I wish also to thank particularly Rick and Namiko Greatting for their efforts to help me understand Wilson's Japanese (sometimes only Japanese-sounding) terms.

I would like to thank friends who have put up with some rather random-seeming questions in recent months as I have striven to make twenty-first-century sense of a number of Wilson's comments. It was clear that Wilson thought any contemporaries who read his manuscript would understand him. However, the passage of a century has obscured much. For example, no one at the time would have forgotten the scandal surrounding the murder by Chicago sausage maker Adolph Luetgert of his wife, whose body he apparently disposed of by making her into sausages. (Her jewelry later was found in one of the Luetgert sausage factory's vats!) However, a century of scandals have superseded this particular sensation, and thus it required a bit of research and explanation. Similarly, the jargon of hoboes of that era was far more developed than present-day Americans might imagine; Wilson knew that jargon well and employed it in his log.

Especially, though, I offer my thanks to Fred Wilson himself, for providing a richly rewarding account of his experiences. Through this project I have obtained many new insights into enlisted life in our navy of a century ago. I am indebted to him for the time and effort he took to leave this invaluable record.

Finally, my wife, Middy, has for several months become a "widow" each evening, as I disappeared into my study to continue work on "the Wilson manuscript." For her patience and forbearance, particularly as I read interesting passages to her when she really didn't want me to, I am everlastingly thankful.

It has been my goal in this work to preserve Wilson's original manuscript as he left it. The reader doubtless will notice errors in grammar and punctuation. These have intentionally been left in the log in order to retain the original flavor of the work. Wherever I have found it necessary to inject a word or phrase, those additions to the text are enclosed in brackets or added as footnotes. Wilson used "there" and "their" and also "to" and "too" interchangeably in the text. Wherever correction was necessary, I have done so without notation, as these changes do not alter the sense of the prose but only facilitate reading. Wilson paid scant attention to sentences and paragraphs; for the sake of readability, I have taken the liberty of ending sentences where I thought appropriate and of dividing the text into paragraphs as I thought the sense warranted. At the publisher's suggestion, I have omitted certain passages written almost exclusively in pidgin English. Such omissions are noted in footnotes.

The reader will note that Wilson uses racial terms of the day, such as "Japs," "Chinamen," and "Chinks." It is clear from the text that he attached no derogatory connotation to them, as his comments concerning the Chinese and Japanese people were uniformly complimentary. Further, Wilson uses the now-infamous "N word," but not to describe African-Americans. Rather, it is the term he, and all American servicemen who fought in the Philippine Insurrection, assigned to the Filipino insurrectionists.

The text that follows is essentially as Wilson wrote it. In a sense, this approach is unfair to Wilson, as in a normal publishing process for a living author, an editor, working in conjunction with the author, would have corrected most shortcomings. In this case, lacking Wilson's concurrence, I have not felt free to make any substantive alterations to the original text.

Introduction

Writing in *The Forum* in 1899, Capt. Henry Clay Taylor, president of the Naval War College, and Boiler Tender Frederick Wilson's commanding officer on the cruiser *Minneapolis* during the war with Spain, concluded that he was certain the United States had become "the imperial republic of the world." He asserted that Americans now "must realize . . . that plans for the future must be made by minds willing to acknowledge that imperial resources may be needed to preserve these possessions that have fallen to us." Congress proved willing in the postwar years to provide the ships, and Wilson, as "a cog in the machine of Uncle Sam's Navy," became one of the early guardians of the new American empire, though he clearly did not agree with America's colonial enterprise.

Fred Wilson joined the navy—probably because of the continuing economic depression following the Panic of 1893—at a most exciting time. His enlistment in 1895 coincided with the commissioning of the first modern battleship of the U.S. fleet, and on board her he first learned the profession he would follow for the remainder of his working life. By 1898 he had become an experienced hand, a petty officer. Only the randomness of fate ensured that the ship to which he was assigned did not participate in either of the two great naval battles of the war with Spain. In reality, the brevity of the war meant but few navy men shared the glory, and in the Atlantic-Caribbean theater of operations, that glory was greatly tarnished by the subsequent strife concerning which commander, Winfield Scott Schley or William T. Sampson, should receive recognition for the victory at Santiago on July 3, 1898.

The advent of American empire in the Pacific—the acquisition of Guam and the Philippines from Spain and the annexation of Hawaii as a territory—developed a large, new role for the U.S. Navy in the Pacific and East Asia. The deployment of a significant naval force to the Asiatic Station following the victory at Manila Bay, May 1, 1898, ultimately brought Wilson to the Asiatic Station, on board the cruiser USS

New Orleans, at the end of 1899. Subsequently transferred to the battleship *Oregon,* Wilson, it seemed, would have an opportunity to participate in the relief of the legations in Peking during the Boxer Rebellion of 1900. Unfortunately fate once again intervened when his ship, rushing to the theater of war, ran hard aground on an uncharted reef in the Gulf of Pechili—not once but twice—and was sent to Japan for repairs. Wilson's record of that cruise, the subject of this book, ends with the return of his ship to the United States at the time of the assassination of President William McKinley in September 1901.

Wilson's active service continued for another decade and a half after the end of his log, including the period of expansion of the navy during the presidency of Theodore Roosevelt. Few people were better prepared or more willing to wield America's growing naval strength than was Roosevelt. Conditions in Asia dictated a continued strong American naval presence there, and thus Wilson again served on the Asiatic Station, 1904–1905, aboard the torpedo boat destroyer *Chauncey* during the Russo-Japanese War, the resolution of which was largely the result of President Roosevelt's diplomatic efforts, for which he was awarded the Nobel Peace Prize for 1906.

Wilson also participated in the culminating naval maneuver of the Theodore Roosevelt era, another event motivated by continuing tensions in East Asia: the world cruise of the U.S. Atlantic Fleet, more popularly known as "the Great White Fleet." Sent to the Pacific coast on board the newly commissioned cruiser *St. Louis,* Wilson, by now a chief petty officer, was transferred to the battleship *Wisconsin,* then completing a major overhaul at the Puget Sound Navy Shipyard. The *Wisconsin* was ordered to join the Atlantic Fleet when the fleet reached San Francisco in May 1908, and thus Wilson completed the famous circumnavigation of the globe with the sixteen white-and-buff-colored first-class battleships, a cruise that captured the imagination of the American people. To the best of our knowledge, the fleet's October 1908 visit to Japan was Wilson's last visit to that country, whose people and culture—and particularly women—so enchanted him.

Wilson's active overseas service ended with a cruise to the Caribbean in 1914, during the American intervention in Mexico. From then onward, persistent medical problems kept him ashore until his death in 1924.

Wilson's career encompassed the rise of the predreadnought battleship fleet and its full maturation in the world cruise. However, by the time of that famous cruise, the advent of HMS *Dreadnought,* with its main battery of ten twelve-inch guns, spelled the beginning of a new era of battleship design and construction. The first-class battleships of the Theodore Roosevelt years, each mounting only four twelve- or thirteen-inch guns, rapidly became obsolescent. By the time of Wilson's death, all of them had been consigned to the scrap heap as a result of the Washington Naval Arms Limitation Treaties of 1922. Thus, Wilson's naval life closely paralleled the rise and fall of the predreadnought navy.

"This is to be the true log, [the] common place log of a common place bluejacket, his vices and his good points, the log of most all bluejackets," wrote Fred Wilson of the story that follows. This assertion probably is the least accurate statement in Wilson's remarkable account. The very fact that he faithfully kept a log marks him as extraordinary among his shipmates, and not "common place." Indeed, of all the thousands of enlisted engineers whose hot and tedious labor propelled the ships of the coal-fired turn-of-the-century fleet, he is the only one to offer an extended and detailed account of life in the engine rooms. In this respect alone, his story is noteworthy and important.

Elsewhere, Wilson said of his log that it was "written in a plain way, but every word is truth, plain and unvarnished." Wilson was a highly perceptive and articulate observer of the passing scene. When he went ashore, he was confident that "nothing was lost" on him. He observed everything with a keen sense of detail: daily events, scenes, the most common of the people he met. "I was very much interested in everything I saw," he wrote of Nagasaki, Japan. More remarkably, he recorded detailed accounts of the places he saw, the people he met, and what they said to each other. He even learned and recorded the names of some of the Chinese and Japanese rickshaw men he hired while on liberty. In some of his dialogue he recreated the pidgin English that was the lingua franca of sailors on the Asiatic Station. While in Japan he picked up some Japanese words and phrases, and he developed his own variety of pidgin Japanese. When he went ashore for more than a single day, Wilson often carried portions of his manuscript with him, to make timely entries of events as they unfolded. In this manner he preserved otherwise ephemeral perceptions of events he witnessed.

Unfortunately, we know little about Fred Wilson's early life. When he enlisted in 1895, he reported that he had been born on November 23, 1868, in Dalington, Pennsylvania, a village three or four miles southwest of the site of George Washington's famous 1776 crossing of the Delaware River. However, there is no record of his birth in Bucks County, the county in which Dalington is located, or in any of the adjacent counties, nor does he appear in the 1870 census. When his daughter Muriel was born in 1911, he listed his place of birth as Baltimore, though his official navy records continued to report Dalington. His early life probably was rural, as at various points in his log he evokes very romantic images of such youth, though he carefully disguises them as third-person accounts. It is possible that his youth was not spent in Pennsylvania. At one point he describes an idyllic scene in Maryland, "a scene most men look back to with regret after a lapse of years." At any rate, at the time of his first enlistment in 1895, Wilson listed a Baltimore address for his mother Rebecca, identifying her as his next of kin. It is very easy to picture him as "the boy with the short, black, curly hair and laughing, half-serious, dark eyes" who in one story had a goat as a pet; an early photograph of him portrays just such a youth. He tells us too that as a youth, he used to steal away with a chum into the woods to practice acrobatic tricks, a profession he followed for a while after leaving home.

Wilson saw some service on merchant ships prior to enlisting in the navy; however, we have no details about that service, other than a passing comment that he had "been on a few merchant ships that steam[ed] easier" than the cruiser *New Orleans*. It is equally easy to imagine Wilson experiencing hard times in his early independent years. Following the Panic of 1893, America experienced a deep economic depression that continued for several years. Wilson's extensive knowledge, evident in his log, of the specialized jargon of the hoboes and tramps of that era strongly suggests that prior to enlisting he spent some time as one of the knights of the open road. Possibly too, the "fictitious" young man in one of his stories who had fallen on hard times—"He was simply a good hearted, ordinary fellow, like some you know, not too good, who drank a little [and] was free with his money"—was self-descriptive.

At the time of his enlistment he presumably was as yet unmarried, although subsequent enlistment forms identify at least three—possibly four—wives as next of kin.[1] This frequency of marriage was unusual in this period. Perhaps Wilson partially explains this in his log when he observes, after discussing "Japanese Mary's" ability to separate bluejackets from their money at her waterfront "dive" in Nagasaki, "Yes! Yes! Poor Jack indeed has lots of troubles and is easily led and beguiled by rum-sellers and women. That [is] one of the reasons he gets married so numerously. Poor fellow, its his only way of enjoying himself, and he likes to have a home in almost every port where he may touch for any length of time." Despite his many liaisons in the Orient and his numerous wives, Wilson apparently met his match in Miss Nellie E. Townsend, whom he married in Cape Charles, Virginia, in February 1909, just five days after the Great White Fleet returned to the United States from its 'round-the-world cruise. She remained his faithful wife for fifteen years, until his death in 1924.

Although Wilson never consciously described himself in the pages of his log, we can discern quite a bit about the man from his activities and observations. The picture of Fred Wilson—"Wils" to his shipmates—that emerges is very complex. He was appreciative of art, so much so that a scene he observed near Nagasaki triggered memories of a painting he had viewed much earlier at the Metropolitan Museum of Art in New York. Not only does he describe in detail the scene in the painting, but he also recalls the artist's name. This aspect alone would place him in a very small minority of American sailors of a century ago—and probably today, as well. He was very sensitive and appreciative, too, of Chinese, and particularly Japanese, culture. Complimentary comments about the Japanese and Chinese abound in his log. His admiring attitude toward the Japanese—"I was never among a people I felt so much at home with in my life"—and the "considerate and sociable" Chinese is particularly remarkable when measured against the general tenor of racial intolerance in the broader American society.

One searches in vain for any derogatory comment about the black sailors who served on board Wilson's ships. We know that at this period in the navy, blacks were concentrated in two areas: stewards and cooks, and the engine rooms where Wilson also labored. We know that he worked with black sailors, yet on the few occasions when Wilson identifies any black by race, his treatment is sympathetic. In one case Wilson describes a fight started by a white bully in which the black beat his antagonist, an event concerning which Wilson recorded, "I was glad he [the bully] got his just deserts." In another case, a black oiler (a second class petty officer) confounds an acting warrant machinist by refusing to admit that he was running forced-draft blowers in an unauthorized way. Wilson's silence on the broader topic of relations between blacks and whites in the navy of his day is regrettable, as we would have benefited greatly from some discussion about his attitudes and the general nature of relations between races on board our ships of that time. On the other hand, Wilson and his contemporaries in the armed forces in the Philippines regularly used the now-infamous "N word" to describe the Filipino insurgents.

Throughout the years of Wilson's service, naval officers generally concluded that desertion had nothing to do with failed leadership; rather, the excessive desertion rates, many officers argued, were caused by, among other things, the need for white sailors to work for or with blacks, a situation then quite rare in the broader American society. The presence of a black oiler, a second class petty officer, on board the *Oregon* meant that a fair number of white sailors—coal passers and firemen—would have been required to work under the orders of a black. Had the attitudes the officers described actually prevailed on board the ships on which Wilson served, it is reasonable to believe they would not have escaped his keen eye and pen. Wilson's lack of comment thus provides an interesting insight into the nature of lower-deck acceptance of blacks and of officers' misperceptions of the enlisted force during the period.

Wilson identified himself as a molder (iron) when he joined the navy as a coal passer on board the receiving ship *Vermont* at the New York Navy Yard in Brooklyn on October 30, 1895, at the relatively late age of twenty-six years, eleven months. He was "duly examined and passed by the doctor, was sworn in, and became a cog in the mechanism of Uncle Sam's Navy." Wilson joined the navy just three weeks before the navy's first modern battleship, the USS *Indiana*, was commissioned on November 20, 1895; he and many of his fellow "rookies," or green recruits, on board the *Vermont* were drafted to man the new ship.

In July 1897 Wilson was transferred again to the *Vermont*, where he spent six months before being assigned to the newly recommissioned cruiser *Minneapolis* in January 1898. The *Minneapolis*, a 7,375-ton cruiser, was assigned to the Northern Patrol Squadron at the outbreak of war with Spain and thus operated along the North Atlantic coast. In April 1898 she was assigned to scouting duty in the West Indies and searched unsuccessfully for Adm. Pascual Cervera's fleet as far as Venezuela. She was in port at Key West, coaling, on July 3, 1898, and thus did not participate in the Battle of Santiago. Of those days, Wilson noted, the crew had all drills "down fine, and if the occasion had of arrived, we would have rendered a good account of ourselves.... But unfortunately, we had no show to distinguish ourselves." Wilson's first enlistment expired at the end of October 1898. He reenlisted and continued serving on board the *Minneapolis,* then "in ordinary," a condition somewhat akin to being "in mothballs" but with a small caretaker crew.

In March 1899 Wilson was transferred to the auxiliary cruiser *Prairie* at Philadelphia when that ship was placed in reserve commission and assigned to cruise with naval militiamen off the Atlantic coast. In October of that year, *Prairie* went into the yards for a major overhaul and to have her gun mounts removed in preparation for carrying the U.S. government exhibition to France for the Paris Exhibition, and thus Wilson once more was available for reassignment.

Not until he reached the cruiser *New Orleans* did Wilson fully appreciate that service on board the *Prairie,* a 6,620-ton converted merchant ship, had been good. In fact, Wilson recorded at the beginning of his log, she had been a "home." But by the time he reached this conclusion, he was on board the *New Orleans* and headed for Asiatic Station.

Wilson's initial enlistment experience wasn't pleasant; indeed, it has several threads in common with those of virtually all recruits of the period. The initial shock, one suspects, would be that of entering the world of a receiving ship, which served as an enlistment center, boot camp, and personnel distribution center, accepting and training new recruits and then dispatching them to meet individual ships' requirements. Wilson reported on board the *Vermont* at the New York Navy Yard in Brooklyn. At that time, many wooden sailing ships remained in service; however, even among the old wooden ships, the receiving ship *Vermont* was aged. Laid down as a sailing ship of the line in September 1818, she hadn't been actually completed until September 1848, when she was placed "in ordinary." In 1861 she was fitted out as a stores ship for service during the Civil War. The *Vermont* was later converted to a receiving ship—or "guardo," to use the jargon of the day—with an additional deckhouse as accommodation for about four hundred "rookies." This addition also gave her a remarkably arklike appearance. She served as a receiving ship from 1864 to 1876 and again from 1879 to 1901. Thus, when Wilson first stepped on board her in 1895, more than seven decades had passed since her keel had been laid, and she was nearing the end of her long and undistinguished service.[2]

Generally, "rookies" were the targets of a number of well-organized scams common to receiving ships. The ship's yeoman, as with Wilson, generally palmed off used or poor-quality uniforms on the new recruits, while another "old salt" relieved the rookies of their civilian clothing and disposed of it for his own financial benefit.

Introduction

The official navy ran its own scam. Polished recruiting officers routinely promised recruits a free set of clothing upon enlistment. This promise was true only in the sense that the men did not have to pay for the uniform issue in advance. The reality, generally not understood until after one had been sworn in, was that the uniforms were issued freely enough but the new recruits would be allowed no liberty (free time ashore) until they had repaid the government in full for them. For a coal passer earning twenty-two dollars per month, this took several months, and for a landsman at fifteen dollars a month, even longer. During those initial months, the recruits, lacking any money, were required to subsist on inadequate and unappetizing government rations. This harsh, indeed fraudulent, arrangement understandably turned a great many recruits against the navy right from the start. "I don't like to look back on those days," Wilson wrote. "They weren't pleasant by any means."

On board cruising ships, the crew was divided into messes of twenty men each, who then elected their own cooks and treasurers. This was a system that worked reasonably well if the individual messes managed to find a cook who actually took an interest in preparing the food. Further, individual messes levied a monthly sum from each member for the cook to augment government rations with items not provided by the navy, including such basics as salt, pepper, and butter. In essence, American sailors were required to subsidize the government by spending their own money to obtain a bare subsistence diet. A monthly mess bill of five dollars could amount to 25 percent, or more, of a young sailor's pay.

A great many elected cooks were incompetent in the galley and unqualified to handle mess funds; others were crooked and absconded with their messmates' money. While in port, the mess cooks frequently went to market ashore to acquire fresh vegetables and meat. All too often a mess cook would never return, leaving his messmates in the lurch. While he was on board the *Oregon*, Wilson noted that his mess was particularly poorly run: "You often go hungry in the navy, sometimes through a rascally cook or caterer who rolls you, but generally thro' the miserable ration served by Uncle Sam."

In 1901 the navy began phasing in the general mess system, by which each ship was assigned a number of trained cooks who were to prepare all the meals for the crew. Under this "revolutionary" new arrangement, the mess cooks were reduced, by and large, to delivering the cooked meals from the galley to their individual messes. The general mess later was expanded to include a central facility at which all enlisted men would take their meals. At the same time, the navy ended the practice of individual sailors' using their own mess gear; thereafter all mess gear belonged to the ship and was cleaned by the mess cooks after each meal. But these developments came after Wilson's cruise to Asiatic Station. He had to survive the inadequate system that had long "served" the navy.

Wilson's account, like all enlisted accounts from this period, is replete with mentions of the unacceptable quality of meals. The protein mainstay of the diet was "canned willie"—canned corned beef. Unfortunately, the system of canning such products had by no means been perfected. The meat often was green in color and the smell appalling. The other mainstay of the diet, "salt horse," or salted beef in brine, was even worse. Wrote Wilson: "It carries with it an aroma of the days of Paul Jones, of 'wooden ships and iron men,' when bilge water and weevils and cock roaches were much in vogue, of seamen with long queues done up in rope yarn and tar, who gave and took hard knocks, and who, if all accounts of those days are correct, w[ere] ninety percent brute. . . . As for myself and others, I would make a meal from hardtack and coffee any time, in preference." Given the nature of navy food at that time, it is not difficult to appreciate Wilson's consuming interest in huge meals during his infrequent runs ashore, when an artery-clogging dozen soft-boiled eggs often constituted a "side" dish.

The log contains frequent reminders for those who have served in the navy more recently than Wilson that certain aspects of the navy-enlisted experience remain the same despite the passage of a century. The recent recruit of Wilson's day could easily be discerned, Wilson reported, by "his nautical air and general 'salty' appearance. . . . What a wise weather-eye he casts about him, and what a roll! He is a heavy weather man, all right. What he doesn't know about the briny isn't worth knowing." When the "salty" recruit reports back on board after liberty and safely passes the officer of the deck's scrutiny, there is a transformation. "Just for'd of the smokestack he will begin to roll and gives the impression that he has got a terrible jag on when, in reality, it is only a 'smoke stack' drunk and assumed for effect." The term "smoke-stacking" was still in common use forward in the late 1950s and early 1960s and one supposes continues to be today. Fortunately, as Wilson also concluded, the recruit "outgrows all this in time, . . . and makes a good hand."

No one who has served on board a ship in our navy—or any navy—will soon forget the sheer pleasure of a liberty in a foreign port and the preparation of an appropriate "liberty uniform" in anticipation of the great event. The passage of a century has not changed those very human emotions. "What brushing up and overhauling of clothing the evening before [liberty]," Wilson wrote. "Jacky is very scrupulous in his appearance going on liberty. But, hmm . . . coming off liberty, that's another story." When liberty finally was granted, "It was with a happy heart [that he] went over the ship's side into the steam launch."

Unfortunately for Wilson and his shipmates, liberty was granted only rarely, and it was even further restricted by an onerous system of "liberty classing," yet one more of the punishment systems in place in the navy at the time. Few sailors qualified as "Special First Class," the one category that enjoyed full, regular liberty. Even then, Special First Class men, under ideal circumstances, could expect liberty only once every fourth night, when liberty was granted. However, such frequent liberty rarely occurred. Wilson, in fact, averaged far less liberty—perhaps once every other month. This was not uncommon. Seaman Charlie Fowler, who served on Asiatic Station a few years later, reported in July 1906 that his cruise thus far had not been very exciting—"six days at sea out of six months, with a total of three liberties in two ports."[3]

When the battleship *Oregon* reached Woosung, the deep-draft anchorage near Shanghai, a full month passed before the captain granted any liberty. Earlier, prior to the *Oregon*'s arrival in Kure, Japan, her commanding officer had given no liberty for more than three consecutive months, during two of which the ship had been at anchor in Hong Kong. Further, when the *Oregon* returned to Manila Bay after visiting Kure, the commanding officer granted no liberty, because he believed the men had had enough liberty while in Japan. The concept of a ship in port for a month or longer without granting liberty is so alien to our modern navy that it requires explanation. The crew of the *Oregon* was not being punished; it simply was not the practice to grant much liberty. The *Oregon*'s record regarding liberty certainly would constitute "cruel and unusual punishment" in today's navy. "Oh, how we longed for liberty, which was so slow in coming," Wilson wrote in Kure. "You who can put on your coat and hat and go where you please, where fancy pleases, don't know what freedom means."

The officers' excuse for not giving liberty in Hong Kong was the presence of the plague. However, Wilson noted sardonically, "There wasn't any plague for the officers, the Chinese stewards and mess attendants. Nor was there plague for the monitor *Monterey*'s crew, who went ashore regularly." In a similar vein, when the *New Orleans* was in Colombo on the way out to Asiatic Station, the crew was restricted because of the presence of small pox ashore, but the officers permitted people "from the lowest haunts of the town" to come aboard and also sent out wash. "So," Wilson concluded, "I should judge the case of small pox was manufactured for the occasion." The reality was, as Cdr. William G. Miller advised Secretary of the Navy Truman H. Newberry in February 1909, "The men are allowed to go ashore only when there is no excuse for keeping them on board."[4]

So it was that the men on the ships on which Wilson served rarely got ashore, which was the principal reason they drank to excess when they finally achieved a brief moment of freedom. "You get ashore about once every two months, then you try to cram all the enjoyment you have missed for that length of time into 12 hours' liberty. You get drunk, spend what you have saved in that time, and are a madman in action. You can't have any enjoyment in a rational manner."

Wilson's account is replete with mentions of sailor "dives" along the waterfronts of the ports he visited. The reader will be introduced to McGurk's Saloon in the Bowery, also known as Suicide Hall, and to Sailor Liz, Marine Jenny, Red Maude, and the other "soiled doves" who inhabited that place. Their profession notwithstanding, Wilson found them "poor unfortunates, . . . good hearted and willing to share their last pence with the man who has treated them good. That is their code of honor." In Japan Wilson describes the Maintop Saloon in Nagasaki, Japanese Mary's, and many other such waterfront establishments, and he reflects on the wiles of Eva, the popular barmaid of the Maintop. How expertly she would string young sailors along in order to separate them from their hard-won salary is a story that might easily be repeated today in seaport bars around the world; most certainly, this was the case in the Mediterranean and Western Pacific (or WestPac, a later generation's Asiatic Station) in the late 1950s and 1960s and 1970s. Chinese establishments described in Wilson's accounts included Black Mary's in Shanghai, a place "much frequented by men-o-warsmen in search of a square meal," and Mrs. Dale's, a similar establishment geared for bluejackets. Wilson also visited Ship Street in Hong Kong, at a time when it was at its height as a wide-open red-light district. Here, he reported, "Everything goes. Next to Port Said with its brothel in Arab town, it is probably its nearest rival in wickedness." But the same account that embraces Black Mary's and Eva's activities also contains wonderfully sensitive accounts of the lands and the peoples he visited.

~ ~ ~

Wilson particularly loved the Japanese, and he worried that in their rush to adopt Western ways they would lose the essence of the tranquility they then enjoyed. At one point Wilson comments, "They are advancing, getting civilized according to European ideas. Soon they'll be bolting down whole wedges of mince pie and milk at the quick lunch counter, making wild rushes for the subway or elevated, reading their papers on the fly and the thousand and one other rapid-firing, nerve destroying devices of modern civilization." Unfortunately, Wilson's fears, and more, have become the hectic reality of life in Japan today.

Thus Wilson's nearly two years of service on Asiatic Station passed—long periods in port, with very little opportunity to get ashore. Indeed, the ships on which Wilson served, unlike in today's navy, spent very little time at sea, with the exception of the long passages between American home ports and Asian waters, and back. The remainder of the time was usually spent at anchor. Under the circumstances, the crew members suffered deadly boredom, as a result of the unvarying routine. As Wilson noted, "Inaction is one of the things that try the soul; routine is another. The two placed together form a combination that will eventually drive one mad. Routine saps all the individuality from a man." Further, if they had the misfortune to be swinging interminably at the hook off Cavite in Manila Bay, excessive heat without effective ventilation—let alone air conditioning—made the enlisted men's life even more miserable. Therefore, they always hoped for, but only infrequently received, relief from the weather by a tour to northern waters and Japanese ports.

In due course, Wilson was transferred to the gunboat *Concord*, which was scheduled to leave Asiatic Station for duty in Alaska. This departure stirred Wilson to write, "It wasn't so much in leaving China that the shoe pinched, although I had enjoyed myself immensely amid her quaint and strange scenes. Nor the prospects of leaving the Philippines; that, at least, was a relief, to get away from the rainy season and misery of life aboard ship in that hot clime. But to leave Japan, sunny, dazzling, mystic Japan, with all its beautiful coloring, its picturesque setting, the people, and above all, the girls of that wonder land. Aye, there was the rub, to lose all this, perhaps never to see it again for years, if ever. That was the pity of it, the regret."

By the time the *Concord* had reached Alaska, Wilson was experiencing another aspect of service in the navy. He was becoming a "short-timer." All who have experienced this phenomenon will well recognize his symptoms. As Wilson noted, "a sailor with only a short time to do to finish the cruise is a very nervous and skittish critter. . . . Time flies on leaden wings. . . . You lose all interest in the things that formerly made up your life. . . . You are full of the time when you are to get your few dollars and are free—free to blow it in [to spend your money as you wish], to go where you please, and to stay as long as you please."

~~~

Some time before his enlistment Wilson had acquired a taste for tattoos, which he had had applied rather liberally to his body. His initial enlistment form reports that he already had a necklace tattoo, his initials on his left arm, and a crucifix on his back. The examining surgeon further noted that his arms were minutely tattooed. When Wilson reenlisted in 1898, the receiving ship's surgeon noted, "back all in ink." Tattooing was a far more common practice in Wilson's day. In 1908 Surgeon Ammen Farenholt completed a study of 3,572 navy men who had enlisted or reenlisted on board the receiving ship *Independence* at Mare Island, California, during the preceding eight and one-half years. Dr. Farenholt determined that 23.01 percent of the men enlisting for the first time already had tattoos, while 53.61 percent of men reenlisting had tattoos. Further, he estimated, about 60 percent of all men with over ten years of service were tattooed.[5]

By the time of his fourth enlistment in 1906, Wilson had extensive Japanese tattoo designs covering his right arm; a dragon, spider web, four butterflies, and a spider across his back; a snake around his neck that had covered up the original necklace; another snake across his chest, with a dragon on the left side; an eagle and monkey on his left shoulder; clasped hands, a lizard, a woman, and his initials on his left arm; a fish, eagle and shield, anchor shield and flags, a woman and a lizard, and ship and flags on his right forearm; and flags on the backs of his hands.[6]

~~~

Wilson was an engineer—a "snipe," to use the term common then, as now, in the navy. By the time he began his log, he had risen rapidly through the ranks of the engineering force from coal passer to fireman second class, to fireman first class, then directly to water-tender, a rating that carried the rank of petty officer, first class. This in itself was a noteworthy achievement and says much for Wilson's professional skill and

Introduction

ability to handle rough men in the even rougher fire rooms and engine rooms of ships. Wilson lived and worked in a harsh and challenging environment where, as he reported, he had to deal with loafers and shirkers. "If they, being bigger men and stronger, try to slug me, I simply use a twelve or fourteen inch monkey or Stillson wrench and lay them out."

His description of the trials and tribulations of new coal passers was written from the heart, colored by his own personal experiences on board the battleship *Indiana*, 1895–1897, and cruiser *Minneapolis*, 1898–1899:

> When on watch, his duties consist of getting out, or passing, coal to his firemen, and in some ships it is no snap to handle 40 or 45 buckets of coal, each weighing about 145 or 150 pounds, in a temperature of perhaps 150° to 175°, & has to haul the ashes from the ash pans and load and send up buckets of ashes. He is put to work also at cleaning bilge strainers when they become clogged up with coal dirt and ashes. At times he is put on the fires when a fireman plays out. He has to stow coal in the bunkers when they coal ship. [He] has to go in the boilers and knock off scale and scrape out mud and scale and clean out bilges in port. [He has to] scrub paintwork and paint, clean off pumps, polish bright work, and do any work he may be put at. [He] goes in the back connections of the boilers and cleans out the soot and ashes from there and also in the smoke pipe, [and] any old place that is hard to get at and is dirty. It is hard and awful dirty work, and it is work that is never done.

Wilson's navy was struggling to adjust to the provisions of the Personnel Act of 1899, which, among other things, abolished the engineer corps as a staff branch of the naval officer corps and amalgamated all current engineer officers with the line. This was the culmination of a long struggle on the part of engineer officers—derisively called "mechanics" by their peers in the line of command—to gain military titles, respect, and prestige. Prior to 1899, engineer officers used titles descriptive of their positions: assistant engineer, passed assistant engineer, chief engineer, and others. While these titles met the needs of the service, they separated the engineers socially from the officers of the line, who held more exalted military titles, such as commander, captain, or rear admiral.

As one officer confided to Lt. Cdr. Albert Key when he was aide to President Theodore Roosevelt, "Every man and woman in my home community . . . *knew* just where socially and officially to place a man whose title was 'lieutenant,' but they did not know where to place a man whose title was 'passed assistant something.'" Key, a line officer, passed the message on to the president but added that he thought the officer's position was "hysterical and exaggerated."[7]

"The line or executive officer, proud of his past achievement and prestige," Engineer in Chief [later Rear Admiral] George W. Melville wrote in 1898, "withstood steadfastly the engineer, who strove to secure rightful recognition, in rank and title, as an element of the combatant force."[8] A line officer writing two years earlier had put the problem a bit more succinctly: "I suspect that the real bitterness of the Engineers' fight has lain in the feeling that he belonged to a body of men who were expected to do the dirty work, accept danger in the dark and get none of the credit of success."[9] Yet the engineers' quest for rank and title was ridiculed by many line officers:

> I hate to talk, yet I'm the cock of the walk
> And a Chief En-gi-neer.
> But I've a bill to change my name
> And make me something more;
> With sword in hand I'll take command
> And be a Com-mo-dore![10]

These sentiments also were reflected on the mess decks, where Wilson routinely recorded the general worthlessness, in his view, of the seaman branch, whose members he believed were useful only for swabbing decks and shining brass work. Conversely, the men of the seaman branch, in general, treated the "snipes" with disdain, despite the fact that in the new steam-and-steel navy the snipes' role was critical, for no longer did the seamen control the ship's propulsion through the skillful manipulation of sails.

With the Personnel Act of 1899, engineers obtained their coveted military titles, but at the same time, the enlisted engineers lost their specialized shipboard leadership. From this point onward, in theory, every line officer was to be qualified in engineering; however, the reality was that the engineer officers fled to the bridge, but very few of the original line officers moved to the engine rooms. Toward the end of 1899 the *Army and Navy Journal* reported that only five original line officers were serving as engineers, while eighty-five former engineer officers were in line duties. Congress had created a hundred new acting warrant machinists to help ease the transition. In consequence, the Navy Department directed that all watch duties in engine rooms be performed by the warrant officers.

Some of these new warrant officers, neither commissioned officers nor enlisted men, supervised Wilson's work, and while he admitted some warrant officers were excellent, the ones he encountered on board the battleship *Oregon* in 1900 were, in his opinion, incompetent. Even the *Army and Navy Journal* noted the acting warrant machinists' limitations: "These men are competent within their limitations, but they are not the trained, skilled, theoretical, and practical engine experts, and should not be expected to assume the same responsibilities" as the former engineering officers.[11]

One problem with the new warrant officers, Wilson correctly observed, was that they were appointed from the ranks and then continued to serve on the same ships on which they had served as enlisted men. The men who worked for them knew all their personal weaknesses, due to their earlier close association as messmates. Thus, when one of the warrant officers, who as a machinist's mate had been noteworthy for his lack of personal cleanliness, criticized the cleanliness of the enlisted men now under his command, he generated nothing but contempt. "It cuts us deeply," Wilson recorded, "to be told that we have to get another shirt, etc., by men who when of the common herd couldn't muster enough clothing together to dust a fiddle." Wilson argued that upon appointment as warrant officer, the individual should be sent to a school for several months to acquire military skills and some sense of etiquette, and then be assigned to a different ship, where his past would be unknown to the enlisted men. This was sound advice and was the course ultimately adopted. But in the meantime, Wilson and his shipmates suffered the attentions of these warrant officers whom they derisively labeled "bolo-men."[12]

"The men grew to hate the very sight of the 'bolo-men,'" Wilson recorded, "and if one of them passed along, someone would shout 'bolo!' and it would be taken up by everyone, along with catcalls and hisses." On another occasion at quarters, the entire engineers' force "stopped in the midst of 'setting up' drill and yelled 'bolo!' at the top of their lungs." Given the high professional standing of, and consequent level of respect accorded to, today's warrant officers, it is difficult to imagine the enlisted men's attitude toward them a century ago.

An important part of Wilson's "plain and unvarnished" truth about his experiences dealt with the commissioned officers of the ships on which he served. The enlisted men's difficulties with the acting warrant machinists were quite understandable. The warrant officers were new and their collective position in the engine room not entirely clear. However, the enlisted men's relationship with commissioned officers was considerably more troublesome.

It was clear to most officers that the nature of the enlisted force was changing. The skills required to maintain a modern warship meant that men with skills—or the ability to learn them—had to be recruited. The navy now needed turret captains and many more technicians. In effect, these recruits represented a new class within the navy. The great majority now had at least a public school education. They came, Cdr. William G. Miller advised Secretary of the Navy Truman H. Newberry in 1909, "from the same class of people from which the officers are taken, and [their] average intelligence is equal to the average intelligence, less the superior education, of the officers of the navy."[13] Indeed, increased technology demanded such men. As Wilson noted, "Steam, hydraulics, electricity, pneumatics, etc., have [replaced] the simple routine of former years, and from being a mere machine that pulled and hauled [a rope] at the word, [Jack] had to do some thinking of his own."

Having recognized the changing nature of their men, the officers, one might anticipate, would adapt their leadership methods to meet the changing situation. That, unfortunately, generally was not the case. The executive officer of the battleship *Oregon*, Lt. Cdr. Charles A. Adams, regrettably typified a significant class of officers. It seemed to Wilson that Adams's "especial mission [was] to harass and make miserable and unendurable [the enlisted men's] already uncomfortable condition." The men knew Commander Adams as "Jack the Ripper." Wilson clearly pitied the man, but he also recognized that he could be dangerous:

> "The Ripper" was around looking for men out of uniform, and everyone he saw he would pounce on with a roar. Poor, useless, old man. [His is a] wasted life of no earthly use, a life spent in abusing men for petty trifles.
>
> "Jack the Ripper" represents a class fast dying out: men who all their lives have abused men who have no power to resent the abuse. He had even gone so far as to strike men with an umbrella he carried, of course, knowing his man. Some men would report him and cause him to be censured. To his equals he was as affable as his nature would allow him; to his superiors, cringing. Poor old stiff! Hysterical old woman.

Wilson always carefully watched his officers. It was a common practice then, as now, because the officers were an enlisted man's connection to the naval bureaucracy. This dependence influences all aspects of enlisted lives, from the granting of leave or liberty, to promotions and transfers, to the everyday comforts of life aboard ship. In Wilson's time, that interest, that concern, was rarely returned by the officers. In reality, enlisted men rarely ever were mentioned in officers' correspondence and diaries from this period. It is almost as though they did not exist, as far as the officers were concerned.

Chief Yeoman Fred J. "Bunny" Buenzle observed in his classic autobiography, *Bluejacket*, that in the U.S. Navy, "it was felt that too often a graduate of Annapolis believed that gentility of speech and kindliness of manner were somehow incompatible with the duties of a naval officer."[14] Wilson, who at one point refers to his officers as "government-educated asses," observed, "They look like gentlemen, act like gentlemen in the glare of the lime-light, but not one half of them have the true instinct of a man." Further, Wilson and his shipmates were convinced that the officers profited at the enlisted men's expense through markups of uniform prices or kickbacks from vendors of food for the crew. They also believed that the officers involved received kickbacks to accept poor-quality coal, which resulted in considerably harder work in the fire rooms. Concerning the paymasters and commissary stewards, Charlie Fowler wrote, shortly before he received his appointment as a warrant paymaster's clerk, "Some of this gentry are prone to dishonesty, and wax rich at the expense of the enlisted men, and some are honest, but incompetent."[15] Either way, the enlisted men suffered.

There is no sense, throughout Wilson's log, of any spirit of cooperation—of common cause—between the senior petty officers of the ships on which Wilson served and their commissioned officers. At one point, Wilson reports that, seriously ill and on the "binnacle list" (sick list), he was berated by an officer: "Why the hell ain't you in sick-bay, damn you, etc." His own reaction constituted a stark condemnation of officer leadership:

> I didn't reply, and it did not make any impression upon me, as that is one of the things you rapidly get accustomed to in the navy. You can't answer back, even if you are on the report and go to the mast, or "stick." There is no use in trying to clear yourself. It is all cut and dried for you. You are bound to be punished. If you talk, you only augment your punishment and are put down as a 'sea-lawyer' immediately. So the old hand, knowing how it is, never explains. Asked if he has anything to say, it is always, "Nothing to say, sir."

Before naval officers reading this account dismiss Wilson's observations as biased or uninformed, it is important to remember that these criticisms were not written by an embittered raw recruit. Wilson was at this point a first class petty officer on his second enlistment—a career man. Further, although the specifics of individual complaints differ, there is sufficient evidence from surviving records of the enlisted men of the period to support the conclusion that their officers failed in their leadership role and ill served the men under their command, and thus the nation. This failure might be attributed to the sense of "class," which was much stronger in American society then. It is equally likely that it is one of the negative aspects of the officer procurement system of the time, in which virtually all line officers were graduates of the Naval Academy, and thus indoctrinated by the older line officers who were their instructors. The officer class was, in essence, a closed system that tended to perpetuate outdated attitudes and preclude new thinking, particularly as regarded leadership of enlisted men.

While he was in sick bay on board the cruiser *New Orleans* at Singapore, Wilson was fortunate to receive a visit from a chaplain. This officer, William T. Helms, was remarkable to Wilson because he "dropped his quarterdeck stiffness for the natural man" in his talk with the men in sickbay. This was a rare occurrence in the navy of the day. As Wilson further recorded, he had seen many chaplains "who will not go among the men at all, but generally keep aloof, and it is just as well, for they generally have not the good feeling of comradeship that would make them popular among the crew." Put simply, as one of Fred Buenzle's shipmates commented of the chaplains, "The trouble with all of them . . . is that they live aft, too hell-an'-gone far aft."[16] Reporting the departure of the chaplain from the USS *Lancaster* during a cruise to the Mediterranean, Buenzle noted, "He was not missed from among us, for during his month aboard the *Lancaster* he had never, so far as I knew, spoken a single word to one of the enlisted men of the crew."[17]

The men thus saw the chaplains first as officers and only secondarily as men of God. In a navy in which the officers' role—as seen by the men—principally was unwarranted harassment and the enforcement of unnecessary petty discipline, the chaplains' insistence upon an officer's rank and privileges, however well warranted, ensured the preservation of an unbridgeable gulf between them and the men to whom they were expected to minister.

~~~

Today's navy personnel might derive a number of lessons from Wilson's account of his cruise to Asiatic Station. Technologically, the world, and with it the navy, have changed in most remarkable ways. However, though the material aspects today bear little resemblance to the fleet of a century ago, the human elements—the human relationships—remain essentially unaltered. Thus, when one of the hated "bolo-men" on the *Oregon* admits that the chief engineer trusted no one in the engineers' force, Wilson offers guidance as valuable today as it was then: "It's a poor policy for any man, no matter his position, not to place a certain confidence and reliance on those subordinate to his orders, for men, knowing they are not trusted, as a general thing don't render very good service. Any man, no matter what position he is placed in, has to rely upon someone."

Concerning the negative impact of mass punishment, a common practice in the navy in his years, Wilson reported from Manila Bay that his ship, the *New Orleans*, was getting no liberty, nor was the flagship, the armored cruiser *Brooklyn*. From what he had heard of the *Brooklyn*'s officers, Wilson reported, "they had stopped all liberty, wouldn't serve out any money to the crew, wouldn't allow the smoking lamp to be lit, and took all other privileges away from the crew as punishment for not manning the boats' falls with the alacrity the captain thought necessary." Concluded Wilson, "Such is naval discipline in this case, though I understand the many innocent suffered for the few guilty. If the guilty few cannot be punished, why punish all the rest who are innocent?"

"Of course, it is hard, you know, but in order to reach the guilty, we will have to punish the whole ship's company," he suggested was the officers' excuse. To this Wilson responded, "That only makes matters worse. It makes us all feel a strong sense of injustice. It makes us dissatisfied. It is no argument to make us do our best."

~~~

Introduction

"In them days," recalled one sailor of the period, "you so much as winked and you were clapped in double irons."[18] Any member of today's navy would be utterly staggered by the frequency and severity of "petty" punishments in our navy of a century ago. Poor living conditions, poor food, harsh discipline, and officers insensitive to the needs of the enlisted men all contributed to a crisis in manpower in the navy. "I don't see how they are going to keep a man in the navy and make him stay when they will not grant him the slightest favor," Hospital Apprentice Deane C. Hartley wrote of his ship, the cruiser *Minneapolis*, in 1904.[19] This was an oft-repeated sentiment in Wilson's log.

Statistics support this criticism. For the fiscal year ending June 30, 1905, *Minneapolis*, with a crew of 477, enlisted (probably reenlisted) four men, discharged sixty-four, and had fifty-six deserters, for a net loss of 116 men, or 24.3 percent of her crew. She also had one general court-martial and sixty-eight summary courts. Under the category "petty punishments," her commanding officer reported that 114 men spent a total of 668 days in double irons, another sixty spent 250 days in solitary confinement on bread and water, and 188 men received extra duty. The total number of desertions, courts-martial, and "petty" punishments in a single year (487) exceeded by ten the number of men in her crew![20] Yet these figures were not remarkable. The battleship *Massachusetts*, with a crew of 561, during the same period reported eleven enlistments, fifty-five discharges, ninety-nine desertions, nine general and 159 summary courts-martial, and a staggering 2,559 "petty" punishments. *Massachusetts* thus had a total deserters/punishments figure of 2,812, or an average of five punishments for each and every member of the crew. And those figures were for but a single year.[21]

Wilson's frequent reference, then, to the fact that people were choosing to "jump out," desert, were natural to the environment. The officers, who seemed to be in a state of denial about the failure of their leadership, regularly found excuses for the growing numbers of desertions. Many, like Rear Adm. John B. Coghlan, ascribed the high desertion rate to "the ordinary restless spirit bred in the boys by our general life, in which we are constantly engaged in jumping from one place or position to another."[22] Desertion thus was simply a unique aspect of the free American environment. As one officer attempted to explain his own ship's problems, "the attractions of [the Pacific] coast are so great, the wages so high, the people so friendly, the cities so 'wide open,' the climate so mild, and the opportunities so numerous to rise and make money that 'the men before the mast' cannot resist the temptation to 'run.'"[23] Thus, the men themselves, and not their officers' failure in leadership, were responsible for their desertion. This was a conclusion doubtless most reassuring to the commanding officers. Unfortunately, it offered little actual explanation, and, as these causes were deemed intractable, it offered no remedy.

A few officers judged the situation more accurately. In 1902 Rear Adm. Henry C. Taylor, the chief of the Bureau of Navigation and the officer responsible for the recruitment and retention of the enlisted force, advised Secretary of the Navy William H. Moody that much of the desertion problem would be resolved if the senior officers could "ensure the constant interest of the commissioned officers in the men's comforts, amusements and interests." The fundamental leadership defect, Taylor reported, was that "we do not sufficiently urge our officers to devote themselves to the enlisted men, but rather encourage them to do other things . . . and in other ways [tell] them tacitly that honor and profit lie in caring more for other matters . . . than for the efficiency of the enlisted force."[24]

The high levels of desertion placed further strains upon the recruiting effort and led recruiters to accept men who in one way or another were unfit for duty. In 1899, the year Wilson sailed for the Asiatic Station, 2,023 men deserted from a total enlisted force of only 14,502, a desertion rate of 13.9 percent. By 1901, the enlisted force had grown to 18,825, but the desertions had grown even faster: to 3,158, or 16.8 percent. In essence, one in every six men deserted from the U.S. Navy in fiscal year 1901. A 16.8 percent desertion rate in the navy of 2001 would have meant 52,593 desertions in a single year—a truly catastrophic level that doubtless would trigger congressional investigation.[25]

One enlisted man on Pacific Station in 1902 advised the editor of the *Army and Navy Journal:* "The loss of continuous service men, the great number of desertions of late and greater number of courts-martial are apparently without reason to the department officials and general public, because they never get through that circle drawn by the officers around the inner routine of the modern man-of-war."[26] There is no evidence of a "circle drawn by the officers" regarding enlisted affairs. Rather, and perhaps more damning, the record amply proves that the prevailing attitude toward enlisted men in the wardrooms of the fleet was one of near-total apathy. Most officers, conscious of their social status, simply made no effort to discern the needs of the men they commanded and thus made no effort to meet those needs, except in the rare cases where excessive desertions focused the Navy Department's attention on specific ships and their commanding officers.

Wilson and his messmates of the engineers force were actively interested in world events. This is a topic rarely touched upon in any other published accounts of enlisted life in this period; thus Wilson's diary affords a rare and valuable insight. On board the battleship *Oregon,* when cooler weather allowed the men to return from their makeshift sleeping arrangements on the weather decks to their assigned berthing area on the orlop deck, Wilson and his friends formed what Wilson dubbed "The Orlop Deck Debating Society." "Not a question of any moment, not a leading topic of the day, but was discussed in its entirety by these sages of the fire and engine rooms. The situation in China was discussed in its every aspect," Wilson recorded, "as well as the Transvaal" in South Africa.

Wilson most certainly was an anti-imperialist. As for American motives in China, whence the battleship *Oregon* rushed shortly after Wilson joined her in an abortive attempt to arrive in time to assist in the relief of the legations during the Boxer Rebellion, Wilson was exceedingly critical—indeed, very cynical.

The Boxers "raised a revolt, but as in many other cases, how was it repaid?" Wilson asked rhetorically. "At Pekin[g] and Tientsin, houses were looted. Innocent Chinamen were shot down. Any Chinaman in sight, whether friendly or not, was shot. Women and children were killed and ravished. And all this by civilized, enlightened people, the elect of God Almighty. Down with the chin chin joss! Open their heads to *our* religion and civilization. . . . And, incidentally, as a side line, grab a few cities and ports. What hypocrites we are!"

Wilson believed that in the end the great powers "would jump in and take hold of what they could, just as any other footpad [thief] would, simply by the law of force and might." His assessment was not far from correct. The ultimate collapse of the corrupt Qing dynasty and the establishment of a republic in China in 1911 under Sun Yat-sen, as well as the increasing European focus on the arms race at home that was to lead up to World War I, helped avert the ultimate division of China into European/Japanese colonial territories, though the European powers and Japan did carve out "spheres of influence" in that weakened and troubled country.

Wilson also opposed the American involvement in the Philippines, where Emilio Aguinaldo ("Aggie" to Wilson) continued his armed struggle against the imposition of American rule. "Under the name and cloak of protecting our American subjects and interests, we are trying to accumulate more territory," Wilson wrote, "having broken the Constitution of the United States in Porto [*sic*] Rico and the Philippines, not to speak of Guam. And New Jersey. We are rapidly becoming as rapacious and greedy as the mother country (or step mother country), 'Bloomin Hold Hingland.'" The inclusion of New Jersey probably is a reference to the change in corporate laws that facilitated the creation of huge and sprawling monopolies, such as Standard Oil of New Jersey, which was established as a holding company in New Jersey in 1899. It suggests that Wilson also was interested in the domestic political issues of the day.

Wilson was convinced, and correctly, that the efforts expended in the Philippines would not yield concomitant benefits for the United States. "I often wonder about the policy of the Philippines," Wilson recorded, "what use they are to us. They will never pay us for the trouble." This was not a common opinion. As Lt. (and much later Vice Admiral) Albert P. Niblack recorded in May 1899, "I am a warm believer in our guiding star. We will not regret the Philippine wind fall in twenty years from now."[27] The eventual reality was much closer to Wilson's view, with which in a few years President Theodore Roosevelt would come to agree. Following the Japanese defeat of Russia in the Russo-Japanese War of 1904–1905, and the revision and renewal of the Anglo-Japanese alliance in 1905, the balance of military power in the Pacific shifted to favor Japan. In the changed circumstances, the American Philippine territory became a strategic liability. By August 1907 Roosevelt confided to William Howard Taft that strategically the Philippines had become "our heel of Achilles."[28]

The fighting was still going on when Wilson arrived in Manila Bay in December 1899; indeed, the first boat to hail the *New Orleans* upon its arrival in Cavite carried news of the death of Maj. Gen. Henry W. Lawton, killed by a Filipino sharpshooter at San Mateo shortly before the ship's arrival.[29] As the cruiser swung at the hook off Cavite in the weeks that followed, Wilson recorded some U.S. Army operations against the Filipino insurgents. The army was, to use Wilson's phrase, "making the niggers hike." It is informative, too, that Wilson used the now infamous "N word" only to describe Filipinos; nowhere in the text does he apply it to American blacks. One inference that might be derived from this is that he used the term exclusively in a derogatory context. He did not experience those feelings toward his black shipmates, but he did toward our then-enemies, the insurgents; thus for him they were "niggers."

Wilson's observations about the fighting in the Philippines bear haunting parallels with America's later counterinsurgent effort in Vietnam in the 1960s and 1970s. Ashore in Manila, Wilson met an American soldier whom he had known in Baltimore before he joined the navy. "Among other things, he told me . . . [a] Filipino would fire at them and then run and hide his gun and pick up a hoe or something, and be industriously working when you next saw him. The very ones who would carry water for the tired soldiers one day, the next would be fighting against them." "Vietnamese" might easily be substituted for "Filipino" in this passage to describe the method of operation of the Viet Cong local force guerrillas encountered in Vietnam six decades later.

In a distant foreshadowing of the debate over "rules of engagement" in Vietnam, Wilson believed that the U.S. government was being "a little too lenient in dealing with [the insurgents], our troops not being allowed to fire unless fired upon." He concluded, with a cynicism worthy of the 1960s and early 1970s, that "the [McKinley] administration trends toward prolonging the war as there are obvious reasons for doing so. Among other reasons, not by any means the least, are the 'sons of somebody' who hold commissions in the volunteer army drawing fat salaries for comparative[ly] little labor, Army contractors, etc. The men themselves are heartily sick of it, and hail with joy any prospects of getting home again."

Ashore on liberty in Manila, Wilson noted the phenomenon of the appearance of the newly arrived troops, the equivalent of the "FNGS" (f—ing new guys) of the American Vietnam experience: "Dusty looking soldiers from the front were out in force, and also a large sprinkling of a new regiment who had just disembarked a day or so previous[ly], their nice, clean uniforms [were] in sharp contrast with the well worn ones of the men who had been thro' it all and were waiting to get relieved from the fighting for a while."

Wilson even hinted at the possibility of "fragging," a practice that received considerable publicity during the Vietnam War: "Some officer may take a dislike to [an enlisted man] and make it hot for him upon every occasion that offers. 'Officers and gentlemen' are not above those things, you know. Perhaps this same thing would account for the mortality among the officers in the South African war on the British side. Not all these 'sons of somebody' were shot from the front, boldly facing the enemy."

Wilson and his shipmates also watched developments in South Africa, where the Boers were fighting against the British forces. Wilson recorded that "most of us sided with the Boers as any fair minded bluejacket who loves fair play generally sides with the underdog in a fight." The American newspapers, he felt, had sided heavily with the British and paid little attention to the heroism of the Boers. Indeed, Wilson felt the American press coverage of the British in South Africa even eclipsed their coverage of the work of the American forces in the Philippines; he hoped—in vain, it turned out—that some day the heroic deeds of the army in the Philippines would be sung in the American press. In this respect, too, there is some similarity with the American Vietnam experience and the press's perpetuation of grossly inaccurate stereotypical images of Vietnam veterans for many years after the war.

Wilson also decried the fad of aping the British and affecting British accents and mannerisms, a practice popular with a number of senior naval officers of the day. "Everything is English now. Americans find them very good to pattern after. They are the vogue, the criterion in everything. We must cultivate their accent, using a broad 'a,' or else we are an uneducated, uncultured people. Some people forget that we can lead the world in most everything and only show where our weakness lies by imitation. We should stick to America and all things American, and instead of imitating, let others imitate."

For Wilson's keenly perceptive eye, and his willingness to record and preserve his images of our navy on Asiatic Station during the period 1899–1901 we should feel deeply grateful. He has left us a unique, sensitive, and detailed account of life in the Asiatic Fleet that will immeasurably enrich our understanding of our navy, and particularly of enlisted life, a century ago.

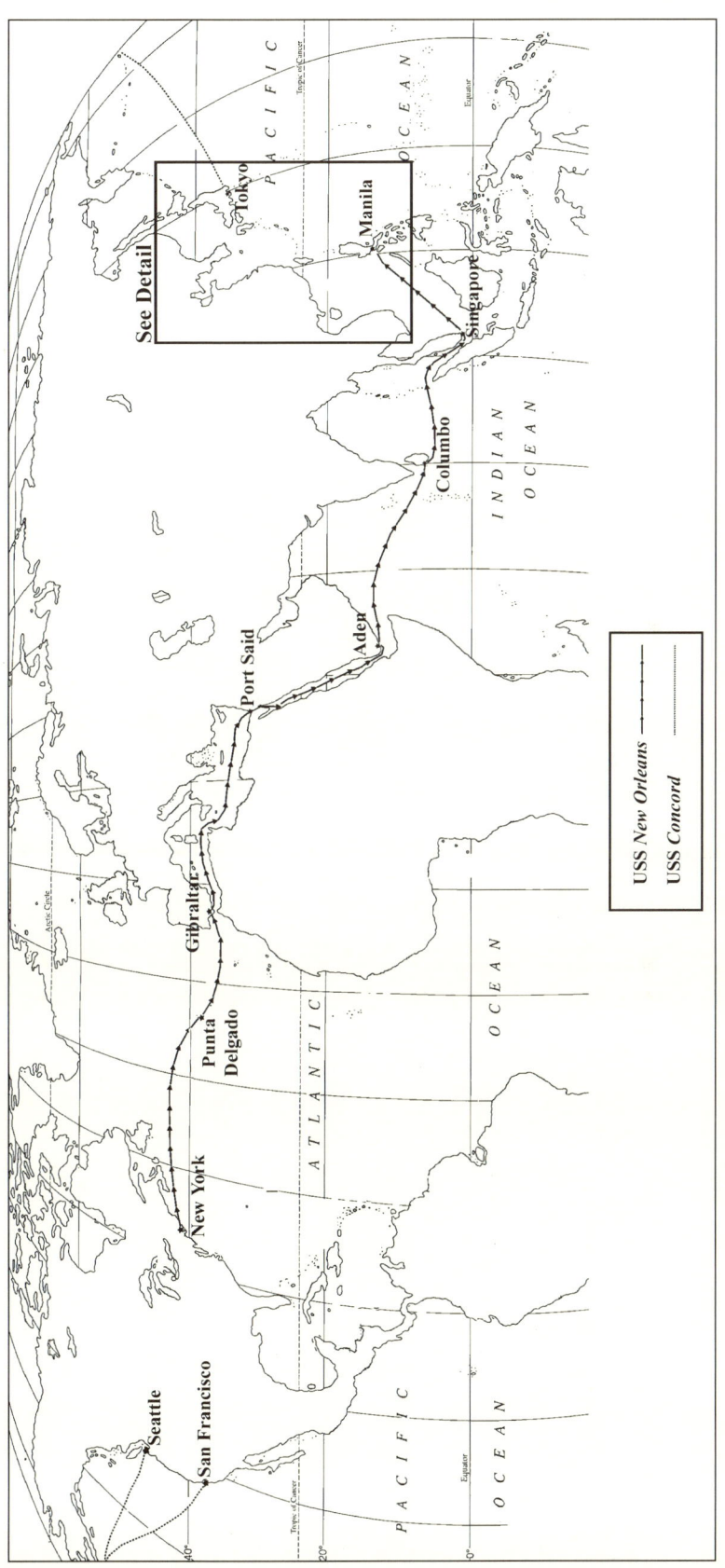

Track of Wilson's cruise to Manila aboard the USS *New Orleans* (1899) and from Japan to San Francisco aboard the USS *Concord* (1901).

Wilson's travels on Asiatic Station, 1899–1901.

PROLOGUE

~

To Asiatic Station

"Holy smoke! What a fierce looking ballyhoo."
"So that's our future home, is it?"
"Yes. That's the lemon peelers' gold brick."
Yes, she was dirty and grimy from the coaling that wasn't yet finished.[1]

FRIDAY, OCT. 20TH 1899

The *New Orleans*, great ship! Was this day transferred from the U.S.S. *Prairie*,[2] a home, if I had only thought so,[3] but all sailors after their first cruise [are] born growlers.[4] It becomes a chronic complaint, so to speak. It is our privilege. I had been cruising all summer on U.S.S. *Prairie*, taking out Naval Reserves from every state that had Naval militia, and we finished up in Boston and was ordered to the New York Navy Yard for a thorough overhauling and to have her guns taken off prior to filling out with exhibits for the Paris Exposition, and it was while lying there that I was (having just two years to serve) sent aboard the *New Orleans*, a ship having a hard name all thro' the navy, and from what I see of her, she deserves it. I, with ten others, [was] sent aboard. My first impulse was to drop my bag & hammock & ditty-box and take to the woods, for I don't believe I ever beheld a ship in a worse condition. Coaling, she was the dirtiest ship I ever beheld.

Well, I went aboard and I never felt so down in the mouth in a long time. One man jumped ship in our draft and stayed away, leaving his bag & hammock aboard. A young lady came to see him just as he was leaving the *Prairie*, and being a fine looking girl and the idea of parting and the looks of the ship and trip before him soon decided him. Can't blame him. Myself, [I] would have probably done the same.

I have got a rough old trip before me. There have been quite a number of desertions from the ship. Some came as far as the dock and then looked at her and sloped (deserted), leaving bags [and] hammocks behind. Others jumped at night. I saw one

1

The USS *New Orleans* about the time of Wilson's service onboard. Navy Historical Foundation.

man grab up a bucket, cross the gangway as if he were a cook dumping slops, and keep on up the yard, where [he] would have no difficulty in getting out the gate.

She is the most uncomfortable ship as far as accommodations are concerned I ever saw. Just imagine sleeping on top of the coal-bunkers, piled in anywhere you can get room, everybody from chief machinist to coal-passer. No place to put your clothes. No place worth speaking of to wash. Then you have an idea of this ship. Well, I have concluded to make the worst [best?] of a bad bargain. Duty is duty, and we can't have our own choice or else nobody would go out in her.

The largest part of the boys from the *Prairie* came aboard on a visiting party to see the ship and us tonight, and gave us the laugh and generally [commiserated with] us who were so unlucky as to catch this ship. Well, I see lots of old shipmates aboard and sailors easily become acquainted. Must make the most of it. Dead tough, tho'. Only consolation I have, I can make quite a little pay day of it. Only wish, tho', I had a chance to bid 'em all good bye up at McGurk's. Am 4th class, to[o], for breaking my liberty 37 hours.[5] Well, let her go.

SATURDAY, OCT. 21ST

Left for the Philippines today at about 3:40 P.M.[6] Finished coaling this morning. The ship's sides haven't even [been] repainted where they were chipped and red leaded, so she presents quite a mottled appearance. [They] wanted to get us out in a hurry.

Prologue

Well, we left with three cheers from the *Chicago*[7] and the *Prairie* which we [answered] from the rails and rigging, and amid a waving of handkerchiefs and hats from those on shore, we slowly dropped away from the dock and under the Brooklyn bridge en route to Manila. Thought we would stop [at] Tompkinsville, S. I. [Staten Island] and clean ship, but instead kept out to sea.[8]

Am getting a little more reconciled and may in time like the ship a great deal better and not find her as black as painted. Had quarters tonight and kept us standing in a cold wind for about three-quarters of an hour. Couldn't hear a word of what was said, but it don't make any difference. Its all right, I guess. Was glad to get below where it wasn't so chilly. Didn't look quite as dismal as before. May get accustomed to it in time.

SUNDAY, OCT. 22ND

Quiet day today. General field day. Crew cleaning ship. Myself and another old water-tender who came aboard the same day and number of the old crew of the engineer's force and men off watch taking it easy, knocking around in dungarees. Easy ship for uniforms, any old thing goes. Collared a locker and put a bottom in it, and stowed some clothes away in it, which I will use instead of breaking out my bag so often. Like her a little better. Might not be so bad after all. Will probably call in at the Rock [Gibraltar] and coal ship again, or else Port Said. We are living pretty good in our mess. Hope we continue so. Plenty of fresh water also, to wash in. That's very good. Will have to write a letter from the Rock to those at home.

MONDAY, OCT. 23RD

Nothing of any moment today. My first day below. Started cleaning the after fire-room, myself and the two other water-tenders of [the] watch. Had trouble pumping out the bilges, full of coal and ashes. The men got their stations at "abandon ship" today, all but the second section (to which I belong). They remained below on watch. Had "setting up drill" and "double quick." "Hoochie Coochie" run around. This sort of thing makes us all weary. As if the engineer force doesn't get enough exercise without that! This is the first time I have had it in four years. No wonder so many men jumped. Found K——'s ditty box tonight (the lad that jumped from our draft) and appropriated its contents as spoils of war. Gave the box to the water-tender who came aboard the same day I did and kept [pair] of scissors for myself. Will have to look around for his bag. No use letting anybody else have it. He would like to see his old shipmates get it, sooner than any stranger. Well, sorry he didn't have nerve enough to make the trip. It is getting considerably warmer. We are no doubt in the Gulf Stream, doing pretty good speed with two boilers, about 10 or 11 knots, 75 and 80 revolutions of the engines. Very good indeed, a nice speed to travel at without forcing.

Prologue

TUESDAY, OCT. 24TH

Nothing of any note today. Weather has been very mild. Looks like a slight blow tonight. Had fire quarters and collision drill. Missed both of those functions as my division was on watch below. The third section is catching it all this week. Pretty nearly all a new crew. I suppose that is the reason they are having all of these drills in a bunch. Was working all day cleaning and fixing a bilge strainer. Same old disgusting job I have had many a time before. Funny they can't build a man-o-war in which they can get a perfect suction from the bilges. One of the most important things on a ship is to keep bilges pumped dry. We are still bowling along at the same old gait.

WEDNESDAY, OCT. 25TH

Pretty heavy seaway running for the last twenty four hours. The *New Orleans* behaves very good, despite the reports I have heard to the contrary. I should judge people on this side are prejudiced because she is English built, built originally for the Brazilian government, by an English firm. She was purchased at the outbreak of the Spanish-American War by our Government. Of course, almost everything in her is different as regards machinery and all spare parts would have to come from England. It struck me as funny to see all the valves, etc., marked in Portuguese. I feel still as if I am on a Dago cruiser. At [Meridian (noon)] today we had reeled off 920 miles. As we are on a direct course, we will pass the Azores about 1200 more miles, and then straight to Gibraltar. Some of the crew felt rather tired today, I noticed, and indisposed. Haven't their sea legs on as yet. Bet they will be seasoned by the time we reach the Philippines. Turned out of my hammock this morning and went aft on the berth deck near the entrance to the engine-room hatch. Got there just in time to get under a sea that broke over the waist from the port side. She certainly can take over a lot of water. Sea is moderating now [considerably]. Hope I have a better night's sleep than last night. Never heard such an infernal racket as they made last night calling the watch. Most of the crew are "rookies," or recruits, and they must imagine when they are awake that every other mother's son is the same. I had the satisfaction of rebuking them in a forcible way and then rolled over as well as I could in my hammock to secure what few hours of sleep remained before all hands were called. Oh yes, there is plenty of comfort in going to sea. Give me the land, tho' in mine. I can read about it in Russell's[9] or Marryat's[10] novels, lying back in an easy chair after I get this cruise done.

THURSDAY, OCT. 26TH

Well, we ran right into it today. Been shipping seas continually. Fire room, bilges are full of water, and all strainers were so choked up with coal and ashes that they cannot be pumped dry. Been working at 'em all day with no success. Still, we are making good headway. But its pretty rough, all right. I believe we shall lay over at Algiers for

Prologue

repairs. Well, we need 'em badly as we were hurried off half finished. Still, she is a better boat than I thought, for from all accounts she was a floating hell and caused more desertions than any ship in our navy. She is uncomfortable and there are no accommodations of any sort. After putting this run in on her a man can stand anything. Sleeping on cold iron isn't conducive to health tho', and you cannot sleep in a hammock. The decks are sloppy & slushy from shipping seas. Altogether, she is most damned uncomfortable.

SATURDAY, OCT. 28TH

Nothing out of the common run happened yesterday. I go on watch from 6 to 8 P.M. They are putting on an extra boiler in a hurry to reach St. Michael's, I believe, in the Azores, for coal. Had the usual trouble this morning with the bilges. Same old story. Scrubbed and washed a few pieces of clothes yesterday. That's one of the most important items on shipboard, keeping yourself clean. I pity these poor "rookies."[11] When they first come aboard a ship they do not know in the least how to take care of themselves. They present a most dismal appearance. They are not used to the food nor anything else. In fact, the navy is something entirely different from what they imagine it is. I remember my own experience when I lived for two months on "Government straight."[12] It was something fierce. Also on the *Minneapolis*[13] during the war, when nearly all of us would "cork" off on the decks with nothing but a piece of newspaper under us and our shoes for a pillow. The eight hours we were off watch seemed like so many minutes, and the four on seemed about twenty-four. And then the grub and the water. It was a break to get a drink of cool water. I never wish to undergo the same discomfort again, nor would I for a thousand, if I knew such was the case again. I don't [respect] an administration that feeds its soldiers and sailors on [Eaganized] beef,[14] etc. But I suppose it is human nature to make all they can for themselves whilst they have the opportunity. Still, I [do] not do much growling about what is past. I have only to do with present ills or joys as the case may be in this journal, in which shall be recorded honestly events of this cruise as they take place.

SUNDAY, OCT. 29TH

Still bowling merrily along. Went on watch yesterday afternoon at 4 P.M. Had my first introduction by connecting the 3rd boiler. Something new to me to be working under blowers all the time, but it has to be done on this ship as [there] is no direct ventilation from the deck. Had quarters this morning and kept us standing at attention for three quarters of an hour before retreat sounded. This seems entirely different from any man-o-war I was ever on. In fact, she is different. The officers don't seem to have the same smart, natty appearance as most I have been with. There is a vast difference somewhere.

Prologue

MONDAY, OCT. 30TH

This is a regular home. Who'd leave her? At last I have found the only ship where it is possible for a bluejacket in the navy to be contented. After coping for four solid, long, and weary hours below from 4 to 8, then to come up on deck and do the jumping jack act for nearly another hour. As if a man didn't get all the exercise he needed below, especially a poor devil of a fireman or coal-passer, not to speak of the water-tender.[15] This is the first ship I was ever in where they depend on blower engines for all their draft. When your blowers break down, down goes the steam. And the horrible racket these blowers make sounds like quarry crushers. I'll be deaf before I am done with this ship. Its all right for me tho', I can mount a soap box and keep out of the way of the bilge water and floating floor plates and coal buckets and such gear, and take a squint at the water-glass, but not so the firemen and coal passers. They have to work right in it.

It has been a continual roll all the way out. They say, who know, that she will roll while moored to a dock, but I rather doubt that. But at any rate, I picked myself up off the deck last night where the rolling flung me. I thought I was on the *Indiana* and heard the roar of the secondary battery. [I] came to [and] I found out it was paymaster's stores, hard tack cans, canned willy or beef, and all kinds of canned stuff had come adrift, and spilled all over the deck.[16] It woke old Jack up also, who was in his hammock. Old Jack thinks he won't hold out in this ship as his lungs are not in the best of condition. The blower in the fire-room don't agree with him and he is rather timid about the ship also, having heard so many tales about it. Still, we can manage to exist thro' the run. Then it might be a little easier altho' they run the blowers both at sea and in port. Well, we hope for the best, altho' I think if all the ships in the navy were like this one it would be a hard matter to man them.

WEDNESDAY, NOV. 1ST

Yesterday just one year ago I shipped on the *Minneapolis* (or re-shipped) at League Island, then lying in reserve.[17] Yesterday we dropped anchor in Porto La Garda,[18] island of St. Michael's, Azores, a Portuguese settlement, coaling station. I came off watch at 8 A.M. and was, with 3 others, put in charge of the coaling. The natives were to place it aboard and stow it. We [were] to see it done properly. Well it was a red hot time. I never want to see the like again. We got thro' at 2:30 this morning, [having] put aboard 500 tons. Soon as the natives came aboard then the crew commenced to get full and, of course, it wound up in the usual way: a free fight for all. What started the scrap, I went below and found in a top bunker two men who were stowing. Instead of stowing it properly, they had built walls with lump coal and would then bank coal up against it so as to look as if the bunker was full. The other bluejacket along with me, being half-full [half-drunk], let a roar out of him at this and chased them out the bunker. When they got on deck, they resumed argument and finally

Prologue

went at it. Then began a general mix-up between some of our crew and the Portuguese, in which shovels, fists, and lumps of coal were freely used. No one was seriously hurt, but fully an hour [passed] before they would resume operations, and then only by dint of hard coaxing and driving by the bosses.

Well, we started off again and was fairly under way once more when one of the poor devils poked his head thro' the bunker hole and was hit in the face with a lump of coal and knocked out. Then commenced the same trouble over again, and so it continued all thro' the night. I never was so glad to get thro' a job in my life. Then, to cap the climax, just to show how they appreciate labor on a man of war, after turning in in my clothes full of coal dust, they sent for me to turn to at 4 A.M. to get some coal down that was left over and would not go in the bunkers. But I distinctly refused. I said I would see the doctor first, about having some rest, whether it was required or not after 24 hours hard, solid work. Well, they let us alone.

This is an old, picturesque looking place in the style of all Portuguese or Spanish towns. It looks very old. They are rebuilding the breakwater, where it was washed down by the sea. All the buildings are square and painted white, or a sort of a banana color, with green blinds, and it rises right out of the sea and has a number of vineyards and plantations on the surrounding hills.

They done a lot of our crew up who went ashore and no doubt they deserved it. One or two were seriously cut up. Yes, there is no doubt the *New Orleans* is a home, to those who like her. But I don't. And I doubt if I ever will.

FRIDAY, NOVEMBER 3RD

Got underway from St. Michael's yesterday morning at 10 A.M. Our next stop is Port Said at the entrance of the Suez Canal. That's if our coal will carry us that far. [We] were to go to Algiers, but received notice of a bubonic plague there. American Consul's representative [was] aboard yesterday with a Portuguese wine-shop keeper. Wanted to identify some of the boys who broke some of his windows and did other damage. Well, he caught them: 1 cadet, 1 ensign, 1 warrant officer, and a couple of enlisted men. So you see, it is not always the enlisted Jack that is a rowdy and a bully. $1 or $2 of our money covered all damages.

Well, I don't like this ship any better by any means. I have pains across my back from lying on cold iron. There is positively no accommodation aboard this "hooker" whatever.[19] No place to wash your clothes, and I never was so dirty in any other ship I was in as this. You get full of oil, grease, coal dirt blown around the fireroom by the blower engines. It is something fierce. Never saw the like. If I finish my cruise aboard this one I shall be good and sick of the navy. No use of a man putting in his life without any of the comforts that go to making up life. A convict gets better food, and better sleeping quarters than are to be obtained in this ship. I am more and more disgusted every day.

SATURDAY, NOV. 4TH

General field day today. Scrubbed hammocks. Had a fierce old time finding mine. When I did find it, somebody had wiped their feet all over it. You can't imagine what trouble that small piece of canvas is, and how difficult it is to scrub it when there [are] about 400 men and boys beside yourself all engaged at the same time. It is only a farce serving out clean hammocks on this ship as they are just as dirty five minutes after you get 'em, as the ones you turn in. You can't keep clean on this ship. Impossible to do so. The moment you step below you get filthy. The blowers in the firerooms only help to stir the dust and fling oil around over everything. Still, they say the longer you stay, the better you will like it.

I think, myself, the first 4 years are the hardest. After that if you re-ship on her you must like it. No way to keep clean. No place to sleep. I can't kick about food tho', our mess is doing pretty well. I have fared worse in that respect many a time. They gave us a bit of infantry drill yesterday morning, about one hour's worth. [If there's] anything [that] makes me weary it's that, especially when you are mixed up with a lot of rookies. "Fours right," and "fours wrong," generally the latter. Why don't they drill "rookies" in an "awkward squad"? That's wot I'd like to know. If *She* had saw me then with the look of patient resignation and disgust on this classic "Phiz" of mine, she would have gave me the "horse laugh" for fair.[20] The idea of a first-class pettyofficer getting rawhided around with an awkward squad! Bah! Decidedly it is tough. Somebody swiped three or four [pairs of] socks from a fellow's bag and he is making the air extremely blue. Those are some of the things you have to contend with.

SUNDAY, NOV. 5TH

Had general muster this morning; that is, all the men are mustered aft on the quarterdeck and as their names are called, they answer with their respective ratings, and walk around the deck in front of the officers and captain. This is called "going 'round the stick" or mast.

Well we have had pretty smooth weather since leaving St. Michael's and as I write this, we are going up the Straits of Gibraltar. We are now flying signals for the Rock. I hardly think we [will] stop unless for orders, or to send a cablegram. We have just [passed] the entrance to Trafalgar Bay, where Nelson won his immortal victory over the combined fleets of France and Spain.[21] It is now between three and four bells [between 5:30 and 6 P.M.] in the evening, and this ship has stopped rolling for the first time since leaving New York. Here in the Strait the water is like a millpond.

I just witnessed a most beautiful sunset, the land of Italian skies far off on the port quarter. I can discern the light around which you go to the Bay of Biscay. All this is historical land, the land of romance. We can just see the Rock of the Lion in the distance. I shall go up on deck and take a good view of everything.

Prologue

MONDAY, NOV. 6TH

Well, I did go up on the deck and take a look, but it was nearly dark then before reaching the Rock. We passed it about 7:30. We could only see the lights of the garrison and town and only discern dimly thro' the darkness the form of the peak. Many were disappointed at not passing in the daytime, as they may not get an opportunity of seeing the greatest fortress in the world again for years; perhaps never, as some will come back to the States by way of "'Frisco." Well, we are gliding up the Mediterranean, and it is very smooth. We expect to continue straight to Port Said at the entrance to the Suez Canal, expect to reach there by [Saturday] or Sunday next. Have the mid-watch this week and it will about carry us thro' the Mediterranean. I should like to stop over at Naples and get a glimpse of the bay.

TUESDAY, NOV. 7TH

Put on a new boiler, C, last night. Think they are going to let one die out. Still jogging along at the same old gait. Nothing of any note or out of the common takes place. Same old routine for us: after coming out of a dirty, close, badly ventilated fire-room where, if a blower stops from any cause it will almost roast one, we are taken on deck for "monkey drill," or other drills, and kept standing around nearly all the forenoon or afternoon, where we should be taking what rest we can. Instead, on this ship they make things just as uncomfortable as possible. What sleep you get is broken and troubled at best and your bed is a blanket thrown upon the tops of the bunkers. God knows what it will be when we strike hot weather. The weather still holds fair and is pleasant.

WEDNESDAY, NOV. 8TH

Nothing of any note taking place. Time fully occupied in routine of the ship, and right here a word in regard to that routine will not come amiss, that is, by the engineer's force or "black gang" as they are known by those on deck. And right here let me observe that the "black gang" is generally looked down upon and despised by the rest of the crews of all men of war. Even the Personnel Bill will not do away with the distinction between Line and Staff.[22] I, being a member of the despised "black gang," will state right here that there are more duties connected with, and more brains to be found in, the force below than on deck, by a long shot. There are not so many foreigners below, very few "Square heads" (as all Scandinavians are known) as in the force on deck where most of the seamen are of that race, mostly all Swedes, Norwegians, or Russian Finns.

The duties of the men below "who feed the fires" and look after the great engines with [their] myriads of valves and pipes, manifolds and pumps, are very onerous.

Prologue

Machinists, water-tenders, oilers, etc. have their hands full and if they make a mistake it is generally a serious one. All the work in a ship now-a-days is below; there are only a few seamen required on the modern man-o-war. The rest of the crew, except Gunners mates and all idlers, as the Carpenter's mates, painters, etc., are known, are generally employed scrubbing paint work, decks, etc., all engaged in keeping the ship clean. That is their work outside of their drill.

The engineer's force is divided into three watches, or sections. First, second and third sections of the engineer's division. They take their respective watches in rotation. Say the first section has the four to eight, the second has the eight to twelve. The third the twelve to four. Four hours below and eight hours off. At least it is supposed to be off, but you are mostly always occupied by drill or something else. The section that comes off watch last is known as the second relief, and if it happens to be the four to eight coming off at 8 in the morning, they are generally drilled all the morning, either at the great guns, boat or infantry drill. Well, in this ship they keep us at it nearly all the time.

I am in the second section and this week I have the mid-watch, i.e., twelve to four. You get two sleeps on this watch: from hammocks until about 11:45 when you are called, and from 4 to 7 A.M., or six bells, when you are relieved at 4 A.M. in the morning. It is the most miserable watch on board ship. After breakfast, or "mess gear," comes quarters. Sometimes we are dismissed, then we are off until 11:30, or 7 bells, when we eat, change, and go below at 12:00. After coming off at 4:00 in the afternoon, we go to quarters, have "setting up" drill and double time around the ship. That occupies about three-quarters of an hour.

Today after breakfast we had quarters at 9:30 A.M. After quarters we had fire quarters, which was repeated. Then came "abandon ship." That occupied all this morning. We are gaining about 20 min. per day, so we were just dismissed in time to eat and go below, having no time to ourselves. That's the way it is all the time on this "wagon." They make it hot for us all right. No wonder so many men run away; there is no rest for us. We have got to get almost knocked out below and then come on deck and get "raw hided" all the time we should have off. Your eight hours off is only a farce in this boat. Well, it will be so hot after a while that some will have to go on the sick list, but time will tell.

We have just passed a beautiful island here in the Mediterranean. I must find out the name. Quite a high peak to it, and thickly inhabited.

THURSDAY, NOV. 9TH

Since we entered the Straits of Gibraltar every thing has been smooth sailing, hardly a ripple on the surface of the water. Weather very fair. Nothing but calm skies and magnificent sunset effects. All is serene. Well, we had the same old thing again this day. Came off watch, went to quarters, mustered aft and listened to the reading of a court-martial, the first since leaving New York. The man was caught smuggling liquor aboard. Serious offense on a man-o-war. Listened to the finding of that. Then they sprung "general quarters" on us. We of the second section being first relief had to "stand fast" and there we toed the seam[23] from 9:30 A.M. until 11:30. Retreat [went] just in time for us to eat, change, and get below in time. Talk about your ship for drill. This "Portuguese hooker"[24] beats the old Nick.[25]

Had plum duff[26] for dinner, and coffee. Nothing else. And we had to bolt that in order to get below in time. Yesterday I forgot to mention they had "bag inspection." That is, the bags of the men were brought up on deck and inspected by their division officers to see if they had everything required and that they were clean, neatly rolled up and "stopped," that is, tied on the ends of each roll with what are known as clothes stops, pieces of cord or strong twine.[27] Everything has to be extremely neat. Yes, they always have something up their sleeve for us. Boilers are acting a bit cranky. Engines are lifting water over just enough to make us water-tenders keep on the hop all the time. And then the same old dirt. Am taking two baths a day, and can't keep clean at that.

Held auction on deck today. Sold the contents of the "Lucky Bag," men's clothing and different articles that belonged to men who deserted, etc., or else was found adrift around the decks and confiscated by "Jimmy Legs" (the Chief Master-at-Arms). Articles like that are merely bid for in a nominal way. Everything goes for a few cents, and the proceeds go toward the Hospital fund. Thus, "Legs" will hold up probably an old shirt, flat cap, [pair of] shoes, mattress cover, etc., in a jumble and ask "How much?" Somebody starts it at 10 cts, raised to 15 cts, or 25 perhaps, but not over. Very rarely exceeds that sum. It is optional with the master-at-arms to throw them to the first bidder, or any man who comes and tells him he has lost just such an article. If there is an article similar in the "lucky bag," he will get it. If you have anything and it is found around the deck it goes in the "bag," if by carelessness. You must go to the officer of the deck to get it, and then you are put on the report. For instance, a great many cases are late hammocks. If not off the deck in the allotted time, in they go.

FRIDAY, NOV. 10TH

A little better this morning. We were dismissed about 4 bells [10 A.M.] from quarters after having "setting up" exercises. Well! Well! We were dismissed this evening at quarters without any "setting up drill" and the run around. Wonder what is going to take place. Must have something up his sleeve for us. I believe he will give us the "wig-wag" or signal drill before long.

SATURDAY, NOV. 11TH

General field day today, cleaning up ship for tomorrow's inspection. That's where the deck hands come in. That's all they are needed for outside of their drill. The ability to handle a swab and sling a 6–0 paint brush is the full requirement of seamen on the man-o-war of today.

Prologue

We are rolling considerably. Quite a swell on. Plates, coffee kettles, and everything loose sliding around deck. Just now a landsman [is] over in the port passageway gathering up tins of hard tack and other stuff that scattered all over the alleyway. Came off at 4 P.M. and go on again at 8 P.M., the other two sections have the dog watches this week.[28] Glad we are done with the 12 to 4 as it is a miserable watch. No drill of any kind today.

SUNDAY, NOV. 12TH

Dropped anchor here in Port Said about 11:35 A.M. Beautiful weather. Was immediately surrounded by Arab bum-boatmen of all description with all kind of wares to sell.[29] But you can get just as much and just as cheap in New York. They are all rascals and swarm all over the ship. Keeps Jimmy Legs busy chasing them with a club. The kids over on the other bank swim out to the ship and dive for small coin[s].

Received news that the *Brooklyn* went thro' this port Friday. We will stay here about four or five days. Ready to coal ship now. I am on auxiliary[30] watch this week. That lets me out of the coaling; am glad of that as it is a most miserable job.

The dog men [bum boat men illicitly selling alcohol] are in their glory selling bottles of gin, Jamaica rum, etc.[31] The gang will be full of booze tonight. Took several snap-shots of some of the Arabs. Quite picturesque. Just came down from the spar deck; was listening to the music played alongside by three Italians, 2 quite pretty girls and a man. They sang and played and reaped quite a harvest. Their singing was of the indifferent quality. Just over on the shore, about a hundred yards distant, we were treated to quite an acrobatic performance by four boys, one very small and an excellent acrobat. He is losing time here. Wonder some enterprising manager hasn't picked him up. He is excellent and I know what I am talking of in that line, as I have practiced considerably myself.[32]

It is dark now. Everything looks strange. The buildings are outlined in silhouette against a narrow ribbon of gold along the horizon. There is something in every strange land I see that brings an indefinite feeling of sadness over me, and I long for I know not what. Not homesickness, surely, for I have been long accustomed to being away from those ties. I suppose it is the streak of melancholy in my make up, always longing, always hoping for something better, a dream of the future. Will it ever be realized?

Quite a large liberty party has just left the ship. Nobody knows when they get liberty in this ship, and they don't see anything of the towns. Just get drunk. That is all.

MONDAY, NOV. 13TH. PORT SAID

Native Arabs coaled ship today. I took several snap-shots at them. They were all small sized men, but they can carry the load of a Mexican burro. They are like the burros in that they also have drivers. They carry about 70 lbs of coal on their shoulders in a basket, and go at a dog trot all day; great endurance. But they are just as touchy as the

Prologue

Portuguese at St. Michael's at Punta Delgado, but the difference in the work they do is largely in favor of the Arabs of Port Said. The crew, or part of them, got liberty last night, and the other parts go tonight. I don't go. Am 3rd class; broke my liberty in N.Y. for the first time in over 3 years, and I haven't any kick coming. Lots of dog men around today. All kinds of curios for sale, but as we are outward bound, I am not on the buy. It will be different when we are homeward bound. Haven't rec'd any news of the Jeffries-Sharkey fight yet.[33] A large German steamship came in today and proceeded thro' the canal. Immediately after, an English cruiser followed close at her heels, thus confirming a rumor we heard early this morning that the cruiser was lying in wait for a German ship supposed to be filibustering for the Boers,[34] but why she would go thro' the Suez is unaccountable. It took my suspicion all the same.

Well, we finished coaling today. I did not have charge, [Wilson had been in charge of coaling in the Azores] and glad of it, altho' they finished in good time. Am glad I am on auxiliary watch. The same acrobats and the four Italian musicians were around again this afternoon at mess gear and reaped another small harvest, but the man who does the largest biz is the man (dog man) who sells his bad whisky, gin and rum on the quiet. They are adepts at [it] all right. Will soon leave here now, and I may never come back by way of the Suez again. There is no routine to this ship. It is the worst I have ever experienced. I shall drop a few cards home to let 'em know I am thinking of them.

TUESDAY, NOV. 14TH

Busy cleaning ship today, and are going to paint ship, as we left New York with the sides of the ship unpainted, and this is the first opportunity we have had. Will pull out of here tomorrow A.M. perhaps. Just rec'd news of the Sharkey-Jeffries prize fight. Quite a number of encounters on this ship last night, as the booze was getting it its fine work. Lots of it aboard, so I don't care whether I can go ashore or not. It helps relieve the monotony of the ship. I believe there is liberty for men who have not been ashore and are entitled to go, that is, classed men who have jumped or come up a class. I have jumped a class myself. Will have to find out if I am in it. This is a queer ship.

Well, apropos of that, I believe I secured a good bargain in a curio today. I bought two Turkish fez's, 3 oxydized silver bracelets in antique style of old Egyptian style, a paperweight of olive wood from Jerusalem, and a book of flowers of the Holy Land with olive wood back. Paid 9 shillings for the lot. Would not take $10 for the book of pressed flowers, as they are fine. They ask all sorts of prices here, and you give 'em just about one third what they ask. They try to do you in every way. If you get mixed up in the different moneys in vogue here, they give you the wrong change every time. They are all rogues. The most of the stuff they have for sale is all cheap, tawdry articles that you can buy in New York very cheap. It is well enough to buy curios that are representative of the country, and not too much of them, especially on an outward bound voyage, as you have no place to keep such articles. I'll do all right coming home. They do anything for money here, are a nest of beggars. The boys swim out to the ship and dive for small pieces of silver and always contrive to get what they dive for. You find it very interesting to look and size up everything even if you are kept aboard ship.

WEDNESDAY, NOV. 15TH

Well, we are getting steam up to get underway from this port at about 6 or 7 P.M. Took in all fresh water this morning. Primed furnaces and started fires on my watch, 8 to 12. I rather like this for its novelty and the stir about it. When those Arab peddlers come aboard, they turn the port side of the spar deck into a regular bazaar. What with their chattering and gesticulation, the noise reminds one of a lot of parrots. They are not backward in charging all sorts of prices, and as I said before, come down about two thirds. They are worse than Jews. In fact, nearly all the articles they sell are made by the Jews in Jerusalem and surrounding places, and the cheap tinsel stuff are of cheap French manufacture, such as beads, mirrors, soap boxes, pipes, etc., nothing genuinely Oriental about them. They charge more for those cheap articles than you would pay in New York or any American city. The dates you buy are fresh, the oranges are more lemon than anything else. The cigarettes are good, but quite a different flavor from ours. All the underwear, towels, etc., are just what you would expect to find in a second-hand Jew shop. There is an old cobbler here who goes around to different ships in a small boat, rowed by a boy. This boat is his workshop.

Well, I am perfectly disgusted with the drunks on this ship. As soon as they get a drink or two, they want to fight their friends and everybody else, just to see how hard they can hit. They mostly always know the men they pick out as easy marks. Lots more men jump ship and go ashore than are in the actual liberty parties.

Yes, I have been thinking seriously that the navy is no good. You have no privacy. You are thrown into contact with lots of roughs. The 5 years I have been in the service has been a continual fight and trouble. Lots of drunks in the passage-way are wrangling now. It makes me dead tired, and weary, and what's worse, I used to be just as drunk and quarrelsome myself. But I am getting over all that now. I think I shall have to buy some views from some of the peddlers, as I have seen some very good ones suitable for framing.

The *Nashville* is here and has just finished coaling.[35] She is also ordered to Manila. The *Marietta* has not shown up yet.[36] We passed her, I believe, the night we passed thro' Gibraltar. They are both good little boats and do very good time.

THURSDAY, NOV. 16TH

Left Port Said at 8:30 last night and started thro' the canal, one of the most perfect sights I believe I ever beheld. They talk about Egyptian darkness, but last night belied it. A perfect full moon [was] in the heavens. It was a night to make one think of

Prologue

home, and quiet moonlight rambles with your best girl. Instead, we are 5000 miles from home, and it knocks all the romance out of a fellow when he has to go below and face the music for four long hours amid stifling coal dust, dripping hot oil from blower engines, and howls from the machinist on watch for more steam, etc. Yes, it knocks all the sentiment out of a fellow.

Well, today as I write this we are going thro' the canal yet. It is a wonderful, vast undertaking. You are amazed at the magnitude of this feat of engineering. [On e]very side are desert lands, with [no] human habitations except signal stations, few and far between. Nothing but telegraph poles, two lines of 'em stretched along the right bank of the canal coming from Port Said. We have tied up for several ships to pass us, and one, or rather two, passed us just at 12:30, after I came off watch, one an Englishman from Glasgow and the other a big Russian troop-ship going home, I suppose, as her decks were lined with soldiers. We are going thro' at a pretty good speed, about 10 or 11 knots in some places. Where the canal runs thro' a body of water called Bitter Lake, we speeded up as much as possible. The channel is marked off with buoys similar to any other channel. The stations are very pretty places and neatly taken care of.

Have been on deck since writing the last, as we were nearing the end of the canal [and I] wanted to see all that was taking place. Nothing in sight for a while, but the banks of clay, sun-baked, and the desert. Was watching a camel train slowly leaving a little village near Suez, and the Arabs and camels presented the same dusty, muddy look as the landscape, children and men in rags that looked as if they laid in the soil and wallowed around, mud huts, men, children, women and camels all lying around. Also along the banks Arabs [were] working repairing the embankment in places.

And at last Suez came in sight. It looks to be about 9 miles distant from the canal and [there] is quite a mountain behind it. Another sheet of water separates from the canal embankment. Further along toward the end as we came out into the Red Sea, are lots of dredging and the works of the company. There is quite a grove of trees along the waterfront, and from there stretches a long road, all made of ground, to the village of Suez. Looking at Suez thro' a glass [telescope], some of the houses are very old and some are very modern. But it is all very picturesque. I noticed a number of boats that looked like floating pavilions out in the mouth of the canal, noticed a small yellow flag on them, and judge they are floating hospitals.[37]

Well, we are underway again and at last in the dreaded Red Sea that is disliked by all firemen and everybody that has to work below. But it is excellent weather now, quite chilly for this climate, and if it just stays as cool as this, there isn't any kick coming on that score. This is holy land, or water, here. We will cross the part of this sea where Moses led the Jews across from the clutches of the pursuing Pharaoh. Our next stop no doubt will be Aden, Arabia [Yemen], there again to coal ship. I believe we are going to have a tough old run with this coal we got at Port Said, as it isn't very good and all the life is taken out of it by lying exposed to the sun so long. If it is no good, it will be hard for us all below, especially for coal passers and firemen.

Prologue

And here a word about these two ratings will not come amiss. An inexperienced young fellow generally ships as a coal passer in the navy rather than a landsman, as the pay is more, being $22 per month, and the landsman only $16. The [civilian] person hasn't anything but the idea that all a bluejacket has to do is to look neat and just drill. He will be much wiser when he reads this. When on watch, his duties consist of getting out, or passing, coal to his firemen, and in some ships it is no snap to handle 40 or 45 buckets of coal, each weighing about 145 or 150 pounds, in a temperature of perhaps 150° to 175°,[38] & has to haul the ashes from the ash pans and load and send up buckets of ashes. He is put to work also at cleaning bilge strainers when they become clogged up with coal dirt and ashes. At times he is put on the fires when a fireman plays out. He has to stow coal in the bunkers when they coal ship. Has to go in the [secured] boilers and knock off scale and scrape out mud, and scale and clean out bilges in port. [He has to] scrub paintwork and paint, clean off pumps, polish bright work, and do any work he may be put at. [He] goes in the back connections of the boilers and cleans out the soot and ashes from there and also in the smoke pipe, [and] any old place that is hard to get at and is dirty. It is hard and awful dirty work and it is work that is never done. If he has any time off, he is at drill, either in the battalion [ship's landing force] or any other drill as the case may be.

You have to wash your own clothes and you must be clean for inspection. All this and more a fireman or coal passer has to do. For this he gets a magnificent $22 per month, 20 cents off for hospital dues, and his ration which, as served out by the Government will not be sufficient to keep him alive, and he always puts $2 or $3 extra in his mess per month. Buys his own clothes, which cost more than they are worth, and there is just about enough left for a good drunk the first chance ashore. After a while, if a good man, a coal passer will get rated to fireman, 2nd class, $30 per month[;] and then fireman, 1st class, $35[;] oiler, $37 (second class petty officer)[;] water tender $40 (first class petty officer). I worked up to the last named rating. That's about as high as the majority ever reaches. The higher the rating, the more trouble.

FRIDAY, NOV. 17TH

Port Said, with its acrobats, its money changers, Arab fruit and date sellers, curio venders, Italian music girls, and cosmopolitan population and Oriental picturesqueness is but a memory of yesterday, just as I suppose the very pretty Italian guitar player is in the minds of some of our susceptible bluejackets. The little rogue, how demure and coquettish! She would gaze at me over the edge of the umbrella she held up to receive the offerings of coins, and what a sweet smile she would bestow upon the Jackie who would drop a half crown or coins of a larger denomination in the umbrella. Yes, all that is a pleasant memory, but I noticed the little rascal would smile only in proportion to the size of the coin. "Monee! Monee! Pay! Pay!" I'll bet she stirred more than one pulse to beating harder by her bright glances and pretty ways than by all the music she or the rest rendered, which in the language of the modern man-o-warsman, "was decidedly on the bum."

I forgot to mention we finished painting the ship's sides at Port Said, and she looks considerably better now. Also had a fight the other night on deck, between an Irish water-tender and [a] colored coal-passer who is cooking for the coal-passers' mess. The water tender was full [drunk] and in a fighting humor and was after the other fellow all day, thinking he had an easy mark. At last it became unbearable and they adjourned on deck. It took the coal-passer about 2 minutes to knock the big thickhead out. I was glad he got his just deserts. I always like to see a bully and a [blackguard] knocked out. There are lots more would-be toughs who deserve the same fate. So far, they have contrived to pick out cripples and old men to get a reputation on. They always almost invariably make an awful howl when instead of licking their man they get licked themselves. They are an awful lot of curs. Nearly every ship in the navy has its full quota of such scum.

Well, we are now bowling right merrily along thro' the Red Sea. It is decidedly warmer today, and we have changed the uniform from blue to white. [We] are falling back in the routine again. Food is getting scarce, had to fall back on government straight [rations] for dinner today. Hard tack and canned willie. Of all the vile stuff in the world, I should judge naval canned beef is the worst. It is known familiarly by the name of "Canned Willie." That and canned mutton, canned sausage, canned ham, etc., as served to us, is something fierce. I couldn't eat it at first, and I have never acquired a taste for it. Cooks try to make 'em palatable in every way, in rope yarn stew, blanket stew, hash, meat balls, but no go. It still retains the same old flavor. Poor Willie! It has been cursed and damned and the manufacturer or inventor of it has been consigned along with it to h[ell] for a diet unlimited numbers of times. But it still holds forth as the staple article along with "salt horse."[39] At this moment, the master-at-arms just passed the word for the engineers force to draw "small stores and clothing." [I] am only down for 2 bars of soap this month. Well, I will just hop aft and get 'em.

SATURDAY, NOV. 18TH

Getting warmer and warmer every day. If it keeps up this weather, the Red Sea will have nobly upheld its reputation as the hottest sea of all. Nothing of any note today. Usual routine.

SUNDAY, NOV. 19TH

Weather is getting fearfully warm. Beginning to tell on the men below. Had articles of war read to us on the quarterdeck today. The uniform was dress white. Just imagine men coming off of the 4 to 8 watch below, as black as [chimney] sweeps with coal dust and perspiration. Then to take a bath in a crowded wash room where one can hardly turn around, and if you are cleaned, someone who is not will rub against you and dirty you up in spots. Then to get at your bag and break out a spotless white uniform for quarters. Why, it's almost an impossibility to keep the body clean in this ship, let alone white dress. Never heard of such a thing, especially on steaming watches at sea, and that sea, the Red Sea. Then to be kept at quarters standing in the sun for over two hours. A horse couldn't stand still that long. No wonder this ship acquired such an awful reputation. If I were in New York, I would be tempted to leave her for good and all. They are beginning to howl for steam. They want the speed and after you are knocked out below, you come on deck and drill all day and no place to sleep. Uncle Sam is very good. He gives his enlisted sailors a bed to sleep in, but no place to sling it. The hammock hooks in this cursed ship are about 12 inches apart, in the alleyways and over the coal bunkers, and most of the room is taken up by Paymaster's stores and other material. [That's] why we have to sleep around the decks. Coal passers or firemen coming off watch fling themselves anywhere, down on the decks, in the alleyways. I have groped along coming off watch and stepped upon a man's face or arms without eliciting even a curse from him. Yes, you can get used to anything. The mess tables for the engineers force are in the alleyways and resemble nothing so much as troughs in which the food is thrown almost any way. I shall never like this ship, as I foresee nothing but discomfort and misery ahead of me for the rest of my time unless I am transferred to some other ship. Thank God they are not all [like the] *New Orleans,* or the *Amazonas.* I can't think of her as an American ship. She was built to herd brutes, and these are the sentiments of all.

MONDAY, NOV. 20TH

Have been see-sawing with a French steamer on and off since yesterday afternoon, quite a race. He is faster than us, I believe, but we have managed to hold our own. Of course, we [would] leave him astern if we had all boilers going. They have been shaking us up below for more steam, but the boys will not work with the vim they would show if they didn't have a morning's drill ahead of 'em after doing a hard steaming watch below. Just as my section came off at 8 A.M., the Frenchman was just off our port quarter, then he forged ahead as the section that relieved us had to clean fires and the steam [pressure] will drop about 20 pounds [per square inch]; consequently, less speed. Well, had only a short drill this morning, was merely given our stations at the great guns. I am 1st captain of an Armstrong 4.7 (four point seven), No. 1 man. We usually get the same drill in all the other ships, so I am well satisfied at that.

Well, we are leading the French steamer again. I think we shall beat him into Aden. We are now in the [straits] of Bab el Mandeb, out of the Red Sea. We have only had a couple very hot days so far. I secured a snapshot of a large rock right at the entrance of the straits. There were three of them, and they loomed up grandly out of the sea.

Prologue

Had for breakfast this morning bread, butter, and coffee of very indifferent quality; no such a breakfast as a man should face hot fires with. Had the usual scrap between two coal passers last night, one a good deal smaller than the other. The youngster managed to hold his own tho', and would have won out in the end. Both pretty badly banged up.

TUESDAY, NOV. 21ST

Arrived at Aden, or just outside of Aden, at 2:30 A.M. this morning. We are coaling ship. Can just see the white houses of the city in the distance. Across from us lies the fort, on a rocky hillside. We are surrounded by the usual swarm of natives. Those coaling ship are the most repulsive lot yet met with, dirty in their rags, yet picturesque. They are mostly all undersized. They carry the coal in bags with about a bushel in each one. It comes alongside in lighters already in gunny sacks. It is quite a sight to see these small, wiry little rascals carry load enough for a Mexican burro, and keep it up all the [day]. They are tireless. Like all the rest of the natives who coal ship whether Italian, Portuguese, Arab, etc., they have to be driven. The drivers talk with their lungs, hands and feet. Such a jabbering you never heard.

There are lots of black boys here. I do not know their nationality. They are also small, but as trim[ly] built as an arrow. Mostly all their features are very regular and pleasant looking. I noticed one boy in particular who is very straight and lithe, his hair, bleached by the sun, is nearly white, and looks as if it were a powdered wig. That, in conjunction with coal black skin and very regular features, and snow white teeth, make rather a handsome picture, and I couldn't help thinking what a handsome, odd looking "Buttons" he would make, or flunkey of some description. He struts about on the gunwhale of the coal lighter as if he were vain of his appearance. "Allee same one peacock, John."

You can get some fine ostrich feathers here, also horns, and sawfish blades. The boys here also dive for sixpences, but will take nothing smaller. Will throw pennies, etc., back indignantly on the deck amid a perfect Babel of protest. You can see their tawny, glistening bodies a dozen feet below the surface of the clear, limpid water.

The *Brooklyn* [had] left here about 8 hours before we arrived.[40] We leave as soon as the ship is coaled. The next stop will be Colombo. Last night, as I came off watch at 8 P.M., it was quite dark off on our port bow. There was a soft, diffused glow, and slowly the moon made its appearance. I never saw it quite so plain before, nor assume such large proportions. It looked for all the world like a big fiery balloon, and in ten minutes, where all was darkness before, you could see to read plainly by its light.

It is very hot here. The natives dress any old way. I noticed one particular savage who sat perched in the [stern] sheets of his boat like a big crow, clad only in a string of glass beads and his dignity. Charming simplicity. Bring up a fist full of hard tack and you have the whole raft of them around you. One poor old Arab had his toe cut off by a coal shovel. Had it dressed in the sick bay after he was scrubbed good and clean, so they could get at it, and was carried down the gangway and placed in a boat and sent ashore, probably never so clean before in his life.

WEDNESDAY, NOV. 22ND

Once more we are underway as fast as brawn and muscle can force us thro' the water. Left Aden at 7:30 P.M. last night. We are thro' the Gulf of Aden, out in the Indian Ocean. We are endeavoring to make all the headway possible. I should judge our captain's purpose is to overtake the *Brooklyn* and pass her, but if the captain of the *Brooklyn* finds out we are after him, we won't see him until about two weeks after we [they?] reach Manila, or I mistake the man.[41] This ship is doing excellent, considering the condition of her machinery. The [forced-draft] blowers in the firerooms are always breaking down, and everything depends on them. I wouldn't want to be a second-class machinist on this dago. They are continuously repairing blowers, and on the grating where the blowers are, the temperature reaches about 170 or 180 degrees. They can't stand to work on them very long.

They have soaked us with this coal. It is all dirt. We can only hold [i.e., maintain] 75 or 80 pounds of steam with it, work as we may. They had a queer way of tallying coal in Aden. Every tenth bag that came aboard, the native tallying would tie a knot in a string, and when they would come for his tally, he would pull out a pocket full of knotted cord. They know how to steal on the count, also, always about 10 bags ahead on every hundred. While in Aden, I also saw some very pretty basketwork, very cheap, and the ostrich feathers I spoke of before were also very cheap. You could get about a dozen nice, assorted plumes for 4 shillings, or a dollar, American money. You have to watch them, tho', as they are as tricky as their more civilized brothers of the West. The feathers are tied in bunches of 4 or 5 together, the finest always on top, some bad ones beneath. But you can always get the worth of your money. The trouble with us for curios [is] we are outward bound, and [there's] no place to keep anything we could buy. Too much trouble to keep track of them as it takes all a man's time to look after his bag of clothes, etc.

The natives wear an iron bracelet on their right arms to protect them from evil spirits. Most all of them chew a stick of wood of some kind that keeps their teeth very clean. They make a lather of the same stick and apply it to their hair and let it dry and stay for a couple of days; that is, those that have wool long enough [do]. It bleaches it almost white. Like all Mohammedans, they will run at the sight of pork. You can clear the ship of them quicker by chasing them with a piece of pork than with a club.

Yesterday, some of the British garrison came aboard to look around, most of them belonging to the Royal Artillery. They are a fine looking body of men, judging by those who came aboard, dressed as they were in khaki uniform with cork helmets that they all wear in hot climates. Very neat appearing, indeed. Still, a man-o-warsman

Prologue

has to be just as neat as any uniformed body of men in the world for captain's inspection every Sunday morning, and it is a much harder job to keep clean aboard the modern war-ship than ashore.

I have mentioned before in this log about bag inspection and how everything is stowed a[nd] how kept. It will not come amiss here, whilst in the Indian Ocean with only the routine of the ship to keep track of and that hardly of any note, to name the articles a sailor in the U.S. Navy is required to have and the relative value he pays for same. Each and every man is required to have the following articles of wearing apparel:

1	Pea Jacket, or overcoat	$11.00
2	Pairs, blue cloth trousers	each $3.00
2	Overshirts, blue	each $3.75
2	Cloth caps	each $1.00
2	Watch caps	each $0.45
2	Undershirts, blue	each $1.60
2	Drawers, blue	each $1.50
2	Drawers, white	each $1.00
2	Undershirts, white	each $1.00
2	Working clothes, white	each $2.80
2	Mustering suits, white, with blue collars and cuffs	each $3.75
2	Pairs, shoes	each $2.40
1	Pair, leggings	$0.60
2	Neckerchiefs	each $1.20
2	Mattress covers	each $0.60
1	Mattress	$4.00
2	Blankets or pair	pair $4.50
2	White hats	each $0.45
2	Pairs, socks, woolen	each $0.35
1	Sweater	$1.60

In addition to the above, if a deck hand, you can place a lanyard (for knife), knife, oil skins, sea boots, tobacco, needle, thread, soap, towels, comb & brush, etc. [on the list]. If of the engineers force, add blue dungarees to work in, but no storm clothes.

It takes a young fellow that ships as landsman about four months to get out of debt, at $16.00 per month, and a coal-passer about three months at $22.00.[42] You cannot go ashore on liberty until you are free of debt, and before you can draw monthly money, you in addition have to have a month's pay on the books. You are only allowed to draw a month's pay; nothing exceeding that (unless by special permission). So, if you are classed for misconduct any money [that] accumulates on the books, there it stays until you are paid off. You are allowed to make an allotment in favor of any person, leaving them so much of your pay per month, not exceeding

Prologue

over two-thirds. And that is a good thing, because if you are moving about, it relieves you of a lot of trouble. We have the best paid navy in the world, but even at that, it is small pay in comparison with the work you have to do, and the annoyances you have to put up with. Look at this ship, for instance. She is the meanest below I have ever been on. The pay I get I consider small compensation for the services rendered, or any other of the men below.

Well, this is a field day today, cleaning up after coaling ship. There's where your seamen and landsmen of today [are] right at home—scrubbing ship. The weather still continues fine. It has not been so exceeding[ly] hot today. We are making good time so far, over halfway to the Mecca of all ships of the navy in these days. Four of us steaming across seas as fast as we can force them. The *Brooklyn* ahead of us. The *Nashville* and *Marietta* behind, all bent on arriving and putting out of commission a miserable half-breed, [Emilio] Aguinaldo by name. Ag., old boy, you don't know what trouble and misery you are putting lots of us at.[43] If we could only get a whack at you, we would put you to work tending water on the boilers of the *New Orleans*. That would make you jump around like a monkey on a hot griddle. From my own experience, first you see it [i.e., the boiler water level in the sight-glass, which must not be allowed to go too high or too low] and then you don't for about half an hour. Keeps us guessing all the time.

THURSDAY, NOV. 23RD

Had fire quarters last evening, and also read out three more court-martials. Same old offense: drunk on duty and jumping ship. 2 months' pay lost and fifteen days double irons was the highest penalty. Yet Jack will get drunk in spite of all. They have stopped all beer in the navy here some time ago. Then they would bring the beer aboard at mess gear, dinner & supper hours, and serve it out in line, a bottle apiece, to each man, but hardly ever over two. Four bottles for a quarter. Back then a man coming off liberty knew he could get a bottle at noontime, and he would save a few pennies in order to buy a couple bottles. Now, when he wakes up in the morning after a night's carousal, knowing he can't get a harmless bottle of beer for an eye opener or bracer, he spends his last dollar in buying a bottle of whiskey and smuggles it aboard the ship, and in consequence, he gets drunker than ever and is probably reported as such. Sometimes he is caught smuggling whiskey aboard and that is a court-martial offense.

Now the powers that be have proclaimed that beer is not good for the enlisted man. Consequently, the enlisted man considers whiskey is. The powers proclaim that beer tends to the destruction of discipline and good morals and in general affects the whole personnel of the navy. Still, we always had beer served out to us until shortly after the [Spanish-American] war. There was nothing wrong with the splendid personnel and deportment of the men who won off Santiago and at Manila, and endured all sorts of hardships without a murmur in their country's defense. After the war, it was suddenly found out that Jack was to be made a good little boy of; must be led

Prologue

around by the hand. Now there are more courts martial than ever before for drunkenness. Why don't some of these old hens or tabbies of both sexes go to the front in time of need, not sit at home in luxurious ease, and debate wisely what is good for Jack? Jack of today is no fool. He is just as saving, just as prudent as his brethren on land. He always knows how to take care of himself and that, too, in all ports of the world, without chaperone. So they stop his vulgar beer. It is not good for him. They prefer champagne for their own use. Still, the powers that be impose no restriction upon the people of the quarterdeck [i.e., officers]. They have unlimited supplies of eatables and drinkables, and from most of them I have seen they need it, especially the drinkables. I once heard of a first luff [a ship's first lieutenant] who asked a seaman who was brought before him for coming off under the influence, "why he couldn't drink like an officer and a gentleman?" Jack replied, "No sir; I can't do that for if I did, I'd be dead."

But Jack can drink anything he can lay his hands on if he is a tank, from alcohol to red ink. See 'em stand by to swipe a pot of shellac and carry it to some convenient spot, pour water in it and stir it with a stick until the shellac forms in a ball. Then pour the alcohol off and strain it thro' a thin rag of some kind. The rest is easy. The sugar, condensed milk and water and they can mix a shellac cocktail with a squirt of Venetian red in it for a flavor, or whatever coloring they have in the pot of shellac. Sometimes they get away with the contents of an alcohol chest. But you mustn't infer from the above that all are drunks. Oh, no. There is just about the same proportion in the navy as ashore. Jack is getting wiser and saves his money. And there are lots that do not drink at all.

The principal reason they act so wild ashore is because they haven't perhaps a liberty in a couple of months. Then we are inclined to be boisterous and will perhaps drink a little too much for our good. But if we go ashore quite often, you will notice we conduct ourselves with the same decorum that a good citizen would. It is only the first splurge, then we "pipe down." Jack has his haunts to go to and seldom bothers anywhere else. You can see him rolling up the Bowery at any time in New York at Coney Island and nearby resorts. But the most of the drinking bluejackets repair to McGurk's in the Bowery, known as "Suicide Hall." There he is in congenial society, with its Sailor Liz's, Marine Jennies, Red Maudes, etc., who are only too willing to help spend our pay and incidentally lay a train [to deceive us] for our "pay day." It is a common occurrence for a paid off bluejacket to spend probably $400 or $600 in a short while at these dives, then ship over after their little fling.

One thing about McGurk, he never puts a sailor out. He can hang around as long as he pleases after he is broke and the girls, poor unfortunates, are good hearted and willing to share their last pence with the man who has treated them good. That is their code of honor. But still, when you are broke, you may as well "get up Jack, and let John sit down." I have been thro' it all, and when broke I would make tracks as quickly as possible back to the ship. Very few bluejackets but have visited McGurk's or any of these "sailors' hangouts," even if only for curiosity alone. Perhaps they get disgusted on the first visit and never go again, but the chances are two out of three that they will.

Prologue

Did you ever see the "rookie" ashore? If you haven't, you can easily tell him by his nautical air and general "salty" appearance. In fact, he has quite an aroma of tar, "Shiver me timbers," and "dash my tarry top lights" air about him. His clothes are generally Paymaster's, with a wide, ill-fitting collar, large lanyard, the largest he can get, cap with a decided, most decided, list to port. What a wise weather-eye he casts about him, and what a roll! He is a heavy weather man, all right. What he doesn't know about the briny isn't worth knowing. He thinks with pride that he is "the limit," the only article that every happened. What a glance of disdain he casts on land lubbers.

That's ashore. See him aboard the ship engaged in the manly occupation of scrubbing paint work, he is a different bird. Or see him come down toward the ship from liberty, and come aboard after reporting to the "officer of the deck." Just for'd of the smoke-stack he will begin to roll and gives you the impression that he has got a terrible jag on when, in reality, it is only a "smoke stack" drunk and assumed effect. Thinks he isn't a sailor until he gets drunk, gets in the "brig" for a few days in irons. Has a court-martial. Has a picture of a pig tattooed upon his foot[44] and in other ways emulates the example of the bluejacket of the old wooden ships. He outgrows all this in time, tho', and makes a good hand.

Well, had general quarters today, was at it all the morning. My station was at the for'd 6" gun, ammunition whip getting up shell. I don't mind that so much. Weather has certainly been very fine. It is nice and cool, which is a blessing in the Indian Ocean. I wonder where they got this coal from we are using now. It is composed entirely of sand, slate, and rocks. "Couldn't burn it in H[ell] with the blower on." This I heard one of the firemen say.

FRIDAY, NOV. 24TH

Had small arms instruction this morning for about an hour. Shoulder Arms. Port Arms, etc. Try to make a soldier out of a sailor and a sailor out of the fire-room and engine room people. This infantry drill looks all right in parades, reviews, etc., and it is good enough to learn as a finishing touch to a soldier, a gloss, so to speak. But what they should teach, also, in the opinion of your humble servant, is, for the recruit or any person unacquainted with the arm he is drilling with, its mechanism. Familiarize him with all its parts, and how to replace and repair any portion that becomes fouled or broken. 'Nough said. That speaks for itself. We are having glorious weather, cool breezes blowing, just enough to refresh one. The ship is rolling and pitching but very little. In fact, she has encountered nothing but a smooth sea since we left the Atlantic. That adds a little more comfort to this life.

Well, I don't find things very monotonous on this run, as I have plenty to keep me busy, and any leisure I do have I enjoy to its fullest bent. The hours simply fly and it only seems a few moments from the time I come off watch until it is time to go on again. The dirty watches are the drag. They seem very long. You do not find much amusement on a long sea run like this. It is all routine and business. The amusement comes in port, when we are cleaned up both on deck and below. I have been in ships where they have good minstrel troupes, good bands, and all sorts of talent, boat racing, baseball clubs and football elevens galore.

We are just beginning to fit into our places in this ship. Where there are so many new men, it makes things very uncomfortable, not that this ship will ever be comfortable, she isn't built for that. I'll bet they were glad to get rid of us on the other side [in the United States]. I know lots of men who would not ship over until they heard the *New Orleans* had left. She is disliked by naval officers and men alike. They [the officers] have poor accommodation themselves. The second section, of which I am one, made a spurt on watch last evening. Happen'd to strike some of our old coal and brought the revolutions from 80 or 82 to 92. Didn't think they had it in 'em.

TUESDAY, DEC. 5TH

Since writing the above, I have been completely knocked out. I came off watch the evening I made my last entry in this log with a dull pain in my knee. That was at 8 P.M. About 11:00, I judge, I was nearly out of my mind with pain and misery, and this is the first time I have felt like writing anything down. I tried hard to go on watch the next morning, and managed to change into my dirty working clothes and get below. How I did it, I can't tell. I only know five minutes after I went to the machinist of the watch and had to come up. When I got to the top of the engine room hatch, I had to lay down completely exhausted, and lay there for 2 hours before I could pull myself together enough to wash up and change clothes. I went to see the doctor at sick call and was told to take a rest. Got no treatment and had to lay off on the top of the bunker. One of the men loaned me a mattress to lie on. God, how I did feel as if every bone in my body had been broken on the rack. And my head! Well, I lay around about four days, eating nothing, and chased from one [compartment] to another by the master-at-arms, until the doctor came to the conclusion there was something the matter with me. My leg was swollen and inflamed a great deal. It turned out to be an abscess of the bone, and it was so serious looking that but for the American Consul at Colombo, I should have been sent to an hospital there. But the American consul didn't want the trouble, so I was slung in a cot in a sick bay, hotter than any place you can imagine. Must have been about 100 or 105 degrees. No ventilation of any kind in it, the air ports being closed at sea. And there I laid, cooped up in hell. I never felt so miserable in my life. Happily, I am on the road to recover[y] now. I was operated upon twice. I have never experienced the misery in my life before that I have undergone on this ship. It is awful. I can just imagine what a dog an enlisted man is from this one, this being the first time I have ever been on the sick list in 5 years in the navy. I was compelled to get in uniform of the day to see the doctor. You can imagine the pain of that; a man hardly able to move, crawling along on my hands and knees (on one knee, rather, dragging my other leg after). I was sent with the two nurses to get into white mustering clothes and when I was changing the master-at-arms came up and wanted to know what the hell I was doing there changing after hours. And being sick as I was and not in the mood for any trifling, I gave him such a calling down as he never had before in his life. The poor miserable cur who would try and bulldoze a sick man! Well, enough of that for the present.

It has been nothing but drill from morning to night, day in and day out. The men have had battalion drill and heavy marching order galore, with the thermometer around the hundreds. It has been one continual performance such as I have never seen before. We stayed a couple of days at Colombo. The ship, as usual, [was] overrun with all kinds of fakirs [peddlers]. I couldn't get around much to see what was going on, but things were lively, I can assure you, from the chatter I heard on deck.

WEDNESDAY, DEC. 6TH

I forgot to mention that we had been running under one engine for about 57 hours. The stud bolts holding the piston in place had almost all carried away, which necessitated shutting down that engine (the port). Well, yesterday it was drill all day, battalion in the morning and heavy marching order in the afternoon, together with air bedding and "arm and away" drill. Today it has been raining all day and that has kept us out of drill so far. Of course, me being sick, I am excused from all drill. I can't walk, that's the reason. My leg is getting better, a mighty quick cure for an abscess of the bone, which might result differently, and is quite a serious thing at times. If it heals up and is all O.K., I am a mighty lucky fellow.

Thanksgiving has past whilst in Colombo. We got in there on that day. Our Thanksgiving dinner was composed of bad bread, canned "willie" of course was the piece de resistance, as usual. Slops, called coffee. I spent my Thanksgiving in the "sick bay" under a temperature of about 105 degrees.

We had "clear ship for action" the other day. It took 'em all day to strip her, and I don't know how long to assemble everything again. Well, at Colombo, one of the baymen, or nurses, bought a monkey. When they brought him in the sick bay, they had to break out some carbolic acid to purify the atmosphere. Of all the loud smells, Mr. Monk was the worst. He was very wild and wanted to bite everybody. They say the way to keep a monkey from biting is to bite him back, but nobody seemed to want to bite this monkey back. Mr. Monk bit the ship's corporal and was promptly flung around in a circle around the sick bay by the end of his string and brought with a flop on the deck. Mr. Monk was out for about half an hour, and we thought he was dead. But he revived and came to, but he was tame, would eat out of your hand. He has been very quiet ever since.

Talk about fakirs at Colombo! Well, you could buy anything. You see the same Arab kids diving for small coins. They also sell lots of different kinds of stones, but you have to be a judge to keep from getting cheated. They sell a stone which they call a white sapphire [that] more often turns out to be glass or crystal than anything else. Cat's-eyes also are common, but hard to get the genuine [item]. You can get good

Prologue

opals, topaz[es], etc. It is cheaper to sell the genuine of those than any imitation. You can get some fine opals, my favorite stone. Some people claim they are unlucky, and would not have 'em at any price. Moonstones, tourmaline, etc., are also cheap and plentiful. The settings they sell are not gold, most all settings being an imitation of Roman gold, or a dull finish. Ebony work is also cheap and plentiful. You can buy carvings quite nicely done, very cheap, such as elephants, writing desks, canes, etc. I bought a pair of carved ebony elephants for 2 shillings; could have got 'em cheaper, but being outward bound, [there] is no place to put 'em. Coconut wood articles, also. They sell boxes made of porcupine quills and bunches of quills for penholders. Fruit is plentiful and cheap. Bananas are very small, not much larger than your thumb, but good. Oranges are not so good. Everything is very cheap. Labor is cheap. They pay the men who coal ship about 10 cents a day.

There was also some snake charmers aboard; one in particular gave an exhibition of a fight between a mongoose and a cobra in which the mongoose would get the better of the cobra every time. I noticed some of the crew getting tattooed by some of the native tattooers. They are not very good at it, as a general thing. Their drawings in their books of designs are only good as it related to birds, butterflies, snakes, cranes, flamingoes, etc. They cannot draw figures in any degree of proportion. Their work on the arms, etc., does not look good when finished.

In fact, there are no tattooers worthy of the name outside of America or England, with the exception of Japan, where they also are good at dragons, snakes, animals, etc. It takes an American with an electric tattooing machine to do real artistic work. I have seen some men who could work a portrait on your arm, and who do really beautiful designs from an artistic point of view, as different from the tattooing of years ago as the half-tone reproduction of a drawing now-a-days is like the old chalk drawing of a few years back.

Tattooing is an art that should be popular moreso than it is, if it were not associated with drunken sailors, etc. People only think of it, if they think at all, as being a crude sort of way of putting pictures on sailors' breasts and arms, most all of which designs are very crude in drawing. I have seen some beautiful Japanese work of dragons, etc., and also some beautiful work by electric needles, in different colors of dark blue, red, yellow, green, and brown. With those colors it is possible to get quite a combination, and do really artistic work, such as flowers, etc. I believe this art will become more popular as it becomes more advanced, and by electricity it is not at all painful and does not get sore. Of course, lots of people think it a barbarous practice, but there are all sorts of people in the world, and I have noticed lots of people with [tattoos] on.

THURSDAY, DEC. 7TH

Well, we are just entering the beautiful Straits of Malacca. There is beautiful mountainous scenery on both sides of us. I noticed a lighthouse situated far up on a

Prologue

mountain side in quite a fine situation. It is very warm, as we are now drawing nearer the line [Equator] every day, and will be nearest it at Singapore. From Singapore we take a northeasterly course thro' the China sea to Manila. My leg is getting better day by day, and I am a lucky man that it turned out no worse, as an abscess of the bone oft-times turns out to be a very serious thing. So, after all, if all goes well, I will not have to go to an hospital. I am glad in one way and sorry in another. By going to an hospital I am free of this ship, but on the other hand, I am getting well and with returning strength I can but laugh at all the inconvenience they put me to. And perhaps when we get to Manila, if we are any time there, we will be under the Admiral and then we will get just the same drill as the other ships, which will be quite a relief, as I never have seen in my 5 years service as much drill as on this ship, especially at sea. We have had nothing but smooth seas right along from Colombo.

I could not see much of Colombo, as I was slung in a cot. There was no liberty allowed any of the crew. The excuse was a case of small pox ashore, but they let anybody come aboard from the lowest haunts of the town and also let washing go ashore. So, I should judge, the case of small-pox was manufactured for the occasion. I wonder what is the excuse at Singapore. I don't care myself, as I cannot go. I am only second class in conduct class, and besides, am on the binnacle list, or sick list. But it just shows what the navy is.

We have not sighted the *Brooklyn* yet. She is jogging along at about ten knots per hour. The chaplain of the *Brooklyn* came aboard us at Colombo and visited the sick bay. I found him quite the gentleman, who dropped the quarterdeck stiffness for the natural man in his talk with us. They are very scarce in the navy, but as yet, he is unspoiled, and I trust he will continue to be as he was when I saw him. He is well liked by all. I have seen lots of Chaplains who will not go among the men at all, but generally keep aloof, and it is just as well, for they generally have not the good feeling of comradeship that would make them popular among the crew.[45]

FRIDAY, DEC. 8TH

Last evening we had collision drill & abandon ship. I was lying in my usual place on the bunkers, hardly able to move around. I couldn't have gotten to the sick bay, anyhow, thro' all the water-tight doors, they being all closed, when an officer came down and seeing me lying on the bunker top, roared, "What the hell are you doing there?"

"On the sick list, sir," I replied.

"Why the hell ain't you in the sick-bay, damn you," etc.

I didn't reply, and it did not make any impression upon me, as that is one of the things you rapidly get accustomed to in the navy. You can't answer back, even if you are on the report and go to the mast, or "stick." There is no use in trying to clear yourself. It is all cut and dried for you. You are bound to get punished. If you talk, you only augment your punishment and are put down as a "sea-lawyer" immedi-

Prologue

ately. So the old hand, knowing how it is, never explains. Asked if he has anything to say, it is always, "Nothing to say, sir."

I was on the report for not airing bedding yesterday, but of course when they found out I was on the sick list, I was excused. But four or five others were punished for the same offense, among them two men who should not have been as they were on watch at the time, and the men who relieved them were supposed to get their hammock and air it for them, that being always the rule in the navy. Your relief, that is, the man who relieves you on watch, has to get your hammock, etc., for you whenever you are below as you cannot get it yourself. Still, even that excuse won't go. You are reported and that is enough. Officers will not believe an enlisted man unless they are officers you work under and know you as a responsible man, and I cannot say that I blame them, as the navy is largely composed of the riff-raff of different cities and countries. I have seen good men in the service, well educated, well-born and raised, but they are about 20%. The rest you would no more invite to your home than you would a mad-dog. So, the majority of officers have a gruff way of talking to all enlisted men alike. You are even insulted by some. If you were to bring your sister, wife, or mother aboard ship to show her around, they [would] make you feel your position even then.

Well, we are having infantry drill this morning for the second relief of the engineers force. It is getting very warm as we are nearing the line, but I must say it has been a good, cool trip so far, and it is nearly over. I woke last night to find a puddle of blood under me from the incision in my leg. It was bleeding very much and I had to go to the sick bay and get the bandage changed early in the morning. Truly, I am having a tough old time of it, but it might have been worse. I'll have to "grin and bear it." It will come all right in the end. Should judge we will be in Singapore tomorrow, as we are making excellent time.

SATURDAY, DEC. 9TH

Still pounding merrily along. We shall soon be in port again. These Straits of Malacca are thickly studded with innumerable small islands and that makes navigation rather risky. Was working the engines by signals from the bridge all last night, as I could plainly hear from my couch on the cold iron of the bunkers. Suppose we will be in to-day or at least early in the morning. We had general quarters last night at 9:30. That is the first time we have had any drill at night since I have been on this ship, but God knows we have had nothing but drill and work during all the daytime—one continuous performance, in fact.

I hobbled up to the sick bay last night at the imminent risk of getting knocked down and run over by the rabble in their wild charge to get to their stations. I got there, however, very leisurely; took my time, and sat there with three others on the sick list for about an hour and was nearly parboiled. The sick bay comes closer to my conception of hell than any place I have ever been unfortunate enough to have been in. It would make a perfect oven in this climate. There is no ventilation in it, and the ports have to be closed at sea, except by special permission, and the steam and exhaust from the ice machine run directly thro' it, thus superheating it, as it were. Fierce! Ye Gods, there is no parallel to it.

I have often been overhead on [i.e., on top of] boilers opening the main steam stops [outlet valves], but it is not as hot as the sick bay, where I and dozens of other poor devils had to lay and suffer and only relieve their pent up feelings by curses, not loud, but oh, how deep! Our beds on the bunker tops are another Hades. Occasionally a breath of cool air comes down the skylights and refreshes us, but it is seldom. No sleeping on deck as this is the rainy season and if you get to sleep on a "corking mat" on deck, you will only be aroused to find yourself soaking wet, as the rain descends in an instant.

Lots of the crew bought "corking mats" and "pillows," as they are called by all sailors, mats of light woven grass something like our matting at home, only so soft you can double them up in your hand, and the pillows are made of the same material, filled with grass or straw. You can sleep very [comfortably] on them. No sleeping in hammocks [in] this weather.

My leg is getting rapidly better, I find, and if no after complications set in, I shall be a lucky man getting off so easily. Several of the men are suffering with abscesses and boils caused by bad food. I have never had occasion to eat such bad food before. In our mess, we have had five or six cooks, and none of 'em know their business, and the way food is prepared and served to us would kill a dyspeptic in a week. I haven't had a piece of well-baked bread since leaving New York, except what we had in port from bakers ashore, and everything else is on a par with the bread. Soggy potatoes, slops for tea & coffee, and "horse meat" or salt horse, and navy canned meats. I never could eat any of that stuff.

SUNDAY, DEC. 10TH

Arrived at Singapore this morning. Laid outside at anchor all night. Passed the *Brooklyn* as we came in the harbor. She was coaling at one of the coal-docks. We have to wait, I believe, until she is thro' coaling and have to coal alongside the same dock. It is a rainy, drizzly day. We passed some beautiful scenery coming in. It looks very tropical, with its palm trees, beautiful fronds of which you can see all along the beach, and also some finely situated villas stud the higher places. It speaks of comfort and of ease. You can easily see that a few thousand dollars would be a competence here, where everything is so cheap, especially labor. Coolie labor costs almost nothing. I see lots of "rickshaws" drawn up on the beach at different landing places, and you can also see them with their coolies scurrying along the roads.

We are getting out of the way of the Arabs and Mohammedans now, and among the Chinese. As I write this, I look thro' a port and see that the most of the bum-boat

Prologue

men are mostly all Chinese, interspersed with a few Malays and other races. As usual, the ship swarms with them. Fruit is plentiful and cheap: oranges, pine-apple, bananas, etc., of the same inferior kind we have gotten all along this route. Lots of cheap catch-penny stuff from the states and from Europe. It costs as much and more than in New York or any other American city. Cheap underwear, soap, tobacco, perfume, pipes, and all the miscellaneous articles [were] brought aboard to sell to the bluejackets who will buy anything. Lots of them were stuck in Colombo and stuck hard. All the jewelry they bought has tarnished and lost its brightness, and you can buy anything you want for a mere song from the disgusted owners. I notice some fine shells here, and cheap. I haven't seen any coral like you can get in the West Indies, but the shells are peculiar to this country.

Talk about cheap money. This currency takes the biscuit. An English [sovereign] is worth $10.40 Singapore money, something like Mexican money. Looks for all the world like big medals made of aluminum, and it feels almost as light. Money changers with a big bag slung along their sides dish it out to you. They will cheat the eyes out of you, slip in any old thing that looks like money. You have to watch out for counterfeit money. It is a very easy money to counterfeit. They will not take Mexican money here, or Chinese coin. It is [not?] good in Hong Kong. You have to watch yourself here. The money you get here is only good here. Can't spend it elsewhere. I believe we are going to get liberty here. The uniform was white working clothes this morning, for a wonder, and no inspection, too busy coming into port, and besides, it is raining; altogether, a dismal day.

MONDAY, DEC. 11TH

The *Brooklyn* pulled out from the coal pier this morning at 8 A.M. Thought she was going straight thro' to Manila. Was saluted by the shore-battery and answered. We also saluted. She hove to and dropped anchor quite a distance from [us]. I also see an English man-o-war in here. Hardly any port in the globe, tho', that you can enter without encountering one of the "steel walls of old England." They are everywhere. The sound of the *Brooklyn*'s saluting 6 pounder came to us about 1 moment after each flash of fire, no doubt reminding the different shipping on the harbor and the people of Singapore of how those same guns spoke a short 18 months ago off Santiago at the other end of the globe, wiping another navy off the water, almost. She is the only ship in here with a war record, we of this ship not being in the Naval Battle or, at least, the ship was not. The *New Orleans* simply figured in bombardments.[46]

This is one of the finest harbors in the world outside of the magnificent Bay of Naples. There is room enough and to spare to float all the men of war in existence. Food is cheap here, beefsteak selling for 4 cents per pound, and other meats and poultry in proportion. Last night I had the first appetite I have had since being in the ship and, I will add, the first opportunity of appeasing it. I certainly did lay in a supply of fried eggs, meat hash, good bread, butter and tea, and topped it off with about a quart of tapioca pudding. Not so bad, that. I have eaten of bananas about two dozen and three large pineapples. I felt better after that performance, sort of laying in sea-stores for the run to Manila. Had beefsteak for breakfast, pretty tough. Reminded me of Bowery sirloin or some I got in Boston on Tremont Street. Poor old cow must have died a natural death.

The crew is getting liberty here. I suppose my name will come out in the drawing tomorrow. Sorry I can't go, being on the sick list, as liberty is very seldom on this ship. It is worse than that on the *Brooklyn*. I understand that there hasn't been any liberty given to the men since leaving Hampton Roads. I hear bad rumors of that ship, also. Perhaps it is only idle rumors, tho'.

This is a fine place, Singapore. Chinese tailor came off "the beach," [i.e, out to the ship] yesterday and took orders for lots of dungarees and white working clothes, and brought them all off this morning. Quick, quick work. I do not see any curios in this place yet, except the money; that is curio enough. Most all the articles in the curio line come from different parts of China here. The coolie boatmen row standing up in the stern of their boats. They earn their money coming to and fro to this ship as we are lying about five miles out. They live, sleep and eat in their boats, pull a matting over them for protection from the weather. It rains every day or night here, now.

One of our warrant machinists got frisky ashore last night and was promptly knocked out, and that, too, by a woman. It seems some of the boys were in this restaurant eating and drinking and conducting themselves quietly, the place being kept by an Austrian woman and her two pretty daughters, respectable people, when Mr. Warrant Officer with his jag blew in and insulted the lady of the place by asking her an insulting question which she did not understand at first. But when he repeated it in a more insulting way so she couldn't misunderstand, she promptly hauled off and let him have a straight jab in the solar plexus that put him down and out. He was assisted out a sadder and wiser man. Was drunk and lost his bearings.

Had abandon ship this morning. Lowered all the boats this time. Was all the morning at it, and at 7 bells (half past eleven) had "arm and away." Well, I never mind a drill in port as long as I am not standing watch because a man may as well be on deck drilling as working below. You put the day in just the same. It is raining pretty hard now.

TUESDAY, DEC. 12TH

Still laying out in the harbor. *Brooklyn* left yesterday about 11 A.M. I did not see her depart. I have not heard yet when we shall leave, or yet go alongside the dock for coal. H.M.S. *Centurion*[47] came out from the harbor yesterday afternoon and came right across our stern in an oblique direction, a fine ship. The name of the other cruiser is the *Hermione*.[48] She is painted black, and no doubt is part of the Mediterranean Squadron. The *Centurion* is white and belongs to the Asiatic station. She is flagship. There is one of our colliers laying off from us. I think she is bound for the States.

Prologue

I hear bad rumors of the treatment of the men of the *Brooklyn*. Seems strange how they are treating men on our men-o-war since the Spanish-American war, and especially on a foreign cruise or station. There is no living any more aboard some of the ships. It may be for the benefit of discipline, but I fail to see it. And enlistments are becoming scarcer every year. [The] majority of the men will not re-enlist for four years, altho' the four months out, and four months pay offers a large inducement. The American Navy, I am sorry to say, is no place for an American, and the officers do not want Americans. They would be entirely satisfied with foreigners that will stand all sorts of ill-treatment.

We are undergoing minor repairs while we are lying here. The ship below is in an awful state, every valve in her wants overhauling. The bilges are full of water, and no way to pump them dry, and no doubt we will have to go on blockade duty the moment we arrive at Manila. The crew are having a good time ashore. This is a nice place, they all agree, to go ashore in. Not so many moons ago, they used to have huge fires burning at night to keep wild beasts away, and signs up along the roads [to warn] "Beware of the Jungle," and at times yet, an occasional tiger will show up along the outskirts of the city, looking out for a meal. They can swim from the adjoining islands, this being nothing else but an archipelago.

Well, they are having infantry drill upon deck with the auxiliary watch, second relief. What a farce, there being but six men! The rest of the deck force are having boat drill, but the idea of drilling six men? What is the navy coming to? My leg is a little worse this morning. It might turn out a serious thing after all, but I hope not. We can sleep more comfortably these nights, as it grows cool enough for a blanket toward morning, but it is hot enough during the day.

Four or five men are breaking liberty. Probably thinking it will be the last they will get for some time, they wish to make the most of it.

WEDNESDAY, DEC. 13TH

This is an extremely hot day; begins to remind one that we are only a couple degrees removed from the line.[49] We are still lying in the roads. Have the Marine guard on the quarterdeck continually to receive the officials in this port and from other men-o-war. Nothing but bugle calls for the guard and roulades[50] and salutes when any important personage comes aboard. Keeps bugler, drummer and marines and side boys on the jump. American Consul must have come aboard this morning as he was greeted with the salute he rates.

Didn't have any drill right at quarters, for they expected a visit from one of the exalted personages, so they postponed drill until just about 11 A.M., and then, when we thought we were out of drill for the morning, they sprung "fire quarters," "collision drill," and "arm and away" in rotation. Thermometer about 99 or so in the shade. Yes, it is nothing but drill on this ship. Have "setting up" drill every afternoon and run around or "double quick." Thank the Great Spirit I only have 22 months to do in this hell! Even the officers are disgusted. There is no necessity [to] have so much drill in this climate, and there is a clause to that effect in the "Blue Book" governing the drills, etc., of the navy. Still the captain or first lieutenant are their own "Blue Book," and do just as they please. They have their own hobbies and follow just the bent of their own minds.

As regards uniform at Sunday inspection, one captain will have a hobby to see if your flat cap is on straight and the streamers not [too] long and in the right place and the cap about regulation size, 10″ in diameter. He won't see anything else. You might have dirty clothes on, but he won't see it. He is all intent on looking at caps. Another wants you to be strictly regulation, wear paymaster's clothes, and you must have a paymaster's undershirt on while that's all he looks at. I have seen him pass two coal passers in the section I am in, the "2nd," standing right opposite me in line with no neckerchiefs on! Others look at your shoes [to] see if they are neatly blacked, and thus it goes. A new ship, new regulations and uniform.

You can hear nothing in the American man-o-war but the pipings of boatswain's mates who are all "square heads."[51] You can't make out what they say, "scrub and wash clothes," something or other. The worst mixture of chewed up words imaginable. I have seen people come aboard ship and look puzzled and perplexed when they would ask questions of these people and receive a blank stare or a mixture of Swedish dialect in reply, wouldn't believe they were on an American ship. This navy is a farce in some respects. Do you think the different nationalities of which this navy is composed would fight against their mother-country? *Nyet.* We would have to recruit a new navy or fall back on naval reserves. Almost every, or I will say three-fourths of, the deck petty officers in the service are "square-heads." That looks bad for the American born lad, doesn't it? But it is so, and I defy anybody to prove different. They can't. I know just what I am talking about from long experience. You find your good-bred American on the quarter-deck [i.e., as an officer]. Very seldom [does] a foreigner creep in there. They take care of that. A well brought up American lad will not stay in the service. He is humiliated too often.

A boy who is apprenticed to this life is ruined forever unless he is a remarkable lad in many respects. They learn all badness they didn't know before. They have got to follow it up for a living as that is their trade. In the navy they may get a warrant officer's billet such as gunner, boatswain, carpenter, but how few out of the entire number of apprentices attain that! They may become in years, a Chief Boatswain's Mate, Chief Carpenter's Mate, Chief Gunner's Mate, or Chief Yeoman, etc., get as high as $60 per month. That's the highest, or $65 as Chief Master-at-Arms. Wouldn't they have more comfort with a trade living ashore? Yes, a thousand times yes. Only the very roughest like this life, but there are scores of good, manly men in the service who would like to break away and live a natural life ashore, but hard times and circumstances won't allow them. But as a rule they get away in time.

I forgot to mention about the Spaniard during the war who was on the *Columbia*. The Navy Department, out of regard for his feelings, placed him on the *Richmond* at

League Island, the receiving ship, and kept him there all during the war on full pay. Would have been a shame to make him fight against his fatherland and uphold the flag of his adopted country. Good thing there wasn't many Spaniards in the navy. If it had been Sweden or Norway, I shudder at the consequences.

Well, I saw some nice India shawls on deck at noon, very nice indeed. The jewelry fakirs are still around. There is a great absence of noise here compared with the other ports. John Chinaman does business in a quiet way, but he gets there just the same. I also saw some nice views of this place, of Japanese girls, etc.

THURSDAY, DEC. 14TH

What a beautiful sight it was last night. There were lots of us up on the forecastle, sitting around in groups listening to the music from mandolin and guitar, such tunes as "Old New Hampshire" theme, "Green Fields of Virginia," etc. Made us think of home, now thousands of miles away, and not to be thought of for perhaps years to come. Some of us will be homeward bound before others. Others may stay out here their entire cruise of four years. Some of us will go home via Honolulu to "Frisco"; others will not, perhaps, return at all. Yes, it brought back thoughts of home and of the Christmas time they would have there and the Christmas we will spend here at the other end of the globe. Far out across this bay were thrown the long streams of light from the search-lights of the fort, illuminating the shipping in the harbor wherever its rays fell. Everything was still. Myriads of lights from the distant city and here and there the red and green lights of some rapidly moving launch darting like fireflys hither and thither over the dark water. [It was] a beautiful and peaceful scene. These are the times when one is a[t] peace on a man-o-war.

But the quietness and romance was rather rudely dispelled by a drunken fireman who came from liberty drunk and was still "hitting the booze" on board. He wanted to sing or dance or any old thing. Cries of "sit down," "Will you keep quiet or shall I make you?" "Pipe down!" "Put a stopper on that gab of yours," etc., greeted him and he got mad, and the hotter he got, the more he was jollied, until at last he offered to "lick anyone for drinks." Seeing nobody took him seriously, he growled and roared some more and then concluded to move, which he did in a most unsteady manner, having quite a heavy roll on. No doubt he thought he was a great man at the time, and owned the ship, but when I saw him this morning and saw the large, aching "head" he was carrying, he didn't look quite so fractious.

Well, we lay around the forecastle until "taps," and then dispersed to our different places of rest. Didn't rain yesterday or last night for a wonder. Well, had general quarters again this morning and the captain came around to inspect himself. He came up around the sick bay and made them send a man down the canvas [chute] from the main, or gun deck—he was supposed to be wounded—and was promptly picked out of the chute by the hospital apprentice and carried in and laid out on the operating table where everything was prepared: rubber blanket and pillow and case of instruments. Thus they kept up the drill all the morning. Ye Gods, the drill we get in this ship!

I notice some of the tawdry gems and showy rings bought in Colombo are disappearing. Most of the white sapphires have been crushed to dust between two coins, and stamped upon to see whether they will stand the test. Good sapphires will stand all that. Sailors will buy anything. It seems funny to see some of the most ignorant running around with their big, misshapen and warty feet stuck in sandals of different kinds, and gems on their fingers that are bigger than the Kohinoor [diamond] and would cost as much if they were the real thing. Poor Jack! Some of his 1812 innocence [i.e., innocence of a bygone age] clings to him yet, altho' the majority are pretty wise, but they are the ones brought up in big cities and who learn to be fly before they strike this outfit.[52]

I believe we are to go alongside the dock tomorrow. Wish we would get out of here. I like to be on the move, or else settled in one place. Want to hear how Ag [Emilio Aguinaldo] is coming on. Wonder if he sees the futility of struggling against the U.S. by this time? I hope he has, as he causes lots of trouble. The *Brooklyn* must be nearly to Manila by this time.

FRIDAY, DEC. 15TH

Today the first lieutenant has monkeys on the brain. It seems he has just got wind of the four or five aboard. One of the painters went to the mast and asked for liberty. The "first luff"[53] says, "I believe you are the man who owns those monkeys."

"No, sir," replied the painter. "I don't own any monkeys."

"No matter. You can't go ashore. I don't care if you are special first class, as long as those monkeys are aboard."

He told the same thing to another man. Accused him of owning the monkeys also. Had the master-at-arms chasing them up, but one old fellow with a fringe of whiskers like an Irish nestie [nester?] made a short arm jolt at him, and the others threw "straight jabs" and "upper cuts" so numerously that Jimmy Legs, being the cur he is, was glad to escape. The monks still hold forth on the uptake of the for'd smoke-pipe. They show up occasionally under the hood for something to eat, but when you go after them, you'll have a hard job. I believe the first lieutenant has offered to let any 4th or 3rd class man ashore on liberty who will bring the scalps of the aforesaid monks or their persons before him. Wonder he wouldn't take 'em and drill them when he can't drill the crew, or teach them to scrub paint work, etc. Up to date, nobody has taken advantage of his offer. I would like to go ashore myself, but I am on the sick list. When I am three months aboard ship, and in a port where they are giving liberty, I will go up and let them know I am aboard ship. Otherwise, they forget your existence.

We were to go alongside the dock this morning, but the gasket on the top manhole plate blew out of the boiler they were raising steam on, and it has put us back for some time. Didn't have much drill this morning on account of expecting to go out.

Prologue

SATURDAY, DEC. 16TH

Came alongside the dock about 4 P.M. yesterday afternoon, and coaled all night long. Finished coaling about 9:30 this morning. These Chinese coolies don't hurry themselves as at other coaling places. Two of them carry a basket of coal weighing 160 pounds on a bamboo stick on their shoulders. They have quite a distance to go and come; still, they come along with their funny little dogtrot in an endless stream. They pass a man who gives them one penny (Singapore money), half-cent in our currency, every time they pass with a full basket. The front man receives it. They must be pretty tired by the time they carry a hundred or so baskets. Still, that is pretty good wages for this country. Some of them work just long enough to get the price of a good drunk and they are off, emulating the example of their Western brother in that respect. Some of them are muscled like bulls and active as cats, but they are not in it with the Arabs at Port Said, who can beat anything in the world coaling ship.

They had the crew pretty well corralled here at this dock, tho', right under the glare of the electric light, with a marine sentry at both gangways and a middy stationed out on the dock. Still, a few got away for a night's frolic. They forgot the port side of the ship. Lots of men swam ashore with their clothes in a bundle, and others swam to sampans and were picked up. Not much trouble to "jump" ship after all.

From the ship's forecastle we had a good view of the street right off from the dock and an endless procession of bullock carts, ricksha men, pony carriages, etc. Here last night an endless panorama was unfolded before our eyes, going and coming on the docks: native soldiery in different uniforms, and generally puny looking men they are, too; Hindoos and East Indians in their dress that looks for all the world like pajamas, with great white turbans wrapped around their heads, John Chinaman with all sorts of dress, some with European head-gear, and others with their wide wicker work hats as large as an umbrella, gaudy colors on lady-like looking men, with high combs in their black hair. In fact, [it was] a dream of the Orient. There are all sorts of nationalities here, with here and there an Englishman ("Ah, there, 'Arry old man.") off of some liner or tramp steamer in the China trade, looking cool in their white clothing and pith hats. An old Chinese woman, must have been about 117 years old from her looks, hobbled slowly up the dock on her stumps of feet that looked as if her feet were cut off flush with her limbs; looked like she was walking on stilts [her feet were bound]. It was painful to look at her. Also passed in review some quite good looking Malay women in cool, white draperies. Yes, it is the East, with all its mystic appearance and romance, tho' no doubt common enough to those accustomed to it. Everything goes here as far as costumes go. You suit yourself. Some are in European dress; others a mixture of both; and still others are dressed in half a yard of muslin, or a ten cent towel.

John Chinaman does most of the peddling and from what I see, most of the work. I can't accustom myself to a country where men take the place of animals; have a man hooked up in the shafts instead of a horse. But it is all custom, no doubt. Most

Prologue

of the bluejackets treated their rickshaw men like human beings. Every time they took a drink, the rickshaw man got one also, and in numbers of cases, the man was as drunk as his fare.

An American man-o-war is a gold mine to these people, and they know how to take advantage of you, also. Had some amusement looking at the naked Malay boys diving for coin. Yes, I thought at first they at least weren't here, but they bobbed up serenely soon as we reached the dock, all ages and sizes of them, in canoes. They are as quick as their other brethren in other ports and better natured. They flounder in and out of their small canoes without capsizing, tho' how they do it is a wonder.

The gang on the forecastle had some fun this morning with two side painters who were working on a small stage. Let the lines go and dumped them in the water and floundered them around to their hearts' content. When they got up again on the stage, somebody lifted up the paint pot by its line and spilt the contents over one of 'em, a big square-head. That made him properly hostile, and he cursed and damned and fumed to our great delight until he was dropped into the water again with the stage. They left him alone only after they got tired and [were] attracted by something else.

Last night was literally the hottest I ever put in. Not a breath of air. I thought I was melting. We are now about to get under way. Had quarters about twice already. All hands are cleaning and washing down ship. The monkeys are still at large. Like Aguinaldo, they defy capture.

SUNDAY, DEC. 17TH

Once more underway, thro' the blue waters of the China Sea. Our course is now N.E. and this is the last leg of our course. Next stop will be Manila. All out for Manila. Eastern America. The waters of the China sea, I find, are as deeply, darkly blue as the Mediterranean. Not so the Indian Ocean; that is almost the color of the Atlantic and as we approached the Straits of Malacca, became a clear, translucent pea green, and that was the color around Singapore and until we got an offing in the China Sea. We have had land all along on our starboard beam since leaving, and in some places we could see shallow places in the water, which makes the China Sea a hard one for navigators.

There has been a large single-stack steamer gaining on our port quarter ever since daylight. She will pass us, no doubt. We are not making over 75 revolutions; another case of bad coal. They certainly can soak you, both in price and quality, as well as quantity in these coaling ports. Altho' coal is inspected before being purchased, it is only a farce, as you have Hobson's choice (not the Hobson of osculatory fame) and have got to take just what they give you.[54]

We left Singapore about 3 P.M. yesterday afternoon and came right out. Had quarters sounded just four times prior to leaving. You know, in coming in or leaving port you are all supposed to be at quarters, but on this ship they somehow are sounded about four or five times before they get things straightened out. Yesterday was field day, Saturday, you know. General cleaning up, same as wash day in ordinary families. Everything slushy and sloppy. No living for one. No place to go if you are on the sick list or coming on or off watch. Miserable. You know just how it is. Of course, we had to have drill on the *Amazonas*. Couldn't do without that. Field day too. Sprung collision drill and abandon ship at 7:30. Delayed the 8 o'clock relief from going below. Kept it up for about three quarters of an hour. This morning the uniform [was] white mustering clothes, or "white dress," according to new regulations. Read out articles of war. You couldn't hear the executive [officer] five feet away. Then inspection of the ship thro' about quarter to twelve, just in time for the watch to change and eat (in haste) and get below. Captain inspected below this time. Must have seen quite a mess. Must have got dirty if he went out in the fire-rooms, just as the men were cleaning fires. I'll bet he thought he was in hell from the heat and general look of things. First time he has [gone] below since I have been on the ship, and I can't ever remember the strictest commander of a vessel going below to inspect at sea. But this is the *Amazonas*, you know.

On the quiet I hear the captain, first lieutenant and chief [engineer] had a slight altercation, "a run in." [Captain] wanted to know from the chief why we didn't make more speed and chief replied, "It's a wonder you get the speed you do from the way my men are treated. They are treated like dogs, worse than coolies." And more in the same strain. But it don't do any good. We are at the mercy of two old ladies. The entire crew have no confidence in them. How different on some ships. I have been under the strictest disciplinarian, where the men have every confidence in their officers and consider everything all right, as long as the "old man" orders it.

Well, we shall not be long out now, will soon reach our goal. Perhaps we will have it better; perhaps worse. At any rate, I am sick of this life with its eternal quarrels and petty strifes, uncongenial companionship and discomforts. A man or boy in this outfit is continually on duty twenty-four hours out of twenty-four. You never know what will happen next. You cannot relax your vigilance one moment. You are always subject to call. You get ashore about once every two months, then you try to cram all the enjoyment you have missed for that length of time into 12 hours' liberty. You get drunk, spend what you have saved in that time, and are a madman in action. You can't have any enjoyment in a rational manner. You have no ties of home. You forget any refinement of manners you may have possessed before leading this life. You are made to feel your inferior position every moment of the day in some way or other.

No, it is no place for well-raised boys or men. You are looked upon as a failure who has entered the service as a last resort. Too often that is the fact. Wherever you are seen with this uniform on and are not drunk, people wonder why you are not. It is an adjunct that goes with the uniform, that of drunkenness. People are more surprised to see a sober sailor than a drunken one. We are the best paid service in the world, yes, I grant that. But our money is worth just about as much as a fast woman's—

about 7 cents on the dollar. You know of some bluejacket that that will not apply to, I hear you say. Yes, very good. That is the exception, not the rule, and I am speaking of the majority; of myself, as well.

But there comes a time in every man or woman's life when they start to think, and I have done some pretty tall, old thinking, mostly of what a big chump I have been. However, no regrets. Never in my life ashore have I went thro' what I have aboard ship. Here it is always the longing for something better to turn up. Always living in hope, thinking of what good times you will have in the future. Perhaps they will never come. And then the monotony of the life: drills, your work, and all the routine. [You] soon lose the power to keep your mind employed. As you soon learn to do them as a piece of machinery would, your mind [wanders] somewhere else. Such is naval life. Mind, I do not want to discourage anybody from this life. It is well liked by some. I am only writing my impressions, and writing the truth as I see it and experience [it]. Everything you read about the navy is by some writer who has got a good flow of language and sees everything from a "quarter-deck point of view." Or gets his impressions and notes from some officer in a ward-room over the cigars, or "walnuts and wine." A W. Clark Russell view, not Dana's in *Two Years Before the Mast*.[55] There is always a seamy, underside to every view. Seen from afar it has some glamour about it, like a lofty mountain rearing its head above the clouds. But when you are upon it, it is probably ordinary soil you are on, and is divested of its enchanted appearance, just as in the navy at inspection you will see canvas cloths covering a number of dirty places, for instance, clean hammock cloths covering nettings that are dirty and stowed full of dirty hammocks, or the men's black clothes bags hung on jack-stays. Such is a man-o-war, a farce in many respects.

Whilst lying in the cot in the sick bay for captain's inspection, they brought out a nice, clean sheet and placed it over me and took one of the dirty ones and made a pillow slip of it by wrapping it around the pillows, which had no slip on all during the week. The captain came thro' with his retinue and staff, and looking at me lying there with such a critical look that I actually felt as if I was imposing upon them by being sick, and felt guilty, altho' at the time I was in a fair way to lose my leg. That's the way all well-disciplined bluejackets feel while in the "presence." Enough of that for the present.

Here's two landsmen kicking because they have to go to work and scrape the shellac from the deck here, this being Sunday, when there is an order against doing unnecessary work. It couldn't hold over until Monday. It's very important, that is, seeing the deck has been in the same condition since I have been aboard. "Six days shalt thou labor and do all thy work" and on the seventh, scrub paint-work on the modern man-o-war. "Sech it is" and yet we roar.

MONDAY, DEC. 18TH

El Capitan was below quite a time yesterday, and in just the right time o' the watch also. In the firerooms he and the chief became wedged in between sweating, hard working firemen and coal passers. They were just cleaning fires and there is not much room to move around as all the place is taken up by the men. They have hardly room to work in comfort; just room to turn their hoes and slice bars in. Everything is filled with coal dirt, ashes and steam from playing the "wetting down" hose on hot clinkers and ashes. Captain asked the chief how often we cleaned fires. "Every watch" was the reply. Well, the steam fell lower and lower and even the "presence" in all its awful majesty couldn't have gotten those stokers to budge it the fraction of a pound. Wanted to know if the steam always dropped as low as that every time fires were cleaned. Was told yes, that there was no help for it, no way to avoid it. Suppose he went up on deck considerably wiser, but it won't diminish our drill one iota.

We are having beautiful weather, fine breezes on deck. Rains most every day. In fact, it is a little chilly toward evening on deck. Wish we could only get some of the breeze below. Pity they couldn't rig up more windsails for us,[56] but no, that would be too much comfort. They have lots of breeze aft [in officers' country], and electric fans in their rooms. This morning, infantry drill after quarters and bag inspection. Same old bag with same clothes. From this on, it will [be] "bags and hammocks" and clean and paint ship, etc., clothing cleaned and overhauled, and neatly stopped and marked. Same with hammocks, for we will have to be inspected by the Admiral after we arrive and join the assembled squadron.

I have been thro' numerous "Admiral's inspections" and after about a week of preparation, hurry-scurry, and bustle, it is all over in a few moments. It is very seldom an inspection at all: a mere glance, and perhaps a man selected from a division, at random. But it is always best to be prepared, as the unexpected might happen. By the way the doctor looks at me, I think he contemplates putting me to work, cut up as I am. Well, I am ready at any time, but it will be some time before I can do any "monkey drill," any jumping around. I will have to take things easy, but I am glad I am nearly well. I didn't lose any of the bone, as was surmised by the doctor, and after getting off so lucky, I can cope with any misfortune and discomfort, even the *Amazonas*.

TUESDAY, DEC. 19TH

I forgot to note yesterday that we had another court-martial read out. A Marine caught "jumping" or leaving ship without permission. The usual punishment: 15 days brig, double irons, loss of two months' pay, amounting to $25.60. Couldn't reduce him in rating, as he is a marine. Couldn't even make a landsman of him. There are a few more court-martials to be handed out yet.

We are having beautiful weather, nice cool breezes all the time. But you have to be on deck to get the benefit of it, as there is no system of ventilation below the main or gun deck. Well, it is battalion drill this morning in light marching order: leggings, canteen, and cartridge belt and bayonet, and of course, rifle. Heavy marching order, in addition to the above, you carry a knapsack and haversack and all that pertains to it, mess gear, knife, fork, spoon, cup and plate, blanket, rubber blanket, extra shoes,

Prologue

change [of] underwear, extra socks, extra trousers and overshirt, comb, brush, tooth brush, soap, needle and thread, etc., all rolled up and stowed neatly in proper place. You can imagine how you would feel under that load on a rolling deck, thermometer about 99 or 100. It becomes labor then. Then go below if you are of the engineers force.

Very seldom I have ever saw these drills at sea on any other ship. But then, this is the *New Orleans.* Beg pardon, the *Amazonas.* We never got such drill on the *Minneapolis* during the Spanish-American War. The most of the drill there was general quarters, which was perfectly right, and was done to perfect a green crew to their duties and stations so they could man their respective guns in [the] quickest possible time, or be at their stations at magazines and ammunition hoists. And I tell you that the gang had things down fine, and if the occasion had of arrived, we would have rendered a good account of ourselves, for all the small battery we had. But unfortunately, we had no show to distinguish ourselves. We done our duty. We were in dangerous places. We lay off of Santiago alone, not knowing that the Spanish fleet were in that harbor and hardly knowing how near we were to them at times. We made a run out of St. Thomas thro' what was reported as the Spanish fleet, every man at his station and prepared for the worst. Fortunately, we found out afterward the lights of the supposed Spaniards were tramp steamers. But the will was as good as the deed, for at the speed we dashed out of the harbor at, we would have cut anything in half we struck. We were going a good 22 knots. Nothing could have stopped us.

We are having more trouble at the mess again. Hardly anything to eat this morning. Hard-tack and potatoes and cod fish, with bad coffee was the fare. The codfish & potatoes would have been all right, if cooked right, but they wasn't. We'll get a good cook if we keep on trying them. This one we have is about the 10th man we have had, going from bad to worse. No trouble for a good cook to make good money on a warship. Beside their pay, if in the engineers force, they are coal passers at $22.00. They get two rations, $18 more, making $40 per month clear for them. Beside, they have a "striker" or helper who gets his own ration of $9. Good cooks at times are much in demand and can sometimes get 3 rations, $27.00 or more. Any young fellow can do all the "cooking" that has to be done in a man-o-war. Only thing he must know is how to make bread. Everything else is of the simplest, mostly baked beans, beef stews, soup. But the acme of the cook art is making up "canned willie" so as to disguise it and render it appetizing, whether in rope-yarn stew, cracker hash or blanket stew or sea pie, blanket stew or sea pie, meaning a stew that [has] a cover on it. Ye Gods! What fearful and wonderful messes I have run up against in my time in the outfit. Would make a dyspeptic run away or drop dead.

WEDNESDAY, DEC. 20TH

"Well, Wils," says old Jack the water-tender to me yesterday, "notice anything about the alleyways and top of the bunkers?"

"No, not particularly. Why?"

Prologue

"Oh, nothing much. Only I see they are managing to clear away all the paymaster's stores and gear from them now that we are drawing to a close getting to the end of our run [and] getting ready for the Admiral. Wouldn't do if he asked where the men's sleeping quarters were, to point to the place where it should be and find it all taken up in stores."

He was right. That's just exactly what they have done. They couldn't manage to stow this stuff any sooner and thus give us more sleeping room, but they can manage it when they have to. Ever since leaving New York, as I mentioned before, one half of our sleeping quarters have been taken up with stores, hard-tack tins and spare gear of every description. Yes, getting ready to receive the Admiral, everything will be cut and dried for him. They are laying down strips and lengths of shellacked canvas in the alleyways, painting the ship, and cleaning out bilges and holes and corners.

Had collision drill and abandon ship again this morning, and at collision drill they acted like madmen. I was sitting in the sick bay and could take it all in. The gunner has charge of the compartment outside the sick bay, and he was roaring and bawling at the top of his voice, driving the men on deck after the water-tight doors were closed, and in general making an 18 carat ass of himself. Bad enough for an "officer and a gentleman" to abuse men, let along a young sprig of a "warrant officer" who is neither officer nor enlisted man. As far as their title to a gentleman is concerned, they can be that if they are born into that instinct. Congress can't make them. Thank heavens I have ran up against lots of men in the outfit who are gentlemen, both as regards officers, warrant officers, and enlisted men. No position can spoil a true man. As for the others, I leave them to their own besotted ignorance. They always give themselves away before you are thrown in contact with them very long.

Having the usual fine weather, no sea of any account running, only a long undulating ground swell thro' which we are running [at] about 12 knots. We are getting nearer and nearer our goal every day, every hour now. I don't know what lies in store for us there. I trust that Mr. Aguinaldo will soon be brought to bay. Would like to see him captured alive and tamed and brought to the States as a curio. Put him in a monkey cage at Central Park. Would attract lots of attention. Or else, let him go on the stage. At any rate, will be able to hear some news from home and the latest news of events that happen there, and thus relieve this tedious monotony. Life becomes rather irksome after a while on ship-board. Time hangs heavily on my hands as I am still on the "binnacle list."[57] I trust I shall soon be able to get to work as the days will go faster. As it is, I don't know what to do half the time; nothing to take an interest in. We have had considerable trouble with the port engine and its auxiliaries. This ship needs a thorough overhauling below, and it has required some good engineering to carry us thro' this far in such good time.

Jack laid in a good supply of oranges and pineapples before leaving Singapore, and they have came in all to the good. Been living on them almost, myself, and such luscious oranges and pineapples as they are. I have nowhere tasted any better. [I] eat hardly anything at the mess table; hardly anything *to* eat. But I can make a meal off most anything. I don't suppose people would wonder long how hoboes and "the other half" manage to live and wax fat on "free lunch" if they could see the food we eat and manage to work on. A Bowery stiff wouldn't eat the food we have [had] to put up with at sea on this trip: sour, half-baked bread, badly baked beans that have no taste, canned willie that nobody eats and is finally thrown thro' the slop chute. A good drink of coffee or tea is a God-send, even a drink of cold water from the "scuttlebutt" is a luxury we don't often enjoy. It takes all the time of the men on the "ice machine" to manufacture ice for the people aft [the officers]. It was a hard matter to get enough to put on my knee (as I mentioned before); [it] almost had to be stolen.

And yet, people who read this will think I am a chronic fault-finder and "growler." Well, I am as far as this ship is concerned, but not of others. It is true we sailors do lots of growling, but we have cause to growl. Any good point about this ship I am only too glad to speak highly of, but they are damned scarce. I have cudgeled my brains to pick out one good point for the crew of this ship, but failed to find any. I fail to find any officer (that is, those that have the power) looking out for the welfare of the men. The chief [engineer] has fought for us, but has been promptly sat upon and squelched for his pains. I plainly perceive we are cut out for a hard time of it as long as we have the present administration.

A shipmate, an oiler, has just called me telling me dinner is ready. "What is it?" I asked.

"Guess," says he.

"Canned willie," says I.

"Right!" says he.

I knew I could almost hit it the first time, and I am no mind reader, either. Will knock off writing now and go up and see what I can rake up in the eatable line. Got some oranges to fall back on, anyway, but they are unsatisfactory when you crave for a large steak.

THURSDAY, DEC. 21ST

Served out clean hammocks yesterday afternoon and scrubbed last night and this morning. A whole chapter could be written about this piece of canvas, but I have mentioned about it before. I always pay $1.00 for getting mine scrubbed, unless I feel like doing it myself, but it's very seldom I feel that way. I managed to find my hammock and bedding in the netting without much trouble, first time I have seen it since I clewed it up and lashed it last, after leaving St. Michael's. [I] was more surprised to find it than I would have been if I had lost it, as the men, some of them, have a habit of "swiping" anything like that and using it to cork off on around the deck. Some of them will steal any old thing like that. Your towel, pair of socks, dirty or not, tooth brush at times, don't make any difference to them. [They] were raised that way, I suppose. But it's a good thing they are in the minority and when caught, everybody takes a kick at them.

Prologue

Had fire quarters last night at 7:30. Captain came around and inspected himself, followed by the first luff. Came in the sick bay. I was there, as that is my place while sick. Another poor fellow [was] slung in the cot, a marine private. It registered 101 degrees by a thermometer that the apothecary took from a cool place in a drawer. First luff said, "Whew! Its hot in here," and was it. Ask me the hottest place on earth or on the seas, it's the *Amazonas* sick bay. They say Muscat, Arabia is hot, but it isn't comparable with this sick bay. It is a crematory, a dry house. I pitied the poor marine. I could sympathize with him. When I was in that cot I thought I should go mad, I was tortured so. You could dry clothes in there in fifteen minutes.

Well, the first and third divisions are racing each other again, [trying] to get the most turns out of the engine. This is a cut-throat ship for that. The people aft only laugh at poor devils of fireman and coal passers killing themselves trying to beat each other. If we have anything to eat, and any inducements to work hard, it would be another story. Let me tell you, I used to try and have a section that could beat any of the others, and had one. What credit did I or the section get? One twelve to four watch we happened to fall back a few turns on account of cleaning tubes and fires, and I got sheol[58] for not keeping up the same high standard. All the previous good watches were forgotten. Since then I have been content to do my duty and just keep up with the band, and not strive to get beyond.

We are having a beautiful moonrise every night, about two bells [9:00 P.M.]. Last night the moon arose like a huge ball of fire. [It] looked as if it were standing in relief from the Heavens. We were steering a direct course almost for it, and it seemed as if the ship was following a silvery path with the moon for the goal. No sea of any kind running, simply a swell. We can see the Southern Cross very distinctly at about 12m [midnight]. Can also distinguish the North and Dog Stars. Will be in tomorrow morning, if all goes well. We should be sighting some of the numerous small islands by this time. We have been making rather good time.

Had a fine breakfast of hard bread and worse coffee this morning. "Willie" was [there] in all his glory, but I reneged. I can't. I can't do it. Later. Just finished general quarters. Seems like the more we have these drills, the more confusion and noise we have. This crew has had drill enough to know their stations and duties in the dark, without any confusion. I think the officers are more to blame for this than the crew. They must needs bawl at the top of their "lungs of brass" unnecessary orders, and cause confusion and disorder.

They sent another man down the chute into the sick bay, supposed to be wounded in the leg. In first aid to the injured you are supposed to use a tourniquet improvised from anything at hand, your silk neckerchief and a jackknife, to "set up" on with if you have nothing better. We are taught that on some ships, but I did not notice it here. The "skipper" came around on a tour of inspection. Suppose he found everything O.K. The first luff didn't like the appearance of the first relief of the engineers force standing idly, so he made them get rifles and act as a reserve to the riflemen already detailed. That's not a bad idea; wonder it didn't suggest itself before. There isn't any lack of drill on this ship. I'll bet my two little ebony elephants we get more than any ship in the service.

Had a most epicurean luncheon at noon. The "cook" was trying to hunt up a "duff bag" last evening. Don't believe he succeeded in getting one, as we were the only mess without "duff" today. The spuds were black as tar when broken open, and the coffee was no coffee at all as far as taste went. But the meat!! Salt horse of Revolutionary birth, and the vintage of 1776. It made its presence known by its aroma. Thought I was in a soap factory or fertilizer place. It looked dubious last evening. I saw several cooks taking theirs to the galley on strings. Looked for all the world as if they were going to feed an alligator or lion, or bait a shark hook. It was green in places. Yes, this is the modern navy with its old 1812 ration.

Every time I see this "salt junk,"[59] I think of sailors with plaited cues worked with tar and rope yarn; sailors with a forelock to touch and pull for a "salaam" while they scraped with their bare feet upon the deck. Those "iron men and wooden ships" of the old navy, who knew not the meaning of fresh meat and "soft-tack" aboard ship, who only received a liberty at the end of their cruise, and then got beastly drunk and remained so till they were shipped again. Yet we get their ration; the wooden walls are now steel walls; and [there] is required to man these steel walls 99% more brain than the old wooden ships required. Everything has changed, but the ration remains as it was in the last century.

Just witnessed a scrap on the fo'castle between an English seaman of the 3rd division and an apprentice boy. It was "nip and tuck." The skipper witnessed it from the bridge, but said nothing. Neither one was hurt, and they will perhaps be better friends after it.

I mentioned before in this log how many ways you can increase your monthly stipend. Here is an example in the fellow who clipped my hair last night. He is a coal-passer in rating, at $22.00 per month, is cooking, $18.00 more, and shaves and cuts hair besides—a good many irons in the fire. He makes good wages for a man-o-warsman.

Had a pretty fair supper tonight. Cook made some biscuits with some jam. They tasted very good. [I] must have eaten about 15, more or less, with a couple bowls of tea to wash them down. Like all sailormen, I flatter myself on being a good trencherman, and can always enjoy a good, square meal, doubly so when we only get one about every week. Also found out what became of the duff. Turned a dark purple color on the cook's account, was spoilt, so he gave it a passage over the side. He is young and no doubt will learn, but meantime, we grow thin.

Old John, two machinists and myself, with hundreds of others, were lying around on the forecastle in the cool evening breezes and watching and pointing out the different stars, jollying each other and trying to convince one of the party which was the Southern Cross and making a bet that the foot star of the Cross would appear before 8 P.M. He seemed doubtful, however, that it was the Southern Cross, but the lower star making its appearance, tho' very dim, convinced him.

Far off on the horizon appeared a flashing light and we knew that we were fast approaching Manila Bay and that our long voyage would soon be over. Soon we were up to the light and we steamed swiftly by and past Corregidor, thro' the same channel in the starlit night that a long grey line of warships, not quite two years ago found and stole softly thro' in the dusk of a May morning, past the forts and over [the] mines, and lay before the eyes of an astonished city in the early dawn. The rest is history.

As we steamed swiftly up the bay, we signaled the flagship. The lights of the city and the numerous shipping in the harbor were in sight. The moon arose over the dark edge of the city in all its majesty, illuminating the scene almost as bright as day. Our signals were answered by the flagship. We glided by craft after craft to our anchorage. "All Hands bring ship to anchor," came the terse command from the bridge. "All Hands bring ship to anchor," piped the Boatswain's mates in chorus. And we knew that our voyage across two oceans and three seas to the other end of the world was over. All hands were called to quarters.

"Bugler, call away the gig," came the order from the officer of the deck.

"Let go the anchor," and through the hawse pipes sounded the rattling of the chain.

I went below from where I was standing on deck as retreat from quarters was sounded, to seek my "caulking mat" on the tops of the bunkers, and as I went, I heard the word from the Boatswain, "All secure, sir." And then, "Pipe down," and all was silence.

The End

The Cruise to Manila
Fred T. Wilson
U. S. S. *New Orleans*
Manila, Dec. 22nd, [1899]
To Asiatic Station

Prologue

CHAPTER ONE

Manila

The United States Cruiser *New Orleans* left New York Oct. 21st 1899 and arrived here in Manila Dec. 21st 1899 after quite an exciting and interesting trip. After our arrival here we first heard that we were racing across the globe to see which ship should arrive first, the *Brooklyn, Newark, Nashville* and *Marietta*[1] having started from different ports in the States a few days ahead of us. The *Newark* left San Francisco about the same time and of course arrived in Manila considerably ahead of us. We of the *New Orleans* rapidly overhauled the *Brooklyn* and would probably have arrived in Manila first best but for an accident to the port engine between Colombo and Singapore which necessi[ta]ted a lay-over for repairs at Singapore. However, we made the best time across, being exactly two months on the trip, but at the time we knew nothing of the interest taken in the States to see which ship would beat in the voyage half around the world. I only know we were pushing the *New Orleans* for all we were worth, that is, not full power as there was always one boiler in reserve. And I suppose the other ships were doing the same.

We were all naturally anxious to reach Manila both on account of being at the end of our journey as well as to satisfy our curiosity as to the place. We wanted to see the principal places we had read so much about in this far away place: Cavite, Corregidor, Manila, etc. From all accounts that the most of us had received from shipmates and newspaper accounts, the entrance to Manila Bay was about as narrow as Santiago's channel where the *Merrimac* was sunk by [Naval Constructor Richmond P.] Hobson and his crew.[2] But I should judge that the people who compared the two entrances had never seen Santiago, for we judged the entrance to Manila past Corregidor about 4 miles in its narrowest part. And Manila Bay itself would afford room enough, and to spare, to float all the navies of the world.

Well, we arrived and reported to the flagship *Brooklyn,* and after being at Manila a few days we were ordered across the bay to Cavite for a few repairs. From Cavite we can just barely discern the flagship laying across the bay, it being somewhat difficult to discern signals from here. Well, after getting settled down to routine we were allowed shore leave from 9:30 A.M. until sundown, as our part came around to go ashore, which is generally every fourth day. It was only on [Saturdays] and Sundays that we could catch the ferry for Manila, it leaving every morning at 9:30 and only on those two days were we allowed to leave the ship early enough to make this boat, the *Taaleño*, which was or is the Government boat. There is another ferry line [run] by the natives that used to leave Cavite at 10:00 A.M. Sundays, named the *Filipino*, and that was the boat I took on my first liberty ashore. Just barely caught it in time one Sunday morning. Just paid my forty cents Mex and secured a ticket in time.[3]

The ride across the bay is quite a long one occupying over an hour, but it is well worth the passage from Cavite, there being many sights to engross one's attention. Everything in the shipping line seemed to be an Army transport; more transports than war vessels, in fact. Here and there they could be seen discharging cargo in[to] the *cascos*[4] along side or embarking soldiers for their homeward bound trip, which is the best part of Army life to them. Beyond the breakwater and close to the entrance to the Pasig river were numerous natives in *banca*s[5] fishing away in a stolid manner. I watched them closely but did not see one of them secure anything whilst we were going past. But it is quite an animated scene along the Pasig. You plunge [into] it almost immediately from the bay, by an abrupt turn to the right, and you can see nothing but *casco*s filled with inhabitants as far as you can see, steamers and shipping from different parts of the Orient, life and bustle everywhere.

They, the house-boat dwellers, seem to live a happy, contented sort of an existence. They take life in a very easy manner, content with little; enough to eat of the plainest kind, principally rice, and any old article of clothing to cover their nakedness suffices. They are like fish in the water. Young girls and women are as expert as the men, living as they do on the water all their lives. It is almost as much their native element as dry land. As a rule tho', they are pretty modest. Only the youngsters are clothed in the "altogether." The brown houseboat maidens are fond of gaudy colors, and you can see them decked out on gala occasions with brilliant hues of all descriptions: reds, blues, yellows, etc., of the crudest coloring, smoking the inevitable cigarettes. They go bare-footed and bare-legged around the decks of their *casco*.

The ferry stops opposite the Captain of the Port's office, and here also there is plenty of bustle and excitement, what with native officials of every description. Some of them, I noticed, had a band around their white caps with "Captain of the Port" in gold letters upon it. Sentries were walking to and fro and here and there an Army or Naval officer could be seen. I noticed upon this wharf hundreds of coffins, each with an inmate. Poor fellows. It meant war to them and to their relatives and friends. They were waiting to be taken aboard an Army transport and thence home. Homeward bound! There must have been sorrow in many an American home over the husband, the brother, or the son who went forth seeking for glory and adventure only to find a death in a far-off land, perhaps to get shot down at the last moment by an insurgent bullet after months of hardship thro' swamp, rice field and jungle, in trench and on hard fought fields. That was their longed for home-coming.

I strolled all over Manila, looking at places of interest, taking in the sights. It is much like any other old town that Spain has possessed. It shows the same style of architecture that is associated with Spanish rule. It is an old, old city reeking with bad smells, burning bamboo fires that the people cook with. In the quiet streets you can see the Filipino women washing in the streets. And the wash isn't hung on lines, but laid on a piece of matting in front of the dwelling, each piece in a loose heap. It looked to me at a distance like a flower-vendor's array of different colored flowers. It doesn't take long for the tropical sun to dry them out.

The day being Sunday it was pretty quiet for Manila. Along the business portion of the town every shop was open, but all saloons were closed. But of course it was like a Raines-law Sunday in New York.[6] You can get drink in any portion of the globe, at least I have found it so. I dropped in one Chinese restaurant and bar and ordered a bottle of beer, and one of the waiters says, "No sellee beer alone. Got to makee bluff allee same Malican man." He knew. He had been in Frisco, Portland and other Western cities. So I ordered a wedge of pie (a great combination, pie and beer), but it was only by thus doing that I got the beer, which was very warm and cost 40 [cents] Mex per pint bottle. My first impression of Manila wasn't very favorable. In fact, I voted it a mighty dull place, different from any other Oriental city. I came back aboard the ship and was glad to do so.

We had a marine from our ship who went on liberty with quite a sum of money for a marine, getting drunk and making a display of his coin as some men will. He was last seen taking a *banca* to come aboard the ship, having missed the launch from Cavite. His body was recovered a few days after and identified, the badly decomposed part of the face eaten away. He was murdered while in the boat and thrown overboard. It doesn't pay to trust Filipinos to[o] far. They are too handy with the deadly bolos, and often, under the disguise of friendship and posing as "amigos," they are only too willing to murder you for a few Mexican dollars.

I only made two visits to Manila whilst there. On my second one I changed my opinion of the place considerably. I had a good time. Being Saturday, every thing was lively and in full blast. The streets were crowded in the business portion of the town. Along Escolta it was a continuous procession, the narrow street being crowded with pony coaches, carabao carts, cavalrymen on horseback cantering along, the majority I seen being mounted upon the native pony. They are hardy little things, sort of a cross between a mustang and our own horse. It looked like cruelty to animals to see a big cavalry-man or officer mounted on one, his stirrups lengthened out so they nearly touched the ground. They present anything but a martial appearance thus mounted. Put you in mind of Don Quixote on another Rocinante.

Carabao carts are another object of interest to the casual visitor. Carabao, or "water buffalos," are something like our oxen in the even gait they strike. You can hit them with a bale stick or pick handle and they simply pay no attention at all. The driver can tug at the line he holds attached to a ring in their nose but not a muscle does he move from the same old gait. They absolutely refuse to work harder than a settled pace. It must be understood among them. At certain hours of the day he must be driven down to the water where he can wallow in it and get refreshed. If the driver for any cause neglects this important function, Mr. Carabao will make a steady lope for the nearest place to bathe, taking cart, cargo, and driver in with him. There is no stopping him.

Along the Escolta and across the bridge of Spain there is quite a traffic. You can see Filipino women in their native dress which is not according to the latest Parisian fashions, no doubt, but still is very picturesque. With the yellow piña waist and black skirt wrapped closely around them, bare feet in high sandals, they go mincing along with fan and sunshade. They wear no head gear. Some of them are quite good looking. In the pony coaches you can see the socially up to date army or navy women shopping, their smart, up to date appearance in great contrast to the Spanish women or other types.

You see all nations here: Japanese and Chino and their women. French and Spanish women. But the American women [threw] them in the shade completely. About the queerest sight I saw was a Filipino woman dressed in a straw sailor [hat] with shirt waist and black silk skirt, like "Mericano." She presented quite a startling appearance thus gowned, with her comical looking "Phisiog" [physiognomy] with its high cheek bones and slant eyes under a straw sailor. Anyway, the motive was good, no matter what the result. She was ready to become Americanized as soon as possible. Strolling along, I went in the best saloon I could see, "The San Miguel," which is carried on in quite American style. It was filled with soldiers and sailors principally, with here and there Frenchmen, Spaniards and natives. You get the coolest glass of beer in Manila there, 20 cts. Mexican. I made my way thro' the crowd to a vacant table and sat down, looking at the varied scene around me. Dusty looking soldiers from the front were out in force and also a large sprinkling of a new regiment who had just disembarked a day or so previous, their nice clean uniforms in sharp contrast with the well worn ones of the men who had been thro' it all and were waiting to get relieved from the fighting for a while.

While sitting there studying the scene around me and inwardly thinking what a martial appearance it presented, and incidentally quaffing a generous quantity from the large "geyser" on the table by my side, I was touched on the shoulder while a voice inquired, "Excuse me! But what ship are you off of?" Turning, I saw a soldier of the 21st Reg[iment]. The face seemed familiar to me but I could not place it.

"From the *New Orleans*," I replied.

"Do you know anybody by the name of W[ilson] on the *Brooklyn*, a water-tender?"

"I am a water-tender and my name is W[ilson]. But I am from the *New Orleans*," I rejoined.

"Great Scott! I know you now. Don't you recognize me? Joe H——from Baltimore. Remember the time we were together in a circus?"

Manila

Then I knew him. "Shake, old man! I am glad to see you. How are you making out? Join me?"

"No. Take a drink with me. Come over to my table? By Gad, I am glad to see you."

"Same here."

And then began a series of questions and answers and recollections of bygone times when we were both "kids" doing a tumbling act in a small circus. And inquiries about mutual friends and acquaintances. Gradually as the beer flowed we got more and more reminiscent and in a mellow mood. He had been out quite a while and it was all active service, had been on the "hike" after "Aggie" [Emilio Aguinaldo] since the arrival of his regiment nearly a year past. In fact, [he] had just come in from the "firing line" the day before.

"I am sick of it all," he said. "I never was so weary looking at dead bodies before. Dead Filipinos. They keep us on the hike all the time. We have been in several stiff fights. It has got so now, a force of a dozen Americans can start a regiment of the 'niggers' on a run. I don't want to fire a gun off anymore. Don't care if I never handle mine again. Would just like to stay here in Manila until we are relieved and sent home."

Among other things, he told me of the bamboo cannon the insurgents used, [and] how they would reload empty cartridge shells. A Filipino would fire at them and then run and hide his gun and pick up a hoe or something and be industriously working when you next saw him. The very ones who would carry water for the tired soldiers one day, the next would be fighting against them. Now they only wanted to fight when they felt like it. They wanted to knock off fighting on Sundays and go to church. Says he saw a detachment go boldly out in front of the American line to go to services in a church that was nearby, thinking that the Americans would not disturb them. And they were might[i]ly surprised when they were shelled and dozens of them killed. Couldn't understand our method of warfare.

Well, we began to feel rather good under the influence of numerous "beers," just enough to feel contented with life under any circumstance. Didn't care a cuss whether we were in Manila or the North Pole. Somebody proposed to sally forth and take in the town. We left the saloon and pushed our way along the narrow sidewalks thro' the crowds. We went into a nearby cigar shop to get a few "smokes" and while purchasing, Joe noticed a small statuette holding a drinking horn up in its right hand.

"Shay G——, 'hic,' chancht to buy curio, send 'im home. Fine work of art. Hic. King Gambrinish eh? What'ell."

I looked at Gambrinus and he looked (so it seemed) at me in a knowing way.[7] A sort of sympathy seemed to exist between us. "All rightah," says I. "How much, old man, for the King?"

"60 Mex," says he.

So the King became mine, tho' what in thunder I wanted of him in the curio line I could never tell, he being made of very base metal indeed, a little pewter King on a marble base. But cheap at 60 cts. Mex. If they had charged me ten times that amount, no doubt I would have purchased just the same. A sailor or soldier will buy any old thing, you know. I have the King in my possession still.

Leaving the cigar store with our lighted cigars (and you can get good cigars in Manila very cheap, and they are the only article you can get cheap there) and the King tucked in my only pocket (the one in my white dress blouse. We go ashore in white uniform in these warm climates), we passed from the busy streets across the Bridge of Spain and were soon in a more quiet neighborhood. Here they were very old streets indeed, in old Spanish style. Hardly anybody was visible, probably taking their "siesta" as I should judge it, too, about the noon hour.

Yes! Manila is a very old city indeed. For instance, take the old fort along the Pasig, [covered] with moss and gray with age. And also the Walled City. You would imagine you were transposed by some subtle influence back into a bygone age, and would not be surprised to see men in doublet and hose with rapiers at their side, men at arms in steel corselet and halberd and all the varied costumes and customs of a bygone century strolling along those old quiet streets. It is true there are men at arms about, for almost every few squares we would run across a soldier, but in the brown khaki uniform instead of corselet of steel, and with a belt loaded with ammunition and Colt revolver instead of halberd or pike. The old city being under martial rule, soldiers are doing police duties as well as the force of native policemen, who, by the way, render good and efficient service to the conquerors. We also ran up against groups of released Spanish prisoners, because at this time they had not been sent home, and all were on parole, smoking their cigarettes and taking life philosophically. No doubt they feel keenly their position, for here they were only a short time ago all powerful. But the fortunes of war, you know. The long walk was sobering us up a bit, so we proposed a halt until we refreshed the inner man once more. There happened to be a small shop close by that sold bottled beer, so we sojourned there for quite a while. We were getting noisy but in a good-natured way; felt at peace with all the world.

Coming across a large church we went thro' that. It was open, as all churches are in Manila, and an imposing looking structure from the outside, but moreso when we entered it. It had been newly painted, chiefly in imitation of porphyry and onyx. It is very lofty, and inspiring enough to look from the tessellated floor to the naves so far above. In fact, you felt that you were in a church, and we, who were feeling very good indeed, recognized that fact. The only occupants it had at that hour were a couple of Filipino scrub women and two or three men, probably the caretakers of the church. We went into the vestry, which was a large room hung around with costly oil paintings of the orthodox religious order but otherwise bare with the exception of a few chairs and a table. The windows were all of stained glass. I was afterwards told it was the finest church in the Philippines. There is one thing about all Oriental and European churches: they have that about them that makes one realize by their vastness and furnishings that they are indeed places of worship, moreso than the American church style of architecture does. It is the magnificent reach from pavé to dome that gives that feeling of sublimity to them, and that [which] the American churches all lack, unless the Mormon Temple at Salt Lake [City, Utah,] is an exception.

We took a turn thro' the Tenderloin situated on the outskirts of the city. These unfortunate women are all kept in one quarter. They occupy two streets each about half a mile in length. They are the off scourings of Russia, Sweden, Norway, etc., with a sprinkling of Spanish. I don't doubt in that small space you can find almost every nation represented. I know we got enfiladed by a choice selection of cockney slang from one dissipated hag. Don't believe in all my experience in different parts of the globe I ever heard her peer. She was simply a model in her own peculiar class. A trooper or sailor would appear an amateur in contrast with her. I did not see many native women in this section. In fact, I can't recall one face. They generally keep aloof and to themselves unless selling fruit, etc.

We quickly left the Tenderloin behind us, and our ammunition beginning to give out, we voted with one accord there was only one place to quench our overpowering thirst, and that was back at the San Miguel saloon again. So back we started. Joe had some photos to get on the way back and when we stopped there we had to get ours taken in a group, of course. So the artist posed us as best he could, telling us in broken English to look pleasant. No need to tell us that, as we were very happy and in a beaming state. We tried to look sedate enough and partly succeeded. I know when the pictures were rec'd, Joe had a particularly benign expression of countenance. For R——and myself, least said the better.

We reached the San Miguel, and as it was getting along we only had a few moments to stay together, they having to report by 5:30 and having a long distance to walk to reach their quarters. We bid each other good bye with numerous hand shakes and protestations of eternal friendship, all three in a maudlin state, but happy. [Then] we parted, they for their camp and I down to the Captain of the Port's to get the *Taaleño* across to Cavite.

On the wharf one will meet many old shipmates, friends he may have not seen for years. I ran across many such, and we had quite a lot of news to unfold to one another on the trip across, inquiries about shipmates and reminiscences of times past in other ships and in other parts of the world. In both my trips to Manila I did not see a drunken bluejacket or marine or soldier. It is true the bottle was passed frequently but was lightly touched. Bluejackets are not saints, you know, and not many years ago, Jack's liberty ashore wasn't complete until he was stupefied with liquor and badly beaten in several fights. We of the new ships are wiser now.

On the run across the bay the *Taaleño* stopped at the different ships to return libertymen. The *New Orleans* men were carried to the Navy Yard in Cavite and we there caught our launch to the ship. There at Cavite we would have another chance to meet old friends whilst they were waiting for [their] respective launches. I met an old friend of mine on this last trip to Manila. I have met him often in different places.

A Sailor's Log

The last time I had the pleasure of meeting him was in [Philadelphia] when we were both paid off, and this time in Cavite. It is not such a large world after all is said and done. I only had a chance to exchange a few words with him. I was talking to some of the boys at the launch landing and somebody tapped me on the shoulder. I say "tapped," it sounds milder. In reality it was a smash between the shoulder blades that took my breath away and jarred the King from my pocket.

"Hello, old man! When did you come out here and what are you on?"

"That you old sport? Glad to see you. The *New Orleans,* and you?"

"The *Glacier.*[8] Come and see me some time on a visiting party to the ship. We can talk it all over."

That was all. The greeting between two chums who had not seen each other for a year and a half. Wonder where the next meeting will take place? We never correspond with each other, but we will eventually run up against each other at some future day.

Well, I came aboard the ship feeling good, the King and I, with the memory of a good day's liberty in old Manila, not too much to drink, and the satisfaction of meeting some old and dear friends in this far off land. A man is none the worse off for a little sport. Anything to relieve the tedious monotony of a man-o-war. We are thrown far too little in contact with the world. We are kept too long aboard. You see a bluejacket ashore. He is drunk. You blame him. He has perhaps twelve hours liberty to enjoy himself in. And he has no doubt been kept aboard ship three months, perhaps six or more on a foreign station. That is all. He is not necessarily a drunkard because he breaks out after coming almost out of prison. Well, I put the King in my ditty box and there he is to this day, a souvenir of a delightful liberty in Manila. Eh, Gambrinus, old boy?

Close by us where we laid at Cavite are the sunken, blackened wrecks of the [*Reina*] *Christina* and the *Castilla,* their charred and battered remains mute witness of what war is, and what war must have meant to them on that memorable day of May First, 1898.[9] They have been literally stripped of every thing removable. Even pieces of brass have been chipped away by curio hunters. They are indeed a pathetic sight, but not one half as pathetic as that other blackened, charred hulk that lies at the other end of the world in Havana harbor.[10] A few of the crew received permission to visit one of the wrecks, and taking a small boat they rowed over to the *Castilla* on a Sunday morning after morning inspection. Being good swimmers, they dived for anything in the curio line in and out of the wreck, but the only articles them could obtain were a couple of 4.7 shells and an old rusted rifle, part of which, the stock, was missing. And that the Captain made them throw away for fear it was loaded, and being rusted so, it would be dangerous to remove the ammunition. But they still had the shells.[11]

Over from us at that time lay the *Oregon,* the *Monterey, Marietta, Nashville, Helena* and *Newark.*[12] The last named has just arrived from a tour around the Islands where they had taken a town. She was flying the yellow quarantine flag when she steamed into Cavite, having a couple of cases of small-pox aboard (which is a very common thing among the Filipinos, mostly all of them having their faces pitted). We were also quarantined at that time. Two of the crew, being suspected of the bubonic plague, were removed to a small building on the extreme end of Cavite and there isolated from contact with the world in general.

One of the quarantined men had deserted from the ship and getting beached in Manila and unable to get a ship back to the States, enlisted in the Army and still had on the uniform of a soldier when apprehended and brought aboard the ship. He was supposed to have contracted the plague during his months in the city.

The *Brooklyn* had gone to Hong Kong and it was current news that we were to leave for Nagasaki immediately upon her return, but you can never rely upon any news you hear in the outfit. Of course we were all anxious for a change, as it had grown horribly monotonous lying at Cavite with nothing to look forward to except routine. The daily grind of a man-o-warsman's life [is] only relieved by monthly money being served out, when the games of chance would start up in full blast. In No. 3 Fireroom, I remember, [there] were two games in opposition to each other, one being a sweat game, and the other joker dice. Talk about "dobie" dollars,[13] you could see about a peck of them lying around, principally in front of the dealer, the man who ran the game. Also poker partys in quiet parts of the ship. They only last a short while tho'; in less than a week one or two parties would have all the money and the rest, having borrowed all they could, would be broke and looking forward to next payday.

All Mexican money [is used] out here and almost every month it fluctuates in value all the way from 43 cts. to 50 cts. It was a common sight to see the crew as fast as it was served out to them ringing it on the bunker's top and deck. I remember the first batch of coin served out to us. Out of 31 Mex, I found 3 lead dollars. I was lucky, as some of the men found a dozen or so. It is the easiest coin imaginable to counterfeit. They counterfeit a special brand of Mexican dollar for the drunken soldier and sailor trade. It is such a flimsy counterfeit that a five year old kid could detect it. It is made of iron and covered with tin, purely and simply just that, and it goes with a drunk without the least trouble. Other dollars they will drill full of holes for the silver, honey-combing them completely and plugging the holes with lead. It is beyond a doubt the worst looking coin in the world and I wonder WJB——while out here as a colonel of a regiment didn't get disgusted at his ideas of a silver standard.[14] In these countries you require a belt to carry your month's pay around with, or else a carpet bag or basket.

I had heard much about the Far East and how much one of these "dobie" or "dungaree dollars" will purchase: a land where you get paid two for one and where you double [your] pay (sic). [That is only] another illusion quickly dispelled, as much of the romance of the East is also, when you come in actual contact with it. Why, everything out here costs a "dobie" dollar! Buy a meal, and not a very good one at that.

One Mex. If you are a drinking man, treat a friend. One Mex. Buy a trinket, no matter how flimsy or common. 1 Mex. "Allee samee," and thus it is thro' the whole gamut. I never saw much change while here. [Your] Mexicans slipped from you, if you just opened your face. "Gone where the woodbine twineth." There is one consolation, however; we never looked upon it seriously as money. In fact, I have [seen] hundreds of them thrown in a locker or ditty box that wasn't locked and nobody would think of stealing them. Too much trouble to get away with. Takes a whole sock-full to pay for one liberty ashore. "Nay! Nay! Pauline," the coinage of the U.S. is good enough for me just as it stands.

We have always had trouble more or less with this ship on account of its narrow beam and top heaviness, it being the easiest matter in the world to list her over a few degrees. And when she would become listed there would be one continual roar from the captain. Orderlies and messengers would be kept running to the chief engineer galore telling him to get her on an even keel. Of course the fault always lay with the engineers force. I remember one night she had a decided list to port and the captain was foaming at the mouth and kept his [orderly] on the trot running to the warrant

The *New Orleans* as she appeared on her delivery to the U.S. Navy in 1898. Navy Historical Foundation.

Manila

mach[inist] who had charge of below during the "chief's" absence. "The captain wants the ship on an even keel, sir." "Take the list out." Everything was trim below. The three boilers were equally filled with water, also the steaming one for auxiliary purposes. The reserve tanks in the double-bottoms were filled completely, and we had been taking coal from the port side right along, but of course, the fault was "below."

The orderly kept carrying his message, telling the mach[inist] "to fix that list" until the mach[inist] waxed sarcastic and said, "What list? Fix what list? Tell him to tell me which list and I will try and have it fixed." Whether the orderly carried the answer to the old man is not known, but finally the "old man" came and jumped the machinist himself. And such a "jacking" up! The Mach tried to explain, but it was no go. The fault lay below. He wouldn't be convinced that it might [be] the way stores were stowed in [the] paymaster's department or anything of that kind. So, after a bitter tirade, he ordered a gang of men below to shift coal from one bunker to the other, from port to starboard. It had to be done of course, no appeal.

So, the two clean fire-rooms were filled with coal in transferring from port to starboard, keeping twelve coal-passers and firemen busy for at least four hours. In order to help out on this occasion I pumped D boiler's water over into C. Otherwise the gang would have been occupied at least four hours more, [but I ran] the risk myself of getting reprimanded for using my own judgment. No matter what the occasion is, you are in doubt whether to use your own judgement or not. That is inculcated in you from the start. I have found that out long since and have learned not to be too zealous in my duties.

~~~

We were the recipients of the news one day that there was to be a skirmish between the troops and the insurgents on the extreme end almost of Cavite province just a few miles distant from Manila, and not so far from Cavite village itself. So we watched from the ship and every once in a while we could see a slight puff of smoke arising from the brush along the beach, and gradually those puffs of smoke became more numerous and were coming nearer and nearer to Cavite as our troops gradually got the natives on the "hike" and kept them moving. By the aid of a strong pair of glasses I saw three or four natives break from the brush and lope along the beach at full speed, so I judged that the boys had them going. No use trying to catch them. You couldn't catch them with a switch engine. They would stop just long enough to pillage and burn along the way. I felt sorry for the boys who were on that "firing line" that day for you could fairly see the heat simmering over the distant beach with not a breath of air. The hospital ship had worked its way as close as possible to the scene of action and continued to lay off there for two days. I believe from the reports we heard afterward there were not many casualties among our troops, but among the "niggers"[15] it was pretty severe; [however,] that charge effectually cleared the province.

The whole trouble lies in the fact that we are a little too lenient in dealing with them, our troops not being allowed to fire unless fired upon. It looks, from what I have seen and heard, that the administration trends toward prolonging the war, as there are obvious reasons for so doing. Among other reasons, not by any means the least, are the "sons of somebody" who hold commissions in the volunteer army drawing fat salaries for [comparatively] little labor, Army contractors, etc. The men themselves, one and all, are heartily sick of it, and hail with joy any prospects of getting home again.

We had quite a dry old "square head" for warrant machinist on the *New Orleans*,[16] and the way he would murder the English of his adopted country was simply something fierce. Every time he transferred an order to me in person it was all I could do to restrain myself from laughing in his face. His station was the firerooms and all auxiliaries connected with them. Every warrant machinist [has] stations under their immediate supervision to keep up in repair. They have taken the place of engineers as provided in the new Navy Personnel Bill. He was known to the gang below as "Whiskers" on account of a large pair of ecru lambrequins attached to his face.[17] I suppose he imagined he looked like one of the old Norse Vikings of his country, but he was almost an exact counterpart of the King Gambrinus, minus the costume and drinking horn of course.

His favorite hobby was the blowers in the fire-rooms. He would keep the machinists under him continually repairing them, and was always at the water-tender of the watch about them, giving him his orders to see that they were properly oiled and not running too fast. He happened to have the duty one Sunday, and making his rounds thro' the department discovered the blower in no. 4 fire-room running as fast as an express train, and making about as much noise. The oiler of the watch, a colored man, was full of "vino" or alcohol and started it up to cool his throbbing head. There he set, calmly enjoying the breeze as it cooled his fevered brow. Whiskers was almost paralyzed with the audacity of the act. Running a blower without permission was simply an act of sublime nervine. Striking an attitude like C. Columbus in the act of discovering America, he roared, "Who was de man, und who vas de reason which was dat blowers started up, aind it?"

The oiler looked up as wise as an owl and denied all knowledge of the crime. Whiskers fumed and roared but could not shake the assertion of the oiler in the least. "Some oof doze days I stop dose plowers altogedder aint id, and put 'em on de repord."

One day at quarters in the morning he asked me, "Who ist standing vatch for you?"

I looked at him. "Nobody is standing watch for me. I am standing my own watch and have just come off."

"No. No. You cann ifka boosta. I mean who ist standing vatch for you?"

"I tell you nobody is standing watch for me. I am standing my own watch."

Then he got hot under the collar, and in a tone intended to contain a great deal of sarcasm, asked me, "Do you shoffel your coal? Do you go mit de fire a slice bar fly? Pull dose ashes py a hoe und plow dose oilers? I means oil dose plowers? Got damn! I mean who stands watch for you? Are you de firemans or de coal-passers, aind id?"

"Oh," I replied. "I savvy. You want to know the men who are standing watch *with* me!" And I told him. Well, he went directly to the other section and asked the other water tender the same question, in exactly the same way, received the same answer, and then foamed at the mouth and cursed us for not understanding English as she is spoken in broken Norwegian. Truth, our modern men of war are composed of many nationalities. There will be no room for an American after awhile. The deck petty officers are nearly all foreigners, as I have said before, and some of the "words" they pass on deck are truly wonderful and would lead a wondering visitor to guess what he was up against.[18]

~ ~ ~

Our quarantine was kept up for quite a while, and we were even closer prisoners than we commonly are aboard the ship. That is the rub in a sailor's life. No wonder we are unsociable and rough in our ways when we do get ashore, and no wonder we break out and drink a drop too much when we get the chance. Show me any person who will not and I'll show you a cold-blooded milk-sop with "cold feet," one who is the exception, not the rule. We are put down, both soldiers and sailors, as failures and drunkards by the world at large. We are not all that tho'; not by any old means. Take this army and navy here in the Philippines, perhaps over fifty thousand men. Go among them. See how many drunks you will find and how many disorderly ones. I'll guarantee you will find more disorder among the same sized crowd in civil life. You will see more people acting the "hard mug" and being disorderly and drunk at a large camp-meeting or at any place where the masses congregate. I'll wager that nowhere in the world will you find for the same amount of people such an orderly army and navy. Does Army discipline and Naval discipline and fear of punishment keep them in check? It might in some cases. But in an Army of occupation there is almost an unlimited opportunity to loot and commit all sorts of depredations, but such cases have yet to be reported. "No?" No.

The American soldier or sailor goes and passes away his spare time in the only place where he is sure of getting entertainment, and of meeting shipmates and comrades. He will drink, I grant you, and get jolly, but seldom quarrelsome. What the devil would you have them do on a run ashore after months aboard ship in dull routine, or leave from lines after duty well done? Get a tract or Bible and get off in some quiet corner and read the same with a long, puritanical "phisiog" and go back to duty "hiking" the "niggers" feeling much refreshed after his recreation? We know how to enjoy ourselves, and we do it in our own way. If so, as long as we tran[s]gress no laws and interfere with nobody, why, it is our own look-out. People who don't like

A Sailor's Log

it can do the next best thing. We can't bring them to our way of thinking, and we shall leave them talk about the war and what they would do if they had charge of the campaign. Meanwhile, they stay at home keeping their own precious carcasses out of harm's way, where, if they are inclined to think the soldiers and sailors of the Spanish-American or Philippine wars are such an extremely horrid lot and beyond reformation, they can no doubt seek consolation at some old maids' meetings, and [there], over unlimited quantities of tea and cake (which these same duffers have a large and generous capacity for), discuss what is best to do for the poor, degenerate soldier or sailor. Or they can steal our girl away from us whilst we are gone. "That's all fair, etc."

Meanwhile Jack, old shipmate or comrade, we'll drink our beer or something stronger in some retreat among congenial company, thinking of the time when we can see mothers, wives, and sweethearts once again. But in order not to lose all the enjoyment of this life, we mustn't think too much of the "girl we left behind" because that same duffer with the sanctimonious case of countenance and generous opening for tea and cake or cream might be "culling us out in her affections" while we are here. We are all right for souvenirs and cap-ribbons and soldiers' buttons. Fans and jewelry are cheaply purchased at the expense of a letter telling us how much they love us, sic. And would we please not forget to send her some souvenir to remember her absent boy with? Of course we do, bless their dear little scheming heads and hearts. Of course these little epistles make us feel good, you and I, Jack. But it doesn't hinder us from making love to some dusky Filipino maiden or little Jap, while Katie or Mae, if you please, not May, are being escorted to some church sociable (where they serve cut cake and cream) by the stay-at-home who is working his fine points. We will wander down some leafy bower amid tall bamboo and lofty palms with the dusky maiden of our choice, remembering all the time that "absence makes the heart grow fonder," remembering also that "absence brings forgetfulness." And we can't indulge in too much castle-building as it is of too ephemeral an architecture. Let the future look out for itself. Only the present is ours. Let us drink when we can and make love when we can. Do you *"sabe"*? *"Mañana"* never comes.

Speaking about the gals, whether dusky or not, we had a debating society that used to compare notes on topics of all kinds from how we [would] run the campaign if we had our way, down to comparing our ideal ideas of what an American girl should be. We would meet on the top of the bunkers about 7 P.M. These were our sleeping quarters. We would spread our "caulking mats" and make a pillow of a "dungaree" jumper, and thus, if undisturbed, we were fixed for the night and would hold rather lively conversations until "Taps."

A young fellow from Mass[achusetts] held forth on the mat next to mine. Another chap from New York, one from Indiana and another from Phila[delphia] also slept in close proximity, and we would have some pretty hot arguments at times. If one man expressed an opinion on any subject, the rest of us would throw him down just as if we were trying to "enclose" him in a game of cards. Mac, the man from

Mass[achusetts], started to fall away in flesh when we left New York. You could see him dwindle away in front of your gaze. We would try and rally him. "What's the matter, Mac?" said one of the gang one night. "Why that solemncholy case of countenance? You look like you have been crossed in love, or are suffering from a severe attack of homesickness."

"Yes, don't take it to heart s'much old man. Just as good girls to be caught out here. You can buy a little Jap when we go to Nagasaki and she will love you better than the girl that threw you down."

"You fellows make me dead tired. You're talking rag-time. I don't care for any girl or wasn't threw down by any, and I have been to sea long enough to not be homesick. I can't eat this stuff we are getting, and I'm sick."

We insisted that he was homesick and in love until he got so mad he wouldn't speak to us. "What's the matter with Mac," says the lad from Indiana, "[is] he's been looking for his ideal girl and can't find her."

"That's so," I chimed in. "I believe I did hear something mentioned by Mac about his ideal. The trouble of it is when he finds his ideal, he'll fail to be his ideal's ideal. And he'll be worse off than he is now."

"That's the way with you mugs. You give everything away you hear, can't be trusted with any thing," roared the man from Mass.

"By the way, Mac, how is this last girl of yours, the one you are writing to?"

"None of your biz."

"Do you think she'll wait for him and be true to him all this time?" asked one, addressing his remarks to me, so Mac could hear.

"She might," I rejoined, "but I doubt it. But the question is whether he'll be true to her. You know how fickle he is. He's a proper sailor."

Mac prides himself on being very faithful, but it is only a delusion on his part. He couldn't be content with one girl if his life depended on it. The way he has jumped about from one to another would keep a person busy keeping tabs on him. But he takes a great deal of comfort to himself on his faithfulness, and if you want to get him mad and indignant you have only to tell him he is fickle-minded. He will not see himself as others see him. And we, knowing his weak point, always harp on it to get him mad. Why, it was only [a] week that he was acquainted with the girl he corresponds with before leaving New York. Prior to that he was madly in love with a girl in Phila[delphia], and before that one in Boston. He was inconsolable each time he broke off his engagement, but it would only last a week and he would bob up serenely with another ideal or as near to one as he could get. Fickle! Why, he's as fickle as I am.

Sailors are all susceptible; fall in love easily and out just as easily. We can love an Esquimoux just as easily as we can an American girl. That's adaptability. We adapt ourselves to circumstances and slight nothing that comes our way. But the American girl is preferred, muchly so for a hundred reasons.

Many and many a time have we held bunker conversations over every conceivable subject. We would have some hard arguments over the Boer war, being divided in our sympathies. From all indications, the majority were in favor of the Boers' cause. And at that period also, the other great cause for discussion was whether we were in the twentieth century or not, more people being interested in that problem than us. We never came to no definite decision on that point, and referred it to 1901, when there would be no doubt about the century.

Manila

CHAPTER TWO

Nagasaki

At last the long expected and oft delayed day arrived. Feb. 19th 1900 at 8:30 we [upped] anchor and left for Nagasaki, and I, for one, and lots of others, expressed the hope that they would never see Manila or Cavite or the Philippines again. Just before our departure for the North Asiatic Station, our old first-lieut[enant][1] was detached, as was also the boatswain.[2] The least said about the pair of them the better. The former was a fiend for drill and I should judge from the way he [treated] us, a dyspeptic or else troubled with liver complaint, for he certainly would give us of the engineers division a fierce deal at times. As the log shows on the run to Manila, he kept us at it from morning until night and no matter how hard we were worked below, after handling hoe and shovel and slice bar thro' a heart-breaking watch, at quarters he would give us "setting up drill" [calisthenics] and double-quick just as if we didn't get exercise enough. Peace be with him. I hope never to run against his like again. It seemed to be his especial mission to harass and make miserable and unendurable our already uncomfortable condition.

As for the Boatswain, he was cordially disliked, and systematically "cussed" (in an undertone, of course) by all hands. His was a most severe attack of abnormally swelled head. Despite frequent "call downs" from the "old man" and the other officers, he imagined he was the "real thing" and a "criterion to pattern by." He had been acting boatswain for over two years and had only an acting appointment in all that time. He should have rec'd it after acting a year. It was a frequent remark of his. "I don't drink, I don't chew, and I don't smoke, but I certainly do like the ladies." And it was this extreme liking for the ladies that caused his downfall. He was taking lessons in Spanish from a "lady" in Cavite, who besides instructing him in that language, presented him with a souvenir of their many lessons which landed him high [and] dry in the Naval Hospital in Cavite. "*Adios, Señor. Wie geitz, mon ami. Au revoir*, scat." 'Nuff said. The first luff who came before we left seemed to be of a different caliber, as also the Boatswain.

We were all glad to get away from Manila with its sickly climate. And we got away in a good time before the rainy season set in. There were several cases of bubonic plague, yellow fever and small pox there and we were quarantined for a full month before we left. All of the crew were vaccinated. What a blessing it was to come up on deck after a good hot watch below and breath[e] the cool breezes of the China sea. We could feel ourselves braced by it when only a few hours out, and in forty-eight hours the uniform was changed from white to blue. I don't like these hot climates, especially aboard a man-o-war, as there isn't much comfort under the most favorable conditions of the weather, and they are veritable steel hells in a hot climate. I would come up on deck from the mid watch below at 4 A.M., just before day broke, and look at the dark expanse of swirling waters and lowering skies, and the salt breeze would put new life in me. A man must be very stolid indeed who can look out over the vast ocean and remain unmoved. There is nothing finer, to my mind, or more sublime than such a sight: a wild surging sea and far off in the eastern skies a narrow strip of light, the approaching dawn. Or the same sea tipped with golden light from a full moon making the crests of waves look like molten gold, and perhaps off in the distant horizon silhouetted against the skies a ship in full sail. Such is the poetical side of a sea-faring life. I have been on many seas and oceans, and [have] seen them calm as a sheet of glass or as turbulent as a violent gale of wind could make them.

We ran into quite heavy head seas on the way to Japan, keeping the decks submerged for almost forty-eight hours. Sea after sea would break over our bow and dash fore and aft over the break of the fo'castle and run the length of the waist to the poop, clear thro' the freeing-ports. It seemed to be all head seas; we did not do much rolling, [instead] pitching all the time.

We were quite soft from our two months lay at Manila, and the first two or three watches went pretty hard with all of us. If you have never been called up on a midwatch [midnight to 4 A.M.] to go below and face three or four roaring fires with one to clean, you cannot form any conception of what a fire-man's life is in the service. A stoker's life is, as we all know, a short lived one at best on a great ocean liner. It is just as hard in the navy, only at times our runs are far between and we get a chance to recuperate. But take a long run, such as from New York to Manila: watch after watch, and you'll think you are in [hell]. I have saw many a man knocked out. These big warships don't steam none the easiest. I have been on a few merchant ships that steam easier. You have got to be poking a fire continually from the time you come on watch until relieved, and [there] is always a howl for more steam. You can't manufacture fog fast enough for the engineers. They can grind up more than you can give every time. On the *New Orleans* four boilers (all she has) will not furnish the engines all the steam they can use up. Neither will the eight twenty foot boilers on either the *Columbia* or *Minneapolis* furnish enough for their three engines.[3] If they could, there would be some chance to take it easy at times. The "man with the hoe" has a hard old time of it at best.

Here on this ship they won't allow us enough water to wash in. We have to get water to wash in any old place we can, from the feed pump while at sea, and from reserve-tanks and boilers whilst in port. Of course, that is stealing it and subjects you to punishment if caught, but we have got to have water, and will get it by hook or crook.

The weather continued to get cooler and cooler as we advanced, and the exhilarating effects could be noticed in the men. We felt better in every way. That "tired feeling" even disappeared, and we didn't mind the watches so much. The speed was increased to 85 revolutions. As we got clear of the China sea and out into the North Pacific Ocean, the heavy head seas had almost entirely disappeared and we were bowling along merrily. We had to soon get between blankets and there was no more "caulking off" on the fo'castle and waist. The cool weather made the fellows take to their "dream sacks,"[4] only among the engineers force we still held forth on the bunker top, but wrapped up snugly in a blanket.

Washington's birthday found us in the North Pacific. It being a holiday, all unnecessary work and drill was dispensed with, but we didn't have the dinner we bargained on having. We [had] put in a dollar Mex. along with our mess money to have a spread on that day, but as the fates ordained we were at sea, and our dinner consisted of "salt horse" vintage of '68 [1868], Minneapolis Creamery butter (put up especially for bluejackets' use), plum duff which was all right, as we had a good cook, stewed tomatoes, "spuds," and coffee which wasn't by any means bad, and we all managed to stow away quite a good "feed." The cool weather also done away with the "dobie itch" with which a great many of the crew were affected.

Just before leaving Manila, one of the warrant machinists went over to the yard at Cavite on duty after some stores and spare-parts of machinery, and while there had a run-in with an officer. Being full of "vino" at the time, he didn't act a bit mealy-mouthed or use select language, but calmly offered to put the officer out with the gloves or any weapon. The officer made a report of it. The mach[inist] was pretty full on coming aboard and feeling at peace with all the world. In relating his tale of woe to the gang around the machine shop he said, "Why, I wasn't drunk, hic! Only had so much gin," indicating about a pint with his hands apart, "and just about seven bottles [of] beer to wash it down," he concluded with an appealing glance at the gang for sympathy. This statement overcame one of the fellows so much that he went and lay down on the vise bench completely exhausted, letting a wild yowl out of him at the same time.

"That's the way it is with some people here. They are living on the flat of the land and still never satisfied! Only 7 bottles and so much gin! Whoop! Wasn't drunk! Oh, my!" It took him, I may say, all the afternoon to recover sufficiently to resume work.

There is an officer on board in charge of the powder division who is very strict on his men and never lets an opportunity slip by of calling a man down who is out of uniform. He is one of those who are continually looking for trouble and is never seen to wear a pleasant look. I should judge there must be something wrong in his physical make-up, as he is continually finding fault and growling and making things in general very unpleasant. I nudged the man next to me one morning at quarters, "Look at H[ines]. The uniform is all blue and he has a white cap on."[5]

"Yes," said the man I nudged, "and just watch him call some of the men down. If he would see anybody in his division with a white cap on, down he would go for a chance. Watch him jack them up."

We watched, smiling inwardly. "Division attention! Front rank, two paces to the front; march! Front rank, about face! Take your dress from aft. Come up in the centre. You there, toe the same seam. Steady, front. Why haven't you your shoes blacked, sir? Where is the flap of your shirt? If you come to quarters in that condition again, sir, I will put you on the report." And thus we could hear it all along the line. But his men were all smiling, knowing he would get "called down" when he went back to report his division to the executive officer, and sure enough he did. The executive said a few sharp words to him and Mr. H[ines] hustled back and changed his cap with his ears tingling. A little thing like that counts for a great deal in the outfit, especially where the officer has no use for himself or any body else, and takes a delight in making life unpleasant for any poor devils who are unfortunate as to come in direct contact with them. And they [the officers] can make it very hot indeed. They make many a poor wretch run away simply because they don't like his face.

I don't know how it is with other men, but the less I always had to do with my superior officers, the better off I always considered myself. I always kept out of the way. My idea was, they were always looking to find fault, but that is the way we have in the outfit. The admiral calls the captain down; the captain makes it hot for the first luff; the first luff for the watch and division officers, those officers for the ensigns; the ensigns for the "middies" and warrant officers (who are neither officers nor enlisted men) and everybody calls down the "engineer's force." Is there a foot mark on deck? Blame it on the engineers division. Is there a dirty spot on the paint work? Blame it on the engineer force. Any old thing? The engineer's force. The navy is a system of fault-finding and throat-cutting all thro,' and the petty fault finding of the men and small fry is emulated by the very top notchers of them all, as was made clear by the bickerings of the different commanders during the Spanish-American war. It may be necessary; it probably is, this system of fault finding. And then again, it many not be. Who can decide?[6]

~ ~ ~

We arrived at Nagasaki the morning of Feb 25th, [1900,] Sunday. On our way we stopped twice for target practice, the marksmanship not being very good on account of the heavy swell. We found inside [the port] two Russian men-o-war, one I believe, from the looks of her, must have been listed as a first class battle-ship. But I shouldn't [think] her from all appearance to be modern. Looked like an old iron-clad. The other was a powerful first-class cruiser with four funnels, and an immense battery. Looked strange to see them in this port, they being on the verge of war.[7] Also, an Englishman and an Italian. The Englishman left the evening of the day we arrived and the Russians the following day.

Nagasaki

I liked this port. I should think I could live here forever among these strange people. We are all O.K. with them. They are a contented lot. Look at the sampan people. In the small house [the sampan] a whole family will reside, having just enough clothing to cover them, and enough to eat. That's all they want: an idyll[ic] sort of existence. Women here are about on a par with a billy goat in the States. There is quite an absence of morals. In fact, the word morals is unknown and has no equivalent in their language. It is almost no disgrace at all for a family to let out any of their daughters for immoral purposes, and is thought nothing of. But once married they are true as steel, and hardly any of them ever break their marriage vows. In that respect they can set a good example for their Western sisters. As one married woman told me without any prudery (which is another word without any [Japanese] equivalent), that once married, "All same dead. Finish. How you call him?" Much has been written and said of these queer little people, and there is no use of going into any description except from a bluejacket's standpoint. This is only a common sailor's log, written in a plain way, but every word is truth, plain and unvarnished.

My first liberty ashore, how shall I forget it? Old John and I went together. It had only been five years since he was last out here, having gone home on the *Baltimore*. We took a sampan ashore, the officer of the deck dividing the liberty party up into parts of about seven men each, thus giving every sampan man a chance, the fare being only five cents or five sen.[8] Reaching the beach we jumped ashore and were immediately surrounded by rickshaw men. Talk about your New York cabbies! These rickshaw men would make them look like amateurs. They would insist.

"Come on Jack, let's take a rickshaw," I said.

John didn't want to, but I insisted and we jumped in and away we sped on a dogtrot. You never see a rickshaw man walk, always jogging along. That was my first ride behind a human horse. I felt almost ashamed, and if I had had a few more drinks aboard would no doubt have gotten out and hauled the rickshaw man. But one soon gets used to them. They are tireless. Some of the hills at Nagasaki are very steep and they would have a good drag of it. Descending they brace themselves back until they are leaning backward at an angle of sixty degrees. They are all, let me say, damn rascals, and will charge you treble the price, American bluejackets being very good things in their estimation. Jack gave one of them directions w[h]ere to go and he started off "around the creek" and stopped in front of a native wine shop and eating saloon with the sign, "Centennial House and Happy Home Saloon" above the door. Jack opened the door and walked in. The little Jap woman ran up to him at once exclaiming "Hully gee" (which I afterwards found out was the name he was known by, meaning "Old Man").[9] "Me very glad see you. What goin tek?" and bustled around to entertain us, calling her husband down, who recognized Jack. In fact, they made us feel quite at home.

Jack enquired where "Moriya" was, Moriya being another married woman who kept a wine shop and eating place. We finally left after numerous drinks, feeling very good indeed, to look for Moriya's place, which we found only a short way up the

A Sailor's Log

street. Our rickshaws had only hove in sight when a little woman came running down the street recognizing "Hully gee" at once.

"Hully gee me ver glad to see you. How you been? What you have drink?" In fact, a series of questions, shaking hands [at] least half a dozen times. This little woman we found to be quite a hustler. There wasn't anything too good for us. She seemed to take pleasure in doing anything to make us comfortable. It was, Jack afterwards explained, a favorite resort for a few of the *Charleston*'s[10] crew, when there before, Moriya being very reasonable in her prices and strictly honest. We ordered supper here. First fish, [then] steak and onions, fried potatoes, radishes, coffee and Japanese cakes. Port wine or "saki." Before we were thro' with our supper we were feeling very jovial indeed. "Hully gee" and I were both very chilly and shivering, owing to the change in climate from Manila. He proposed hot whisky. I was surprised at that as he is generally very temperate. "I'll go you. Moriya, give us the best you have in the house, will you?"

"You can take choice."

So Hully gee went to the shelf and selected a fat bottle of Cyrus Noble and Moriya fixed us up with numerous hot whiskies. How many, I wot not. As we got more mellow under its generous influence, it soon drove the chill out. Moriya cannot help but be well liked. She is so obliging and has an "off handed" way about her, as Jack says. Every time we would compliment her she would smile and bow, "Tank you, tank you, vera mooch. Tank you. Me like American vera mooch."

All this time the two rickshaw men had been drinking at our expense. Mine approached me. "My want get chow," bowing and smiling.

"What?" I asked inquiringly, looking at Moriya.

"Rickshaw man want somting to eat."

"Oh, I savvy," putting my hand in my pocket for a Mex.

"I fix," says Moriya. "I give rickshaw man ten sen piece. Dat 'nuff for chow," whilst she did, and they, knowing they couldn't get any more out of her, accepted with such good grace as they could muster up.

We had quite a long chat with Moriya and her husband. He only knows a few words of English, while she is conversant enough with the language for all necessary purposes. Everything was spotlessly clean and it is almost sacrilege to step on the matting they have on their floors with your shoes on. I tried to make love to the servant girl but it was no go.[11] Moriya said, "No good. She married, all same finish." And that settled it. "You want buy girl? Japanese marriage," Moriya asked.

"You can bet your boots I don't," I replied.

"Bade your boots. Me no savvy dat," looking puzzled.

"All same, no want," I explained.

The rickshaw men had their "chow" and finally came back and we left Moriya's for the bazaar, promising to come back again about 9 P.M.

Leaving, the rickshaw men hustled along on a dog trot past groups of Japs, Italian men-o-warsmen, English bluejackets, some of our own boys, Japanese girls clattering along with their queer gait on wooden shoes. Their wobble would strike dismay

Nagasaki

to the heart of the most swagger American or English girl. It is a cross between a dog-trot and double-shuffle caused by the wooden sandals, if they were to try to walk like a European they would drop off.

Some of the bluejackets were enjoying themselves on "wheels"[12] hired, of course, for forty-sen per hour. Tho' some of the streets are impossible with a wheel, nevertheless there are plenty of good roads, especially the "Oura" which runs along what is known as the "creek" and is very level and smooth.[13] As for Nagasaki's side streets, a New York goat would hail them as the "seventh heaven" of "goatdom." They are a Chinese or Japanese puzzle in their tort[u]ous windings. Be slightly under the influence of liquor and straggle around them in the dark, [and] after about four or five hours of it, you will finally arrive from where you started.

We brought up finally at the door of the bazaar and entering (followed, of course, by our "rickys") we found ourselves in a place something like our closed market house at home, only instead of provisions it is all fancy goods. It was very quiet inside, it being about 9 P.M., not any crowd at all. All good Japanese [are] tucked away between heavy mats at that hour. I could have wandered around for hours there, and it would have required an unlimited purse to satisfy my wants. Everything Japanese the heart could wish: silk handkerchiefs, very cheap; exquisite ivory carvings and tortoise shell works, beautiful fans of tortoise shell, ivory, silks, cunningly devised jewel[r]y and lacquer-ware and inlaid works, small boxes with secret recesses, bronzes of all descriptions, cheap and dear, in profusion. It would bewilder one to choose. You simply want everything you see, from an exquisite tea set down to a set of chop-sticks. Everything is so odd.

I wanted to get some ivory sticks to set tattooing needles in, and seeing some chop-sticks of ivory, I began to purchase. I purchased so many chop-sticks of different variety that they must have thought I kept a "chow house" or else had a mania for collecting them. You can buy at your own price. I was looking at some pipes and priced a couple, not particularly wishing them. Asking him how much, he said, "Four yen" (Two dollars). I walked away not wishing to buy at all, saying, "I'll give you one yen." And I had to take them at that price. It is very foolish to pay their first price. They don't expect you to.

I secured enough ivory chopsticks and other stuff at last from the different stalls, and Jack and I started back to Moriya's again to find a good hot American supper awaiting us: rare done steaks, soft boiled eggs, fish, radishes, onions, bread and butter, Japanese cakes, oranges, etc. Their tea is excellent but they cannot make good coffee. We done justice to a great meal. I consider myself a fairly good trencherman, but "Hully gee" can place me in "Class B." But we finished at last, having washed it down with about a gallon of Port wine which was excellent, also some sake. So you can judge of the miscellaneous assortment of "boozes" we had to carry around.

Moriya directed the "rickys" to the place where we were next to go to turn in for the night, as all good bluejackets do, and others who are not bluejackets. They started off in the right direction but mine says, "You wantee nice girl?"

"Yes," I replied.

"Allee yight," and they immediately turned around to go in the opposite direction. At this I let a wild howl at him and he stopped as well as Jack's man. We made them turn and ride us to Moriya's again, which they did with bad grace enough. We explained how it was to Moriya and after a sharp talking to, they took us to the proper house. We'll here draw a line. Sufficient to say we paid the two "rickys" off and dismissed them, they promising to come around for us in the morning, which they didn't. Moral: don't pay your jinrickshaw[14] man until you are thoroughly thro' with him. They like American bluejackets who spend money with a lavish hand, but they will try to have their own way about it. You get one and leave it all to him, and he will simply run you up to the bazaar and then to some house from which he is getting come-shore [cumshaw] or commission. That is the usual routine. And he will try all his power of persuasion to keep you from deviating from it. Well, all I can say is we were finely treated in the house we were in. All Japanese girls as a rule are easy to get along with and easily pleased. They won't so much as let you light a cigarette for yourself, but are eager to please. Only one thing, you mustn't touch their hair. They are very particular about their coiffure as it is a work of art and has to be put up by a professional hairdresser. That's the reason they use the block for a pillow, as everyone knows.

Moriya awoke us about five o'clock in the morning, coming all the way from her place for that purpose. Getting another "rickshaw" apiece, we were quickly whirled thro' a drizzling rain down to Moriya's where we found a good breakfast awaiting us. But I wasn't in much of a mood for breakfast or anything else as I had one of the fiercest "heads" on I ever recollect, as well as an internal commotion from the excess of the past night. Ye Gods, 'twas fierce! I was weak as a sick kitten when I got thro,' the kindly little Jap holding my head. As soon as I could catch my breath I managed to ejaculate, "Me very sick man, Moriya."

"Oh, yes, me see. You ver sick. You feel betta now?"

"No. Bimeby [by and by] I feel good."

However, I managed to go a couple eggs. And numerous hot whiskies and lemon placed me on my feet, all except my head, which I imagined was swollen to abnormal proportions from the fierce pain.

We left for the landing to catch the launch for the ship, being due at 6:30. It was a very cold and drizzly morning and very dark. You could see shadowy forms flitting around, some groping their way along with a lantern, and the only noise you could hear was the clatter of wooden sandals, their wearers indiscernible thro' the darkness. It seemed as if one was back in a past age from the surroundings, and the crooked streets and absence of electric lights, the queer sounds, and the vague forms seemed fitting part of a century long since past. But from the state of my head I knew I was living in the nineteenth century. It was practically up to date. We ran up to another "rickshaw," its occupant hailing us. We recognized the voice and nothing to do but have another round or two of drinks. So we stopped at another house on the Oura,

Nagasaki

Japanese Mary's, a house much frequented by bluejackets of English and American extraction. But I wasn't looking much at surroundings at this time, being handicapped by that awful "head." I managed to down a plain soda and we left for the landing only a short distance away. Paying the "rickys" off, we came aboard the ship clean and to all intents sober, with another experience added to my already long list in many lands and under many skies.

One day not long after, "Hully gee" and I found ourselves once more in Japanese Mary's. We were both feeling considerably better; had become "acclimated" to the different brands of drinks, so to speak, and in consequence were in good condition to look around and observe things as they really were. Mary is a great jollier in her Japanese way, and as soon as Jack and I came in, she immediately deserted the other sailors from different ships and came over to our table and sat down. She seemed to be quite taken with me, and bestowed many amorous glances from her narrow slits of eyes upon yours truly, which I returned with interest. Mary immediately "set them up."

"Dis time me treat. Dis on me," said she.

"All right," says I. "Here's happy days, Mary, old girl. Drink up Jack and let's have another one."

We had several others, Mary always bestowing those same bewitching Japanese glances upon me, which I always returned with compound interest.

"You can hab anyting you want in dis house. Any ting you want, you savvy?" with a meaning glance and edging up closer, upon which, being a true sailor, I immediately wound my arm around her ample waist and proceeded to make love to her in the most approved American fashion. But I wasn't to be fooled by Mary. I saw it was a case of jolly from the start. Her idea was [to] keep us there so we could spend our coin with her. Altho' she treated several times, she always was careful in computing how much we owed her for every round of drinks. Well, as the crowd commenced to pour in we concluded to take a slope and go up to Moriya again, which we accordingly did.

I only dropped into Mary's once or twice after that and then only in the early morning before coming aboard, to have a drink. "Mary," says I one morning, "I think you one great jollier, savvy?"

"Me savvy," she replied. "But me tink you de jollier all same."

"How do you make that out?"

"You plomise me to come round see me and no do. Me wait at night for you."

"All right Mary, I'll come and see you the next time I come ashore."

"You say dat but me no believe any more. You tell Mary damn lie. You one damn fool dat you no come. Me tink you one very fine man."

"Yes! And me tink you one fine woman. Me marry you when you no hab Japanese man. All light?"

Mary tried her fascinating powers upon several of the boys with the result that some of them were on the verge of "jumping out" and taking charge of Mary and

A Sailor's Log

her rum-shop, and some of them did really break their liberty ashore, and [went] broke in her place, only to have her affections wane as soon as their yens gave out. I have met many sweet women in many parts of the globe. Poor Jack, he almost always comes off a sadder and wiser man with his dreams shattered and only his vanity hurt. Yes! Yes! Poor Jack indeed has lots of troubles and is easily led and beguiled by rum-sellers and women. That [is] one of the reasons he gets married so numerously. Poor fellow, its his only way of enjoying himself, and he likes to have a home in almost every port where he may touch for any length of time.[15]

Mary told me one night, or rather in the early evening while I was in her place, "See dat man?" pointing to where her liege lord and master lay coiled up like a big house dog between two heavy mats. "Dat man very drunk. He no do notin. He no work. I do all work, hustle and tend ever'ting. He just hab chow. Make sleep all time and getting drunk. Me no like him. Allee same he master. He no care for me and I no care for him. He hab me. Two, tree girls he go see. Me gottee keep him. Dat's de law Japan."

Which is the truth. All the time I was ever in there I always saw him sitting around on his haunches smoking and eating around his charcoal fire. He knows what a good thing he has and from his actions I should judge [he] takes it as his just due. Even Moriya's husband at [her] little eating house takes life very easy. But he is of a different caliber altogether: a very polite and gentlemanly little Jap, and Moriya herself is a great little hustler in her way. I always found her the best of all. As long as she was treated right you were all right. And if you were ever short, you could always borrow from her and she would loan you the money in such a way as to make you believe it was a pleasure to her. Yes, Moriya, you are all right and I would recommend every American bluejacket to give her a call at her little restaurant on the Idsumo-machi.

O-ji-ji (Hully-gee) and I often went ashore, and one afternoon we started out for the bazaar and then I really had a chance to fully appreciate Nagasaki and ascertain some idea of its size, which is misleading from the place where we lay in the harbor. It looks very small from the harbor. It is built on tiers one above another and it is all hills, places where a rickshaw man cannot take you, and an impossibility on a wheel [bicycle]. Passages in some parts are cut through the solid rock and every part of the city is full of interest and new surprises crop up on every side. The harbor itself is practically impregnable, land-locked completely as it is, with its tort[u]ous winding entrance. It is very picturesque, crowded with junks, sampans, U.S. transports,[16] mail steamers, men-o-war, etc.

All along the Oura and the other streets around the water-front are gin mills, of course, to catch the sailors. How they contrive to make a living I can't imagine. They are conducted by Russian-Jews for the most part, Italians, etc. There is almost invariably some dissipated looking hag at the door with "Come in Jackie, this is the place." Most of them have nautical names such as the "Main Top," the "U.S. Navy Club," the "Columbia," "The Dewey," etc, the "Italia" and others to[o] numerous to mention. I never, when I passed them, saw them with any customers, so I should judge [they] were not very popular. The "Main Top," I understand, does a good business principally on account of a young girl who had several of the boys on a string. She was quite a belle among them here. At home she would be very ordinary indeed. Hully gee and I never patronized any of those places, always being more content and surer of better treatment among the Japs. The Europeans are all robbers from my standpoint. They will tell you plainly they are not out in Japan for their health, and, from the prices they charge, I judge not.

We almost walked over the entire town that afternoon. I was very much interested in everything I saw. The quaint shops and the quaint customs of the people have a charm all their own. For myself, I go wild when I seen a curious bronze or carving of ivory or bone or any curious design of jewelry. I could wander around indefinitely among these crooked streets, looking at the window displays and at the carvers in ivory and bronze workers, and workers of designs in silk, the dyers, etc., who work openly, the entire family sitting around on their matting having their "chow," everything scrupulously clean. You must kick your shoes off before walking upon their floors because their floors [are] covered with matting [that] is table, chair, bed and everything else to them. It is only among the most civilized, according to our standpoint, who use tables and chairs. None of them will do without chopsticks tho', and all of them, men, women, and children, smoke, filling their tiny pipes repeatedly from their tobacco pouch hanging from their girdle or stowed away somewhere in the folds of their kimonos.

Most of the workmen, especially in the machine shops, etc., have adapted themselves to the European rig, as it is no doubt handier to work in, but they will shift while at home [into] their native garb. Shoes, however, come a little higher than they care to pay for. So they almost invariably work with their feet clad in *tabi* and *zōri*, the first a form of foot covering that leaves a space between the big toe and the rest so they can catch the string of the *zōri* [straw, thonglike shoe] which is made of woven straw. Cost about 18 sen. Looks like a cloven foot thusly clad. Of course on the street they adopt the *geta*,[17] the wooden high shoe. And they can travel with these stilts on without any trouble.

Jack and I lost our way in [the] narrow, winding streets and went about three miles in the opposite direction before we discovered our mistake. We wished to get down towards the water's-edge so as to get our bearings. We wandered on lost in the sights before us until it began to get very dark and the small shop keepers began to light up. Some of the more pretentious shops are well lighted by electricity, but the majority have the ordinary kerosene lamp, and the dimly lit streets are lighted in the same way. We just began to realize that we were lost when we happened to espy one of the Japanese peddlers whom we had noticed aboard the ship, and upon inquiry, he quickly told us in which direction to travel to get towards the harbor front. We might have wandered on for hours as in a maze thro' those old, crooked, unpaved streets.

After we struck the main streets we recognized where we were at and then everything was plain sailing in front of us. We passed the post office and the different gin-mills along the river-front and went on up the creek to Moriya's where O-ji-ji and I put away in great style one of the largest meals I ever sat down to. To say we were hungry after our long walk is to put it mild[ly] indeed. Jack, for an old man, [and I] bolted an awful feed consisting of 2 fried soles of good size, ten soft boiled eggs, each beside rare done steak and onions and fried potatoes, bread and butter, radishes, and onions galore, and cooked in the most wholesome and palatable style, everything scrupulously clean. In fact, Moriya's cooking puts me more in mind of what we are accustomed to get at home, than any restaurant I have yet been in, and as far above the ordinary eating houses at home as the Waldorf-Astoria is above Beefsteak John's on the Bowery.

O-ji-ji and I will remember that meal with pleasant recollections for a long time to come, as it was tempered with the best sauce—hunger—[and] a good, strong active sailor man appetite. Moriya always treated us to the best in her house as we were the means of bringing nearly all the ship's company up there for their suppers and a few drinks. She made us each a present of a tortoise-shell hair-pin before we left Nagasaki. I have seen some of the fellows off the ship go ashore without a *sou*[18] in their clothes and go up to her never having been there before, and beside standing her off for the meal and drinks, borrowing ten or fifteen yen besides. But be it to their credit they always paid her when the monthly money was served out. The "joints" kept by the Europeans didn't pan out so well, as the gang, seeing they were all on the do themselves, wouldn't hesitate about doing them out of money in return.

The Main Top saloon, I believe, was about the most popular of the European places. The bar was presided over by a buxom damsel by the name of Eva. She was quite a belle among the sailors from our ship and the others, and she would flirt judiciously with all, without giving either man cause to believe he was more favored than the others, or, to put it in another form, she continued to make each amorous "Jackie" believe he was "it," which he was undoubtedly. They each and every one sincerely believed they had made an impression on the fair Eva's heart, and I know she made quite an impression upon their pocket-books. Landsmen, etc., would go up there and blow in their meager month's pay to make themselves "all hunk" with the fair [Eva] behind the bar. Kids of eighteen, etc., very impressionable to the darts of Cupid, would "treat" the gang with a rakish devil-may-care air. The gang would consist of about 20 or 30 at times. They wouldn't last long at that rate. The next liberty they would go broke and Eva seemed to be more distant. Poor devils!

We have all had the same experience. I know it took me a long time to learn my lesson. And yet, at times I am as susceptible as a boy where women are concerned, but that is most always when I am in a slight degree under the influence. At other times I am very skeptical about them as they are a very curious and unknown quantity to me. I don't "savvy" them at all, and I would like to see the man that does. They don't "savvy" themselves. And the dainty little Jap girls are the same as their Western sisters.

As for myself I much prefer the girls of Japan to girls of the fair Eva's ilk, who is perhaps a fair sample of all bar-maids in foreign lands with her coquettish airs.

Nagasaki

Sometimes Eva would be out on her wheel when some of the boys would arrive at the Main Top. Then the "old man" would rush out of the door and call, "Eva! Eva!" at the top of his lungs of brass, jumping up and beckoning like a ringtailed monk[ey] at the same time for her to come quickly. And Eva would ride up on her wheel working the pedals like a pair of connecting rods on a high-speed engine in order to get back quick enough, before the prey had taken another notion to go somewhere else. She would come swiftly up and say ["Come in"], with a graceful nod and sweet smile for each in turn, calling some by their first name (causing the one who was familiarly known and accosted to swell out his chest like a toad and the others to look at him with jealous eyes).

In dismounting, she would contrive to show about 12 inches of ankle, but I have seen many better turned myself. She would walk in like a queen surrounded by courtiers and the drink would flow. I would go up at times and watch the game. It was as good as a circus to an interested spectator. There are many Eva's, and many Japanese Eva's also, for instance, Japanese Mary, who is a past mistress in the art of jollying bluejackets to buy "booze." Ah, O-ji-ji! You and I were well onto their little game of jollification. We were wise Zulus and kept strictly to the native Japanese, letting the Russian-Jews and Russian wallahs[19] alone. I believe myself we were more than half Jap because we could eat their "chow," drink their sake and smoke their queer little pipes, as much at home as themselves. Getting alongside a charcoal fire with our sake warming in the tea-kettle, our pipe and perhaps our *O Komisano,*[20] we were well content to let the rest have their little fling at their Main Top and Eva's, their Flags of All Nations, the Portsmouth Arms, the Prince of Wales, etc. Time flew by with us when ashore all too fast.

Kenzo[21] was our washerman, and a curious little old fashioned cuss he was, and is, with a fine sense of human[ity] not often found in the Orient. We would go up to his house on the Na-ga-ta and have a good, quiet time. Lots of his Japanese friends would always drop in, and oft times it would be a jolly party gathered there around [him] drinking sake and eating and having a good time generally. O-ji-ji knew him from a former cruise, and knew his father who was a stern old Jap of the old regime. Jack used to tell me about old Kenzo and his ways. He was prosperous in many ways and had accumulated quite a lot of property, and was the cock o' the walk around the hill; was greatly feared as well as esteemed by his neighbors. He took a great fancy to O-ji-ji, and many's the time the pair of them would have in old Kenzo's place. The old fellow, as stern looking as a carved stone Buddha, would contrive to put away a great quantity of sake, helped in no small degree by Jack. Then, oft-times, the two would lock arms and take a stroll to different parts of the town in search of a general good time. None of his friends would dare approach him, or any of his family for that matter, unless called for, and then only by salaaming continuously from the time they reached his door until he unbended from his stern dignity graciously enough to receive them. Well, he died and was buried upon the hills not far away from the place where he lived and he left his numerous family all provided for, Young Kenzo's house, for a washerman's place, being about the best on the hill. And Kenzo, Jr., bids fair to pattern after his father. You can see that he is boss in his own household. Jack and I were always welcomed up there, as it helped to relieve the dull monotony of Kenzo's general mode of living. I used to stay, often all night after a pretty fair bout at the sake, and at times we would send for a dancing girl or two to entertain us. And at any rate, [we] would almost invariably have a good time.

When I was first taken up there I thought I should not be able to find the place again, as Nagasaki's streets are anything but easily traversed, and it was a perfect Chinese puzzle to either find one's way back or to the house. One night especially, after a good night's supper at Moriya's, a little later than usual I started up to Kenzo's. It was dark as pitch and raining, and Moriya loaned me a *kasa*,[22] or oiled paper umbrella, for the occasion. Well, I stumbled on thru darkness and turned the wrong way. I remember I retraced my steps a dozen times to start anew, always winding around almost to where I started from. I know I was about to give up in disgust and return to Moriya's to get a guide when by chance I happened to make the right turning, and groping along, cursing and splashing in the mud, I felt my way up to where the house, I thought, should have been. I always used a fountain that supplied the people in that neighborhood for a landmark. Yes, there was the fountain sure enough; then I looked for the house. Surely that couldn't be Kenzo's place? It didn't look as I remembered it. But that was the same fountain, O.K., no getting away from that. I pinched myself and thumped my head with my fist, and blinked, and looked wise. And looked at the fountain. Yes! That was all right, it was the same old fountain, sure enough. But the house, beyond a doubt, was altered completely.

"However, here goes," thought I. "I [will] raise the neighborhood and find out if I am dreaming or awake and completely muddled." So I battered at the nearest door as loud as I could, calling out, "Kenzo!" at the height of my lungs. Somebody stirred and I called again loudly and there was the noise of someone getting up with a bad grace. The door flew open and a Jap came out without a word, dressed only in a shirt and [a] paper lantern. Grabbing me by the hand he half pulled and hauled me around two or three corners, up to another door, and knocking on it and calling "Kenzo!" went away without a word. I suppose he was too full for utterance at being routed up at that time of the night, it being very late for them, about 10.20.

I heard Kenzo stir and answer my call, "Get up," and then a few doors were pushed here and there and the place was completely tran[s]formed. It was then as it should be, the house as I had been accustomed to see it. The simple fact of enclosing the house entirely by a few sliding partitions changed its whole aspect, and no wonder I was fooled. To this day I doubt if I would recognize it under the same circumstances.

At another time, while going up the steps leading to his place, I made a misstep and dropped down between the stone steps and a house, a distance of about twenty feet. However, I was feeling too good to be hurt much by any fall. If I had been strictly sober there is no doubt I would have cracked my collar bone or done myself serious damage. Howbeit, I picked myself up and crawled up another way. John rushed after a lantern the moment he heard me fall and disappear from sight. When he and two Japs got to where I had dropped, I was up the other way, and all they found was my hat. I will admit I was pretty full on that occasion. I had not drank so much, either. I always blamed my condition at that time to a brand of Japanese beer. I drank probably three bottles of it [at] Japanese Mary's, having struck a particularly congenial crowd of English bluejackets. Mary is not noted at any time for the excellence of her stock of spirituous liquors, quantity rather than quality seems to be the result aimed at. The beer being flat and very heavy soon had me *hors-du-combat*. In fact, I wasn't myself until two or three days after coming aboard. I learned my lesson, however, as I always avoided beer after that and confined myself to sake, which has no evil after affects, no matter how freely partaken of.

There had been numerous fights between sailors from the different ships. A number of our fellows had a "run in" with some German sailors from the *Irene* and *Jaguar*,[23] and the English and French and Germans had "mixed it up" on several occasions, but nothing resulted seriously with the exception of a Russian sailor getting hurt pretty badly. I never liked to mix up with any crowds and that is partly the reason I always avoided the Main Top and other European "joints." The Main Top, especially, had been the scene of a number of fights and bills for damages were made out by the proprietor. The whole shack wouldn't exceed two hundred yen in value, but the bill was made out for about twice that amount, another method of doing business. Where the fair Eva was at the time of the rumpus I could never ascertain.

Kenzo used to have the greatest variety of girls come up to his place to see us, good, bad, and indifferent, but all of the same indifferent morals, and all anxious to earn a few yen, which is perfectly legitimate in Japan and doesn't hurt a girl's prospects of marriage in the least. Women are not looked upon as toys in Japan, but they are helpmates in the true sense of the word. That is, among the middle and lower classes, [where] they have to work oftentimes harder than the husband. It is no uncommon sight to see a woman in a sampan sculling, with a *chishi*[24] slung on her back while her Lord and master is "corking it off like a big marine" or house-dog in the cabin.

You can see women here coaling ship in thousands, and pulling heavy loads like horses. They all work, and hard at that. They have absolutely nothing to say at all. The husband is supreme. The wife owns nothing, can have nothing, although she may be the "rice-winner," as take Japanese Mary, for instance. Mary does all the work and is bar-maid and business manager at the same time. Her Master does nothing but sit back and take life easy, collecting all the receipts and putting them to his own use, is openly unfaithful and she cannot murmur. Still they are happy with the happiness of ignorance. Women suffrage hasn't caused any discontent there and it would take a century of agitation to get them to revolt against the rule of custom.

One of the daintiest of all the little Jap maids I became acquainted with was O-ha-na. She was about as dainty as one of the quaint figures on their own porcelain, yet despite her daintiness she, like all Japanese girls, was very strong. She, like all the rest I knew, weren't especially noted for their morals. She was a waitress in an eating and drinking place much frequented by transport people. All over the wall were the names of returning soldiers and sailors homeward bound from Manila, all transports stopping at Nagasaki on the return to San Francisco, for coal. As I have before noted in these pages, I used to stop at this place very often. In fact, no liberty ashore would be complete without going up to see O-ha-na and having a good chat with her and a few drinks. I would ask her if she knew or heard of New York, but she always didn't savvy New York. San Francisco she had heard of. Also Manila. But New York and other large American cities were beyond her ken.

She confided her love affairs to me also. It seems some bluejacket from the *Bennington*[25] had made quite an impression upon her heart, and so she poured out all her quaint little love affair to me and begged me to write a letter to her friend. It was quite a masterpiece of Oriental broken English and if it reached its destination, must have been preserved as a curio. It seems the bluejacket had promised to take her with him to Yokohama, and she not knowing the *Bennington* was homeward bound, and taking the Jackie's promise in earnest, believed him. I didn't think it worthwhile to inform her otherwise, but offered her such consolation as I had at hand, which seemed to please her very much. She sent the letter, but when I left there she hadn't rec'd any answer up to date, and I think she was recovering from her slight attack of love-sickness. She told me in strict confidence not to tell the "Missus." "She make plenty bobbery[26] for O-ha-na. She no like see me go, all right."

Replied I, "I no speak."

"Dis piecey man my frien'," says she. "You my sweet heart, how you call 'em in English?"

"No, no, O-ha-na. He's your sweetheart and I'm your friend. *Ni?*"[27]

"Two mens I like. He my sweetheart and you. *Ni?*"

"Yes, yes, that right, little one."

But as time elapsed, I noticed that her sweetheart who was absent seemed to worry her less and she seemed pleased enough to accept me for a sweetheart in place of the absent one. In fact, she told me she had forgotten him and told me also one day, "If you go Manila, I go you want. You go San Francisco, I go. All right?"

"Yes, O-ha-na, I'll see. If I stay at Manila, I'll send for you."

"All right. Me come."

At last the time drew near for our departure from Nagasaki. Our old captain was detached and our new captain having arrived, we soon found out where we were to go on leaving Nagasaki.[28] Reading his orders before all hands assembled at muster, we found out the point of destination was Manila, that hell-hole, and that we would leave inside of a week. So we endeavored to make as good a time as possible, realizing that for us our good time in Japan was at an end, and that [there] was nothing in store for us at Manila but hardship and deprivation of all that makes life worth the living.

Nagasaki

So, only having about one more chance to get ashore, and feeling a little bad at the prospect of leaving such a nice little girl behind half heart-broken, I went up to see and spend another evening with O-ha-na. She was glad to see me, as she always expected me every fourth day. I told her we would leave in another week and I was doubtful if I would be able to see her again before the ship left, but that I would write and she could get someone to read my letter for her and that if there was any possibility of staying in Manila for any length of time I would surely send for her. She expressed her sorrow and regret at my leaving so unexpectedly, assured me of her undying affection, and with many a caress and exclamation in her pretty broken lingo, bade me good bye. I did feel a slight qualm at leaving her, knowing that I hadn't the slightest intention in the world of sending for her or ever expecting to see her again.

"Poor little trusting Jap," I mused. "Here she evidently believes all I have told her." And it was, as I have said, with a slight feeling of regret that I bid her good-bye until we met again, and tore myself away, as I had lots of places to visit and lots of friends to take leave of. So leaving her disconsolate I went on up the narrow street to the bazaar where I made a few purchases and stopped into a couple more saloons to drown my sorrow and brighten up my spirits for "parting is such sweet sorrow."

However, I had occasion to come back the same way, and going by I could not resist looking in once more to see O-ha-na, and if possible stopping to cheer her up once more before I left. Ye Gods! When I got to the door, O-ha-na was sitting in the lap of a big, brutal looking soldier from one of the transports and looking transfixed and soulfully into his eyes from her own bright, almond shaped orbs. My dream was shattered. My idol was, after all, of mud. With a wild yowl I flung myself into [the] outer darkness without disturbing the sweet scene, or myself being observed. I drowned some more sorrow. It was a case of "diamond cut diamond." An hour afterward I had fully recovered from the severe blow to my vanity and was sitting in Kenzo's house, seeking consolation from a bottle of hot sake and making violent love to little Su-na-wa, my other girl. It pays to have a stock on hand in case you are disappointed. I think, no doubt, all my girl friends missed me. At least, they missed the *yens*.

But not so Kenzo, the little washerman. All he done for both O-ji-ji and I was done out of pure good heartedness. No trouble too great to put him to. Nothing he wouldn't do for our pleasure. I honestly missed him, and he was about the only one in Nagasaki I was really sorry to leave, and I knew he felt our going keenly. The last morning he came aboard, the morning the ship was to sail, he lingered as long as possible aboard. He hated to bid good-bye. There is none better than that same little Jap. He was all right.

"Well, Kenzo old boy, we go today."

"Yes, me savvy. Me very sorry, Kenzo very sorry. Nudder time you come again. Den you remember Kenzo."

"You bet we'll see you again. At least, I will come again, but I think O-ji-ji no come again. So good-bye old man. We'll see you before long, and we won't forget."

We shook hands and the little fellow turned away with rather a sad countenance. As John remarked to me, "He feels it all right. You can see the way he hates to leave."

I could see it. The little Jap, after a hand clasp, turned, and went sadly up [down?] the ladder without looking back. You could tell he was dejected and sad by simply looking at his back. He wouldn't look back for fear of breaking down, which would be unmanly to a high degree. And yet the Japanese are a race accustomed to hiding all emotion. I was never among a people I felt so much at home with in my life before. After I knew them, I was treated as a brother, and nothing was to[o] good for me. Especially was this true of Kenzo.

Yes, Kenzo, we shall come again. [Although] our natures and our aims are as wide apart as two poles, still friendship such as yours is appreciated and never forgotten. The kindness shown us at your house will always be a pleasant memory. And should we have the good fortune to meet again, it will be a joyful occasion. You above all others do I regret in leaving. No, old fellow, we shall not forget....

Moriya gave John and I each a photo of herself and gave Jack also a gaily flowered kimono and a pair of sandals, or *zōri*. We were indebted to her and her estimable husband for a good many kindnesses. We rec'd nothing but the finest treatment at their hands. They were very fond of Jack, or Oji-san, whom they had known before, and there was nothing they wouldn't do for him. They were particularly Jack's friends, while Kenzo was mine. Moriya herself came off in a sampan at the last moment bringing the kimono to Oji-san. Several of our fellows left many an aching heart behind, and no doubt many a little Japanese bosom felt heavy as lead for the time being, until they rec'd consolation elsewhere.

I hated to leave Nagasaki, especially to Manila, the abhorrence of every bluejacket who is compelled to endure there the fiercest heat and deadly climate cooped up in a steel cage heated up to away in the hundreds by a fierce tropical sun. It was like leaving Paradise for Hell. We left a fine climate at Nagasaki where a blanket was a necessity at nights, good food, our washing done for the cost of soap, almost—the three things that makes life endurable on a man-o-war—for a climate almost unendurable and comparatively nothing to eat, and where if you give your washing to a Filipino, he will bring it off about two weeks from the day you sent it, or else not at all, and charge you fancy prices for it. As one man forcibly put it, "There are only two places that are on a par with hell; and that's Manila and Guam," and I believe he is right.

We bowled along merrily over a sea of glass with scarce a ripple upon its surface as far as [the] eye could see. Here and there a solitary flying fish would dart out of the water and skim along for a flight of a hundred yards or so. Was it hot? Well, rather! We felt the change not twenty hours from Nagasaki and the uniform word was passed for white. Hot, a sea of brass with the unchanging white heat of a tropic sky above. We lay around the deck like fish out of water, trying to get the benefit of a capful of air. And yet lots of the boys were glad to get away from Nagasaki and get back to Manila. Well, I am glad they had their wishes gratified, but I noticed they were invariably the biggest kickers when the heat struck them.

Nagasaki

We had quite a smooth trip of it, everything worked well below. The new chief engineer tried a few experiments with the boilers. At first we steamed with only the lower fires burning in one end of each of the four boilers. We then changed again and let the lower fires die out and steamed with only the wing furnaces. The speed at first was seventy turns or revolutions, then 73, then 80, then 90 and 95, a habit they have in the service of raising the ante every once in a while. Then the port eng[ine] broke down, but was quickly repaired and underway again. And again the [starboard engine] was disabled for good, so we had to reach Manila on "one leg." However, we managed it all in good shape and arrived in Manila on my watch, the eight to twelve, about 11:30 A.M. and found it a scorching day.

The same old Filipinos surrounded us. Everything looked the same. We, as it happened, was senior ship and the pennant was hoisted according[ly]. The *Dixie*[29] lay off from us, also the *Culgoa*[30] and a couple of the captured and repaired Spanish gunboats. The same dull, deadly old place of Cavite. Nothing to vary the monotony whatever, only an occasional trip ashore to visit some cock fight at Cavite or to Manila to stow away a few cool lagers at the San Miguel saloon. The ferry boat crow[d]ed with sailors, soldiers, etc., makes [its] daily trips as usual, a few *banca*s here and there with Filipino washermen and bumboat men and women, looking like overgrown monkeys with their pock-marked faces, and shirts flapping in occasional hot breezes. Over across the bay, seven miles away, the white houses of Manila glisten in the sun. Near us are the white walls of Cavite standing in relief to the tropical foliage behind, and far beyond lost in haze, the blue fringe of mountainous country.

The *Dixie* was also in Manila when we reached there, having on board about five-hundred landsmen in training for ordinary seamen and seamen. It seemed the fellows aboard of her were all of the opinion that they were "shanghaied." They all bit at alluring advertisements in some of the Western papers, picturing in glowing phrases and terms what a fine thing in general a bluejacket's life is on one of Uncle Sam's steel ships. [They] were promised a clothing outfit free, good food, and a trip around the world. Some of them hadn't the slightest conception of a sailor's life. And what a disillusion[ment] for some of them when their eyes were opened to the real thing. I do not speak for all, but at least 70% were seasick, homesick and on the verge of insanity before they clear[ed] Fire Island and they were only awaiting a favorable opportunity to "jump out" at any cost. They were taxed double price for what clothing they drew, and even at Manila, after being out about 4 or 5 months, were still in debt for their outfit. They deserted in droves all along the route. One fellow even jumped over board in the Suez Canal and swam ashore and made his escape. And pretty hard lines he must have found in that desolate stretch [of] desert land before he could reach a place where he would be rec'd. Probably at Ismailia. They were a disgusted, discontented lot when they reached Manila and found they were to be distributed among the fleet to take the places of short-time men. And no wonder, in this fierce climate three or four years of it would kill a government mule, let alone a human being. Take even the deadly monotony and routine, in a good climate it is bad enough.

A Sailor's Log

But little shore liberty and being cooped up is not what people think it is until tried. Take men working below and they are easily disgusted when they are compelled to be diving in bilges and cleaning boilers and other work in a temperature of about 102° and above. A fellow becomes crabby and irascible. Everything seems to bother him. He is enervated. At the end of a couple of years he isn't the same man by any means.

Jack was transferred to the *Petrel* two days after we arrived at Cavite.[31] It wasn't when he expected to go by any means. He was hoping to get sent home from the Philippines altogether and was [not?] expecting to be transferred for a long time. Finally he was told he was to be [sent] to the naval station at Cavite. But the Commandant there, having no orders relative to him, sent him aboard the *Petrel*, which was station ship. It seems a shame to keep a man as old as him and with the service he has in this infernal climate. I missed him very much indeed. He was always the same way, a rare good shipmate, and many a good days we had together. But the exigencies of the service are no respecters of personal feeling. You go where you are sent and that's all there is about it.

"If you don't like it, why there are transports leaving every day," is what you hear as good advice very often when you have a growl coming. We are not the only ones who have hard lines and harder deals. The *Bennington*, for instance, left us at Nagasaki flying a "homeward bound pennant" half a mile in length. We cheered her off for she was homeward bound loaded down with short time men and curios. But—to our surprise—about a week after our arrival at Manila, the *Bennington* came steaming in. Gone was her long ribbon of silk and deep were the curses muttered by her crew. Curios could be bought at a discount. Gone were their expectations of a fine trip home to 'Frisco. They had stopped at Kobe to buy silks, Yokohama for China ware and porcelains and all sorts of curios, and it was there the dread order to about face and return caught them. Such is life in the service. For my part, I never knew where I was going until I arrived there.

The *Glacier* came in port also, from Sydney with a cargo of mutton and beef. I went ship visiting on her as I have some good shipmates aboard her. They had had a fine time of it in Australia, were treated fine by the people who very seldom see American bluejackets. While aboard of her I couldn't help thinking of how uneven things are divided in this comical old world of ours. Everything was cool and any amount of room.[32] Room enough and to spare for 5,000 men to lay about the decks in comfort, while we aboard the *New Orleans* considered ourselves lucky for the night if we could get a place to throw our frames on deck. Even a small kitten wandered around looking for a place to "caulk off" at without curling up between some of us and getting crushed in the night. Again, we started to get stores aboard and again were our sleeping quarters between decks occupied by pickle barrels, pork barrels and hard tack tins. Such is the sleeping accommodations aboard our ship.

Our first lieut[enant] went ashore and was overcome by the heat and was assisted aboard about midnight and died shortly afterward. He was very fair in his treatment of the crew, and we were sorry enough at his death.[33]

Nagasaki

We lay at Cavite expecting the flagship *Brooklyn*, which soon came in. We had received orders, or such was the rumor, to leave for a trip around the Islands. But owing to repairs to the st[arboard] eng[ine] we were told to await the flagship's arrival, and were expecting at any time to get orders to leave, but our duty and destination were unknown. But we were hoping to go north, hoping almost against hope to get away from this climate.

There were a great many conjectures going on about this time as to the ship's future course. All sorts of rumors were rife about the changes to be made. All men considering themselves "short-timers" (i.e., having under a year or so) were looking forward to being transferred. In fact, this living in hopes was the only thing to relieve our monotonous lives, our existence there being deadly dull. We got no liberty, the "skipper" saying we had "had plenty of shore leave in Japan, enough to last us for awhile."

Officers were continually changed about. This ship cannot be recognized by the department as being healthy for officers, but for us poor devils any old thing would go. The magazine temperatures were away above what is considered the danger point, so much so, that the cordite stored in the after magazines became spoiled and there was continual danger from that source. On that account we were expecting to be ordered further north. This ship is no good in a hot climate. We have no ventilating blowers worth the name. There were only a couple to cool the magazines and they were totally inadequate. The rainy season had set in. The bunker tops, our sleeping quarters, were filled with stores, so when it rained we had no place to go. Even the unbearable and stifling heat of the berth deck was denied us.

The stores we got aboard were of rather better quality than is usually allotted to the navy, but I found out afterward they were Army stores and secured from the Department of Subsistence. Canned beans without tomato sauce, also canned ham sliced, and a good quality of beans were among them; quite different from the horrible mass of unknown material we were used to having served out to us. It is usual to open some of our canned "willy" and then clear out until the worst of the smell is over. In *fact*, any of the food served out to us wouldn't pass muster in a pure food show. But as an oiler, a Russian, used to remark, "Good for bluejacket. Anyting plenty good for sailor."

As for our sleeping accommodations, I can only quote what fell from the lips of one of our officers and was overheard in a conversation with a brother officer. "Never in my experience of the navy did I see the like before. I happened to come on deck just as the rain began to fall, and I saw the entire crew gather up their 'corking gear' and huddle like a flock of sheep under the forecastle. And later on I saw the men after the rain had subsided swab down places on the deck and spread their mats again. As for my own men, Lord knows how they exist at all. I have seen a few of them stripped naked lying on the floor plates of the fire-rooms."

His words were true. Whenever it would pour we had to scurry for cover like a lot of frightened cattle, and come back again after it was all over. If we went below we would nearly suffocate from the closeness and intense heat. I used to get up in the morning with a head feeling like I had been on a drunk for a month.

Oh, what curses we would heap on this ship, especially us below! Our work wasn't hard, no fault there. But the discomfort! We were heartily sick of the Philippines. An issue of the *Manila Freedom* in an editorial spoke in glowing terms of the climate of the Philippines, claiming that for white man, brown, yellow, black, or any other color, search the whole world over, nowhere on the face of the globe would such a salubrious and glorious climate be found. We read the article in its entirety and heartily cursed the writer of it, and dozens of the men swore they wouldn't buy that paper under any circumstance again. From his account of it, we judged him to be a Filipino or else a person with an axe to grind. Probably wanted to sell some real estate. Another paper, the *American* came out directly opposite to his esteemed contemporary's point of view, and claimed it was the worst in the world and wasn't fit for a human being to live in. Of course we took sides with him. The climate is all right as long as you have some good, soft easy billet ashore, with a "punka wallah"[34] to keep you cool and numerous cooling drinks to refresh the inner man. But if you are a poor devil of a soldier, officer or man, hiking after the niggers thro' rice paddies, swamps, and jungle racked by fever, hungry and ragged, or a poor devil of a bluejacket cooped up in a steel ship, with the temperature around the hundreds, it is the worst climate in the world. It's just the point of view from which you size it up. Many a time have I lain and cursed myself for being such a fool in enlisting over the second time and being sent to serve in such a climate, lying on top of the bunkers, near a port trying to get a breath of air, with cock-roaches crawling all around.

This is the worst ship for cock-roaches I have ever had the misfortune to be shipmates with. It literally swarms with them between decks and as you lie perspiring freely, they crawl all over you, as anything wet attracts them. Such a nice sensation it is, and such comfortable quarters as we have on the *New Orleans*. The persons who designed the sleeping accommodations of this ship should be prosecuted as criminals.

We were getting no liberty. The flagship wasn't giving any either. And from tales we heard about the flagship, they had stopped all liberty, wouldn't serve out any money to the men, wouldn't allow the "smoking lamp" to be lit, and took all other privileges away from the crew as punishment for not manning the boats' falls with the alacrity the captain thought necessary. Such is naval discipline in this case, though I understand the many innocent suffered for the few guilty. There is nothing [that] justifies this. If the guilty few cannot be punished, why punish all the rest who are innocent?

"Of course, it is hard you know, but in order to reach the guilty, we will have to punish the whole ship's company." That only makes matters worse. It makes us all feel a strong sense of injustice. It makes us dissatisfied. It is no argument to make us do our best.

The ship's company organized a minstrel troupe and ball team, and rehearsed in no. 1 fireroom. There was one man in the troupe in particular who could be heard

Nagasaki

above all the rest, bedlam tho' it was. His lung power was something wonderful. Combined with lungs of brass, he had the endurance of a teething baby. Somebody, I suppose, at some previous time while under the influence of mixed ale, had told him he could sing, and he felt bound at every conceivable opportunity to show us all the "timbre" and range of his voice, especially in the high notes. I used to hear this fellow and think of all that perverted talent going to waste, for if ever a man was endowed with a voice to peddle fresh fish, he was the one.

Later on in our sojourn here at Cavite the captain allowed us liberty. But what a difference from the old regime! There were only twenty allowed to go ashore at a time, and there would be a great rush and scramble to reach the writer's [the ship's writer was the predecessor of today's yeoman] office in order to be one of the lucky twenty. It caused a great deal of dissatisfaction among the crew, and a great deal of bitter feeling was engendered. And the crew made life miserable for the writer whom they accused of all manner of crookedness in putting down the names. I know that I went up one Sunday to get my name down for the following Monday's liberty party. The party always left the ship about 8 A.M. in the mornings, allowing ample time to get to Cavite and there catch the Government ferry boat, *Taaleño,* for Manila. So the liberty list was always made out the evening before. I inquired of the ship's writer this Sunday as to the time and place of putting down names. He told me promptly at 1:00 P.M. turn to at his office. I made it a point to get there, but even ahead of time. As i[t] was, I found seven men ahead of me. Of course, as soon as the rest of the men who wanted liberty saw us line up, they made a grand rush for position in line, to the number of a hundred or so. I felt sure I was safe on account of being well up in the line, but to my surprise and disgust, the writer only took four names, and then closed, saying he had the full allowance: twenty men. Then I tumbled; took a great drop, in fact. I saw the game wasn't on the square and that his favorites, what are known as "politicians," etc., were getting their names placed down quietly by him. The other men, seeing how it was arranged, got "hot around the collar" also.

"Well! The only way to right this," I saw, "is to go to the mast, and explain how things are run." The thing was so plain a case of roguery and crooked dealing that we couldn't help kicking about it. Well we went to the mast and saw the "first luff." Did we get satisfaction? I hear you ask. *Niht.*[35] We got a calling down. I explained just exactly how the list was made out, an[d] how we would get no show. The executive [officer] wouldn't listen, only saying, "Well, you must take your turn, you know. I haven't many boats to land a larger liberty party with."

In vain we tried to tell him [we] were perfectly willing to take our turns. In fact, that was what we came to see him about. But he didn't want to be bothered, it seems. And he stopped his ears and told us to go for'd again. I knew we wouldn't get any satisfaction at the mast. In fact, it is only in very rare cases you can get your wrongs redressed at the mast. I have never yet, this is the solemn truth, ever gone aft[36] for anything without looking for a refusal and call down. And all Americans are of much the same feeling. No matter what your record, as for any privileges, you get none. I felt so disgusted at the time I could have torn my rating badge as a first class petty officer from my sleeve and cast it on the deck.

These are the little petty trifles that sting, that make you feel your position keenly, feel how helpless you are, and how you are considered by your superior officers. In fact, the mast is looked upon as a place of punishment in all ships, not a place where you can obtain justice. Probably the officers didn't feel good that Sunday, as there was quite a lot of beer drunk at a "smoker" they had the night before. There wasn't any use to growl and tell your troubles to any one, as you would [be] told, "Well, you know there's plenty of transports leave here." However, shortly after, the writer put another fellow's and my own name down, and came and told us it was all right, as two of the names he had already placed on the list were those of men who were on the report, and not entitled to liberty, and we were the next in the line. But I made a resolution then and there not to bother with any more liberty as long as it was run in that fashion, but to settle down aboard ship and make the best of a bad bargain, and learn better next time.

But still by this unexpected act of Providence or the ship's writer, I had again the very great privilege of another run ashore in Manila, and it was with a merry heart I went over the ship's side into the steam launch along with nineteen of the elect for that day's run ashore, looking forward like a boy let loose from school, to a day's holiday, or better still, like a sailor let loose ashore. How quickly do we forget in the excitement of the moment the dullness of our position for weeks and months! At the prospect of a run ashore we forget all wrongs and the petty trifling annoyances of a sailor's life and live only in the present, which is well, as the present only belongs to us. The past is dead and no more real than a troubled or a pleasant dream. The future never comes. It is only the present for poor Jack. Of course we do look forward to the future and build castles in the air, and live largely on hope, hoping the next port will be better, only to reach and find it just as bad or worse.

We conjecture where we are going at. It is a common saying among us, yearning for a change, "Anyplace as long as it is away from here. I am sick of this." And thus Jack welcomes any change to relieve the tedium of his dull life. Many are the dissatisfied Jackies laying for months at Cavite or some God forsaken place around these islands, or at Guam, hoping against hope for a change; hoping the ship will be relieved and they are transferred somewhere else. We get dull and listless in these climates with the eternal grind of routine. We have exhausted all of [our] shipmates' powers of entertainment. Their conversation and actions no more interest us, and we look forward to something turning up. Generally it does, but only when your patience is taxed to the utmost limit. In these places a man should have a limited time to do, so he could look forward to that time. And when his time had expired in that particular place he should be promptly relieved. Now you can only look forward to being shifted from a place at the end of your enlistment of four years, and then

Nagasaki

Wilson ashore in white service uniform with two other chief petty officers. Place and time unknown. Courtesy Muriel Wilson MacFall.

with the not remote prospect of serving a month or so overtime, which is provided for in a clause of the articles you ship under.

Well, I was comparatively a happy man when I set foot ashore at Cavite in the Navy Yard there. What a relief to set foot on land after being cooped up aboard ship for a long time! The *Taaleño* shoved off at the usual time and I quickly found out that you could purchase numerous large, cold bottles of beer for $1.00 Mex aboard her. Of course, this is strictly under the rose as there is an order prohibiting the sale of intoxicating liquors aboard [any] vessel of the navy or any yard or station. But, suffice to say, some progressive fellow knew just how to conduct this. I know I went below ostensibly to see the engine and found numerous sailors and marine[s] gathered around a nice, large ice chest that would refresh you [just] to look at it. I was quickly in possession of a nice, large cold bottle. Talk about your Nectar of the Gods! I don't know when I enjoyed such a treat. I took one long drawn breath, applied the nozzle of the quart bottle to my lips, and let her go. When I removed the bottle I felt like a man who had taken a long dive. The tears stood in my eyes and with a long drawn breath of satisfaction and content, I placed that bottle aside, feeling indeed a new man. Beer drunk in that way never injures any man, let those carp about it who may. I like a good, cold drink of beer. Whisky I haven't any use for, and I claim I am not a drunkard by any means.

Well, we reached Manila after stopping numerous times, once at the flagship, and quite often in the Pasig river, in order to get to our stopping place in front of the Captain of the Port's offices. The same old scenes. But Manila struck me this time as a town that had experienced a boom and had suffered a consequent relapse. Before, the place was over run with soldiers. At that time the greatest number was in the islands and about forty thousand were stationed around and in Manila. But now on this visit it was different. Of course there were quite a number around the streets and in the barracks, but the main streets like the Escolta & Rosario, and the Plaza de Cervantes, etc., were noticeably clear of people. Everything was dull. The novelty of the American occupation was over at last, and I imagined Manila had fallen into its old rut of listless apathy. I noticed the absence of hustle and bustle since I was there a few short months before. Then, if I forget not, all the stores and saloons were open continuously all day, to supply the business demand, but on this visit Manila was the sleepy old Spanish town. Everything closed from twelve to two. Nobody hardly on the streets, except those whose business called them there. It was a sleeping town, a dead town at midday. Even the saloons were without their custom, which I noticed had fallen off to a great extent. Around two P.M. the shops commended slowly to open up, but they opened in such a manner as to lead you to think they realized that business was about finished for the day.

Even the English and American shop keepers have fallen into the custom. 'Tis the climate. Any American who imagines he can come here and put life and hustle into any business will find out his mistake. They may do it for a while, but eventually you will see them relapse into the custom of the town. You can't expend any surpluss energy in this place. The climate will find you out if you do. Shopkeepers here wait on one as if they didn't care a rap whether they made a sale or not. They look sleepy. They are not awake. It's the climate. Even the Filipinos with curios to sell on the shady sides of the streets are half asleep. They will hold out canes covered with snake skins, or stuffed lizards, and models of the different weapons used by the different tribes of the islands with the "tired feeling" you read so much about in patent medicine advertisements. They are content, wanting little.

The only energetic natives are the *cocheros*, who show a little animation in looking for fares. A large number of Filipinos, women and men, attracted our attention, the women as well as the men smoking cigarettes and here and there an occasional one with a large villainous looking cigar stuck in his or her mouth. Some of the women were quite pretty (for Filipinos), but never a look do they deign toward an American. They won't flirt much. We found out it was the noon hour and they were the employees of a large tobacco factory.

We were then nearly on the outskirts of the town and were attracted by the picturesqueness and tropical luxuriance of the scene. Here and there was a fine mansion in a clump of palms, in striking contrast to the nipa huts clustered around it. But to me the nipa huts were the most interesting.

We wandered quite a distance along this road, passed now and then by a native riding on a "wheel" of the "ice" variety, and a coach now and again containing a couple of soldiers out for a lark, until it commenced to rain and we had to make a bee line for one of the nipa-shacks and stay until the rain stopped. We found a couple of women and a man inside, and neither of the trio were noted for good looks or even

Nagasaki

cleanliness. They were squatting on their haunches on the bamboo floor around two or three large bowls containing some of their messes. Rice I could make out, but the rest of the food was as much a mystery to me as the canned beef and mutton that are served out to us. I noticed the absence of knives and forks, and even chopsticks. Nature was good enough for them. They would dig their hands in the rice and transfer it to their mouth and then dip in the other bowls according to their needs. They didn't invite us to eat and we didn't care for the invitation.

They soon made known to us that they had a commodity to sell, either "vino" or anything else, but we didn't care to purchase under the circumstances, and flipping them a silver coin, the rain having stopped, we hailed a *cochero* and told him to land us on the Escolta, which he did in front of the San Miguel saloon. We paid him half a Mex, which was cheap for four men, and strange to say, all he asked for. But he appeared perfectly satisfied.

Didn't seem to be much business doing in this, the best and largest saloon in Manila. The waiters were careless. The beer, at ten cts. gold a glass, was warm. There were only a few customers scattered around the place, mostly soldiers. I saw no one I knew. Being hungry, I ordered some sour-kraut and sausages—something to remind one of a different clime. A very small plate of kraut and two sausages with some mashed potatoes were all they would serve to you for sixty cents Mex. Any bar in America would give you more for a lunch, but then you have got to pay for everything you get in Manila. Ham sandwiches were 30 cts Mex apiece and everything else in proportion. However, in some of the Chinese restaurants you get a pretty fair ordinary meal served for $1.00 Mex.

After satisfying the inner man with numerous beers we strolled around the town at random. Manila is pretty well over-run with Chinese, or Chinos as they are called here. They occupy numerous streets and they are all in business along a distance of the length of an American block. There are hundreds of them. They occupy small stalls and a small part partitioned off serves as living quarters. Many of them have all their stock in a single showcase, mostly cheap soap, razors, buttons, cheap jewelry, etc., of American manufacture. Others have gents' furnishing goods, dry goods, silks, etc. Very few Japanese places are to be seen and they are on the Escolta or Rosario. I seen very few Filipinos engaged in business of that kind, or any kind, in fact. I also noticed very few American women on the streets, possibly one or two in my day's outing.

I went into the Indian Bazaar on the Escolta and took a look around. That was about the most reasonable place to buy [that] I ran across. I became particularly enamored of some delicately carved card cases of ivory. They were exquisitely carved with many figures in bold relief and ridiculously cheap considering the workmanship and the labor expended. I paid $16.50 Mex for one elaborately carved in ivory Budd[h]ist temples and foliage, altars and Budd[h]ist priests, over a hundred different figures, some almost carved in entire relief. I was shown others of sandalwood and ebony, very cheap. Sets of ivory chessman, beads, cashmere and Indian shawls and silks. You can't leave such [a] place without becoming a purchaser, especially if you are a lover of curios, and I confess I would spend my last peso in purchasing anything that appealed to me in this line. Naturally enough, altho' a sailor, I tried to reduce his price, but haggle as I would I could only get him to deduct $1.50 Mex from my purchase. I left the bazaar thinking he would call me back but he didn't, so I concluded I had better go back and close with his offer, which I did.

In Japan or Egypt or almost any other Oriental country you can generally get what you want by paying one-half what is asked. I have even bought articles for one-third the original price. But in Manila, no. They don't care whether they sell or not. They hardly care to wait on one. They must be in business simply as an occupation. They must be all millionaires. How they pay the salary of their salesmen and clerks I can't surmise, as in one day's stroll I saw but very little business done and that only in the most prominent shops. How the Chinos make out is a mystery, but then they can subsist on the simplest dishes and other wants are few.

We were having a most enjoyable time, at least I was. But at last the day was drawing to a close and we were due at the landing at 5:00 to catch the *Taaleño*, so we commenced to realize that our good time was over for an indefinite period. There's the rub. In going on liberty you lose sight of everything but the holiday in store for you. But [on] the return you are about as joyous as a boy returning to school after a vacation. You all know how anxious he is to get there and start the old routine again. Well, a bluejacket returning from liberty is just about as anxious to get aboard ship. So it generally is with very serious faces that we return, unless we are loaded up to the muzzle with bad booze, and then you are happy until it commences to die out.

We started back toward the ship meeting shipmates at different places on our way down. Very few were drunk. I only noticed one man in particular who was drunk. He was in the condition known as "ossified," drunk and dirty. A nice looking object is a drunken sailor, especially in a port where you go ashore in white dress and roll in the dust and mud. This man was brought down to the boat by one of his shipmates, but in waiting for the boat to shove off he wandered off again, lost the boat, and broke his liberty. He came aboard the next day. Of course, he got punished for breaking his liberty. In some ports a reward is offered for your return, and taken from your pay.[37]

Waiting around the landing we were besieged by the Filipino girls selling fruit, peanuts, candy, etc., and for lack of something to while away the time, made love to them. They are adepts in the art of flirting quite as much as their sisters of the Occident. You can't resist buying when they throw you a coquettish look from their dark eyes. More often you buy in order to start a conversation and you find them not averse to a little by play on the side. Some of them are young and very good looking, but the old ones are miserable looking hags. You can look at the pretty ones and see what a few years will do for them. Our amusement was finally cut short by a warning whistle from the boat and we climbed aboard for the long hour's ride to Cavite. There were [only] a few of us returning, ma[n]y having gone back on the former trip. There were no drunks aboard, for a wonder. A few officers [were] on the top deck and here and there a mail orderly.

Nagasaki

At Cavite we hurried over and got in the cutter in tow of the steam launch, and for a finishing touch got wet as it commenced to rain as soon as we shoved off, and we had no awning. We reached the ship [and] were mustered. Two men were absent. Went below and changed, and our day's outing in old Manila was over. I had rather a good day of it, and no bad effects from drink, and in consequence, no "swelled head" and "blue devils" the next day.

About the 15th June the rainy season started in with a vim. The few rains we [had] had previous to that date were only preliminary affairs, "curtain raisers." But when the regular performance started it left no doubt in our minds that it was here to stay for an indefinite period. The only word we could hear passed on deck was "Squee-gee down the decks." The seamen and deck hands were kept busily engaged "swabbing" and "squee-geeing" in watches, another proof of their seamanship. For myself and several others, we much preferred the rainy season to the dry, as it was a great deal cooler, plenty of breeze blowing, whereas in the dry season we were continually bathed in perspiration. Of course, everything became damp and soggy, and everything was miserable, but so is the normal climatic conditions.

Of the two evils, we considered the rainy season the least. We would spread out "caulking gear" on the bunker tops and lay back and read papers, perhaps a month old, or the Manila publications. It was pretty comfortable between decks. If you were fortunate enough to get a space next to a port, then you would get the benefit of whatever breezes were blowing. In the night you would also get the rain as it blew in in fitful gusts. Many a time I awoke with my mat thoroughly soaked and had to carry it below and hang it over the boilers to dry.

Many days the bumboat people couldn't get off. Oftimes they would come off shore all night, then have a hard job on the return. I used to watch them battling with a rather choppy sea, making poor headway, and the little buxom Tagal[og] girl wet to the skin, bailing out their *banca* as fast as they would ship a sea. She took to water as naturally as a duck. Sometimes when extremely rough they would have "outriggers" of bamboo to steady their slender craft, but more often they dispensed with them. This little Tagalog girl was one of the prettiest Filipino bumboat girls I saw, but she must have possessed a devil of a temper. About the only words of English she knew were "ten cents," the price of a few bananas or a couple of mangoes, and "go to hell." The latter she would fire at some "Jacky" who would try to get fresh. All attempts at familiarity she would cut short with a slap and that phrase. She didn't like to get fooled with and was there expressly for business. And they have quite an eye for the main chance. You could buy a Turkish towel like you could get in the States for 5 cts. from them for 80 cts Mex, and other articles in proportion. Cigars, bananas, mangoes and oranges are the only reasonable articles sold. Cigars are cheap and good, but not so good as Puerto Rico or Cuban cigars and [there] they are just as cheap.

I was reading an article in one of the New York papers explaining in what trades and lines an American would succeed [in the Philippines]. The only persons that will succeed either in the large cities or the interior are people with [capital]. Small peddlers, with cheap jewelry and different American goods might make a living, but I doubt if the Filipinos would take kindly to any innovation of their manners and customs. They don't like Americanos and they don't take any trouble to conceal their dislike. They like you just so far as they can derive any benefit from you, but rightfully we are regarded as intruders. I like to hear from these people who don't know what they are writing about, who speak of the fine climate and tell credulous people what fine opportunities await them in the Philippines in different trades, about the undeveloped resources, the good chances that await carpenters, bakers, butchers, shoe-salesmen and every other walk of life. But they don't settle there themselves, I take notice. I often times wonder why they do it. They make a flying visit and perhaps like the editor of the *Manila Freedom,* get filled up with dope or "vino" and dream dreams. I'll bet if the editor of the *Freedom* would strike a crowd of soldiers or man-o-warsmen, he would change his views regarding the "magnificent climate" in a jiffy.

At last the long looked for casting arrived on board and was placed in position.[38] It took the Filipinos quite a while to finish the job, but it was done in better shape than was expected. So once again the magnificent cruiser *Amazonas* was in condition to go wherever sent. We were all hoping to be sent to China, on account of the trouble up there.[39] All sorts of rumors were rife as regarded our destination. We were "coaled" to the full capacity and had aboard stores for three months or more, and everything in the machinery line was [as] good as could be expected. We were built originally as a twenty-two knot ship, but any man aboard would bet a month's pay that the *Amazonas* couldn't make 16 knots for a four hours run without a breakdown. Rumor had it that we were to convoy the transport *Logan* to China, she carrying soldiers to protect American interests, and to assist in the breaking of the unfortunate nation. Oh, how we wished that that particular rumor would come true! Anything to get away from Cavite and these islands.

Everybody was deeply interested in the South African war, and I judge that we were, at a conservative estimate, about equally divided in our sympathies. Perhaps the most of us sided with the Boers, as any fair minded bluejacket who loves fair play generally sides with the underdog in a fight. The papers as we read them seemed to be making a bid for the English. Every paper lauded British bravery and heroism and mentioned very little about the Burghers, excepting now and then, about their firing upon the Red Cross flag and hospital corps. You could see plenty of reading about the besieged in Mafeking, Ladysmith, etc., and the unequaled bravery of the Britons at the Tugela [River], Modder River [November 28, 1899], Spion Kop [January 24, 1900], Elandslaagte [October 21, 1899] and Colenso [December 15, 1899], but only a short account of the heroism displayed by [Gen. P. A.] Cronjé [at] Paardeberg [February 17–27, 1900], where only about 2,000 Boers held at bay fifty thousand Englishmen, and even then hesitated about a surrender until they managed to get their ordnance safely away.[40]

Nagasaki

All the papers we could [buy] in Manila were full of news of English doings. The American papers were also full of the South African Affair, of Brittish valor. They quite overlooked the doings of their own soldiers in the Philippines. Where does British heroism compare with the defense of the small garrison of thirty-one men of the [U.S.] 45th Infantry at Daet, where they held a church against hundreds of the insurgents? The captain shot thro' both legs, even then cheering on his men. The roof burned and falling in on them. Many of them killed and wounded. About the artificer who escaped in the night and brought back reinforcements for their relief? How about the march made by Maj. [Peyton C.] March after Aggie [Aguilnaldo]? What of the fight near Monyagaray, where the 35th Inf[antry] ran into a force of 250 natives and were surprised? One man, a musician, fell shot thro' the groin from hip to hip. Falling on his back in the water, he coolly proceeded to load and fire up the hill at the enemy, firing 29 rounds before being carried from the field. How about . . .

But we will let it pass at that. There are a thousand instances. They occur every day. Perhaps these deeds will be sung in future years.[41] Everything is English now. Americans find them very good to pattern after. They are the vogue, the criterion in everything. We must cultivate their accent, using the broad "a" or else we are an uneducated, uncultured people. Some people forget that we can lead the world in most everything and only show where our weakness lies by imitation. We should stick to America and all things American and instead of imitating, let others imitate. Instead of the American press holding up things British for our approbation, let them laud American bravery and heroism. Don't let us lose sight of our own troubles in the Far East. War is war, whether carried on between handfuls of men, or between armies. The Spanish-American war by the navy was war in all its horrors to the Spaniards. One life lost in warfare alone carries grief to some family or friends.

CHAPTER THREE

Aground in the Yellow Sea

The scene shifts again. Since writing the [preceding], I am one of the crew of the *Oregon*[1] bound for Taku, or some other point on the Northern Chinese coast.[2] Everything happens that is totally unexpected, I find. I was resting myself in my usual place on the bunker tops of the *New Orleans*, reposing peacefully upon my luxurious bed and sleeping the sleep that only a man with the consciousness of duty well performed can enjoy, when I was rudely awakened from my siesta by the messenger from the clerk calling me, bidding me report to Mr. Somebody or other, a young middy who lately landed aboard, in order to have my census taken.

I knew they were taking the [decennial national] census aboard the ship, but as yet they hadn't reached the engineer division. "Strange," thought I, "that they have selected six men from the division at this time in the afternoon. Must be something up. Wonder what 'tis? Can it possibly be a case of transfer in a hurry?" I asked myself these questions and was speedily answered upon reporting to the middy. I was asked if I was one of the men about to be transferred to the *Oregon?* I replied, "I did not know, having not been informed upon that topic."

Well, after answering the usual questions from the middy, who acted as a census numerator, I was taken in hand by the messenger to get my clothing list, which I gave them. Then I knew I was to be transferred. Upon asking when, I was told immediately after supper. It was then five P.M. Supper at 5:30. In half an hour I was ready, bag & hammock lashed securely, ditty box alongside, ready to bid *adieu* forever from the *Pelican*.[3] I was glad of the change, of course.

In the packing up there is always a lot of useless gear you find you have to leave behind, gear that accumulates almost without your knowledge. Your bag is limited. You find something in your hurry you discard. I left behind an ebony cane I got at Colombo, and some turned wooden boxes from Nagasaki. Also dungarees, shoes, etc. All this I gave away to my shipmates. At once we were sent for by the paymaster, and signed accounts clear of the ship. Then I bethought me of some mess gear, and went to the cook of the mess for it, and had to stow that away. You have to carry your mess gear, i.e., knife, fork, spoon, cup and plate, to another ship with you to place in your mess there, or else you have to buy it when you reach there.

At last we were piped to lay aft on the quarter-deck, and after bidding good by[e] to numerous shipmates, we put our bag & hammocks in the cutter and was towed alongside of the *Zafiro*, the boat that Dewey had for a dispatch boat.[4] This packet was to take us to Hong Kong, leaving the next morning at 10:00 A.M. We were the first draft aboard. We were wet to the buff, being caught in a shower coming over in the open boat. When we had safely stowed our gear away we discharged the cutter [i.e., unloaded their sea bags and ditty boxes] thro' a cargo port of the *Zafiro* at the risk of our neck. A choppy sea running made us hustle. Finally, we pulled our way aboard, the six of us, and looked around to see what comfort was in store for us.

It would have been comfortable enough for us, but they kept pouring them in. Two other drafts came that night, one from the *Brooklyn* and one from the *Glacier*, about ninety men in all. For the first time in eight months, I slung my hammock and slept in it by the open cargo port. The next morning another big draft arrived from the *Monadnock* and *Petrel*.[5] There must have been about three hundred men aboard the small *Zafiro* in all. We were jammed like sardines, and I knew what was in store for us. At breakfast, which we had about 9:00 A.M., the gang went in swimming. For breakfast we had hard-tack and coffee. Yes, I could see our finish. I knew what was in store for us. We pulled out about 10:30. We had no work to do about the ship, she carrying a Chinese crew on deck and below, with English officers and master, with, of course, a naval officer to supervise. We were crowded. It reminded me of the steerage of an emigrant ship, [with] the stench between decks, as all ports were closed. We were called aft and divided into messes by the officer in charge, and told we had about three days' run ahead of us, and to make ourselves as comfortable as possible under the circumstances. Of course, we all tried to do that, but we had our hands full.

The rations issued by the paymaster to all hands were beef, potatoes, coffee and bread. Each man is supposed to get of beef, one and a quarter lbs per day, two ounces of coffee, one lb of bread, and a small allowance of vegetables. You can see what a paymaster can make off of Jack, who is allowed thirty cents a day for food. The food issued to us, each man individually, came to just about ten cents. Caterers of messes could [buy] meat from the government, that is, fresh beef or mutton from the *Glacier* or *Culgoa* for five-cents a lb. The paymaster paid about three, and perhaps less. Bread is worth about five cents or less a [pound] loaf, and the coffee and potatoes didn't amount to three cents worth. We didn't have enough to eat, but there wasn't much kicking. The common expression was, "No use kicking, it's only for three days. We can go without eating that long."

The poor fellows detailed for cooks done their best, of course. We would eat breakfast, of coffee & bread, at 9:00, dinner at 10:00 and do without for the balance of the day. It would have been a boon to get seasick; then we wouldn't have wanted to eat.

A Sailor's Log

We would make the beef & spuds into a stew and make out the best we could. Of course, there wasn't enough to go around, and some of us got left occasionally, but we didn't kick. We knew we were against it. The paymaster needed the money. However, we of the *New Orleans* managed to swipe about forty lbs of beef and cut it into steaks and broiled it on the one small galley for all hands' use. I saw men [eat] some of the beef raw. Must have been hungry.

What a shaking up we got! The *Zafiro* proved a mighty lively small packet, and the dancing around she did for those three days made me wish I was on terra-firma once again. The sea hath no more charms for me. My bed was the hard planks of the top deck, my pillow a pair of shoes. Oh, how sore I was! I was sandpapered and rolled around the deck from the motion of the ship. I felt sore all over. No sleeping in the stench below. Fresh air was what I wanted, and plenty of it. In fact, I lived solely upon ozone the entire trip. Twelve of the first-class petty officers, myself among the number, were detailed as policemen to preserve order among the rest. I am happy to state there wasn't any disorder. We were engrossed in our own misery too deeply to make any trouble.

There wasn't an insult passed or a blow struck the entire run. It rained nearly all the time and we huddled under the awnings. We washed and scrubbed clothes to make ourselves respectable looking, only to get as dirty as a pig when we transferred again.

Some of the fellows, as usual, ran up against some "vino" or a decoction equally as vile. Bought it off a "Chino" for three Mex a bottle. I tried a couple of drinks of it and had enough for about forty years. It was about the vilest stuff that ever passed my lips. A chief machinist with our crowd kept hitting the bottle pretty lively and it commenced to show. He swelled up perceptibly before your very eyes, and I could see that he was gradually getting more complacent and filled with the idea of his own exalted importance. In fact, he got the hallucination in his brain that he was the very greatest article that ever happened, the only gazabo[6] that blew down the pike. When the ensign called us aft to detail us to keep order among the men, I knew that something was going to carry away. I could feel it coming. Pressure on the "brass bound" fellow was getting too high. Something must give. The ensign mustered us, "all hands," and read our names to the draft, and told them while he didn't anticipate any trouble among them, still it was in accordance with the regulations of the navy to appoint men for police duties, and to act in case of emergency, etc., etc.

That was the C.P.O's cue.[7] He stepped up to the ensign and asked permission to speak a few words to the men. The ensign looked at him and, as everything went aboard the *Zafiro*, "acquiesced." The C.P.O. was in a mellow state. He puffed up like a pouter pi[d]geon. Maudlin tears swelled up in his eyes, and placing his cigar on the rail for safe keeping, struck an attitude à la Napoleon, or Daniel Webster, [and] commenced. "Men. I shansh detain you, hic, long. We're all hearsh bound for unknown, hic, waters, some us'h p'raps never to return. All I ask and pray ish, hic, be a man.

Aground in the Yellow Sea

Remember to obey yoursh shuperior officer." Here he wandered off on another tangent. "I'm shentleman my sef. Once a shentlmen always a shentlmen, I, hic, saysh." And looking around with a belligerent air, "Anybody doubtsh my words can, hic, see me any old time. Uphold the flag, that glorious old emblem" (pointing). "An, an . . ." He floundered completely.

I came to his assistance by starting a cheer, which drownded him out. As he had got rid of his surplus steam, everybody joined in with a laugh. With a gratified smile and a great air of importance, he moved away like a "line-of-battle ship." Ten minutes later he was sound asleep on the for'd hatch, with a half burnt cigar clenched loosely between his teeth.

It rained steadily the last day, and glad indeed we were at the prospects of leaving the *Zafiro*. If the rest of the men felt as sore and as hungry and disgusted as I did, they had my heartfelt sympathy. Well pleased we all were when we hove in sight of the entrance to the harbor of Hong Kong. We found it to be quite picturesque, but [we] weren't in the mood to enjoy the scenery for we were leaving bad quarters, sore, and hungry, and the prospect before us was unknown.

The morning we left Manila we weren't quite so hungry, and as we followed the coast for the entire day, we were in the mood to enjoy nature's handiwork. We were always within a cable's length of the Islands until late in the afternoon, when we left them behind. The entrance to Subig bay is a beautiful spot.[8] I noticed hundreds of mountain streams of clear, sparkling water flowing down the rocky fissures of the mountains. The whole coastline we passed was mountainous country somewhat similar to Cuba. It is all very interesting, and the trip, if one were only a tourist with nothing to do but lay back and enjoy life, would well repay one. I noticed a few lighthouses, all seemingly deserted. I should judge they have not been tenanted since the American occupation.

Just as we had entered Mirs Bay at Hong Kong about 3:30 P.M., the dinghy of the *Zafiro* carried away from its davits and fell with a crash into the water, turning upside down, thereby causing a delay of over an hour. Finally they succeeded in righting her and without much difficulty a strap was passed beneath and we got immediately underway again. We expected to find the *Oregon* in Mirs Bay, the lower bay in the harbor of Hong Kong, but she was farther up toward the city.

Hong Kong is another such place as Nagasaki, surrounded by hills. It nestles at the foot of, and is built upon, several hills, very prettily situated, but not as pretty as Nagasaki. All this we had to take in at a glance, for we soon sighted the *Oregon* with the *Monterey* close in to the city. I saw at once that the *Oregon* had been loaded down to the water line with coal and stores, in fact, lower than she usually was when prepared for sea. I could distinguish light smoke from both stacks, and remarked to a water-tender who had just left her when she was laid up in ordinary[9] and was now going back, a man whom I had been shipmates with on the *Minneapolis*, "I'll bet a sou that all boilers are lighted, and that she will pull out almost immediately."

"By Gad, I'll bet you're right. We'll hit a watch for tonight [for] sure. I can feel it coming." They were washing down decks and she was in a perfect mess. We could see nothing but work ahead of us and no rest after our tough experiences aboard the *Zafiro*.

The *Zafiro*'s signals were answered and we were ordered to pull alongside, which we did, coming up on the port side. All the men for the *Oregon* were mustered on the *Zafiro* and ordered to pack their bags and hammocks aboard the *Oregon*, which we done, and quite a lot we were. Everything was dirty and full of coal dust and that with the rain, that had settled into a drizzle, made the outlook miserable enough. Some of the old crew were returning and were greeted by their shipmates. Questions passed and answered.

They of the *Oregon* hadn't rec'd any liberty while in ordinary in Hong Kong, six weeks of it. "And how is things at Manila? Same old rain? etc." Eager questions about absent shipmates, what ship they caught, and a hundred other questions fired as from a millimeter gun, and as hurriedly answered, everything confusion.

Men placed their bags one place and ditty box and hammock in another, and were hunting for them thro' the ship. I had been on the *Indiana*, a sister ship of the *Oregon*'s and I had not forgotten her general plan. I noticed everything was almost the same, the details only being different. I placed my bag and hammock where I knew they belonged and followed S——, the water-tender, to our mess. They were just having supper. I gave my mess gear to the cook, and immediately proceeded to fill the "vacuum" caused by the three days trip on the *Zafiro*. Perhaps I wasn't hungry! I don't like liver in any way, shape or form, but I didn't discriminate that night. I just bolted about three lbs together with fried potatoes, coffee, bread & butter with a nice thick gravy. Finally, even I was gorged to repletion. And no sooner than [that] I was told I belonged to the third section and was to go on at 8 [P].M. having the 8 to 12 watch,

We were going out at 6 P.M. sharp, and we shoved off at just about that time, bound for Taku, the scene of the war, where the combined mercantile powers, England, Russia, Germany, France and the United States, were bombarding the forts and raising Cain in general, all anxious to divide poor John Chinaman up in sections and secure all his ports for their own use, using the missionaries (mischief makers everywhere, who are trying to convert a nation that doesn't want to be converted, and who have a religion of their own a thousand years older than our own) as a pretext.[10]

I have often wondered if a missionary, or any number of them, were killed in the heart of some out of the way place that wouldn't be worth the taking, if the "powers that be" would take such an interest in them. Missionaries are a nuisance. It is my candid opinion that they are in the business for a good, easy time, that is, with a few exceptions. Father Damien and others who literally followed in the foot-prints of the Master are, of course, exceptions.[11] The others are all rogues. They get the best of everything. They interfere with people that don't want them around, trying to convert them to their own idea of thinking. And, incidentally, as a side line, making

Aground in the Yellow Sea

quite a good thing of life. Talk is cheap and with a good gift of gab and a long, sanctimonious expression, you have quite all the stock in trade that is required to follow that profession. How hard some of them labor in the vineyard only they can tell, and are only too willing to tell. They don't mention what a good time they have in these far away countries, where labor and all the necessaries of a luxurious existence are to be had for a trifle, where women are cheap, and a coolie servant or any number of them cost only a few sou by the day.

I wouldn't mind being a missionary myself under the circumstances that I have seen surrounding most missionaries I have seen. They make lots of converts, especially the pretty teachers of Sunday classes. The Celestial[12] is a pretty "nifty" rooster at times, and if [there] is anything to be gained, he will profess any old thing in order to obtain any advantages for himself. What I say, let these people alone, and others also. There are enough at home that need looking after, and of our own religions, too, which makes it all the easier for our would-be missionaries to foreign lands. Let them stay [at] home and teach the word of God to people that speak the common tongue and have heard about Christ, not try to convert anyone who wouldn't "savvy" them or the religion or the God they tell them about in a thousand years, who simply profess religion like a parrot would. They have religions and beliefs of their own, and most races have had theirs before the Anglo-Saxon was even heard of.

∼ ∼ ∼

As I was saying, the *Oregon* was steaming out of the harbor of Hong Kong before we were aboard an hour. What our exact destination was, we couldn't find out at the time. I met ma[n]y men I had known in other ships and in other climes. It didn't take us long to find out that the *Oregon* was another mad-house. How long it was to remain one, we couldn't surmise. After we struck her there were about fifty different "words" passed in so many moments. I never worried my head about such trifles. I am pretty well used to them by this time. I know exactly what my rate called for aboard her; all I wanted was to get acquainted with my station, that is the machinery, the touch of it, and how everything would act.

And so I went below to take my watch. A glance was sufficient to show me that I was in one of the best-equipped ships I had ever served in. The boiler feed pumps were the best I had ever handled. Everything was where it should be, and where a practical man would naturally look to find them. I knew the run of the different leads of piping at a glance, and was perfectly at home as far as my work related to the machinery. The men were all new, and had to be placed, but that was soon fixed. The other water-tender "put me on" to the men he knew, and told me whom to watch.

We steamed along nicely at 50 turns my first watch, all boilers, four big double-enders, under steam. They gradually increased the speed, but only by watches, as they were afraid of the engines and thrust bearings running hot. We took life easily

USS *Oregon* as she appeared while Wilson served onboard. Navy Historical Foundation.

up to 85 revolutions and all was "merry as a marriage bell," but things changed. They always do change, I find it so often. And on my fifth watch in the morning they worked all the auxiliary machinery, and whooped her up to 90 revolutions at the same time. The steam commenced to drop and when we left at twelve, we were carrying only a hundred lbs, dropped from 150. From that [point] on, it was the same old drag. "Bolomen," the warrant machinists of the watch, bawling for steam, "jacking" us up, and expecting us to rawhide the watch. The men complained of getting nothing to eat, which was literally true, tho' more the fault of the cook than anything else. All they managed to get to eat in our division was a few [biscuits of] hard-tack, and coffee. I told the "bolo-man" of the watch this, and also told him I didn't care to "bulldoze" men who weren't getting enough to eat, and weren't treated any too well. He said it seemed pretty tough, and that he would speak to the "chief" [chief engineer] about it.

But from what I seen of the "chief," there wasn't any prospect of relief from that quarter. He didn't have the least bit of interest in his men. Didn't trust them; in fact, had no use for the enlisted men at all. We were put thro' drill after drill when off watch. It was a case of the *New Orleans* all over again. But all the drill was in order to break the new men into their stations. Mine I knew before I set foot aboard the ship. The water-tender I mentioned before informed me. At "general quarters" my station was the "after 13" hydraulic pump room," there to run the big hydraulic pumps that worked the turrets and ammunition hoists. I made it my business to get good shipmates with these pumps at once,[13] and we were pretty well acquainted with each other after I had worked them once.

Aground in the Yellow Sea

This pump room was also my cleaning station. It had been very nicely cleaned before, but had been neglected for some time while the *Oregon* was in ordinary in Hong Kong, but I knew I could get her in slick shape in about a week's work, and then by keeping the gang from hanging out there and washing clothes and drying them around the room, always keep her clean. If you wish to keep a station clean on a man-o-war, you have to put your foot down at once and keep people from loafing [there], otherwise you become a flunky for a few of your shipmates who think nothing of dirtying up your paint work and spitting and throwing "quids" of their filthy weed around. I told them from the start that they [would] have to stand clear. I wasn't cleaning up after them. I was cleaning up after the government. They kept clear after that.

We had fire drill, general quarters, abandon ship, collision [drill], etc., thrown at us in rapid succession. It was drill, drill all the time. But I surmised that this would wear off in about a month or so. They sprang "heavy marching order" and battalion the first thing. That was all well enough as there were to be landing parties, and every man jack should know how to pack a knapsack. At "abandon ship" it was laughable to see the "first luff" (known as "Jack the Ripper" from the artistic manner in which he could lay you out) trying to get the Chinese servants, ward room stewards and boys to learn their boat to abandon in. He would swell up in the face like a red turkey-cock, and fume and froth at the mouth.[14] Everything was confusion, bustle and excitement. But the real excitement was to come later.

"Here, writer!" he would bawl out at the top of his lungs, "Come here. Where the blazes does these fellows belong? What's your name? And yours? Ning Po, eh? You belong to the third cutter, savvy? Three-pieeee cutter," holding up three fingers. "Get!" hustling the frightened Chinks this way and that.

"What's your name?" said a middy to one of the frightened Chinamen, who didn't know what all the row was about, and were standing in a bunch on the superstructure.

"Chow Lee, sir."

"All right. 2nd cutter, over here. Ah Lung! Where is Ah Lung?" One of the Chinos started to say something. "You Ah Lung? Run along here."

"No, sir. Me no Ah Lung. Ah Lung, he go to Manila." This raised a laugh. Ah Lung is going to Manila yet, I suppose.

We had bag inspection, and then fire quarters and general quarters at midnight. I had just come off watch, just stripped and [was] washing up when the alarm went. Away I jumped into dungarees and, full of soap and water, hustled below to my station, being second relief then, to put pressure on my pump. It lasted about half an hour when "secure" went and I returned and finished my interrupted bath, and tired out, turned in on the deck and slept the sleep that comes to the tired and weary body, dreamless, and awoke greatly refreshed. These *Oregon* decks are softer than the *New Orleans*, being covered with linoleum, and make a good bed.

The 28th of June dawned with a thick fog. When we went below, we were running at about 50 revolutions, then full speed, then slow again. We had encountered thick, foggy weather for the last two days. The day before, being near our destination, we had cut out boiler D on my watch. We expected to reach Taku on Friday morning. Steaming along on three boilers they wanted all the revolutions we could give them. It was set at 75 at first, then increased. Coming off watch at noon Thursday, the engines were stopped and the anchor was dropped shortly after. We had had general quarters all the watch. At noon the word was passed for hammock inspection, and we brought our hammocks from the nettings and spread them on the fo'castle.

The chief told his "bolo-men" not to take any man's word for the cleanliness of his bedding, but to see for themselves that every mattress, blanket and mattress cover was re-marked with each man's name. It wasn't the words he used, but the tone, the inflexion on "not take any man's word," the contempt he threw into it, as if we were all dogs, liars, and not to be trusted under any circumstance. And all over such a matter as hammock inspection!

We had then ran off our course and as I said, were at anchor in a group of islands, about as dismal as I ever beheld, with a lighthouse on our port bow. Bearing about three points beyond we could see the streak that betokened a reef. How we managed to get in there without running aground was a mystery. During the hammock inspection, two officers were out in boats taking soundings. You could see yellow spots in the sea that showed shoal water. About 2:30 they started to get up anchor to get out, the fog having lifted. Somebody made the remark, "What a narrow escape!" to which somebody replied, "This ship will get it yet," and get it she did.

While they were getting up the anchor I went on the orlop deck forward to the handling room where all the firemen had a hang out, and had just lain down for a "snooze" when I heard a grinding, rasping noise. The ship shook from stem to stern, trembling all over. She listed over to port [starboard?]. The traveling purchases for handling shell started around to the port side of the travelers with a wild run. We jumped up in a fright wondering what the matter was. I thought the anchor chain had parted.

"What's the matter? What's wrong now? Did the chain carry away?"

"Chain, [hell]! She's got it at last. We are in it for fair this time."

Just then the siren sounded for collision quarters, and we ran to our stations. We started pumps on secondary drain and bilges, and fastened all watertight doors to different compartments. The ten thousand tons of the *Oregon* lay on the rocks with a heavy list to starboard, where she settled when the water filled the forward compartments. Ten thousand tons of the finest battleship afloat, the acme of mechanical skill in naval architecture, was fast aground, grinding her life out on the rocks.[15]

Everything was in an uproar as she began to settle. Soon we were down to the ports of the berth deck on the starboard side. Men prepared to leave the ship. Some gathered up a few belongings and placed them in their ditty boxes. Some had life

Rushing to the Taku Forts to support the allied forces in the relief of the legations at Peking during the Boxer Rebellion, USS *Oregon* ran aground near Howki Island, Gulf of Pechili. Navy Historical Foundation.

preservers on, and some had two. Yes, they were expecting to leave the ship. Others went rapidly to work and help[ed] wedge compartment bulkheads, shoring them to keep them from bursting in. After the first excitement was over and we knew she couldn't settle for being held up by the rocks, divers went below to ascertain the extent of her injuries. All sorts of rumors were current as to the nature of the holes stove in her, but not any were true. We were kept busy below using all pumps wherever we could get them on [line up suction from] a compartment. The fires were started under D boiler again. The forward boiler fires were hauled, the boilers blown down under pressure thro' the bottom blow [overboard valve] to lighten the ship forward. Coal was started over board from the forward bunkers and everything possible done to lighten her forward. On deck, bucket lines were formed. Handy billys were rigged to pump her free, but she gradually settled deeper on the rocks.[16] All pumps going, we could just hold our own.

She seemed to be resting with a rock under her port bow. The rock was reported up through the bottom, and some of the seams were started. The compartment B92, under 5 & 6 fire-rooms, buckled in during the morning following the disaster and water oozed in freely. Some of the other compartments were also bent in, buckling the angle irons badly. As luck would have it, there happened to be a wrecking company close by that [was] working on one of the Maru[17] steam ships and then came and secured the job of raising us. And in spite of being hampered by suggestions and interference from the officers, they succeeded in clearing us of the water in the different compartments. They brought with them two wrecking pumps. One was sufficient to get the water under control in conjunction with the pumps below, which were running constantly. About sixty five hours after we struck, we were afloat on an almost level keel, so with a tow from the *Nanchang* and *Kwongchang,* two of the wrecking company's steamers, away we started, also using our own engines.

A channel had been sounded previously, and men were in the chains taking soundings. We pulled clear of the rocks, and feeling secure, the skipper took things in his own hands. The *Nanchang* happened to swing across our bows. This was on account of the swiftly running tide, and couldn't be helped. Thro' it all I will say the captains of the wrecking company's steamers handled their boats like tugs, but, of course, the Naval officers didn't think so, by the way they acted.

"Get out of the way there, or I'll hit you!" bawled the captain, steaming ahead four bells and feeling secure once more, now that she was afloat.

The *Nanchang* just cleared our bows with her starboard quarter in time. We didn't hit her, but we hit something just as bad. No sooner were we clear of the *Nanchang* than bump, bump. We got it this time. We were high and dry. It wasn't a rasping, scraping sound this time, accounted for by the diver who made another investigation and reported us on sandy bottom. We made attempt after attempt to back off.

Heavy-duty wrecking pumps provided by civilian salvors helped save the *Oregon.* Navy Historical Foundation.

All men were chased aft on the quarterdeck. Wire cables parted in the effort to get us off, but with no success as the tide was running out swiftly. Another attempt was made about one A.M. Monday morning, July 2nd, for about 3 hours, to get us off. No success. Then they started to lighten her up forward. The sheet anchor was hoisted aboard the *Kwongchang,* more 13" shell taken out, more coal and stores hoisted in the effort to lighten ship. Such a yelling and confusion I never heard before. The merchant officers were disgusted. Men were worn out from excessive work, working in watches, Port and Starboard. Many of the gang got drunk from liquor bought aboard one of the steamers. Eight or ten were confined in double irons under the [sentry's] charge, and should be punished severely, for it is a serious offense to shirk work and get under the influence of liquor while a ship lies in the condition of the *Oregon.*

The water gained steadily again in the fore-hold and to make matters worse, the wrecking pump broke its valve-stem and the men pumped by hand, only keeping the water back a little. And thus we lay nearly 90 hours on the rocks.

Sunday, type written telegrams were posted up on the bulletin-board giving details of the recent fighting in "Tien Sien," [Tientsin] about [Vice] Admiral [Sir Edward H.] Seymour's brigade being cut off, Captain [Bowman H.] McCalla being wounded, the brave old man. [He was one of the] best-spoken-of captains in the navy by all enlisted men.[18] A list of American killed and wounded [also was posted], among the names, some shipmates that we knew who had died doing their duty far from their native land. This caused excitement. We all cursed our fate in not being able to get to the seat of war. Who among us could read these bulletins with a feeling of indifference? I know almost every man chafed under the forced detention of lying here idle, no, not idle, we had more work than was possible. But we longed to be at the front.

The [HMS] *Endymion,* English cruiser, came to our relief. They also had lost a number of men. A Russian cruiser was also on the scene of action. Also the *Yorktown.*[19] The evening before, a Chinese man-o-war came into the bay w[h]ere we were fast aground and besought the protection of the American flag, which was granted, and which he hoisted at his fore.[20] From what I could gather, he was chased by an Englishman and was followed [into] the bay by a big Russian. I did not know that they were waging war against the Imperial government, altho' we heard a number of Imperial troops had sided with the rebels, the Boxers. But, of course, I had an idea that the different nations would capture everything in sight, and then fight among themselves for the lion's share of the spoils. A number of Chinese sampans came alongside and some of them reaped a harvest of coal. They would catch it in baskets as we dumped it thro' the ash chute. Some of them carried away a ton in a load. This coal cost as high as thirty dobies a ton in Hong Kong. The men amused themselves by throwing old beef cans and empty bottles over the side, to see the Chinks hustle for them, the boats often coming together with sufficient force to mix them all up. Then they would talk and jabber and gesticulate like monkies [*sic*], pull off and line up for another rush.

No tables were spread for mess gear. We ate as well as we could sitting around, and slept the same. Any clear corner free from traffic made a good bed. Some of the men would sleep on a row of ditty boxes. Others flung themselves on the deck exhausted, and fell asleep as soon as they struck.

~~~

Never on any ship was I ever cast with such an engineer force. A bigger pack of hoboes, or aggregation of loafers, never struck a man-o-war before. If selected for general laziness, you couldn't have hit it better, except at the mess table. Then they were all alacrity, and what each man would eat [would] keep four horses alive. If you wanted to insult them, just ask them to do something. You should hear the roar they would put up. To hear them talk, you'd think each man had done all the work in the ship. I didn't get quite onto them at first. I thought they were getting a hard deal from the tale of woe they would spin. I found out their cook was put in irons for being drunk, and that they kicked and growled so much nobody would cook for them.

I treated them kind at first, just as I treated any other men that worked with me in other ships, but they only laughed at me for being soft. I tumbled, and put the screws on them accordingly. Of course, they were doing hard duty, but what has every man but hard and long labor in front of him with a ship aground? Work and hard work had to be done. You couldn't keep them below five minutes at a time. I got tired of coaxing them to work, the big lazy duffers, loafing on a few good men who did their own work and theirs, too. The [height] of their ambition was to get full of "booze" and any hour you could see the same old gang, one at a time, making a quiet trip to the *Nanchang,* where they could obtain a bottle of fierce stuff for three Mex. If the messenger or any one of the men were sent for them to turn to, they would bluff him or want to slug him according to the booze they had aboard.

In every ship you find a gang of this kind. They are agitators. They are useless. They either can't do their work or won't, and persuade other men not to do theirs, telling them they will get just as much credit for not doing it, as for working, tho' I never saw yet where a shirk ever rec'd any credit. Most of these hoboes get paid off with a "postage stamp," or very small discharge.[21] Then they howl and want to know how it happen'd. The *Oregon* had even a worse crowd of these bums than the *New Orleans.* It took an [invitation] from the warrant machinist to get them to work at all. It is among these men that a water-tender's troubles commence. They will bluff you if they can. If you are naturally a good hearted fellow and don't rush them, you are soft. If you keep them up to the mark, you are something worse. When you, as petty officer of the watch, muster your men and find them absent, and report them absent, they want to slug you. I have never expended any useless strength or wind on these big curs. I simply report them for what they are: shirks and loafers. If they, being bigger men and stronger, try to slug me, I simply use a twelve or fourteen inch monkey or Stillson wrench and lay them out.

Aground in the Yellow Sea

I had one chronic "chaw" in my section. It was a continuous growl from the beginning to the end of the watch. A first class fireman he was, tho' the Lord knows how he ever become one. I had a dozen coal-passers who were better than he. Every order I gave him he would want to know the ins and outs of it. I didn't mind his growling, that was his business, unless he got personal. I never yet interfered with a "chaw." It pleases them and don't hurt me. Finally, seeing he couldn't spoil my temper or get me mad by growling, he started to loaf and pile up his fires with green coal, what is known as "crown-sheeting" a fire. Shuts off the air from circulating over the top of the fire. I called him down quietly for this. That was his cue. He started into chaw and wound up in abuse. Says he, "I'll be [damned] if I'll do any work with a man hollerin' at me. You won't get any work from me, you or any other [damned] water-tender. I was on this ship two years before this last time and I guess I know my business better than any —— jay that's just come to it. I won't give any steam even to the chief himself if I am going to be hollered at this way," winding up the old song with a few nautical swear words as a proper sailor-man should.

I wasn't even ruffled. I expected this tirade all along. "Well, look here, old man. Its true I'm new on this ship, but not new in the navy, and I've met your like before. I've listened to your old guff for three or four watches now, and as long as you do your work, just the bit that holds your end of the boiler up, you can chaw 'til doomsday. But let me tell you, now, once for all, if I catch you slighting your fires in any way, I bring you right to the chief engineer for a shirk and loafer. That's for not working. For the personalities you indulge in about me, I'll grab you by those whiskers (he had a full beard) and wrap that infernal —— head of yours against the bulkhead until I dislocate your spinal column. Mind that now!"

I never heard any more chaw or guff from this fellow since, but he couldn't do his work at all. Many times I felt inclined to put him in the coal-bunkers and put a coal-passer in his place on the fires.

Another miserable little cur full of vino called down the ventilator and when the fireman sitting under it answered back, "Who's that?" dropped a marline spike[22] down, nearly striking the fireman. I ran up to the auxiliary boiler room as quick as possible, as also the fireman, but could find no trace of him. However, we nearly guessed our man from his voice, and [from] the fact of seeing him drunk around the wash room. A whisky bottle followed the marline spike later on. This miserable cur was a cleaner on the orlop deck, but as there wasn't any cleaning going on, on account of being on the rocks, I made it my business, as did also the other water-tender of the watch, to have him brought below and put to work with the rest of the watch, getting out coal and hoisting [it] to clear the ship. This was perhaps the worst punishment that could be given him, the very mention of work to some of these hoboes completely prostrat[es] them.

I forgot to mention about our friend the chief machinist who made the speech aboard the *Zafiro*. Meeting some old ship mates aboard the *Oregon* when he came aboard, he was rapidly introduced to a good many bottles. By continuous visits to his friends, he became more and more mellow, an[d] kingly in his feelings. About his third watch out, he was in such a state that he concluded he could run the whole machine, both above an[d] below, without any assistance. So, going below, he told his oiler to stand by, that he was going to stop the engine in a few moments, and before the oiler could prevent him, he did stop her, and stopped her dead on the top center, from full speed ahead, so that she reversed. One of the machinists first class jumped quick as a flash and threw the engine over and speeded up again. It was hardly noticeable from the bridge. They tried to get him out of the engine room, but couldn't do it except by force. So the "bolo-man" called upon "Jimmy Legs" for assistance. The next I saw of this mighty individual, he was languishing in double-irons under the sentry's charge. I do not know what disposition they made of his case. They released him when we went on the rock, and he redeemed himself by good work. He was O.K., as they all are, when sober.

I also had a narrow escape from getting into trouble thro' my friends.(?) Going on watch Sunday night, I was invited to go up in the evaporator room by an old shipmate. I knew it was a drink, and feeling bad from the *Zafiro* trip, concluded a good, big "dose" would do me good, sort of take the kinks out. I went, telling my mate to keep an eye to the water, she steaming along very easy. My friends were noisy from the effects of continued libations. I took two drinks and broke away, pleading duty. I went down from the evaporator room hurriedly, when who should I pass looking up squarely at them but the chief. He was standing right in the door of the engine room hatch. Thought I, "All is lost. He'll catch them for sure." I couldn't warn them, so making a pretense of wiping off my manly brow with a sweat rag in order to cover my face, I darted by and below as quickly as possible, knowing they were old foxes at the game and even if the chief caught them red-handed they would lie out of it, as after events proved. However, I resolved to be more careful in the future.

The morning of the Fourth of July, 1900, dawned upon the coast of China with the prospect of a drizzling rain, which, however, was dispelled partly by the sun. It was the second anniversary of the battle of Santiago in the United States, we here in far-off China being a day ahead.[23] [It was also the] second anniversary of the *Oregon*'s famous fight and cruise around the world in time to be in at the death blow of the Spaniards.[24] This day two years after, the *Oregon* lay hard and fast upon the rocks, a doubtful proposition at best. Everything possible was being done to get her off. Working night and day until exhausted, men would fall out and be replaced by others. We had help from quite a number of different races. Men from the Russian [man-of-war were] working with bulldog tenacity, tireless. When these Russians took hold of anything, either it or a piece of it would have to come. There was also a Russian diver at work. Our Chinamen also willingly lent a hand and a fine body of men these Chinese men-o-warsmen looked, with their pigtails neatly plaited and coiled under cocked up straw hats, dressed in blue-dungaree with blue sashes, they were as neat as any of those among us, handsome men some were, not like the opium eating and smoking Chinamen of the States, but bright and intelligent looking fellows. Their officers [wore] neat uniforms, blouses of brownish silk, faced with black satin and braid, the Imperial Dragon swallowing the Sun of Japan worked in gold relief upon their cuffs.

The Japs from a cruiser recently arrived also furnished their quota of men in watches, those sturdy little men from the land of the Rising Sun doing mighty work.[25] They are English in their uniform and tip-top sailors. The ship swarmed with foreign bluejackets. It is there where you see the good fellowship that distress engenders. Russians, Japs, Chinamen, all sworn [enemies], their enmity forgotten in the common cause of raising the mighty battleship from where she lay. The coal was being hoisted out of her as rapidly as men could work. The 13" shell was all removed and transferred to the *Nanchang*, as was also the heavy sheet anchor and [starboard] anchor davit. One anchor was disabled, the fluke broken off close by the shank. The two for'd 6" guns were being removed from their mounts. The pump [was] working rapidly upon the lower hold, but alternately [it was] losing and gaining water. Everything was being done that human ingenuity could devise, and it was all brute work that these sailors from foreign ships were doing, nothing but lift and pull all day long.[26] We decorated ship and fired the National Salute at noon, but altogether it was a dull 4th. Still, I would rather be where I was than at Manila on the *New Orleans*.

Besides, wasn't it the Glorious Fourth, a day propitious in the history of the United States? What day more fitting than this to float the pride of the American Navy and gladden the hearts of those interested in her at home? This was to be the day. We hadn't made any trial the day before. Every effort was made to lighten ship. The two steamers were alongside, but they were pointed the same as ourselves, so they would have to go astern as we also were to do with our own engines. We were moored by two anchors astern and were to use our winches.

We started. The steamers thrashed the waters with their propeller blades. We backed, at the same time starting the winches and putting plenty of strain on them. The 13" turret aft was also worked so the big pistols would list the ship. All to no avail. We only pivoted around. Move back one inch with the terrible strain we did not. We danced "double quick" to the tune of the bugle to vibrate her and possibly shake the ship loose. We were tired. It was kept up alternately until long after we went on watch. We of the four to eight [watch] got a hack at keeping up the steam on the two boilers while the two engines ground it up faster than we could make it. They stopped the engines several times to let us bottle the steam, which fell below 80 lbs. When steam was raised, away went the engines again. About five P.M. it was given up in disgust, and everything quieted down for the night. No one worked that night except the regular watch. The *Nanchang* hauled off for the night. The next day was to be another trial, but there wasn't much hope. And we were just as badly off as we were the first day.

A Sailor's Log

About this time the news reached us that the *Concord* was lost in a typhoon while en route to Cebu from Manila. We, however, placed very little faith in this rumor, but it seemed as if the hand of Providence was against us in our undertakings in the Far East.[27] First the *Charleston*, in a series of accidents.[28] I often wondered about the policy of the Philippines, what use they are to us. They will never pay us for the trouble. China is different in a certain sense. She has to give way before the advance of civilization. As "Mike," a wardroom steward told me. "Chinee man no change, no damn good. Chinamen no fight any how. No more China now. French, English, Russian, Amerca take everting. Empress [Tsu Hsi] she no damn good. Make plenty trouble." Mike is ahead of his race, and although serving in an humble capacity, has more brains and energy and broad mindedness than a good many mandarins of his own Celestial Empire.

The Fifth of July came at last and the hour appointed for our next trial.[29] About 2:20 or 3 P.M. [July 5th, 1900], everything was in readiness for the grand coup. This was to be the time she (the *Oregon*) was to come off the rocks as everything possible had been done to lighten her forward. The *Nanchang* came alongside again, this time with her bow faced aft, as these steamers can, or any steamer can, exert more power going ahead than astern. Everything was again in readiness below to use the main engines. Hawsers were again ready for towing and they were to apply all possible power to pull us off.

About this time, [there] was great excitement forward on the forecastle, occasioned by an accident to the diver, a Norwegian I believe, Petersen by name, and a man who did valuable work.[30] He had made many descents without accident, but this time he crawled completely under the ship's bottom and came around to the starboard side when his line became fouled in some way, and he couldn't signal properly to his assistants on the port bow, they all being in the sailing launch, at the lines and pump. The air pressure became greater and greater, and he, receiving no answer to his repeated signaling, turned on the valve that regulated the pressure to a certain extent, letting more air in, and he quickly arose to the surface on the starboard bow, where he lay helpless, stretched out on the surface of the water, threshing his hands about in order to grasp a line or obtain a hand hold somewhere. He was immediately noticed by someone looking over the side, and a great cry arose, "Something wrong with the diver! Something wrong with the diver!"

One of the ensigns, a young sprig, ran aft in a flurry to the quarterdeck, yelling out at the top of his voice, "The diver! The diver is drowning! etc., etc." Possibly he was going aft for orders from the captain as that was the last I saw of him until the trouble was all over. This young ensign was as useless an article as I have ever saw aboard ship. He was very consequential. He would overhear someone during the trouble on the rocks giving an order, then he would go over to the men and repeat it, as if it originated with him. He was full of those tricks. I have seen him look around furtively to see if the skipper or first luff's eyes were on him, then he would "throw an awful bluff," chasing the men away, "Get out of here. Move back there! Damn you, out of the way!" he would yell at the top of his lungs, pushing them back at the same time. I used to watch this fellow in his clean ducks, afraid of getting his hands or clothes soiled. He amused me. I was always interested when I saw him around the decks, looking with interest for the next funny break he would make.

If matters had been left to him, Petersen would have suffocated in his diving suit. As it was, he had a close call, and but for a young seaman by the name of James, would have "lost the number of his mess."[31] James jumped to his assistance. The men's shoutings attracted a number of the Chinamen close by in sampans, and one of them came at full speed to where the diver lay struggling in the water. Petersen thro' it all preserved his presence of mind, and kept tapping the face-plate of his helmet. The Chinamen and others who had jumped in the sampan [were] holding him up in his cumbersome suit as best they could, whilst James with great difficulty unscrewed the face plate, James and the diver bobbing a number of times beneath the sea until they got a round turn around the [by] then unconscious man. During all this, the wildest excitement prevailed. All sorts of advice were hurled from the forecastle. The first luff came to the scene, and having his usual allowance aboard, commenced adding to the general excitement by cursing and damning everything in sight. "Get out of here! [Damn] you dogs! Get back to your work. Who the [hell] told you to knock off? Clear this fo'castle, every mother's——, or I'll punch your infernal heads [off]. Get out of here, you firemen. When I wanted you to go in the bunkers to work you wouldn't go, but [damn] you are always around when you're not wanted, in the way," with a volley of curses. [He presented] the picture of a poor, old man, with violent passions, screaming around in futile wrath, his red face leading one to expect an apoplectic stroke.

They sent to the sick bay for brandy, but [sick bay] sent up "spirits of ammonia" instead. Finally, the marine officer came forward with a bottle, and poor Petersen revived, not much the worse for his narrow squeeze, and [was] willing to go down again. If this accident had culminated fatally, I don't know what should have been done, as this man rendered incalculable service, and would have been hard to replace. After he recovered he said that the *Oregon* was only resting by about three feet of her bottom on a ledge of rock on the starboard beam, and it would be an easy matter to float her.

The *Kwongchang* went around about 2:30 so as to face aft, the same as the *Nanchang*, and in working around using a steel cable fastened from our port bow to [her] port quarter and also fastened by her port bow to our port quarter. The moment we felt the strain, the *Oregon*, much to everybody's surprise, slid gently off the rock and was afloat once more, without any assistance, you might say, practically, and entirely unexpected[ly]. It was a strain in the right direction of a few pounds, whereas bullhead[ed]ness and power of fifty thousand horses had failed to budge us when applied in the wrong way. A seaman standing by seeing the *Kwongchang* moving around, made the remark to me, "If the *Kwongchang* was going ahead with a line from our port bow to her stern, she could pull us off without much trouble, that is the direction in which we have to be moved," and his words came literally true before he had finished speaking. So easily were we afloat that we didn't believe it for some time. Thus was the *Oregon* floated once more, just exactly seven days on the rocks, coming off at about 3 P.M., July 5th, 1900, after many futile efforts.

The next day we changed our position, moving over in[to] a calm spot where the tide wasn't so strong, to give the diver a good chance to work on the bottom without getting fatigued and having to come to the surface so often.

The place in which the *Oregon* now found herself was on the other side of the island where we ran aground on a rock. The distance from the other side was about ten miles, and it took us nearly all the afternoon to make it. You can imagine how carefully the journey was made. We follow[ed] the *Kwongchang*, with the *Nanchang* still made fast to our [starboard] side, and arrived without any more accident, and let go the anchor. The next day we moved nearer in toward the island, as the current was still too strong for our diver to work with comfort, and less undertow was found nearer inshore.

Our diver worked nearly all day, only coming to the surface for a slight blow and a fresh supply of wooden wedges and gear to stop the holes. As the leaks were stopped and the seams wedged and caulked, the pumps made perceptible headway upon the waters, but they still had their work cut out for them and were kept at full speed all the time, and great work one of these pumps did. I often expected it to fly in pieces from the knock that developed as the bearings wore and loosened up, but an occasional setting up [adjustment] renewed it once more and off it went, full tilt. Bad, indeed, would have been the *Oregon*'s state if those pumps had became disabled permanently.

The spot where the *Oregon* now lay, close inshore, contained a pretty fair sized Chinese town, and was cultivated and contained plenty of shade trees in the principal clusters of long, low, rambling Chinese houses. The town itself was scattered along for about three miles. It was an oasis in about as barren a spot as I ever beheld. The rest of the islands [were] nothing but rock and sand. The crops, whatever they were, seemed wrung from the unwilling soil by sheer force. The only commerce we could see carried on was a few junks passing now and again, I suppose from Chefoo or Port Arthur. We had a bumboat come off, or rather, two of them, with an assortment of most everything the bluejacket requires: apricots, English walnuts, sponge cakes, candy, eggs, beef steak, towels, soap, cigars, cigarettes, etc., etc., all at reasonable prices. The eggs [were] very cheap: 1 cent Mex apiece. Steak 12 cts Mex per lb. These bumboatmen ferreted us out a couple of days after we ran ashore, and to some of the fellows was a Godsend as a number of messes had pretty tough living, having exhausted all the sea-stores laid in at Hong Kong, and "Government straight" even when plentiful is bad enough, but when one has to spar for it, it becomes unbearable. Plenty of these men couldn't obtain a drink of coffee or tea, or even a hard tack, if they happened to be late at mess gear.

My own mess continued feeding very well indeed, having stuff laid in [in] abundance, and beside, having a good cook, a German, steady, and to be relied upon. We even had pumpkin pies, puddings, etc., at this time for dessert. The only thing we lacked [was] vinegar, which we could do without well enough. And right here let me add, I regained the appetite I [had] lost in the miserable climate of Manila Bay. I could put away three neat, square meals a day, and still have an appetite. The sun here is very hot during the day, but is tempered by cool breezes. At night it is very cool, and especially so toward morning. To eat well, and sleep well is quite an item, and I done both. The only trouble [was] in getting an equable temperature to sleep in. Some parts of the steel deck, being very hot, you would get toasted sufficiently on one side, and then roll over on the other. In another place, you would chill out before morning. I used to shift positions. Going off watch, I would select another spot that somebody had just vacated going on, and in that manner pulled thro' the night pretty comfortably for a man-o-war.

These Chinamen up here in the northern part of China are for the most part a fierce looking lot. They wear mustaches [and] goatees, but seldom a full beard. Piratical looking enough are they, and from what I see of the nest of islands we got mixed up in, and the number of wrecks around, must have been in the olden days a source of profit for them. I still believe yet that any helpless merchantman driving ashore there would always remain a mystery of the deep, no one living to tell the tale. I saw at a distance what I think was the remains of a small barkentine, her two sticks [masts] still standing, the whole fabric high and dry upon the beach. And the *Maru* steamer being aground there and ourselves in the same fix, all this in the last year of the nineteenth century when navigation is down to a fine point. What must it have been years ago when these lands were infested by hordes of Chinese pirates, whose loot rivaled the spoils of their more famous brothers of the Spanish Main? The Chinese Morgans, Blackbeards, Captain Kyds, etc., reap a rich harvest from the shipping engaged in barter in the Eastern world.

The *Nashville* came in shortly after we were afloat, but only remained a short while. The *Kwongchang* also left, being dismissed, the *Oregon* having no further use for her. The *Iris*[32] came alongside and all valuables, money, etc., were transferred aboard her. She also supplied us with fresh water, the two forward boilers being refilled and ready for steaming. All the coal in the forward bunker was packed aft by the men of the different sections, a heart-breaking job, the "bolo-men" always after them and trying to drive them faster.

These "bolo-men" of the *Oregon* were about as incompetent a set as I have been with, always pulling against each other. Not having any idea of routine, and less of discipline, they demoralized the whole "black gang." It was useless for a petty-officer to try and get work done by the men. The "bolo-men," who are taking the place of engineers, are not respected by them and not having sufficient will power and force, couldn't enforce any discipline whatever. If you, as water-tender, reported any man for loafing, the man would talk to the "bolo-man" on watch in a manner that would never be tolerated one instant by an officer. And, ten to one, the man would be told to go back to his work with a reprimand that hurt his "*amour propre*" about as much as a pea-shooter would hurt the armor plate of the *Oregon*, only to repeat the offense time and again. We got so ourselves, we concluded not to care, saying to one another, "Well, what the [hell] can we do? The men can give these fellows any old con and are let go; consequently, we are laughed at. As long as the warrant mach[inist] is satisfied, all right. Let it go. We will worry thro' the watch as best we can. But ooh, for the old regime when a petty officer was a petty officer, and men would do their bit!"

This was the substance of it all. This personnel bill of '98 is largely responsible for the condition of the navy today. The most of the bolo-men are heroes of '98. The machinists of years of experience in the outfit were cast aside and thrown down when they went up for exam for warrants, and the young sprig, who in several cases was not a machinist by trade, was granted a warrant. It used to amuse me to have my bag inspected by a "bolo-man" who, it was a notorious fact, used to turn in at hammocks with greasy dungarees and shoes on, and was the comment of the whole ship for his dirty appearance, and was threatened oftimes with a complete scrubbing with sand and canvas.[33]

"Let's see your clothes," said this B.M. to one of his former mess-mates. "Spread them out, and lets get a look at them. Are they all marked and stopped?" [he asked] pompously.

"Yes, you bet they are," sarcastically replied the man. "I'm not ashamed to show my clothes at any time. *My* clothes are always clean and ready for inspection, and that's more than some people I know can say."

Of course, this shot told, but the B.M. preserved his usual expression, this being a sample of the remarks the most of them received. The great majority of them did not know how to keep themselves clean until they received their present appointment. Indeed, it seems [un]natural for some of them yet to do so, even with the assistance of Chinese servants. By these remarks I do not want anyone to think I include all warrant mach[inists]. Such is not the case. Some of the squarest and most capable men I know are warr[ant] mach[inists], too good men for their position in the navy. It is not an enviable job. They are being continually called down by their superior officers and laughed at by the men. In fact, [they] haven't many friends on ship board. Someone even corralled one of these fellows' shoes aboard the *Oregon*, causing a loud howl and [an] indignation meeting among them.

These shoes were left around the engine room hatch and when they were looked for by their owner, were among the missing. The men who had been working around the hatch during the day, scrubbing paintwork and cleaning, were called to the engine room and closely interrogated, but the theft remained a mystery. This was carrying the war into the enemy's country with a vengeance. There was nothing said or done when we would lose clothes or shoes. Any time going on watch men could be heard swearing as only a man can swear who loses anything in this line. I lost a new overshirt I cut down for a "steaming shirt." Only used it one watch, and hung it up in the aux[iliary] boiler room, where we were allowed to hang our wet clothes coming off watch. When I went to look for it, it was gone. Others lost clothing they hung up in there, time and time again.

There [is] generally a lot of petty stealing done in a strange ship's company at first, until the men know each other. But some of these "scum of the earth" are so used to wearing cast off clothing ashore, that they can't refrain from doing it aboard ship. They steal your soap, towel, tooth brush, even a dirty pair of old socks, anything that comes their way. They are a miserable lot of thugs, and make it decidedly unpleasant on board ship. The trouble of it is, you never can catch them, and if you do, they say, "It was a mistake. I thought it was mine." The idea of a man wearing another man's shoes by mistake!

A large Russian wrecking tug belonging to the navy came from Port Arthur, but as we were afloat, and the pumps we had at work were adequate, she returned whence she came. There wasn't enough water for this powerful tug to get at, she having two manifolds to her two pumps, with 15 suction hoses to each, of about 8" diameter apiece, so that thirty different compartments could be pumped out at the same time, a suction hose placed anywhere it could be used. All thro', the Russian Navy rendered us all possible service as well as the Japs.

Some miserable rat about this time threw the captain's dog overboard, or such was the supposition. This was done, I presume, to show the esteem in which the skipper was held by some of the crew. But however much he himself was obnoxious, it was a small way to get revenge, and met with general condemnation by the majority of the men. By doing such dirty tricks as this it makes it much harder for the men on board, and both innocent and guilty suffer alike.

A funny incident happened while we were around in the bay getting patched up. Early one morning Jack the Ripper came around the berth deck, looking for somebody to abuse in order to relieve his mind. He found him in the shape of a big, husky coal passer, who, having a night watch, was sleeping in. He was half in and half out of his hammock and the first luff coming along [at] six bells [7:00 A.M.] "seeking whom to devour" ran up against this fellow's not overclean foot dangling from his hammock. Plump in the eye was planted the big toe of the sleeper, and such a bellow of rage [issued] from the Ripper that all the sleepers in until six bells, awoke by the infernal noise made by the irascible old man.

"You infamous scoundrel, you scum of the earth!" he roared, wiping his injured optic with his handkerchief, "What the —— blazes do you mean by kicking me in the eye with that dirty foot of yours, you, you damned scoundrel? What do you mean by sleeping half in and half out of your hammock, sir? Either sleep in or out, you skunk, you. . . ." Here his feelings almost overcame him and exhausted and swelling with rage he almost collapsed.

Here some other sleeper awakened by the racket and not knowing, and if he did, not caring, bawled out in a hoarse voice, "Why don't you run away?" And then all sorts of advice was hurled at the old fellow. Someone unknown asked him if he "thought he'd ship over?" Another, with his head well down in his hammock, advised him "to try and stick it out," etc. Then the Ripper started in to abuse the entire deck until, exhausted from his passion, he left in a rage amid a chorus of groans and cat-calls. Doubtless he sought and found consolation from his private stock. But he effectually awoke all hands that morning.

We had our troubles below as well as the men on deck. Every watch we were standing in watches as usual at sea. And all the coal was packed back from forward, and wet coal it was at that, the bunkers forward being full of water. This was a heart-rending job, and I pitied the poor coal-heavers who had all they could do to keep enough coal on the plates for the watch's use on the two steaming boilers. After the coal was all back, the extra men started in to cleaning bilges, another nasty job at best, but a fierce one at this time as all the bilges were full of coal and ashes, and it is always a mean job to get dirt from beneath boilers. However, it was all accomplished at last. The chief crawled thro' all the double bottoms and found them in a pretty bad state. All the cement [ballast] would have to be taken out and the indentions [dents in the hull] jacked back in place, and twisted and bent angle irons straightened. Evidently there was an immense amount of work in store for all hands in the near future.

Every watch almost would we have a "chaw" with the "bolo-men" about the men. They want[ed] the men to do more and faster work and we contend[ed] that they had their hands full as it was. They wanted to go so far as to put a fireman only apiece [i.e., a single fireman] in each fire room, which was all right at first when the coal was brought back to them and running from the bunker doors where they were working. But when the coal got back too far in the bunkers of the two after fire rooms, I insisted that two coal passers be placed again on watch, and only gained my point by persistent "chawing." These B.M. haven't any idea what work a man can do. [They] seem to think a fireman or coal passer is a mule to be worked for all there is in him. Fires were cleaned every watch and tubes blown and everything kept in readiness for a move at any moment. They transferred all the 8" shell and ammunition aboard the *Nanchang*. They replaced the large anchor and anchor davit on the [starboard] bow, another bit of double work.

I started in also to give my cleaning station a touch up, although I didn't expect to remain on the ship very long. Still, I thought it best not to neglect it too far, but while on watch, a few moments devoted to cleaning it wouldn't go amiss. In fact, I rec'd a gentle hint from the B.M., the one known as Clarence by the petty officers and called "Flying Jib" by the firemen.[34] This fellow was an apothecary, but had read and had taken a cruise, I believe, in one of the State Nautical schools. But as far [as] practical ability was concerned, [he] couldn't take the knock out of a grind stone. Upon a gentle reminder from him, I gave my station a rub up. I had touched it up before he told me, and I told him I had already been at work upon it. "Oh, all right," replied Clarence, "I didn't look at the station."

I went out there once more, it was Sunday afternoon, and started in to clean up, wiping out oil trays that had filled up with oil, polishing a lubricator here and there. Clarence, all of a flurry, looked in. "We are going to get under way in a few moments. Go out and shake the steam up."

"All right," I replied, and started to put away my gear.

He looked in again, "Put pressure on the aft 13" turret at once. I will tell the other water-tenders to look after the boilers."

"All right, sir."

I put the pressure on, when the other water-tender poked his head in, "Better send for the 2nd relief man, and let him look after those pumps. I'm not going to look after everything out there."

I told the messenger to get the 2nd relief water tender down at once, as I had to go to my station in the fire-room. Nobody had notified the men to work the steam up, and all auxiliaries being slapped on, air pump circulators, steam on the jacket, big hydraulics running, the steam fell and I came near being in the hole [i.e., the boiler water level nearly fell below safe limits]. The chief came out.

"Water-tender, can't you raise your steam higher?"

"Yes, sir. It is going up now."

"You should have had it up long ago."

"No, sir. We were just notified that we were going to move the engines."

"How long ago? Twenty minutes?"

"No, sir. Not quite that long."

"Well you should have had it up in that time anyway."

Such it goes. I could have told him why, but what would be the use? It went up in a jiffy and we moved and it was over in about ten minutes, as they only shifted around a bit to give the diver a chance to work better.

~ ~ ~

"God created the Heavens and the earth, the skies and sea and all that in them is." Congress created the "bolo-man," but for what use we men of the "black gang" could never ascertain. Everything that lives and has breath and being is placed upon earth for some purpose. But what of the bolo-man?

Echo answers, "What? Damned if I know." He is with us in all his glory of sword and gold lace. He derives his name, that is, his slang *nom-de-plume,* from his compatriot of the Philippines. He is likened unto him in that he is a sort of social outcast, a pariah, abhorred by all, jacked up by the chief engineers, called down by all his superior officers, damned by the men. His is a most disagreeable position. Men hate to have a man over them who has been one of them, has slept, eaten, and worked side by side with them, and upon their sudden elevation, gotten the "swollen head" and come the high horse over their former mates.

We hate to have our bags of clothing, our bedding, inspected by men who were notorious for being dirty when common sailors. It cuts us deeply to be told that we have to get another shirt, etc., by men who when of the common herd couldn't muster enough clothing together to "dust a fiddle." In his exalted position he forgets all this, and makes a very strict task master. If he isn't competent, the men who worked with him formerly know it, and despise him according[ly]. Like all warrant officers, he is neither "an officer [n]or a gentleman," but comes in on neutral ground. Perhaps time will remedy all this and the "bolo-man" will be recognized. At present, he doesn't command the respect and obedience he should. This will wear off, but it will take almost a new [ship] to do it. But to us at present, the B.M. makes it mighty unpleasant. But we'll have to do the best we can. Stick it out, old man. "*O tempera. O mores,*" 'sic.'

We at last got underway, on the morning [of] July 12th 1900, about 9 A.M., after a stay of nearly two weeks, one week for repairs. Almost as soon as we got under [way] the added pressure made us take more water and all the pumps were kept continually running at full speed, and even then could just barely cope with the water. We ran at about a seven knot speed and were partially towed by the *Nanchang*.[35] Such an infernal screeching and screaming from "Jack the Ripper" was never head aboard this ship before. I often ask myself the question, how is it that naval officers do so much shouting and bawling in order to get a ship under way, to bring one alongside another vessel, or to dock a ship? I never heard yet any undue noise from skippers of vessels in the merchant service, or commanders of other men-o-war. It makes some of the American officers look very cheap and small, beside incompetent. I could see the looks of disgust upon the skipper and mates of both the *Nanchang* and the *Kwongchang*, as well as the Russian wrecking tug officers who would handle their vessels like small boats with no excitement, while the officers of this ship ran around like madmen, shouting and gesticulating in an unnecessary manner. There isn't any excuse for this at all. There is no need whatever for all the noise and confusion of orders. I have heard a dozen orders shouted in a jumble to the skippers of these two merchant vessels, the *Nanchang* and the *Kwongchang*, and no attention paid to them, for they weren't understood.

About 6 P.M., we were somewhere off Chefoo, and were looking for the *Nashville*, which was to accompany us to Nogi, or where we were to go in dry dock. We whistled continually, and fired several six-pound blanks to attract them if they were in the immediate vicinity. Just as I was going on watch at 12 [midnight], I believe we overtook her, for I dimly remember hearing her crew give three cheers upon finding us afloat and steaming along right merrily. Everything was easy below for the firemen, turning as we were at forty-five, so that we were remarkably free from molestation by the "bolo-men." Only one B.M came out in the fire rooms, just after we came on, and had just finished cleaning our four fires. He started looking in under ash-pans and at fires. I asked him what was the matter. We were carrying 120 lbs full. He told me he wanted the steam raised to 140 lbs. I asked him why he didn't say so at first, as it was just as easy to keep 140 as 120 lbs, the way the engines were turning. He said he didn't know that he thought she was steaming hard and he started in to look at the fires. The steam was raised according[ly], and Mr. B.M. didn't bother us again the rest of the watch.

Somebody threw a lighted cigarette butt in some open powder that was on the fo'castle and "Jack the Ripper," smelling it, came forward in his usual rage and started in abusing what few firemen he saw around off watch, as was his usual custom. "There you go, you damn whelps! You scum, etc. Just like you, you damned mean ———. Nothing to do but throw lighted cigarettes purposely in that powder out of pure cussedness. You infernal hoboes and bums! Get out of this!" Poor, old man. He is going fast.

A fireman throws him into a fit whenever he sees one. "Look out for it, here he comes," is sufficient to break up a party of coal passers and firemen. They know he will stop and abuse someone of their number, and while they are used to it, still they think the easiest way is to disperse. I always like to watch him, at a distance of course, to see what funny break he'll make next.

They corralled and "brigged" in double-irons three of the hard characters, and what a blessing it was. What a feeling of relief when they put these fellows away. Such a miserable trio I suppose never trod the forecastle of a man-o-war. One of them happened to be the man I suspicioned of throwing that marline spike and empty whisky bottle down the ventilator, one of the meanest, most contemptible [cusses] I ever ran against. [He was] the kind that would beat his old mother if she didn't furnish him the price of a pint of mixed ale when he wanted it. Not one solitary good trait in his whole makeup. Any mean deed or action was his forté. It was written on his face. To look at his face was enough to convict him. He was a shirk, a liar, and a thief, and a drunkard. And the other two were fit mates. He was the smallest of the trio, a pilot fish for two sharks. He was caterer of his mess. How they elected him caterer, God knows. He spent all the money [entrusted] to him in whisky of which there was a plentiful supply aboard the *Nanchang*. When the mess's money was gone, they tried to beg, borrow or steal the wherewithal for more booze. They gave a "song and dance" to a good-natured, easy going fellow who told them he would loan them 2 Mex, but only had a $5 Chinese note. They promised to give him his change, but drank it up as he should have known they would do. When he asked them for his money, they slugged him and laughed at him. They all three posed as pugs and had acquired a cheap reputation by knocking out cripples and Chinamen. We prevailed upon the fellow who lost the money to report them thro' the proper channels, which he was loath to do at first. But [he] finally did so and the outcome was the three "gentlemen" were safely [landed] in "limbo" with a court-martial awaiting them. The skipper was hot against them and promised to make it warm for them. The small, mean cuss had spent half his cruise in the brig and why they kept him [so] long, I couldn't surmise. He wouldn't do any work, was a disturber and agitator. The other two had been fired off of every other ship they were on, and were taken from the brig and sent to the *Oregon*. They were deserters, had never finished a cruise, were always classed,[36] never drew any money, but were always drunk. Sucked up men's money who [were] foolish enough to satisfy their insatiable appetite for "booze." Neither one would work.

I had two of them in my section and had resolved to report them the first opportunity I got. I expected trouble in this, and know that with my fists I couldn't hope to be successful against the big fellow, but had resolved to even up things with a monkey-wrench of suitable dimensions. Oh, the fierce look I would get from the two I had when I mentioned work to them, and I knew it was only a matter of a few days before the big, black, muzzled hound would try and punch me. Of course, the little cur would assist. I intended to get the big fellow, no matter how. I didn't intend to [be] done up by them if possible, and was glad when they were brought up with a round turn.[37] Everybody was glad. There was some [peace] after this, for altho' the force was still handicapped by a few "tough mugs," they kept pretty quiet.

Meanwhile, we steamed quietly thro' the Yellow Sea, trusting that the good weather would continue and that we would be fortunate enough to escape the sudden and violent blows so frequent in this sea. A rough sea would play havoc with the wooden wedges and plugs in the *Oregon*'s bottom.

"Jack the Ripper" again came to the front. A few of us were standing up by the compartment in which the scuttle butt[38] is situated, on the port side of the superstructure, leading out to the fo'castle. A few men happened to be standing almost blockading the gangway. I heard a snort behind me and we looked around and there was the "Ripper" looking for some poor fellow to abuse, as usual. He pushed them aside, and singling out a marine for his mark, he spoke very sarcastically. "See this opening?" pointing to the door and [throwing] out his chest and spreading his arms apart. "This," with a withering look of scorn that almost froze the poor marine, "this is a door! DOOR! A gangway. A place for people to move to and fro about their business, not a place for loafers and bums to congregate in. A door, do your understand me? A DOOR!! A DOOR! DOOR." Here he swelled up and expanded so, I felt alarmed as to his condition. "Get out of here you loafers! You damn rascals. You infernal scoundrels, You. You.———." Then he passed on about his business feeling, I take it, very much relieved. Poor old man. Poor old fellow. Only a few more months before a board of survey takes hold of him.[39]

Oh, the trouble we had on a watch. We came down and found about 125 lbs of steam. When we cleaned the fires, the steam dropped below 120. About 2 A.M. the "bolo-man" asked me to shake up the steam to about 140, what we had [previously] been carrying. I tried, but it was no go. Try as the men did, we could only boost it up to 130 lbs. It would have held at that if they had continued at 45 revolutions, but no. The orderly came down and said, "Captain wants 50 turns." That settled it for the

Aground in the Yellow Sea

two boilers. Every pump in the ship was running at full speed on the compartments, [and the] two wrecking pumps [were] running as fast as they possibly could to try to keep down the water, which was gaining. The evaporators were on full tilt. The ice-machine and hydrokinetic valves [were] open on A & B boilers heating up the water in case another boiler had to be put on. The boiler being overtaxed, the steam fell lower and lower.

The chief engineer was broke out of his comfortable couch to come below and [ascertain] the trouble. Then the roar. My troubles commenced. Then the chief personally inspected the fires, the steam dropping all the time in spite of his roars, and the "bolo-man's." They could do nothing. They tried to make the fifty turns with the engine, but the wrecking pumps almost stopped and the water gained. They wouldn't slow down until they were compelled to. The order was given to put A boiler on, and fires were started and hurried along. But the steam was down for that watch and nothing would get it up except the slowing of the engines, and they wouldn't do that until they had to.

I was exhausted running around attending to a thousand orders at once. "Blow tubes" [blow accumulated soot, with steam, from the outsides of the watertubes in the boiler], so we blew tubes. No use. "Hurry up getting those ashes up. Put those two auxiliary pumps on the secondary drain. Shake those fires up, etc., etc." A thousand and one orders at one time. No use. On deck they were cursing about the pumps not doing their work, but they wouldn't order the engines slowed. When I was relieved at four A.M., glad indeed was I. I never put in such a dispiriting watch, and never stood so much abuse. I heard that "Jack the Ripper" made the remark that "every damned one of the firemen should be court-martialled. The worthless curs, etc."

But the men done the best they knew how. No one could do better. The steam was used up faster than it could be made. It was only on the four to eight watch that they managed to raise it once more, and then only when they had to slow down and were making about 20 turns for nearly an hour. At 6 they had the steam up and the other boiler, A, was connected, and then our troubles were over as far as steam was concerned. That is, unless they raised the number of revolutions according[ly] and overtaxed the three boilers. But we did not look for that because at the speed we were making the vibration loosened everything up and there were rumors about dropping the hook in a suitable place and sending the diver down to make an examination and repair the injuries.

We were in a hurry to get out of the Yellow Sea. It looked squally and a cold rain with sullen, dun colored clouds obscured the sky. We could make out dimly once [in] a while the rocky eastern [western?] coast of Corea, along which we were skirting. We were speeding as fast as possible for a ship in the condition of the *Oregon*, but the water would alternately gain and decrease, all depending on the two wrecking pumps. If they failed, we would have to take chances of sinking or swimming. They had done an immense lot of work running continuously at full speed.

Well, well. Wonders will never cease. It has came at last. Three ensigns have taken charge of the watch below. Seems the "bolo-men" have been superseded. I could almost have cried aloud with joy when this change took place, just to have the old regime back again. It seemed like old times once more. I could always get along with engineer officers, but the trouble I have had, and all of us have had, with warrant machinists are legion. I knew one of the ensigns, having been shipmates with him on the *Minneapolis,* and a perfect gentleman in his treatment of the men. Men were willing for such men. But for an ignorant lot such as most of the warrant machinists have proven themselves, no one will do any more than they have to. I have submitted to more ill treatment and bull-dozing from these men in a year than I have in all my previous service put together. They are not competent to take charge of a big force and the machinery of a modern man-o-war. In fact, as I have said before, most of them are not machinists at all, and those that are machinists are shop hands, men who had had no previous experience at marine engineering.

Many of the old chief machinists of the navy were barred from the warrant by the age limit of 35 years. Those old hands are the men who have had the practical experience, but they are not trained or fitted by education to take the place of a trained engineer who, coming from Annapolis after years of training, theoretically and practically are fitted for this duty. It was a great relief even to have these engineers back, if only for a short time.

I reported everything direct[ly] to the engineer of the watch and ignored the B.M. completely. Some of them were standing around not knowing what position they held, but the majority confined their services to the fire-room, about which they know as much as an educated pig would. They think they do. One of them even had the nerve to tell me how high I should carry water in my boilers. I, who have had years of experience at it and in different ships! I admit I always can learn, but I will not willingly accept many bolo-men for a teacher. Everything went along swimmingly. An absence of growling and confusion marked these watches with a new hand at the helm. The revolutions were increased to 60. Everything steaming nicely. On the 8 to 12 watch one Sunday morning, we came to a full stop from full speed ahead. This was on account of a Chinaman falling overboard from the *Nanchang.* The phosphorescent life buoy was dropped immediately, and catching that, he was quickly picked up by the *Nashville*'s life boat, and we proceeded on our way.

The 3rd division, mess 15, had their troubles about food, getting almost nothing to eat. This was our section. Some wag drew a picture of the menu provided for this mess. It was a sketch of three hardtack, labeled breakfast, dinner, and supper. That was literally all they got. One man, an old timer, said Sunday morning, "There is no excuse for this at all. We had a few beans for breakfast, and they were spoiled. When you can't get beans, beans cooked right, on a man-o-war, what are we going to do? Here was I, looking for a couple of days towards having my beans, only to find them spoiled." This was his moan. If he could only have filled up this morning on beans, he would have withstood the pangs of hunger for another week without any kick. You often go hungry in the navy, sometimes through a rascally cook or caterer who rolls you, but generally thro' the miserable ration served by Uncle Sam. It's infernally small when it reaches the enlisted man, and hardly keeps him alive. Yet there is no let up on the work.

The berth deck was in a fierce condition from the wrecking pumps. Oil, water, slush filled with steam which, as it condensed, dropped from the deck above like rain. Everything [was] damp, hot and miserable. We never got down the mess tables at all, but filled our plates with whatever was going and selected the best place around the deck for a place to sit and eat, tho' who couldn't find a place to eat sitting stood up and filled in. Everywhere muck. The linoleum torn from the deck. You had to be careful how you walked. If the ship rolled, you would skate across and bring up on the other side. Where we would sling our "caulking mats" on the orlop deck we would find ourselves swimming from the water that washed down thro' the hatch leading to the berth deck. When this would happen, we would move and take up another station elsewhere. A number of ditty boxes placed in a row made an excellent bed, but there wasn't enough ditty boxes to go 'round. But if you were lucky enough to get them, you were sure of being clear of the water. Some other jokers wrote in chalk over the passageway leading to the fire-rooms, "No place like home." Perhaps he enjoyed the company of the "bolo-men." It was home with a step-mother. You were sure of a growl the moment you put your foot in the fire room, until the engineer officers were placed in charge.

This continual performance disgusted me more and more with a bluejacket's life in the navy. I always lived in the future, trusting that something would turn up, living on hope, looking forward to what the distant future contained, dreaming of home and friends, oftentimes of an old sweetheart, and wondering what they were doing at the other side of the globe and if they gave a thought toward the absent one. I knew that at least one did and always would as long as life remained. That She thought far more of the one away than he did, perhaps, of her, such being the law of nature, and such the unselfish affection of a mother. Sweethearts I often thought of, sometimes with a smile, picturing them as settled down with a few children and no waistline to speak of. It takes very few years, indeed, to make a change with sweethearts, friends and wives. Perhaps the best of it all is the memory left to you of a by gone affair of the heart, or a friendly [relationship], long since severed. When we are far removed from the scene of such by distance and by time, it affords one a pensive sort of pleasure in the retrospect. If we perhaps were there and sought to renew the broken threads once again, it would lose its glamour and enchantment.

Yet many a time I have caught myself dreaming, living my past over again, and building castles in Spain for the future which never comes. The past, with all its joys and sorrows, has belonged to us, and is part and parcel of our beings. We have profited by it and its lessons taught, that being our store of experience. I know of no life so conducive of dreaming as a seafaring one. Your duties done for a time, in the stillness of a watch at night I have oftimes found myself leaning on the rail or stanchions looking over a wide expanse of moonlit sea, seeing nothing, my mind far away over many seas, think[ing] of those at home, or a dreamy review of past joys and sorrows.

Your mood is often in accord with the mood of the sea. Gray and sullen, the swirling seas illuminated at times by the light of a moon half obscured by sullen looking clouds, the more of sorrow than of pleasure in your dreams. In same accord, your mood [is more positive] with a moonlit pathway of molten gold from a clear, star-studded sky, the dark sea-line sharply cut against the blue sky, and perhaps a ship sharply silhouetted on the faraway horizon. That is the poetical part of a sailor's life. But we of the fo'castle are not supposed to be alive to the beauty and grandeur of the sea. I know we get it knocked out of us for a time when we have to go on watch. Then we descend from the clouds, with a large, dull thud that jars you, all right, and [we] find ourselves face to face with the common, prosaic duties of our lot. By the time you are thro' contending with the B.M., the growling of firemen and coal passers, the howls for more steam, you are glad enough to turn in any old way, so long as you can forget the petty troubles in dreamless sleep, leaving star-gazing for a more propitious time.

Aground in the Yellow Sea

CHAPTER FOUR

Kure, Japan

At last, we reached the entrance to the Inland Sea of Japan, after quite an uneventful trip across the Yellow Sea, in which we were making better time than the *Nanchang* and *Nashville*, the former supposedly towing us, and the latter acting as convoy. But owing to the choppy sea, we cast off from the *Nanchang* and proceeded alone at about 70 rev[olutions]. We soon left the two far astern and arrived at the Straits of Shimonoseki before the other two were properly started. This was on the evening of the night of the 15th July [1900], Saturday. Here the *Oregon* hove to and came to anchor.

About noon Sunday we started thro' the Straits into the wonderful Inland Sea of Japan. In this strait the *Wyoming* under McDougal silenced the guns of the forts of Shimonoseki and opened up the eyes of the Japs, and they have been open ever since, and a wonderful little people they are today and very friendly toward us.[1] The town off which we anchored is a beautiful little place. All places are picturesque in Japan, until you are right in the place itself, and then it [loses] some enchantment. But the view at first sight is certainly a lovely one.

All through this wonderful sheet of water, which is more of a wide strait or lake than a sea, we steamed around tortuous bends, close to the rocky shore at times, now running at full speed and now barely turning over, the *Oregon* always in the lead—a shipwrecked battleship running away from her escorts. It seemed funny, but boilers and engines were practically intact and the *Oregon* always had the reputation of being a good steamer, for didn't she distance the fleet at Santiago and chase the [*Cristobal*] *Colón* to a finish?[2]

We steamed along having our usual troubles with the bolo-men, only not so much so, since they were not in supreme command. All along this sea are mountains of volcanic origin. Here and there are seen pretty little villages with their terraced rice paddies at the base so as to be sufficiently irrigated by the streams that are continually flowing. On the higher tiers are vegetables of all descriptions, tea, radishes, onions, etc., all [growing] from the bare rock, almost. Some of the higher peaks are crowned with a twisted, grotesque shape of a tree, giving an aspect to a landscape unlike any other place in the world. Clusters of houses [are] snugly tucked away in crannies. Around each hill some new surprise awaits one, and you wonder if you are not looking at some toy landscape, but you remember you are in Japan, where everything is strange. You can't help but admire the perseverance and toil that have made these volcanic hills what they are. In places, the mountain slopes are bare and of an ochre tint, in contrast with the green verdure and sienna tints of the earth. [This] makes a pleasing harmony of colors. The light and shade caused by a passing cloud completes the picture, one that an artist would delight to paint,[3] and these varied tints are very successfully portrayed by the Japanese themselves in their colored prints. I have seen scenery at home more beautiful, but none more strange, nor that appeals to one's imagination more. It is a fairyland, an enchanted picture thro' which we float, looking for the new view in a beautiful panorama.

On the 8 to 12 watch the morning of 17th, Monday, we speeded up as high as 76 rev[olutions] for about half an hour. We had dropped anchor at about 11:00 P.M. the night before, and [had] gotten under way at about 6:30. We were either stopping, slow ahead, or making all we could. It was steaming by signals from the bridge all the time, something every fireman hates. It is ash pan drill, putting up dampers and taking them down. You are no sooner getting everything in good shape than you hear a jingle in the engine rooms and you see the engines slow down or stop, and on goes all dampers again. Despite [the use] of the dampers, the steam was very hard to hold and only by bleeding all the time could the boilers be prevented from blowing off. Lifting a safety valve in the navy is a crime, but the *Oregon* came near doing it all the time. One of the B.M. told me that "I would get myself in serious trouble if I let a boiler blow off."

He didn't like me, nor I him, and I told him with a sneer that I didn't think the trouble I would get in thro' him would prove very serious to me, and that from what I saw of the bolo-men, they'd have all they could do to avoid serious trouble themselves, to which he made no reply. This was the watch [when] they were relieved from the charge of officers and the ensigns put over them, and they felt this change. I could see [from] the way they would confer together that they couldn't exactly tell where they were, or what they were to do. One of them told an oiler on our section, "that was what should have been done when she first ran on the rocks. We should have been relieved from the strain of excessive duty and placed in charge of the pumps in the fire-rooms where experience was needed. Anybody could look after the engines and take charge of the watch. A coal-passer even."

That was his way of looking at it. I hardly think he expected anybody to believe, really believe, that old "con" of his. The very fact that they placed first-class firemen on those pumps (the for'd aux[iliary] pumps) showed that not an exceeding amount of confidence was placed in their experience. They were relegated to the fire-rooms and took the part of "leading stokers" or firemen, special class, I hardly know which. But they didn't bother us much and we water-tenders reported everything to the engineer [officer] direct.

Kure, Japan

We moored at Kure, the place we were to get [dry-]docked, about 3 p.m. Tuesday the 18th July, and a beautiful place it proved to be. Here are big government ways and dry docks, shops built of brick in European style.[4] In fact, it looked to be the most progressive place in Japan, having more of a European appearance than Yokohama, Nagasaki or any other seaport in Japan. I didn't see any other flag but the Japanese. [There were many] torpedo boats and cruisers and a big battleship of 14,000 tons. Yes, Japan is getting together a mighty navy. Here, where no foreign powers are allowed, and I heard no other warship ever came, are ships galore. We were allowed here only by courtesy, the friendly act of a friendly nation. We were surrounded by boats containing Japanese sailors, "rookies" (recruits) out for boat drill. We could tell them by their new duck uniforms and especially by the ragged stroke they pulled. They came from the shore and pulled all around the *Oregon*. Nor was the inevitable "compradore" and bumboat man absent. They were alongside immediately, having come from Yokohama and Kobe, knowing what a mint an American warship is. But there wasn't much money aboard the *Oregon*, all the collateral having been placed aboard the *Iris* with other valuables. Prices were very high for Japan, occasioned by the large body of troops that pass through the larger cities on their way to Tientsin to assist in the smashing of the China shop.[5] We saluted the ships and the forts as usual, which was returned. So, at last the *Oregon*'s run was over for a while. A fierce, miserable trip it had proven to be.

Kure is a most beautiful spot. It was misty, foggy and rainy weather for the first two or three days, but one afternoon the clouds rolled away and the sun came out, and then we beheld this beautiful village in all its glory. It nestles at the base of the greenest mountain chain I have ever seen outside of America. It has more of an European aspect than most Japanese ports, caused no doubt by the appearance of the ships, of which [there] are a great many, mostly all new, ideas taken from the different naval powers of the world.[6] They have a number of ways for torpedo craft and other small fry. I noticed a submarine boat, cigar-shaped, red-leaded, hauled up on the beach. There are, I believe, three dry docks, and any dock that can accommodate a ship of the *Oregon*'s class has got to be a large one. We have only three at home that can do so, one at New York, one at Port Royal [South Carolina], and the other Port Orchard [Bellingham, Washington].[7]

The big three stacker we took for an armored cruiser turned out to be the big battleship that Japan purchased from England some time ago, over 14,000 tons displacement.[8] When she swung with the current, we noticed what an awful beam she had, as large, if not larger, than our own. She also had run up on a rock, and had just come from the dry dock. Japan is getting a navy that will place her among the powers of the world if she keeps on increasing as she has since the Japan-China War,[9] but as yet, I hardly think she could cope with Russia. Because they whipped a part of China, that is no sign they can whip a power equal with their own in the Far East, and a nation that can fight. But Japan has ports that any nation would find impregnable. For instance, no fleet could get up here in the Inland Sea, or in Nagasaki. But this lovely spot especially is well protected both by nature and by man. There are a number of forts to be passed, and it is a narrow channel that has to be navigated. Guns placed upon the mountain sides could pour a hail of steel that nothing could withstand. There is a training station here also, for "rookies." They are out on the water in the afternoon for boat drill.[10]

There is one thing about the Japs—they are all uniform, especially in size, no foreigners among them, and they do not want them. You can tell it is a Japanese Navy, but I'll be darned if you can tell whether ours is an American Navy or not. A stranger not conversant with our ships wouldn't know whether he was on a Danish, Swedish, German or Russian, because if he asked anybody for any information around the decks, he would be answered in a language he wouldn't understand.[11] Well, no matter, we are a cosmopolitan nation. But it does seem queer that more good billets couldn't be given to Americans who spend the greater part of their life in the service, and who are fitted to hold a warrant officer's billet, than is now given them. Nearly all the good billets in the Navy are filled by foreigners.

The *Nanchang* was discharged of the shell and gear taken from us by the Japs. The gunner, acting under orders, went with our men to discharge her and wipe and store the ammunition in the Japanese arsenal, but the Japs wouldn't permit it. It was not permissible for any foreign power to visit their yard and shops, etc. They said they would take care of all that for us. And another thing, the *Nanchang* was given three days to clear after her cargo was discharged and the *Nashville* was to shortly follow her. One thing that galled us and made us choke under the restraint was that the *Nashville* gave liberty and we had none. That's what jars you: to see a party go ashore from one ship and you have to stand by and bear it. The *Oregon* had given no liberty either in Hong Kong or any of the other ports she was at for over three months. The regulations call, it is true, for liberty whenever feasible. But your captain can use his own discretion, and sometimes if sore against his crew, will not give any for months.[12] The officers [are] going ashore and having a good time; you, Jack, can lay back and look and envy them.

At Hong Kong, the excuse was the plague, and the *Oregon* men were kept aboard, but there wasn't any plague for the officers, the Chinese stewards, and mess attendants. Nor was there any plague for the monitor *Monterey*'s crew, who went ashore regularly. This also creates quite a little dissatisfaction. "Well, if you don't like it, why don't you run away?" you ask. Well, some men haven't the money together to run away in a foreign port; others resolve to stick it out at all hazards. Others want the discharge that shows good service. Many do run away, regardless. I'll bet there is more desertions in the American Navy than any other. The dear public is not interested in this matter and consequently such a small item is not noticed. But I have seen one third of a crew on different ships steal away like the Arab, their places being filled.

These boys and young fellows from the interior know nothing of discipline. They imagine, and are helped in their imagination by a suave recruiting officer, that they are going on a pleasure trip to ports of romance and of song and story throughout

Kure, Japan

the world. They know nothing of the hard work, the rawhiding and abuse, the bad food and insufficient ration, the months they are in debt to the government for clothing. They awake from their "pipe dreams" to find out that they have been "shanghaied" in the truest sense of the word. "Do they stay?" Echo answers, "*Nyet.*" They jump out in droves wherever they get the chance. Most young Americans who are well raised won't stand it at all. Take a young chap who has everything he wishes at home. He gets disgusted when he finds what he has to contend with in the Navy, where he has to scrap to get a place to swing his hammock, spar for something to eat, has to mend and wash his own clothes, jump out at a call and work like a dog, is called down by an "officer and a gentleman" for some slight discrepancy that the officer commits himself daily. Then he rebels and wonders how he got in the Navy, why he is there, what use is he, and just at the time, "where he is at." His patriotism and love of country is crushed out as far as serving the country in time of peace is concerned, and knowing he is up against a bad bargain, and knowing he will be no better off if he served his time, but infinitely worse, he jumps. Who can say he is wrong? It is like getting a bad place to work in. If the man or boy don't like it, if it doesn't come up to his expectations, he quits, that's all.[13]

News reached us by the *Kobe Chronicle* that the Boxers and Imperial troops had allied and were playing havoc with our forces or rather, the allies; also that the Marines from the *Oregon* were strictly in it, completely cut off, but no definite information could be obtained. It also stated that the Boers were slightly to the good in South Africa and England was "still on the fence." We had lost all track of affairs. Being so busy with our own troubles, we had no time for any others, no letters from home. We were out of it altogether. We lived in hope. What was to be the next move? Were we to get temporary repairs and proceed to Taku or San Francisco? We didn't care which; anything for a change. That's what your bluejacket lives on, hope.

"Papa!" asked little Rollo one morning at breakfast, "What is a bolo-man?"

"A bolo-man, my son?" queried his father in surprise at this unusual question, but not so much surprised as to prevent him from carefully buttering his fifteenth consecutive muffin. "Hem. . . . A bolo-man, my son, is of two species. The name properly belongs to a class of Filipinos or *Ladrones*[14] who go about armed with a knife or short sword known in the Philippines as a bolo. It has a curved blade not unlike a Turkish scimitar. They use it much as a native Cuban would use a machete. It is as indispensable to the Philipinos as is the machete to the Cuban. These bolo-men, from their guerrilla-like tactics, have proven a great annoyance to our troops in the far away Philippines. They are as stealthy, treacherous, and fatal in their work as is canned corn beef. In fact, it has yet to be proven which has killed the most men. The term 'bolo-man' is synonymous with all that is treacherous, mean and snake like."

"But, Papa," exclaimed Little Rollo, "isn't there another kind of 'bolo-man'?" You know, during our visit aboard that large battleship at the Navy Yard last Saturday, I heard one of those common sailors make the remark as an officer passed by a group of them, 'There goes a bolo-man.' So there must be bolo-men otherwise than the native Filipino."

"Ah, yes, my son!" replied Rollo's papa, as if a new light had dawned upon him, which new light didn't prevent him from reaching over and selecting the brownest and most crisp rasher of bacon, which was his ninth slab. "Ah, yes. I believe it is a term applied in derision, as Mr. Thirdly, the chaplain, explained to me, to the warrant machinists of the navy. You know, my son, that warrant machinists have only recently come into being in the United States Navy, in fact, only since the Spanish-American War. These men are made to pass an examination, much as an engineer would in applying for a certificate of his calling ashore. Many of them do not require to pass an examination, merely—to use a vulgar phrase—'having a pull' is sufficient.[15] Many of them are not machinists at all. The only acquaintance some of them ever had with a machine shop, even ashore, was to carry large tin pails full of beer on a stick to the mechanics of the shop, where they were employed as floor sweepers and at chipping castings, etc. The practical men of the navy recognize the comparative uselessness and incompetency of these men, and from their methods in dealing with their former shipmates and messmates, which are not unlike the method employed by the bona-fide bolo-man, gave them that name, and they are generally known by it throughout the navy."

"But Papa," persisted little Rollo, "how did the name first originate?"

"The name originated, my son," Reginald Rollo's dad [answered], carefully cracking and opening his sixteenth egg and helping himself to four lumps of sugar and about a pint of cream to his sixth cup of coffee. "The name originated among a party of our bluejackets in faraway Manila, as my good friend Mr. Thirdly kindly explained to me. It seems a number of our sailors were returning from liberty, where they were allowed to go ashore about once a month, all feeling convivial and jolly under the influence of those vile and intoxicating liquors which our sailors will persist in partaking of to excess, despite our efforts to lead them into better paths. These rude men, after a day's debauch ashore in Manila, would all return by the government ferry boat to Cavite, where our ships all lay. Meeting each other as they did, men from different ships, they would compare notes and inquire about each other's welfare, ask about old acquaintances, in the meantime partaking freely of strong, vile drink from numerous large, villainous looking bottles, which every sailor always provides himself with when returning from a liberty ashore. These bottles of vile stuff are, by the way, known to these vile, uncouth men as 'dogs,' and when empty, as 'dead dogs' or a 'dead marine,' but I digress. 'Where is so and so?' asked one bluejacket of another. 'Oh, he's a warrant machinist now,' replied his friend.

"'Well, I'll be [damned], a warrant machinist! You surprise me. Why, I knew that chap before he shipped. He's no machinist, no more than I am. His trade is that of a

Kure, Japan

shoe-maker. He joined in '98 because they wouldn't enlist him before that time. Lord knows he tried often enough, but failed until they needed the men. And so he's a warrant machinist! How does he treat the fellows? Is he any good?'

"'Good? Good [God!]' roared the other fellow. 'He's a regular "bolo-man."' The phrase was so apt, and so expressive of the warrant machinists as the men knew them, that it was taken up and spread like wildfire, and they are known better by this sobriquet than their own rank. And that is all I know about 'bolo-men,'" finished Rollo's papa, at the same time finishing his breakfast and preparing to go to his office with the air of a champion pie eater who has dined well.[16]

∼ ∼ ∼

The poor bolo-man. He would abuse those under him and was abused by the chief [engineer]. They still continued standing "sea watch" when the auxiliary watch was started. That gave them four hours on and sixteen hours off duty, so you can see they were not by any means overworked. They had their trouble in mustering the men. Instead of mustering all hands at "turn to"[17] in the starboard engine room by calling out the names, they had every man in the force report to them and get his name checked off, a roundabout way of doing business. They haven't the slightest idea of routine. The most of them were new to the service and did not have any engine room experience.

It seems to me, if I may criticize the "powers that be," that they take the wrong way in making these men. To make an officer requires something else besides a knowledge of machinery. Men should know their drill before being placed in charge of a division of men. I have seen the senior "bolo-man" get all mixed up when trying to pace a section. They cannot give the command because they do not know it. An apprentice of six months before leaving the "Island" at Newport[18] can handle a section. It is laughable to hear such commands as this: "Form yourselves into two lines, you men. Here you are in six. Can't you get into shape?"

Yes, the men can get into any shape at all at the proper word of command. What they should do is to train these warrant machinists and make them a little more military. Learn them the manual of the sword and small arms, not the manual of the monkey wrench. Not one out of fifty can give a command as it should be given, and this helps the men to guy them, make them look small.[19]

The *Nashville* left Kure and the *Nanchang* was to follow as soon as [its] cargo was discharged. Our pumps were going all the time while we were laying waiting for the dock, which we were to enter at spring tide.[20] Small stores [issue clothing, etc.] were served out at last, for a wonder, soap being especially wanted. This time I had to draw another cap ribbon, making about four so far in the cruise. Also, two white hats. I forgot to put down for shoes, and [didn't care] particularly as I thought I could buy them without any trouble. But I found I had to get them made to order, as the Jap who brought off shoes brought the loudest collection I ever saw. Bright yellow, red, and olive green, the loudest hues, and they not being allowable aboard, I had to get measured and had to wait. This shoe man came from Kobe, that being the nearest city to us.

Oh, how we longed for liberty, which was so slow in coming. You who can put on your coat and hat and go where you please, where fancy pleases, don't know what freedom means. I resolved this time, being so long aboard, to get a good jag on when I got ashore, not knowing when liberty would come again. Anything for a wild fling at the beach, something to break the monotony. I used to make resolves to myself when aboard ship, saying to myself, "I am going to buy some silk, a piece of tortoise shell work, or some curio when I go ashore the next time," only to change my mind when I did get liberty. It seems as if there is an entire change takes place the moment you see the shore looming up. You forget all the resolves made aboard ship and your thought is for amusement first and last, and the first place you make for is a bar of some kind. You lose no time in getting there, either. You know your time is short and you want a run for your money. Poor Jack!

The decks of the *Oregon* were still in a mess from the pumps, and we had to take our meals "picnic" fashion from the deck. I used to wish I was a Chinaman or Filipino on these occasions, so we could squat down on our haunches and take our "chow" with the same degree of comfort. But we were living pretty fair, and our mess had no complaint to make on that score, and as long as we had plenty to eat, we didn't care how we ate it, either standing, sitting or lying down.

I found out the name of the place where the *Oregon* went ashore. It was near Howki Island, in the Straits of Pechilli, and the channel we were in is known as the Changshan channel. I rec'd this bit of information from a clipping posted on the bulletin board, which clipping expressed doubts that the ship stranded there was the *Oregon*. And a later clipping said that the ship had sank, but all hands were saved. This was the first bit of news we rec'd about the *Oregon*.

I was taken off watch when the auxiliary watch went on, and the next morning "turned to" on my station, the big after hydraulic pumps and pump room used for turning the aft turret and ammunition hoists. This station hadn't been touched or cleaned for about three months, and was a mess. But by dint of hard work and sweating, I finally got it into shape. The oil trays were filled with oil drippings, and I cleaned them first. Then I scrubbed down the paint work and next day I cleaned the bilge. That was the hardest work of any. I hadn't done any of this dirty work since I was a fireman. Instead of taking the floor plates up, I crawled and worked under them, and I was all gummed up with oil and dirt, but I got it clean and my hardest work was over. The rest, such as shining bright work and using emery cloth and polish, was child's play, and I soon had the station looking bright. It was clean, at any rate. These large pumps carry pressure up to a couple thousand lbs to the square inch. The only fault I found was the way salt water would come down thro' the two ventilators that led to the quarterdeck. This was done by the deck hands washing down with a hose in the mornings. The ventilators being short, the deckhands wouldn't miss them. Anyway,

Kure, Japan

give a Jack a hose and he'll wet down everything in sight. Give him a pot of paint and he'll paint until it's all gone, piling it all in a space a foot square, if necessary.

Lots of salt pork was ruined by the salt water and oil as well as other stores, and had to be thrown overboard. Pity lots of "canned willie" wasn't destroyed also, but you can't destroy it. It refused to be downed.

~ ~ ~

Anent "Canned Willie" or Eaganized beef, there is quite a pathetic little story attached showing that nothing goes to waste in this world, and that canned beef isn't all beef at all.

Many years ago, far away among the hills of sunny Maryland there stood, surrounded by picturesque shade trees, a small white farm house. All around stretched broad acres of wavy grain, reaching back to the base of the lofty mountains that formed part of the chain of the Blue Ridge. To the right of the little white house enclosed by a worn fence was an orchard of fruit trees wherein peach, apple and pears vied with each other in abundance. Along this worn fence stretched a shady road, or lane. Far off on sunny slopes and hillsides, cattle could be seen grazing, or lying in the shade of chestnut or oak, whose green foliage and far reaching boughs afforded refreshing shade from the heat of the noonday sun.

The entire scene was one of peace, of happiness, and of plenty; a scene that almost all men look back to with regret after a lapse of years; a scene of waving grain, broad acres, and rich meadow lands, of gurgling brooks, and here and there a glimpse of silvery water, all the brighter as seen thro' the interlacing boughs of dark green foliage. Morning, noon and night, when the shadows began to lengthen at the close of long, hazy summer days, along this lane a handsome sun-browned boy, the only son and child of the farmer who owned this place, could be seen driving the cattle to a far slope. [He was careless] of the future, happy in his ignorance of the world and the struggle for existence outside this earthly little Paradise; care free, his wants few, as happy as the butterflies that flitted to and fro among his mother's flowers. His only regret [was] the brief schooling he received in the short winter days. His constant companion and attendant [was] a merry little creature that [had] belonged to a dead aunt, a married sister of his father, who upon her deathbed left it with a dying request that she would be taken care of.

The boy and his little companion became almost inseparable. They missed each other and grieved when separated even for the shortest time in all their gambols together, to [go to] school, which the boy hated with the healthy hatred of a boy unused to restraint and discipline, except by loving hands. [It was the] dislike that a boy leading an outdoor existence has for enforced confinement; a dislike that his companion did not share, so long as it kept her near the handsome lad who was the object of her love and adoration, [whom she] looked upon as her protector. [She was] content only where the boy with the short, black, curly hair and laughing, half-serious, dark eyes was. Thro' long summer days, the dying days of the autumn, and the short days and long evenings of the winter, the pair were inseparable.

One day in childish play the boy presented his little playmate with a silver ten cent piece with a hole thro' it, and placed [it securely] around her neck, so 'twas almost impossible to be lost. And thus perhaps three or four years rolled by. The boy, having a dislike of the dullness of life on a farm, asked for and obtained permission from his father (his mother having passed away during those few years passed) to seek his fortune in the neighboring city.

The father was only too glad to give the required permission, as times of late had not gone well with him, and beside, he contemplated presenting the growing youth with a stepmother, a way that fathers have, and it would be an easy way of breaking the news to him, at a distance, over a telephone, as boys have a dislike to see any stranger usurp their mother's place. So, with a few belongings and a few hard-earned dollars in his pocket, the sum of all his worldly wealth, the boy once more wandered down the lane, followed by the accompanying [pet], the confidant and ally of all his boyish joys and troubles. An affecting parting at the pasture bars, and the boy passed out of the old life into the era of a new existence, leaving behind him one staunch friend, the memories of a passed life, and an unbounded hope and ambition for the future, passed out with the happy ignorance of life, and passing, smiled.

The scene changes. Along one of the principal thoroughfares of a big city, a young man wanders aimlessly. By his general appearance one can see at a glance that all has not gone well with him. One can see by the aimless way in which he moves along that he has had his share of the world's hard knocks. He has striven hard and has failed. In him it would be hard to recognize the growing young boy who [had] left the old home with such a confident air as if the world was to be at his feet in a few short years. The confident lad who was to conquer, and instead failed, was now broken and vanquished, was now a man, with a man's experience and but a slight trace of his former self remained.

His father, married again, had died, leaving all to his widow, and the old home had passed into strangers' hands. Of Esmeralda he had heard but little, and that in a desultory manner after the first two years of his absence. She must now be grown into maturity. Pleasant and bitter memories chased thro' his brain and were reflected in his face as he walked with dejected tread, not knowing where the next meal was to come from. He had tried everything. Had been a railroad man. Had been a waiter in a beer garden; had managed to go to the Cape Nome [Alaska] gold fields and all he brought back was a broken constitution. Had, in fact, turned his hand to anything that came. The boy so confident had found all the good positions filled, and as this is not a story for good little boys, didn't wax rich and become a money-king. He was simply a good-hearted, ordinary fellow, like some you know, not too good, who drank a little [and] was free with his money. In fact, [he was] just an ordinary young fellow.

Kure, Japan

Wandering along, he was attracted by the sight of an American flag waving from a window overhead. The mere sight of Old Glory alone did not affect him, but the soldier standing in front of the door leading to the room in which the flag hung from the window, and the advertisement, "Recruits wanted for the United States Army," did, and the thought struck him, "Why not?" And he did.

In the faraway Philippines, [there was] a company of soldiers, tired, hungry, and dusty from a long "hike" after the rebel Filipinos under Aguinaldo, whom they had chased for long, weary days over mountain paths, thro' rice paddies, swamp morass, and jungle, and now in the glow of a dying tropical day, [they] were about the pitch camp and partake of a meager meal. Small fires were quickly started. Hard tack and canned goods were broken out, and the coffee made. The ragged groups in khaki fell to as only half-starved soldiers can, each man, with his tin of bootleg[21] and handful of hard tack and "canned William," threw himself upon the ground in the most comfortable position they could find. This was their only means of relaxation from the almost constant watchfulness they always had to maintain. But pickets being out, and no immediate sign of the so-called "rebels" in the vicinity, care was thrown to the four winds of Heaven, and the laugh and joke, and jesting remarks as to the quality and quantity of their rations [were] passed around, remarks and jests good natured in the main, from men who, tho' exhausted in mind and body, still had the courage to find a spark of humor in their hard lives.

"And where does the canned beef come in?" you ask. Right here is where it comes in, you bet. This pathetic little story has to do with canned beef, as I said in the beginning. But canned willy properly comes in at the last moment, and when it gets its work in, something has to drop.

"Great Scott!" suddenly roared a hardy, ragged corporal. "What the devil is this I am chewing on? Here, Dick. Here is a ten cent piece I found in my beef. Queer place to find money. Almost any old thing can be found, but coin, this must be a particular brand. Pity we ain't some place where we could get a couple of large cool 'geysers' of the foamy for this. My, I couldn't do a thing to a large, able bodied one!"

The soldier addressed, a tall, handsome fellow with curling hair and large, black eyes, [was] handsome in spite of the evident fatigue and hardships he had undergone, and with the three white chevrons and diamond on his ragged sleeves that bespoke him a first sergeant of his company. "Tops" glanced carelessly in the direction of the speaker and caught the coin as it was flipped toward him. Immediately, a changed expression came over his handsome face. (This is where the graft comes in.) One emotion after another passed over his mobile countenance. The sight of the coin brought back to his memory recollections of a small, white farmhouse situated at the foot of the Blue Ridge in old Maryland, a barefoot boy with curling hair, and a prattling merry childhood companion passing along the shady lane that led to the meadow and to sunny slopes beyond, where cattle grazed. Lost in reverie, his mind soared back to the past, caused by the sight of the little coin, when suddenly he was recalled to the present by the voice of his companion.

"Why, what's up old fellow? Wake up. You're rambling."

"Where did you find this, Jim?" he asked with a husky voice.

"Why, must have been in this can of canned corned beef," answered Jim.

"What? My God, can it be possible? Can such things be?" Yet the evidence was indisputable. The very presence of the coin was sufficient evidence to convince any sane person on "God's green footstool." The coin was there. What of his companion of "boyhood days down on the farm"? Was she there, too? Was there no respect for age? Is nothing exempt from the rapacious maw of the contractors who furnish the army and navy with canned corn beef? No, the proof was there. The ring was there and the remains of Esmeralda must have been in that very can of "willie."

"Horrors!" you exclaim. "Another Luetgert case?[22] Can such monsters exist?" Nay, nay Pauline. Gentle reader, not on your imperial autograph. Nothing so horrible, for you see Esmeralda was a goat of the female persuasion, and must have attained a ripe old age at the time of decease, for the box said, "Canned in 1899."

One night before quarters, I was leaning on the chain that forms the life lines around the forecastle, carelessly watching the Japanese diver as he donned his suit and prepared to descend below. You have no idea how elaborate a toilet a diver has to undergo before he can descend to the depths below, and having nothing to do at the time, I watched him perform his dressing act with the aid of the other Japs who assisted him.

He first divested himself of his half European garb, and leisurely pulled on a heavy white wool sweater and heavy drawers of the same material, also a pair of heavy, long woolen socks extending to above his knees. He then filled his small metal Japanese pipe with tobacco from his pouch and quietly took a couple of whiffs, knocked out the ash, filled up again, repeating this operation several times. This wasn't a necessary part of his toilet, but only the leisurely way the Japs have. Next, he was assisted on with the rubber suit proper, putting his legs in and having it drawn up, completely enveloping him so he could put his arms in the sleeves, the rubber suit being all of one piece. Next, the shoulder piece to which the helmet is screwed was placed in position. This is screwed down with thumb screws to a rubber gasket so as to be perfectly water- and air-tight. Next, his assistants adjusted the rubber cuff of the sleeves around his wrists. This was done by wrapping a soft strip of chamois skin several times around each wrist. The tight-fitting rubber cuff pulled down over the chamois and two rubber elastics slipped on over the cuffs, holding them securely in place. (Here he smoked some more.) Next the heavy shoes with their copper toes and thick leaden soles were strapped on and secured with the rope lashing attached to each shoe. Then the life line was slipped around his waist and made fast. (Here a few more puffs.) A few directions to his assistants, and the helmet was placed on over his head and given the turn that secures it in place to the shoulder piece. Two little Japs

Kure, Japan

started up the pump. The one he had this day was of the old-fashioned kind and worked like a "handy-billy," just an ordinary pump.

Mr. Jap clambered out on the ladder that was attached to the side of his sampan, and at the word, his assistant screwed on the face plate and down he went with a splash, his aides looking carefully after the life line and air hose. Just then, the call for quarters went and we had to muster.

~ ~ ~

This was the auxiliary watch [that is, the engines secured and steam being supplied only to auxiliary machinery]. Our chief came out and looked at us and spoke a few words to bolo-man no. 2 and said something about "cleaning stations and work." Then turning to us, said, "You men shift yourselves, and go below and clean your bilges. Dismissed." That is the first time I ever heard such an order issued, and I make note of it here as an unheard of proceeding. A man having an aux[iliary] watch is not excused from keeping so much iron, steel and brass clean upon what is known as his "cleaning station," but I never heard a man ordered to go below and clean it after coming off watch, Saturday morning being the [normal] time, and Sunday morning before inspection was always deemed sufficient for this purpose. But I found the *Oregon* one of the worst run ships of any I have been on. We all know that this "chief" hates himself and was no friend of his men. In consequence, he got less work from them than any officer I have seen. Men knew they would have to be below most all the time, and concluded to do their loafing while below. And there is no such thing as forcing a man to work in the navy.

Promptly at about 6:00 A.M., Tuesday morning July 24th, the *Oregon* was towed over and docked. There was room enough and to spare in depth and width in this magnificent stone dock.²³ The Japs are away ahead of us in yards and docks, from the specimen I see here in Kure. This dock, a fine granite structure, will accommodate almost any ship afloat and they have more like it. The accommodations [ashore] are all right for the men. There was an absence of shouting and yelling. The Japs worked very quietly, thoroughly understanding their work. We have got a great deal to learn in this respect, working quietly.

The "poor old Ripper" started into yelling and screaming, sounding for all the world like a drunken woman in a patrol wagon. But the Japanese commander, I should judge he was captain of the yard [likely the dockmaster], shut him up by quietly turning to him and saying, "These men no understand you when you yell and make noise. I talk to my men and tend to the docking." And he did. A few questions here and there and the ship was docked as quietly as anything of the kind I have ever saw done. The Japs have a way of working uniformly together. One man will sing out and the mauls all fall together in rhythm and the ship is shored up properly. Hobson of *Merrimac* fame then took charge for the American side of it.²⁴ From what I have seen of Hobson, he is a plain, unassuming young man, smart, and a man who thinks and acts for himself and is not easily swayed by others. I first saw him walking around the dock in white, with a sun helmet and umbrella, goggles protecting his eyes, business like and thoroughly the Naval Constructor.

The crew were allowed to descend the dock and view the bottom of the *Oregon*. I was on watch at the time and did not get to see it at that time, but before going on watch at 4 P.M., I set on the fo'castle and watched the moves of some of the officers and warrant officers. I remarked to a shipmate alongside of me, "Keep your eye upon that bolo-man. He'll fall in the water presently." This was no. 4 bolo-man, known familiarly to the "black gang" as "Dopey."[25] This fellow shipped as mach[inist] 2nd class during the war and those that shipped [with him] or saw him aboard the *Franklin*[26] said he was about the seediest bum they had beheld in a long time. But now he was hobnobbing with officers, wearing a dressing gown, and waited upon by Chinese servants. But [he] had not contrived to get rid of the hang-dog, hunted look that came from a long series of cold refusals from good housewives that had showed him the back gate or a wood pile.[27]

He was "doping" along the dock with his usual sleepy manner, when he tripped over a line and nearly pitched head first into the dock. Then he went down the steps and contrived to get punched in the eye with a bamboo rod a Jap was using to draw some wedges toward him. He was in everybody's way. I went below and watched. The next thing I heard, Dopey had fallen overboard and everybody from the skipper down had given a large, hoarse guffaw, after which he "pulled his freight" and got aboard out of sight. More of the B.M.'s were strutting around the dock like real officers, looking wise, and casting a critical eye at the docking. You'd think they were in sole charge from the pompous strut they put on.

They reminded me of a certain carpenter in Phila[delphia] whom we called "Admiral Chips." This fellow was short and stout and pompous. When a ship was being docked, he would run here and there among the men shouting unintelligibly, especially when any of the officers were looking. Sometimes an officer would call him and send him on an errand. He had no say at all in docking a ship, but after the ship was safely shored and all secure, then Mr. Admiral Chips took supreme command, and the way he would order scrapers and painters around was a caution. I used to see this fellow coming along with his pompous, consequential air and prepare to give him a good salute. Drawing myself up to attention, I would throw my hand up with the precision of a machine. This did him good, and I believe I could have asked and rec'd any favor in his power to grant. But ignore him and he would try to imitate some officers and call you down; it worked well with "rookies," but not old timers. They would laugh in his face. Our big carpenter put me somewhat in mind of him. Two years ago he was a machinist "corking off" any old place around the ship, spreading all over the deck like a huge crab or jelly fish, occupying enough space for five ordinary men. Now one morning I heard an awful howl from him and he was ramping around in a big dressing gown, looking for a mess boy. He found him in the passageway acting a "punkah-wallah" pulling the punkah over the other warrant officers,

Kure, Japan

bolo-men, etc. "Here, you belong to me!" he roared in a voice of thunder. "Drop that d[amned] punkah and get my bath ready. You've got nothing to do with those mugs. You're mine!"

This was addressed to the Filipino boy who was mess boy for the warrant officers. Get his bath ready! Two years before he was content to take a bath in a condensed milk can when he got the chance. Oh Heavens, 'tis a wonderful world. All this large, obese party did at the time of the *Oregon*'s mishap was to make a terrific noise to give the impression to the officers that he was the "whole cheese." That and abusing the fireman or oiler who ran the pumps was all that he did, but what a fierce noise it was! Of course, hitting up the "booze" at regular intervals helped keep up his steam. The Navy is composed of just such large "bluffs." Getting right down to good competent business they are unable to do, and what they lack in brains and competency they make up in noise.

I had to laugh at the big fellow. The airs he gave himself after the ship was successfully docked! He and a few officers were looking at the ship's bottom with a critical eye when some of the men came below to get a squint at it. Some of them jostled against his Imperial Jiblets and he let a roar out of him.[28] "Get out of here!" he yelled at the men, turning to Hobson, who stood near. "That's the way with these fellows. They are always in the way."

Hobson answered him quietly, "I can't see that they are doing any harm or in the way. Let them all come down and look." And that's just how the crew happened to get below that afternoon.

The *Oregon*'s bottom was in a bad way. It reminded me of a battered old tin can. The keel was bent in three or four different places, one indentation fully fifteen feet long, and three feet deep. The work that Petersen the diver did was excellent, putting on two patches about three foot square and wedging and caulking the seams. The patches were of wood, rubber and waste, the whole clamped on by a bolt. It was truly a hazardous undertaking to cross the Yellow Sea as we did. None of us expected to find the *Oregon* as bad as she actually was. Hundreds of indentations marked the entire forward section of the hull. This was to be all patched temporarily, the places filled out with wood knees or braces to conform with the lines of the ship. Then plates [were] placed over these. Of course, these repairs, when finished, would last for years, but what the *Oregon* needed was at least a year's work to bring her back to her previous form.

Good for the skipper! We were given five days' liberty and allowed to draw our two months' pay due us. One half of the entire ship's company, regardless of class, went ashore, all except fifth class, this being a class established by the skipper himself and not according "to Blue Book" regulations.[29] [A fifth-]class man received no privileges whatever, wasn't even allowed to handle his mess money, but signed for it and it was turned over to the caterer of his mess. You were fifth class until the Captain saw fit to make you fourth. Of course, the three prisoners were allowed no liberty, those in for a general court-martial. Just imagine, a whole, five days! I did not go in the first half. But five days! Five whole days away from the routine of naval life, away from the bolo-men, and the petty annoyances and meanesses of our life aboard ship. Why, I nearly jumped like a kangaroo when I heard of it, the highest [*sic:* longest?] liberty I [had] had during the cruise being from four in the afternoon until 6:30 A.M. the next morning, and sundown liberty at Manila.

How patiently I waited with the other half of the crew for our turn to go! And how the other fellows lucky enough to go in the first part gave us the laugh. But we knew they would come back "broke" for the balance of the time here at Kure, that they would be sick from their long debauch, at least some of them, and that we, laughing last, had the best of it. But the work the bolo-men tried to put on us! They wanted to make the men left do the work of the men on liberty in conjunction with their own. Such a mixed up affair it was below. Bolo-men as represented on the *Oregon,* were about as competent to handle a force of men as a monkey would be to play a nocturne on a violin. Government schools [should] take these men from civil life, give them a course of training fitting them for officers and engineers, and *then* and not until then, will the men respect them. As they stand at present writing, they are a farce, but an unpleasant farce for the men.

As the case stands at present writing, any landsman or coal passer can give better commands than these men, who have had absolutely no military training whatever. What the government wants is a school of application [as army training centers for cavalry, artillery, etc., were known] for the training of warrant machinists. They appoint your warrant machinist from civil life, take him from the ranks of marine engineers, men who can pass a good, strict exam for marine engineer. And, of course, like all applicants for the Navy, they must be qualified physically. Six months at a school of application will learn them the duties required of an officer in the service. Then the warrant machinist coming aboard a sea-going ship has simply to get acquainted as any other person of whatever rating has to do to learn the ship, the valves, etc. But do away with the gang that occupies the center of the stage at present. Men won't obey men who slept on the same "caulking mat," worked with them, messed with them and lived as a shipmate with them. The men know the failings of these men, and hate to take a "calling down" from a bolo-man who, when he was a M2c [machinist 2nd class] or machinist of whatever class, would be the last man to turn to willingly, were "shirks" and loafers as enlisted men and couldn't even keep themselves clean. The whole scheme at present is wrong, and the department will find out its mistake sooner or later.

Men commenced dropping back from liberty after the first 24 hours, tired out, "busted." Some held it out as long as possible, by any means, begging, borrowing, and standing people off for their money. The most came back disgusted, said the town was no good, etc. These people cannot get along anywhere. They quickly get tired. Many get drunk and blow their coin right and left, while others more wily hold

Kure, Japan

back and let the "easy" ones do the spending. Of course, the town is small and hasn't any European places, and everything is strictly Japanese. Others will break their liberty as long as they can obtain "booze."

Everybody had to be in uniform [of the day] on the ship. You couldn't go out to the dock or even work unless in uniform. Men coming up from below to get a drink of water had to change from dungarees to white. Some of them would take an hour to do this.

The "Ripper" was around looking for men out of uniform and everyone he saw he would pounce on with a roar. Poor, useless, old man, [his is a] wasted life of no earthly use, a life spent in abusing men for petty trifles. Before the *Oregon* ran aground, he had a cheap reputation as a "sailor man." But he showed his lack of competency and made it apparent to all that he was only in the way in sudden emergencies, screaming and roaring at the top of his voice, pulling men here and there, cursing them. He made himself an object of disgust to all hands. We did not blame the skipper so much for running us aground the first time. It was a desire on his part to reach Taku as quickly as possible. And even when we hit the second rock it was impatience to be off and doing. "Bull headedness" if you will. But still no one would accuse him of not being a "sailor." A man of action he showed himself, and if even he himself wasn't disgusted at the asinine antics of this poor, red faced old woman, why he was less observing than the majority of the crew thought.

"Jack the Ripper" represents a class fast dying out: men who all their lives have abused men who have no power to resent the abuse. He had even gone so far as to strike men with an umbrella he carried, of course knowing his man. Some men would report him and cause him to be censured. To his equals he was as affable as his nature would allow him. To his superiors, cringing. Poor old stiff! Hysterical old woman! What an unconscious clown he was to some of the men who were on the "qui vive" all the time to see what funny stunt was next on the stage when the poor old clown occupied the lime-light. The name of "Ripper" he gloried in. Even I have seen the Japanese size him up as an unknown quantity with looks of mingled amusement and disgust. To these quiet, polite and observing people, he was a phase of American life of which they "wotted" not.

Well, let him rest for a while, poor, old, drunken sailor.

How anxiously we awaited the return of the first half of the crew enjoying their five days' furlough, and what rumors were rife among us left aboard the ship! It was reported that the *Newark* was coming up to Kure and that numbers of us would be drafted to Taku, and that the other half would receive no liberty in consequence. This rumor gained credence and [there] was a number of downcast countenances to be noticed among us in consequence. But it proved to be as unfounded as most ships' news generally is. The five days rolled around with leaden wings and at last the last few stragglers came aboard. Some did not show up at all, but they had gone to Kobe and thence home by way of some tramp steamer. They didn't intend to come back. The last were aboard, and that night the list came of the other half posted on the bulletin board, and we read our names for the five days' liberty, like children loose from school. No bolo-men. No irksome ship's tasks. To sleep in as long as we wished in the day. To do a thousand and one things that discipline aboard a ship will not allow. To be free. Free to do as one pleased for a whole five days. Why, that seemed a life time to us, cooped up as we had been for months. We never gave a thought to the flitting of the five days and the return. We only thought of the vacation. Why, it would prove a veritable August outing. We could run to Yokohama, to Nagasaki, where I could see old acquaintances. To Kobe. To Hiroshima, a few miles below Kure,[30] or stay in Kure and enjoy its beautiful scenery and surroundings.

What brushing up and overhauling of clothing the evening before! Jacky is very scrupulous regarding his appearance going on liberty. But, hmm . . . coming off liberty, "that's another story," as Rudyard K[ipling] would remark. And for five days, five whole days, it required a few extra touches. The brushing up, the careful arrangement of every tie-tie, the seeing that everything was just as it should be. The paymaster served out monthly money to the last half. Two full months' pay to those that had it on the book to their credit, and what was due them to the others. Everybody had a plentiful supply for five days in Japan, Japan of the Inland Sea, the very interior of this strange land and stranger people.

The other half that came back had diverse tales to tell. Some liked the place and some didn't, but no doubt the place was all right. It must have been the men themselves. How long the night seemed! We were to leave the ship at 9:00 A.M. the next morning. But at last the momentous moment arrived, and clad in blue we stood around the forecastle until the welcome word, "Lay aft on the port side of the quarterdeck all the liberty party," was passed. We lost no time in doing so. There are some calls we like to answer with alacrity. We formed in two long lines of blue and were inspected by the officer of the deck and passed over the starboard gangway, down the dock, and into sailing launch and cutter which we filled up to overflowing. Then, in charge of an officer, we were towed across to Kure and landed and left, each man to follow his own desire, to go whither he pleased for a large, whole five days.

We were met at the landing by the usual rickshaw men, also by a number of "runners" for the different drinking houses of which there was not a few. "This way for the *Oregon* House" or "Star House," was printed on flags and on placards. But jumping into a rickshaw apiece, I and a comrade made our escape up to the town. We went quickly along up the main street known as Washagamato, to the "Joe Bush House," which a couple of shipmates of ours were interested in, and they having gone on the first five days leave, were still there, in consequence, breaking their liberty. How they came to be [there] was that they made a bargain with this particular house, which was in no wise different from the usual run of Japanese "joints," to secure the *Oregon*'s trade for a share of the proceeds, which after working for [them] about four days after [they] arrived ashore, they did not get. When they demanded a division and percentage, the master seeing that the trade was about over, held fast to the money, a way your Jap has, being a regular Shylock in a trade. Of course, they

Kure, Japan

threatened to break up the place, etc., but he only salaamed and no "savvied" until they gave up in despair and all they could do was to take down the sign and cover their names with ink, and tell the boys. And the next day the place was deserted, where before was a curious crowd of spectators and rickshaws in front of the place, all was deserted. But they had made their money and were perfectly contented. But the evening, or rather, about noon, when we first came in, the place was in full bloom, filled with drunken sailors from the former five days' leave. They were lying around in all conditions. Some had lost their shoes; others were clad in simply a kimono and *zōri*, a straw shoe. Most of them showed the effect of a hard week's drunk.

I did not stay long in this place. Ordered up a couple of bottles of beer and proposed to my comrade to go out. I always like to roam around and take a look. We went. I first went and bought a pair of trousers, very thin stuff, must have been made of gingham, but very comfortable they proved after the heavy blue flannel suit. Clad in my thin white undershirt and a straw hat and light trousers, I felt like a new man, and ready for anything. I left my uniform at a place on the corner, kept by about the nicest old fellow I ran across in Kure, and jumping in a rickshaw, we started around, bent on doing the town.

Kure is like all Japanese towns. The streets are narrow, as all Japanese streets are, except one or two, which are extremely wide and has shade trees on both sides. I noticed a number of curious signs among which was the most noticeable, of a Jap restaurant, "Drink and Kook Shop. Selling by Chep," another, "American Chop Chop Hab Got. Flesh Heggs and Bear," comical mistakes at which we lay back and roared. Kure had never had any intercourse with Europeans before. Every place where they sold anything at all had bottled beer displayed where it could be easily seen. Must have all been put [there] for the occasion by some big firm, perhaps by agents for the different breweries.

Japs don't drink beer, and the price, 40 cts Japanese, per qt. Ice *(kori)* came extra, and to get a cool drink we had to crack it up in your beer or else get a bucket full of *kori* and half a dozen beer and put them on ice and always keep some ahead. Everything was dear. Talk about Japan being cheap. The Japs would naïvely tell you, "Beer 20 cts. Japanese man; American, forty cents. American plenty money." Tax you. Well, if summer resort prices didn't prevail in Kure, then they don't rob summer boarders in the United States. Open your mouth and you had to pay a yen. Give a rickshaw man less than half a dollar and see the look of disgust with which he regarded first the coin and then you, until a crowd gathered around. But mention "police" and see him quickly fly. Of course, we took in the "Yoshiwaries,"[31] and turning off into that direction, the sign that attracted our attention was "Welcome, honorable American man-o-war. Dis house keep by nice girl."

Yes, all Kure had turned out to welcome us with open arms, and to relieve us of our money. Flags were flying and Japanese lanterns were illuminated in our honor. Such a windfall had never before struck Kure as the *Oregon*'s crew with their pockets lined with yen. Never before had such fabulous prices been paid for anything in Kure.

A Sailor's Log

Of course, the Kure people had been told what an American sailor was accustomed to pay by their Kobe brethren. Many had come down from Kobe to get their share of the *Oregon* spoils. Every house in the Yoshiwara, if you asked where they came from (that is, the inmates), would bring the invariable reply, "Kobe." All the eating houses such as the "Oregon Houses" and the "Star Houses" were kept by Kobe people. If I could have thought in time, I would have written Moriya and got her to come down and cater to our wants in the eating line. But in spite of the high prices, I managed to have a fine time.

The first night, I lost control of myself altogether, and got in a beastly state of intoxication, which I intended to do. I confess it. I intended to get drunk after the fierce experience aboard the *Oregon*. I don't know how many bottles of beer and other stuff I consumed, but it must have been a great old quantity from the state of my head the next morning. I know we were taken in hand by the women in the house in which we staid and given a bath in hot and cold water, and clothed in a kimono. Our own underclothes were washed and dried during the night. One of the women started to manicure my fingernails, and if I hadn't stopped her, [she] wouldn't have left any of the nail at all, with the result that my finger tips were sore for the whole five days.

These were the proper Japanese dolls. All they could do was to smile and nod, a perfect type of the girl sold for immoral purposes, if you can call it immoral in Japan, where it is perfectly lawful and legitimate, and a source of revenue to the government. They keep these houses in bounds and the girls are not allowed to go beyond the limits without a permit. God only knows what sorrows and love affairs are concealed behind these smiling, expressionless countenances. They look and act as if they were contented with their lot, and perhaps they would rather be an inmate of the Yoshiwara than pulling a freight car around, for all Nippon girls have to work, only the aristocracy being exempt. There are no drones in the Nippon hive. They have an easy life, these girls, and often marry good men from these places. Unlike their western sisters, there is no shame connected with their calling. They are a product of Japan, necessary, and recognized as necessary. Give one of them a quarter or a half-a-dollar and they are pleased as punch and will talk about it for an hour and show it to their sisters.

We were well settled in this place, clothed in a cool, light kimono, lying back smoking a fair cigar for Japan, price ten cents, with a bucket full of quarts [of beer] fast getting ice cold, and fanned by the girls, enjoying all the luxuries of life, and fast getting hilarious and jolly. Toward night we were pretty far gone and the girl I had took me by the hand (afraid of losing me, I suppose) for a walk, and a walk it proved to be. We were also joined by the daughter of the master of the house, a *"chishi"* about 9 years of age also destined to be a Yoshiwara doll and fast being educated for that life.[32]

My *Okamisan*[33] led me directly toward a Japanese shoe shop and with child like simplicity selected the best pair of *gaita* in the whole shooting match. Lacquered they were, and had elaborate trimmings, as coquettish a pair of little Japanese

Kure, Japan

Cinderellas as I ever saw. These she thrust her little brown pedal extremities in and glanced archly at me from her narrow, slitted eyes. Of course, I knew the expression, had long been shipmates with it in western lands as well as in the East. Feeling generous from the good wine and beer I had imbibed, with the air of a millionaire I dived down in my kimono sleeve and brought up the purse.

"How much?" I questioned the dealer. Gravely taking a piece of chalk, he marked the price on a slate, $2.50 yen. This I paid. It was cheap. A curious crowd had gathered around, about fifty of them, to look at one of the "Honourable American Men-o-war so liberal with his gold," and glances of envy was directed toward the girl. [For the] little girl, I selected a pair that looked like toy clogs and gave [them] to her, price, 80 cts, while the wondering crowd looked on. Then the "Honourable, etc." stalked forth in his majesty and a kimono with the *chishi* by one hand, dangling a pair of *gaita* and the *Okamisan* by the other hand, also dangling a pair of *gaita* (price $2.50). When we reached the house, the little girl ran and showed them to her father and the other little girl, who got jealous immediately and also wanted a pair, making known her wishes by catching hold of my hand with both of hers and pulling and tugging and nodding in the direction of the shop.

The *Okamisan* was also very profuse in her praises of the "Honourable, etc." The old man salaamed so often and was so polite and profuse in his protestations of thankfulness and regard that I had a notion to take him out and buy him a pair. Finishing up a large cold bottle with a sigh of satisfaction, I took the whole three girls and the mother over and before an admiring audience, I let them select the best in the shop. My Cinderella selected a pair with red lacquered trappings, and a pair for each little girl and the old lady. Price, I believe, for the whole lot [was] about $4.00. Then, with a heart bursting with pride at a good action done, we sallied forth, the little girls jumping up and down like a pair of small puppies, full of delight. Again was the old rogue profuse in his thanks and praises of the "Honourable, etc." With another bottle, I succumbed, and soon toppled over with a sigh of contentment, at peace with all the world.

The next morning I awoke with a start and wondered what the deuce was the matter with my head, it felt so queer. Looking around, I thought the place looked strange. I expected the sound of the bugle in "Reveille" would soon sound. Everything was as yet dark, but gradually I gathered my scattered wits and realized where I was. My tongue was parched and dry, and I had a most violent thirst and horrible headache, bespeaking of the night's debauch. I looked at my watch. It was about 6 A.M., rather early for a man that turned in about 2 A.M., so with a sigh of satisfaction, I realized that this was the morning of the second day, and that I could sleep as long as I wished, and I did so. Rolled over and was soon fast asleep again.

I was awakened about four hours afterward by someone moving about fixing up the room. The sun had long been up and the girl was straightening up the room. Then I remembered the shoes, and wondered what the Dickens I had bought, if the man had been bought out. But counting my money I found with all my extravagance I had not exceeded what I intended spending per diem. But I was sober now, and regarded the picture in a different light. The girl was about as handsome a Nippon girl as I had ever seen, but I wasn't in quite the mood to appreciate beauty of any kind. My first break was for a large, cool bottle. Then I had a bath, and throwing off my kimono, I put on my snapper outfit once more. Then, by signs, I broke in on the master of the house's profusions of thanks by asking for my friend, whom I thought had stopped there also for the night. But to my surprise he made known by signs that he had wandered off during the night. So, bidding them *Sayonara* (good-bye), despite their efforts to detain me, I wandered off in search of other fields to conquer.

I did not find my other companion, but I ran up against Ken,[34] clothed like myself in a summer rig, and asked him where he was going.

"Nowhere in particular."

"All right, let's go and get a cold one, and then some chow, and then we will take a look see."

So we went down to the place where I had left my clothes. This place, as I said, was conducted by about the best old fellow in Kure, a queer old Jap joker, making all sorts of funny remarks trying to learn English. His beer was kept rather nice, and it was about the coolest den in town. There were two different families in this place. The old fellow had a boy about fourteen and a girl of twelve, but well developed for her size, also a married daughter who followed the old custom of blackening her teeth with betel-nut.[35] But the boy and girl were as handsome a pair of Nippon kids as you could find throughout the island. The girl, a regular little Japanese beauty with "the beauty of budding womanhood," standing with reluctant feet where the brook and river meet. (Laura Jean Libby)[36] And accommodating. The boy would anticipate your every want, an obliging youngster if ever there was one. At first, the little girl was shy at the "foreign devils," but soon got better acquainted and would wait on us with a rush. The boy would blacken your shoes and do anything for one, and would refuse "komshir" whenever offered.[37]

It was about the only place where we could get anything that approached an American meal. Our first meal was composed of fish, a small piece nearly raw, potatoes, cold and soggy, a cold slab of steak that had been parboiled in the pan, and some fierce stuff for coffee. We would make this place our terminus on one end of the town and always stopped there. It was occupied by a decent crowd of four or five marines, decent fellows who were enjoying their five days in a quiet manner. I shall never forget this place, nor will Ken, for it has many pleasant recollections for me, and the old man and his healthy children deserve our thanks for the many kindnesses shown us. We made out as well as we could with the indifferent meal, looking forward to something better later on. Meanwhile, we were getting back into normal shape once more, and I know I was feeling a little sorry for last night's debauch, and resolved to take it easier for the rest of the furlough. And I will state here that I did not get drunk again.

Kure, Japan

Ken and I started out for a walk and we dropped into the "Yokohama Hotel," kept by Joe Bush, and there met the usual gang of drunks. I met my companion of the night before in there. This place was filled to overflowing with drunken, jolly bluejackets. They were coining money, and the usual crowd of curious Japs were all around the door and in the place having a look at the "Honourable American Men-o-war," seeing his method of enjoyment, etc. Some of them commenced to talk about the battles of Santiago and Manila Bay, and they were getting into quite a heated argument, some of them arguing about the *Oregon*'s position and the chase of the *Colón*. Others who were not on the *Oregon*, but on other ships, were turning the *Oregon* down, and finally they commenced drawing diagrams to illustrate their argument, and diagrams they were. It was the usual sailors' argument, and but by somebody starting up a song, would have ended in a battle royal free to all comers.

It was then getting toward the cool of the evening and Ken proposed taking a swim, which was seconded, so we gathered up a few fellows who were in favor of the motion, and getting a "ricky" who knew where to take us, we started. The "rickies" stipulated 60 cts for the run to take us out and back, and it was well worth it. We started out a whole cavalcade in all sorts of rigs.

Along the Wasagamato went the whole procession, Ken's big straw hat in the race, past curious crowds of gazers and on out the street until the limits of the town was reached, and there the "rickies" had to slow down to a walk, because the ascent of the beautiful, winding, white ribbon of mountain road was steep. This was a most beautiful place. The road wound around, forming a complete horse-shoe. The route lay along green rice paddies with here and there a picturesque group of people ankle deep in the water of the rice fields. Everywhere we were greeted with a smile, past teams of oxen with the ox in front and some old Japanese in the shaft, guiding the cart that was loaded down with grain, or other products. Groups of working men and girls all passing along, everywhere greeted [us] with a laugh. People would rush to the doorways to see the Americans going by. Naked children everywhere, and half naked men and women trying to keep cool, stretched on their matting enjoying the cool evening breeze.

We were curios to these simple people. Never before had they seen so many foreign devils together in one bunch, and we enjoyed it just as much as they did. Just outside of the city there was a large spring of cool water, situated at the base of one of the high hills, and we ordered our "rickies" to draw up there, while we quenched our thirst, which you will imagine, no doubt, was a rather severe one after the spirituous refreshments we had indulged in. We lolled and rolled around in the cool grass in this shady spot, and our thoughts no doubt wandered backward to some such spot we knew long ago. It isn't often a bluejacket gets the chance to rest under green boughs and refresh himself with a drink of clear, cold spring water, and we took advantage of it all.

Here we rested and cooled ourselves from the hot sun. Japan is the land of the rising sun, *Asahi*. And when *Asahi* is fully risen, everybody knows it. Hot is no name for it, but the atmosphere is dry, with scarcely any humidity, and you do not feel the effect of the sun's rays as you would in America. The "rickies" were laying off in the grass with us. We hated to make a start, but finally tore ourselves away from the lovely spot. Someone with an eye to business, a true bluejacket, saw the value of the cool spring water for cooling beer, and proposed to go back to the town and get four or five dozen quarts and sink them in the spring. Not a bad idea, but we wanted a swim, and jumping each man in his "rickshaw," away we started up the ascending mountain road. Just above the spring, the ascent became steeper and our "rickies" soon showed it. From the usual lope, they leaned forward, breasting the bar of their "rickshaws," getting right down to their work, a long line toiling along the winding country road.

At last we got out, some few of us, and walked along until we reached a stone image of Buddha that crowned the apex of the hill, and then from the summit we caught a glimpse of the Inland Sea beyond, beautiful beyond words, a glimpse of silvery water, the white strip of roadway winding down in innumerable curves. Above the road up the mountainside, [lay] terrace after terrace of rice paddies; below the road, the same. Here and there a quaint Japanese house [stood] in some out of the way place. Below us were the pools of water used for irrigating all this land.[38] And jumping in our "rickskaws" again with a whoop, away we started down the steep hill, the man in the shafts lying back with all his might to keep from getting run down by his own rickshaw.

This was all easy riding, and we were soon at the pond in which we were to swim. There was a wayside inn just at this point, and the inmates jumped up with wonder to see so many Americans together, and gazed at us in wonder, as with a yell like a lot of boys, we rushed along the bank, divesting ourselves of clothing on the fly to see who would be first in. Ken and I made it about the same time. In we plunged and swam over to the other end, about half a mile across, with some of the fellows following. We forgot our dignity as bluejackets and yelled and cavorted, and splashed to our heart's content in the cool water. Soon a crowd of people lined the banks. Men, women, boys and girls, and catching the spirit of the scene, threw kimonos aside and plunged in also. The "rickshaw" men did the same, and it was a merry party that splashed around in that pond that hot August day.

The day would have been marred by an accident, however, but for the quickness of two of us. One of the fellows, a little the worse for the beer he had imbibed, was staggering around the bank, trying to disrobe. He had a white working suit on and was just pulling the jumper off over his head and tugging at it in the effort to get it off, overbalanced and fell in. Ken and I were just then at the farther end, and happened to see it. At first we thought the fellow was doing "stunts," showing us a disrobing act, [but] the way he was rolling around with the jumper still over his head like a bag, [convinced us] that it was no joke on his part. So, letting a yell that reverberated among the hills, we attracted the attention of those nearest him and they, seeing that he was in a bad way, quickly came to the rescue. Pulling him out, they laid him on the bank and pulled the jumper, the cause of it all, from over his head, and

Kure, Japan

worked the water out of him by the method employed in such cases. But the load of water he had shipped had fully neutralized the cargo of beer he had aboard, and when we reached the other bank, he was a vastly sober man. But he summoned up courage enough to finally go in the water again, and enjoy himself.

It was getting rather toward the dusk of the afternoon and crowds of people were stretched around the banks and on the roadside above, watching us, some of them workmen from the Navy yard, who walked all this distance to and from every day to their work. Getting tired, we came out of the water and donned our clothes, watched curiously all the time by the Japs who are very inquisitive. Men, women, boys and girls alike, it is all the same to them. No false modesty among these strange people. We went up to the inn and tried to find some beer, but there were only a few bottles of lemonade, and warm at that. Also some few cakes and candy. We bought the man out. Such a windfall never came his way before. His bright eyed daughter served us up some tea, and such bowing, smiling and salaaming the Honourable American Men-o-war hardly ever received before.

As it was getting late, we started off once more. With numerous *Sayonara*'s (goodbye) away we sped toward the city once more, very much refreshed from our bath. People were coming along the road from work and once we passed about ten girls in a group. We were going down hill to the town and speeding along swiftly. They looked at us with wide open, surprised eyes which soon changed, however, to a giggle and laughter as we saluted them. ("*Combawa*," good evening.) "*Combawa onaga, combawa.*"[39]

"*Combawa, combawa,*" returned they in feminine chorus with little shrieks of merriment. Poor little maids! What a narrow life to be sure, but they are not unhappy by any means. [A] very little [thing] pleases them. A new hair pin. A pair of *gaita*. A kimono. A silk *obi*. And they take more delight than a woman suffragist would upon her election to the United States Senate. As we swept around a break in the road far below, we looked back and they were still standing in the road, waving hands and fans at us, picturesque little Nippon maidens looking for all the world as if they had posed for the painting on some sumptuous lacquerware box or fan.

We were getting close to the spring, and had a good view of Kure, which, with many twinkling lights as it was just turning dark, lay stretched out before us in the green valley below, a beautiful view, [with] the Japanese fleet in the distance. In the center, almost, of Kure, there is a big rice field. It looked like a huge green carpet from where we were. Kure is a beautiful spot. We jumped out at the spring and had a drink of the cool water, and then kept on in [to] the town, down the street until we reached the "Yokohama House," where we paid and dismissed the jinricksha men. I gave mine a dollar, which was twice the amount, but he was a sturdy young boy, and so willing that I considered him well worth it. I often had him on the same trip. He put me in mind of a little Shetland pony, the way he would work in the shafts. At the "Yokohama House" the Japs were in front of the door. Beer was flowing like water, and the gang showed the effects of it, but were jolly and not a bit quarrelsome. I did not see a fight the whole five days ashore. Ken and I soon left the "push"[40] and went down the line farther to our eating place on the corner, where we ordered up as good a meal as could be gotten together. The usual eggs, and beefsteak, and cold potatoes, with tea. We made a meal of it, however, and washed it down with a few cold bottles of beer. Large quarts, 40 cts per bot[tle], if you please, dungaree money. Then we sallied forth up the line again, looking for what might turn up. Out of the "Yokohama" came sounds of revelry by night. Wild howls pierced the stillness, and we knew the gang would soon be chasing the [Cristobal] Colón or arguing the position of the respective vessels upon which they served. We didn't care for any of that and kept on, passed by many places where we were invited to "come in" and buy something to drink. Every shop in the town had beer to sell.

We enjoyed ourselves looking at the sights, at the Japanese out in the cool of the evening. Many curious costumes we remarked, but everything went, and nothing but the Americans attracted any attention. Everywhere we went we were the centre of attraction, and if you espied a group of Japs, you could be sure that there was one of us in the midst of it. We turned into the street leading to the Yoshiwara and were called in by a couple of girls that were in a small shop filled with Japanese notions.

"Say, say, come here," waving her hand toward us. Nothing loath, we leisurely walked in and took a seat on the matting, having plenty of time at command. We found out that the two of them and an old lady wanted to practice their little knowledge of English on us, and incidentally, tried to get us to purchase Japanese hair pins, ornaments for the hair, etc. We compromised by buying a couple of bottles of lemonade for them and for ourselves. The smallest one of the two, a little, round, buxom Nippon girl, limited her conversation in English to the following remarks: "Shay, shay," plucking me by the sleeve to attract my attention, "You—" a pause to think, and looking very wise and shy, "me—America go. You—me—America go, all yight?" blowing in the direction in which she thought America lay, from the palm of her hand. Then, to be entertaining and vary the conversation, she would substitute Hong Kong, Manila, Shanghai, Kobe, Yokohama, San Francisco, New York, for America, to which proposition I gave a grave assent, which seemed to satisfy her, but, bless you, she didn't believe a word of it. She was a quaint, little jollier.

We left there and went in the Yoshiwara to the house "Keep by nice girl" and secured quarters for the night. Ken's policy and mine was to sleep wherever night overtook us. We had no especial plans, and wandered as the wind where we liked, followed fancy's dictates. We were of one mind. It was in this house, "Marimoudo's"[41] ("Keep by nice girl" as the sign read), that Inouye, a Kobe tattooer, hung forth, so I sent for him, and taking a look thro' his books of designs, and finding him one of the finest Japanese tattooers I had ever seen, had him do some work for me. I saw some of the work that this man had done on a few of his friends. One of them had a most elaborate design traced upon his back, arms and thighs, fish interwoven with scroll work, dragons, female figures, warriors, etc. A Japanese fairy story told in India ink. They were most elegant specimens of Japanese tattooing. Inouye laid me out on a mat and commenced work on my shoulder, upon which he placed quite an elaborate

Kure, Japan

design. It kept two *musmee*s[42] busy fanning us, both on account of the heat and the mosquitoes, which tho' smaller than the Jerseyman, are of the most venomous kind. However, we managed to get thro' the work, with the fanning and numerous cooling drinks. The pain was not so very severe, considering the size of the design, which covered my entire shoulder. For this design I paid the large sum of 7 yen ($3.50). The same job executed by one of the Manila tattooers would cost about 20 yen or more.

In the morning, Ken and I arose, and after the usual morning bath and rub down, felt fit to eat a horse, hoofs and all. So we sallied forth to see what we could devour. We came across the Japanese restaurant with the inviting sign, "Meal and eat house, selling by cheap," and concluded to try what sort of a meal they could produce in this place, our usual place being at the other end of the line, and we didn't care for the exercise of walking or "ricksha" riding to increase our appetite, already of abnormal dimensions. So in we went, greeted by the proprietor with a series of salaams that would have done credit to a Chesterfield.[43] The table was covered with a soiled sheet that had seen previous hard service, and from its battered and soiled look, must have had quite a war record. However, we couldn't afford to be dainty in Japan, and expect spotless linen and an immaculate service in a town that had never catered to the gastronomic needs of the "foreign devil." I made the remark to Ken, however, that "I wished Moriya was here, then we could get something to eat," to which Ken said, "Amen."

The menu was brought forth, cold, half-boiled potatoes, sloppy coffee, a piece of meat that had seen better days, bread, and that was all. We tackled it. We were hungry. We tried our best, but couldn't do much with our appetite suddenly palled. I ate about an ounce of the meat. I took time to masticate it, then, driven to desperation, I called for a couple bottles of beer and "*Kori, kori!*" (ice) and we filled up on beer. We paid the price, 60 cts apiece, for food that a dog would refuse at home.

"It's no use," said Ken. "If we want to chow, we will have to turn cook ourselves."

"Good. That's what we will do as soon as we regain our lost appetite," rejoined I. "But at present, it will take at least half a dozen cold bottles to wash the taste of that breakfast from my mouth."

"Let's take a stroll down the line again," which we accordingly did, stopping every once [in] a while for a cool bottle. Passing a barber shop, we concluded to have a shave and went in, where we excited a great deal of curiosity among a crowd of young Nippon youths who were idling about the shop. The barber was quite an old man and had a very pretty girl assistant. He pointed to a chair. He had selected me for the first victim. I sank in it with a groan. "Good bye, old man. Just break the news to Mother," I said screwing my head in Ken's direction. I noticed him making eyes at the girl. Strange how all petticoats appeal so strongly to all Jackies, no matter what nationality they may be.

But I was agreeably surprised. Instead of getting a scrape that would discount the Bowery two for five, he went over my face very easily with his small, no-handled razor. They use no lather, just plain soap and a little water, which they rub over our

A Sailor's Log

phisog with their hand. After he had finished shaving, I was turned over to the girl, which operation I rather liked. She led me over and set me in a chair and telling me by signs to bend over, gave my head a thorough shampoo and sousing in cold water, after which by signs she bade me wash my face and then setting me in another chair, cleaned my ears with their queer looking instruments, a steel fork with a bulb on one end made to vibrate by a smart tap, causing a sensation like the buzzing of bees. This I liked, especially at the hands of this *musmee*, a very pretty specimen of her kind. Finishing me, I watched Ken undergo the same treatment. This cost 32 cts. Ken gave the old man half a dollar for his part and more of our fellows, seeing us in the shop, came in and the old fellow forgot Ken's change in the excitement of so large a crowd, and as Ken didn't bother him for it, we went out.

We stopped at the "Yokohama House" and it was full, as usual, the gang just getting underway again, after the night's [orgy]. We tried to get some of them together for another swim, but none cared about going, so Ken and I hailed a pair of "rickies" and went. I had the same boy as on the previous occasion. We stopped at the spring for our usual drink of cold spring water. The people along the roadway had grown to know us by sight and greeted us with many smiles, and "*ohayo's*" (good-morning). I don't know of anything during our entire stay in Kure I enjoyed more than these long rides thro' the beautiful, strange country, and the swimming.

There were three large ponds, something like our mill ponds at home, and we tried all three. But the centre one was the best, and beside, the wayside inn was close to the second one. The man of the house greeted us with the usual salutation and pointed with pride to an array of bottled beer, which he was fly enough to get.[44] But not having any ice, we didn't purchase much from him. We much rather preferred his tea and cakes and the company of his pretty daughter than warm beer. After our plunge, we would sit and talk, sipping our tea and idly watching the passers by along the road. The girl [was] untiring in her attention to us, everyone pointing to different articles and naming them in Nippon, asking for its equivalent in English. This caused great merriment on their side.

From where we sat on the straw matting of this inn, or tea-house, we could catch a glimpse of the sea beyond, a silvery strip of quiet sea beyond the mountains. The road wound down to the beach. We were beyond the graven image of Buddha that marked the summit of this mountain road. Truly this stone Buddha must have seemed a God indeed to many a weary rickshaw man, as after a hard pull he reached it from either direction. Then he would heave a sigh of relief as all else was plain sailing for him. The same may also be said of the weary horse or bullock with his driver in the shaft. Also the boy or man whom I often saw along this road hauling a load behind him that would shame a mule, or else pushing along a wheel barrow loaded down. Truly this was Buddha, this little graven God of stone that marked the apex of the mount, and no doubt was placed there by some grateful native.

Kure, Japan

In the Metropolitan Museum of Art in Central Park, New York City, hangs a painting that has always appealed to me more than any other among that costly and superb collection of art. There are paintings there that are worth many times their weight in gold, canvasses by the famous artists of all countries, superb gems that fairly sparkle and glow with color, masterly in draughtsmanship, small bits that are as clear cut as a diamond of the first water,[45] and as costly. Among all this riot of art, I say there is one painting above all others that, had I my choice, I would choose, passing by all others, Meissoniers,[46] Boughews,[47] Corots,[48] Sabigny,[49] Rosseaus,[50] and our own artists' productions. It is called "Broad Acres," and it is broad in every sense of the word. I have stood before that picture so long at times as to attract attention, when gazing around with a start, I would find people looking curiously at the man in Uncle Sam's blue shirt, who seemed engrossed in gazing at this one painting and oblivious to his surroundings. And annoyed at being lost in reveries before this picture. I would move around the galleries only to be irresistibly drawn backward again. It is by the artist "Gay," "Broad Acres"[51] of waving grain, softest greens tipped with golden browns, the wheat fields fast ripening under a glowing sun. In the middle distance a brown farm house, a road that winds past the house and thro' the fields of grain, an old coach lumbering along, just a suggestion of a clump of trees around the small farm house. But the sky! The sky is magnificent, with its soft, fleecy clouds and subtle gradations of color. It is suffused with light and atmosphere. The entire canvas is aglow. It stands out above all others in this particular part of the Museum. The other canvases look brown and dingy beside it. An art critic or connoisseur might pick flaws in it from a purely academic standpoint, but it has that mysterious touch of nature about it, that touch that makes you think that you have seen somewhere just such a spot. You get lost gazing at this canvas and your thoughts turn backward in memory of these same wheat fields, the sun-kissed ripening grain, the little brown farm house, the lumbering old coach, and the clump of shade trees and rippling brook. It is the same. It appeals to every American heart, for it is a typical American landscape. We all retain memories of some such. This picture brings it back possibly to you. You gaze for miles into a painted bit of canvas, forget yourself, and are gazing at the same thing in memory. This is what I call true art, art that appeals to the common herd. It is an American landscape.

The landscape that we gazed at in the early morning, at noon, and at eventide in Kure was as typically Japanese as the above is typically American, and I used to enjoy it might[i]ly. I know I felt like a boy again, and Ken did also. We would gaze and gaze and hardly realize that we were in the country, and we would roll around in the grass, frolic around among bushes and wild creeping vines, and go in swimming to our heart's content. At least twenty years rolled off our shoulders, away from the dreary old prison routine of the big, steel ship with its incessant, wearisome old grind, the eternal discipline, the fault-finding, and abuse. No wonder we appreciated the country and would consider the day as lost if we didn't have our usual ride and swim, and come in, stop at the big, cool spring and dip up a huge bucketful of clear, cold, sparkling water, and fling ourselves down by the side of it with a sigh of contentment, living in the present. No thought of returning to the ship, of the ship's doings crossed our mind.

We got sunburned, scratched up with brambles and rocks, and were sore, but happy. The strangeness of it all, two bluejackets making these junketing trips to the country to get near to nature's heart. Why, it wasn't often we ever got any nearer the country side than some beer garden or other place artificially made for that purpose. Jack generally has to be content with city haunts. Isn't often he has the time to gambol amid green things and under green boughs. But here in Kure he had the chance, but only a few availed themselves of the golden opportunity. Ken and I actually caught a glimpse of a small field of corn, but it is true the rest of the landscape was rice. The trees were in some places curiously twisted and gnarled, grotesque, purely Japanese; the land broken in terraces, mountainous and rocky, the crops wrung from the very rock by patient toil. But things were green, the landscape not like the American one, but purely Eastern, but beautiful in all. Compare the lights and shade on mountain sides, sparkling water beyond a perfect August sky. Why shouldn't we forget our troubles for the time being and be kids again?

Ken and I, feeling the pangs of hunger gnawing at our vitals, made it up that we would buy out all the American or Japanese produce we could get that appealed to our taste. We couldn't appease an appetite that yearned for corn beef and cabbage with queer little Japanese confections that were a sugared disappointment when you crunched them between your teeth. And Nippon *cohee* (tea)[52] is all right, but it can't fill the spot. Ken is noted as a trencherman, but of my own prowess he knew but little. But as we were built on the same general plan of human architecture, being both of extreme elevation, lean, lanky, and above the average height, he could only surmise that I would prove to be a worthy shipmate at the mahogany.

"By gum!" suddenly exclaimed Ken. "I am as hungry as a goat."

"Ditto," quoth I. "Let's buy some old grocery man out, and as you have been telling me how good a 'chef' you are, we will go to the old fellow's and you can cook it."

"All right. I'll go you. But I don't know as one grocery store will have enough."

"Well, lets hit a cold bottle up first, and look around."

We stopped and got a bottle of beer at one of the places we were opposite and bought the ice to put in it.

"We have got to have a big, large fish," said Ken. "And about ten [pounds] of the best steak we can find."

"Do you think half a peck of tomatoes will be enough?"

"Hardly. But we will have to make out with that many. Don't forget the 'spuds,' and plenty of onions."

Kure, Japan

"Bully! How are you on cucumbers? Do they agree with you?"

"You bet! They never touch me. Three of them will be enough." (In Japan they are about a yard long.)

"We will broil the steak with butter and season it as it broils."

"And have French fried [potatoes]."

"And slice the tomatoes and cucumbers."

"And bake the fish until it is nice and flaky."

"Hello, we forgot something!"

"What's that?"

"Why, eggs."

"That's so, by gosh. A dozen apiece ought to do. Make 'em soft boiled for me."

"Make mine sunny side up."

"And——"

"And what? We'll wash it down with about four bottles of Kirin beer and about four more after that."

We got hungry as bears talking about it, and it being well on toward the afternoon, the fierce breakfast that left such a bad taste had disappeared. We told the "rickies" to *hayaco* (hurry up) and were soon in front of the old fellow's place. Dismissing the men, we soon ascertained what the old fellow had in stock. We sent out for more steak, eggs and fish. Ken rolled up his sleeves and prepared to do the "chef" act.

"Gawd bless the day that mother made me do chores around the kitchen. I am going to put my knowledge to good use on this occasion."

He soon had a good, hot charcoal fire going in the old battered-up American range, and the entire family gathered around the "chef" to get pointers on American "chop-a-chop" for future reference. Ken put them all in use. They were all flying around. Even the old fellow, *O-ji-san*, stood by with the pepper and salt, the little *musmee* with the butter, [and] the healthy, husky, Jap kid with a large slab of steak about three feet square.

With a wide flourish, Ken heated the pan and the aroma of a well broiled steak soon permeated the place. If any other hungry bluejacket had passed at that moment, they would have charged our laager [Afrikaans (the Boer language) for "camp"] and it would have been another Spion Kopje. It was the first real, American aroma of cooking that greeted our nostrils in Kure. The steak was done just right, and covered and laid by. I waited with tears in my eyes, nearly famished. Next the fish was baked to a turn. I sliced the tomatoes and cucumber, set the table, sent the girl out for a bunch of flowers, got a white cloth and by the time Ken had completed the omelette, the table was spread in style. The fish was excellent. We finished it all. And the steak was all an epicure would desire.

We were just getting deeply interested when in came a couple of our folks. They sniffed the air and then glanced over toward the table with a hungry glare in their eyes. We thought 'twere better to invite them. And they fell to with such a right good will and proved themselves such mighty trenchermen that it 'twere well for us that we had about twenty minutes start of them. They swore Ken was the best "chef" in Japan. And Ken responded modestly but with the consciousness of a duty well done. I watched him swell up near to bursting, but whether from the flattery or from the vast quantity of food he had devoured, I couldn't tell. But any way, he fell to bragging of what he could do if he had the material. I don't know whether he meant in the eating line, or as a chef. Everything was excellent, and hunger proved the best of sauces. Everything disappeared; nothing was left, excepting a few pieces of broken bread. And with a deep sigh of thanksgiving, we settled back to discuss [over] a few cold bottles and a cigar, full to repletion.

"I care not what happens now. I have dined. I can last until we have to go aboard ship."

"I thought you were laying in sea stores," said Ken, so full he could hardly talk.

It was a pretty even thing between us. As for the other fellows, they weren't considered on account of not starting with us. But we all had enough. The bill for the raw material amount[ed] to $3.10. *O-ji-san*, I think, charged us for the privilege of cooking it. Nothing like a Jap for holding onto coin and making a sharp bargain.

After that, Ken was in demand as a cook. The old man made him cook for the other fellows when they came in. But Ken soon tired of the job and proved indifferent. It was all right cooking for only us two, when we were to eat it, spurred on as it were by anticipation. That was the best meal we got in Kure, and although Ken did the "chef" act afterwards, it was with but indifferent success, and I "joshed" him about it, as being an unreliable cook, and swore by all the Gods of Japan that he was drunk, which he indignantly denied. And [he] reiterated by all that was holy, that [there was] not another cook in Japan, or the Far East for that matter, that could beat him at any old kind of cooking, providing that he had the provisions, and nothing could shake him from the firm stand he took. And after imbibing a few more bottles, we let it go at that, and to please him, we fully concurred with his view, which completely mollified him.

Again back to the Yoshiwara, to while away another night. This was the liveliest place in Kure at night. All kinds of noises rent the air: the tinkling of *koto*[53] and *samisen*,[54] the noise of some Japanese street fakir, of which there are not a few in Japan. [There were queer] little shooting galleries where you use an air rifle and get a prize according to the score you make. I made a couple bulls-eyes and was presented with two bottles of lemonade. Another attraction was a ball that rolled down an inclined spiral and through the doors of a small model European house. This being too tame, we didn't patronize it. We patronized the phonograph man and listened to a few Japanese airs of which we knew nothing. We also grasped a huge wooden maul and tried to smash the ball up to a certain mark, but didn't make much of a success at it. There is quite a knack in striking the wooden peg squarely in order to score high, and although I determined to do or die, spitting on my hands and grasping the maul and swelling up until I was nigh to bursting, and brought it down with a tremendous force, still the little joker failed to bob up over a couple feet, much to the amusement of a large crowd of Japs who had assembled to see the American knock that ball so high it would never come back. I tried again and must have hit it squarely with not half the force and that ball scored the highest of all, and the Japs expressed great admiration for my prowess. I let it go at that. I didn't try again. I couldn't spoil that last score with another try, so I rested upon my laurels.

The streets of this Yoshiwara at nights are filled with Japanese bluejackets, and they make an awful howl when under the influence of sake. It is then that they show their Malay blood. They tried our patience several times by grasping us as they intended good naturedly, and trying to get us to go with them. This grew monotonous after a while, and we shoved them off as quickly as we could. To hear one of these Jap sailors making a noise when drunk, you would think someone was running a "muck,"[55] but there is more noise than harm in them. It is a way they have.

We had several "geisha" girls to sing for us, and altho' we didn't "savvy" it, still it was entertainment to watch the singer if she happened to be pretty, which was nearly always the rule. And we applauded generously and looked wise as owls not to hurt the poor little singer's sensibilities or professional pride. On one occasion, a group of three—two men and one girl—gave an exhibition. The girl took the part of the forlorn maiden, and stood off at one corner of the room. One of the men made an impassioned appeal in the usual Japanese sing-song way, accompanied by the other one on the *samisen*. He made some very eloquent gestures and the two of them indulged in one of the most extravagant sword-plays I have witnessed. The way they postured and made sheep-eyes at the girl and clashed their rusty looking *katana*[56] together would arouse a pang of envy to the breast of the worst "ham" that ever strutted along the "Rialto."

Thro' it all, the girl remained unmoved and didn't seem to favor either adorer. It all ended peacefully, however, and the two warriors returned their swords to their scabbards and pulled their two small black mustachios off and put them away for future reference. Then again, we had three men. One did the sword act, one sang, and the other played the *samisen*. The one with the sword acted the words and deeds of the verse, and the way he lopped off heads, thrust, parried, and cut his way thro' the enemy was fierce. Once, after a most magnificent spurt, he held up both hands to show how many "bit the dust." Then, wiping off imaginary blood from the blade, [he] returned it to its scabbard with the most elaborate gestures. He could handle the blade to perfection, and we got tired following the whirling blade with our eyes.

From other parts of the Yoshiwara would come the refrain, *"John Keno, John Keno, Nagasaki, Yokohama, Kobe man, hoi, hoi, hoi."*[57] Then a burst of laughter. The sound of *samisen* and *koto* is very pleasant, but then seems to our untrained ear to be the same strain repeated continually. It may be there are fine notes too fine for our senses to grasp that we know nothing about in Japanese or Chinese music. As it is, every tune is the same to us. Our music would seem meaningless to them also.

A Sailor's Log

And so we whiled away our five days leave, taking our regular ride for our daily swim. All to[o] quickly the time rolled around. Some of the fellows who had went to Hiroshima nine miles below, commenced to come back by two and threes. The time was drawing to a close, when, like boys returning to school from a vacation, we should return to the ship.

The uniform ashore just about this time was blue, and hot enough and uncomfortable enough it was. Of course, the crowd that came down from Hiroshima had left their kimonos and other cool rigs behind. We still had ours and had them on up to the last two hours before returning to the ship. About the coolest costume we ran across on any of our people consisted of a big straw hat, a paper umbrella, or *kasa*, and a neckerchief. A pair of straw sandals completed this unique full dress. It didn't attract any comment or attention in Kure. You go as you pleased in this part of Japan. If you don't want to wear clothing here, why, you go without. Of course, meeting each other this night before going aboard, we had a regular sailors' uproaring time of it. It became a common drinking bout and soon the old fellow's place was filled with a crowd of noisy, jolly bluejackets, but it ended in no fighting, the *Oregon*'s crew being the best natured crew I have ever seen ashore. It was all noisy jollity. Songs were the order of the night, and it was kept up until morning.

Then the fact stared us in the face that our time was up at 1:00 P.M., and with sober faces we doffed [our] outing rigs and donned the blue. The fun was over, but a good five days it was, and [it] ended all too quickly. Putting the finishing touches on our toilets, we left our vacation clothing to the old man [in] a big heap. We drank all the cool beer he had in stock, and at the last moment, just as we were preparing to leave, we heard an uproar up the street. It happened to be about fifty [bluejackets], all marching, each man armed with a paper parasol, and all singing, coming down the line. Of course, we had to tail on behind, and bidding good bye to Ojisan and his *Okamisan* and the two youngsters, we hustled out and marched down with the crowd almost to the navy yard gate. But we didn't go in as it lacked over an hour of the time. A few of us dropped out and had a few more cool ones, and at last we could delay no longer, so the three of us strolled along and came over the gangway, [and] saluted. "Returning from liberty, sir." We were marked in "O.T.,"[58] clean and sober." It was just one o'clock.

Of course, the bolo-man on watch sent for us all to turn to. I didn't go myself. I couldn't have went very easily. What I wanted was a good sleep, and as soon as I changed my clothes and got in dungarees, I crawled off and stowed myself away, and as luck had it, he didn't need my services very much below. But the majority of the men had to turn to. Our troubles was on, you see, from the very moment we passed the gangway, and we were "hounded around."

The Japs had made rapid progress with the patch, and a good job they were making of it. The *Oregon* bid fair to be herself once more. At last the day came and the dock was floated [flooded]. We were to go out, but the ship still leaked. (The day we came aboard, the ship settled forward and sprung the angle iron and the longitudinal bulkheads in the fire-room considerably.) The dock had to be pumped out again,

Kure, Japan

and it was a week later that we made the next attempt, [on] Tuesday evening at about 6 P.M. Aug. 21st [1900]. We found when the dock was floated that all was well. We were towed out in the stream, where a few extra touches were made [and] more cement placed in the double-bottom compartments. After anchoring in the stream, all liberty was stopped, but whilst in dock we went in parts, first-class men every fourth day, and several good times we saw on these night liberties. The prices of beer, food, and other commodities were reduced in proportion as the money grew scarce. Beer from 40 cts was reduced to 25 cts., etc. The *Oregon* gold-mine had run out. Every man, almost, had spent his two months' pay.

Of course, the old gang jumped ship. The French [unauthorized] liberty party would leave promptly at about dark, and any old time on Sunday after quarters. They would go without any money to speak of, but always continued to have a good time. They always returned "slopped up" at all events. Jacky forward must have his beer when he can get it, the same as the gentlemen aft, who make an awful howl if they have to go without. "Beer good for officer, no good for men. Mr. [John D.] Long, he savvy."[59]

The brig was full of ship jumpers and all of them were mulcted of two months' samoleons of the realm and sentenced to confinement in double-irons, full ration every third day, etc., etc. Seven men of the engineers division ran away in Kure. I couldn't blame them. I felt like doing so myself, for never in my previous naval career did I meet with such abuse. We had to work at least an average of fourteen hours per day and the rest you were being continually disturbed. I don't know the cause of this. The ship itself is all right, but I shall always have a horror of the *Oregon*. I blame it to the bad management of the "bolo-men." I never on any ship beheld such a discontented force below. The chief himself had no earthly use for any of his men. [He regarded] us all as rogues. [He never] liked to see any of us standing around, even if we had just came off watch. He would have us "turned to" again at something. My station, as I have said before, was the after 13" hydraulic pump room. After coming off watch (this was after we left the dry dock), I would have to go below and put pressure on the turrets or ammunition hoist. There I would stay for four hours. This was a continual happening and I used to curse the day I ever shipped over [reenlisted], and vow to myself if Providence would ever let me get clear with clean heels this time, the "bolo-men" would never get a chance at me again.[60]

We worked Sundays, Saturday afternoons and all the time. Graft. Nothing but graft.[61] Saturday evening, clean bags and hammocks were served to us in time we should have had to ourselves. We didn't even have a chance to write a letter or scrub a piece of clothing, or do any mending. Nothing for ourselves. An oiler with nearly nine years service in told me, "Nothing they can do can square things with me. If they would let me live in clover the next ten months I have to do, they could never make me forget the treatment I have received on this ship."

One instance, for an example: the men had been painting bilges, scraping and scaling, of course, and the plates were being screwed down after being inspected, of course, it being nearly knocking off time. The bolo-man on watch waited until the last screw was secured and then made them take them all up again and do part of the work over. Whenever the auxiliary watch list should have been put up Saturday evenings, it was kept back so the men couldn't tell who were going on watch, and being "turned to" almost every Saturday evening, they had to muster and work with the rest, and when their names came out for the watch, they had to put their watch in also. This was a favorite trick to get more work from the men. As far as the work done by the men was concerned, they would stay below and [do] it, but they were disheartened, disgusted, and horribly sick of it all. If this treatment of the men had taken place in the States, they couldn't have mustered enough men to man a "handy billy."

One of the "bolo-men" had charge of the fire-rooms, and whenever the day's duty would fall to his lot, he would always take one [man] from my station and make me work on my own, in the fire-room. There are six water-tenders in the *Oregon*. Four of them have a boiler apiece, with pumps and fire-rooms, etc., for their cleaning stations. Of course, they each have a number of men to help them. Two water-tenders have a pump room apiece, forward and after hydraulic. These pump rooms are kept clean by the water-tender alone, with no help. They are a big station. Of course, all cleaning stations extend from the double bottom to the deck above. These hydraulic stations are the largest stations in the *Oregon* for any one man to keep clean and look after. You can't neglect them. It was always the custom to let the water-tenders strictly alone on these stations, except when standing watch every other week. This gentleman, I fancy, never liked my style, which feeling on his part I fully reciprocated, atho' I always obeyed with alacrity any order and made no demur, except to myself, no matter what I thought. One day, Mr. Bolo told me to "go out in no. 6 thwart-ship bunker and scale and paint that secondary drain pipe and place the cover over it."

Now, this was a coal passer's job and was given me to humiliate me. I said nothing at the time, being too full for utterance. He continued, "I will send you a man to help you." I went, [and] he sent the man. I was talking to another water-tender about the job.

"Did you ever do anything to——?"

"Not to my knowledge," I replied. "At any rate, I am going to see the chief. It won't do any good, I know, but I'll see him anyhow."

The bolo-man came out just then. "Did you get that man?"

"Yes, sir," I replied. "But one moment. Do I understand you to say that I must scrape and scale that pipe myself in person?"

"Did you get that man?"

"Yes. The man part is alright, but do I do that pipe myself? That's what I want to know."

He wouldn't tell me definitely whether he wanted me to do it personally or not. At any rate, I said to him, "I'll see the chief about it."

"Go up and see him now," he retorted, "and when you have seen him, hurry down and resume work on the pipe."

Kure, Japan

I laughed, a bitter one it was, tho'. "I'll see him anyway and have some sort of an understanding. I know I'll have to do the work tho." Going up on deck I found the chief about to come below, and accosted him at the machine shop door leading to the engine room hatch.

"Chief, I would like to speak to you one moment." He assented with a silent nod. "Mr. H[ammond][62] has taken me from my work on my station and has put me to scraping and painting the secondary drain pipe line through no. 6 port thwart-ship bunker. I want to ask you if you want me to do that kind of work?"

"What is your rate?" he questioned.

"Water-tender, sir."

"Well, the reason you are put to doing that kind of work is because you do not understand a water-tender's duties thoroughly. You know you couldn't grind in a valve and do some other work that was asked of you the other day, and you have to be put at something you could do."

At this, I nearly fainted. "Sir! You have evidently gotten me confused with some other man. Nobody in this ship has asked or ordered me to grind in any valves, or asked me to do anything that I haven't done a marine,"[63] I exclaimed. "[I] can grind in any valve you have in the ship. Another thing, chief, I didn't come to the *Oregon* to learn to tend water. This is the easiest and simplest ship I have ever been on to tend water in. My station is the after 13" pumps, and if there is any painting and scaling to be done, the bilges there need it badly. All I want to know is do you want me to neglect my station to do a job that the lowest rated man in the force can do?"

At this he asked my name. I told him, and he looked wise and considered for a moment. "Well, go and do the job in the bunker. It is more important at present than your station, and I will look into the matter later."

That was all the satisfaction I rec'd. I knew that I would have to obey the bolo-man. The chief, of course, would uphold them. That was necessary for discipline. But I wasn't so much disturbed by this party afterwards. The chief had been willing enough until I mentioned my name, to throw up another man's shortcomings. The same bolo-man had told the chief about the water-tender who the day before, when told to grind in his Kingston valve, had made a kick, telling the bolo that it was a machinist's duty to grind in all valves and that he knew practically nothing about it and that if he ground it in, he wouldn't be responsible for it if it leaked, etc., etc. The water tender was right. It was a machinist's work, and is done by machinists in all ships. But it doesn't require any ability to do it. The water-tender made the kick on the principle that it wasn't his work, that if he started in on that kind of work they would find more for him to do and keep him at it. But the sneaky "bolo-man" didn't lose any time injuring him by carrying a big tale to the chief detrimental to this water tender.

CHAPTER FIVE

Woosung, China

The *Oregon* left Kure about 6:00 A.M. Wednesday August 29th [1900]. We had coaled up with 300 tons of Takas[h]ima coal and steamed with three boilers. Takashima coal is like oil. The smoke that pours from the stacks is as heavy and thick as if it came from a burning tar or pitch vat. It makes great steam if [the fire is] kept clean, but you have got to clean it every watch. With this coal the *Oregon* made 87 turns for over an hour, with three boilers. We reached the Straits and town of Shimonoseki about dark. All day long we had gazed at the beautiful scenery of the Inland Sea. We had stopped, slowed down, and changed our course to test compasses in the afternoon.[1] The run was a quick one. We arrived at Nagasaki at about 10 A.M. the next morning. Before leaving Kure, a collection was taken up to endow a ward in the navy yard hospital, and a considerable sum was amassed.

I was glad to see old Nagasaki again, but didn't hope for any liberty as we had orders to coal and provision and proceed to Woosung, and we had no hopes in the order being revoked. My division brought her in on the 8 to 12 watch. Coming off at twelve, I went up to my dinner. Looking around, I espied Kenzo come aboard for washing. He didn't see me until I gave him a call and then he looked as if he couldn't believe his eyes. However, it didn't take him long to recognize me thro' the grime and coal dust, and I thought he would never let go of my hand. "O-ji-ji?" was his first question. I told him I last heard of him on the *Petrel* at Manila. I had lots of questions to fire at him, told him to tell 'em all that I was here on the *Oregon*, to tell Moriya and little Sunawa. "Yes, yes. Me speak. Me tell everybody. Vely glad. When you come shore?"

"No can tell, Kenzo. Think we leave in one, two, three days. No can tell." I scurried up the fellows and he carried away a load of washing that a pack mule would stagger under. I was glad to see Kenzo and he I, but how much more pleased I would have been to set foot on the beach, to get ashore and visit my many good friends in Nagasaki. I gazed longingly at the town, or at least up the bay toward it. We were anchored far down the stream. We could see that the skipper wanted to get out of here as quickly as possible. I should judge he wanted to get to Woosong before an order could intercept him.² We had been expecting orders to proceed to 'Frisco. The ship was in a bad condition, badly strained, and was in no condition to use her big guns, but we had to take it as it came. We could look toward Nagasaki, but we may just as well have been in the heart of the Sahara as far as [any] prospect of getting ashore was concerned. That is the service. Once at Baltimore, while on the *Prairie* engaged in taking out Naval Reserves, I could look at the shore and the city, but as far as getting ashore and visiting my people, I might as well have been at sea.

Kenzo told me the next day, "Sunawa like see you belly much. She glad you here. Bimeby, you come shore."

But I only answered with a mournful shake of the head. "No use, old man. Can't be did."

While in Nagasaki, the *Corunna,* U.S. transport, came out and as she passed us, the regiment gave us three cheers and their band struck up some gay tune that reminded us of home. We manned the rail and returned it with a vim. I don't know where these soldiers were going, whether to Manila or China. We know nothing out here. The folk at home are better posted than we who are on the scene. Why, I had to wait for a two months old paper before I could find the name of the place we went ashore in, Pinnacle Rock, Straits of Pe.chi.li [Pechili] near How Ke [How Ki] light, forty miles from Chefoo.³

I was hoping against hope that something would intervene so as to prolong our stay at Nagasaki, but it was not to be. At first, it was reported that we were going to get under way at dawn Sunday morning. The coaling was finished by Sat[urday] night. We took aboard a thousand tons, and all stores, excepting fresh provisions, were aboard. Fresh provisions were to be taken for two days' rations. They were brought aboard Sunday afternoon. Kenzo brought all our clothing back Sunday morning. All did not have money to pay him [as w]e were waiting for monthly money then. I told Kenzo I would collect the balance due him and send it by mail from Woosong. To this he was satisfied, as he knew he could trust me. Even the messes hadn't all paid up, and we had no money to lay in stores, but as the distance to Woosong was only a short run, it was best under the circumstances not to serve out monthly money in Japanese yens. We would only have the trouble [of] getting rid of them at Woosong at a discount. You lose on a Mexican dollar in both Japan & China. In Japan you can only get 90 cents Jap for one, sometimes only 85 cts [sen]. Provisions were reported cheaper at Woosong than at Nagasaki. All Chinese ports are free ports and there are no exorbitant duties to pay, as in Japan where subjects, even sampan & rickshaw men, are taxed. No calling is exempt from taxation. They are striving to maintain a large army & navy away in excess of their size and population.

I gave Kenzo two envelopes addressed to me at Woosong so he could return an answer letting me know if he received the money.

Being busy all day Sunday, there was no quarters. But the Ripper sprung them on us at about 3:10 Sunday evening, when we least expected it, the first time I have ever seen Sunday quarters in the evening since I have been a bluejacket, so you can see we can always learn.

We got under way about 5:45 A.M., Monday morning Sept. 3rd on my watch, the 3rd section having the 4 to 8. Getting clear of the harbor, full speed ahead with the three boilers, bowling along about 13 knots, a slight sea running. We were making about 86 or 87 revolutions, the skipper never being satisfied unless tearing along at torpedo boat speed. The *Oregon* can make good time after the four years and over she has been in commission and the vast amount of sea she has covered in that time, and the hardship she has endured. But three boilers wasn't fast enough, and the other one was lit and hooked on. It looked squally and I suppose the skipper feared bad weather and wished to make all haste. But men-o-war are always in a hurry. There was some tall swearing done by the water tenders of the 2nd division, being relieved by us at four. They had no sooner planted themselves for a snooze on their mats when they were hustled out by the messenger to put [hydraulic] pressure on the 13" turrets. The air was sulphurous for a while, but this is a common occurrence on this ship. Water-tenders on the *Oregon* can always look for eight hours on and four off instead of vice-versa. When you are second relief you are always available for the hydraulic pumps. The only thing you can do is to curse. Or run away.

The big, modern steel battle ship with its five and six hundred inhabitants has its petty jealousies and ambitions and competition as well as any other large establishment. In this run to Woosung, the bolo-men were striving mightily to get ahead of one another in revolutions. The captain desired to make a record run from Nagasaki to Woosung, and he was in a fair way to accomplish it. We were squeezed for the last drop of blood for the advantage of these fellows. Every watch we had to clean every fire and still for all that were making all the way from ninety to ninety-six and -seven revolutions. I must say the third section done its part well on this run and averaged more than the other two divisions. After the fourth kettle [boiler] was hooked up, the second section got all the best of it as this boiler was clean thro'out. They made as high as ninety seven turns. We came on and the steam was on the drop. Cleaning fires, the steam dropped to 100 lbs. We only made 90 [turns] that first hour. The B.M. of the watch then came out to make his usual howl. He made it. He knew as much about a fire as a pig would. Two years before he was selling ribbon and yelling "cash" at the top of a high soprano voice. Did the steam go up? Echo answers, "Nay, Nay Pauline," it did not. It went down. This nearly drove him insane. To think that the other bolo-man should make more revolutions than he. After a while, when he had retired to the engine rooms, the steam arose to about 120. He opened up. We made 94 that hour. The next hour was the hour for hoisting ashes. Then, of course, the men couldn't do their fires justice. The *Oregon*'s ash hoisting gear is one of the worst features on her, the worst I have ever seen. It takes time to hoist 60 or 70 buckets of ashes. Out came Chauncey again.

"What in the devil is the matter with that steam, W[ilson]?" He appeared real agitated.

Woosung, China

"Well, I'll tell you. The matter with the steam is we are hoisting ashes in the first place. In the second place, the steam will be lower than it is at present. I have been carrying low water [i.e., a low level in the boiler sight glass] all the watch to help you out with your revolutions. I will have to pump up for my relief, so he can have a chance to slow down his pumps while he cleans fires. In the next place, the boilers are getting dirty [the watertubes are being coated with soot, interfering with heat transfer]. The watch coming on will not average as much as us."

At this he went away. We made an excellent run and average for the four hours, so much so that an ensign who had the bridge and must have had a bet on, sent the machinists, oilers and the water-tender each a bottle of beer with his regards. I never thought Asahi beer could taste as good. It was nectar of the Gods, ice cold. I pulled the cork out and never took the bottle away from my lips until it was drained.

My words proved true. The watch that relieved us never came near our mark at all. At twelve all hands went to general quarters. I rushed to the after pump room as I was still second relief until twelve m[idnight]. There was just 85 lbs of steam on the gauge and that, too, for a relief coming on. We left them 115 lbs. I couldn't start both pumps on account of lack of steam. The next watch done better. The ship came to a full stop for 25 minutes on account of an accident to the steam steering gear. This gave the watch a start with the steam and helped them out while blowing tubes. They managed to knock out 95 turns with a start of 153 lbs of steam. Left us 125 at 4 A.M. and the third section made a fine run again, ahead of all. I was troubled with firemen's cramp during the night, but on any stiff watches you often get these from drinking too much water.

About as cruel a deed as I have saw done was the placing of four prisoners who had terms of thirty days to do in solitary and irons. They were placed in two magazines over the boilers in a temperature of about 125° or 130°. It was fully two hours before they were ordered out of these ovens. Much more time would have driven them mad, especially one whose constitution at the best wasn't very rugged. This was as asinine and criminally careless an action as was ever done in the navy. My section was composed of a number of prisoners awaiting their turn at the brig. They were sentenced to terms in the brig of from 15 to 30 days in double irons, loss of pay from 1 month to three, beside extra police duties and, of course, reduced to fourth class [liberty status]. All this for jumping ship, breaking liberty, and other offenses heinous in the eyes of the naval officials.

The poor, imbecile "Ripper" ramped and fumed along the decks one morning and we watched him furtively, wondering who would be the unfortunate devil he would jump on first. He contented himself with an occasional explosion of "Filthy! Filthy!" while inspecting the berth deck. We watch[ed] him. Just as he passed inside the compartment containing the prisoners, he swelled up and grew as red in the face as a pompous turkey gobbler, and the roar that came from him caused all the bolomen and middies within hearing distance to crawl beneath their bunks in affright. I don't know what aroused his ire, perhaps a prisoner was lying down when he came thro' and did not see the august presence of His Imperial Jiglets, the Grand Vizier of the *Oregon*. The noise he made drowned the noise of the engines. After heartily cursing all hands within reach, he collapsed and retired to the sacred precincts of his den, where about a dozen good, stiff "horns" considerably mollified him. "Here comes the Ripper," is generally passed along the line, and people dive out of the way as if they were guilty of some misdemeanor and he was a policemen. Poor old stiff. Your kind are rapidly dying out. Poor, useless, abusive, old curmudgeon.

We dropped anchor off Woosung light about 2:30 P.M. Sept. 4th, and in the morning watch got under way about 7 A.M. and ran out to sea for target practice with the big guns. So, after all our speed, we laid over a full night without going in to Woosung and coming to anchor with the rest of the ships. I think it was an order from the Admiral that sent us out for target practice, for we were signaled from the lighthouse and a whale boat of ours shoved off and returned with some order.

Sept. 5th was a regular *Oregon* day with all hands, especially below in the "black gang." I went on watch at 4 A.M., came off at 8 A.M., had breakfast, went below as second relief and had pressure on the turrets and ammunition hoists at 9:30, after quarters. Staid there until 12 m[eridian (noon)] when I was relieved by the watertender coming off watch. I went to dinner [then] went below again as first relief at general quarters and tended water on C boiler from No. 5 fire room (or would have tended water if that boiler had been steaming, but at any rate, had to remain there at my station). Left there at 3:30 for my supper. Went below on watch at 4. Came off at eight. That constitutes 16 hours [of] good, hot and hard duty, and at night was woke up by the rain beating down on me thro' the hatch near which I was asleep on my mat. It beat down on me and run under my mat in little rivulets and streams, so I had to hustle out of that, and it took me half an hour to find another place to "flop."

This is the general routine of the *Oregon*. What is it, bad management that makes so much work for us to do, or are our ships undermanned? I know that I have worked harder and longer hours in the service than any man would have to work ashore. A man, to earn a living, wouldn't have to work sixteen hours per day, and then look forward to a drill at midnight. No wonder the crew of the *Oregon* has a horror of her. It isn't the ship, but whenever the *Oregon*'s name is mentioned, it will cause a shudder of disgust to the man who was aboard her from the time she left Hong Kong.

We ran out to sea, and instead of launching a target, the skipper used a rocky island for one. We steamed past at good speed and [maneuvered], firing as we ran, using 8", 13" and 6 pdr [pounder]. On the whole it was the most disgraceful exhibition of marksmanship I have yet seen in the Navy. Shell struck the water a mile short and ricocheted over the island. I don't remember seeing one good shot. A whole island to fire at, half a mile in length, and a hundred feet high. Evidently, the skipper has a grudge against all rocks in Chinese waters. It's the first time I have ever saw anything of the kind used for a target. I thought at first they were bombarding it, and expected to see

Woosung, China

the "Ripper" land with a party and hoist the Stars & Stripes and take possession in the name of our glorious republic. It would have been practice, anyhow. He could have addressed an imaginary conquered people and abused them to his heart's content.

After expending the ammunition and shell, we steamed back as hard as we could drive the *Oregon* to our former position, where we came to an anchorage once more. Under way again at 8 A.M. the following morning for more practice, [this time] with the secondary battery.

Instead of having secondary battery target practice, they swung ship all day; that is, maneuvered the *Oregon* in every conceivable form, circling and swinging from port and starboard. It kept the men at the throttle jumping around like monkeys on a hot griddle. Full ahead starboard engine. Full astern port, etc., etc., and nobly does this ship answer her helm. She is a magnificent piece of mechanism, the one battleship without a peer in the world. But still.... Well, one can't be content where one is ill-treated and abused. Another thing, we got tired of lying off Woosung. We wanted to get in and get something to eat, to draw money and fix up our mess. We left Nagasaki without any stores of any kind and before we reached here we were even out of salt, and salt and pepper are not issued by the paymaster. The caterer asked about some pickles for the mess, but was told they were reserved for the officers. Everything is reserved for the officers, especially if it happens to be a prime article, and these pickles were very good, some we got in Nagasaki.

It was like some of the stores I mentioned about on the *New Orleans:* sliced ham, etc. These articles of food struck the officer fully and they corralled the whole cheese. All officers' rations are commuted [received as cash rather than kind], and they get their 30 cts per day, the same as any of the common herd, even the Admiral is only allowed $9.00 per month ration. But, of course, they can purchase any stores from the pay department. They use the ice machine turned with full pressure upon the cold storage room, cooling the beer for the "gentlemen aft." "The gentlemen aft" have to have their beer, and they have to have it cold, or else a roar would arise that would jar the whole of China. Right here I will say that the navy is no place for an American boy or man who has any pride or manhood about him. The only place for an American is on the quarterdeck. And you have got to come thro' the Academy. If you don't, you will be made to feel your position and your social inferiority. There are a number of "Mustang" officers [commissioned from enlisted service] in the service that can vouch for the truth of this statement, Mustangs high in command, and generally they are the best officers, for having been slighted and snubbed and made to feel a sort of ostracism on account of not being Academicians, they are more just and kindly disposed toward the ship's company and are stern disciplinarians toward the officers under them. It is only when they attain command that they can square themselves for past slights.[4]

The waters of the Yang-tse-kiang and the Woosung rivers rush with tremendous force far out to sea. We lay twenty miles from Woosung, and the waters around us were of a dirty yellow, muddy color part of the time, and the water is brackish only this far out at sea. We were waiting for the neap tide.[5] [We] expected to cross the bar on Sunday, the ninth of Sept[ember]. Friday, the *City of Pekin* crossed our stern and hove to about five hundred yards off our port bow. She was bound for Shanghai, and she lay there until about 7:30 when she went in. We boarded her for mail, but she had none aboard for us, excepting a few papers. I believe they brought news of more Chinese troubles. That the uprising was general thro' out China, a well organized movement. The rumor was that old Li Hung Chang had thrown off his cloak of diplomacy and stood revealed in his true colors, a Chinaman of the Chinese, which I consider well of the old sinner.[6] Under the name and cloak of protecting our American subjects and interests, we are trying to accumulate more territory. Having broken the Constitution of the United States in Porto Rico and the Philippines, not to speak of Guam, and New Jersey,[7] we are becoming rapidly as rapacious and greedy as the mother country (or step mother country), "Bloomin Hold Hingland."

~ ~ ~

We think a great deal of our missionaries and their good work in carrying a religion nineteen hundred years old to a nation that was civilized when we were swinging by our tails and chasing each other with a large stone ax in the neighborly fashion of Primordial days. Just about two hundred years ago in the most intellectual centre of America, Massachusetts, they were burning people for witchcraft. They are doing it yet in some parts of our own *civilized* country. Why not save some souls at home? It is true we have plenty of missionaries at home, but there is yet room for all these and more that are strolling around Japan, China, India, and other far-off countries. But a missionary don't see as much on the "home station" and have so good a time as he does on the "Asiatic station," where women are cheap and service of all kinds for the asking.

Yes, weighing it impartially, if I were a missionary, I would prefer the "foreign station." My, what a nice time I could have. When I came back on a visit to the home country, with a long, sanctimonious phisog, I could tell of the good work, how many converts I had made. I could interest my audience by descriptions of the habits, customs, and scenery of the country. The cozy home I had in some lovely spot waited upon by hand-maidens of easy virtue, every luxury of good living, wines and liquors, donations of neighbors, having my own "rickshawman," and sampan man, all this for a "gift o' gab" that would hardly obtain me a livelihood peddling corn salve on some street corner [in the United States]. I would forget to mention this last, of course, and when in the end of my discourse I would state that I was only home for a short time, had been recalled on some business matter, and was going out once more to labor in the vineyard, and there was still work for a man to do and I felt that my life would fail to be complete until I had brought more souls, etc.

The credulous "yaps" and "yahoos" that know nothing of the true state of affairs would murmur and purr among their dainty selves, "What a dear, good man, Brother

Woosung, China

Congame must be, and how devoted and in love with his work among those horrid Japanese and Chinese. Only think, he is going to leave dear America, to leave home and friends to live among those queer people. How devoted, poor soul, and with his talents he might do anything in America." And they knit him numberless socks, embroider numerous slippers, wish him God speed upon his long, weary(?) journey.

If they could only see him in the sacred precinct of his cabin, with his feet at an angle of forty-five degrees about his head, with a large jug of old Cyrus Noble, or Old Crow, reading one of Zola's latest, or a novel by Albert Ross,[8] they would change their opinion. "Yes, he could do anything in America with his talents." He is doing them right along, but his talents, I don't know so much about them. He may have the ability to back a hod of mortar up a ladder. All this twaddle about "poor, dear missionaries in foreign lands" makes me weary. It makes me weary even to write about it. In fact, I am so overcome that I will have to get out my mat and sleep it off. "These 'yere misshunaries ain't all Father Damiens and John Stornes, not be a bag of beans." W'ot'ell. Just forget his salary and watch the large, voluminous howl that rends the midnight air. You would think that some irate parent were beating his hopeful with a bed slat.

~~~

The battle-ship *Indiana* went into commission just about five years ago from the date of this writing. I was one of the fortunate, or unfortunate, "rookies" that made up her crew. She lay in the Delaware abreast of League Island. I had just shipped as a coal passer a fortnight previous, in company of hundreds of others, upon the receiving ship *Vermont*, duly examined and passed by the doctor, was sworn in and became a cog in the mechanism of Uncle Sam's Navy. I don't like to look back on those days. They weren't pleasant by any means. I, with a number of others, w[as] sent below to report to the Yeoman for our outfits. The Yeoman, we found, was quite a nice sort of a chap, and evinced a fatherly interest in us, so much so that he palmed off the bummest shop-worn goods that he had in stock. They at any rate were very dear, that first bag of clothes. We being of the greenest as far as the navy was concerned, allowed him to palm off on us articles that were not required. They do this to all "rooks," the object, profit or "comshur"[9] for the Yeoman and his assistant, "Jack of the Dust."[10]

The outfit secured, we were taken over to the bath house and after a bath, donned our sailor "togs." The clothing we wore was taken charge of by a nice, old man who had us in tow. This was another source of revenue for this old "stiff" [hobo, or tramp]. After getting in uniform we reported back to the "officer of the deck" and were told to go above with the rest of the men on the spar deck, which we did. I had no sooner struck there than a petty officer put me to work "teasing out canvas" to make "swabs." He sighted me for the very newest "rookie."

At "mess gear" we formed in line on the deck, and at the command, filed over the gangway past the officer, but once past him, we lost all discipline and order, and the flying wedge that shot down those ladders would do credit to a Yale-Princeton game.

The receiving ship at New York, USRS *Vermont*, had been laid down as a 74-gun ship-of-the-line in 1818. Rigged to accommodate large numbers of sailors, by 1895 it had a decidedly arklike appearance. Navy Historical Foundation.

The wild charge on the tables in order not to get left was of the fiercest kind. On the whole, the entire push were good-natured enough about the food set before us. [It] was of good enough quality, but insufficient quantity. That accounted for the rush. Pandemonium reigned. Yells and curses were plentiful. You got down the ladder without getting crushed. You couldn't fall in such a jam.

You sighted a place only to reach there and find it taken. Finally, on your first attempt you picked up a plate here, a cup there, and knife and fork elsewhere. Then you went for your food, only to find it all gone, that is, the choicest of it. You couldn't get enough to eat on your first day or so, but gradually you didn't hesitate about a point of etiquette, and you got as proficient in sparring for your rations as any old "shell back."[11] If there was pie at the places at table, or apples, you grabbed up anybody's you came across. After a while you learned to take a sneak away from such jobs as swabbing or squeejeeing down the deck, scrubbing paint work, and other "guardo" work.[12] Of course, if you were listed in a working party, you had to muster and go with them. I was always selected for most working parties. My first attempt a[t] swinging a hammock was on someone's hook; you always are, you know. I was hustled here and there and finally secured a billet that nobody would have, right under some hot steam pipes.

Woosung, China

I was heartily sick of the navy in those first few weeks, but I got so I could hold my end up with the best of 'em. I never got left at table and always secured a good swinging billet for my hammock. Always secured a deck bucket and had a good wash as soon as an old hand. I was wishing and always saying to my mate, as he also to me, "I will be all right when we are out of this beastly hole and settled down on the *Indiana*."

Finally, the day came. We were read off in the draft for the *Indiana* the evening before we left. Great packing of bags and making ready. It took me over two hours to get everything secured. I have done so several times since in about 15 min[utes'] notice. Next morning, most of us "rookies" were up bright and early, afraid we would get left. The old hands slept in until the last moment. Finally, the word was passed to "lay below all the *Indiana* draft." On[to] the main deck we filed and as our names were called, passed aboard the tug with our bag and hammock. The tug carried us to Jersey City, thence a special train to League Island[13] over the P.R.R.[14] We got into busses and were taken down to the yard, and on a lighter to the *Indiana*.

～～～

On the *Vermont* with us also in the draft for the biggest battleship and first one of the navy was a young fellow by name, let's say Quinn, in absence of his right one. I understood from talk I heard [that] he was a married man and had marital troubles of some kind. He appeared melancholy and blue at times, but we were all blue enough from getting left at meals, and the drills and working parties. I never spoke over half a doz[en] words to him, but was answered pleasantly enough and noticed nothing unusual in the man, except his desire to brood and be alone. I know he regretted the step he took in enlisting. He was of the same exalted rank as myself, coal passer: $22.00 cold plunk per month. A coal passer is on a par with a marine, about the last rung in the social ladder.

Quinn didn't like the navy, didn't like the "Guardo." That wasn't strange. I didn't myself. However, I looked for better days. (I have been and am still looking for them and that is five years ago.) Quinn's wife came to the *Vermont* to visit him. After that happened he [was] more homesick than usual. It wasn't as homelike and comfortable as he would have wished. He regretted the step and brooded more. That was his nature. Some wouldn't have brooded, but being up against the wrong proposition would have jumped the outfit without a qualm. He looked and evidently felt that he was in a prison from which there was no escape. Four or five others were awaiting their opportunities to skip out as soon as they were clear of the Cob dock.[15] The navy was too strong for them.

We were crowded on the tug. Quinn looked very glum, indeed. I was watching him. On the train he grew more morose as the City of New York receded from view. His thoughts were all there. Before we got to League Island, he was on the verge of insanity caused by God only knows what. It looked to me as if his wife was glad to part from him. She appeared gay and chipper enough, and had the look of a silly, easily swayed working girl of the common class. It looked as if they were trying to shove him off against his will, that he had shipped on account of no work and that he knew almost that his wife didn't care to have him around as long as he helped her with his miserable pittance. They preyed on his mind. He went around like a man in a dream, dazed, like a dumb animal.

On the *Indiana* all was confusion, incidental to putting a ship in commission, of course. Men from Cramps,[16] machinists, painters, caulkers, riggers swarmed all over the ship. There was no place to go, no place to sit down. The master-at-arms told us to take our bags to the bag room, and stow our hammocks in the nettings. Quinn obeyed like an automaton. About this time dinner was piped. Owing to the confusion, nothing could be had but some hard tack, canned willie, and slops of coffee. You had to wait for a cup. Everything was quickly gobbled up by the hungry gang. Quinn, moving like a man doped, got left. He didn't seem to want to eat anyhow. At turn to, we were mustered and given our billets. We went hither and thither looking for our hammock billet numbers and washroom lockers, etc. Quinn didn't evince any interest. He tried to find a place to be by himself. Finally, he sat down in an out of the way nook, but was in the way of some workmen. He leaned up against the bulkhead and was told to "get off the paint-work." Wandering down on the berth-deck, he was jumped by the master-at-arms and told to get above on the fo'castle. "Clear this deck."

Badgered and bewildered, he went below, but it was hot there and he was in the way. We were all in the way, it seemed to me also. Coming up from the lower regions, he sat on one of the bit[t]s[17] in despair, when a roar from an irate boatswain-mate told him to move "t'ell out o' that." And thus it went until it came time for hammocks. Poor devil! He had the glare of a hunted, dumb animal in his eyes, too miserable to curse back and hold up his own, he was giving away under the strain. At hammocks, his troubles only commenced. Some [hammocks] had to swing low and some high. There were quarrels and finally a fight between a couple of fellows. Nobody would swing without a quarrel from someone else. Poor Quinn, too apathetic to bother, was wedged in between two hammocks, getting the worst of it as usual. He began to look mildly surprised that he was allowed to be alive at all, and this surprised look grew into a look of wonder that his numerous enemies had allowed him to live so long.

Doubled up like a jack knife in his hammock all night, unable to sleep as were we all, from our cramped position and the intense heat of the deck, what queer thoughts must have come to this miserable being, in the way, badgered to madness, imagining that he was wanted by nobody, [that there was] no hope for him. His mind must have snapped under the continual brooding and strain. Poor Quinn, last up in the morning. Last to lash his hammock, abused by the master-at-arms for being late, getting left at breakfast, a meal like the previous night, hard tack, willie and bootleg.

Then we were sent for with the rest, to "turn to" below. We were mustered and given our stations by the engineers, detailed for different jobs. Quinn was put to

Woosung, China

work in the bilges, had just started to work there in a queer kind of way when he was sent to another job scaling a boiler, not even allowed to work undisturbed. The poor devil was going fast. His actions became noticeable to all hands. He broke away from his work. He hadn't even taken the trouble to change his uniform and was still in his best and only suit of blue. He crawled up the ladder to the berth deck and going into one of the drum rooms, stowed himself away. All he desired was to be away from his imaginary tormentors. He wanted to be alone to brood and mope. Looking at vacancy, he thought of God knows what. There he sat, crouched in a bunch, in the corner of the drum room.

He was missed, staying from his work for so long a time. The water-tender reported him absent and soon the engineers messenger was shouting his name and looking for him around the ship. Finally he was dragged forth from his hiding place and told to report to the engineer on duty. With dull, hopeless, hunted expression, he went below to be asked sharply where he was at all the time he was absent from work. He looked queerly at the engineer and answered only with short nods of the head. The engineer reported him for shirking. Quinn went slowly back to his work.

That night the whole berth deck was aroused by his shrieks and cries. They found him cowering in a corner with his hands over his face, whimpering and crying like a child. "Don't take me to that place! Don't take me to that place! For God's sake, let me alone."

The man's mind was gone. He was taken in charge by the ship's corporal and placed under the sentry's charge, moaning like a whipped hound. The next morning before the Doctor he was pronounced hopelessly insane. Two days later he was led in single irons over the gangway into a tug and sent to the hospital. What became of him, whether he went to the asylum for the insane at Washington, or what became of him, I do not know. What his trouble, the primary trouble, no one knew, but him. But secondarily, the cause of his insanity was the misery of life on ship board, no companionship that was congenial, no sympathy, nothing to cheer him up. Poor Quinn never went to the mast about shirking. The other fellows quietly walked aboard the tug with the rest of the workman and were absent at quarters the next morning. They have been absent ever since.

Those were fierce days, all of us mostly "rookies" and in debt for clothing. No money to put in the mess. We lived on hard tack, bad coffee and canned meats for nearly four months. We learned to detest canned articles of food then, and do so yet. That period was five years ago. Many a rough old time have I seen since, but that was the worst because unused to it. Poor Quinn!

Sunday morning, Sept. 9th [1900] at about 7:30 we up[ped] anchor and steamed toward Woosung. We went full speed thro' the swift-moving, muddy, yellow flood that reminded me more of a wide river at home after the spring freshets than a sea. Soundings were taken clear up until we dropped the hook again, the lowest sounding "quarter less five" (28 feet), and then the lead must have plunked at least a foot in the soft mud, which we stirred up all along the bar. The soundings were almost the same for almost the entire distance across, "half six" [39 feet], "quarter less six" [34 feet], etc. We passed a lightship at the bar coming in, the *Tungsha,* and one at the other side, the name of which I didn't quite catch. The land is all low lying country bordering the Yang-tse. We anchored pretty far out. We found plenty of warships here, French, English, German, Russian. The smaller craft were over nearer the forts. We were passed by plenty of Chinese junks, all with eyes painted on the bows. "So can see. No hab eyes, no can see." They evidently are thoroughly conversant with this rapidly moving flood of water. They do some rather pretty [maneuvering]. It was quite a treat to watch the Chinese bumboatmen swing in toward our port after gangway.

No American men-of-war were in evidence. I went below on watch at 12, having the mid-watch. When I was called up on deck I went and there was the *New Orleans* launch tied to our [boat] boom. I was surprised, but agreeably so. The last I [had] heard of the *New Orleans,* she was at "Hungry Gulf" in the Philippines. There was a message for me that a bundle I had left in my hurry on leaving the ship would be sent me. That suited me O.K. I was told the *New Orleans* had been there two weeks, that she "was a home" under the new captain. Just my cursed luck! Everything comes too late. But any amount of homes wouldn't make me forget the fierce deal from New York to Manila. The wound is healed, but the scar is there.

I have stated before that I have never beheld such discontent among a crew as among the crew of the *Oregon.* To quote a blacksmith, "She is a hell." I have been on seven ships, but this is the culmination of them all. Men below, the "underground savages," were treated like convicts, watched like rats by the "bolo-men" and the chief [engineer]. No reliance w[as] placed on petty officers or any of the men. The men grew to hate the very sight of the "bolo-men," and if one of them passed along, some one would shout "bolo" and it would be taken up by everyone, along with catcalls and hisses. Let a bolo-man show himself below and the word was passed thro' the entire department. "Bolo! Bolo!"

"Where away?"

"In no. 7 fire-room."

One night at quarters the whole force stopped in the midst of "setting up" drill and yelled "bolo" at the top of their lungs. They tried to detect the culprit, but met with no success. Every man apparently was attentive to the word of command. The "top bolo" complained to the chief, but the only satisfaction he rec'd was "Find any of them that does it, and I will have them punished."[18] If any of them had the least spark of manhood in them, they would have sent in their resignations. But all the spirit had been crushed out of them by hard times on the road as "hoboes." But we were watched like convicts, and woe betide the man that fell by the way. The slightest infringement of any rule and up to the mast we went. Let me cite one case to show in what light the chief held his men.

Woosung, China

It has always been customary in the navy, if a man is standing watch and his name appears on the liberty list, for him to get a relief before going ashore. Some times, the yeoman asks you the name of the man who volunteers to stand your watch while you go ashore. This is the proper method. But in ships where you get a liberty in parts and you happen to be on watch when your part comes, the yeoman has to find you a relief. At least such is the custom with most commanders of vessels.

The man I have in question secured his relief as he had often done before, but he didn't tell the yeoman the name of the man. It had not been the custom to do so. He went ashore. He had the mid, or 12 to 4 watch, an oiler watch. The oiler whom he was to relieve knew whom to call in his place. No. 1 bolo-man [Acting Warrant Machinist John F. Green] happened to have the mid watch and refused to allow that man to be called, and the oiler on watch had to stand until 2 A.M. and then call the oiler that had the 4 to 8. That caused all the trouble. The "bolo-man," it seems, had a dislike for the oiler in question and took this method of obtaining a small revenge, by making a howl to the chief, saying T—— had been ashore without obtaining a man to stand his watch.

This was just suited to the chief; anything to get a man punished was his hobby. He determined to push this case to the utmost, to have the man "hung or keelhauled" was his wail. "How I would like to give 'em all, damn 'em, a good two dozen [lashes]!" The case was taken to the mast, but the oiler explained so clearly and lucidly, I have so stated before in this journal, that it was referred to the captain. But he was brought up a month later and told his punishment was 10 days extra duty—80 hours extra work.

Thus, this man with a record of only three reports for minor offenses against his name in eight years, the holder of a good conduct medal and two excellent discharges, [was] punished wrongfully because the chief engineer "requested" that an example should be made of him. Thus was this young fellow, as square a man as I ever knew, spoiled as a willing worker in the service. Knowing he was punished wrongfully and smarting under a sense of injury, he became disgusted and careless, and indifferent. That was not only the case with him, but with nearly all the rest, men whom I had known, men who did more than their duty, who were all good workers, and willing and more useful in their humble capacity than the Government-educated asses[19] that hadn't the ability or necessary judgment to deal out justice with an impartial hand. By these very same incompetents were hundreds of men made disgusted with service under the flag.

I rec'd my packages from my friend on the *Pelican*. Among other articles, it contained a fine pair of field glasses, and I had long wished that we might accidentally run against the *New Orleans* so I could obtain them. We just arrived in time, for the *New Orleans* left for Taku on Tuesday. The *Nashville* steamed past us and turned up the Whang Poo river and continued on up to Shanghai.

Where we lay at anchor in the Yang-tse, the Whang-poo emptied its waters just above in the big river. The current was very strong, forming all kinds of eddies in the yellow flood. I never saw ships turn and swing so swiftly before. The steam launch men had their hands full. There wasn't much rest for them, even when tied to the boom, as they were dashed around like a chip, and under way they were submerged at times. The Chinese handle their junks with great skill, and it would do you good to watch them bring these craft alongside. Far up the Yang-tse the broad bosom of that noble river was studded with brown sails, sailing into lands unknown to most of us. Up the Whang Poo fourteen or fifteen miles lies Shanghai, the fairest and most cosmopolitan port in all China, with a market unsurpassed, everything cheap, with its European hotels, clubs, race course, etc. It [has] American, English, French, Russian, German and other nationalities' concessions. How long we intended to lie in this place we had no idea of. All our hopes of the *Oregon* returning home [were] knocked in the head. It is good policy to keep the *Oregon* in Chinese waters as long as possible, so time will bring forgetfulness and everything could be smoothed over.[20]

While lying at Woosung, we got "setting up" drill twice a day, at morning and evening quarters. The same future admiral(?) that ran shrieking back to the quarterdeck for advice or orders about rescuing the drowning and almost suffocated diver had been assigned to duty in connection with the engineers force. A clause in the Navy Personnel Bill [of 1899] provides that all commissioned officers must fit themselves for duty in both engine room and the deck as well. This bright, promising young man was sent by the chief to inspect a boiler that was being sealed. All the manhole plates were off, of course, and the men were inside working. The grate bars were out of the furnaces and false ash pans removed. He was overheard to tell the chief that he had thoroughly inspected it. "Oh yes, chief, I went all through the boiler. I went in thro' the furnace and came out at the top manhole." I can't exactly say what the chief thought. He simply looked at the young person. It was enough to wither him.

This young person took quite an abnormal delight in giving us "setting up" exercises. All firemen like this drill? He would give us the full limit and we would be put thro' a course of sprouts that would make us swear for an hour afterward. "Full stoop. Go down all the way!" he would yell. "Lift your heels up there. Kick up! Kick up!" prancing up and down like a dancing master. Then he would look for approbation to the master and he generally got it, for anything the old fellow liked was to see his men doing something they hated.

The sampans had a hard and most difficult time making [reaching] the ship, often having to put back on account of the swift current and high winds. The Yang-tse rushed toward the sea with irresistible force, and while lying out in the river it was "dollars to doughnuts" whether we ate or not. On one occasion, the boat with fresh provisions reached the port gangway all right, but the line carried away while the cooks were discharging the provisions. The Chink put on all sail and made for Woosung, carrying cooks and all.

Everything was dear for this country. It is all a fairy tale to imagine that you can buy as much in these countries for a Mex as you can for a dollar at home. When you

Woosung, China

hand over a Mexican [dollar] here, you don't look for any change in return. Perhaps the prices were steep on account of the many men-o-war and transports that were lying all around.

England and Germany seemed to vie with each other in sending troops, no doubt preparing for trouble. It looked to me as if they intended to divide up China between them, but Russia wasn't behind by a long shot. England's hands were full in the Transvaal, where she had "bit off more than she could chew," a bitter but wholesome dose that she deserved.

We had received no word from the flagship and were awaiting orders. We were anxious to get inside as far as possible. Something was wrong with the lines and telegraphic communication was entirely cut off at times, and so we lay, waiting for developments. We were always waiting.

~~~

"Oh, Mama, look! There goes a sailor."
"Where? Is he drunk, pet?"
"No Mama, he doesn't appear so."
"Then he can't be a real sailor, darling. Possibly he is one of those naval reserve sailors."

Little Elsie's Mama only voiced the real sentiments of over two-thirds of the good citizens and citizenesses of the great and glorious Republic. It has only been since the advent of the new navy, with its steel ships of complicated mechanism, that the personnel of the navy has undergone a change. Time was when Jack considered a liberty on shore a dismal failure unless he got "bilin" ["blind"] drunk and considered he wasn't keeping up the prestige of his calling and uniform unless he did so.

Time[s have] changed in the last decade. Once [in] a while Jack gets drunk, but it is more the exception than the rule. Added machinery brought added responsibility, and Jack has to keep his wits about him, or else he might make a mistake that would cause whole oceans of trouble. Steam, hydraulics, electricity, pneumatics, etc., have surpassed the simple routine of former years, and from being a mere machine that pulled and hauled at the word, he had to do some thinking of his own. You can't run blindly these days in a man-o-war and open a valve or pull a lever. You have got to ascertain if all is right along the line, if every valve is right, especially so at fire, collision, and general quarters. You are woke up by the bell or "siren" in the dead o' night, not knowing what time it is. If you are in a hammock, you take three turns of your lashing around it and have it on one hook for fire drill. If you are a "smotherer," you take it with you to smother the flames. At general quarters they are supposed to be used as a protection along the top deck. At the bugle call for "general quarters" or any of these drills at night, you must get the sleep from your eyes on the run and find out the time, so you know what relief you are, and then you know where to go.[21]

It is a lovely feeling to be turned out at an unearthly hour and run below and put pressure on a turret or hoisting engine, to see that everything is right so you won't get about five or six hundred lbs of pressure against some pipe that will carry away. I used to like general quarters at night and be "second relief" and rush below and prepare and start both pumps, with the engineer asking if you have pressure two moments after you get there, on a pair of [vertical reciprocating] pumps that would require at least 10 minutes to drain and warm up! If you are particularly sleepy and are in a hurry for pressure, you open up your steam too much and if you don't watch like a hawk, up one goes with a thump and down with a crash that threatens to blow the bonnet from the cylinder. I found this often the case with the pumps on the *Oregon*. You weren't allowed any time at all to prepare, and the ill usage those pumps used to get would have put less carefully constructed machinery out of commission long ago.

Jack doesn't spend so much of his money for "booze" as formerly. Many look for advancement and are generally found taking a course in some school of correspondence. They also place quite a bit of money away for a "payday." Most of them don't want to be in the navy all their life. One or two cruises suffice. Thirty years and retirement isn't much to look forward to, altho' many old timers will tell you that the first thirty years is the hardest. [They j]ust look forward to doing thirty years in the service under strict discipline, which is necessary, and ill-treatment and abuse, which is unnecessary.

No wonder men on their second and third cruises are cranks. It's the petty trifles that count, little sands that make the mountain. These trifles wear on the temper of an ordinary man and he becomes a "chaw," or chronic kicker and growler. After fifteen years' service he is hopelessly unfitted for civil life, would be lost in society, and has developed into the regulation type of continuous service man, expecting no other mode of living. Not contented with his life, he is anything but that, but resigned to it. He knows he will never have any privacy or comfort aboard ship; that he can count no moment of the day his own that he is aboard ship; that he is liable to duty all the time, in fact is on duty, for he is "stand by" when asleep. Some officer may take a dislike to him and make it hot for him upon every occasion that offers. "Officers and gentlemen" are not above those things, you know. Perhaps this same thing would account for the mortality among the officers in the South African war on the British side. Not all these "sons of somebody" were shot from the front, boldly facing the enemy.

We had bag inspection. The auxiliary watch, of which I happened to be one, of course, had to bring up their bags of clothing. This is dreaded by all bluejackets, one thing especially I hate above all others when it happens to catch you unprepared. In spite of all the care you take of your clothing, the name you stamped on each piece time and again will wash out, and you neglect to roll and stop the pieces as the regulations require. There were only a few of us that morning, and the young ensign I have before mentioned inspected. He unrolled piece after piece, something I never before saw done in the navy, altho' it is allowable. But the majority of officers doesn't

Woosung, China

take advantage of their privilege. While waiting for him to get to us, the "Ripper" loomed up on the horizon. We heard him before we could make him out, and knew he was shotted to the muzzle for b'ar. He didn't waste much time with the division on the starboard side of the fo'castle, but came with a snort to the port side where the "firemen" were. On a coil of line an Irishman had thrown his bag indiscriminately, not an article marked, and none stopped up. All were clean, however. With a wild snort and roar of rage, the "Ripper" spotted this wardrobe.

"Who owns these clothes without any marks or tie-ties on them?" he roared in a voice of thunder. No answer. The fireman they belonged to was safely concealed behind a friendly ventilator out of the "Ripper's" line of sight.

"Does anybody know whose bag this is?" he questioned, looking around with a wild glare. Of course, no one knew. Not being able to find out, he turned to another fireman. "Dump that bag out. Dump it out!" pointing to this man's bag, that was half emptied. "Let's see what you have in it." The fireman did so.

After criticizing it, his eye landed on my bag. "Dump it out!" he roared. I did so. Out rolled a miscellaneous assortment: part of this manuscript, safely tied up; another white canvas bag inside my black one; an album of views of Japan; a short Japanese sword; and a Kodak.

"Ha! What's that, a camera?"

"Yes, sir," I answered meekly.

"Did you take any views when we were in dock?" he asked with a half smile, the first I had ever seen.

"No, sir," I replied. "No films."

"Too bad, you should have taken some pictures." Then he moved on, first asking me why I didn't put my black bag over the white one, and then suspiciously asking me if the white bag was one I didn't turn in when we changed from white bags to black. I told him I got that white bag three years ago on the *Minneapolis,* so he moved down the line seeking a new victim to expend some surplus ire on. Poor old chump, your kind are rapidly dying out, but not too rapidly.

~ ~ ~

While laying at Woosung, we had the usual flock of fakirs and curio-venders, curios made expressly for just such trade, like the Japs, who brought aboard genuine(?) Satsuma ware and guaranteed it to be over two hundred years old. It looked old enough for all antique purposes, seamed and cracked and discolored as it was. The Japs are very handy at this sort of thing. There is also a good imitation of iron made from rice. It will deceive almost any one but an expert. The Chinese brought aboard small live tortoises, opium outfits without the opium, very curious and elaborate carvings from a soft stone, something like our own soap stone, josses and figures of monkeys, unnatural looking dogs, interlaced with foliage. Some were very elaborate.

You could purchase at your own price. The guileless, bland Chink will charge you ten times the amount he expects to receive and will come down to a ridiculously low figure. For instance, one very large piece of carving he asked twenty-four dollars for. I didn't want it, having no place to put it, and assuredly wouldn't carry a stone quarry around with my kit, so I offered him two dollars for it, Mex, of course. He wouldn't hear of it, but slammed the carving down with great force, taking care not to break it, and regaled me with a volley of pigeon English. But just as they were packing up, he came over and offered it to me after a little haggling for the two dollars, and would have sold it to me for fifty cents, I verily believe, but I didn't want it at any price, having no place for it. Handsome pieces of silk, and silk embroidery; different colors of Chinese inks, mostly common, cheap kinds; and the rest of the stuff [was] the cheap bumboat material common in every port in the world. Curious daggers made of Chinese cash interwoven together with wire could be had for a song. Carving knives of all descriptions for carving in wood and other materials, curiously shaped little teapots with a place inside to place the tea before steeping, carved tobacco jars made from bamboo, fans, all very nice, no doubt, and I could have bought a large assortment, but then, I recollected, you get tired of lugging these articles around, and they are left on the ship when you are transferred.

A bluejacket is known by the trail [he leaves behind] of Colombo ebony canes and ebony elephants and elephants of cocoanut wood, shells of all descriptions and sizes and colorings from Aden, Singapore, etc., baskets from Aden in the Red Sea and Koodoo horns,[22] canes from Manila covered with snake skins, bolos, ostrich feathers, bamboo canes with curious Oriental carvings, and a thousand other articles too numerous to mention. At first you swear you are going to carry them from ship to ship, but the order to transfer you to another ship comes too quickly, and all your energies are spent on getting your bag of clothing together, and you let the rest go, caring nothing about them. And thus on your trip around the world from New York to Manila, from Manila to San Francisco, especially if made on different ships, [you] leave a trail of curios behind. What becomes of them you know not; neither do you care. You can get more.

Nothing of any importance took place or was to take place as far as any of us in the fleet knew, but that is always the case. People at Podunk Centre or Ran Ha Hee are wiser than any of us, on the spot tho' we be. We still had received no word from the flagship. We knew, or had an idea, that she was still at Taku and that the *New Orleans* had left for there. Three of the German ships also left for the same place. German troopships and English transports were the order of the day. There was evidently some move contemplated by the powers and possibly by the United States. I should judge they were preparing quietly for the Chinamen's downfall under some other pretext than the massacre of missionaries, the missionary part of it not being sufficient cause in itself for war and only a poor, flimsy excuse. They were trying to invent some other cause for a demonstration and wild howl and if all protest was of

Woosung, China

no avail or none forthcoming, they having sufficient force already at hand, they would jump in and take and hold what they could, just as any other footpad [robber or thief] would take it, simply by the law of force and might.

The Chinese have some desirable ports upon which these bloody freebooters have long cast envious glances, and like the American Indian, [the Chinese have] got to take a back seat. But only the pretext, and the excuse, it is too flimsy to even deceive the most obtuse mind. Cast off all pretext as England did in the Transvaal and make it a war of conquest. "Your country is rich, and we want it; and in the interest of Christianity, we are going to take it."

~~~

Chill breezes came sweeping down the Yang-tse these days, and at evenings, the uniform was blue. Being the last days of September, it would not be long before winter would be upon us. The climatic change was very sudden and a number of us caught bad colds. Some had to go upon the sick list. But even at that, the cool weather was a welcome relief from the intense heat of Manila. Lying in the stream as we still were, there was no liberty given yet, and it grew very monotonous. Even few of the officers [were] going ashore, as it was an uncertainty when they could return. Beside, the cost of coming off to the ship amounted to a great deal. The ship began to look shipshape once more, painted almost all over. Thro' out the different departments she looked even better than when I first came aboard at Hong Kong. The only uncomfortable thing was the absence of linoleum around the decks. This hadn't been replaced. The engine rooms and shaft alleys were painted as also the for'd and aft 13" pump rooms. I painted mine and gave it a thorough cleaning so that station looked as well as it ever did.

On account of the cool weather, the engineers force sought their winter quarters, the forward handling room on the orlop deck, and the Orlop Deck Debating Society was soon the vogue. Not a question of any moment, not a leading topic of the day, but was discussed in its entirety by these sages of the fire and engine rooms. The situation in China was discussed in its every aspect, as well as the Transvaal affair. Nothing escaped the impartial criticism of the society, from the greatest society [issues] even down to the bolo-man's last eccentric move, all were discussed and commented upon. Sometimes the comments were of a sort that would place the men who uttered them upon a par with the worst nihilist or anarchist that every annoyed a crowned head or drank deep draughts of the foamy in a Hoboken [New Jersey] saloon.

Particularly notable in their [forceful] remarks were a couple of Irishmen. Let the Boer war be brought up and you would hear a tirade against England that would drive an Anglo-maniac mad. These two men used to take an unholy delight in annoying a Britisher, [who was] also a fireman. They would make some disparaging remark about the English so he would be sure to overhear, and finally, unable to bear more, he would chime in indignantly. At this they would bait and goad him all the more, until he either had to move off in a mad rage or else fight, which he knew was useless.

"D'ye mind, Paddy!" H—— would call to his running mate, "How many Boers stood off those fifty-thousand lime-juicers at Modder River and the battle of Colenso?"

"I did [hear], but I forget the exacht noomber," answered Paddy.

"Just 987 av them at Modder River and 756 at Colenso. An th bloody bloomers that was there was at least two million av thim."

Here the "juicer" would prick his ears up.

"Yis," continued H——, "the juicers ar all right, alright in foightin savages, but what 'ell did th' iver do wid a civilized foe? Niver were they known to run from any country on equal terms wid themselves. Whin it comes to massaycrayin a lot of pure savages or defenceless people, they ar th greatest thing that iver happened, But look ————."

"Hits a bloominh loie!" roared the Englishman, unable to contain himself longer. "Hits a loie, I say, han hi can prove it. Hingland never was whipped at any stoige of th' game. H'er Majestie 'as the foinest h'army h'in the world t'day. Bloind me hif she 'asnt."

"Thin why the divil didn't ye stay in it, ye bloody son av a gun. Why didn't you serve yer Quane yer full siven years and not run away if ye loiked it so well? D'ye moind th time ye was strutting around the Rock wid yer little red jacket on? Ye wid yer little red coat an yer little red cap, and yer pretty little breeches on. An whin ye seed an American bluejacket ashore twas yerself that was only too glad to do a song and a dance fer some beer? D'ye mooind how ye all thried to rin in so as to get your tank full? Niver a wan of ye ever had the price to buy yer own drink. 'Tis only too glad ye air to sing a song or do a clog for a 'blooming bowl,' ye bloody lime juicer, ye!"

"Hit's a loie. Hi never jumped 'er Majesties service. Hi never wore a red coat or took the shilling.[23] But, Hi say, Hengland's harmy is as good hand has brave has hany harmy hin the world t'day, the finest generals."

"Yis, they are all Irish, an it's the Oirish that's doin all the fighting in South Africa today, being used as the cat's paw for England's chestnuts, an well ye know it. How well the Quane knows it. Arrah: risking her delicate health by a visit to the ould dart[24] bringing a plentiful supply of shillins wid her to purchase raycruits for the red coat army. Ye bloomin rat-faced weasel, well ye knows it. Woud ye foight agin yer own country if there was war declared bechune America and England? Would ye? I doubt it! Ye wouldn't jump out quicker than ye did from Gib[raltar]? Ye all talk of an alliance; prate about bein cousins. Cousins is it? Foine cousinly love ye showed on plinty of occasions when ye could have shown it. Yes! Yes! In the Revolution when bounty money was offered to the Injuns for iviry scalp of man, woman or child that was a rebel. Foine! Foine! Whin in 1812 you boarded American ships and 'Shanghaied' American seamen rought from under the American flag, just for an excuse for another war to try and retrave what ye lost in the Revolution. Very brotherly ye war whin ye shilly-shallied

Woosung, China

about recognizing the Union during the Civil war, and fitted out th *Alabama* complete with English gold. English built ship. English men. English everything. And agin jurin the administration of President [Grover] Cleveland about Venezuela,[25] whin yer bloody lion's tail was twisted into a Turk's head.[26] Arrah! An alliance ye are all harping about. A foine alliance it would be. Foine for England, I mane. Ye bloomin 'bleeder.'"

And thus it would continue, the Irishmen "stringing" the "lime-juicer" half in jest and half in earnest until he was nearly frothing at the mouth with rage. But happily it never culminated in anything more violent than a war of words, of which the Englishman always got the worst, there being two to one. But they told him some unpleasant truths, I think.

About this time the "skipper" corralled about seven of the junior officers having a quiet little game after "lights out." It was just getting interesting, a "jackpot" was about to be opened and was won by the "skipper." At least I believe he claimed it, and I never heard of any dissenting voice among the seven unfortunates. They were placed under immediate arrest, relieved from duty, and confined to their rooms. That is, confined as an officer generally is, merely in name. Just the same as giving them a furlough. Of course, being of superior fine fibre, the disgrace is supposed to be sufficient punishment. They were recommended for court-martial to the admiral, but I believe it was disapproved, as the following Sunday they were all restored to duty. So you can see that an officer and a gentleman can gamble just the same as any ordinary soldier or sailor, but if caught, even shooting an ordinary game of craps, the Jackies get a couple of months' pay taken away and a term in the "cooler."

∼∼∼

An order was posted up to the effect that everybody had to be in strictly regulation uniform by the 30th of Sept[ember]. If not, they would be put on the "report." We awaited this day anxiously, hoping that we would be able to pass the rigid inspection all right, and that those of us that had our uniforms made to order and that had passed on plenty of other ships would pass inspection on the *Oregon*. But we reckoned without being right this time. The American Navy is about as lenient in regard to uniform, or I should say, more so, than any navy in the world. Men can draw cloth from the paymaster and give it to the ship's "sheenies," or tailors, to make up.[27] And the uniform is not uniform by any means because hardly a suit is made alike [*sic*]. Some have fancy crochet work on shirt and trousers, tie-ties here and there, and all of this is not uniform with the clothing served out by the department. A bluejacket that takes an interest in his clothing doesn't care about the clothing served out by the paymaster. It doesn't fit well by a long shot, and is not put together as well.[28] The cap is too small, they think, and they get theirs made according to their own ideas. Some of them are a wonder of needle work.[29] Now plenty of "skippers" and "first luffs" like their crews to wear neat-fitting, tailor-made clothing, but at any time you are liable to run against a snag in the shape of a captain that wants his crew to be strictly dressed all alike in uniform, collars, tape, caps, buttons, tie-ties, every item just so, as it is served out by the Government.

After passing thro' half a dozen ships, I struck this snag on the *Oregon*. It was a sudden order. Men had been wearing "tailor-mades" ever since the *Oregon* went in commission. Then why the change? Why, the paymaster had a large stock on hand and wanted to get rid of some of it. They work together, these "gentlemen," in "doing" Jack. There is lots of profit in selling clothing to the sailor. The Government, you say, don't countenance any thing of this kind, but sells to its sailors without any profit whatever, sells at just what it costs. Yes, my innocent, but the Government is [not] expected to get any of this profit, and is not even expected to hear of it. And it doesn't. Prices, as every bluejacket knows, vary on all articles. A pea coat that cost you $9 at one place costs you $11 at another. According to the contract, the paymaster can set any little advance he wishes about the contract price. That's his profit. His accounts balance. You have paid and signed for the article and that's the end of it. This is also done in foodstuffs, as I have noted before. Rascally paymasters can juggle with even the men's food, and they do it, have done it, and will continue the motion down to the *finis*.

So this Sunday at morning quarters we were put thro' the mill. Every little detail of uniform was looked over. Capes of shirts were measured; hats were measured; nothing escaped. The young gentleman who "went through the furnace and out of the top manhole of a boiler" did for us, and very thorough he was. This was the same young man that ran back to get permission to rescue the diver. He was particularly zealous this beautiful Sunday morning. He wanted to show his superiors what a good, zealous and competent officer he really was, partly, I judged, on account of being just released from the "coop," he being one of the seven. He and the chief were so engrossed in this labor of love that they didn't see the "skipper" and his retinue approach for inspection, and the captain was half thro' the ranks of the engineers division before they saw them. It was too late then to give the proper "salute" to the "old man." We were commented upon very freely by this enterprising young gentleman and put down in his book in what respect we were out of uniform. The "bolo-men" stood off and made remarks and giggled among themselves. This pleased them vastly, for are they not "officers"? Small ones, 'tis true, but still they were above the common herd who were being measured and harassed and treated like a gang of convicts. The whole business was humiliating enough, the Lord knows, without being laughed and giggled at by "bolo-men," especially the *Oregon*'s "bolo-men," who when they were of the common herd were noted as coming to quarters out of uniform and dirty, and had been called down by the engineer. These men were known as "bums in luck," "can-house bums" and "stew bums," tho' what these inglorious terms wot of, I wot not. "Gadzooks! By my halidom." Were it not common repute among the lads that most of them hadn't the wherewithal in their wardrobes when of the rabble, whereof to flag a hand car.

Woosung, China

About a month after arriving at Woosung, liberty was given special class men. Seven was all [that were] allowed each day from the engineers department, and of these seven allowed liberty, only two or three would go. These men were in the navy strictly for a payday. They were planting every solitary "dobie" they could. Others that wanted to go very badly couldn't, simply because they weren't special first class. To be a special first class man aboard the *Oregon,* you had to be on probation or more brutally on "parole" for six months. They took you on probation for that length of time. If you remained first class and were never reported or committed yourself, you were, if the administration saw fit, advanced to special class, "star first class." Men who had been special first class for perhaps two years or all during their present cruise and all during the last one on other ships, on being transferred to the *Oregon* had these privileges taken from them, and were simply first class. This was a most enormous crime. The idea of a man not being on the *Oregon* for six months was punishable, you see. That is a specimen of naval justice. These men, who thro' no fault of their own were transferred from other ships, were thus deprived of their special privileges, and had to stand back and watch any number of "punks" getting all kinds of privileges. This kind of treatment is small. It makes a man disgusted. Another thing that made us more disgusted was the posting up of a notice forbidding sailors, soldiers and marines entrance to some of the hotels and bars of Shanghai. A man in uniform wasn't welcome in these places, but oh, how welcome they must have been at Tien-tsin and Pekin! Nothing [too] good for the man in a blue shirt then.

Our marines were brought down on the *Zafiro* from Taku. A few of them had lost the number of their messes at Pekin, but the mortality was very small among the American forces there, ridiculously so. They were heartily welcomed aboard. They had had rather a rough experience of it, but so had we on the rock, for that matter. They brought all manner of loot with them. Some of them had some valuable articles, such as gold-embroidered robes, rugs, bracelets, etc., but the most of it was cheap junk. These articles they disposed of to members of the crew at good prices. Jack will buy anything at fabulous prices if he has money and has been aboard ship for any length of time. Most of the articles sold were rings of the most approved Chinese designs, made of white metal and silver and some of brass. Looking at these cheap articles, I opined that some Chinese five-cent stores must have been in the path and were looted in a charge, but not all was of this order. Some of the loot was very valuable, both intrinsically and as a curio.

After the special class men had all rec'd liberty (there were about 24 out of a hundred and five of the engineers force) first class men were allowed to go. Here our noble chief engineer showed once more his parental affection for us, the scum. Once again, he wouldn't allow anyone having an auxiliary watch liberty, nor would he allow the boilermaker and one of the coppersmiths shore leave. The former was scratched [from the liberty list] so viciously that he tore the list completely across with the point of the pencil. The excuse for not allowing him liberty was that the other boiler man was at the time on the sick or "binnacle" list with the Shanghai fever. The latter was also "scratched" and told he couldn't go until he had completed a job of work he was employed upon (perhaps the job would last a month or so). I, who was one of the aux[iliary] watch unfortunates, [was] cursed by fate in being compelled to remain aboard. So we had to content ourselves as best we could aboard. We received the usual allotment of "knee stoop" and "double quick" at setting up drill without stint. We were snarled at, barked at, and in general, treated as "Boxers." Oh how we cursed, not loudly, but oh, so deeply, at the fate that had placed us under such a mean, drunken and miserable administration! I am afraid that I must have nearly forfeited my hopes of Heaven.

But the unseen hand that watches over the sailor came to our rescue. The last part of the first class men had gone, and the next day the word was passed for "all special and first-class men who had not had a liberty in this port" to put his name down at the ship's writer's office.[30] Perhaps we didn't take advantage of this! Of course, we of the engineers department were about the only ones that hadn't rec'd any liberty. We promptly filed up to the yeoman's office and told him to put our names down. The chief couldn't hold these names back and had to submit the list to the Ripper, and then there was an uproar. The Ripper, I heard, wanted to know why all these first-class men hadn't went with their parts. The old curmudgeon hemmed and hawed, but he had to leave us all go, about 27, and a complete watch list had to be made out.

Woosung, China

CHAPTER SIX

~

Shanghai

I felt like a boy at the prospects of a liberty. The same old story: wild to get ashore once more, more especially so as I had never had a liberty in a Chinese city before, and there was plenty to be seen. We were all ready and in uniform to leave the ship at 1 P.M. for our forty-eight hours leave. As usual, we went loaded down with Mexican [dollars]. It takes a gunnysack to carry enough for a bluejacket's liberty.

We were towed over to the landing at Woosung and purchased our tickets for Shanghai at the ticket office of the Chinese Imperial Railways. We paid for second class passage, the run only being fourteen or fifteen miles. This little station was pretty well filled with passengers of all classes. Of course, the majority of the gang made a descent on the bar. I refused several invitations to partake, but I was content to wait until we reached Shanghai. I didn't see much of interest around the station while waiting for the train: a few Chinamen of the better classes and some Chinese section hands, and a few neatly dressed Chinese women and the usual horde of fruit, peanut, and bar booze vendors.

The most interesting object I found was a large Sikh soldier clad in black whiskers and turban and khaki. He was the ticket taker at the gate. For side arms he carried a large ticket punch. These Sikhs present a most imposing appearance. They, I found later, were doing their work all along the lines, and also police duties. The Chinese hold these Sikhs in great fear. They [the Sikhs] are not chary in manhandling any coolie they catch in wrong-doing. It is a common sight to see them marching one along, driving him ahead by his cue. Sometimes two or three Chinks will be noticed with pigtails tied together with a nice, large Sikh holding tightly the cues with [one] hand and a bamboo cane with the other, the blows of which he distributes with equal impartiality, the poor Chinamen jabbering and protesting, and the Sikh cursing and driving his charges. This is about all they are good for. As soldiers they are a dismal failure. They can't face the music. They are all right mauling Mongolians. There was a regiment of Gurkhas, little black men, very homely, that are the reverse of handsome and imposing, but they can fight like devils and don't fear death. The Sikh is ornamental; the Ghurka, useful. However, I digress, as usual.

The train at last rumbled up to the little station, with English-style engine and American-style cars marked first, second and third class respectively, counting from the engine. If there was this kind of classification in the United States, the first class would be the last, the hind end. But there has to be classification in China. The Sikh punched our tickets at the gate, and the Chinese conductor did the same aboard the train. We passed, quickly enough for this kind of a railroad, some fine farm lands, [with] men, women and children of both sexes working in the fields.

The country from Woosung to Shanghai is very level, and villages and farm houses dot the entire landscape. The entire distance is dotted with little huts containing their dead, and the bones of others are heaped up and covered with mounds. Long dead Chinamen whose habitation has fallen in course of time, whose bones have been turned up by the plow and heaped up here and there in heaps until all has disappeared into the soil. You can see at a glance that it is an old, old country, the oldest in the world. Everybody seemed industrious. The farm house[s] are compounded off, long, low and rambling in structure. Plenty of breathing space. The farms are in a high state of cultivation. The oxen are used for plowing as well as the water buffalo. The oxen struck me as all shoulders and peculiarly fitted for the yoke. Anything they are yoked to pull either comes or something has to give way. I saw drove after drove of these, all well fed and sleek looking. In fact, but for the build of the cattle, the landscape is not unlike an American one, only there are more people working in the fields. They stand still and watch the train as it passes, viewing the foreign devil, as he has his head out of the car window, with either a pleasant smile or with stolid indifference. If you are inclined to be friendly, you are greeted with plenty of pleasant looks, and as I was feeling pretty happy at my relief from the iron discipline of the ship, and no doubt wore a pleasant cast of countenance, it was reflected on the faces of most of the inhabitants along the line.

We stopped three times from Woosung to Shanghai, but at last we arrived at the last-named place. This being the terminus, [it] had quite an imposing depot, and it was crowded with a cosmopolitan class. We jumped from the train, passed in our tickets at one gate, and the liberty men came in at another, that is, the returning liberty party. Pretty well used up they appeared, but on the main [they] presented a creditable enough appearance after forty eight hours of the usual dissipation. We gave them the "high ball" as we passed them. Their fun was all over; ours only started. We hurried out of the station as fast as possible thro' the crowds of China-men. But great Moses! What a wild horde we were beset by: sellers of bamboo canes, blowers, squeaking toy dogs, and the ever present, muchly present rickshaw man. We couldn't shake them off. An American sailor is a Godsend to them. They refuse to leave until you surrender to one of their number.

"Lickshaw! Lickshaw!" roared one ugly looking son of Confucius, who appeared to have more push about him than the others, and this is saying a great deal. "Me

Shanghai

While in Shanghai, Wilson on many occasions used the services of a rickshaw man such as the ones shown here, providing transportation for a junior U.S. Navy petty officer. Navy Historical Foundation.

very good horse. Me run all day, no tired." He refused to be shoved off without getting killed, and the only way out of the swarming horde was to take him. My companion on this trip was captured at the same time. No. 3285 jabbed and jeered at his less fortunate brethren of the shafts and hustled us over to where his rickshaw was, and in we jumped.

"You want go where?" he queried. "Tom Pow Ching's? My savvy." Now, every sailor is supposed to go to Tom Pow Ching's, he having his store up in the centre of the city. He is the compradore and bumboatman premier of Shanghai. We were no exception to the rule. We knew we could dismiss our horses at this place and walk. At least we thought we could, but then we reckoned without knowing the ever ubiquitous ricky of Shanghai. We were bowled merrily along by our men who showed their delight at capturing two American sailors loaded with a cargo of silver, by seeing how close they could come to every other rickshaw's wheel without taking it off. Mine especially took a fiendish delight in running noiselessly up behind some poor coolie loaded down with a pack of old tins or other stuff and shouting "hu, hu," causing the man or woman to leap suddenly aside, spilling their loads. This caused him untold delight. He also had another specialty, that of forcing others out of his road and then answering their jabber with a torrent of Mongolian abuse.

I remember the string of bluejackets in rickshaws coming up to us. One coolie tried to spurt it and get ahead, but my man must have been watching him out of the corner of his slant eye, for when the other forged up to him, he spurted and cut across his bows, effectually shutting the ambitious coolie out and giving him a laugh in which all joined.

We arrived at Tom Pow Ching's and paid our men and dismissed them. At least we thought we did. After a drink in there, we started out to take in the sights. Shanghai possesses many fine buildings, especially along a street, Broadway Nanking Road, and the Bund, also a fine public garden. A great many men-of-war lay directly off this park. Here on evenings, weather permitting, the city band plays, as in some American cities. It has fine level streets well fitted for wheeling. Swell English women, many of them, I noticed, fine whips in trap [open carriage] and dog cart, with a Chinese tiger perched gravely behind. The solid banker and wife, or some member of the diplomatic corps, as well as the officers of different nationalities were well represented along this handsome drive. You would imagine yourself at home, but for the many Orientals, Hindoos, etc., you see about. A great many of the houses, residences, and clubs are built of glazed brick and are fine specimens of Chinese masonry.

The Bund is very lively and presents an animated scene at this hour in the afternoon: the fine view of the shipping on the river with craft of all descriptions, from the Chinese sampan manned by some Chinese coolie and his family, the woman at the sweep and her lord lolling easily back with his pipe, taking his ease with a most philosophical look upon his classic Mongolian phiz, to the stately man-o-war. Here flap idly in the cool evening breeze the tricolor of old France, the Cross of St. George,[1] and farther down the line can be seen the ensign with the Rising Sun, and in this grand string of war-ships the *Princeton* and *Nashville* were conspicuous among them all from their spick-and-span appearance, very clean and very bright, and with the handsomest ensign of them all waving defiantly.[2]

Truly, the riverfront of Shanghai presented more of a holiday appearance with all the display of bunting, with the band playing selections as usual, children romping here and there, women in handsome dresses, all looking happy and content. No thought of the yellow monster and the terrible peril which had menaced all of the European population. Well can they feel secure for all that shipping, all these soldiers clad in different garb, are here in their behalf.

What disgusted me more than anything I have seen heretofore were the number of Europeans clad in Chinese costume. They were, in the main, missionaries. This adaptation of Oriental costume is done to bring them closer to the Chinamen. I couldn't help laughing at the picture they presented. The men mostly had cultivated the pigtail and they were mostly all light complexioned, a Chinaman with a red cue. The women were a most homely lot, and enhanced this homeliness by the Chinese dress. I looked to see if they had deformed their feet, but none of them appeared to be fanatical enough for that.

Many of these people are in earnest, but they are mistaken. You can't change a Chinaman. They'd sooner be Chinamen than anything else on God's green footstool. Chinamen with about seven thousand years of civilization behind them. Chinamen that believe in Confucianism, Taoism and Buddhism. They can't convert the Chinaman. How many American Buddhists, or Mohammedans do you suppose could be converted? Do you think many could be converted and honestly believe these religions? Some might profess them for a fad. The Oriental mind cannot grasp our conception of religion. Neither can we grasp theirs. They might profess it for matter of gain, but he is a Chinaman still. Five or six thousands of years, Lord knows how many more, of the religions and customs of his race can't be eradicated by a civilization of a few hundred years. They simply don't understand Western ideas, and you can't convince China at the point of the bayonet.

We strolled about, looking at the sights. Nothing was lost on us. We looked in the store windows along Broadway (but this is not as broad as its name would imply) [and] Nanking Road. This is all the European concessions, and the shops are strictly up to date, only you can't tell what kind of a stock they have inside by looking in the windows. The fronts of these shops are very massive and present an appearance more like a business street of banking houses than shops. But you can go inside and get most anything you wish, only you won't find the Chinaman so swift to wait on you in these large shops, as a Jap or an American would. They don't seem to take any interest, and it is a matter of indifference whether you buy or not. Now the Jap, when you go in his small shop, is all bustle. He wants to strike up a bargain right off the reel. He is keen for a possible customer.

We strolled along on the lookout for something or other to turn up, and along this section we almost imagined we were back in some American city. These streets were not crowded by pedestrians. Everything was quiet as if on the side streets of some large city. So we concluded to look for something more lively. Here is where the ever present rickshaw men got their little graft in. They had been trailing us a good distance and we hadn't noticed them until we crossed a side street, when up they bobbed serenely with many bows. "You take lickshaw now? You no want walk. Hab lickshaw."

"No!" I roared. "Get away," with a threatening [tone].

"All yight. All yight. You no want. Bimeby you want mebbe." And they shoved off to a quiet distance.

We strolled some more, and every time we looked around to get our bearings, we met the rascally, bland, childlike phizogs of our shadows, now reinforced by two more ruffians just as dirty and just as ragged and villainous looking as the other two. I laughed at their persistency. "These fellows are going to have us yet, I'll bet," I remarked to my mate.

"It looks that way, by gum," he replied.

A Sailor's Log

"You take rickshaw now," and they came trundling up with a run as we paused again. It was now getting dark.

"I suppose there is no help for it," I said to my companion.

"No," he replied. "When I was ashore here the other day, I had that fellow that is with the one I just had, and there is no escape unless we go in some place and remain there."

"Come here you infernal bum and bring your rickshaw," I called. And he came with a rush, perseverance rewarded, as he well knew it would be if he only kept us in sight long enough. Of course, we could have turned them over to the Sikh and they would have given them the run, but after all, they have their living to make and are necessary.

We went back to Tom Pow Ching's once more and after a short stop, went to a restaurant and had a pretty fair meal served to us. After that, of course, as we were getting full, we had to go to the usual place for the night, as all good sailors do. Here we anchored for the night and dismissed our "horses," paying them and giving them twenty or thirty cents for a "chow." They left, as they knew where to find us next morning.

The house was the usual common place house of its kind, a two story shack, and it was situated down the river front among many of its kind. The girls [were] the usual run of Chinese girls. They are entirely different from the Yoshiwara girl[s] of Japan in that they will not drink anything; no matter how strong[ly I] pressed them, they would not. And what is more, [they] tried to prevent us from drinking.

"You drink. Bimeby you die. What for you drink? Makee sick."

That's the way they look at it and I judge they are right. I only wish to Heavens I had the same view as firmly implanted. But on this night, after being so long aboard, we made quite a night of it. It doesn't take much to make a man drunk after being confined any length of time aboard ship.

I forgot to mention while in Tom Pow Ching's getting ammunition for the night, a bright looking lad of about ten years of age came in to make a purchase. He was clad in a bluejacket's uniform and had the *Oregon*'s cap ribbon on his cap. A bright and winning looking little chap, he spoke to us with quite a foreign accent, very deliberate, as if choosing his words, but [he] use[d] the purest English. It sounded queer to me to hear such pure lingo from such a youngster, whom [at] a second glance we perceived was a half-caste. "What ship do you belong to? The *Oregon?*" he asked, as if he was a man of thirty instead of a young tot.

"Yes, and what ship do you belong to, my young man?" we asked in return.

"Oh, I belong to the *Oregon* also," he replied, showing the ribbon on his cap. "I am an American."

"Oh, you are?"

"Yes. My father is an American, and he comes from Baltimore, where his grandfather lived before. He is an American pilot. I am going back home, and I am never going to leave America again. China is no good."

Shanghai

"So, you want to go to America, to Baltimore. Have you ever been to America?"

"No," he replied wisely, "but it is the best country, my father says, and he says we are all going back to live there, never to leave it again."

"Well, when you go to Baltimore," I said, "perhaps I shall see you. I lived there a long time myself. And America is a big place with great, high buildings."

"Yes, I know. My father has told me and I have read a great deal about it." Then to the store keeper, Tom Pow Ching, "I want a bottle of Mellin's food for my little baby sister."

"So, then you have a *'chisi'* at your house?" we asked as Tom was hunting for the Mellin's food.

"Yes, my little sister," and continued he wisely and in boyish confidence, "I have two little puppies also, and I can give you one if you want it. A little Fox Terrier puppy."

"All right, we will be glad to have it. Here, kid, do you want anything for yourself? Pick out some candy if you want it."

He didn't want to take it at first, but finally we prevailed upon him to select a bottle of candies, and handing the Mellin's food and candy to Tom Pow Ching, I asked how much, passing him a Mex at the same time. Tom took out for the food, but he demurred a great deal, finally he compromised by being allowed to pay for the candy.

"What are you?" asked W——. "You're a half-caste, aren't you?"

He flushed a little, and we could see where the shoe pinched, although we both of us wasn't exactly in the state to study countenances [for] human emotions.

"Yes," he replied, looking up bravely. "I am a half-caste. My father is an American and my mother is half Cantonese and half Portuguese."

Here one of Tom Pow's many retainers around the store chimed in, apropos of nothing: "Yes, yes. Bimeby you see mother and you kiss mother."

My mate turned and gave the Chinaman a black look and started to call him down in no gentle terms. But the mother found an ample, tho' small champion in her bright youngster. With his small fist clenched and mad all over, he started for the Chinaman, looking for some weapon to use on him, and we had to pull him away. W—— grabbed the boy and quieted him down, and I grabbed the Chinese, ostensibly to part him from the boy, but in reality I gave his neck such a twist that it took the breath away from him. But the boy was mad at the remark made about his mother and it took all W—— could do to get him started quietly home again. But we finally got him safely away and well started, and we bade him good bye. [He was a]s straight a youngster, and as manly a boy as I have ever ran across, and one his parents should be proud of. I have often thought I should like to meet him again.

Half castes are looked down upon and made to feel their position keenly. It is worse in these Oriental countries than the same thing would be at home, alto' such alliances are perfectly honorable and conform to the Chinese laws. And any offspring from these marriages are as legitimate as if the union was of the same blood. But then, you know, people love to make it unpleasant for others, and nothing gives such smug satisfaction as the feeling that some people have that I am better than my neighbor, better born, etc.

~ ~ ~

Great Scott! What an infernal head I had the morning we left the house where we had sojourned for the night. It felt almost as bad as if I had gotten full on champagne. In spite of this dreaded head, a man will persist in getting full and with bluejackets it is an old, old story. We drove up to Black Mary's for our breakfast. It was early and only a few of the people were astir. The day was Sunday, but this day is not observed generally in these cities, only a few of the Europeans gathering for worship and perhaps a few Christian Chinamen? Black Mary has been in Shanghai for thirty years, and her place is much frequented by man-o-warsmen in search of a square meal, in preference to the grill rooms and hotels with flash names.

She is a large cullud [colored] lady of the old school, the vintage of before the [U.S. Civil] war, but she knows how to put up a good, square meal at a reasonable price. We arrived there and by that time the ride thro' the bracing air revived us and drove away that all gone feeling, so we managed to do justice to a good breakfast. Of course, our rickys made the usual request for "chow" money which was given them, but they hardly ever went for a chow. They would withdraw around some convenient corner and await our coming forth. I imagine they ate about once a day, and then stowed away a large cargo of rice that lasted for at least 12 hours.

From Mary's we called our ruffians again, and upon their asking our destination, we told them to take it slow, as we wanted to "look, see." So they hauled us with a gentle gait. The only break my man made was running up close to one of those carts that carries two passengers. Built like a wheelbarrow, you have to have two passengers to keep it evenly balanced. He created a diversion for himself by almost taking the lower extremities off of the young Chinese girl sitting on our side, scaring her almost into hysterics. This brought a storm of abuse from the coolie pushing this vehicle, and that is just what my varlet was looking for, so they roundly abused each other. My man must have gotten the better of the dispute, for he laughed and cavorted and left the coolie mad with rage. These little incidents were frequent all along the line.

Finally, some exquisite wood carvings attracting our attention, we stopped and went inside to take a "look, see." I had the buying mania then, and after much haggling, I purchased a finely carved cabinet photo frame, four pieces hinged together, a splendid piece of wood-carving and scroll-saw work. For this I paid $5.50 Mex. I could have purchased any quantity of wood-carvings in the round of exquisite little carved figures typical of Chinese life, modes of punishment, here a small figure of a man hanging by his neck in a cage, his toes barely touching the flooring beneath him.

Shanghai

Another with his hands manacled behind his back and a square board around his neck to prevent him from reaching food, figures of a rickshaw and passenger and man, every phase of Chinese life. They were beautiful, but I had no place to put them.

From there we went to a photographic [studio] and had a dozen cabinet [photos] taken for curio pictures. This is another sailors' habit of getting photos in foreign cities. These were richly tinted, and [it] was beyond doubt the finest studio in Shanghai. This constituted our morning, and back we went at a lope for Mary's to have a chicken dinner, having purchased three chickens before we let for our ride.

After we had done justice to a well-cooked and served dinner or tiffin. (Tiffin is the word in Oriental countries and is the equivalent of luncheon in the States, or dinner for the common herd.) The bluejacket takes dinner at noon. The officers and the smart set take tiffin. The common herd has supper or tea, the smart set and the gentlemen aft had dinner.[3] So you see what little niceties of etiquette and custom divide the two classes, the lower five and the upper ten, the rabble and the elite. If you are bourgeois, but have money, you can ape the upper crust. It doesn't matter that it takes three generations to make a gentleman. Birth hasn't anything to do with taking tiffin; just have the coin and you can call it luncheon, tiffin or dinner. "You pays your money and you take yer choice," see!

There is one officer on this battleship that is known to the crew as "Scum of the earth." He derived this name from making the remark that the men for'd were the off scourings and refuse of the cities and seaports, and one day he told the chief boatswain's mate to "pipe the scum of the earth to tiffin." This same gentleman (?) was also overheard to make the remark, "I can't see for the life of me where all that scum for'd get all their mail. Why, the idea! They receive more correspondence than we officers do. I think really the majority of the correspondence comes from 'soiled doves.'" Shade of the immortal Paul Jones! This gentleman (?) can trace his ancestry back possibly one generation and then I doubt if he would have the temerity to inquire any further for fear of finding his "family thread waxed at the farther end by some plebian vocation." Among the men, he was ever after known as "Scum" and that name will follow him all thro' his naval career. Happily, not all are of his calibre.

This time we went to see a tattooer. That's another sailor's hobby afloat or ashore. Our "rickies" hauled us rapidly to Astor Road to Horishaw's place. Horishaw is one of the most artistic tattooers in all Japan, if not in the world. Chyo at Yokohama was the very best, a man so expert with a needle that on his beautifully executed butterflies and birds, snakes, etc., you could almost detect the dust and feathery down. [Chyo] could tattoo a fly so lifelike that your first impulse would be to brush it off instinctively. Chyo died, and Horishaw succeeds to his mantle according to my view. Horishaw is quite an old man also. We found four assistants in his small shop off Broadway. All of these men were fitted to be master tattooists themselves. When a boy, I had lots of bad work tattooed upon my arms and upper part of my body, and it has always been my custom wherever I meet a good tattooer to get an example of their work to cover these old designs.

A Sailor's Log

I have examples of nearly all prominent Japanese and American tattooers, of which Reilly of New York is the acknowledged head. Now tattooing is more than a fad. More people have tattooing upon them than the general public imagines. Plenty of people are prejudiced against it. Plenty of people are prejudiced against many things that don't exactly concur with their ideas. I am writing for those that are not prejudiced against it, or those that are curious about this custom, that when done rightly is worthy to take rank with other arts. To some people it is a sign of degeneracy, Lombroso the criminologist, so saith.[4] But then, anything can be construed as a sign of degeneracy. Signs of degeneracy in the human race are as plentiful as the symptom blanks of some specialist. Does your ears ring? Have you a sense of fullness after eating? Does everything you eat go to your stomach? Do you like prunes? If you have any of these symptoms you have the "bots," and only Dr. Ofty Gooft's Mague Pellets will cure you. Price, 25 cts., etc.

I like tattooing myself and so do many, many others. I have some splendid examples of the best work. I got Horishaw to prick a large snake around my neck to cover an old necklace that had been done years ago. I gave him the price he asked without any haggling. It doesn't pay to beat a man down at this work. He will only slight the work. Horishaw put a fine piece of work. It took him five hours. Finding out in the course of conversation that I was interested in the art, and [had] done quite a bit of it myself, his first request was for some designs of American faces. The Jap cannot depict European features with any degree of success. I told him I would send him an old book of designs that contained the very thing he was looking for. I drew him rapidly a couple of faces in full and profile, at which they were all pleased. This I did in a very good manner, considering the shaky condition of my nerves. I left him, promising to return the next day and get some work covered up on my arm.

It was then time for supper for us (not dinner). After supper we took a trip thro' the Chinese tea houses and streets more frequented by the Chinese. Leaving the more European streets, we were soon in the midst of them. It was now dark, and the narrow streets presented a most animated appearance. Chinamen love plenty of light. Altho' an ordinary night, it seemed to us as if it was a holiday occasion from the crowds. The rickies left their rickshaws at a stand and piloted us thro' the crowds. Chinamen of every degree and costume, men, women, and children, [were] all chattering gaily, swarms of them going in and out of tea houses, all good natured and regarding us with friendly looks. Lights [were lit] everywhere and the sound of Chinese music.

While looking up at a teahouse, a pleasant looking Chinaman accosted us in very good English. "You want to take a look? Come on, I will show you around." Nothing loath, we followed, as he was of the better class by his looks and demeanor. He explained to us as we went along. We followed him up into one of the largest tea houses. Elbowing our way thro' the crowded rooms, we passed men and women sitting at tables drinking tea or smoking the water pipe. All [were] well dressed and happy; no strife of the Boxers appeared to bother them. They smiled at us good naturedly and in many cases nodded pleasantly. The tables were marble topped, the marble set in

Shanghai

wood. Taking a seat at one of the many tables, tea was served to us. Our guide told us to pay the man who brought the tea. I think it was three Mex. I remember thinking at the time that low prices in China must have been only a myth, for if everybody in this particular tea house paid so much, the proprietors must have been very prosperous. But then, I reflected, these were special prices for American sailors who are lined with gold and lavish of it. This price included our two rickshaw men, who took seats at a back table and were served, as also our guide, who chatted with us and explained the general customs.

All around the big room, or number of rooms, were benches partitioned off. Almost every one of these places were occupied by some Chinamen smoking opium, some in the land of dreams, others just getting into the dreamy state. No one paid any attention to them. It is the custom of a thousand years and more. I made an attempt to smoke a water pipe. I don't care to hit up dope; I have too many vices as it is. I filled the pipe and settled back for a long smoke. The Chinese sitting around laughed good naturedly and all volunteered to show [me]. I handed the nickeled pipe to my guide, who took some tobacco from a jar on the table, put it in the bowl and lit it, took one whiff with his eyes closed, and knocked it out and refilled it. "You fill pipe every time." Something on the Japanese style, I thought.

The tea I found excellent, and quickly poured out what hot water we had. The tea, you know, is in the cups, or rather the tea leaves [are] in a small perforated bowl inside the drinking cup. Upon this you pour your water, and you have a good drink of tea. I can drink more tea than any Chinaman. After exhausting the first supply, the guide called for more, which was quickly brought. The Chinese musicians were all the time rendering selections of music, I suppose their most popular airs. It would have been enjoyable if we had understood it. It was singing and instruments together. The girls of them possessed fine voices, and in this particular tea-house there were about fifty in the orchestra, from very young girls about twelve, up to the fully matured women, all dressed in gaudy costumes of silk and brocade, their faces painted in the highest form of art, more highly colored than even their singing sisters of Japan, the geishas. Plenty of rice powder, and carmine tinted lips and cheeks, the eyebrows penciled black with the ends cut very square where the eyebrows meet over the nose. Some of them are very pretty when they haven't this war-paint on, but this enhances their beauty in Oriental eyes. But they are much prettier with their clear, olive complexions, which all Chinese and Japanese girls possess. We finished the second serving of water, or rather, I did, [as] the two shipmates with me didn't like tea and the guide sipped his very slowly as all Chinese do. So, lighting up fresh cigarettes, we signaled to the guide to make a move.

Passing out of this tea house he led us thro' the crowded streets to another and larger house across the way. This was the same as the other one only on a far larger scale. This also was crowded to its utmost capacity. We didn't take seats in this one, but walked around the aisles where there were the same partitioned small booths with their Chinese occupant[s] under the drug or philosophically smoking away. I didn't see any of the women in these booths. They were either walking around or sitting at the many tables smoking the water pipe or drinking tea. Many of them were very pretty and all [were] well dressed.

Out in the street once more, with its strange sights. Thro' the crowded thoroughfare a rickshaw was impossible and sedan chairs were very numerous. Every once [in] awhile we had to step aside at the call of the chair bearers, and we would peek curiously thro' the curtained window and catch a glimpse of some mandarin, or some Chinese girl or woman of the higher class, I suppose with their feet so deformed that it was impossible to walk. Thro' the dark, silken hangings of one of these chairs I caught a glance from a pair of black slant eyes set in as pretty a face as one would wish. The eyes fairly spoke and sparkled with coquetry. They love admiration as well as their sisters of the Occident. A glimpse of rich silks, and the chair with its fair occupant swept by. For one brief second I held those eyes by mine and an answering smile quickly lit up the dark, piquant Oriental face. Just a glimpse of dark eyes in a crowd, and then on out of one's life, but it left a pleasant thrill behind, and.... But I quickly banished this reverie upon our conductor stopping in front of a brilliantly lit entrance that appeared no different than the rest of the houses.

"Chinese Theatre. You want to go inside?" Yes, we did. So we pushed thro' the chairs and crowd at the door and purchased tickets. Here the rickshaw men were ignominiously fired. They weren't allowed to pass inside, but they were used to that and didn't mind in the least, so to salve their wounded feelings we gave them the usual "chow" money. This suited them better. And going thro' the door we found ourselves in the gallery. It must have been a good play from the size of the house. We secured three seats, and our guide motioned us to take them and he stood. No sooner were we seated, the Chinamen on either side of us making room, than we were served with a cup of tea. This cup was covered with a saucer. I, being the tea drinker of the crowd, sipped mine. Thousands of eyes were diverted from the stage and curiously viewed the three bluejackets, but in not an unfriendly manner.

I looked around the house. It was full. Lord knows how long the performance kept up or had been on; it was then about 11:30. But we were not the only "foreign devils" in the house, for right in the centre, across from us we noticed three Sikhs. "Hindoo men," whispered the guide. "No good." He said this in such a decisive manner there wasn't any room for doubt. All good Chinos hate these people from their overbearing ways. In fact, all are disliked, [and] all Europeans. Americans they don't seem to have such a decided antipathy against. They recognize the fact that the Americans do not seek to rob them of territory or infringe on their rights, but only seek to protect their own. Everywhere we were met with good will and friendly feeling.

After reviewing the house, I turned my attention to the stage. The Chinese orchestra was situated at the back of the stage in plain view of the audience. The business was almost like a Coney Island concert hall. The leading woman (a man) was no doubt a princess from the rich costume of yellow brocaded silk, richly embroidered. I could make out the funny man, or comedian. And the hero. Evidently it was the same old story of a princess in love with some obscure prince, and the undesirable suit of a more powerful mandarin with the sanction of the parent. The same coercion. And objections on the maiden's part, who loved her prince, and finally love triumphed over all and everything no doubt turned out happily.

The [stage] business of the funny man was very good. He would tumble at the appropriate time and in tune to the big tom-tom. His funny business was along the same lines pursued by our own knock-abouts, and was good. It was all clear as to action. The words were unnecessary. It was as if looking at a performance thro' a kinetoscope. The music was very pleasant, and it was all a novelty. Vendors came around with candied apples, very small, about ten of them strung on a stick. I had to try these, of course, and found them delicious, almost melting in the mouth. But sweets didn't agree with me then, not after the jag of the night before. A dose of sour kraut and a couple of lagers would have been more acceptable.

We grew tired of the theatre and asked our guide if he was ready to go, [but] he was loath to leave the performance, and we staid on about fifteen minutes longer to please him. Finally, he, with an effort, [and] knowing his duty to us, drew away and asked us if we were ready to leave, and we left. Outside in the street we found our faithful rogues awaiting us. It was then getting close on to midnight. Our Mongolian friend went with us quite a distance and then left us a couple of "dobies" richer by his few hours work. We wanted to go through the old Chinese city of Shanghai, and made an appointment with our guide to meet us the next morning. This he promised to do, but on [awakening] early the next morning and finding the "rickies" ready, we made a start expecting to find our friend of the night before at the gate, or somewhere, as Chinamen have a way of springing up and finding you on all occasions.

Taking breakfast at Mrs. Dale's, another lady who keeps an eating house for bluejackets and has been long in Shanghai, and making arrangements with her for dinner, we started for the old city. We had been warned by kindly intentioned people that it would be unsafe to go thro' the city on account of the trouble with the Boxers, there being an estimate of three or four thousand of them in Old Shanghai. But we concluded to take chances. We were quickly hauled thro' the French quarter of the town and arrived in front of the old walled city. Here our rickshaw men left their vehicles in charge of the third man and two of them went with us. All around this city wall there is a stream answering the purpose of a moat. Huge cauldrons were strung at intervals all along the wall as far as we could see, for what purpose, I couldn't or didn't ascertain. We crossed the bridge from [the] French town to the gates [of the old quarter] and went inside thro' the narrow entrance. We were in another world. We were to all intents and purposes transferred back centuries. No modern convenience here. All is old, very, very old, even the beggar at the gate, whom the rickshaw men explained had his legs burned off above the knees by quicklime for piracy.

A Sailor's Log

Narrow streets that allow only room for a couple of foot passengers and sedan chairs. The streets [were] lined with shops. Here we were looked at with curious eyes, and on stopping in front of some of the shops and looking around leisurely, we would catch them whispering together. But occasionally [we] would catch the word "Americans" and that seemed to be the magic word that left us unmolested. But we felt out of place. There was that feeling of insecurity. Who could tell what moment some fanatical Chink would make some outcry against the "foreign devils"? It would only take the turning of a hair, a stone thrown from some window or housetop, to start the ball going, and then there wouldn't be any of us to tell the tale. In these intricate passages it would be easy to do away with a larger party than us.

Possibly some one had noticed us going in the old Chinese city, but there wasn't any one [who] accosted us. We strolled along leisurely, looking at the shops. At one place we stopped and bought a couple of ivory cigarette holders. One I purchased had a beautiful dragon carved upon it in relief. They are very good carvers in ivory and bone, these Chinamen, all done laboriously by hand and old fashioned Chinese drills and lathes of wood. Their metal work is the same, finely executed and finished. We watched them making water and opium pipes of metal. A shop of coppersmiths were beating out copper pans and basins equal to our best machine work. Their hardware, cutlery, etc., is of fine steel, but lacks the finish of European goods. It is roughly finished as it comes from the forge and [is] sharpened and ready for the market. [There were little] cups and bowls for opium smoking turned from horn and ivory, crochet needles carved in intricate and Oriental designs, pipes with long ivory stems. Shops galore containing shoes, silks, etc., are on all hands. Vendors [hawked] tiny fighting crickets, each one in a separate bamboo cage about 1" square, the entire stock consisting of trained fighting crickets. Some we saw were enclosed in little round cases covered with glass with a small hole to breathe thro'. Chinamen have cricket fights and wager on the results. What first attracted me to them was the continued chirping. The sail-maker bought and brought off to the ship two of these pugnacious little green insects, and not knowing of their being trained for fighting, turned them both loose in his sail locker. The next morning he found one dead, and the other with his leg bitten off. They had sought each other out and held a fierce battle during the night.

One shop near the gate contained hundreds of birds from jackdaws and parrots down to the smallest wren. Hundreds of wooden cages were piled atop of one another, each with a little winged prisoner. At every turn of the crooked, winding, tortuous street could be seen some strange sight. Quite a crowd followed us and at times they blockaded the streets. The two rickies seemed well acquainted and no doubt explained what we were. At the end of one street we came out on a pond or artificial lake, whose bosom was completely covered with green slime. In the centre stood a large tea-house. Leading out to the tea-house was a foot bridge about three feet in width. This was all of granite. It stood on granite piers. The flagging was of large slabs of granite. The railings were of the same stone. This bridge led out to the tea

Shanghai

house and across the pond or lake in a zig-zag matter. Of course, we went over this bridge and thro' the tea-house, in which quite a crowd were smoking and sipping tea. Our appearance in their midst didn't seem to attract much attention, and we continued on across the bridge.[5]

"Now we go see chin-chin joss. Very big joss," said the ruffian, and he led us thro' more side streets of evil smells and mongrel dogs and dirty Chinamen and beggars. We came suddenly upon a small court and there was the joss house. A monster about twenty feet in height stood in front. He was a fierce specimen of the art. Around him were smaller animals, fearful and wonderful vagaries of the Oriental artist whose design they were. Going inside we found josses of all kinds, sizes and condition, some thousands of years old ranged along the sides of the joss house.[6] In the centre stood another fierce looking big fellow so hideously ugly he would frighten a child or a nervous person half to death. Inside the rail were a number of devotees burning incense or joss sticks in front of this large deity. Our appearance inside of these temples occasioned no surprise. The keeper, as ugly as one of the painted images whose caretaker he was, only looked up at us and then turned to his pipe again. Some of these old josses are in need badly of a new coat of paint and gold leaf. They show signs of age and wear. What stories they could tell of the human heart! What troubles have been carried to these unresponsive wooden grotesques! If they were to spring suddenly into life and could speak of ages a gone, it would [be] a wonderful tale.

"Yes, John. These very big, very good joss. Plenty joss hab got. Twenty, thirty piecee, so," I said to my rickie.

"Yass, yes. Him very big man, this piecee," laying his hand upon the big fellow.

Time was when no "foreign devil" could enter these sacred houses, but now it occasions no comment. The pillars of these houses are elaborately carved with dragons, and small and large dogs of weird aspect guard the entrance to the chamber of horrors where the big fellow holds forth in all his sullen majesty, surrounded by a no less forbidding looking court.

"All right. We look, see nother joss house." And we were led further on thro' another place. This was not as imposing as the first, but was of a different design, and the josses, tho' smaller, were still more horrible and were no doubt the very acme of an opium-distorted dream. The artist simply outdid himself here, for of all the fiercest expressions upon things of wood, these took the palm. If a man with the jim jams[7] was turned loose in here alone, thought I, it would prove his finish. We were tired of joss houses and had been about two hours inside the old city and we concluded to go out, and told the rickshaw men to lead us out again.

"All right, but we take a look-see at police station, then we go."

This was in our road out, and was a square enclosure. Outside, as we were going in, a crowd gathered, as ruffianly looking a horde as I have ever beheld. They looked ripe for the commission of any crime. No wonder, from the look of these ragged, unkempt animals, the Chinese have to inflict such exquisite tortures to have any effect at all upon them. One particularly brutal looking Chink ran up jabbering in an excitable way and pointing at us, he spoke to our guides and they jabbered back and what they said seemed to satisfy them, for they soon subdued their voices and gestures. This was the only time I feared trouble during our visit to the city, and glad enough was I that we were close to the police station.

We went all thro' this enclosure. It looked like a practicing yard for horses, with little houses and cells opening upon the court. We didn't see any prisoners here, excepting one, and he was in a large cage outside the enclosure, and he was pacing up and down like a hyena. In front of the main building there stood an array of old muskets and spears. The guns, some of them were "two man pieces" and "three man pieces," [included] one or two modern rifles among them. The bayonets attached were of all sizes from an old style Springfield bayonet, to the broad spade bayonet. The spears and pikes were wonderful and fearful weapons of war. One had three prongs like Neptune's trident, only each prong was broader than a man's hand and two feet long. Anyone unfortunate enough to get prodded with this would find himself in a dozen sections. This stand of arms wasn't in any degree uniform. They must have been souvenirs of bygone ages, captured from criminals at diverse times. I only saw one solitary officer in the station and he hadn't any uniform on to designate his rank, and only one occupant, and he the occupant of the wooden barred cage. Business must have been dull. There was also an absence of beggars. Perhaps it was too early in the day for the begging element to be up and doing.

We left the police station and proceeded to leave the Chinese city. We had seen enough for that time, at least. The ragged crowd followed us a little distance and then vanished into the holes and corners and mazes of streets. I was glad, for one. I didn't in the least hanker after any of their society. They looked willing for anything and altho' our rickshaw men, who seemed to belong to the same set, had vouched for us as being good "foreign devils," still I confess it was with a feeling of relief that we kept getting nearer and nearer the gate. Ours was an example of supreme faith and trust in our rickshaw men. No man could find his way thro' this old city by himself. He would wander around for a week and be no nearer the exit than at first. He would have to learn the shops to find where he was at. I recognized the shops coming back and knew that we were nearing the entrance. One of my companions had left a meerschaum cigar holder that had the amber mouth piece broken, to be repaired at one of the ivory workers' shops, and I recognized the shop in the distance. We had to wait a considerable time before it was finished, and then it was a bad job. It couldn't be otherwise on account of the hurry.

Everything we bought in the old city cost us more than the same article would at home. The rascally rickies were to blame for this. They wanted largess or "comshur" themselves, and they must have made quite a little profit from our numerous purchases. This is to be expected. It is an interesting phase of the Oriental character. The Chinese will beat you in a trade, but in the whole, have a fine sense of honesty, as also [have] the Japs. I can't find any fault with this. We simply pay for our ignorance. America and England are about the only countries in which a store-keeper will charge

Shanghai

one price to all. If a Chinaman or Japanese went in any of our stores, large or small, he would get the same prices as ourselves, but not so here. There are prices for us, and prices for them, and you would be surprised at the difference.

We finally reached the gate and passed out, having been about three hours inside the old city of Shanghai. What a sigh of relief escaped each of us! We breathed freer, and our rickshaw men didn't appear half as formidable as when piloting us thro' the old city. We had lost our sense of dependence on them. We passed across the bridge into the French sector and took our rickshaws and were bowling merrily along, lying back luxuriously, having seen the old city and fulfilled our duty of seeing all that was to be seen.

This was Sunday, and we were to be aboard at about 4:30 in the afternoon, having to leave Shanghai on the 2:30 train for Woosung. We still had a few hours to spare, and we went to Horishaw's, the tattooer, and let him put a little more decoration on us. From there we went to Mrs. Dale's and had a dinner (not tiffin) of corn beef and cabbage, and then it was all over. During this day we hadn't drank anything and if we had been allowed ashore any longer, wouldn't have touched it. It is only the first break after being aboard for so long that makes one get drunk.

About 1:30 we told the rascals to take us to the station. It was all over, and I had the same "dark blue" feeling. It is just like going back to jail. I knew it would take me a week to straighten out and fall back into routine. We paid our men liberally so that even they, with their insatiable appetite, were pleased. They were all pleased and I know if ever we went ashore in Shanghai again, they would capture us.

We sat down watching the crowds at the station and the wrangling of the rickshaw men who are thick as flies here. The boys commenced to come back, some full as goats, others not so bad, and almost every rickie had a quarrel with his passenger, until [he] saw the watchman or a Sikh coming toward [him], who would lay about him freely with a bamboo stick. There were a few Europeans in the station and a good class of Chinese, and some of these Chinese women were decidedly good to look at. One in particular struck my fancy. She was in charge of a pretty little European miss about six years of age. She presented as neat and well groomed an appearance as any girl of her class I have ever seen, with her raven hair combed smoothly back in the approved fashion, with the usual gilt ornaments. She had more expression than the general run of Chinese women, and I'll wager had more intelligence than her occupation called for. Her complexion was of a clear, healthy, olive hue, [and] contrasted well with the jet black hair and well penciled eyebrows. Her eyes were wider and more speaking than the most. There wasn't any deformity about her small feet. They were as nature made them. In this, of course, she was low born, and the small Chinese shoe and stocking would do credit to a modern Cinderella. Clad as to dress in the costume of her country women with low-reaching blouse falling to her knees, made of light blue silk with dark facings and silken trousers of the same material, she would serve as a model of what the Chinese woman should be, as far as outward appearances go.

With a roguish look upon her pretty face, she would follow her charge about. At the same time taking surreptitious puffs from a cigarette. This only enhanced her charms. Possibly the little lady was well aware of them. No doubt she had been told that she was a very pretty girl, and it was true. She was the prettiest I had seen in a long time. That was only another face that attracted me and then [was] lost in the passing show.

The train pulled in and we boarded it. The fellows produced bottles, but I didn't feel like imbibing. I was getting over mine and didn't care about prolonging the agony. The gang was a merry one and no one was absent. The short run to Woosung was quickly made, and handing in our tickets to the tall Sikh, we passed thro'. The majority stopped at the bar to get a last "ball" before going aboard. We kept on down to the boat, and gradually the fellows straggled down. Of course we were beset by the few Chinks around the landing. Some had beer to sell. Others had whiskey. One old fellow showed a bottle of "Sam Choo" and the drunks made a charge for him. One marine corralled the bottle and, as he [the Chinese man] resisted, the others picked him up bodily and threw him overboard. He swam out and made for a place of safety, heaping all kinds of Mongolian curses on his despoilers. This sort of thing makes me weary. I hate to see anyone imposed on. But the gang's excuse was "He's only a [damned] Chino, anyhow." That's so, but still he is human, and perhaps more of a man than his tormentors were. That wound up the day. We came aboard and the liberty was over for that time.

~ ~ ~

It took me just about one week to get over my usual dose of "blues" after coming aboard. Liberty always affects me in that manner, and the same is true of the majority of my shipmates who, whether hard drinkers when ashore or temperate, are always demoralized upon their return to the ship. After being aboard a long time, and no liberty being given, a bluejacket is more resigned, but when liberty is at last given, as I have said before in this journal (or to be nautical, log), you try to concentrate all the enjoyment in twenty four or forty eight hours, that has been denied you in the past couple of months. And as for enjoyment, we oftimes make a mess of it. At best, it is an unnatural life. Man is a social animal and he likes to be out in the world adoing, associating with up to date people. On ship board, you know your mates. You know them too well, and their powers for entertainment are soon exhausted. And oh, how dull and monotonous life becomes to us! Thus we make asses of ourselves ashore. We are for the time being madmen. When we realize where we are at, and how we are making fools of ourselves, and settle down to conduct ourselves as becomes a good citizen, it is time to go aboard, and the next time is just the same old act, but possibly in a different setting.

The *Brooklyn* had long been expected in from Taku, and great preparations were going on for the Admiral's inspection. Decks were shellacked, the entire ship painted inside and out, and everything was clean as a pin. The *Iris* came in with lots of stores and the balance of our ammunition. Having brought lots of paymaster's stores, especially pea coats, every man who hadn't a pea-coat was compelled to draw one, and this scooped in about two-thirds of the entire ship's company. I have been packing this useless article around for near five years and it has been uniform just twice in that time with me, and that on the North Atlantic Station. But lots of profit for some one is in selling plenty of pea coats at nearly eleven dollars gold apiece. Puzzle, find the man whom it benefited. And maybe someone didn't reap "comshur" from tons of dirt we rec'd for coal. And the chief engineer made a howl because the aux[iliary] watches burned so much of it to keep up steam. This was the only coal I ever happened to be shipmates with that I'll wager was 95% ashes and refuse. A tidy sum can be reaped from five-hundred tons of coal of that kind, but I can't see where the chief had any kick coming. He was supposed to inspect it, and had the option of accepting or refusing. So . . .

The regulation uniform affair that had created such a stir in our midst had collapsed for the time being. The skipper was good enough to be pleased with our appearance, and it dropped thro'. But everyone had to have a pea coat, tho'.

The *Brooklyn* at last made her debut in Woosung toward the latter part of September [1900]. This ship also had the reputation of a "floating hell" among the crew. I can't vouch for it. I can only vouch that the *Oregon* seemed to be getting better, altho' the men sometimes had to go below and scale and paint bunkers on Sundays. This was unnecessary work. Altogether, life for us was made quite unpleasant, but it wasn't half as unbearable as at first. The bolo-man was still as obnoxious [as] of yore, but I suppose "custom makes rule" and you get used to ill-usage.

One cold morning very early, I arose from a rather doubtful couch in Shanghai, on this occasion more from a desire to get out and get a breath of cool, sweet air from the foul odors of the room in which I slept, and also to cool my fevered brain from a rather rough night of it, than from habit or the love of early rising. The place in which I found myself was just the ordinary Chinese shack with its bed composed of the soft side of a plank and a scant quilt for a covering. This was my second liberty in the town [November 1900], fully a month after the first one.

I had come ashore from the anchorage at Woosung the afternoon previous, and had made my usual visit to Horishaw the tattooer and there had more work done. It had proven so cold in his place (Japs aren't much for fires) and the cold and the torture of the needles and the long sitting of six hours under them, had caused me to partake rather freely of large hot potations of sake, of which I am very fond. The cold, the pain, and the sake put me under the weather, and when I wandered forth from his place, I was content to get a bed anywhere, and my rascal of a ricky, the same one I had previously, ran me to the commonest shack his dull wits knew of. I suppose the usual "comshur" was in it. Too tired to haggle, and chilled thro', I tumbled in. But I was bothered by the rickshaw man for his pay. Having given him about a dollar in small change thro' the day for "chow," this angered me. And letting a roar out of me, I paid him and his running mate in full and told him not to let me see his ugly phiz again. This in itself wouldn't faze him, but I went to sleep after securing my belt with the iron money in it, well around me. I had a time getting warmed and had quite a chill from the long sitting under Horishaw and his assistants' needles, but finally I drifted into dreamland, and once more was at home in America, unnagged by rickshaw men and others too numerous to mention that always want "comshur."

It was early, very early, when I awoke. I could hear a cock crow close by. He might have been in the same room as myself, for aught I know. Looking at my watch, it was about fifteen minutes past four. "I'll get out of this anyway," I thought. "Too many odors not of 'Araby the blest' to suit me, and I will walk around until the shops begin to open." It was still dark when I reached the narrow streets. A rickshaw was standing by the door. This, of course, was my varlet's, and something that resembled a bundle of rags was curled up in it. This was my varlet, sleeping the sleep of the just, with his bare feet hanging over the dash board of his wagon. Feeling good, I overturned the rickshaw and him both and left him trying to find out how it happened and where he was, while I turned a corner and slipped away down the street.

The morning was very cool in mid-November and I had to walk rather briskly, being without a pea-coat, in order to get warmed up. Few Chinamen were about. Here and there could be discerned a shadowy shape in the distance, only to fade away. I passed a few stalls where a "pigtail" was bending over a charcoal fire, cooking some Chinese mixture that emitted quite a savory smell, but I didn't care to sample any of their dishes this early in the morning. I tried a cup of tea at one stall and it cheered me up a little. I was in some of the by-streets of the town, and people were beginning to stir. I walked on aimlessly, not caring where I went, as I knew I couldn't get lost. All I had to do was to take a rickshaw man. My desire was to kill time until the larger stores and tiffin rooms opened up.

At last, the first streak of dawn made its appearance. People were rising and opening doors and windows all around. Men and women carrying produce of all kinds were making their way along, presumably toward some market house, possibly one I had passed not long since. Getting tired of wandering at random, I struck out for the European concession. Happily, I was on the right tack for I soon passed down into Nanking Road, one of the great marts of the European concessions. This street is lined with Chinese shops of all descriptions and as one gets down toward the Bund, the shops are almost equal in size to those in any prosperous city at home or abroad. I straggled along, taking in the sights in a very leisurely manner, and in these cities there is much of interest to be seen.

Reaching the Bund, the broad thoroughfare that runs along the Whangpoo riverfront, I turned and continued out, looking at the shipping in the river. People were rapidly filling the street, coolie laborers, the better class of Chinamen, with a plentiful

Shanghai

sprinkling of Europeans, the majority of them English and French. Sampan men were cleaning up their boats for the day's work. Now an English Jackie would pass down and hail one of them and be pulled over to his ship. Men of war were plentiful in the stream, a stone's throw from the Bund. Over in front of the large, imposing banking building paced a couple of Sikhs, clad in blue with heavy capes, not less dignified and imposing looking than the building they were on "sentry go" before. But I trust the banking corporation wasn't quite as big a bluff as the Sikhs are.

A beautiful street is the Bund, and especially so did it appear to me on this chill November morning, more especially so to a man just let loose, so to speak, from school. More especially so, as I had in a large belt above 200 large "dobies" or Bryan dollars of the Mexican breed, for would not all this "*gelt,*" or as we call them "ginkos," furnish the wherewithal to warm the inner man to a superlative degree of warmth? Was I not "panhandling"[8] along this cold, but beautiful street, lined with stately dwellings and business houses on one side, and the Whangpoo river on the other, with all its bustle and life? By choice, couldn't all these "ginkos" (which weighted rather heavily, to be sure) cause me to be smiled upon by some congenial host in any place that my fancy dictated I should go? Couldn't I get in some grill room and lay back with a large hot toddy and a pipe, or even a "hot bidd[9] and a cold bottle" if I wished? But just at the time, I was out for the love of it.

I passed a stand of wheelbarrow men. There must have been half a mile of these vehicles stretched along the street. How they all lived, one could never tell. I saw one come up with a buxom Chinese woman on one side, complacently puffing away at a water pipe as fast as she could fill it, and all her household effects in boxes on the other side to balance it. Alighting, she produced about fifteen copper cash and paid the man off. "Ye Gods!" I thought, here's a go. Suppose all these two hundred "ginkos" in my belt were converted into "cash."[10] Then what a load I would have to pack on a monthly liberty in the Far East.

Finally tired of strolling around, and having by this time aroused an awful appetite, I hailed a passing "rickshaw" man and told him to pull me to the nearest barber shop. I had no little difficulty in making him "savvy" this, but after quite a pantomime, he finally "savvied" and I was soon lying back enjoying the delights of a shave by a good Japanese barber, not one of the Kure sort. Then ho, for a tiffin room and what a quantity of steak I placed to the good, and the soft boiled eggs that followed rapidly on the steak's trail, and the numerous coffee. Mine host seemed surprised at the rapidity with which his supplies vanished. He was evidently unacquainted with an American's appetite.

John, whom I saw sitting patiently waiting my coming thro' the window, I made glad by a few dimes for a "chow." The rogues, they are human, and their legitimate prey is American sailors. But after all, they must eat, and again, tho' they make quite a touch from a bluejacket, they may be quite a while without a job. From the tiffin room, I went into Tom's. Tom's is one of the best tailor shops in Shanghai, C. H. Tom. I had ordered a few things from him in this line. And another thing, I have a great regard for his son, Young Tom. There is a mutual liking between us. He is business all thro', and a square chap to deal with. I promised him before I left the ship that I would take a run under his guidance to do the town, and it was for this purpose I dropped in to see him, so we could make arrangements for the night. He was up and hustling. They have all the work they can do. I told him I would drop in about six in the afternoon and we would start. To pass the time away, I went over into Horishaw's and had some more decoration placed upon me. This pretty well occupied all the fore noon. After tiffin, if you please, I hailed my patient rickshaw man, who all this time was standing by, and took a long ride out Nanking Road on out on the Bubbling Well Road. Here are many fine residences [and] a fine race track. Many of the residences were pointed out to me as belonging to missionaries, so it must be a lucrative business after all, trying to convince the Asiatic mind that their josses are only wooden Indians after all, and the European's God is much better. "More better." There are many fine road-houses up this fine drive kept by Europeans with Chinese help. The Chinese help wants his invariable "comshur."

As the day was very, very chilly, it behooved me to enter the most imposing of these road-house[s], the Arcadia. I thought at first it was an institution of some kind from its immense size, but on going in I was agreeably entertained by Madame, who from her broken English, I took to be German or Austrian. Owing to the cold weather, I moved up to the open hearth fire in the large hall and indulged in numerous hot toddies until once more Richard was himself. I managed to put in a comfortable afternoon, and when I left I was in rather a mellow state and ripe for anything.

I found Tom waiting for me at the store. "All ready, Tom old man?" I asked.

"Yes. All right. Come back and take drink first."

We adjourned to the back room where Tom produced the bottle always kept for customers that want it. He also threw me a large storm overcoat to put on over my uniform, and a cloth cap. I looked into the glass and grinned at the image reflected there. I looked for all the world like a "bloomin' lemon-peeler from old Lunnon," but it was just the article to cover the uniform and keep out the cold.

"Well, let's move, Tom. Have you got a friend to bring along?" I asked.

"Yes, have got." He pointed out and called his friend among the clerks in the store.

"All serene, then. Everything is ready and we'll start."

"Wait. I get rickshaw men." Out he went and three rickies soon made their appearance.

"Hold on. I have my man here," and called him. He didn't know me in my ulster.

After about ten minutes' ride, we pulled up in front of a Chinese restaurant. Here we paid and dismissed the rickshaw men, all except mine. He wouldn't be chased. He was content to stay around and wait. We went up into a private room, nicely furnished.

"Now we have chow," said Mr. Tom.

The waiter [handed] them a Chinese bill of fare and myself a European one.

The drive had rendered me hungry, so I selected about five of the entrées, among them *pâté de foie gras,* Mandarin fish, and some kind of cherry tart. After much

Shanghai

conversing, Tom and his chum selected with great care a good many dishes, Tom saying, "We hab good chow now. I very hungry. What you say to some Chinese wine? Its very good; you like it."

"Get anything you want."

The soup was brought and we fell to. Then came the fish, browned to a turn.

"Mandarin fish very good, Tom," I said.

"Yes, very good," he replied.

I soon found out that I had no mean opponent in young Tom, as far as gastronomic feats were concerned, for I soon was filled to repletion and they were still placing course after course in front of him. No doubt I was handicapped by the liquor I had aboard. Tom didn't savvy the *pâté de foie gras*, tho', and I passed it over to him untouched.

"What you call this?" he queried, taking up some of it on his stick.

"Pâté de foie gras."

"Foy gwaw," trying to repeat.

"It is very good Tom. Try, you like."

It soon went the way of the other dishes. I passed the cherry pudding over to his royal nibs, who was enjoying himself like a kid in the jam closet.

"This Chink knows how to enjoy the delights of the table," I thought, as I watched the contented, bland expression upon Tom's classic phisiog. The wine also warmed him up, but didn't affect me, or at least I didn't feel it. It was colorless and very sweet, more like a syrup than a wine. But no doubt it caused a generous glow to steal over my two Chinese friends. Tom and his friend had in the meanwhile wrote something on a slip of paper and gave it to the waiter.

"Bimeby girl come. Two piecee girl. Both have very small feet. Small feet very nice."

"Ha! Ha! Let the ladies come, by all means, you young rogue."

In a very short time them came, and very small feet they had. Their restrictive mothers closely followed. They have chaperones even in China. Their regard for the proprieties is very strict, each mama carried a water pipe and punk stick for lighting. Tom flushed up when they came in and I chided him about it.

"What's the matter, Tom? You're bashful, you know. Like this girl? What makes you turn red." Here I caught the girl and led her toward him. The girl laughed, but Tom blushed more than ever.

"No," he said. "This girl like you very much. You the first European man she ever talk to. Myself no bother about girl. I got to get married next year."

"So you're going to get married, eh? What's her name?"

"I no savvy girl, and no savvy name. My father, he know and he say I got to get married. That's Chinese old custom."

"Well, Tom, in our country you can go see girl you want to marry long time. Sometime one week, one year, ten years, tho' much better to wait two years and know girl before you catch see."

A Sailor's Log

"Yes, yes. That more better. I think myself more better, but my father he speak if I no do, make plenty quarrel."

"Your girl got small feet too, I suppose, Tom?"

"Yes. I think so. That keep girl from running away. She no can do."

"Small feet are no good, Tom. Makes China girl no walk."

"I no like self, but Chinese custom. Small feet very bad. Self, I like girl have big feet."

"Well, this is nice girl, all but feet, Tom," and so she was, as pretty a little Chink as you could see. She reminded me of the one I saw at the depot on my other visit to Shanghai. "What's her name, Tom, and why don't you make love to her?"

"Her name Chen Jo See. She your girl. I no want girl myself. I catch for you."

The girl kept gazing askance at me from time to time. No doubt I was a puzzle to her with my rig and my actions. "You want makee eat?" I asked, pushing a number of dishes and some fruit and candy toward them. But this seemed to amuse them immensely. This was another "foreign devil's" way that they couldn't understand: the idea of a Chinese woman eating with the male sex. I couldn't even get them to take a drink of the wine. Neither the girls [n]or their mamas understood a word of English, so Tom did all the interpreting for me. His bashfulness wore off, but it was a very decorous party. I couldn't help comparing what a supper it would have been with American or European people. The Chinese are very quiet and take all their amusement very easily. We sat here and chatted, or at least Tom and his friend and the girls and chaperones did. Occasionally, I would throw in a word. Tom soon got enough and the girls and mamas and Tom's friend filed out. Tom and I settled the bill.

"Where are they going, Tom?" I queried.

"They go to theatre. My friend very much struck with girl. I think he have very great 'spense' now."

"Yes, that's so. They are an expense." I remembered plenty of my own experiences.

"We go to one theatre, my friend, he go to another." And we prepared to leave. Tom held my coat, the "bloomin' storm coat, dontcherknow?"

"Why you no wear European clothes, Tom?" I asked as he held it for me to struggle into. At this question he looked at me with surprise.

"I Chinaman. How Chinaman goin' to wear European clothes? Why you not wear Chinaman clothes? All same. Chineeman no can; European no can."

I was silent. But there was a great deal of truth in Tom's simple statement. I think so. And yet we wonder why the Chinese don't adapt themselves to our customs and become civilized as we understand, forgetting that the Orient and the Occident are as wide apart as the two poles. I think myself they are just as good in their habits and customs as we are. Only any others' opinions are not quite as good as our own. They have some customs that appear strange to us, forgetting that we have the same. A few nations or a nation steps in and wants to dictate to this great nation, using missionaries as a pretext for land grabbing. We don't allow Chinese to come to America,

Shanghai

nor does any of the others, but yet we force our way into China where we are not wanted. A stranger's first visit to Shanghai would almost convince him that it was an English city governed all thro' by the English, from the arrogant stand they take, instead of being a Chinese city. I think myself it is all wrong.

It is true that the massacres from time to time that break out are very bad, but who's to blame? They are warned, and then let them keep out or take the consequences. The Chinese use the most fearful tortures among their own people, so I don't suppose they would discriminate in favor of the foreigner. They raised a revolt, but as in many other cases, how was it repaid? At Pekin and Tientsin, houses were looted. Innocent Chinamen were shot down. Any Chinaman in sight, whether friendly or not, was shot. Women and children were killed and ravished. And all this by civilized, enlightened people, the elect of God Almighty. Down with the chin chin joss. Open their heads to *our* religion and civilization. If you can't get it into their brain any other way, use a Krag-Jörgensen ball; that is a convincing argument.[11] And, incidentally, as a side-line, grab a few cities and ports. What hypocrites we are!

Tom and I were soon under way for the theatre. Upon arriving at the door, Tom held a lengthy pow-wow with an attendant and we pushed our way up and were shown the best seats in the gallery. Seats are the same all over the house. We did not pay as we passed in. It was fully an hour after we were seated that we paid our admittance fee. The usual bowl of tea was placed in front of us with the program. Also some watermelon seeds. These my Chinese chum soon made large inroads in. This show I enjoyed more than the last. There was more life and vim in it, and Tom explained in his quaint way from time to time. But the audience interested me more than anything else. There wasn't the diversity of costume as in our theatres, but I saw before me a sea of round silk caps with a blue or red knot in the center, and the pigtail. No danger of being out of style in dress here.

"How much one cap cost, Tom?" I asked.

"All price. Dis one I have cost three dollar (Mex). Some Chinamen pay sixty dollars, same kind, but much better silk. All dress alike, but better silk." That's one way they are ahead of us. You don't have to be always spending your wages to follow the fashion.

An attendant would pass around with steaming hot napkins to apply to the face or hands, and the table in front of us was kept supplied with good things to eat. From scanning the people, I soon turned my attention to the stage. No one can accuse the Chinese of lack of humor. Some of their comedy knock about work is as good as any I have witnessed anywhere; it even compares favorably with Coney Isle's favorite ham actors who, when unable to obtain a [performance] date, will sling beer for a livelihood.

The play at this house was the usual rivalry between two mighty mandarins who were "made up" in the most ferocious manner. Their aspect would give even an Apache or Comanche Indian a pang of envy. When it came to the usual passage at arms between them, they each performed mighty deeds of valor. At last, one mandarin engaged them all, taking all comers as fast as they appeared, and at last engaging the whole cheese. There was a mighty whirling of spears, swords, and tridents. The fighting mandarin would dispose of one, and another would throw a succession of somersaults and back handsprings across the stage, alighting on his feet and rushing to the fray only to be disposed of by the ever victorious chief. Another and another would take his place. The tumbling was fine. They keep this up for quite a time. They are hard workers and do not cut any of their acts, but keep it up until the audience is completely satisfied. It is all bewildering. The speeches, of course, I did not understand. To me, of course, it was all pantomime, but a pantomime to be enjoyed immensely. Tom explained such parts as he saw fit, but the tumbling and knockabout work I could understand, and nothing exists that I enjoy better than good acrobatic work, and the Chinese are good at this.

The most grotesque and comic fall was made by the mandarin who, having vanquished all his enemies, mounted the top of a high throne and hurled himself on the back of the neck to the stage, a distance of at least fifteen feet. I have witnessed lots of funny falls, but never any like unto that. He earned his salary doing that stunt, if nothing else.

There was also the small boy who played the school boy, getting off the usual tricks on his teacher. It was all interesting and novel to me. After about an hour at this house, I proposed to Tom that we go to the other playhouse, and find his friend. This we did, pushing ourselves thro' the usual crowd of coolies, chairs and women around the entrance, and went further down [the] street, followed by my ricky, who was always on the trail.

This theatre wasn't as fine as the first. After the usual harangue with an attendant, we were shown to the only obtainable place on the side of the gallery. The tables were all filled in the pit. Tom finally spotted his friend and ran around the walk that is used by the attendants or ushers, with an usher after him, trying to tell him to go the other way back of the gallery. Thomas wouldn't listen to this at all. He continued on his way serenely. His chum occupied a stall with his company. He was as attentive to the little Chinese doll as any American could be. Nature is the same, tho' customs vary.

After a short chat, Tom came back to where I was and we fixed our attention on the stage. It was exactly the same as far as I could make out, only the actions were a poorer class. The same fighting and tumbling and declaiming. The same attendance. The usher came up and spoke to Tom, who turned to me when he had gone. "Girl wants to come up."

"Which is right. Let her come."

In came Chin Jo See and mama with the water pipe, small feet and all. I paid the freight, about eighty cents, I believe. Tom said, deprecatingly, "ver big 'spense, I think."

"Oh, hang the expense, old man. We are out for a good time, and are going to have it. The idea of talking expense to a sailor ashore! But Chinamen are thrifty, which is very laudable.

Shanghai

Chin Jo See was a very intelligent looking Chinese woman, quite out of the usual class, and but for her small feet, of which she seemed proud, to my mind her equal would have been hard to find. She was dressed in the regulation costume, blue silk blouse trimmed with black and blue drawers, or trousers, of the same shade. Her hair was combed smoothly and tightly back and formed into a large coil on the nape of the neck. Two bands of silk the color of her hair held it in place. The usual jade ornaments were in her hair and gilt and jade bracelets encircled her plump wrists. This with her smooth olive skin and black eyes formed a not unpleasing picture. It is a mistake to believe that Chinese girls ar[e] not pretty. They are not according to our standard, but Chin Jo See was a handsome girl and neat. The only drawback was the small tootsies and this only enhanced her value in the Asiatic mind. It is a pity to cripple girls in this manner, but there is no doubt a cause for every effect, and one cause, beside the one mentioned previously is that at one time the Chinese women made the best warriors and in order to prevent the women and girls from becoming Amazons and getting the whip hand of the men, that it was deemed advisable to put a stop to it in some way. And it didn't take the cunning Chinese mind long to hit upon a device for effectually putting a stop to the ambitiousness of their women folk. It is not now so universally practiced, only among the higher classes w[h]ere women are toys and do not have to employ themselves and among the classes where it is intended to beautify and enhance their value for marketable purposes.

Chin Jo See and her mother stood up. I [thought] that Tom would invite them to be seated, but as he did not, I motioned her to a chair. At this she seemed surprised, but took it nevertheless. But mama preferred to stand up all the time, hovering around her handsome daughter, who no doubt was the sole support and source of income and therefore to be carefully ministered to. We sat about two hours at this performance. Tom and his lady friends enjoyed it immensely; Tom especially so. Every once in a while he would emit a wild Chinese howl as a mark of approbation, as all the rest of the audience did. This was in lieu of applause. There is no stamping of feet and clapping of hands as in America, and there are no encores. The performance flows on without interruption and last[s] way into the morning hours.

It was about twelve when Thomas proposed we should vacate. I seconded his motion. He signaled his friend, who immediately arose and came out. I didn't see his inamorata. Possibly she took a chair, as did Chin Jo See. Her mother, not being troubled with small feet, preferred to walk. I bid Chin Jo See good-bye and the last I saw of her was a wave of the hand thro' the door of the chair as she disappeared down the street.

It was now very late, and my two companions were getting sleepy, so they proposed to put me up for the night. To this I was perfectly willing to agree. The part of the town we were now getting into after a rather rapid walk was beginning to get quiet. We had got[ten] out of the crowded thoroughfare. Tom was looking around for a suitable place to put me up, but after several inquiries on his part at different houses [he came up] without any favorable results. They were either afraid of the "foreign devil" or else the looks of the place didn't suit Tom. We had to appeal to the rickshaw man of mine, who was still trundling behind like a big dog. Rickshaw men can do anything and he was looking around at the same time as Tom and his friend and finally his quest was successful. It was too late and too far to go to a hotel, and the other lodging house[s] were to[o] far away and the people would have had to be awakened. And besides—well—I was shown into my room and the word was given to waken me at 6 A.M. [in] the morning. Tom and his chum bade me good night and were soon on their way to their homes. I was tired, and flinging myself on my couch, I was soon in the land o' nod.

The ricky awakened me the next morning, or rather night—it was still dark. He had camped out in front of the house in the small enclosure. He wouldn't let me go to sleep again, either, altho' I roared at him and threatened him with all sorts of punishment. That's the worst of these fellows. You can't bluff them. They are used to getting bluffed and beaten and otherwise treated like dogs. If they think you are a good customer, you can't shake them. They refuse to vamoose. They follow you and stick it out with the patience worthy of a better cause. He sat there sipping a cup of tea, and I became wide awake cursing him until at last I concluded to get up. Everything was intact. My money belt was still under my head where I had placed it, so it was all right. Leaving the place, of course, I had to give everybody "comshur," from the grandmother down. This business of "comshur" makes serious inroads in your pile if you keep it up at a sailor's rate of spending money.

The rickshawman gravely pointed out the necessity of giving mama "cash for chow," etc. At last, all claims satisfied, we got down to Tom's, who met me at the door. He was already engaged in his day's work and was as fresh as a daisy. I felt rather good myself, tho' blue at the idea of going off to the ship. I gave Mr. Tom his storm coat and cap, thanking him for the loan. I put in the rest of my time riding around looking at the sights until it was time to go to the station. The gang was all there, some drunk and others sober, but all jolly. A short ride and we were in the whale boat towed by the launch back to the ship, and it was all over for another month. This trip I brought considerable money back with me, and altogether had a most enjoyable time, so [there] was no regrets.

A few weeks previous to this, the *Oregon*'s minstrel troupe gave a performance which was largely attended by officers from the surrounding warships and from the merchant vessels at Woosung. It was a good performance of its kind, and was enjoyed by all. In a hall or theatre it would have been much better. The singing fell nearly flat on account of the lack of acoustics. All the day the carpenters' gang and others were kept busy rigging up the extempore stage. Bunting was broken out and tastefully arranged forming [a] pro[s]cenium and background. Colors were draped around a large picture of the *Oregon*, which represented her on the famous trip half round the world to Santiago. Awnings were spread and the entire forecastle housed in. Mess benches and chairs were arranged and everything was complete. At about seven, the visitors commenced to arrive. Men from the *Brooklyn* were the only ones that were in evidence from ships of our own flag. The others were lying at Shanghai.

Shanghai

The chief petty officers were the reception committee, and very much to the fore was our old friend, the chief machinist of *Zafiro* fame. I watched him as closely as I did the other performance. He was fast getting a good sized "jag" on, and at every visit aft, he would swell up with importance. I could see, as the jag developed, that he was gradually arriving at the conclusion that as far as the *Oregon* was concerned, show and all, that he was the entire works. I expected every moment that he would have to expel some of his surplus gas in an extemporaneous patriotic speech. He became more polite and bland after every visit to the warrant officers' mess room. This was where he was getting his "bitters" at. He became so solicitous and so pressing in his politeness that the officers began to notice it. For a wonder, though, he didn't commit himself, but he had to be put out of the steerage after the show, repeatedly. The last I heard from him, he was raving because somebody had surreptitiously abstracted a large quart bottle of "sampchoo" that he had hidden under the floor-plates in the aft 13" pump room, my station. I think to this day that he had a suspicion that I was the guilty party, for he questioned me the next morning very closely. Of course, I sympathized with him. He exhausted all his vocabulary in "d[amning] the eyes" of the party that seized his "booze," but he didn't dare accuse me outright, no doubt afraid of a "bawling out" I would have given him. Finally, he concluded to go asleep and that was the end of his performance.

The show ran off without a flaw. The circle was good. We had good end men and a good middle man, or interlocutor. The interlocutor had shipped here in Shanghai. He was in fact a professional "ham fatter," a comedian of the "beer hall" variety, but he bore the hall mark of professionalism. There was a good team of Irish comedians, a good German comedian, some very fine gun juggling, and drilling by one of our men, a good quartette and plenty of buck dancing, singing, and sketches. And also, a very good (for a man-o-war) orchestra to accompany all this. Everybody enjoyed the show. The performers were well treated, had all they could drink, so all was well.

CHAPTER SEVEN

Afloat & Ashore in Shanghai

We had trouble about the coal. The chief [engineer and his] faithful henchmen, his bolo-men, were trying to economize. It was the usual growl with the water-tenders. The five-hundred tons(?) of dirt that had been brought aboard only lasted about sixteen days. And more, six-hundred tons, had been put aboard, this coming in the same quarter so quickly that every means were tried to economize and make it last. We were bull-dozed every watch. They wouldn't allow any more than thirty-two buckets to a watch for the boiler that was now steaming. They had cut the other out some time before. This thirty-two buckets would have been more than enough if it had been coal, but it was dirt. Fires had to be entirely hauled at every watch.

The week I had the 8 to 12 [watch] I would go down to find the boiler cold, the steam dying out, and furnaces filled to the bridge wall and crown sheets with ashes, perhaps a hatful of live coals on top. One watch, especially, I went below at 8 only to find steam at 60 lbs where it should have been 140 in order to do the aux[iliary] watch properly. The feed tank was full of water [not having been drawn into the boiler as it made steam]. The water-tender whom I relieved told me he had burned his allowance and asked for more, only to have a flat refusal. He told the "bolo" that the fires were dying out and the "B.M." told him to let them die. So, having nothing more to do, he came out and sat down, knowing that something would soon be done before I came on. And seeing the condition of things after relieving my man, I made a bolt for the eng[ine] room. The B.M. on watch was the one formerly a "soda watch clerk."

"How about that boiler? Fires are completely out, and the feed tank is almost running over with feed-water. I stopped the pump so as to hold the steam as long as possible. What am I going to do with the feed water? Pump it in the other boilers or let it flow into the bilge, or pump it into the steaming boilers and knock the steam down faster than it is dropping now, or are you going to let the boiler die out?" All this I hurled at him in a jumble.

"I don't know," he started to say.

"Well, it is time you did, or else you will hear something drop. All those fires have got to be hauled and started up, every one. And I don't know as I can save enough live coal. To start with, do I get any extra coal?"

"What's the matter with the four buckets you have on each end this hour?"

"That won't cover the bars of over one furnace. We were now going out in the fire-room."

"You see," said I, pointing to the fires that my firemen were hauling, "everything has got to come [out]. There is nothing left but ashes. We can't keep this thirty-two bucket racket up any longer. If the chief saw this, he would see that it is impossible to hold steam with that allowance. . . ." Just here the chief poked his head around the door. I suppose he had been listening. Coming in without a word, he looked at the steam, which was now at forty lbs and dropping fast.

"Get out four extra buckets," was all he said. Then he went for'd to the other end of the boiler.

"Now is your chance to talk to him," said the trembling B.M. in a whisper.

"What's the matter with you doing the talking? It's your business. Besides, there isn't any need of talk. He can see plainly for himself. What we want is action to get these fires cleaned and steaming, or else we will hear from the deck pretty d[amned] quick."

We got coal. We got all we wanted. I used exactly fifty-six [buckets] that night, and it was two hours before we could work the steam up to a hundred lbs. The ice machine had stopped, the sanitary pump also, and the dynamo pretty nearly so. The chief raised the ante to forty buckets a watch. We could make out on this, and some watches, like the mid, could make out on much less. It was this same old growl, each B.M. vying with each other to save the most coal, but I burned as much as was necessary to keep the steam up to 120 lbs. It required that much in order to hoist a boat, which might happen at any time during the day. I could do it on the allowance of forty buckets without much trouble. At general quarters on Thursdays, when every pump in the ship almost was in use, all the turret turning machinery, air compressor, etc., I used much more and then the steam couldn't be kept from falling. I burned fifty buckets the morning we had general quarters, and when I came on at night the B.M. with the day's duty wanted to know who authorized me to use "fifty buckets of coal." I told him the chief had passed the word to use as much coal as was necessary to hold the steam. The other water-tender, who was there and had turned that order to me corroborated this. The B.M. said he didn't know anything about it, and if anything was said, I would have to take the responsibility. I said I was perfectly willing to do so.

I never heard any more about it, but the same night I had another "chaw" with the B.M. that had the 8 to 12. This fellow knew as much about marine engineering as an owl, but hadn't the sense to keep his mouth closed and look as wise, so he thought he would lecture me also about such a sinful expenditure of coal. He wanted to know how I came to use fifty buckets. I showed him the fires that were being cleaned, and explained all to him. He had the nervine to tell me that the turret turning eng[ine]s and pump didn't make any difference in the steaming of the boiler, that it wasn't any harder to hold the steam with all that machinery on than it was without.

"Yes," I said as sarcastically as possible. "Under your theory you could also put the main engines on and it wouldn't make any material difference, is that it?"

"No! You don't understand me. I mean to say that it is a great deal in the firing and the way fuel is used. Some men can use less coal. For a given number of inches of furnace space there should be . . ."

"That's all right, young feller, in books. But your experience is nothing but theory. Along with this theory you want good practical knowledge. Book learning is very good, with experience, and as for skill and brains, there is just as much of it on this watch as on any of the others, d'ye see? This pound of coal turning so much water into steam is all right when you are using, let's say, ordinary coal. Just ordinary, that's all. This is dirt. Let me show you the condition of the fires when we clean."

"Oh, I understand that. But in cleaning you have plenty of fire to build upon."

"Yes," I queried, "that's your idea of it, is it? Look at this!" And I showed him all the ashes that was being hauled with no fire at all. "Does that look like we have much to build on? We have to start with live coal from the other fires." That convinced him, and he left.

All this trouble was caused by "comshur," and we were being used as the cat's paw. I don't know how many people got "comshur" out of this. Talking about "comshur," the price of provisions w[as] very exorbitant for a market like Shanghai, even taking into consideration the expense entailed in bringing provisions from Shanghai to Woosung and delivering aboard ship.

Tom Pow Ching, who had the monopoly of the men's messes, told the caterers "that he had too much 'comshur' to pay." [Number] one man, of course, he had to have his profit, and the more that the Ripper squeezed him for, the higher he raised the price. Twenty per cent was the Ripper's commission. And he was known as "Old Twenty Per Cent" by most of the crew. Tom Pow Ching didn't know he was letting the cat out of the bag by telling this, because among China men, "comshur" is legitimate business, that's all.

Thanksgiving being almost upon us, great preparations were being made. Each cook vied with the others in making cakes, pastry, and in the array of geese, chickens, turkeys, suckling roast pigs, etc. The galley was thronged from morning until late a[t] night, and an odor of good things pervaded the air. Jack always makes a showing upon holidays whenever circumstances will permit. Lying in a port like Shanghai, where every good thing almost was obtainable, it behooved us to spread ourselves. So at dinner (not tiffin), the mess tables were laden with an immense array of good things to eat, and at every man's plate those that wished it had a quart bottle of beer, the first I have saw aboard ship since beer was denied Jack. This cost us 42 cts Mex. There wasn't many that failed to avail themselves of this opportunity.

Afloat & Ashore in Shanghai

After dinner, there was boat racing between different divisions of the ship. A whale boat race [was run] between firemen and coal-passers in which shovels were used instead of oars. The coal-passers won handily, and could afford to crow over their opponents. There was a tug-of-war between men from the deck force and men from below. The tug-of-war was won by the deck; this was something unusual. There were sack races, obstacle races, pie-eating contests, all taking place on the quarter-deck. After supper there was an impromptu concert by members of the minstrel troupe and others.

Like every other occasion on men-o-war, there was plenty of "booze" floating around. The warrant officers treated their favorites to bottled beer and punch, and a few naturally made a day of it. But there wasn't any quarreling or trouble of any kind. Our friend, the chief machinist, just got enough on board to make him wish for more, and he received permission to go ashore. He came off full as a goat and lay around useless for a couple of days. When the cargo died out that he carried aboard, he combined forces with the "King of the Orlop Deck" in order to secure more whisky. The "King" was a coal passer in charge of the orlop deck and one of the biggest drunks in the service. Nothing he wouldn't do for booze. He had been court-martialed time and again for drunkenness and "before the mast" times innumerable. Gifted with wonderful conversational powers and a sublime "crust" when taken to the mast, he would talk them to a stand-still, and very often this would get him off without punishment. When unable to obtain "sampchoo" he would manage to make out on shellac. Half of the shellac he drew for his deck went far toward quenching his thirst.

The machinist was *hors du combat* from too much dallying with the fierce stuff that was brought aboard and was lying around the orlop groaning like a big, fat hog when I brought my "caulking gear" and threw it down in my usual place. He was floundering around and keeping everybody awake, and I suppose [he] got cold lying on cold steel, for he tried to stick his feet under my blanket. Not liking this, I braced myself, and planting both feet in the small of his back, I threw him up against some lockers. He let a roar out, but rolled over and adjusted himself to another position. The King had just staggered down from the boom where he was awaiting another bottle from the steam launch men. He came along in sections, cursing and bemoaning his sad fate and the unfaithfulness of shipmates.

"Mother of Moses! Will it never come? Five dobies a bottle for booze that they can get for 40 cts at the landing and stillsh don't want to bring it off to shipmates. They're like bolo-men. No goodsh. You can't make [a] race horse out of a mule. Guessh I'll turn in. Game's all over tonight." Here he went along the armor belt passage and pulling out his "gear" he threw it down with great force upon the machinist, who let out another howl and rolled over and floundered around some more. The King, not liking to give up, went prowling around to see if he couldn't connect, and failing, came back and started [to] turn in, cursing shipmates and steam launch crew in particular. He started to unroll our fat friend, thinking he was the caulking mat. At this, duff bag let another howl from him. The King staggered back. "Watsh h[ell] this?" and turned on the light. There sat his nibs with a dazed expression, blinking like an owl.

A Sailor's Log

"What's you try to do, Paddy? Anitsh got no respect for superior (hic!) officer? I think I have to lick yer."

"Lick!" roared the King at the top of lungs of brass. "Lick? Lick who? Whoever told ye that you could fight, you walleyed mongoose! Fight? Do me ears deceive me or is it yerself that speaks wid the front part av your face? The only thing you can lick is a bottle o' booze. The best thing you can do is to roll over an go t'sleep, or its meself will have you run to th stick fer insolence to a coal passer, so lay down and be nice, my little man."[1]

All righth, Paddy. No 'fense. You know old Dick didn't mean any 'fense, hic." And, blinking like an owl, our fat friend collapsed like a balloon all in a heap.

The King spread out his caulking gear first one way and then another. Finally he threw the entire outfit down in disgust and rolling Sir Richard over like a bale of merchandise, laid down himself, and pulling the blanket over his head, was soon in a troubled, drunken doze. The pair of them kicked a[nd] rolled so much that at last I had to trek and take up my position on another *kopje* farther up the deck. All this commotion was after "pipe down," and it was a wonder it didn't attract the master-at-arms' attention. They awoke everybody near them. It was fully five days before the King exhausted all his money and shellac, but he wasn't detected. And what is more to the point, it would[n]'t have made the least bit of difference to the King, who was an old offender and old hand at shellac drunks aboard ship. In fact, anything with a bite would have proved acceptable, from red ink up to Cyrus Noble, a brand of whiskey that the bluejacket takes an especial delight in.[2]

～～～

With a boxing match coming off between the self-styled champions of the English and American fleet, [we organized] a performance by the *Oregon*'s minstrel troupe for the benefit of the families of the marines killed at Pekin. Payday very near. A collier alongside coaling us. Things were humming.

There was trouble aboard the collier. The entire crew were against the skipper. They were unanimous in declaring him the meanest old —— that they ever had the misfortune to sail with. No liberty had any of the crew received since leaving Lambert's Point, Norfolk. The crew was a mixture of Philipinos, Spaniards, Italians and only a few Americans. They had no liberty and no money and nothing but the very worst fare. The first mate, engineers, every officer and man w[as] against him. They were continually quarrelling. The crew got hold of some booze when alongside of us and they went after the "old man," who came aboard us for protection, but was told to regulate matters aboard his own ship.

When aboard, the mate and he became involved in another quarrel, and the second engineer came up. "What the devil do you want up here," asked the captain. "What do you want up here?"

"I came up here to decorate that ugly face of yours, you —— cur. And I'll do it now," squaring off in true pugilistic fashion. The skipper decamped. They kept this

Afloat & Ashore in Shanghai

up for quite a while. The next day the skipper did get hit, a beautiful sock in his port lamp that did decorate it.³ And that, too, by one of the men! In fact, the whole crew had offered to fight him any way. Finally, in disgust he went ashore for a time.

This is a common occurrence aboard all tramp ships. The skipper and men are always on the outs. The captains of these ships will take any kind of back "guff" as long as they have the advantage from a monetary point. By cruelty, starving the men, running a "slop chest" where they charge fancy prices for articles of wear that a Baxter St. Jew wouldn't handle, giving no money, and no liberty, they hope to drive the crew to run away, thus losing their money, which, after accounting to the agents for as suits the case, and himself, he pockets the lion's share. If the men jump in foreign ports, he can secure a cheap crew. This fellow in charge of the collier *Saturn* was one of this class, in it for all there was to [be] gained.

The day set apart for the fight came around at last. Our man "jumped ship" in order to be on hand; thus, he staked everything. The fight was stopped by the municipal authorities and our man, who had risked so much, lost all.⁴ There was over two thousand pesos up. This was all returned and divided among the men that had bet. A purse of five hundred was quickly collected for R——. R—— wanted to take the Englishman out in the open field and decide it, but to this proposition the Englishman demurred, claiming that his officer wasn't to be found. R——, unable to get satisfaction in any manner, broke down and cried like a child. The Englishman has every attention given him aboard his ship, and had the entire crew of the *Centurion* behind him, from her commander down. But our captain refused to sanction what he termed "rowdyism," and so R—— had to leave the ship without permission, and there was nothing but a court-martial with loss of three months' pay and confinement for thirty days staring him in the face upon his return to the ship. It was owing to our captain's efforts that the fight was stopped.

The minstrel troupe made out much better. It was a success from a financial standpoint. The attendance was large, and would have been much larger, if (as is usually the case) other bluejackets from the *Princeton* and others hadn't circulated the report around Shanghai that "shows composed of ship's talent didn't amount to very much, and were generally a fake." But the people that went considered their time and money well spent, and were lavish in their praise. They were agreeably surprised, and such remarks as "I didn't think it was in them," and "How could it be possible for bluejackets to give such an excellent performance?" "I am surprised. It is the best thing of its kind we have had here in many a day," etc., were rife. And I'll wager if the performance had been repeated, there would have been "standing room only." And it was, of a truth, a very good and creditable performance.

One morning on the 4 to 8 watch, the "bolo-man" known to us as "No. 5 Stew Bum,"⁵ feeling slightly chilly in the eng[ine] room, came out to no. 5 fire room to warm up in the early hours before the force "turned to." Planting himself in front of the furnaces, he prepared for a general conversation. This was a thing I didn't care about at all this early in the day, feeling pretty sleepy from being broke out from a warm "caulking mat." And another reason, I never could talk to an officer, because I never felt on equal terms and at my ease. The uniform forbade that, and although this particular B.M. had been a "panhandler" prior to slipping into the naval service during those "lucky days of '98," when war was on and any article would come in as machinist and pass through during the rush. And when the new Personnel Bill had passed, this "No. 5 Stew Bum" had went up for a superficial examination as warrant machinist. There had to be one hundred made, and much to their surprise, this one and a few others had been appointed. This was so far in excess of their wildest ambitions that some of them pinch themselves to this day to find if they are really awake or is it all a dream. This fellow planted himself for a conversation.

"I've come in to get warm," he said. "It's pretty chilly out in that engine room this morning."

"Yes," I replied without any interest in the matter at all and in a tone tending toward discouraging any conversation whatever.

"How's this coal? Fine ain't it? You fellows want to use as little of it as possible; you want to economize."

"Yes," I replied. "It is pretty good."

"It's a d[amned] shame we couldn't get away with that other stuff before the collier came."

"Yes," I said. "There was enough kick made about burning so much of it."

"That's so," he admitted. "The chief gave orders to that effect."

"Yes," I questioned, "and yet when there was any trouble about steam not being carried high enough, he told us there wasn't [any] limit to the coal, but to keep up steam and not mind the saving of it. But that was after we had been caught with low pressure, and couldn't hoist a boat or do other necessary work."

This fellow had been one of the foremost in annoying the watches and trying to reduce the amount of coal. By so doing, he hoped to curry favor with the "old man." None of them had received permanent appointments then, and there were any amount being given to other warrant machinists in different ships.

We were all silent for a short time when I chimed in, *apropos* of nothing, "I used to think myself, and it was the general impression thro' out the service when comparing engineer officers for all around meanness and hardness toward their men, to award the laurels to Mr.———," naming a certain eng[ineer] officer. "But he is outclassed at last and made to look like an amateur."

"Yes. You bet he is outclassed," chimed in the coal-passer, who was sitting between us. "Why, he wouldn't be one, two, three."

"How's that?" questioned Mr. Bolo, looking for information, his ears pricked up to drink in our opinions greedily. This information I felt like giving to the full. I wasn't inclined to tint it, either. I felt just in the humor, and by this time was thoroughly awake and ready to do justice to the subject.

Afloat & Ashore in Shanghai

"Why, the present gentleman whom we have the honor to serve under can give him cards and spades. Mr. So-and-So isn't to be considered in the same category for general, all-around meanness, petty spites and vindictiveness and venom. We have the prize 'umbria' with us."[6]

"What?" said he, trying to look surprised at our opinions and making a flat failure of it. "What? Do you mean to say that you don't like the chief?"

"Like him? Like what?" I roared in a tone of disgust. "Does the devil like holy water? Does anybody like him, except a few 'white mice' who hope to curry favor by carrying tales and in general trying to convince him by plausible lying how good and faithful they are, and what a mean lot he has under him[?]"

"Why," he continued, "I don't see anything wrong with this old fellow. He is strict. He wants to know everything that's going on himself, to see for himself. He won't take anybody's word for it. He's a cool man. You never see him excited about anything."

"As for his 'coolness,'" I replied, "I have seen him get in such a passion over trifles that I expected him to burst a blood vessel or fall in a fit of apoplexy. And that was on a couple of occasions when he bawled me out."

"Yes, he does fly into a temper sometimes, but no doubt you deserved the bawling out you got."

"Well, if I had, I'd [have] taken it like a man. I don't mind a reprimand as long as it is my fault. But on both of these occasions, it wasn't my fault and it was undeserved. And I explained the matter to him, but he wasn't man enough to admit that he was in the wrong, like a great many naval officers I know." Here I explained the two occasions that the chief had given me the hauling over the coals, once being about the open bunker door and the other time about pressure on the aft turret.

"I don't suppose you minded the 'bawling out' much," said he. "It didn't do you any harm."

"It didn't do me any good, either," I retorted. "I don't know how it is with you, but I always have a feeling of injustice and resentment toward a man that accuses me unjustly and in such a manner without first finding out whether I deserved it or not. In both of these cases I did the best I knew and the ripping up I got was entirely undeserved."

"No doubt you think so, but how was the old man to know whether you were deserving or not?"

"He should have enquired and not jumped so rapidly at a conclusion. You don't suppose a man would deliberately disobey an order or be lax about doing his duty, do you? Another thing, as you admit, he trusts no one. It's a poor policy for any man, no matter his position, not to place a certain confidence and reliance on those subordinate to his orders, for men, knowing they are not trusted as a general thing, don't render very good service. Any man, no matter what position he is placed in, has to rely upon someone. Why isn't he like other officers? I have had officers give me orders to carry out time and again, and that would be the last of it. The orders would be carried out and reported to him as carried out. That was all there was to it. Perhaps in the course of a tour round the dep[artmen]t the officer would casually look to see if it was carried out, but he wouldn't stand around and nag and worry himself and everybody else about him. If, in the course of this inspection, he found everything as it should be, well and good. If not . . . then came the bawling out process. But I never had it used on me yet, and I never heard of a case. Here it is all fault finding, nothing done right. Men stand over you and nag. They want to show you how to open and shut a monkey wrench. It's disgusting."

"Yes," he admitted, "there has to be a certain amount of reliance placed on men, but this man doesn't do it. You see, he don't know his men, and you admit there are plenty of good men in this dep[artmen]t and plenty of damn bad ones, but the chief don't *know* them."

"Well, he should know them. Other officers know their men. He shouldn't treat all as if we were convicts, for in so doing, he spoils the entire lot."

"Well, hmm. That's so. But then you know . . ."

"Yes, I do know. I know that it's men like him that do more toward driving men from the service than anything else. Why, a recruit running up against such a person wouldn't stay no longer than it took to make the nearest port. He simply couldn't stand the pressure. Look at the old hands that have ran away, and that on this station. I know plenty of men who[se] time would be mighty short if they ever sighted home once more, isn't that a fact?"

"No doubt about that at all. But I can't see anything bad about him, as I said. I would rather have him that way than any other." Here Mr. Bolo stood up, yawned, and stretched his arms. "Well, think I['ll] go out to the eng[ine] room. It's nearly 'turn to.'"

After he had gone, the coal-passer turned and gave me a knowing and most elaborate wink. "Be—gosh! Plenty good for a rook, eh? Pretty smooth."

"Yes. There's evidently very few high spots on him. He's a pretty wise gazabo[7] for his first cruise. He wants to find out our opinion and heap his own, I think. Eh, Ed?"

"You bet your boots. I didn't think he had it in him. He will put your ideas, his own and anybody else's together and sum 'em all up and be rich by the amount."

"Well, well. I hope he retails the whole thing to the 'bloody old tyrannical Russian,' as D—— calls him. I don't care a d[amn]. If he can make a little capital from it, he is welcome to it."

"Yet," said Ed, "the same, the very same jigger will let the whole thing out of him about the old devil when he is drunk."

"Well, it's a long road that has no turning. Something has got to drop some o' these days. Anyhow, we'll have to stick it out as best we can. It will come all right in a hundred years or so, and our present enlistments can't last forever." So, with a sigh [I] went out in the s[tarboard] eng[ine] room to get my litmus paper for testing the acidity of the water in the boiler [to control precipitation of impurities in boiler tubes, impeding the flow of water].

Afloat & Ashore in Shanghai

Three long, weary months now lying out in the Yangtse. Long, weary months. Nothing to break the monotony. The same sickening, dull routine. The same tiffs with the bolo men, the same drunks ramping around the decks with the same "jag" produced by the infernal decoction for sale by the Chinese boys, smuggled aboard ship for that purpose. Pay day and after a long wait, another liberty ashore. I enjoyed this one more than any. More fine work placed upon my already well-decorated anatomy.

I had been feeling badly, dull and dispirited, and cursing my fate, and growling for a month past, cursing my luck in ever shipping over, the circumstances brought about of my own free will that condemned me to life aboard a man-o-war. And it was with the intention of getting a good "pot" on ashore that I went this time. So, after getting off the train at Shanghai, I looked for the usual "ricksha" man. I didn't have long to wait. There were about a thousand seized upon me at once, the former rascal among the number. I waved him away time and again, until he nearly went frantic at the prospect of losing me. I had no intention of dismissing him; I only wished to learn him a lesson. He wept and raved, but I continued firm.

"You no good," in pidgin English.

"My good. My very good piecee man."

"You savvy. Last time you have two piecee men and wanchee pay. Every night you makee bobbery."

"My no! No two piecee men. Dis time you takee my. My be belly good man."

"You no speakee true. You makee big lie. You act all same last time. I no wanchee." And I tried to shake him off, but he clung frantically and tried to carry me off bodily. They know bluejackets are invariably good pay, and they don't always have a job.

After stringing him long enough, I jumped in his rickshaw. Even then I had to chase the "no. 2 man" away. He had hooked on.

"Where you going, W[ilson]?" yelled a mate as we pulled thro' the push of vehicles.

"Up to the tattooers first. Jump in one of those rickys and come on," I yelled back.

"How long are you going to stay there?" as his man came up close to mine.

"I don't know, perhaps six hours or so. I can't tell how long it will take to do the work I want."

"Well, if you are going up to the Grill, I will get the room and put down for the meals for the two days."

"I don't know how soon I can be up there. It may be too late to get in. Better wait until I come up and then we will fix things."

So he continued on his way to the Grill Room on Canton Road, and I to the Jap's. But first I went up to Tom Pow Ching's store for some "sea stores" to see me thro' the night and the ordeal of tattooing. I purchased two quarts of Cyrus, warranted to be the "pure quill." They are all warranted pure in China. "This will see me thro for a while," throwing down the Bryan money [silver—reference is to William Jennings Bryan] for the same.

A Sailor's Log

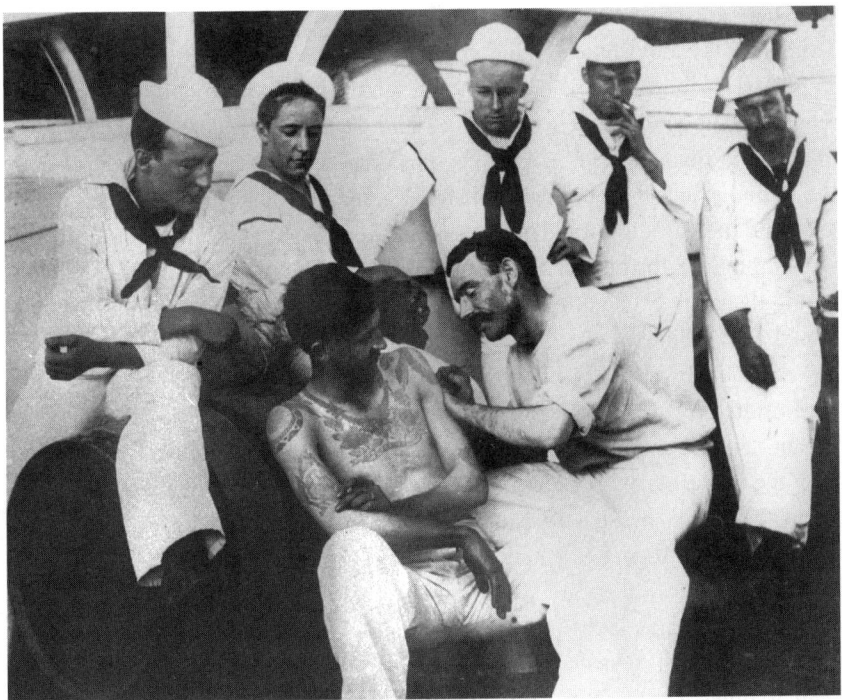

Tattoo being applied to a sailor onboard the cruiser *Olympia* in 1899. Wilson made frequent visits to tattoo artists on Asiatic Station to cover earlier rough tattoos. Navy Historical Foundation.

Putting them under the seat of my horseless carriage, we were soon at Horishaw's. To be sure, they were glad to see me. I found Horishaw and his friend gone. They had went home to Nagasaki, finding a falling off in business. Ohashi had a great many new designs to show me. They were drawn on silk, a long roll about four foot by one, in shape of the old fashioned papyrus scroll of Egypt. This I thought a very good idea. The designs were all very elaborate. Nothing too minute or ornate to escape the painstaking [attention] and patience of these Japanese tattooers.

As I have mentioned before, tattooing in Japan is an art, as much so as painting on china or in water color or oils, and it [is] made as much of. The designs [are] of dragons, snakes, eagles and birds, butterflies and all animal life. The gaily kimonoed and *obi*'d geisha girls or *musmee*s, are as artistic as any you will see worked on silks or any medium, and the material they are worked on, the human skin, is a far more difficult texture than either silk, canvas, or china. It is an interesting sight to behold a really good Japanese tattooer etching a design. With them it is a serious art; with us it is fallen in[to] disrepute because it is practiced only by the lower classes, and the designs are simply hideous to behold: anchors, Jack's last port, Jack's farewell, etc., seem to be about all that the tattooers(?) of our own land can conceive and execute. No wonder people are disgusted and consider it degrading. It is degrading because it shows no taste, no skill, and no art. Happily for this art there are still a few exponents

Afloat & Ashore in Shanghai

left. There are a few American and English tattooers that are artists in their line, peculiar as it is, and whose designs are beautiful.

But the Japanese excel. The art seems peculiarly their own. It is an object lesson to behold a really good Japanese tattooer with his delicately set needles in carved ivory sticks, his curious dishes of colors, his small brushes for tracing the design on the arm or body, the light touch with which he gathers up the slightest touch of ink, or color, and the way it is pricked in, there is almost no waste of ink, and no smear, and no blood follows the needles. True, it is painful. Some tattooers can work with less pain to the subject than others, but if it wasn't for the pain, most people wouldn't [would?] get tattooed.

Very many tourists in Japan have been tattooed by Chyo, long considered the foremost in the world. Among them, many women, who satisfied their curiosity and love for the curious and odd by getting delicate, tiny figures of storks or birds etched upon the whiteness of shoulders, a fly so minute and perfect that at first sight one would endeavor to brush it off. Not many Japanese women favor it. The only tattooing I observed on them was a mark, the brand of the Yoshiwara, to show whom they belonged to.

This visit, I had a large dragon etched on my back in order to cover about the vilest attempt at the Crucifixion that I had ever beheld. It took Ohashi just about six hours to finish it, and it was a case of Christianity or the emblem disappearing before the royal four-clawed dragon of Japan. There was nothing in this to alarm one, or to cause one to exclaim in horror, "down goes the cross and up goes the Yellow Peril." It was simply an artistic, barbaric, Asiatic, fantastically conceived monster obliterating about as puerile an attempt at depicting our Great Teacher, an attempt about as picturesque as primeval man away back in the Stone Age could scratch upon a soft stone with a piece of flint, a spear head.

Ammunition gave out, in the shape of Cyrus, and as we had visitors continually dropping in, it behooved me, therefore, to get more of the same brand. First came three sailors from the *Brandenberg*.[8] One, a boy, haggled about the price of a pair of clasped hands, with the German ensign and the English crossed for a background. This he had changed to an American ensign after I had thrown a few jolts of Cyrus at him. The "schnapps" seemed to go to his head and soon he commenced talking volubly to me in a mixture of German and English. His favorite term of addressing me was, "Yankee man." At last the fumes of old Cyrus became too much for him and he dropped asleep while under the needle.

His two companions went out for a walk, but soon came back. I had made them all feel pretty comfortable by this time, and soon three marines from one of the English ships came [in] and we were a jolly party. Old Cyrus leveled all national disputes and placed us on a friendly footing. A Japanese who had been a wardroom steward in our Navy and had been recently paid off came in, and I had him go for more, which he willingly did. I pressed drink upon Ohashi, but he refused to touch it on account of the work he was doing. As a rule, the Japs are an abstemious race, but

A Sailor's Log

they have no idea of [the effects of] drinking whisky. They will fill a glass to the brim and dash it off the same as water. The steward's *Okamisan* came in after him and nothing must do but she should join us in a bumper, and it was a rather large one. Then the respective wives of my two tattooers came in, and soon it was a jolly crowd. Jollity was the order of the night. They were my guests. There was no quarrelling of any sort. Drink only made them jolly.

It was late when I said goodbye that night. Even the rickshaw man came in for his share and was feeling good when I concluded at last to go.[9]

I awoke [the next morning] with the usual bursting head, and for about half an hour it was dollars to doughnuts whether I would get up or not. This is the punishment of the drunkard, the aftermath. I don't advocate drunkenness; far from it. Aside from the "ten nights in a bar room" aspect, a person is foolish, very foolish, to introduce anything into his system that he knows will make him sick, and from which he can derive no earthly use whatever. It is foolishness to make oneself sick. There are good, long lapses where I can leave it alone, but if kept up, you become a slave to the drink habit, as much as to the opium habit. This is to be the true log, common place log of a common place bluejacket, his vices and his good points, the log of most all bluejackets. A man under the influence of strong drink is temporarily insane. His reasoning faculty is dulled. He becomes simply a beast. When I am sober, I always move away as quickly as possible from a drunken man. I don't like them around me. No one else does, even if they are your friends. You don't know no more than the "drunk" himself what moment he will turn on you.

There never was a more fallacious saying, "What's in a man sober will come out when drunk." Not so. The reasoning faculty is gone. Without reason, the human being is simply a brute. He is without soul. The immortal spark is quenched with strong drink. It is reason that places us above the level of the Digger Indian or the clay eater of Georgia, or any other brute. "When drink is in, reason is out." So, don't let any man, or woman for that matter, get offended at the antics of a drunken man. Of course, they have a right to get offended at the mere matter of his being drunk. But at any action that he does caused by the curse of drink, let them exercise forbearance. He or she are not themselves.

I have no excuse to offer. I am, or was, a sailor cooped up aboard ship for months at a time. I am dull and listless aboard from discipline and the horrible routine that wears on a man and is worse than solitude. We get ashore for a short, very short, period. We don't know when we shall come ashore again. And we proceed to get as full as possible to drive away the blues. We are no more fit to be turned loose than is a prisoner, but it is a noticeable fact that there is less drunkenness among soldiers than sailors for the simple reason that a soldier is in contact with the world more, and is leading a comparably healthy life, more like a rational human being. Hic.

"Oh, the miserable head!" I thought it would burst. My tongue was fast to the roof of my mouth. I was burning for a drink of cool water, not for Cyrus Noble this early in the morning. It was about 6 A.M. I hate to lie abed late, so with a groan, I struggled to a sitting position in the bed, grasping my wildly throbbing coconut in both hands. It was the usual little, barn-like Chinese brothel shack. Of its occupant outside of myself, the least said, the better. There was plenty of cold water, and the way I doused that aching head would bring envious glances from a Polar bear. I reduced the swelling considerably, and managed to get my tongue from the roof of my mouth with an effort. I got out in the fresh air as soon as possible. John had just uncurled himself like a big Newfoundland from his bed, the bottom of his ricksha.

"Hello, John. How you feel?"

"My feel belly good. No me."

"How would a big 'geezer' go, you think this morning, John?"

"No savvy geeser."

"Booze. Old Serious Trouble. Fire water. Any old thing. Hardwater. Red eye."

"No savvy any ting yo spek."

"Whisky. Whisky, John."

"Now me savvy," with an expectant smile.

"All right then, John. We try and find Grill Room, and we catch whisky."

And then, as I was sober, albeit, gadzooks, a little dazed from too much imbibing of old sack the night before, a ray of light flitted across the cobwebbed cells of memory in this crown of mine and Godwot beseems by me halidom,[10] I remembered the fair maid of the Grill had given her address to one of my messmates, who had prided himself on the conquest of the fair ladye's heart, and had thereby bee[n] mulcted to the tune of about forty dobies coin of the realm. Bryan money, scads, to wit, drinks of divers sorts for the maiden and self. Principally for the maiden, who was possessed of a large thirst, almost as large as Percival, the Bowery Pan-handler. No. 8 Canton Road. "Ha!"

"No. 8 Canton Road, John. Grill Room, No. 8 Canton Road. Now you savvy, you imp of Confucius, you Boxer?"

"Me savvy. No. 8 Clanton Road. Why you no speak ploper last night? Me can do. No. 8. All light."

We found it this time, sure 'nuff.

"All's well, John. I won't be out for some time. What?" I exclaimed as he approached, "Money? I'll pay you off now. No wanchee any more. Catch 'nother piecee man. You no good."

"No, no! No wanchee money. You all light. Pay no want. Just now, money for chow."

"Oh, chow. You must have the appetite of a goat. Here you are, tho'." And I tossed him 20 [cents] Mex and away he went smiling, half rogue and half fool.

The Grill was open, but nobody [was] astir, except the Chinese servants. I went into the bar. Nobody there except the Japanese behind the bar. No barmaid. Taking her beauty sleep, no doubt. She needed plenty of sleep.

"Give me little gin, little lime juice, and lemonade." My morning beverage to take the kinks out after a night of it. "Is there [a] small, weasoned up [wizened?] rooster in here? Came last night and took a room," I asked, tossing off the eye-opener.

"Yes. He sleep, I think, just now. You go up to room."

"Give us another one of the same first," tossing the coin for the two drinks on the bar. I went up and found the room. There were two of my mates there, a large, commodious room with three big double beds in it. They were just getting up and looked rather rusty.

"Hello, you plugs. Are you going to sleep all day?"

"What time is it, my Lord?"

"About 7 A.M. What's this, do me eyes deceive me, or is that the real McCoy, the only Cyrus I see before me eyes?" pointing to a half emptied bottle of Cyrus Noble on the table.

"The coffee is just coming up. I['ll] ring for the boy. What you want is a café royal."

While I'm waiting for the coffee, I['ll] take the royal now." Clutching the bottle by the neck, I took a good bumper.

The boy made his appearance with the coffee and while sipping it, we compared notes of the night.

"I like the looks of things here. Think I'll pay for the balance of my time for meals and a bed here."

"We are going down to breakfast now. Come and join us."

The meal was well served, good service. The Chinese beat the world in this respect. Over the coffee we made plans for the day.

"Where are you off to this morning, Wils?"

"The old Chinese city, after I go to the tattooers to get the money I left with him for safe keeping last night. Then back here for tiffin. Then a ride out to the Arcadia, out Bubbling Well Road past the race course, to the German camp. They have a canteen there, you know. Good German beer. Then back for dinner. Then Too Cho Loo's Tea House and any other tea house, and the Chinese theatre or any place at all, if you are agreed. How do you like that itinerary. Eh?"

"All right. Can do. Just now."

"Good! Good!" they both roared. "Bring us three bottles of auld ale. That's the ticket, just the thing. You're a good guide, W[ilson]."

"Well, I should smile," I said with becoming modesty. "What your Uncle Dudley don't know about Shanghai, for the short time he has been in it, why. . . . What he don't know," sez I, "my rickshaw man knows. Bring forth the ale." The ale came. Good auld ale. Burton-on-Trent, said D———. "Burton-on-Trent. Well 'tis meself that knows the place. I tell you there's nothing like a glass of Bass's, or a drink of musty auld ale, for 'tis yerself that will be drunk for a week. You know yer drunk, but ye can't help yerself."

"Here's to good auld ale," I roared, holding up a flowing glass of the sparkling liquid.

"Ease it into ye," roared D., the wild Irishman, with his strident voice that could be heard a block away.

"Here's a go," said S———.

Afloat & Ashore in Shanghai

"This is what ye call hoigh loife. 'Tis better than the prison ship, with the tyrannical Russian. The Great White Czar with the absolute conthrol of the underground savages, the power of loife and death, wid the sneakin' way he has o' watchin' his men to see if he can't get them on the report and get 'em hung to the signal yard before mess gear in the morning."[11]

"Yes. Here's to freedom, if only for a day, from the prison ship. We have got to have a good time before we deliver ourselves into the hands of the enemy. Some more old ale. This is on me. Then we'll finish the Cyrus, and that will hold us for a while.[12]

"An' we'll be back in time for 'tiffin.' Tiffin, tiffin. 'Tis a mighty foine word, is 'tiffin.' The idea of a savage havn tiffin. 'Pipe the scum o' the earth to tiffin.' 'Me Lord Algernon De Rochelly went to tiffin fresh from the hands of his *walley de chambree.*'[13] Whoop! 'Twas me Lord Algernon that went to South Africa to conquer the poor Boer, wid his decorations and his orders. And his *walley-de-chambre.* And his thrunks and his tub. Was himself and the other gold-plated show soldiers wid thir great reputations, that were goin' to scoff the poor Boer and thrust him off the face o' the earth. But the whiskered, common-looking farmer ginerals made things so warrum that he hadn't time to take his tub. In fact, he lost it at Colenso, where three hundred and fifty Boers defated 85,000 Britishers. Whoop! 'Tis meself that knows it." D—— hates a "lemon-peeler," but doesn't carry his dislike to individuals, but to the nation as a whole.

The inner man satisfied, we sallied forth on our tour of inspection. My knave was engaged in a wordy altercation with some more of his kind and was munching an orange when he could find time between his rapid-fire vocabulary. At the same time, he had his eye upon the entrance to the Canton Road Grill and Tiffin Rooms (as you please). The moment he discovered us, he made a wild charge, followed by more of his kind. The Irish Agitator and S——, the machinist, picked out their men before John had an opportunity to choose, so this time there wasn't any "comshur" in it for him.

"Chinese city, John. . . . Or, stay. Tattoo man first."

Down Canton Road we went, turning off into the Bund, the beautiful drive along the river. Up the Bund to Broadway and thence to Astor Road No. 1, stopping in front of the tattooers. Ohashi was just getting up and looked fresh enough after his revel of last night. I got my Bryan money, and promising to come back at night for some more work, we were off again, first taking quite a swig from a half emptied souvenir of the night before. This time along the Bund, carriages were rolling along in different directions, the occupants going to their different places of business, solid appearing Europeans with the air of the cosmpolité. Chinese merchants and compradores, all solid looking, well groomed, well fed, substantial men. None of the gloss of fashion could be seen at this unearthly hour of the morning, when well-to-do Shanghai was just beginning to stir, and Beauty was taking her refreshing morning slumber after a night of revelry. The cool air fanned our cheeks, and incidentally fanned that large, swollen koko of mine, which was gradually assuming normal dimensions. To my mind, there is nothing like these glorious, cool mornings when the roads are hard and dry as bone, just cool enough to make an overcoat acceptable. And in this part of the world they are to be often met with.

A tall "Hindoo" man doing sentry duty in front of some big building would draw the folds of his cloak close around him. The Chinese "coppers" looked comfortable in their blue uniforms, pigtails hanging at full length but clasped by their belt, as also did the regulation "Bobby" of the Shanghai Municipal Police. Wheelbarrows were plentiful, with a short dumpy Chinese woman on one side and sometimes the whole of her household goods on the other, or else an almond eyed young damsel and her mother. Perhaps only one passenger would occupy the barrow. The coolies [then] by an adjustment of the shoulder strap, would counter balance the weight. [It is] an old, old Chinese mode of locomotion, very cold and slow, but the passenger didn't seem in a hurry, philosophically puffing away and filling and refilling the ever-present water-pipe. The men-o-war were still swinging idly at their berths as on my previous visits. The Public Gardens looked deserted.

"What do you think of the Bund," turning and speaking to the Agitator.

"Foine, a mighty foine roadway."

"Well, you want to look and observe. Take in everything. That's the beauty of going on 'liberty' occasionally. If you miss this trip to Chinatown, your liberty is simply N.G. [no good] You will see enough to talk about for a life-time. There is nothing like it."

"Sure, it's foine as it is. I feel like Lord Algernon de Rochelly already, Me Lud. Lud Algy day Rochelly who turned into the Chang day E-lisay [Champs Elysée], closely followed be his *valley-day-chambray*, Montmorency Pathyrk O'Toole, who carried the dobie money to buy the jewelry he was going to present to the pramier bally dancer, Mlle. Edythe Mayme O'Hooligan at the Bejo. Savvy, ye bloomin' spawn av a horrid toad?" This last to his rickshaw man. Evidently, the Agitator was fast getting up steam.

Soon we reached the limits of French town, the French concession, and alighted.

"How's this?" asked the Agitator. "Is this Chiny town?"

"No. Not yet," I replied. "You see these rickshaw men have only license for a part of the city. Those you see with red and black numbers are allowed in every part of the city. It's only a short distance from here." Soon we were in front of its walls, or at least the bridge that spanned the moat.

I have written about the old Chinese city of Shanghai before in these pages, and it is not necessary for me to repeat, so I will only mention such sights as I omitted before. This time one of the rickshaw men had remained behind to guard their vehicles. The other two conferred together and my man went into a small Chinese "chow" house at the corner. When he emerged he was followed closely by an old, rusty looking Chink, a professional guide. This man spoke very good English. Before, when we went thro', the two rickshaw men had acted as guides. But, no doubt, they would come in for their "comshur" from the old guide. That's the middle man way of doing business in China. No child [is] so small but what largess isn't the very essence of its being. Speak to one or get one to speak to another for you, and see him or her blandly hold out the hand, "comshur." They have the business instinct in a superlative degree.

"Come on," said the guide. "You no hab seen Chinese city."

"Oh, yes," I answered. "I have seen two times before. Now wanted to take long look, see."

"All right. Only two day ago, I take plenty American thro', show everyting. Very nice."

The first thing I espied and pointed out to the Agitator and the Machinist was the lone sentinel standing by the obsolete old muzzle loader that was made more for noise than anything else, in one of the embrasures in the wall. "Looks for all the world," said the Machinist, "like a monkey behind a beer bottle."

"What's the difference?" quoth I. "All guns look alike to the Chinese. It answers the purpose. He could keep all the devils in Shanghai away with that old chunk of iron."

It looked old, hundreds of years. It was old. The wall and moat in parts were comparatively new, our guide informed us. Three or four hundred years; the rest [a] thousand, two thousand, he didn't quite know. Over the moat [and] we were in the city. The guide took us a new route, explaining many things as he went along. He turned into a tea garden.

"Inside," he said, pausing and thumping at a big wooden door, "big Mandarin tea garden. Very old. No people come here, only mandarins, wives, and children. I show you."

The door was slowly opened in answer to his knock by a very old Chinaman, the keeper. A youngster whose curious, round eyes showed no fear [followed] close behind him. We found ourselves in a gloomy court. Everything like a fortress. Signs of age and wear everywhere. Friezes of dragons carved in stone, and drawings in colors depicting scenes in some great Emperor's reign ran all around the walls and partitions. Balustrades of stone, all intricately carved, the imperial dragon in every design. Little nooks with chairs and tables of solid teak, centuries old, and able to stand centuries more of wear before their period of usefulness expired. Signs of age in the very atmosphere. Curious diamond shaped little pieces of pearl shell, quite transparent, set in windows.

"This was used before, long time, no hab glass," explained the guide. Niches in the walls contained the image of some great mandarin, of some metal, whether iron or other material, I know not. All was of a yellowish white. Grotesques, gargoyles, dragons of every conceivable contortion that the Asiatic brain could devise peered from the most unexpected places. At every turn a new surprise, a fantastic monstrosity even more Oriental than the last met our gaze. New surprise followed surprise until the mind was lost in the amaze[ment] at the labor that formed all this for pleasure. I have seen the Pyramids.[14] I can conceive the cause that led to the construction of those massive piles of masonry, but the Chinese were masons of unequalled skill when the Pharaohs were a possibility of futurity.

A Sailor's Log

Human skill could do no more. Nothing was left undone, even the feelers of an immense dragon that capped an arch of solid rock and made of iron, curled to the height of at least six or eight feet, running to a point as sharp as a needle's point. A small arbor looking like a small pavilion contained seats and [a] table carved from the solid stone, or else the masonry was so natural as to deceive the eye.

"This table mandarin makee play. Gamble for big money, sometime have chow, plenty piecee men." Halting in front of a small pavilion, we entered. Back of the usual heavy table and chairs of teak, was a gorgeous curtain of olden embroidery. This our guide drew aside revealing a very old painting on silk of a fiercely bearded, bejeweled and gorgeously robed mandarin. "This picture of very big mandarin. He very good man. Picture four hundred year old. Look, see, very old. China man. Makee all same joss. Pray. Burn stick, have good luck. Picture very old. You see," explained he. "China man no like new thing. Like evything very old. Great respect. American likee new thing. No like old."

"[You're] right, I think, John. About the only old thing the majority of Americans like is old whiskey or wine. Everything else they like new. Even the old sweetheart and friend is no good. In this respect, John, Chinaman much better than American."

"I think so," smiled the old fellow.

"Sure 'tis aulder than the time o' Brian Boru[15] or St. Patrick,"[16] chimed in the Agitator, who was taking everything in.

Thro' a labyrinth of passages of solid rock curiously laid, the art of the mason assisting nature; thro' dark passages, we followed him until we came out on a small balcony overlooking a pool. Dragons and snakes were here also carved of stone, curiously interwoven, their mouths wide open. They were fountains, but when we saw them, no water issued forth. This was reserved for occasions when the mandarins were present.

"Mandarin makee fish here, see," pointing to a number of long, black fish idly swimming around, and no doubt waiting to be caught. Coming out from this passage into the garden once more, we ascended more steps and some of these steps were of soapstone and mighty slippery to the tread. He pointed out a huge slab of soapstone not unlike a huge stalagmite that reared its slender column at least fifteen feet. This was also very old and considering the soft material of the stone, must have gradually wasted away from rains. It looked almost on the point of toppling over. In front of another very old picture of another very old, and no doubt virtuous, mandarin stood a grotesque, gnarled root of wood, varnished to protect it from the ravages of time. It was the exact counter-part of a dragon, when pointed out. I thought it was the opium created fantasy of some Chinese worker in bronze or copper, but a closer inspection and the assurance of the old guide convinced me that Nature could outdo even the Chinese where quaintness and oddity of design was concerned. It must have been a freak of Mother Nature when in one of her most fanciful moods.

A tea tree, somewhat stunted in growth was pointed out, and going thro' more passageways, we came to the exit of this wonderful garden that had exhausted the

Afloat & Ashore in Shanghai

skill of the best Chinese architects and gardeners of many ages. Of their wonderful patience and application, it stands a monument today, as it has stood thro' many ages. Not even the ornamentation on the head of a nail had escaped them. Nothing [was] too small, too slight. And all [so] that a few favored human beings might come and while away a few short hours in the infinitesimal lives that have passed and repassed and will pass and repass within this old, time-stained Garden of the Mandarins.[17]

We passed out to the gate, following our guide as in a dream over the slippery soapstone paving, green with moss here and there in patches. Some children were romping around, curious-looking little Chinese men and women who eyed us as Chinese children will, with a mild curiosity, evidently the offspring of the old keeper of this venerable place. He stood at the closed door, ready to open and let us thro' the gate. As we approached, he held out an old withered claw-like hand. "Comshur, twenty cents, each one piecee man," with an expectant smile. We came out of our dream of a past age into the present one with a jolt, and each hand mechanically sought a pocket containing the necessary small coin, and delivering, we passed out in the wake of our guide once more, into the crooked, noisy, dirty, narrow, yellow cur-infested streets of old Shanghai.

"Sure, I think 'tis ourselves will take a drink of Cyrus after that mope into the past," said the irrepressible Agitator, breaking the silence and dishing out the remnants of a large quart from inside the pea-coat. "I wonder what Lord Algy and Montmorency would say t' each other about the auld garden wid its doraguns and other gugals? Here's luck to the mandarins, hopin' they catch some fish next time they hold a can maker's picnic within the sacred precincts av the auld garden." And he eased a large dose into him and passed the bottle around.

The old guide showed himself not a bit above hitting the bottle himself and "aised a bit into himself with practiced ease." This helped to oil his tongue and he became more voluble. We paused in front of an ivory carver's shop to watch a youngster carving away with a carving gouge. He looked to be about four years old and was as wise looking a little man as one could wish to see. An urchin at home at this age wouldn't have arrived at school age. This young "tacher" gave us a bright look from remarkably sharp eyes set in a round, chubby face, and continued gouging away unconcernedly. He was used to the "foreign devils." I stopped and purchased some bone "chop sticks" and afterwards found when I examined them aboard ship that one of them was in halves, fitted together ingeniously enough. I wouldn't have discovered it then if it hadn't fallen and come apart. In this way they utilize short ends. Truly nothing goes to waste in China.

Turning around from the front of this little shop, I narrowly escaped getting knocked out by a back-hander from a beggar. It wasn't their fault. It was mine. I nearly fell over them as I stepped backward from the shop. There were two of them and they exceeded anything I ever read or dreamed about. "Mother of Moses, will ye look at that," called the Agitator. One of them groveled in the filth of the narrow street, blood pouring from numerous small cuts. His queue [was] undone and streaks of dirt and clay matted his hair, and [his] body [was] clad in rags revealing more nakedness than they covered. There he groveled, putting up such hideous howling and shrieks as to make one's blood run cold.

His companion held a large, flat stone in his hand weighing about fifteen [pounds]. Flinging his arms up and down and exhorting the people with wild cries, he brought the stone down with a resounding thud on his chest. It was a back-hander with this stone that narrowly escaped the point of my jaw. To an unpracticed eye, the way he thumped himself with that stone no doubt appeared fearful. But I had seen many a piece of stone broken on a man's chest, and knew there was a way to manage it without the least hurt to the performer. The guide also knew it, for he shrugged his shoulder. "Chinamen very hard beggar. Make plenty of work for money. He no hurt himself. These men very rich. Makee business."

Up the street from these there were two more. One had exposed the stump of his right arm and was streaked with mud and dirt. His companion could out-howl the other two. I didn't see them gather any "cash." The shop-keeper barely noticed them. But they wax rich. If any American beggar had to work as hard as them, there wouldn't be many of them.

I also purchased a few small opium boxes turned from horn and bone. There are a great many of these shops in the old city. We also stopped at the old tea house, the one that stood in the middle of the pond. This, the guide said, was over four hundred years old. It looked it, and looked able to last a thousand more. The tables and chairs and wood of the house was dark with age and polished from long usage. Some of the old tables had a polish like a ballroom floor. We stopped for tea here and it was the best tea I ever drank. Peanuts were served with it. The cost of those cups of tea for the five was $1.50, not bad considering the few moments we stayed. I drank most of it, mine and the others. An old Chink brought some sweets made of rice and we tried them. It looked and tasted just like the slabs of popped-corn I bought when a boy. The tea would have charmed an old maid. Truly, the quotation is right about the "cup that cheers, etc." There are other nice things to drink beside Cyrus Noble.

Leaving this old tea house that is one of the landmarks of old Shanghai, we wended our way over the old zig-zag bridge and continued our tour.[18] We took in the joss house again, only this time we burned some gilt paper in front of one of the josses. "For good luck," said the guide. The joss house keeper said, "ten cent each piecee man." Some other civilized religions are not so cheap. We went thro' some old teahouses and found opium smokers in all stages of the game, some far gone. Here at their ease lay two well-dressed Chinamen, leisurely smoking, dipping the needle into the black, sticky substance that resembled thick, black varnish, or molasses, and applying [it] to the pipe, filling and refilling after each couple of whiffs until the drug finally put them to sleep and carried them away from their trials and tribulations into the celestial seventh heaven of delight.

Afloat & Ashore in Shanghai

"Spheakin' for meself," said the Agitator, "good ould whiskey is good enough for me," patting the bottle.

"You like try?" asked one of the attendants, seductively holding out a pipe.

I hesitated. "Not just now, no time. Another day."

I have got to "hit the pipe" just for luck some day. It's an experience I have yet to learn.

I watched some of the Chinamen with interest, but I didn't see any wrecks among them, and all appeared to be regular habitués of the place. Perhaps it is true that the drug doesn't have the same effect on them as on the Europeans. Perhaps the Chinese know how to use it. They know how to extract enjoyment out of life. They have the philosophy of earthly enjoyment acquired after thousands of years of civilization, and that philosophy is not to go to extremes. They are temperate in all their vices and amusements. They don't lead the strenuous life. Very rarely do you see one drunk. I never have. I have seen lots of Japanese raving drunk, but then you know, they are advancing, getting civilized according to European ideas. Soon they'll be bolting down whole wedges of mince pie and milk at the quick lunch counter, making wild rushes for the subway or elevated, reading their papers on the fly and the thousand and one other rapid firing, nerve destroying devices of modern civilization. Soon the kimono in Japan will be replaced by stiff and uncomfortable shirts, and trousers that are creased and cause you lots of worriment because they will bag at the knees. The national head-dress of Japan is an oiled parasol. This will be replaced with a nice, new high[ly] polished plug, another source of despair to the man whose prestige is great in society, but whose income is limited, because fashion decrees that the bell of the crown shall be just so and not deviate in the least, if you are to be considered the correct article with the hallmark of correct form stamped upon you. Soon, little snappy brown man, clothes will make the man, and not the man himself. Learn to discriminate my intelligent little friend. Discriminate. Accept the best of what we have to offer you, and retain the best of what years of custom have taught you.

Don't be like a navy yard policemen I particularly noticed in Kure, while in the dock there. He was all in a sweat. His collar, that curse of civilization, our civilization, had got the better of him. It was a tall collar, a very tall one. In fact, it lacked only an inch of being rated a cuff. It had carried away at the back, and despite his efforts, that accursed collar worked up toward his ears. He had lost the button. He tried to look dignified. He had an uncomfortable feeling that we were guying [mocking] him from the ship. He made several efforts to put it back in place. It was a very hot day, an August day. An August day in the sun land of Japan. It was hot. He was hot; so hot, in fact, that great beads of perspiration rolled down his little brown cheeks. The accursed thing had him "faded." It refused to wilt. It must have been celluloid. Plenty of dignified little Japanese visitors walked comfortably around the yard, clad in kimonos of beautiful colors and texture, *kasa* and fan, cool and airy. They looked curiously at the perturbed little brown official. They saw by his hang dog expression that

A Sailor's Log

something was wrong, but they didn't know. They didn't know how a collar should set, as long as it was a collar. They hadn't been initiated into the mysteries of European dress yet. But the little brown man knew. He knew this accursed thing was out of place and was detracting from his dignity. He knew the "Amercans" were sizing him up from the deck of the big battleship and were laughing at him.

Finally, a dignified, stately old fellow accompanied by as pretty a little brown maiden as all that wonderful land could produce, with small, brown feet incased in spotless white *tabi* and very dainty wooden *gaita*, with a glimpse of plump brown ankles just twinkling in and out of the folds of the silk kimono, approached him, no doubt seeking information about the foreign ship. Oh, how he envied the other Japs in comfortable, national dress. He tried to look dignified, but made a miserable failure of it, and he knew it. The old man looked curiously at him, as well as the little maid, wondering what was the matter. He pulled thro' with as good grace as possible. No doubt he vowed by Shinto that he would never be caught in the same fix again. He stalked away as stately as possible, but who, reader, can look stately with a collar up under your ears? He made a miserable failure of it. He looked like a dog caught in the act of stealing chickens. He disappeared. I saw him about two hours afterward, minus the collar. He felt better; he was sure of himself. The accursed thing was thrown in some scrap pile. So you see, little brown man, some things European are strictly N.G. You, little brown man, and you, John Chinaman, are socialistic in your habits, [but] not too much so. You help each other and you organize yourself in companies for protection. You forage for a living in shoals. That's good. Beware of Capital. Beware of the Great American Janitor, and flats where your friendly intermingling would be regarded as intrusion. You have beautiful manners and great niceties of etiquette. See that this doesn't disappear by [the introduction of] European innovations. Weigh it all, little man of the Sun Land, and sift the wheat from the chaff. Yours [is] the opportunity now. It is up to you. Odd's Bodkins, as my friend Amyas Leigh would say.[19] What t'ell. I digress.

Two of the Chinamen smiled when I stopped over them and asked them to show me how they dipped the opium. This they did good naturedly. I would have like[d] to observe the action all thro', but time was pressing, and we moved away, stopping to look with interest at a Chinese weaver working on some beautiful pattern of silk, using a loom, the exact counterpart of those of ages agone. Makers of imitation jade stone, pipe makers, metal workers, all in the smallest of shops. We went thro' another mandarin tea garden, not as fine as the first. In this garden, on a large space of blank wall, thousands of tourists, soldiers and sailors or all nations had written their names. Some were obliterated with time; others were of yesterday. We inscribed ours with the rest, and passed on. We passed many sights I have written of before.

"Sure, it wouldn't have been a liberty at all if we'd missed this," quoth the Agitator. "But as Montmorency would say to Lord Algy, 'Tiffin is served, me Lud.' What do ye say? I'm moighty hungry and want some auld Burton-on-Trent."

Afloat & Ashore in Shanghai

"That's me," said the Machinist.

"Me too," chimed in I.

But we began to recognize where we were at, and knew that we were returning, taking us thro' a large yard filled with big earthen cauldrons and filled with a dark looking liquid. I asked what it was. "This Chinese salt-sauce. No like Americans' salt. This liquid."

"Oh, yes. I know now."

The old fellow led us in different shops and tried to get us to buy different things, skeins of silk, sandal wood boxes, perfumery, etc. But we knew these articles only attracted for the moment and would be cast aside when aboard. All curios seem very attractive and desirable when seen in a shop, but it takes discrimination to select from among so many, and the article you purchased that looked so desirable doesn't seem half so when looked at under a different aspect.

We soon came out at the same old place. This was my third visit to the old Chinese city and I left it with regret. There was so much to be seen, something new at every visit. Across the bridge into the French concession, [where] we paid our guide, "Fifty cents each man, if you please," and cheap at the price, we thought. Going for our rickshaws, my rogue John had something on his mind, and soon he commenced.

"What for you pay guide?" Here he pointed to each man in turn. "Each piecee man pay fifty cents. Why you no give my fifty cents? I good guide. My speak English belly good! Next time, my be guide. My put on good clothes, shoes, go evvy placee. Tea house. Too Fow Loo tea house. My can go. Hab good clothes." And thus he ran on, very indignant and very mad to think we didn't select him as a guide.

"All right, John. Next time, you guide. You makee good guide, eh?"

"Belly good," with an injured expression.

The face he put on made us roar with laughter, he looked so injured.

"Next time, John. Go to Grill Room."

The Grill was only a short distance from the old city and we were quickly there, in ample time for "tiffin." We all did ample justice to the well served meal, and "aised" a couple bottles of "Burton-on-Trent" ale into us. The Grill, as I found it, was a very quiet, respectable hotel. The waiters moved noiselessly around and spoke in muffled voices. They were under rigid discipline. One could see that, and it spoke well for the management. They were very watchful and anticipated your every wish. These Chinese boys make good servants. They only receive from 4 to 8 Mexicans per month; a good steward, about fifteen. The trouble is, they get lazy and shiftless. They are all rascals, and nearly every month they have to be changed. They are very neat and tidy in appearance.

The Chinamen you see in the States are not by any means a criterion to go by, if you want to form an opinion of how John looks. Here in Shanghai they are all fine-looking, well groomed, well dressed young fellows, and all have an insatiable greed for "comshur." Not even a "cash" will be ignored. They are all saving and temperate.

It is nothing for Europeans here to raise them from childhood, just giving them their "chow," not even clothing them. They clothe themselves with what money they receive from "comshur" and always contrive to look very neat, unless brought up in the coolie class. There they are the worst looking beggars in the world, outside of Port Said or Aden.[20]

~~~

Nanking Road is one of the busiest streets in Shanghai. It is lined with Chinese shops of all kinds, of the better class, and it presents a most animated appearance. It is quite wide and well macadamized. You can purchase anything here you wish, from photos to Canton goods, silks, etc. This leads into Bubbling Well Road, which I have described before. It is a beautiful drive way and all the elite of Shanghai's cosmopolitan population can be seen in their splendid equipages any pleasant afternoon. And we ran in the midst of them. Happy as the happiest, your sailorman never gives a thought to the morrow. Time enough to think of the ship and the dismal routine after we have had our fling.

The Agitator made many forcible comments upon the occupants of the carriages. He was a born hater of aristocrats, especially English. In them he recognized the despoilers of his race. When any equipage more gorgeous than the rest passed, he was sure to indulge in a tirade. I do not think 'twas envy in his case, but rather the hatred of race against the English. For myself, I know by experience that money cannot bring happiness any more than it can buy health, and although to all outward appearances these people riding by with liveried flunkies and coachmen have all that life can afford, yet they are not, I question, as happy as the stoical Chinamen lying back with half-closed eyes, looking at his world thro' the blue haze of smoke from an opium pipe.

In all Shanghai, I do not remember seeing over one woman or girl that could be called fair, of the Europeans, I mean. And she, from the way in which she carried herself, exacted the homage due a queen, which no doubt she was by right of beauty. [She was] a perfect blonde of exquisite form, the contours of which were enhanced by her close-fitting riding habit. As I observed her that pleasant afternoon, she was a picture to be remembered. Jaunty, self-poised, well groomed English girl, as undoubtedly she was. She was the center of attraction as she cantered along the Bubbling Well Road, followed [at] the regulation distance by a Chinese groom.

"Be Heavens, look at me Lady Vera de Vere! Wouldn't that jolt ye? If Lord Algy was only here, there wud be a chance for a crush. She is a perfect thoroughbred, ain't she?"

I heartily assented. She was the one bright particular star that outshone all others; a queen by right of beauty.

We stopped at the Arcadia long enough for some more refreshment. Finding no attraction there, we rode on to the German camp. We asked and rec'd permission from the sentry to enter. We found a company at drill, and noted how well drilled they were, the snap and precision with which they handled their pieces, a very pretty picture, very military, no doubt.

"They have got it down fine, eh? Like a piece of machinery at the command."

"Yes. It looks foine, all right, but I'll bet a company of Tennessee Volunteers or any other of our troops could make those fellows 'hike' like Filipinos."

"Our troops would give them a hustle for it, at any rate, I'll bet."

"Sure, loike all European soldiers, they only act at the word o' command. They ain't taught to think for themselves. Why, one of those fellows would no more act without being told by his shuperior officer than they would try to fly. John the Yankee, he goes it on his own hook, but always keeps in perfect touch with the rest av the gang. He's an individual foighter, he is, and figures out his own mode of getting the game he has picked out for himself."

"You're right there, D——. The day of machine-like troops advancing in regular formation is a thing of the past. The South African Affair shows this."

A corporal came up and addressing us, asked about some of our shipmates, naming them, all Germans. He spoke intelligently enough. In the course of the talk he told us he spoke in addition, Italian and French.

We adjourned to the canteen and had some bottled beer, bottled in Hamburg, and a very good brand we found it. The place was half full of "non coms," soldiers, and sailors, all very jolly. The first thing a German does when a little mellowed by beer or schnapps is to sing, and every air is patriotic. A large portrait of the Kaiser occupied a conspicuous position, upturned mustache and all. Among the officers and men, those who could, imitated it. After [we] finished the beer we produced the bottle of Cyrus. "Aise this wan into ye," roared the Agitator above the din, filling a glass to the brim for the corporal. And "aise it" he did, screwing up one eye, and smacking his lips like a connoisseur.

We went thro' the parade ground and watched the men at evening exercises. Here a squad was going thro' a few simple movements on the parallel bars. Another squad [was] jumping over a pole about three feet from the ground. They keep them at it. It is drill, drill, drill, and exercise and fatigue duty from reveille to taps in a German camp or barracks. As the corporal said in his broken English, "Nein goot. Cherman army gif blenty off vork und trill, but nein money." And the way these fellows were put thro' their paces by the corporal in charge was an object lesson, especially so by the corporal having charge of the squad by the pole. Calling out No. 1, No. 1 marched to the pole and stood at attention, and leaped squarely over, alighting very springily upon the ball of the foot, stood immediately at attention, stepped to one side, bringing his heels together with a click, taking up a position to catch the next man in case of a fall. No. 2 man came over and alighted very heavily and clumsily, getting a sharp reprimand from the corporal, who unslung his belt and pushed the point of his bayonet scabbard in the soft turf and went and made the jump himself, showing how it should be done. It was only a very low leap over the pole, but it was a matter of

A Sailor's Log

surprise how heavy and stiff some of them were. We left the men at their exercises and, accompanied by the corporal, went toward the gate. Near the gate the cooks and men detailed were all engaged in getting supper ready, and as it was getting late and time to return for dinner at the Grill, we drank their health and they drank ours in what was left of the bottle, and bidding them *adieu* at the gate, jumped in our rickshaws and were soon back at the Grill.

After a very good dinner, to which we did ample justice, and a few more bottles of Bass Ale, we left the Grill Room once more and in a few moments were in the thick of the narrow, crowded Chinese streets, en route to do the tea houses, and if agreeable to all hands, the theatres. The Machinist and the Agitator were struck with the swarm of humanity. The well-lighted shops and tea houses that lined the narrow streets for miles looked like a revelation of fairy land.

"Be Heavens! This must be a political mass-meeting going on, or a barbecue," commented the Agitator. But no, it was the usual crowded condition of the streets and no gala occasion. And this is kept up all night. The human tide only ebbs at the early hours of the morning and even then the streets are in a more crowded condition than you can see in the majority of American cities. Piercing music and singing came from the tea houses, the good natured crowd flowing in and out in streams from the brilliantly lighted entrances. All was good natured. The Chinese never give the exhibition of rudeness and rowdyism that one would see at home in great gatherings. It hardly ever required a policeman to enforce order. They are by nature and habit easy going and considerate of one another.

We soon had to alight from our rickshaws to make our way through the throng. I can close my eyes and always conjure up a picture of those narrow streets with the brilliantly lighted places of amusement, the contented throngs of Chinese of all sorts and conditions, from the coolies to the well dressed merchant; the sedan chairs that make rapid progress past the pedestrians; the crowded shops with would-be purchasers bending over some article of merchandise. Here a big Chinaman passes by with a singing girl of the tea house, with layers of rice powder and rouge, heavily penciled eyebrows, lashes accentuated by a skillful manipulation of the pencil. Her polished locks [are] held in place by silken bands that take a close inspection in the uncertain lights and shadows to detect from her real hair, so alike in ebony blackness are they. Her brilliant gown of silk and satin [is] covered with spangles and ornaments of silver. Her feet too small to hobble about on, she is carried on his broad shoulder, in lieu of a chair or carriage, perhaps to keep an engagement with [a] Chinese lover. She is a toy of an idle hour, and as far as expression goes, is happy, for has she not all that she desires in the way of silk tunics, bracelets and jade ornaments for her adornments, everything that her dim brain and benighted little soul can covet, even down to the silver water pipe, that all her class affect?

"Hoy! Hoy!" and the crowd parts to the right or left, and an elegant carriage sweeps thro', giving you a glimpse of a very dignified looking Chinese mandarin, clad in costly furs, lying back in luxurious ease. He rapidly flits by with an indifferent glance at the common rabble that is swarming all around him. We stop and gaze at something that attracts our attention in a window, and soon we have a crowd of curious on-lookers around to see what attracts our attention, but all good naturedly enough. My rickshaw man was in his glory. Hadn't he put on his shoes? The moment he placed these useful articles on, he ceased to be a coolie. They were reserved for gala occasions like this, when he felt it incumbent to act as a guide thro' the tea houses and theatres and any other place of interest. He pointed to his shoes and other dress with pride.

"My all same mandarin. Glood clothes. Can go tea house, theatre, no thlink I coolie." This he confided to me with an air that was at once a mixture of pride, simplicity and knavery. Like Solomon, he had arrayed himself in all his glory. He did the best he could. Who can do more? He was pleased at the result, and the prospect of getting the "comshur" that would accrue to some other Chinaman for steering us around. He was in his best, his evening dress, taken from his wardrobe beneath the seat of his jinricksha. But his dream of "cumshur" was shattered. My former guide saw us afar off, and came after us with a sprint that would do credit to a Filipino. You should see the phisiog of John at this unwelcome intrusion. Gone were his dreams of bilking us out of a dobie. At first I thought he would mix it up with the other fellow, but he contented himself with heaping all manner of abuse on him.

"Go ahead, John, mix it up. Poke him in the ear."

"My no pokee. My think I be guide," and he glared at the other man and at the same time gave us a reproachful look.

"Never mind, John, two piecee man," pointing at both, "be guide."

So he had to be pleased with that arrangement, but as they led the way through the busy, pleasure-seeking crowd, John read the riot act in Chinese to the other Chink, who only gave him the horse laugh. We stopped in the same tea-houses I have described before, but the Agitator soon got tired of this, and wanted to get out in the streets again thinking, and rightly, that there was more to be seen in the strange human panorama than in either tea-house or theatre. After taking a good "look, see," our guide led us thro' a dark court, through dark passage ways off the main streets. We squeezed thro' a large picket of bamboo poles that formed a barricade to one of these alleys, and going thro' a dark hall, found ourselves in a well-furnished room.

"What's on now, John?" I asked.

"Bimeby women come, look see," and he went out.

"What kind of a game is this, I wonder?" I asked the Agitator. "Can't be a crib [a saloon or low dive]. He must have something curious to show us."

"What the blazes! We'll see it out. We're fit for anything."

In about a moment, in flocked a whole bevy of Chinese beauties, all small feet, with their mothers and little sisters, cousins, aunts, and all other female relations. I could see our finish in the matter of "comshur."

"Wanchee see small foot?" asked John. "One piecee man," pointing to a buxom Chinese belle who looked us askance out of her slant, sloe black eyes. "She show you, one dollar."

"And cheap at half the price. I'll buy the whole bundle of Chinese femininity for my very own. Can do?" I asked John, winking at the girl, who tittered just like any American girl who is subject to giggles and hobbed behind her mama.

"No can sell. Wanchee look feet, can do. One dollar."

"All right. Here's yer dollar," said the Agitator, who was all curiosity. "Let the performance commence."

The girl, assisted by her very much revered ancestor, came forward bashfully and sat down on the low chair, while with downcast eyes from which she cast a side look slyly, commenced taking off her little pointed moccasins that were elaborately worked, covered with silver ornamentation. Unwrapping the white bandage, she held the little distorted foot up for our inspection, and a curious sight it was, with the instep forced back in a straight line with the ankle, the four toes in a parallel line lengthwise with the sole of the foot, or what was intended by Mother Nature to be a foot. The only toe that wasn't deformed was the large one. This one helped to bring this foot out to a sharp point, so sharp in fact, that it would bring tears of envy to the eyes of a soda-water clerk—one, of course, addicted to toothpick shoes. This foot was not as badly deformed as many are, nor was it as small. When shod, it was more the shape of a foot. Others are simply a crushed, deformed stump that every vestige of nature has disappeared from, toes and all. The girl looked slyly at us, to judge from our looks what our opinion was. We expressed nothing but approval to John, who interpreted to them, at which they seemed pleased. The girl caught a glimpse of the tattooing I had on my wrist, and catching hold of my hand, wanted to satisfy her curiosity by rolling up my sleeve. I playfully objected, "You wanchee see tattooing, can do. 50 c[en]ts comshur."

They all crowded around to see, but didn't want to pay for the privilege. Finally, I let them look at the whole arm, at which they chattered and shook their heads.

It cost us all the small coins we had to break clear from them. The entire crew clung to arms, legs, and every place they could make a grappling, a great chorus of "comshur, comshur." They all had to be satisfied, from mama down to the little tot of a girl just beginning to acquire small feet habit, but who was more clamorous then her elders for largess in the shape of dobie money. At last their insatiable appetites were appeased, and we broke away.

John proposed the theatre. But the Agitator and the Machinist didn't care to go, and I had been there several times, so we concluded to go back to the Grill, as it was getting late and you couldn't get in after 11:30 P.M. Beside, we were sleepy from our rambling and potations and felt inclined to court the God of Sleep. So, giving John the Guide a Mexican for his disinterested attentions, and John the Rickshaw Man orders to lead us to where we had left our rickshaws, we bade him *adieu*, promising to come again next month, if we were here, and making rapid way through the crowds that were getting larger as the night advanced, we were soon speeding away toward the hotel, which we reached as they were closing for the night.

We didn't stay up long, but after a few hot whiskies we were soon wrapped in slumber, lying like a Dutchman between two feather beds, a bed too luxurious for my simple tastes, a bed that makes one lazy, and causes one to lie abed long after the sun has made its appearance.

Speaking for myself, I awoke after a refreshing sleep. It was very early for a libertyman ashore to turn out: about 5 A.M. The Machinist and Agitator were still in the arms of Morpheus. That is, the Machinist was. The Agitator was in the arms of Murphy, and from the way in which his features were contracted and his whiskers sticking out like unto the quills of the ruffled porcupine, he must have been (in his dreams of course) leading a wild charge against the British at an imaginary Spions Kop, and it must have been a success for the features relaxed from their fierce look and a smile wreathed that classic Phiz, with the ecru lambrequins round about. Perhaps, tho', the many bottles of Auld Burton-on-Trent got into actual conflict with the redoubtable Cyrus Noble, and that caused that awful scowl. The Machinist opened his eyes, blinked like an owl at the familiar bottle on the table, and snuggled down in the coverlets for another snooze.

"What's th' matter wid youse plugs? Goin' to pound your lug all de mornin', see? What's the matter wid getting a move on, shakin' a leg, and putting a bit of this under yet belt?" quoth I, feeling as chipper as a Paroquet [parakeet] after my splendid night's sleep. This is modern sailorman's language as she is spoke in the end of the nineteenth and beginning of the 20th century, not the true nautical "shiver my timbers" of the veteran shellback o' 1812, with his queue done up in tar.

I failed to arouse them, and fiddled and fidgeted around until about 7 A.M., when I asked the Chinese houseboy if breakfast was served. He blandly announced that it was.

"So, me boy, bring us up three coffees, strong and black, and we'll do the rest."

"Here you fellows, get up and hit this up before it gets cold," pointing to the coffee in which I poured a liberal dose of the "cratur."[21] "And, me lad, the butler announced that breakfast is served, and Jeems has your 'tub' ready, and the hot water is here, and will yer ludship av th *Times* brought up, and which suit will yer ludship deign to put on that noble form? And will your ludship 'av the wheel or the "auto" this morning? And me lud, Snips the tailor, who savors strongly of trade, was 'ere this morning wid the usual bill."

The Agitator leisurely drew a long leg thro' one trouser leg, sipping his early coffee as he did so. "Sure, I feel like Viscount Algernon de Rochelly after a hard noight wid the drink. What's the programme for this marnin?"

"Nothing that I know of. We have done the town completely, seen from a tourist standpoint all there is of interest. After breakfast I am going around to Horishaw's and get another picture added to my gallery. Then I am going to take a run back to the Chinese city and get a bird to take aboard ship. The game is almost all over for this liberty, and we haven't been so drunk, either. I don't know what we will be tho', before we get aboard."

"There's one thing," chimed in the Machinist. "I don't feel well and I'm going to stay here in bed until after tiffin, or before, if I can eat."

A Sailor's Log

"Hello! You do look sick. What's the matter? Too much dissipation, eh?"

"Yes, I guess that's it."

"Well, let's make a move. Breakfast is ready long ago. We'll send you up a 'bracer.' You look regularly done up, doncher know, old chap? Pretty seedy looking beggar, doncher think? So come on D——," and the Agitator and I stalked out.

"I will speak to 'Sweet Nell the barmaid' and see what she can do for you. Perhaps her womanly presence and sympathy will straighten you out and while away the time that otherwise might prove onerous," I called out. This hit him in a tender spot. I think he was a little "gone" in that direction.

"You go to the devil," he growled, putting his head under the coverings.

The Agitator and I soon finished the simple breakfast of steak and eggs and the inevitable Bass. We stopped in the bar, but Mistress Nell the barmaid had not yet arisen from her slumber. No doubt [she] was dreaming of the "most honorable American man-o-warsman" that would take her to the States, that goal of her ambition. It, perhaps, 'twas just as well, for she would have treated me with a lady-like air of lofty condescension. But I should have sent her the compliments of the Machinist.

John the rickshaw man, and another John, soon wheeled D—— and myself around to Horishaw's. After an hour's work in spreading ink over my anatomy, we went to Tom Pow Ching's for more ammunition, and by the time we arrived at the Chinese city, we were feeling red-hot and about as noisy a pair of bluejackets as you could find anywhere, but not quarrelsome. As we were about going over the bridge, the old guide hurried out and accosted us.

"Only wanch makee buy a bird, savvy? Then come out, not makee much time," I explained, and the Agitator slapped him so hard on the back that he nearly collapsed.

"Good marnin', ye bloomin' auld haythen."

"Glood mornling. Good mornling," rubbing his shoulder. "American vely strong."

"Here. Put this into ye. It'll make ye strong," shoving the bottle at him. This mollified him considerably, and soon he was one of the gang.

"Wanchee catch bird, John."

"All right. My savvy."

"Chow sticks. Ivory, John."

At the first bone and ivory works, I purchased a dozen fine ivory sticks for a small sum. When we reached the bird dealers, I was in a mood to buy the whole stock. There were all kinds of canaries, and other varieties of singing birds, and I didn't know what to choose. I wanted these for the sail locker, as a present to the sail maker's mate, who was fond of pets. Finally I hit on a pair of Paroquets that were swinging and cutting up all sorts of bird gymnastics. These, thought I, are tough, healthy birds and will be able to stand confinement below decks from the sunshine, different from a canary or other delicate singing bird.

"How muchee?" I roared, pointing out the two birds.

"Two piecee, twenty dollar," replies the bird man.

"What?" I roared. "You no speakee proper."

Afloat & Ashore in Shanghai

"My speak proper plice."

"Give him foive dollars and take the birds," howled the I.A. [Irish Agitator]

"Two piecee, six dollars," I offered.

We haggled and wrestled over the price, but I finally secured them for six dollars, minus the iron cage they were in. Putting them in a wooden wicker cage, we started back. I felt very proud of my new acquisition.

"That's the finest pair of birds in the town," I yowled. "Look at 'em! Just alike. Its Nip and Tuck."

"That's a foine name," howled the I.A. "Nip & Tuck."

I exhibited my purchase proudly at the Grill Room, swinging them around recklessly, much to the surprise of the paroquets, who regarded me with an evident look of disapproval from their one eye that was turned upon us. In fact, the booze was beginning to tell. I exhibited them proudly to Mistress Nell. "What d'ye think of them (hic!) old girl? Ain't they a pair of beauts, Mrs. B——? Any message I can carry to your husband?"

"I think your no gentleman," she snapped, turning away.

"That's what they all thinksh, my dear. Sailorman can't be a gentleman. His (hic) uniformsh won't allow it. What t'ell." But she wouldn't engage in conversation with me of my humble calling, and entertained one of her country men with a weak imitation of a Vandyke mahogany beard. So engrossed was she with those whiskers that she accompanied him to the door of the bar, he with his arm carelessly around her waist (of very ample dimensions) and her hand lovingly resting upon his, all the while looking soulfully and trustfully upon his manly countenance, with a Juliet look, balcony scene. Only if memory serves me right, in that scene Juliet looks down upon her Romeo. Such conduct in a barmaid makes me weary, and I turned to the bar for more drinks to console myself. I was gnawed at by the Green-eyed Monster.

Nothing remained to do but have "tiffin." The Machinist came down, looking woebegone about the "gills" and joined us. D—— and I were in our element at this meal, and there wasn't a course that we didn't finish. We went thro' every entrée, much to the Chinese waiter's astonishment, then called for a few extra dishes on the menu. It was time to start for the depot by the time we finished our last bottle. Being in a generous, sailor-like mood, we tipped the Chinese boys, had a parting drink at the bar, and picking up the paroquets, we started.

On the way, we stopped at a poultry shop and purchased several ducks and a brace of pheasants, also another "dog."[22] This was the last straw that broke the camel's back. That dog, of a peculiar brand of Chinese mixture, put us out, or rather, made maniacs of us. I have only a dim recollection of future [i.e., subsequent] events. I only know we were chasing rickshaw men around at the station while waiting for the train. We threw them around and then gave them "ten cents" as a sop.

I hardly remember the ride down to Woosung on the train. I have no doubt we purchased more "sampchoo" there at the landing, the kind that you can buy for forty cents in China, warranted to put you out for an indefinite period. All else is a blank.

A Sailor's Log

I was drunk. They were all drunk. I have only the faintest recollection of coming over the quarterdeck with the paroquets, ducks, pheasant and other purchases. And I know that someone picked me up at the foot of a ladder leading to the berth deck (they told me afterwards), paroquets, ducks, pheasants and drunken sailor all inextricably mixed up. The Irish Agitator made some howl before he went to sleep. So the stuff we bought coming off, the shaking up in [the] train and sailing launch put us about as drunk as bluejackets can become without having the D.T.'s.

Four days later I, with a great many others, went to the "mast" and were cautioned for coming aboard drunk. Since that time I have never been drunk.

Christmas came and went. We had a fine dinner and the [day] passed quietly enough with an impromptu performance by the minstrel troupe and others and stag dancing was indulged in by those of the crew that wished.[23] A year ago we spent the other Christmas in the Philippines; we had just arrived.

The *Solace*[24] was daily looked for in Shanghai by many anxious hearts whose time was up, and the word had been passed that she was to take all men whose time expired at a certain date.

CHAPTER EIGHT

Bolo-Men, Routine, & Discipline

1901 was ushered in in usual man-o-war style. I had the 8 to 12 watch and had to watch the old year out, the dying century and the newly born. I well remember that night. We had general quarters at 10 P.M. and fire quarters immediately afterward. The steam was shut off [to] the whistle and siren below decks so it couldn't be blown by those above. Just before twelve the infernal din commenced, rattling of pans, cat calls, rattles, pounding and hooting. The German ships also observed it in a style befitting the occasion. On board the *Brandenberg* formed of incandescent lamps was the figures 1901, surmounted by a large five-pointed star. Another German afar off had the figures 1901. Their band played some hymns and the full chorus floated across to where we lay, the crewmen singing. It sounded melodious enough to us across the dark water, grand and inspiring. Some German speaking good English and blessed with lungs of brass shouted for three cheers for the United States Navy, his words coming distinctly over that wide expanse of water. These cheers were given with a will, and we returned them just as heartily. Farther astern from us the huge English man-o-war *Goliath* loomed in sullen majesty, not a sound or a light disturbing the grim, warlike hulk of steel.[1] There she lay without a ripple, powerful, silent as the grave, and as terrible.

The New Year came and went. No work was done on this day except the very necessary routine work to keep the ship in condition. The bolo-men furnish[ed] something to drink to those that were of their stations, and a number of the men showed the effects of it, but none so much as K[en], the one who was with me ashore in Kure. After breakfast he was feeling good. At dinner he arose at the mess table and openly declared himself, full steam was up. He allowed, be gosh, he could whup any man in the mess, bar none. Here he glared ferociously at our former caterer, whom we [had] deposed the day before. I don't know why he selected him, but he seemed to be the one at whom his sweeping challenge was pointed. The beer and "beno"[2] was working.

"I don't want any you plugs to think, hic, yer up against an easy thing. I don't care a [damn] for any of you. That's for all." Here he fixed a hostile eye upon [Ken] and we thought he would make a wild charge, only some one at one of the other tables hooted at him.

"Sit down, you big hobo, or I'll come up there and poke you in the eye."

"You will——," he roared. "Come up [and] show yerself, till I swab the berth deck wid ye, you blooming rookie."

"Rats! Put him out!" "Rouse out him." "Shut up, you big chump." And amid a storm of abuse and cat calls, he sat down and soon forgot his troubles in the eatables before him, for [Ken] was a "nifty man" with a set of "mess gear."

However, it behooved him, later on, considering what a big man he was, how important, that he should go aft and pay a few New Year's calls, and incidentally, corral a few more drinks. He was full of business and a very great man indeed. This was the peculiar potency of the brand of liquor he was imbibing: "Green Label, Canadian Club," à la Chinese. So he meandered toward the steerage.[3] Just here he was stopped; stopped in the first round. He didn't even get as far as "wardroom country," nor did he have a chance to pay his respects to the captain. He met "Pea coat," our under secretary for the department of steam engineering. [He was] known as "Pea coat" for the solicitude with which he pressed this useful article of wearing apparel upon the men of the engineer division, $10.30, please. [Ken] was stopped. "Pea-coat" asked him his business. [Ken], being a very great and big man at about that time (beno), told him to "go to Sheol"[4] in language more forcible than elegant. He handled him without gloves, talked like a modern man-o-warsman, "and furthermore," continued [Ken], "you (hic) look after your end of the game, and I'll tend to mine. You look after the Pea coats, and I," great accent on the personal pronoun,

"*I*"—swelling up—"will look after my own affairs." Here he was ignominiously "glommed" (as the King of the Orlop Deck put it) and taken before the Cadi.[5] From thence he was cast into the Bastille.

A few hours afterwards, I saw him pacing up and down under the sentry['s] charge.

"How goes it, old man? Feel any better?" I asked as I went by.

"Lots," he answered. "Say, that's queer stuff, ain't it?"

"Just found it out, have you? I see you are considerably reduced in stature from what you were a few hours ago, eh? You will pay New Year's calls, will you, big man, eh?" sarcastically.

"I don't see any fun in it," he replied, looking as glum as a [Chinese] hairless dog. "You might get it in the neck yourself some day."

"Oh, you'll be all right. You are only in for safe keeping. You might have chased some of the gang around with a battle ax, if they hadn't corralled you just as they did. You know, you were going aft to call on the captain."

"What an 18 carat ass a man is, especially a man, no a chump, by the name of K[en]. New Year's day, too. That's fierce! Nine years' service in, and the first time in the brig," he groaned in spirit.

"So you see, it's never too late, etc. You'll come out all right."

He was released a few days later.

Bolo-Men, Routine, & Discipline

The long looked-for, expected *Solace* put in an appearance the next day, and a number of men were transferred, and a draft came to us, part of the lost *Yosemite*'s crew.[6] The I.A. [Irish Agitator] went with them, without saying good bye to any of his shipmates. "Sure 'tis only a farce, saying goodbye. What do they care about me, or I about them? I won't be missed, and I won't miss them. It's only a farce. Shipmates, bah!" and he stalked away, bag, hammock and ditty box, glad to go, as were all the rest, for as I have stated before, the *Oregon* wasn't a very pleasant home in more ways than one, and nearly everyone aboard would be well pleased at the prospect of leaving her.

The king of the orlop deck went to the mast the same day that I was sent for. But he was a couple of days overtime, with several others who had a fine time of it ashore and were unable to withstand the temptation of sticking it out as long as the money lasted, [including] the money they could beg, borrow or steal, when on their last legs. Black Mary's was the resort known as the "dump." It was from that vantage point they would concoct schemes and strategic moves, and sally forth in pursuit of "booze." Without any hesitation whatever, if you refused them money, would they give you a half Nelson and hold you up for it. Black Mary's place was in the European part of the town, in a row of houses built in the style of architecture affected in Shanghai, very much the worse for wear. The neighbors [were] a cosmopolitan population. Anything could take place, from pitch and toss to manslaughter. Black Mary would never refuse a bluejacket, when broke and breaking liberty, a place to sleep and their "chow," and to the credit of the gang be it said that all debts contracted with her would be promptly paid, and the money was carried ashore. So she never came out the loser. Jack always treats people well, that treats him well.

Her place was always the resort for "beach combers" of all descriptions, whether deserters from the different navies or from merchant ships. If the bluejacket was so unwary as to fall asleep from the effects of his deep potations, and had any "dobie" money about his clothes, it was a hundred to one shot that these "punks"[7] would relieve him of it. We had one of those people to ship with us at Shanghai. Shipped him as a landsman, but he couldn't or wouldn't stand it. He jumped out before he was shipped three months. The men had fitted him out with an outfit of clothing, so that he wasn't long in getting out of debt. This is the class of men they always help out. Any good, deserving shipmate that thro' misfortune had lost any pay or clothing, they would see damned first. This fellow belonged to the class that the King designated "International Punks," "Cosmopolitan Hobos." Men or boys that ship aboard some tramp and finally land in some port in China or Japan. Here they jump out with all they can get safely away with, blow it in, and if a man-o-war happens to be in that particular port, they ship, and when the "wrinkles are out of their stomachs," as the King put it, they jump out again, fetching up in Hong Kong or Yokohama. From there they generally take ship for some European port such as Hamburg or Southampton, then across the Western Ocean to New York. From New York, possibly across the continent to Frisco in "side door Pullman" or some convenient truck.

But "hitting the road" isn't their forte. They are out of their latitude, their element. They are content in making distant ports, working their way in any capacity over the great ocean pathways, in cattle steamer or tramp. They are at home in any part of the world, and generally contrive to have a good time according to their own standard of what a good time is.

The King sallied forth from his *kopje*[8] one day, on a foraging expedition. Tom Pow Ching's was his objective point. Also another objective point, the princip[al] one, was whiskey, Cyrus Noble preferred, but Sampchoo or Chinese gin, "40 cts a quart," wouldn't be despised. Now, Tom Pow is a pretty fly Chinese gentleman, and he "savvies" a bluejacket who is over time, and he knows they come to see him only when they are broke, looking for money or trust. Generally, he shoves them off with a drink, for he also knows when aboard, they will get classed and "classed money,"[9] and his prospects for payment are none of the best. So, when the King hove in sight, Tom Pow was prepared to give him the "liquid air expression."

"Hello, Tom, old man. *Wee geets.* How you *vost?*"

"Good molling," gravely remarked Tom Ching.

"You're looking fine this morning, oh father of the little round pig."

"Feelee fline."

"Will your most imperial dignified *diabulze*[10] deign to trust the humblest of your most exalted jiblets' servants with a bottle of your most elegant booze?"

"No can do," firmly replied the "father of the little round pig."

"What?" howled the King. "Do me auricular appendages deceive me, or do I hear aright?"

"You breakee liberty. No can pay money. Me losee money."

"That's it, is it, ye yellow mugged Boxer? Think I won't pay, do ye? Me the King of the Orlop Deck? To be ignominiously turned down by a Chink! What is Ireland coming to, anyhow?"

"No clan do. Losee money." And T. Pow Ching started toward the end of the shop, signifying that the audience was at an end. But the King had come after "booze" and "booze" he wasn't [was?] going to have, so he cast the critical eye of a connoisseur along the array of bottles, temptingly displayed on the shelves, selecting for his prey a large, fat quart of Cyrus Noble. He reached forth and dexterously glommed it by the neck. A yell from T. P. Ching and the "little pig" and the rest of the relations and retinue of the same exalted personage showed that he was caught red-handed. But that was a small item with the King. He was in possession, nine points ahead of the game.

"If ye bothers me, ye yellow faced monk, I'll break this bottle over that pig-tail of yours." And he assumed a most ferocious attitude.

Tom P. Ching thought that discretion was the better part of valor, so he arbitrated. He could have had the King arrested, but that would hurt him aboard ship as grocery man. If he let the King have it, one chance out of ten, he would get paid. So he concluded to let it go at that.

"Allee yight. You kleep. My send blill," in a tone of resignation.

"Well thin, the top o' the marnin' to ye, oh honorable pie face, King of the monks. *Au Revoir. Auf Wiedersehn.* Among royalty loike ourselves, there should be perfect harmony. Ta, ta."

So the King returned to the "dump," gladdening the eyes and hearts of the "gang" with his contraband of war.

The King told me that he changed his base of operations from Black Mary's to a Chinese joint not far from her place.

"Sure," said he, "Wils, it's the finest place I've struck yet, and my only raygret is that I didn't hit onto it sooner. I was put next [to it] by a rickshaw man. It['s] a Chinese dump. There's a boy there that will run errands any time of the day or night. All I paid was a Mexican for the whole push. The boy asked the others for money, but they didn't have any. So he said, said he, 'All light, all light. You no got. Now calm dlown. Makee sleep.' Sure, you can make all the noise ye want, nobody to call you down. The Chinks below are hitting hop[11] all the time and they don't care if the hull [sic] house tumbles in over their heads. Nothing disturbs them. It's the best place in Shanghai, just the place for [a] lot of drunken bluejackets."

"Besides," continued the King, "we had to quit Black Mary's. The gang of panhandlers and bums became too strong. The dirty lot of contemptible, measly beach combers. We couldn't open our face up there without the whole dirty push ringin' in on our game. Sure, a quart wasn't in it wid 'em. Ye should see th way they would elect themselves bar-keepers in order to con Mary into believing' they were looking after the interests of the house. You couldn't sit down to table without having to feed the whole dirty gang. And how smooth they thought they were, and how easy they think Jack is. 'Great graft.' But the bloomin' lot are mere amateurs at the biz. A good pub handler could give them cards and spades. Ye can't make a thoroughbred out of a mule, and their work was rough, and their game easily seen thro'."

"Yes, we had to pull out. They got too numerous toward the last. But the last dump is O.K. Just the cheese. Ye won't catch yer Uncle Dudley around to Mary's joint again in a hurry."

The King was perfectly right in his views of the case. I was around Black Mary's myself more than once. In fact, being a true sailor, my heart delights in the lowest dives I can find at times. But Mary's place never suited me. You'd have to be a millionaire to stand the game. Her place, or "dump" as she fondly calls it, was always full of beach-combers, punks, and deserters, all ready to greet you with the glad hand, and expansive smile, all ready to sing it without ceremony. Produce a bottle and see how quick it would disappear amid the hungry pack.

When Mary would set the table for "tiffin," Jack, who paid for it all, was crowded out by the same gang of "stiffs." During all this he would look good naturedly on, until it became monotonous from repetition. Then he would leave, and never come back. And as the King said, these "plugs" were congratulating themselves at the easy cinch they were having, and how easy the bluejacket was worked, how "fly," and what expert "con" men they were. Their work was very lumpy. You could tell just exactly what they were a mile away, just con men, "punks." "Bindle stiffs,"[12] the King called them.

Of course, as long as they didn't come too often and become wearisome, your bluejacket, out of kindness of heart and a flush pocket, would good naturedly pay for the drinks and the meals, with an occasional loan on the side, not because he wasn't on to them, but out of sheer kindness. Jack, you can wager, is just as fly, as I have said before in these pages, as the best of them, and can see thro a game. But often he don't care to bother his head how the game goes as long as it don't damage him. I have met lots of men with graft, who have had no doubt to their ideas: easy graft and a mark in yours truly, and [they] no doubt were hugging themselves and congratulating themselves at their own superior wit and wiseness, whereas, they were an open book to be read by those that can. Their work was coarse, no finish. It lacked the polish of your true panhandler. I have let them fellows carry it as far as their repertoire went, and then, just according to my state of mind, have picked a quarrel with him and made a mess of him, or else parted on good terms. It all depended on the particular brand of "booze" and how it worked on me.

Once, some years since, I was "panhandled" while leisurely walking over the Brooklyn Bridge, going toward the New York side, by an especially large, able-bodied "thug" of a city ball park "bum." "Say, Jack," sidling up in the confidential manner that is their custom, and thinking, no doubt, that they are "hitting you up" for the price without attracting any of the passers by's attentions, which is another of their fallacies. "Say, Jack," in a husky whisky voice, "how is it for the price of a bed?"

"I think its all right, Sport. This will fix you, and a couple of 'high hats' thrown in," and I slipped him a quarter, being in the mood. "But, say, how is it you don't go over to the Navy Yard and ship? Coal passer or marine. Any old thing?" I asked.

"What!" he gasped. "Me? Me ship in the navy or become a marine? Do I look like it?" And he drew himself up with dignity. "Nay, nay, Jack. Thanks for the coin. I'll drink to you, but I ain't fallen to the level of the navy yet. That's the last resort." And he passed on, looking for another good mark to batter. It all depends on the point of view.

~~~

Another liberty in Shanghai. Found myself and two companions out at the race-course on Bubbling Well Road during the morning parade of some of Her Majesty's Indian troops. The course was lined with all the elite of Shanghai. Handsome turnouts containing smart-looking women, handsomely groomed, were well to the fore. For their own personal good looks—I will let that pass. All women are handsome, or can make themselves attractive. The Pathan[13] companies presented a very neat appearance, clad in their new bottle-green uniforms. Very trim-looking soldiers indeed, and well drilled, very picturesque and warlike they looked, the morning sun flashing on arms and equipment. Elegant looking officers, veritable sons of Mars, carried themselves pompously and proudly with the air of the conqueror à la Napoleon or Wellington. And that Sikh Regiment, especially the Indian officers, the *Subedar* Majors, *Jemadars*, etc.[14] (the commanding officer, a Prince, Maharajah, or any old thing), with their curled beards and massive turbans, [why,] the gold lace on the resplendent red blouses would make the drum major of a town band turn green with envy. And, I thought, what targets they would be for the Boers. [It is truly] a show army, whose resplendent uniforms would make good costumes for a spectacular performance.

After retreat, the gallant sons of Mars surrounded dog-cart and trap and steed, the popularity of the fair one attested by the size of the group that did homage to her. Nothing like your soldiers to find favor in the eyes and hearts of the ladies; the more gorgeous the uniform, the better. The Hindoo commanding [officer] strutted off like a peacock, followed by his brilliant staff.

All over the town of Shanghai, the English concession, strutted these war lords, with clanking equipment. Toward evening, one especially fierce looking cavalry officer attracted my attention. Very tall, with a large military mustache that gave him a fierce appearance, his tight-fitting uniform encasing about six foot of spare form, [he] put me in mind of a needle roll umbrella. And the saber! What length of blade! It dragged along the pave[ment] suspended by its belt of at least three feet. The rowels [spurs] on his varnished boots were about the size of a Mexican dollar.

I stared in amazement at this figure, the very embodiment of war. He was an officer of high rank. As he stalked along, the admiration of the passing crowds and the particular admiration of the handsomely frocked women who accompanied him, and who were proud of basking in the refulgent gleam of glory shed by this God of War [was apparent, but] I couldn't help wondering what would become of all that equipment if this fellow happened to be ordered to South Africa. And I smiled at the humor of it all, as a picture arose before my mind's eye of this soldier and his like taking it on the "hot foot" before a handful of Dutch farmers. I wondered what kind of a figure he would cut on the hop. He was built like a sprinter, but that clanking sabre would have to be left on the field. How is it that one Christian De Wet, Boer General, plain farmer, knows more of the art and strategy of war than all the gilded, gold bespangled line and staff of the British Army?[15] Strange isn't it? But true.

Just now this fierce looking man was being dragged off to five o'clock tea. "One lump or two lumps? Please, do you take cream? Aw! Aw! Doncha know, old chappie?" This is where he is the one bright particular orb. He shines.

Finding myself in one of the big tea-houses, I concluded to "hit the pipe," go up against the dope, just for an experience. So, seeking out one of the Chinese attendants, I made known my wishes. One of my companions also wished to ascertain for himself the effects of the poisonous weed, and going over to one of the numerous lying off places, we paid the forty cents asked by the attendant, who quickly brought us the required outfit. It was only about five in the afternoon, and the singing girls hadn't made their appearance. The raised platform was deserted, and there were

A Sailor's Log

only a very few Chinese in the large room, and what there was, gathered around to watch the "Amercans," and all eager to give advice to us how to smoke. They were all affable and obliging, and seemed to have a little curiosity how the Americans would make out trying one of their time-honored customs.

One very old man volunteered his services in my behalf, and I signified to him to take the place opposite me. All these lounging places are made for two. The outfit is placed between you. There is a small, hard pillow for the head and you lie back on the hard wood couch, which is not unlike a polished bench, very finely finished. The opium was brought to us in a small horn cup shaped like a miniature barrel, with just the end of it concaved out to hold about a teaspoonful of the dark, sticky mass. In this state, it is all cooked for smoking.

The pipe has a stem of bone or hard wood about three quarters of an inch in diameter and eighteen inches in length, finely figured, and the more costly ones are carved in the Oriental fashion. The bowl is shaped like a mushroom made of metal, with a small hole in the centre, about one-eighth [inch] in diameter. This bowl fits into the stem like a plug. Then comes the small lamp with its tiny globe. The lamp is made of white metal. We had two. The only other article is the needle or piece of wire about as long as one's index finger.

The old Chinaman accepted my offer with alacrity, an old [opium] fiend no doubt, but he didn't show any bad effects from it, being a husky old rooster. He "savvied" no English, tho', and we conversed in the language of signs. He dipped his needle into the opium pot and held it over the flame of the small lamp until it became hardened. This operation he repeated time and again until he had a good sized "pill," or ball about the size of those prescribed by a country doctor. I watched him closely and did likewise with my needle. I only succeeded in melting the bit I had on the point, and it ran off on the lamp, causing some good-natured jabbering and smiling among the envious Chinese who stood around. I had held it too close to the flame. My next attempt I did better, and soon had a good-sized pill on the end of my needle. The old man took the ball he had cooked and pressed it over the bowl of the pipe, making it adhere by skilful working with his fingers. He then pierced a vent thro it with the wire and handed the pipe over to me, ready for smoking.

I lay back in the approved fashion as I had seen thousands of smokers do, and held the pipe to the flame, and puffed away. But the vent would fill up and the pipe wouldn't draw, keeping the old fossil punching it with the wire all the time. A Chinaman standing by soon showed me where the trouble was by making a motion with his lips for me to puff away more energetically. So, I pulled away manfully and it worked like a Manila Perfecto. The pill was soon finished, then another, and another. I smoked until my jaws ached. I felt as if I had been trying to blow a tuba horn. My glands ached, and not feeling any effects, I handed the gear to the old man. The smoke was almost tasteless, but still had the faint, sickening odor of laudanum about it.

A French soldier of the line who was out taking in the sights came up and smiled and gesticulated, and let forth a whole volley of French. He would shake hands. I invited him to smoke, but he shrugged his shoulders and rolled his eyes and exclaimed *"Mon Dieu, le poison! Poison!"* Nothing would induce him to partake. Poison? Yes. So is your absinthe poison, Johnny Crapeau, old man. My companion had desisted after a couple of pipes, and as the singing girls were making their appearance, I left the bench. I know if I smoked all night, that it wouldn't affect me in the least. You have to be saturated with it before you feel it, and that would take a dozen dallyings with my Lady Opium, and more than I cared to stand for.

The old Chinaman accepted the pipe with a smile and my nods, and I left him to finish the stuff. We sat at the tea-table and contented ourselves flirting with one of the "small feet" girls who was not above a little coquettish side play with foreign devils, and who had a whole world of deviltry sparkling in her slant, penciled orbs, who sang to us with Chinese abandon, and no doubt sweetness. But we couldn't "savvy" her sweetest and highest notes. They were wasted on us, but appreciated by the Celestials that occupied the surrounding tables. We couldn't appreciate your notes, but we understood and appreciated your little coquetries, my little Chinese belle, and understood, as far as mere man can, what dreams ran riot in that small head with its dark, polished braids. You are only a poor, benighted little heathen, according to our Western ideas, but a woman for a' that, and we were sailors. We understand. Here's health to you!

About the only other incident on this trip was the trouble I had with John, my rickshaw man. I tried to pay him off and fire him, but he deliberately refused to be fired. This made me mad, and I determined not to take him again under any condition. I resolved to exercise my independence. So, in spite of all his expostulations in pidgin, I refused to be mollified, and the more he persevered, the more "sot" I became.[16] Under no condition would I have him. As I strolled along, heading for no place in particular, he kept trundling his rickshaw along, all the time talking "rag-time." I paid no attention to him. Hailing another one, I jumped in and told him to go to Tom Pow Ching's, and he started off, John and his mate running along and abusing the man I had just taken, who became frightened and rattled, John all the time talking to me and abusing the other man.

"Dis man no savvy. I savvy you. Why you no keepee my? I savvy you. Chlina town. Glill Loom. Tea-house. Cho Too Loo. Ebby placee, my savvy. Why you glet mad?"

The other ricky got frightened and lost his bearings and started off after hesitating, down another street, at which John and his running mate laughed and abused him some more. "He no savvy you. My savvy. He no savvy Tom Pow Ching."

I began to get mad. "Stop!" I yelled to my man. He stopped. It was in a dark, narrow side street. "Get, you Mongolian——before I kick the head off of you."

They sprinted back a safe distance, and I jumped in again and started off. They didn't follow. The man I had kept casting frightened glances to the rear to see if they were following. He was all of a tremble. I don't know what dire threats they used toward him, but they must have been of the most fearful kind, to get him in such a state.

"Now, you no be 'fraid," I said to him. "I fix if they come again. You catch Tom Pow Ching." But I soon saw that he didn't know where Tom's was. He turned off into another dark street leading toward the cribs that faced the river, and he ran into John and his side pardner again. He was paralyzed, half frightened to death.

"This man no savvy you," began John, when I jumped after him, thoroughly mad this time, and landed him a straight jab on the ear that made him groggy. I swung my foot with terrific force and lifted the other fellow where it would do the most good. "Now, damn you, will you be good?"

That settled it. They drew off for repairs, cursing in Chinese and pidgin, and no doubt vowing vengeance. I had no sooner landed on them that I felt sorry. John and his companion were only acting up to their light. After all, it was their method of doing business. I was sorry for giving way to such an extent, for after all I rather liked the rogue, and I hold it a mean trick to hit anything that can't hit back, and this your Chinaman cannot do.

I soon saw that the man I had didn't know where to take me, and getting off, I paid him and dismissed him, and procured another who took me where I wished to go. Before going aboard, John saw me the next day and grinned as he approached me, ruefully rubbing his ear. "Why you mlad?" quoth this innocent and childlike Mongolian. "My likee you, ver glood man." And, of course, I had him to the station, paying him an exorbitant price to soothe his wounded feelings. By so doing I eased my conscience. After all, he was as good as the best of them.

The new captain came,[17] and for a while we were put thro' our paces. General quarters, fire quarters, collision drill, all boat drills, inspections, etc., were the order of the day. At "clear ship for action," he saw that it was done thoroughly. We were a whole day at it. Everything portable was carried below and stowed away. Chests, tables, etc., were properly tagged as they should be, "Overboard." This he seen to himself. The crew and officers found out they had a disciplinarian to contend with and everything had to be done with quickness and dispatch, and with great thoroughness. This was as it should be. Give me the man, for my part, who is strictly up to date; a martinet, if you will, and generally you have a just man. If you are right, you will generally find such a man the same.

A humorous incident happened while the skipper was making his tour of inspection at "clear ship for action." Near the sick bay, he asked two men who had their arm in a sling where the matter lay. They told him. At the moment, the Ripper,[18] who was along with him, with a flourish fished a common five-eighth [inch] nut from somewhere about his clothes, and called the Carpenter, who stood near.

"Hm. Hm, Ah, Carpenter! Here is a nut I found back on the quarterdeck. You had better take care of it." And he handed to over with great pomposity to Chips. This was done to make an impression upon the old man, whom as yet was an unknown proposition to the Ripper. An air of, see how strictly I attend to every little detail? Nothing so small, etc., that it escapes my notice.

This was the Carpenter's cue, as big a bluff as the other.[19] "Yes, Yes. Hm. I know just exactly where this nut belongs," looking at it very wisely and recognizing this particular nut as if he was on very familiar terms with it. "Oh, yes, er ... er ... " in a loud voice. "I believe err ... er ... er." Here he became wool-gathered and yelled fiercely at one of the landsmen who was staggering along under a lot of gear, in order to hide his confusion.

"Where *does* it belong?" queried the skipper, looking at him and sizing the big duff bag up for what he actually was.

"Er ... Yes, sir. It belongs to, ah ..." Here he became stumped and looked initially again at the nut, mumbling something unintelligibly, and looking very red and hot and uncomfortable. He found he was needed elsewhere and rushed off to abuse some poor devil who couldn't resent it.

The skipper looked after him quimsically [*sic:* whimsically?] as if to call him back, but quietly made his rounds followed by the Ripper.

Perhaps in some previous stage of existence that I have no inkling of in this, I may have been an Asiatic, for truth to tell, I can stand a great deal of rest, and nothing suits me better than sitting around a pot of charcoal, dressed very comfortably in a kimono, taking comfort from a pipe, and idly watching some nice little Japanese girl as she bustles around, perhaps tidying the room or else busying herself with the hot sake or getting the "chop a chop" ready.

It suits my Asiatic tastes to watch her especially if she is a very pretty Nippon maiden: the deft touches in the right places; the sake in its china bottle warming up. This is always placed inside the inevitable teapot that is always over the brazier of charcoal. The little dishes and teacups; the miniature table, the chop sticks; the spotless rice kit of hard wood, with its burnished brass bands; the rice that is the staff of life to the Japanese, boiled and tasting as only the Japanese can cook it; the fish, tasting as no other fish does; and the countless other dishes new to our palates that [are] accustomed to Port and mince pie, and other American dishes that would ruin the digestive apparatus of a Harlem goat.

It is wonderful to see how much a busy Nippon girl can find to do in an apartment that is almost perfect in its cleanliness and order. Yes, that is my idea of solid comfort. One feels like a king. Your every wish is anticipated. You feel that it is a very great thing, indeed, and congratulate yourself on being a member of the masculine sex. I [don't?] see whole lots of American girls acting as do these happy girls of Japan. An American girl thinks of almost nothing but dress. The Nippon girl likes finery also, but her tastes are simple and inexpensive, and any little gift, a curiously carved pin for her hair, a new silk *obi*, a pair of highly varnished *gaita*, and she is pleased as Punch, for in all Asiatic countries, fashions never vary. Any articles of attire from those of the vintage of 1812 up to date is strictly *en regle*, and no attire one can don, whether of the feminine or masculine gender, will attract more than passing attention, and then it is all right to their unpracticed eyes. No doubt the advent of Western ideas and customs will change all this, but that will take time. So there is nothing to fear for many years to come; nothing to spoil the charm of the Orient as yet. It gives me the horrors to think of a trolley line in Japan or China.

The passing of our life aboard ship at Woosung grew even too monotonous for my ideas, Eastern as they are. It was almost maddening in its dull routine, and miserable, petty details. The worst to the crew of the *Oregon* was the incontrovertible fact that she contained more "white mice" than any other ship of her complement afloat, from the "bolo-men" down to the commonest rating in the engineers division, each individual vied with each other in carrying tales. At school, boys who told tales were called "tell tales" and "tattlers" and shunned as the devil shuns holy water. Here among so many, it was hard to detect all of the "white mice," but everything that was said detrimental about the officers or the way things were run, was carried aft [reported to the officers].

This system was encouraged by the bolo-men, who strove hard to cut each other's throats so as to bask more favorably in the good graces of his imperial majesty [the chief engineer]. They all put one in mind of school children in the childishness of their tale bearings. Anything went as long as the tales that were told injured the one talked about, helped to make him unpopular, and assisted in getting him disrated. They [the "white mice"] were looking for other men's jobs with a vengeance, and with a most becoming modesty they would put themselves forward as candidate for any vacant rating. The machinists were especially active in striving for the rating just above them, and many heartburnings and jealousies were caused when someone in the "clique" would be made [promoted]. And those that were advanced were invariably the ones that were notorious as "white mice." In fact, competency hadn't anything to do with their advancement. No matter whether you were able to fulfill all the requirements of the rating; that wasn't considered at all. It was given you as a reward for virtue. In fact, you have to be a "sucker," a "pigeon" to further your own interest, to be *en rapport* with the administration. This state of affairs was due largely to the bolo-men, who encouraged it. If you were a man and independent, and exhibited any manliness, you were marked from that [time] on. This was the state of affairs on board of the *Oregon*, and a mighty unpleasant state of affairs some of us found it.

~ ~ ~

Some three years previous to the writing of this "ever true tale," when war and rumors of war were rife throughout the length and breadth of America, from Maine to California, caused by the blowing up of the *Maine*, and when the powers that be had in convention wisely resolved that it would be mighty advisable to enlarge the Army and Navy, two figures might have been seen prowling in close proximity to a certain "water tank" or penstock upon one of our large railroads midway between Salt Lake City and Ogden [Utah], one of the most desolate places imaginable, sage brush and alkali plain as far as the eye could reach. They were the only animate life in that stretch of uncongenial territory known as the "desert" by every panhandler in America. The dreaded inferno of every hobo, tramp, gaycat, blanket stiff, bindle stiff, Prushun,[20] of whatever class these Knights of the Road may be.

The prospect was a cheerless one for any human being and would appall all but the stoutest hearted of the great colony of American nomads. The two figures seen more clearly silhouetted against the blended gold and red of the dying sunset that tinged the long line of rail stretching toward the East with silver, soon resolved themselves into that distinctive class of American "bo's" know as "Bindle stiffs." This was clearly indicated, and needed no Sherlock Holmes to detect by the large bundles that were attached to their backs. In the language of the panhandler, there are known as "turkeys." And the class of bums that carry them are looked upon with disdain by the professional tramp, who generally "flies light." This species of bird generally migrated around the wine belt in California, never very far away from that section of the state, so these two must have had an object in view, in being so far away from their stamping grounds. Arriving at the water tank, they wearily unslung bindles, with a sigh of relief, and sought a drink of water from the pump house, whose occupant had closed up shop for the night, and retired to his bleak looking domicile farther down the line. Then, resting under the tank, they drew from the "bindle" the remnants of a few "lumps,"[21] the spoils of the night before, and fell to with a vim. They ate in silence, so as to lose no time, and not let the other get ahead. The frugal meal finished, the smallest of the two "stiffs," the little tramp, spake thusly to his larger companion, whilst deftly inserting a large charge of "snipe" held between thumb and forefinger into the large and generous opening in his face.[22]

"By gosh, Lem, that was a fierce drill.[23] I never felt so tired in my hull life before. Who'ed a thought that bloomin' shark[24] would darst trow us off on that stretch of track? I tell yer, [if] it wasn't the chanse hov of lifetime, I would quit right yere and make th best of my way back to the land o sunshine."

His companion, about as ugly a specimen of the genus Hobo as one could find in a coon's age, with big lop ears, thick lips, pitted face, and a body that was as ill shapen as a gorilla, a typical stew bum[25] of the can house[26] variety, looked dully at his companion, upon who[se] vacuous countenance could be read defeat, lack of ambition, and [the] hang dog look that comes from a long list of refusals from some worthy housewife who backed her refusal for food by setting a well developed bull dog upon him. The Big Stew Bum spake thus wisely:

"Well, Angus, we're here."[27] This with conviction. "And . . ." batting his eyes like a dying mackerel, "the thing is to get out o' here." This startling bit of information he imparted very sagely and wisely to the "Little Tramp."

A Sailor's Log

"Well, the only thing to do, I s'pose, is to catch the next freight. I s'pose we'll have to take the beans for it.[28] But," he questioned querulously, "I wonder when she'll come along? They run very slow over this pike."

"Wall, she mought come any ole time, and again, she moughtn't. But she'll be here when she arrives." Another startling bit of information imparted by the Big Canhouse Stiff.

"But Lem, d'y think we can make [get on board] her with the two big bundles?" questioned the Little Stew Bum, who evidently regarded his companion, the Big Canhouse Bum, as the criterion of all mental excellence.

"If we can get 'em aboard and ourselves aboard without being spotted by the con [conductor], or shark, we can," vouchsafed the wise one, from the lofty height of his mighty wisdom.

"Well, I only wishes I wuz in Norfolk. We'll have a chance to ship in the navy now. Yer know they ain't so particular now thet the country is on the verge of war," quoth the Little Tramp.

This, then, was their object: to ship in the navy. For this they had braved the terrors of the "desert," "bindle" and all. They were in heavy marching order. Truly, it must have been a mighty inducement to bring them so far afield. From the rest of their conversation, as they talked it over in the glorious sunset glow of that dying day (whose glory, tho', was lost on them, for who lives that can enjoy scenery unless his stomach is comfortably lined with a huge slab of steak and some 'taters), they were going to ship, if possible, to take advantage of the country and foist themselves upon [the] taxpayers. They relied upon escaping the vigilance of the doctors.

They conversed far into the night, building up plans for the future if they were so lucky as to slip thro' the doctors' hands. They became drowsy from their long vigil and their conversation began to wane. At last the big hobo, he of the pock-marked phisiog, pulled himself together with an effort, and started off on a new theme, this in order to keep the little hobo awake, for they couldn't afford to let any chances slip by, for freights were few and far between in that country.

Quoth the Big Grizzly to the small 'un, "I wonder wot we kin enlist as? We'll have to git a few pointers from some one who is next to de game."

The Little Grizzly rolled over and struggled to a recumbent position, squirting about a pint of tobacco juice from the large cavity in the front of his face. "Well," he piped, "I've hear'n tell uv in all [the] books I have read that boatswain mate or fust leftenant is a good billet and good pay. I think that would about suit me."

"You do, eh?" snarled the Big Canhouse Bum. "You don't want much, do ye? Wunder," he continued sarcastically, "ye wouldn't try to ship as captain or how wud admiral suit you? As for meself, I tink machinist would just about hit me. I've heard it's easy to pass for one, and much easier now that the scrap is about on. Barring that, I tink I wud be glad to get in as a moreen. Ye don't have much hard graft at that."

The Little Canhouse Stiff looked at him with admiration shining out from his washed out, bleary orbs, while two distinct streams of tobacco juice ran in a tiny rivulet down the corners of his mouth. He marveled at his side kickers' superior perspicacity and thanked the God of the Hoboes that threw him in contact with such a shining light of his profession. "By gum, I believe that wud be a good graft, but did you ever work at it, Lem?"

"Work! Work!!" roared the Big 'Un. "Work, me work? The idea! D'ye want to disgrace me? No, I never worked anybody but the workers. Thet's work 'nuff for me. I don't go in th navy to work. Wid the elegant 'crust' and nervine that I possess, there is no need to work. I wunst swept up the floor of a big machine shop, so ye see, I hev a pretty fair idear of what's wot. I know a monkey wrench when I see one. But ye don't have to know anyting about the trade. If we did, there wouldn't be any necessity uv joining the Navy." And work! At the mere mention of the word, he fell back completely overcome.

"Don't ye be gettin' mad, Lem. I didn't mean to hurt yer feelins when I mentioned work. I only wanted to find out if ye savvies th trade. I tink I cud pass as a machinist meself. I had an uncle who wuz wunst a machinist, an I ought to know."

"Well, then," replied the Big Grizzly in a mollified tone, "we'll get some pointers from some parties as we go along. But ye don't want to spring about work so sudden like th next time. In me present hungry state, it moight prove fatal. Ye can't always tell, ye know."

Here the conversation was abruptly broken, for down the track gleamed a dull reddish glow, unmistakably to a practical eye, the gleaming headlight of a locomotive. If any doubt existed in the minds of the Big Grizzly and the Little Grizzly, it was dispelled by the vibration of the rails.

"Here she comes. We want to stand by," exclaimed the wise guy. "We can't afford ti take any chances. Truck, bumper, or empty [freight car] goes. Make it as best ye can, on the fly if we have to drop our bindles in the effort."

"Ya don't want to leave me, Lem," from the trembling little tramp. "Ye know I can't pick 'em up on the fly."

"Then you'll have to walk," unfeelingly returned the Big 'Un. "I ain't taking no chances meself. It's a case o' get there. She's crawling up."

And so she was, but she proved to be a passenger [train], to their great disappointment and chagrin. With a whirr and roar, she drifted by, giving the two tramps a glimpse of a comfortable, well-lighted dining car, with men and women sitting at dinner, snowy clothes and glittering service and polite attendants. They watched the hind end markers until they vanished in perspective, then with a sigh the pair of them made a simultaneous rush to the two bindles, and pulled the remnants of food that was left from their mysterious recesses. The Big Grizzly, of course, a little in advance of the smaller and weaker one. Of course, he corralled the lion's share. The sight of the well-appointed dining car had made them hungry.

They sat and munched, and waited, munched and waited. Every now and again the words of lump, poke out, duke outs, squaws, cans, dogs,[29] horsestyle [hostile] sharks, hit the grit,[30] etc. could be distinguished. Finally, near midnight, another welcome light appeared in the distance. This time they were not disappointed. It drew up in front of their hiding place, the tank directly under the hose of the penstock. The fireman jumped up and inserted the canvas into the tank and the "front shark" came quickly hustling up and turned on the water. The engine-man was busily tapping his rods and tightening keys with a copper hammer, and oiling up leisurely. Finally, they were watered. The engineman climbed up into his place and blew t[w]o short, sharp blasts. An answering wave from the "con's"[31] lamp denoted "all right" on the hind end. The throttle was yanked open, the engine on the back motion [rolled backward] to give the cars slack, then thrown ahead, taking up each car separately, and finally all were started.

The front shark jumped up into the engine cab, and just here two shadowy forms flitted like evil spirits across the track and, luck upon luck, struck an empty refrigerator car. Climbing on top of this, they lifted the hatch from one of the ice boxes and dropped down, bindles and all, into its ample depths. And the train pulled out and the engine man "soon had 'em agoing." And safe for the present from "horsestyle [hostile] brakemen," the two canhouse bums stretched out, enveloped in their blankets, and fell asleep, dreaming of the time when they should be machinists in the United States Navy. We will cease to follow them in their journey to Norfolk. Let them sleep.

These two bums are now bolo-men in the Navy, and aboard this ship. The story of how they beat overland and their occupations was given out themselves in moments of confidence and while under the influence of numerous drinks. The Big Grizzly was known by the men of the engineer's division as "No. 6" in the order of his seniority, otherwise facetiously "Cane Bottomed Chair," "Stew bum," etc.[32] The name "Cane Bottom Chair" was aptly given on account of his pitted face. The Little Grizzly was known as "Dopey" and "Chuckle Head," and the tobacco juice still ran down his chin in tiny rivulets. They are now slick and well fed, and the wrinkles are out of their stomachs. They were bums in luck with a vengeance. They put on supercilious airs and grace. They try to ape the airs of gentlemen. They have dinner at seven P.M. and take luncheon at noon. If on the Asiatic station, they call it "tiffin." They wear kimonos and dressing robes, and try to wear evening dress, but the signs are about them. They are bums, pure et simple.

As the King oftimes remarks, "You can't make a race-horse out of a mule." Opportunity came. They made capital out of misfortune and there is a moral to be pointed out, and that is, the Navy of the United States is the only institution where incompetency proves a success. Reader with a large stock of "old guff" and plenty of gall, the navy is the place for you to succeed. All you will have to do is to make a noise and look wise, and what was imbecility in the Little Stew Bum was misconstrued for wisdom. The Big Grizzly possessed the guff and gall, but with a face like that he couldn't look wise. He tried to look judicious and serene, but it was the sereneness and judiciousness of an educated pig. That's all.

Bolo-Men, Routine, & Discipline

Inaction is one of the things that try the soul; routine is another. The two placed together form a combination that will eventually drive one mad. Routine saps all the individuality from man. You have a certain groove to run in from which there is no deviation, a beaten road whose every turn is known. You become a machine. You have certain duties to perform. At first your mentality is part of the equipment in the performance of these duties, but only the first few times. After that, you cease to exercise the brain. Then you become automatic. An automaton is merely a machine for a certain purpose, and when you become a slave to routine you become a machine, a mere cog in the mechanism of the whole, and that whole, the mechanism of a modern warship or a modern army. You fulfill your duties at the word of command without a thought, listlessly, because it is an oft-repeated tale. No interest. Everything works smoothly. There is no break in the monotony. Inaction breeds discontent. The longing to break the bonds that bind you become strong. You want to get away from it all; you want a change. Duties that were once a novelty become irksome and can become inaction, properly speaking, because you act without using the grayish matter that some Supreme Power has endowed every living, breathing thing with. That is the Inaction of Routine.

Oh! those long weary days of routine at Woosung, waiting, always hoping for something to turn up. To lay long, weary months with nothing in sight but a Chinese lightship, a distant glimpse of harbor, and [a] low lying fort in the far distance, German, English and Japanese warships in the middle distance, a muddy mass of swiftly swirling waters, enlivened here and there by a Chinese junk in the foreground, that was all that made our days. True it was that the new captain stirred us up for a time, but it was only routine after all, what we had done over and over thousands of times before, and would do as long as the service held us. Like every new broom, he swept clean and gave us a shaking up that would abide with us many a long day.

The question of uniform was taken up firstly. It seems the new man was what is known as "strictly regulations." I have spoken of this before. He wanted his crew to wear clothing that was served out by the paymaster. The Ripper had agitated this question of uniform with the former skipper with the effect I have before mentioned. It seems when the new broom mentioned the subject of uniform, that the Ripper had placed the "old man" on his mettle by saying, "It's no use, captain, no use. We've tried it before, but it amounted to nothing. It's impossible to get them in uniform. We tried it, but with our old captain it resulted in a flat failure, and the men are wearing the same uniform as before. I don't think it can be done."

The truth was that the Ripper had agitated this question at the instigation of one of the most cordially hated officers aboard the *Oregon,* the officer known as the "Scum of the Earth," who took especial delight in harassing and making his division miserable. The word was passed without the "old man" knowing anything about it, and as our appearance at Sunday morning inspections pleased him, and as he mentioned nothing about it himself, we concluded not to buy any clothing unless we had to. And without the skipper's sanction, it of course fell thro'.

Not so with the newly arrived. "What! Can't get 'em in uniform, in strict, regulation attire?" he exclaimed. "Easiest matter in the world. Have bag inspection and hand every piece of clothing that doesn't conform with that issued by the paymaster to the chief master at arms to be cared for by him. And then report them for being out of uniform every time they come to quarters. That'll fetch them."[33]

When this rumor was floated around, nobody placed any credence in it. It savored of such high-handedness. But as long as some of us had been in the service, we were still to learn. I have always regarded this bag inspection as one of the most disagreeable happenings of my stay in the navy. One afternoon, the word was passed, "Up all bags," and the fun commenced. Such an overhauling of clothing! Whole bags of clothing were condemned as non-regulation. The collar too narrow, a pocket too many, fancy stitching on trousers and shirts, the shield of the shirt not right, and a thousand and one other petty details. These condemned articles of wearing apparel had served the owners on many ships under different commanders, as mine also had. But they were condemned and all were told to turn them in with our names attached, to be gotten when we left the ship, and we were told to get the proper uniform. Men who had only a couple of months to do were forced to do the same.

The couple of Chinese families in sampans alongside reaped a plentiful harvest of clothing that day. Many a man and boy, in disgust and with deep curses, hurled their discarded caps, shirts, trousers, etc., over the side. Many were the curses, not loud, of course, but deep, at this crowning indignity. We bluejackets are chronic growlers and kickers of course; our life makes us so. But we often have plenty of cause, and this proceeding was a little too high-handed. The majority, tho', forget almost as soon as it is over. But not so some. No. 5 bolo-man had the privilege of discarding a blue suit of mine. Himself a disgrace to the uniform he wore, and noted as belonging to the category of the Great Unwashed, when an humble machinist 2nd class, he took especial delight, I think from his expression, in hurting my feelings. How this man ever succeeded in becoming a warrant machinist only an ironical fate can answer. He was literally an incompetent, a "false alarm." But he had the drop on me on this occasion and knew it, and took advantage of it. I gritted my teeth, but I would have cheerfully given a month's pay for a *têt-à-têt* of five moments' duration on equal terms. I could only grin and bear [it] in silence. And wait. Everything comes to him who waits.

Of course, we were all boiling over with rage at this treatment, but it was partly our own fault, and, yes, it is partly the fault of the government also. No other navy in the world has such latitude in uniform as the United States Navy, and this is wrong, and recoils on the men always when least desired. As I have said before, some captains are in favor of tailor made clothing, and will not say anything, no matter how fancy they are made. Others desire the "regulation," and there you are. The remedy for this is to stop all "sheenys" from making clothing aboard ship, or if they are allowed to make clothing, let them make them to conform to "strictly regulations," or let them all be fitted out by the paymasters. Allow no deviation from this rule and you will remove another source of discontent. No other navy has this trouble, and they are always uniform. They have a clothing allowance, and every article is used by the proper authorities.

We had drill after drill. Routine! Routine! We left for target practice, supposedly for four days. This had the effect of undoing five months' cleaning and painting below by the necessity, of course, of lighting two more boilers and getting under way. No trouble at all to undo the work of months by the work of moments. Light up a nicely painted, cleaned boiler and to all appearances, that boiler has been in use for months. We were drilled at general quarters, fire quarters, collision quarters, clear ship for action. Drilled and redrilled, and drilled again, from watch in the fire rooms to the turret pumps and back again to the fire rooms, a few moments on deck, a respite and then "general quarters," a mad rush for your station, pell mell, helter skelter.

The shooting was excellent this time, and considerably above the average, and consequently, the skipper was pleased. We had originally intended to remain out four days, but everything ran so smoothly and swiftly that we were through in two, all our allowance for the quarter of ammunition [was] expended, with many targets knocked to pieces. The ship behaved well, the engines never ran smoother, and it is my firm opinion, humble tho' it be, that the *Oregon* was just as good as before we ran down that rock in the Pechili Straits. The Japs placed that patch on to stay. There was no extra leakage, no perceptible increase of water in the double bottoms, and our new commander subjected the ship to a severe test, the concussion of thirteen inch guns alone putting the ship to a severe test and strain.

Our new skipper, as I have said, was a department man, what is termed a "wall flower," one whom has had quite an easy berth at headquarters and "pull" enough to hold it. This ship was his second, if I mistake not, since the advent of the new navy.[34] A "stickler" for etiquette, as many of the commanders of the old wooden frigates were, he expected every officer and man to be up to date, and sailorized according to rules laid down by the "powers that be"; from these he allowed no deviation. He was a just man. I could see no fault with him. Of course, he was heartily growled at and cursed by the men, among themselves. The change came hard on them, especially in the matter of uniform, and the strict adherence he demanded of all in the discharge of their duties. The ship's superstructure was changed from white to the regulation buff or "spar color"; the guns from being painted white to being bronzed. Inspections and general routine was all changed. But this change was all regulation. And for myself, I couldn't see the justice of any growl at the new man. Rather, the old one was to blame. And altho' I cursed and growled with the rest, it was at the irregularity in the methods of the two captains that caused the discontent.

At the mast, the new captain was just. Here again was a vast difference. Whereas the new skipper brought the drunks up with a round turn and the second offence of drunkenness aboard ship would result in a court-martial for the offender, the former would let them go with five days brig, or five or ten days in "double irons," which was just exactly what they wished, as it meant that much rest and exemption from the disagreeable and dirty work above or below. In petty offenses such as a "late hammock," spitting over the side or on deck, late or missing quarters, etc., the thousand and one things that are offenses aboard ship and no crime ashore, he was lenient, fitting the punishment to the offences.

"I will punish you severely," said he to one unfortunate on the report for a trifling misdemeanor. "Two hours' extra duty," causing the offender to nearly faint with surprise. He was at least expecting the brig or fourth class [liberty class]. Whereas, with our former skipper, I have known one man, and that man if he ever meets [*sic:* reads?] these lines can substantiate it, to be given over 228 hours of extra duty and reduced from special class to 2nd (to be special class one with the former captain had to be six months aboard the ship under him, no matter if he had been special all his cruise on former ships) for the enormous crime of leaning against a wash-bowl in the firemen's wash room. This was the chief's report. No man reported ever got away, whether innocent or guilty. The new captain was very strict about inspection and drills. The old one left all this to his executive, and also the mast cases at times when he was indisposed. Of the two, I will take the new man and let him be as rigid as the regulations call for, as long as he is just. There is no fault to be found, and to those that didn't like it, the old rule still held. Run away.

Oh, what a lovely bawling out he gave to No. 5 bolo or Stew Bum one morning at the mast.[35] This incompetent reported a man for being absent at his station at clear ship for action. The man proved conclusively that he had no station at clear ship. His name or [billet] number didn't appear on the bill that he could find.

"You report this man for being absent from his station," looking sternly at the Stew Bum, whose general get up annoyed him. Before in his whole official career, I doubt if he ever beheld such a "lash-up" as this dirty, little man presented. "You didn't stop to ascertain why this man was absent from his station? Didn't send for him?"

"No sir. No sir," salaaming with both hands.

"Hm. This man may have been called upon to help at another part of the ship. Some unavoidable duty. He may have [gone] to the sick bay, or may have been engaged at something that prevented him from being at the particular part of the ship where you think he should have been. You didn't enquire, did you?"

"No, sir. I—I didn't think as . . ." stammered the bolo.

"No sir. I suppose not. But you must think hereafter. I want no doubtful cases reported and brought before me hereafter. You must know positively that the man has done wrong. In this case this man has proven that he had no station that he knew of. Why didn't you inform him, eh? That will do, my man. You can go forward. A word with you, sir," to the trembling bolo.

What the "word" was, I never ascertained, but it was a crushed, hang dog looking article that slunk away from the mast shortly after. It must have been a lovely "bawling

Bolo-Men, Routine, & Discipline

out." I should think that it partly concerned his filthy personal habits, for he looked as if he had made the acquaintance of soap and water a short while afterwards.

The same thing happened in a number of other petty reports. They were dismissed, especially those of the Czar,[36] who had the usual "quorum" of bad characters up, of course, much to his chagrin.

And thus the monotonous routine continued. We were now five long, wearisome months off the bar at Woosung. The weather [was] very cold, and the ship was cold at times, but on the whole, life was endurable as far as living was concerned. Anything but Manila weather. The rigor of the two poles were preferable to that when one has to be cooped up in a steel trap. One can keep warm, but it's very hard to keep cool in a man-o-war.

At last, the welcome orders came for the ship to proceed to Hong Kong as soon as possible. And at the first high tide we promptly went over the bar. We left about 9 A.M. Tuesday morning, and with steam on three boilers. It was originally intended to steam with four, as the English battleship *Barfleur*,[37] the one it was rumored there was a mutiny on board, was to start for Hong Kong the same time, and no doubt it would be an unofficial race between the two battleships to decide supremacy. There is always rivalry of this sort between nations. The *Barfleur*, tho', left the day before, which perhaps was a good thing for us in our crippled state. The fourth boiler was strained by holding high cold water pressure for too long a time upon it in order to test it and reset the safety valve, causing the tubes to weep [leak, from shrinkage, where they joined "headers"] considerably, and it couldn't be repaired in time. So we put to sea with the three, the section to which I belong having the four to eight watch.

Having good coal, we steamed easily at 80 and 83 revolutions, and if the water tenders of the second section had left well enough alone, it would have been comparatively easy steaming to Hong Kong. But no, no. 5 bolo wagered the beer with the other bolos that he would make more revolutions or turns than the rest, and he started in to do so, giving the water-tenders a hint to understand how he was placed, and asking them to do their best to hold the steam, telling them of the high honor that would accrue to them by so doing, and how good it would make them appear, etc. So, by "bulldozing" and taking advantage of every trick, they ran the revolutions up to about 89.

When I came down to relieve, I found low water in both boiler and feed tank for my end of the deal, and the steam had dropped from 120 to 95 lbs and the engines were still pulling it lower, in order to make a good showing for the last hour.

"How are you making out? Not much gas, eh?" I asked.

"They're pullin' the guts out of her. She's steaming hard," replied the water-tender.

"Yes, I can see that. I s'pose they're after turns? The hell with the steam, all they want is turns. There isn't much steam there, tho'." And I looked at the steadily dropping needle that now registered 95 lbs. "They won't keep this gait up long with three boilers, I'll bet. Go ahead up. We'll do the best we can."

There was, however, a sort of triumphant "beat-that-if-you-can" look upon the Harp's[38] phisiog that belied his disgusted look when he told me they were pulling the "guts out of her," and I thought to myself, "You're wise, all right. You don't care what kind of a dirty watch you leave as long as you have made your point and have been patted on the back like a good dog and told how smart you are." In fact, the entire watch, engine room people and all, wore a satisfied look, thinking that all had been done that could be done with three boilers.

The other water-tender was mad enough at his end, and being what is known as a "chronic chaw," put up a fierce howl at the state in which things were turned over to him.

"How is things?" I asked.

"On the bum. No water in the boilers and the feed tank empty. They're smart, they are. That's your man-o-warsman for you. Racing. Look at that steam. Pull everything out of her. Never mind the relief coming on."

"That big harp has an idea he's just a bit smarter than anyone else, and has a new broom and wants to show what a good boy he is. Turns, eh? We'll give him turns, the dirty big harp informer. He was 'grafting' himself and tried to look innocent when I came down to relieve him."

Never has a bigger loafer ever faced a fire than that same harp. [He was t]he biggest 'stiff' that ever handled a slice bar. If he had to graft [i.e., work] for turns himself, the same as he makes his firemen, we would get to Hong Kong in a month. We had a hot time of it the first hour, cleaning fires and building up, but try as we could, we couldn't raise the steam over a hundred pounds. But the watch did nobly, and we pulled out with a bigger average for the four hours than they did. That made 'em smile on the other side of the face. We laughed now, and they took it very much to heart. I knew the harp would cudgel his wits to beat us on his next watch, and he did. But we made slightly a shade better when we left. And the rivalry became bitter between the two sections. The other [third] section jogged along somewhere near us, but wasn't considered in it. They were sensible men. But the bolo-men were always dogging after the water-tenders trying to induce them to make more speed, but without success. [It was a] happy ship, indeed, and a happy state of affairs.

We were no better than the other section for keeping it up than they were for starting it, but, we argued, if the "Hewers of wood and the drawers of water"—i. e., the firemen and coal passers—were satisfied, we could afford to be. But it is a mighty unpleasant sensation to be watching the needle of a steam gauge and see it gradually drop and more slowly move up a couple of pounds, when you know the men are doing all that is possible and you are squeezing the pump down, carrying the lowest water you can with safety [if too low, water flow is insufficient or interrupted, and tubes can fail catastrophically], keeping an anxious eye always on the water glass and from that to the steam and back again.

There is no necessity for these hard runs, and no excuse in ordinary steaming. The men always respond when there is a call, when necessity demands. When people look at a paper and remark an item that tells that the U.S.S. So-and-So made a remarkable run between such and such a place, they little know what hard work and

At the bottom of the order onboard ship were the coal passers, whose duties included the hottest, hardest, dirtiest, and yet most essential tasks. Navy Historical Foundation.

maneuvering it takes, and they little care. But someone reaps a little benefit from it, or else it wouldn't be done. Someone wants to be patted on the back.

[It] was a welcome relief to once more see the pale green waters of [the] Yellow Sea, away from the yellow, muddy waters of the Yang-tse, that carries thousands of tons of mud and sewerage toward the sea and causes the great mud bar below Woosung. The ship ploughed thro' the buoyant seas that broke in showers of spray over her bows, now rising up on the crest of some high roller, and now burying her nose deep down in the trough. We had the benefit of a three-knot current thro' the Formosan Channel. We had the benefit of Japanese coal to propel us forward, for this coal was on the square, and no more than the legitimate "comshur" was allowed.

Below, it was watch against watch, each vieing with the other for revolutions. Twice on our watch the forward smoke pipe [uptakes to and within the smokestack] caught ablaze, sending flame and blazing soot far astern. Thick volumes of smoke rolled from our funnels, smoke that only Japanese coal can produce, that blackens everything it comes in contact with. The military mast was black with it, as the dense volumes poured against it, when the wind was astern or off the quarter. Truly, we were out for a record run. The bolo-men were dogging us and we were dogging the men. When the funnel caught afire at first, the bolo on watch in his excitement gave orders to throw open the smoke uptake doors, and we had to drop back, of course. But his excitement was our gain, for the steam arose from 85 to 140 lbs to the square inch once more [due to the increased natural draft], causing the incomparable engines to work easier. For a battleship, the *Oregon* is superlative to all. The best of machinery, altho' some of the devices are away out of date and cause untold trouble when in a rush. For instance, the man who devised the ash hoisting engines and method should be made to work them for a while. Ashes would always cause the drop of a few [pounds] of precious steam. And the blue streaks of profanity that they called forth were no doubt excused by the Recording Angel, who knew how trying they were.

The guns were secured for the run, and that did away with pressure on the turrets, for which I was devoutly thankful, thinking I should have more time. But in my optimism, I overlooked the fact that there were many other modes of torture for the tired stoker and his strikers.[39] We had bag inspection thrown at us, the first thing. No, I mistake. The first drill was battalion. "Get your leggings on." This kept the force busily engaged in the very necessary manual of arms. Nothing like keeping two sections of engineers force busily engaged in "Presenting arr-ums," and "Port arr-rums," "Shoulder Hip," "Port Hip," "Order Hip," all thro' the entire gamut of small arms drill. This encourages them to make more speed. You can't make a soldier or marine out of a marine fireman, any more than a soldier or marine can make of themselves firemen. The two professions are vastly far apart, but you can trust the fireman and coal-passer to handle a gun or revolver in the field. He can shoot and shoot straight, as many scores can testify at target practice, but "Present, hip, etc." is very distasteful to him. He would much rather throw his tired frame in sweet repose upon some warm spot along the steel deck, there to remain until time to "chow" and go below for his "bit." Even this was denied him on the *Oregon*. We were still chased from deck to deck, and kept continually on the "hike." We had the handling room of the forward orlop deck for our use, but when the Ripper made his inspections, he would chase us according to his condition, and the effect the particular kind of booze he had imbibed had upon him. And woe betide the unfortunate one that aroused his ire. You could never tell how to find him. He would "bawl" you [out] for being out of bounds or in bounds, just the same.

I[t] must have been a peculiar brand of "sampchoo" he affected. But I always had a secret admiration for him. He could carry an enormous load of "booze" and still be on his feet, but the red, inflamed face gave him away. But he could remember any trifling order that he had given at any time, no matter how much under the influence. The degenerate and worthless offshoot of an obscure branch of a once great family, [only] the accident of birth had saved him from becoming a common whiskey bum, and the same influence has kept him in the service when sentenced to dismissal for drunkenness.

Below, the watches were working like devils. Every fraction of a turn counted. Machinists, water-tenders and all were trying to make more turns than the preceding watches. The harp's watch seemed to be a fraction ahead of the other sections.

Bolo-Men, Routine, & Discipline

He was so interested that he tried to get his men below early so they could clean their fires on the other watch's time, and by so doing have a start for their first hour. We, of course, saw through this very aged scheme, and the man he relieved wouldn't allow his men to start in on the cleaning [of] fires until the whole watch coming on was below. Always, when we came on, the steam was as low as 85 lbs, and still on the downward path. We always left on this run from 110 to 120 lbs, and I always tried to keep my men at it and hold the steam. Men coming off watch, if not kept up to the mark, will generally coal up or slice about 20 minutes of [before] eight bells [the end of their watch]. When steaming hard, in that time the steam is bound to fall, and anybody who has ever stood a watch at sea in fireroom knows how hard it is to catch it up, and how much more difficult it is when you have half of the fires to clean.

The other water-tenders and myself "bawled" them out properly one night. I know if I had left such a relief and received such a calling down, it would have worried me out of a good night's sleep. But not so the harp. He was impervious. You couldn't penetrate his rhinoceros hide with an armor piercing projectile. As the King remarked, "Harveyized steel[40] was putty in comparison with his supreme crust." My partner at first refused to take the watch as it was, until he received orders to do so from the bolo-man. This caused an uproar. I had stood out in the engine room for ten minutes watching the rapidly falling needle. Five moments of eight bells, I went out.

"Don't you think this is getting pretty common? It's getting old," I remarked sarcastically. "How the devil is it we can leave over a hundred lbs of steam when we are going off, and every time we come on we find 85 and still dropping? What's the matter, do you quit firing? I suppose you don't care a damn for the next watch, eh? As long as you have made your point, you're smart, ain't you?"

"Well, your gang is cleaning fires. That's the reason the steam dropped."

"No! I'll be damned if it is," I roared. I stood in the engine room and the steam was dropping the last fifteen minutes. Nobody was cleaning fires then. I'll bet you don't keep your gang up to it. You don't care a cuss about this watch, as long as you are all right. The next time this happens, I'll see the chief, and find out if he can't remedy matters. I'm not going to have the bolo running out here bawling for steam as if it was our fault."

It resulted in a wordy war, and if he had been half a man, he would have mixed things up. But he wasn't that kind. He preferred to get square in a more underhand manner. The bolo came out when we were wrangling and he started to howl about steam as soon as he stepped in the alleyway, but finding how things were, he thought the better policy was to say nothing, or perhaps he wouldn't get any steam at all. Nor did he bother us the rest of the watch. It was the first time that I ever refused to relieve a man on account of a dirty watch, but the case was so plainly evident that it became a duty to roast such a blood-sucker who was making a very small amount of capital for himself by draining the other watches.

The very next watch, my partner put the water-tender of the watch he relieved next to his game of cleaning fires so as to make a good start for himself. The consequence was they fell away behind the mark in "turns" the very next time. They couldn't hold their end up on an honest watch. People ashore can never understand the amount of rivalry and bitter feeling between firemen of different sections. It is the same spirit that animates a person to distance all competition in whatever path of life they may be engaged in.

We made the run in just seventy-one hours. It was on our watch, the four to eight, that the Peak hove in sight,[41] and before the watch was up, we got a bell, and the run was over for us. It only remained to bring the ship to her anchorage in the harbor. We came off watch just in time to wash up and get into the uniform of the day and go on deck.

And in bringing the ship to anchor is just where the deck force and officers shone. The Ripper was in charge, of course, and one could hear his high pitched voice above all others, especially as we passed the *Brooklyn*. This was done to make a good impression on the admiral. (The Ripper was one of the biggest bluffs in the service, a veritable "false alarm.") But he could make an awful noise. The "Red head" officer known as the "Scum of the Earth,"[42] as usual, chased the firemen and coal-passers from the forecastle. The mere sight of a red watch mark[43] inflamed him in a most dangerous degree. He was another "useless article," a big bluff only fit for abuse. Meanness spoke in every lin[e]ament of his homely mug.

"Get out of here, you damned loafers, you bums. Get out!" he screamed, waving us back. These bums and loafers had just brought the *Oregon* from Shanghai on a record-breaking run. But then it was all over and the deck force has about fifteen moments of work bringing the ship to anchor. It is a most pitiable sight to see the majority of men-o-war coming to anchor: the incompetency, the shouting, the unnecessary noise. In the merchant service, a boatswain and two men can bring the biggest "tramp" afloat to an anchorage and you won't hear a bit of noise. But it seems to be routine aboard this style of craft to have half the crew on the forecastle and three or four officers all yelling and gesticulating like a grove full of monkeys. As it was, the Jack[44] was hoisted before the anchor was down, and this occasioned a reprimand from the Flagship.

CHAPTER NINE

~

Hong Kong

The harbor of Hong Kong presented an animated picture that lovely morning, Washington's birthday [February 22, 1901]. The day was as [warm] and balmy as a day in May. Just eight months before, we had left Hong Kong bound for Taku. We saluted the port, the German Flagship, and our own Admiral. The harbor was literally filled with men-o-war and [they] were all decorated in honor of the immortal George. The finest ships afloat were represented, and we were second to none: The *Kentucky,* the most modern and up to date of them all;[1] the *Oregon* and *Brooklyn* that had passed thro' their baptism of fire.[2] The *Concord* steamed in shortly after, another representation that had passed thro' the mill.[3] Of all the modern navies in Hong Kong, we were the only ones that had smelled the smoke of battle. Everybody came on deck to enjoy the sights and breath[e] in the pure, fresh air. I basked the whole afternoon in the sun, feeling a new man for it. We kept below decks at Woosung, as it was very cold, and there was nothing of interest to be seen. Even the machinists and others that were accustomed to staying below, came up from the [propeller] shaft alleys and holes and hideouts where they lived like bats hanging to the ceilings of some cave. [They] came up, batting their eyes and blinking as the sun shone upon them, all having the unhealthy look that one gets from long isolation from the glorious sun. One can understand it when away from its light for a long time.

The ship was surrounded by slipper boats[4] and sampans, bumboats of every description, the whole family living in one small boat and seemingly content. Here a boat came along side and a half-grown Chinese youth held up a pair of canary birds in a cage for our inspection, beside these there was a gaily colored cock-a-too and a couple of paroquets. Possibly the plumage was manufactured for the occasion.[5]

Other boat people were all around us, the young girls looking like the boys. The only difference was the shaven head and pig tail, and you couldn't make them out under the different head gear. The girls are better looking than those of Shanghai, not so hard featured. They are as free and active in their movements as young monkeys. Fancy a young American or European girl as lithe and active at the same age as these young monkeys! They are like dolls. The girls are fond of ornaments, imitations of jade around their wrists and hanging from their ears. No matter how poor, they have some ornament. They swarm aboard with kettles and bags and sweep the tables clean after the men have done eating. [They are q]ueer looking little jokers, always of interest to me, and all active and willing. They help the cook wash dishes and make themselves useful in return for the scraps, and the scraps they gather up will keep the whole family in "chow" for a week.[6]

Other boats swarm around, some of them all filled with women. They also have something to sell, and are on the *qui vive* for a possible customer. Bright eyed, sleek, better dressed, more bejeweled and berouged than their more virtuous sisters, they look more prosperous. Their boats are neater and very clean. They are clad in gaudy costumes. The "mammy" in the boat [is] chaperone for her young "buds." They all savvy English.

"Hello, Jack," sings out one sleek haired, pretty featured "big foot" girl,[7] "Where you come flom? Long time I no see your handsome face. You belly nice mlan. My savvy you, all light!"

"Shanghai!" answered one of the men from the rail. "You nice girl."

"You like? You belly hlandsom mlan. My can do," says Miss Brighteyes. "What time you come shore? Tomollow, seex o'clock, seex o'clock," chattering like a parrot. "Tomollo, seex o'clock," nudging her other companions, "Belly hlandsome mlan. He lovee my. He lovee my. Hlansome face. Hab got plenty mloney. Vey nice. Muchee like. Plenty kiss, more better." This in chorus as they brought the batting of bright eyes to bear on the men that lined the forecastle, looking possibly for a face that was known.

They and others of their class kept around the ship all the afternoon, smoking cigarettes and lolling around the deck of their sampan, and singing their refrain: "He lovee my. He lovee my, can do, hab got more ploper, seex o'clock tomollow" until they reminded one of a bevy of paroquets. They are a necessary evil living on the river. They are of the river and the way Miss Brighteyes could run the mainsail of the slipper boat up would gladden the eyes of any waterman. As it was the Chinese New Year, the boats were all decorated with wishes and prayers and offerings, the different kinds of gilt paper giving them a holiday appearance.

At mess gear, the curio vendors came aboard with their wares, but there wasn't anything new among the goods offered for sale: the same laquerware and cheap imitation tortoise shell goods and views from Japan; the Chinese pipes, common silk stuffs, and cheap embroideries from China; and shawls and scarfs from India offered by Hindoo merchants. Along with all these particular wares of their own kind was the usual common stuff from Germany, France and America, such as cheap scented soaps, pipes and tobacco, etc. You get used to viewing these wares and the desire to purchase soon passes away. They pall from constant contact with them at every port, but they are the only articles that a bluejacket will purchase. The costly curios are beyond his reach and he is generally not a connoisseur in art objects. The bumboat with its fruits, candys and sweets is more liberally patronized.

Washington's birthday in Hong Kong will always hold pleasant recollections for me. The day [was] so splendid, the life in the harbor, the river people, the warships of all nations from the stately American and English battleships to the little gun boat that flew the blue and white colors of Portugal with its golden crown in the center; the Chinese junks flying the gaudy colors and fantastically designed flag of some company, with paper streamers pasted on the stern, invocations and verses dedicated to the new start in the New Year; the puffing launches of the warships, a gig propelled by lusty arms with its long, sweeping stoke; the green sheen of the water, the view across toward Kowloon, where the dry dock is; the houses that looked like so many square boxes with windows everywhere, the simplest type of architecture, built for comfort, rising in rows, tier above tier on the mountainside; the sunset at the end of a perfect day that suffused the sky with a saffron glow as it sank behind the highest peak of all, the one upon which the signal station is; the bands of the flagships at colors; the myriad lights that sparkled like fire flies here and there, and as darkness settled, the refrain from one of the nearby slipper boats, "He lovee my. He lovee my. Seex o'clock tomollow" came over the water distinctly, to our dreaming senses in the unmistakable tones of the "big foot" Chinese siren, queen of the bevy of Chinese beauties aboard that particular boat, the words becoming indistinguishable as the distance widened. They were going to their berth for the night, the sound lost altogether in the other noises of the night. "Seex o'clock, seex o'clock tomollow, tomoll . . ."

There was another parting of the ways. Many old shipmates that I had been with in other ships, both before and after the war, and whose time had nearly expired, were transferred to the *Brooklyn* to go to Manila, thence home by way of the Suez [Canal] on the *Buffalo*.[8] Some were overtime, and some were left behind on account of having no one to fill their ratings, this especially in the mechanic class. They, one and all, lashed bag and hammock together with glad hearts, happy at the prospect of reaching home in the near future. We watched them go, knowing our turn would come some day. I had [seen] many men come and go. One gets used to it. You feel a vague regret at first. It soon wears off and in the course of a few days they are not missed. Some others fill their places, and the dull routine is continued.

The King of the Orlop about this time was in his glory. He had been presented with an old, worn-out sewing machine, whose period of usefulness had expired many moons before. Once the property of a marine, it was being knocked from pillar to post around the ammunition passages. The King had long had his eye upon [it], and on broaching the subject to the marine, it was presented to him with a sigh of relief at the prospect of getting rid of it. The King had previous to this added to his monthly stipend by patching dungarees and different articles of uniform and becoming more ambitious, had determined to broaden the field by becoming a full-fledged "sheeny." To this end, he [obtained] the machine.

With what degree of patience did the King labor to bring the old trap back to some of its pristine glory! He kerosened its running gear, cleared away the rust, oiled it, look[ed] wise, oiled it some more, turned it slowly, trying to move it over the high places [i.e., flaws in its gearing], whereat it got stuck. [He] placed his ear close to it to detect the "thump," then cursed softly under his breath, while we sat around on ditty boxes giving all sorts of advice.

"Why don't you get a bolo[-man] to overhaul it? They understand all about sewing machines," asked one.

"Sounds like a gravel train," chimed in another voice.

"You want to take a set of leads off it."

The King polished away, ignoring all remarks with becoming dignity. After he had thoroughly oiled it and got it free of rust, he tried to sew with it. The shuttle refused to work. There was fire in the eye of the King. He was on his mettle. The needle stuck fast and the machine refused to turn at all.

"Hello, she's stuck on the center."

"Throw her over a little more and give her plenty of steam, then she'll come all right."

"Why don't you take the shuttle out and rewind it? That's what I'd do."

"Youse fellows, you'd do a whole lot. You wouldn't do anything. I'll fix this thing or bust. You're all right at givin' advice."

Taking out the shuttle, he rewound it and placed it back in position. Then he threaded the needle, placed a piece of blue cloth under the "what-ya-call-it," spat a mouthful of tobacco juice in the kit, and prepared to move it with a triumphant air. By this time all the gang was interested and gathered around with all kinds of advice. The King started up "four bells."

"Hello, she's off! Good boy! You're an expert. You're losing time as a coal heaver. You ought to be a bolo-man." "Sounds like a blower. Something wrong with the thrust block," etc., were hurled at him. "How is it to make me a suit of clothes?"

The stitches looked all right on top, and having reached the end of the scrap of cloth, the King pulled it out and looked at it. The thread was all snarled up from the [bottom]. The King cursed loudly, and we gave him the laugh. He was getting madder every moment. There was a dangerous gleam in his eye. He would explode shortly. Seeing how mad he was, we laughed some more.

"Laugh, damn ye! Funny, ain't it? I don't see anything funny. A man can't start anything here without a gang of smart people, that is, who think they're smart, see some sort of humor in it."

Just here the machine worked smoothly for a moment and the King was making elegant headway. The stitching looked all right and looking up with a triumphant air: "Look at that! I knew I could fix it. They can't fool this harp. I am dead out my job

Hong Kong

for fair. What better sewing do you want than that, eh? It takes me to fix yer old machine. Why, I'm a regular expert. Think I'll have to ship as a bolo next cruise"—and—here he lifted up the cloth and looked at the side next to the bobbin. It was a complete tangle. Everybody smiled except one "punk" known as Corregidor Katherine, and he laughed. Laughed loud and long, whereupon the King completely lost control of himself, and the pair of them mixed it up lively enough for a few moments. The boy, of course, was no match for the King, who after wreaking his wrath, became somewhat mollified. The punk vowed vengeance. The machine was put away for the night.

"I declare to goodness, he's such an aggravitin' article, I completely lost my temper. He makes me mad. He will keep away from here now after that. It'll take some of the freshness out of him." This eased the King's mind. He had expended his wrath on something. Many nights he worked over that old rattle-trap trying to get it to work so as to dispose of it to some easy mark, but the machine always burped when he tried to give a practical demonstration with it, so no one would buy it.

The King of the Orlop was again in trouble.[9] It happened this wise: the King was one of the numerous tribe of men known in the navy as "politicians," i.e., in the engineer's department those coal passers and firemen that have jobs outside of the regular department work: wash-room helpers, messengers, storekeepers, etc. Beside these, we had on the *Oregon,* battleship 1st rate, a man that looked after and kept clean a part of the berth deck passages know as "black bag alley" on account of the firemen's and coal passers' black bags that occupied the jack stays placed there for the purpose. Also, there were two coal-passers allotted to the orlop deck and forward handling room, one for each side of them. The King was one. Truth to tell, he kept it very clean.

The ladder leading from the orlop to the berth deck above, the one on the port side, which was the King's domain, was truly a marvel of brass and well-scrubbed oak as white as it well could be. This ladder was the King's chief [concern], the one particular article that he kept up to date. It only went up in position for Sunday morning inspection, unless ordered by the executive, Jack the Ripper, or in his absence, the navigator, acting executive. Then only was it placed in position, under protest. If no excuse was taken, the ladder was placed in position by the doughty Monarch with many curses and growls. "Me beautiful ladder," was his lament. He hated to see it used and desecrated by the dirty hands, feet and dungarees of the greasy coal passers and men of the [engineer's] force, who, knowing his weakness, would leave the imprint of dirty paws all over its well-polished oak.

The King knew his job. He was supposed to scrub this ladder and also a length of web fire hose that occupied a rack in his side of the deck. But being "onto his job," he never did. The ladder he scrubbed with sand paper, and the hose, instead of taking on deck and scrubbing the entire length, he preferred to scrub as it was coiled tight. He only scrubbed the side and edge in full view, the "high spots," like a good soldier that only polishes the tip of his shoes and never bothers his head about the heel.

The King imagined he was trying to be deposed, thought there was a conspiracy against him. "But they can't do it," he confided to me. "They [are] a' thryin hard to get me job, but I'm dead next to the whole cheese. I've got me eye on 'em. Its these compass and square people[10] that want everything for themselves. Shure, they're only a pack of rogues anyhow, and all th' order is for is to keep me and you out of a job. They're all for themselves."

He felt he had a grievance when the master-at-arms 2nd class—he was "one of thim"—made him take his hose on deck one Saturday morning and give it a scrub. "They're thryin to make it hot for me, etc." he told me in the afternoon. "Luk at that hose, hauled all over the deck, dirtier than when it went up. Shure, I know me business, and I told 'em so. But the big 'Booby' (the master-at-arms) made me take it up."

Big Booby was his pet name for that master-at-arms. The 3rd class master-at-arms he called "Tenderfoot," and any time when they were within earshot, he would call out, "Where's the big Booby," or, "Tenderfoot did so and so," in tones of derision. He knew they couldn't get back at him, although [they knew] full well that all the shots were directed toward them. "The big Booby, the newly arrived Mason square and compass man, looking for a first class rate now, had to join the order in China." But at all times, the emphasis was placed upon the "booby." The sarcasm placed upon this word, which indeed was aptly applied, was great. A[nd] the master-at-arms would grind his teeth and wince like the villain at the play as the "booby" came floating to his ears from the King's domain.

Payday came, the coin was duly served out, and the "tea parties" were again in vogue. The King hadn't been ashore since the time he "broke it" in Shanghai, nearly two months. Neither had he drunk anything, not even one of his "beautiful shellac cocktails," with [their] tang of Venetian red. But he succumbed to the flowing bowl. Royalty fell. Numerous "dogs" came the King's way, and he proceeded to get gloriously [drunk]. He became bolder as the drink got in its fine work. In fact, he wanted a wider scope than the confines of his domain. Like all men [of] his race,[11] whisky wasn't any good unless he could talk and fight. And he began visibly to swell up as he reflected upon his own and continuing wrongs. He confided his wrongs to all that would hear his tale and, of course, they sympathized and humored him. What was the use of being a monarch unless he had his rights? He was a very great man, indeed, under the influence of Hong Kong *sampchoo*.

Finally, he concluded to waive all the prerogatives of royalty and go on the hunt for the "big Booby" and "Tenderfoot." So, fortifying himself with an extra large pull at the "dog," he emitted a couple of wild howls and battle cries, and started up through the hatch leading to the berth deck. The Booby and Tenderfoot hadn't failed to hear the commotion below, and by (skillful?) reconnoitering had found out that "Paddy" was drunk, over which they exchanged large smiles. The King had unconsciously "played right into their mitt." This was the opportunity to dethrone him and install a successor. "Tenderfoot, eh?" quoth the 2nd. "We'll gaffle him as he sticks his head above the hatch. We'll surround him. You, Tenderfoot, take up a position on the other side of the hatch and catch him behind. I'll look after his front."

The King, with a roar, jumped on the bench and grasping the sides of the armored hatch combing, swung up with a yell, "Show me the big Booby! Come on, ye square and compass——. I'll lick the whole push," he yowled, his jowls distended and head twice as large as ordinarily. "Ye want me job? Where's he at? Where's the Big booby?" he glared around. "Come forth and get massacred. Give 'em a battle axe! Wow! Wow!"

Just here, the Tenderfoot threw a net over him and snaked him to the deck. He was snared before he could recover from this attack in the rear. The "Booby" had him in front. "Come to the mast. Come on, who's the big Booby now, eh? Drunk, eh? I'll show you all about the square and compass. Come on."

"W-What's the matter?" asked the crest-fallen King. "I'm strictly sober. I ain't drunk. Lemme go. What's the matter wid ye?"

"Matter? You'll find out. You're dead easy, you are. The easiest thing to capture yet. I'm the Booby, am I?" And despite his protests and struggles, they took him to the "stick" where he was pronounced under the influence and put in the brig.

It was a dejected monarch that I saw the next morning, with full "jewelry" in the shape of hand and leg irons, but he had more company in the shape of a couple more drunks. To augment his troubles, everybody passed him in review. "How's the Booby? You will hit the booze and go on the warpath."

"Go to the devil, all ave yuz," said the disgusted King. "You're all glad I'm here. You're all in it."

"I heard somebody say they would pay for all the booze you could drink in order to get you drunk so you'd lose your job. You're a mark, you are."

"That's all right. You can all laugh now. Yer glad to see me in throuble."

To make matters worse, some one told him that the old sewing machine was broken in bits by the 8" turret, and he was asking everybody that passed to see if it was so.

"I know who did it. It's them compass and square ——. I'll get square, tho'. I suppose they'll steal all me shawls and coats-of-arms that I have. It's a foine way to take spite out on a man." He was in deep disgust. At the mast he told the captain that Hostetter's Bitter had caused his downfall.

"I was feelin' sick, captain, and having this bottle of stomach bitters in me bag, I drank it all up and it made me fale queer about the head. Yer honor, sure I haven't drank anything in a long time."

"Go and bring the empty bottle and show me," dryly said the captain. This nonplussed the King, but he went below to find the bottle that never existed, which of course, he couldn't find.

"Some one must have taken it from where I left it, captain. I can't find it anywhere."

"I thought not. Yours is a pretty thin excuse, don't you think so, L——? Beside, isn't it likely a man with your record would drink whiskey, or whatever it was?"

A Sailor's Log

"If ye let me go this time, captain, I promise not to do it again." The King commenced to beg off as the prospects of a "summary" [court-martial] hove in sight, with the loss of three months' pay. "Indade, I'll be good, sir."

"Five days in the brig, double irons," said the captain, and the King brightened up.

On being twitted about "begging off" [he replied,] "Shure, 'twas only diplomacy. Ye have got to take these things easy. I know me graft. Better to cringe a bit than to get a court and lose some pay. It take[s] me to blarney them." But after all, the King didn't lose his job. It was held over for him, so he didn't fare badly at all, considering all the noise and disturbance he created. But the Booby and Tenderfoot had the laugh on him, much to his chagrin.

~ ~ ~

Hong Kong is unlike any other port on the Asiatic Station. There is more English spoken there than at any other port. In fact, it is an English port. It is very cosmopolitan. The first thing that attracted my attention was the absence of the usual omnipresent rickshaw man. They are not allowed to persecute you in Hong Kong. You have to call one before he will notice you. At the same time, tho', he is weighing you up as a probable fare from the corner of his eye. But he is afraid to accost you, [because of] a wise and judicious law that keeps them in subjection. From the landing in front of the Hong Kong Hotel, by a sort of instinct, I turned into the principal thoroughfare, Queen's Road. Queen's Road East, Queen's Road Central, Queen's Road West, Queen's Road Everything. You can't avoid it. It runs "fore and aft." [There] are other streets running with it, across it, and diagonally, but the whole "cheese" is Queen's Road. Everything is here. That is Hong Kong. It is the bluejacket's promenade. You stop in the different joints, the Globe, the Grill, the Stag, and numerous minor resorts. You start away from one and wind up in another at the other end, and then "to the rear, march," and bring up at the other end, and everywhere, you encounter Fusiliers and beach-combers galore.[12]

It is hard to distinguish which have the most crust, the beach-comber or the Fusilier. Either one of them have the "Harveyized nickel steel crust." The Fusilier is the worst "bum" of the two. You can't shove him off. You can the beach-comber, unless he has been a shipmate of yours in the navy. Then you haven't the heart to refuse him, although you know him to be no good and a con man who would "touch" you if he got the chance, quicker than any of the rest. The fact that you once knew him ever so slightly entitles him to numerous drinks and the price of his "doss" and "chow." Altogether, he is making out much better than you, for he is free, and he will tell you how glad he is to have gotten out of the "outfit," and in your heart you envy him his well-fed appearance and all the liberty he has. He can enjoy himself more rationally than you can. He has plenty of time to do it in. You haven't. And you envy him that he can "sleep in" in the morning, as long as he wishes, for no matter how little ability he has, he won't starve in these ports. He would go hungry as a panhandler in America, but not so here.

Hong Kong

The "bloomin' Fusilier," like all other Tommmy Atkins of whatever branch of the service they may be, is poorly paid by his government. In consequence, he is a "panhandler" of the worst kind, for his uniform protects him. The "buggers" will "hit" you up for a "wet" whenever they see you. They are, as a rule, a thick-skulled lot. They haven't as much grayish matter in their craniums as the average rickshaw coolie has, as a general rule. I have never [seen] so much ignorance displayed, so little intelligence, as these soldiers. They are only a degree in intelligence over an educated pig. For a wet, any of them will sing a song or try to execute a few steps, especially for a "shandy," a mixture of "old stock ale" and soda, sweet or plain. Of this they get for ten or twenty cents, doby, almost as much as an Irish woman that hits the growler a welt would get for the same price in New York, that is, a mash boiler full, or in lieu of that, the fill of a horse bucket. Chuckle headed Tommy, our cousin, "don't ye know." Tommy wid 'is little red jacket on, wid his little cap. Tommy the Fusilier. Tommy, the Royal 'Orse Artilleryman. Any old Tommy. But always Tommy the panhandler, the "moocher" for free graft.

I strolled up and down Queen's Road from East to West looking at the interesting sights. The soldiers and sailors, the different types of nations. The European or stray American girl or woman holding themselves with the carriage of a queen in rickshaw or basket chair, looking at the passing throng with proud, indifferent gaze. Handsome? Well, yes, but to my eyes they were never handsomer than the silk kimonoed little figures with the elaborate coiffures and smooth, olive complexions, the little Jap, the most amiable women in the world and the most industrious. [They are] a true helpmate when they are not used as toys. Since being in Japan and other Oriental ports, the European woman doesn't possess the same charm for me. But then, I am no authority, no criterion. I can only speak for myself.

Everybody seemed [to be] coming in from the east. I was going toward the east and had to dart in and out among the many pedestrians in order to get by. I suppose they had all been out toward Happy Valley, as the amusement park is called. It was then the early afternoon, and seeing a sign, with eagle and dragon entwined, and reading the name—Professional Tattooer from Japan—it behooved me to go in and see what kind of designs he had on tap, with the usual result that I had another design pricked among the many elaborate ones that already decorate my epidermis. I have a hobby for this. With the Japs, as I have said before, tattooing becomes an art and anyone ignorant of their art must conflict [compare?] their work with the fearfully executed designs of the majority of American tattooers, or butchers. I added a gorgeous dragon of black, red, green and brown to my collection. The master mechanic proved to be a brother of Horishaw, my friend in Shanghai, but didn't seem to have Horishaw's disposition, as he seemed to be more unsociable after the first flush of conversation wore off, nor did I care for very much conversation myself, for a more damnable prodding I never went thro' before. And if I hadn't had a reputation to uphold, I would have begged off long before the dragon was finished. As it were, I sat looking as indifferent as possible, as if that severe prodding I was being subjected to was a matter of total indifference to me. But ye Gods, what tortures wracked my body and I felt immensely pleased and overjoyed when the little man with the big needles said, "All feenish." I even had the nerve to squint at it with one eye closed, critically, and told him to touch up the end of one of the dragon's claws. What did I care for another extra prod or so after that? Gee whiz! I can remember it yet. I must have been out of form.

This artist occupied about three hours, and it was dark when I found myself once more in busy Queen's Road. Hailing a rickshaw man, I was soon pulled opposite the Grill, and having a few hours yet to kill before turning in, I pushed thro' the door and found myself in the thick of it. There were well dressed and worse dressed beach combers, American and English bluejackets, a few civilians, and Fusiliers galore. The ever ubiquitous Fusilier. One tipsy Fusilier was singing in a husky whisky voice a refrain that went something like this, as I remember it. He was in a sentimental, maudlin state and his dulcet voice would bring tears to the eye of a needle.

"She syled awy one summer dye, h'over th' waters blew-ew. 'Elp! Elp! Was th' bleedin' cry, went 'hup from the bloomin [ship]'s crew. She syled awy . . ."

Here his emotions overcame him and he buried his face in a huge mug of "Shandy gaff," upon which the bluejacket who had no doubt paid for his "wet" slapped him on the shoulder, "Cheer up old man. Don't take it so hard. Have another one on me."

Whereupon the Fusilier, Prince H'albert's H'own, wiped his lips with a soiled paw and exclaimed, "Gawd stryke me h'up a bloomin' crab tree, cousin. Ye are hay mon h'after me h'own bloody styoile. H'old H'england h'and H'america f'ever (hic). H'aint we the bleedin same? But h'I say, matey, the words h'of that song, y'know, fetch the bloomin' tears t'me h'eyes."

And he might have added with truth, to the eyes of his hearers. "We left hold H'england h'on the lee" being rendered by a British bluejacket with a stentorian voice, he was half seas over. Such an aggregation of "juicers" was somewhat of a novelty to me. Even a parrot that was tumbling about in a cage back of the bar would shriek out, "H'eye h'old chap," all he knew, but it was enough.

Just here I espied among the mob an ex-shipmate, who had jumped some weeks before and had swelled the noble army of beach combers, so I hailed him. He also hailed me with delight. Of course, he must join me, but first he must introduce me to his friends. I didn't care much about that, as I knew the introductions would only bring added expense, and I don't find this class of people very entertaining, at least not sufficiently enough to blow them off. Among the number was the heavyweight that jumped from the ship at Woosung to fight the English heavyweight. Of course, I knew him well.

"Let me introduce you to my friends," said the big fellow with the air of a court chamberlain, "the fighters. All these," with a sweeping gesture indicating the group around the table, "are the fighters, the pugs you see billed for the tournament at the Theatre Royal. This is So & So," calling out each man's name and the weight at which he fought. "And this is Mr.——, ex-King of Formosa."

Hong Kong

I shook hands with the "fighters," each and every one. "Pleased to know you gentlemen. What will you take? Nominate your bitters. Take anything." No use holding back, as it was plainly up to me. I could see that I was it.

I took a good look at the scion of royalty, the dethroned monarch, the ex-King of Formosa. If ever there was a pugnacious-looking individual, he was one. Flabby face, flat, rum-lit nose, heavy, battle-scarred features, typical bull dog, hang dog expression, little bleary eyes. The king of beach-combers, prince of pan-handlers on the whole Asiatic station, the battered, weather-beaten water bum. Of course, he posed as a heavyweight. They were all "pugs," but a good, mind you, a good ordinary man could jump in and wallop and trounce the whole mob. They were the lowest kind of fighters, "booze fighters," "samp-choo" and "shandy-gaff" fighters. In fact, any bluejacket that deserts in these waters sets up immediately as a "pug." It is the easiest way to make free drinks and their meals. The boxing bouts that are put on are simply to draw the crowd. There isn't any talent required. All you do is to mix it up, and give the public the worth of their money in "slugging." If there isn't enough beach combers to make a programme, the rest of the bill is made up of Fusiliers and bluejackets from the different fleets.

The deposed king kindly and with dignity took a "whisky sour" for his'n and the rest followed suit. I paid the score. Then I waited to see who was next. Evidently, I was, for all looked at me expectantly, and I was about to set 'em up again, when I espied an old shipmate whom I hadn't seen for years. He also espied me and called me and I excused myself and joined him at the bar, to the discomfiture of the King and the "fighters" who wanted me to introduce my friend. But I didn't take any hints. I saw my chance to get away and seized it. Even at the bar, while talking of old times, I was tapped lightly on the shoulder. Turning to see who it was, there stood a "bleedin' Fusilier."

"H'I sy, moity. Won't ye give us a 'wet'?"

I looked curiously at the vision. There he stood, arrayed in all his glory, pay a "shilling a dye," large white helmet, fancy red coat, blue breeches, belt, and the ever-present "ratty-tan cane," helmet and belt well "pipe clayed," one of "H'edward's H'own" Fusiliers. Tommy the uniformed pan handler.

"Well," I drawled as sarcastically as possible. "I don't know. We haven't the pleasure of your acquaintance. Otherwise, my friend and I would ask you to indulge in a friendly glass."

"Gawd bloind me, mate. Be'ant we the soime, h'all bloomin' in bloody uniform. Do'ant we use the soime langwidge. We be cousins. Stroike me in a bloomin' beer shop!"

"We may be men in uniform, mate, as you say," rejoined my friend, "but as for speaking the same language, I'll be damned if we do. But never mind, name your drink and welcome."

"Make moine a sody, John."

"Oh, you don't want a soda," I interrupted.

"Oi dawn't?" opening his bovine eyes a bit. "Why dawnt hi?"

"No, because it isn't large enough, mate. What you want is a shandy."

A Sailor's Log

"H'I sy, dye chawps mean to insult me?" primping up and starting to unclasp the heavy belt he wore. These fellows have a way of welting you over the crust with the large, heavy buckles of their belts. A well-delivered blow from one will put you out. English Jackies wear the same under their blue blouses when on "provo" duty[13] and oftimes ashore they fill the buckle with lead and it makes a formidable weapon. But English bluejackets haven't any use for their red-coated brethren. They are as diverse as the poles.

"Pretty hard, I take it, to insult you, Tommy," said my friend. "You needn't mind unclasping that belt, if you know when you are well off. Just keep it on and take your shandy gaff. It will do you good. Don't you suppose we know what you want and what is good for you?"

"Blow me h'eyes, moity. H'I believe your roight, you know. H'any way, I'll take a shandy. H'I John! Bring me a bloddy good mug, y'know."

The shandy gaff soon occupied our "cousin's" sole attention and left us free for awhile to continue our talk, but everywhere in Hong Kong we were battered right and left by these licensed beggars. They are pests.

Hong Kong is a pretty "wide" town, but like all Eastern ports, the foreigner has to pay very exorbitant prices, especially the American man-o-warsman. It is a military town, and carries all the numerous callings that are inseparable from the camp: rum shops and girls, and cheap eating houses with high sounding names: "The New York, San Francisco and London Restaurant," where five courses may be had for thirty cents (dobie, of course) and the repast looks like thirty cents. There is a cigar thrown in. It is a most unappetizing meal, badly served. Then there is the "American, England and Paris Restaurant," possibly the perpetrator of this sign had a dim idea that Paris was a country by itself. Other cheap chow houses have wonderful signs with every large city they could think of. Truly a cosmopolitan resort. The Chinese and Japanese girl houses are all confined in a certain district. Here the poor little Japanese "dyo" has more latitude and isn't caged, and there exists great rivalry between the queer little inmates of these places.

When one walks thro' the streets of Hong Kong, especially when the weather is fine, then you can see why all the fronts of the houses have porticos in the heavy architectural style that the Chinese affect. The inmates use them for all living purposes, sleep and have their chow out in the open, dozens of them to each story. They are a social race, like all Oriental people. From these points of view they can see the swarms of people teaming in the narrow streets below. They are part of and in touch with it, an interesting mode of living, much better than our western mode of living, shut up in big, gloomy structures of wood, bricks and stone.

Wonderful are the many sights in the crowded thoroughfares below, as you look from your balcony. People from all over the globe jostle each other, Hindoos clad in the loose white robes and turbans, tall and stately looking, English and American civilians, French and English officers clad in khaki, rapidly moving rickshaws with richly dressed Chinamen lying back, smoking their cigarettes. Many of these Chinese merchants have their own private rickshaws, some very elaborate, with the mark of their house emblazoned on the back. Here are also many Chinese ladies out for an airing, the wife and no. 2 wife together with their hopefuls swathed in bright colored clothing, little round balls of humanity, with round chubby features. In contrast, the women of the poorer class, clad in soberer garb, not silk, leading small mites by the hand, that can scarcely toddle along. Now and again, you see some little mother, hardly able to walk, carrying a still smaller and younger member of the flock on her back. So small is she that you wonder how she manages, and yet the little round yellow face has a look of contentment. Boys playing shuttlecock, keeping the feathered ball up in the air with their feet.

The shops are always open, except at night, always crowded with would-be purchasers, laughing and joking. The shops are always small, and there always is ten or twelve inmates living in them. Contentment seems everywhere, even among the coolies that crowd around, some eating, standing, drinking a cup of tea or [eating] some savory smelling dish that costs only a few "cash." The red coat is everywhere in Hong Kong; you can't escape it. As you walk along Queen's Road, or ride lying in chairs or rickshaws, a glimpse through the open door of such saloons as the "Globe Hotel," "The Land We Live In," and numberless others, you will see long lines of red along the bar or a blur of red gathered around the tables, the ever present pewter mug with its shandy making its frequent rounds. The picture thus presented brings to mind the drinking scenes of old time masters. All is there except the sanded floor. The uniform is there, the pewter, the well-scoured oak, sometimes the pretty barmaid.

The pretty barmaid is the exception, not the rule. A pretty woman soon realizes her value in this country. Most of the barmaids are strong, masculine, husky Polish Jews or Russians, ready to bear a hand and stand a strong "grueling" in a rough house, giving and taking hard knocks. There isn't much attractiveness among them. Frequently among the broad mass of red coats can be detected a note of blue. The English tar growing loquacious and hobnobbing with his brothers of the h'army over their pots. Sometimes the note of blue resolves itself into an American Jackie, indulging in some drink with the Fusiliers. Possibly he is reminiscent of former times before he jumped from the Rock,[14] to take up his residence in the land of the free and to serve under the Stars and Stripes. He is Irish or English, at any rate, a soldier of fortune. Go in any of these saloons and the pewter mug is extended toward you with the same spirit that inspires them to panhandle you for the price of a "wet." On the walls alongside of the numerous and usual placards and posters advertising different brands of beers, whiskies and ales and occupying the place of honor, invariably you note a lithograph of the Queen, then a group of the royal family, usually an old print harmonizing with the other surroundings: old oak, pewter, ale, shandy gaff, soldiers of the king, bluejackets of His Majesty, the King Emperor,[15] typical tap houses, the bon hommerie of the uniform. "'Ave a bloomin wet, matey."

A Sailor's Log

Living out on the balconies are whole Chinese families, the master, no. 1 wife, no. 2 wife, and perhaps, [if] well fixed in this world's goods, no. 3, [and] half-grown pickaninnies. Pickaninnies are proper, queer looking little sedate, dignified men and women, as dignified as their ancestors and duplicates in miniature. The women idly smoking cigarette or pipe. In another balcony above the first, a couple of Chinamen are braiding each other's hair or shaving heads, chattering volubly all the while. Others gaze down below, idly watching the passing throng. Coolies sit in groups sunning themselves on the stone stairs leading up some narrow street, or [they] may be seen seated around some tables, dozens of them, with rice bowl and chopsticks busily engaged. Other savory dishes fill the board. It is [a] free, social open-air existence, weather permitting. At night they seek their holes in the many crannies and nooks and recesses of their complicated houses. These side streets are not over-clean, despite [the fact that] the city is under English control; not half as clean as Manila since the American occupation.

But the Chinese swarm like bees in a hive. No wonder the plague plays havoc with the coolie population, with their dirt and rags and disreputable looking haunts, a fitting place for rats and the rat-like inhabitants, picturesque though they be in their rags and squalor. Talk about Mulberry Bend, its dirt and swarming population.[16] A walk thro' some of the side streets of Hong Kong will show you swarms of people that New York never dreamed of, more so when you suddenly emerge out upon some open square at the intersection of three or four streets. It looks as if the inhabitants had all congregated at those places, so thick are they, but if you look at the streets, they are as full as ever. The markets are crowded and the vegetables, meats, fruit all look inviting. The land of China has been tilled and retilled until it is about exhausted, and the vegetables are forced to grow. They have an insipid taste and are a disappointment to the palate. The fish are good, and are purchased alive while swimming around in [a] tank, but they are not the fish of Japan, nor the vegetables of Japan.

The Chinese merchant will invariably stick the unwary purchaser. They charge exorbitant prices for everything, but after a period of haggling, will eventually drop to the most ridiculous[ly] small price. It would take all the zest from a sale without the wordy war. It is part of the religion. If you go into any shop, rest assured you won't receive any kind of a good bargain without heated arguments on both sides. Without the tremor of an eyelash they will ask you five dollars for an article and sell it eventually for ten cents. That's the kind of country China is, but no more industrious and contented people exist on this earth today.

There are no idlers in China, no drones in the Chinese hive. Everyone has work that wishes to. True, the pay is small, but no smaller in proportion to its purchasing power than the pay of Europeans. The Chinese can all dress well and generally do,according to their station. Four or five dollars (Mex) per month without chow is the pay of Chinese boys. They are all boys, [and] will render you good service. They are willing and obliging. There is a boy working in the Royal Naval Canteen that tends bar from early morning until late at night. His pay, four dollars per month, two dollars of our money, and of course, what comshur he incidentally receives, and no more willing and obliging young fellow exists anywhere. All other help is like this. No small wonder, then, that Europeans like to live in China, where they can possess a retinue of servants on an ordinary salary. They keep liveried rickshaw men and "chair" men who, when not in use, make themselves busy at something else around their employer's place.

I noticed one fine turnout in particular along Queen's Road. Four "chair men," the coolies were liveried in common white muslin with blue facings. The head gear was also painted white and faced with blue. The chair [was] finished in white enamel paint, blue trimming, and the device of the family emblazoned upon it in the same color. The whole rig cost about ten Mexican, but as far as appearance went, [it was] second to none.

Having nothing else to do, I made the ascent of Victoria Peak. The fare, round trip, is thirty cents on the Peak Tramway, a cable road that carries you up about two miles. The cars are drawn up by a cable, and are perfectly safe. From the car, one gets a magnificent view of the harbor of Hong Kong. The road bed overhangs the valley below in places, and you wonder what would happen in case something carried away. The car stops in front of the Peak Hotel, a big, rambling structure situated far above the toiling masses of the city below, away from the turmoil and noise. Here everything is quiet; the air pure. Getting off, I looked around for a couple of chair men to take me to the top, where the signal flag floats, but none being around, I set out briskly. It was very tiresome work despite the concreted roadway. It cost a vast amount of coolie labor to perfect this roadway with its turns and steps. Every piece of building material is brought up by hand labor. I saw a number of them struggling along manfully with a huge piece of timber, only to set it down after carrying it a distance of a hundred yards or so. It was then picked up by another set of men and carried as much farther, the others going back for more. Building materials of all kind [were] being moved in the same way, some of the coolie carriers being women.

As I ascended, I became winded, being unused to this form of exercise, but I stood manfully to it, the perspiration rolling off in small drops. My legs were fast becoming tired, and the small temple that crowned the top seemed farther and farther away, but the engineers that planned the roadway made provision for this, for the roadway skirted along the base of another hill. Being level, this was a relief, and I breathed easier and by the time I reached the next stair, had my wind once again.

There was another stretch of road that was all down hill, past the large brick barracks, in front of which a number of Tommies were taking their ease, evidently awaiting the opening of the canteen. Past these, the top was within easy reach, and taking the road that led to the temple or pagoda (that looks for all the world like the picture you see of the Temple of Fame) instead of the signal station, I passed another hostelry, known by the appropriate title of The Eyrie. I reached the top pretty well spent,

A Sailor's Log

but the view repaid me for my trouble. I sat upon one of the heavy stone railings and removing my cap, let the cool, pure breeze fan my heated brow. "Whew, what a climb!" and I mopped my streaming phisog. "There should be a reservoir of lager or shandy at the top to refresh the weary traveler."

The masonry of the temple was covered with names of the visitors, most of them soldiers and sailors. I didn't bother about placing my own beside the many before me, but gradually recovering my wind, I looked at the panorama spread before me. Far out upon the blue waters, solitary, and almost a speck, was a steamer, evidently a man-o-war, from her cut. Immediately below lay Hong Kong, with its swarming ant hill of human life. The infinitesimal atoms of an hour.

The war-ships were mere dots, no more. I take it [they appeared] in [the] sight of the Supreme Ruler of the Universe as they appeared from where I stood. To me, sampans, junks, and slipper boats were hardly discernible. The cities of Victoria and Kowloon looked small indeed. Far away upon the apex of the Peak across from where I stood, a signal corps of Tommy Atkins were heliographing and wig-wagging to the barracks far below.

No more to be seen, I started down the peak toward the station. What a relief from the climb up. I could have ran down, the only difficulty being in checking one's momentum. I stopped at the water-station in charge of an old Chinaman and had a couple bottles of soda-water and inscribed my name in the book he held out to me.

"You wanchee whiskey?" he asked naïvely, his wrinkled old face put on a sly look.
"Hab got, you like."
"Don't care about any now, John, old man."
"Sloda water?"
"Yes, that will do in place of beer. Beer no hab got?"
"No gottee."

So I paid him for the soda and idly looked at the inscriptions in the book. Some of them were very interesting. One writer from San Francisco had inscribed something to this effect: "Today in company with a party of friends from California we made the ascent of Victoria Peak. Upon arriving at the top after a very fatiguing climb, we considered ourselves amply repaid by the magnificent panorama spread before us. The view was grand and we vowed to come again at a later day, but resolved to fortify ourselves for the exhausting climb by using Germea, the great California Health Food, and we would advise others contemplating the ascent of the Peak to do the same." Even the advertising fiend has found this little book.

Another read, "Today visited the Peak. Found it O.K. and all I wish to say is that the *Don Juan de Austria* is a home," signed, So & So, U.S.S. *Don Juan de Austria*.[17] Right below this, "I also visited the Peak with my friend above, and I also says the *Don Juan de Austria* is a home." Billy Blobbs, Ordinary Seaman, *Don Juan de Austria*. And again, below this: "I hev also visited the peek with my 2 friends above and wot I also wants to say is that the *Don John de Austria* is a home." Ben Bipps, Lds. [Landsman], U.S.S. *Don Juan de Austria*.

Hong Kong

Good enough, shipmates, so the *Austria* is a home, is she? You are all unanimous on that point. That's the law of compensation. The *Austria* is a home, and the *Oregon* is a mad house, or a home—with a stepmother. Lucky dogs, Bipps and you, Blobbs, and t'other fellow. You struck it rich and what is more, you seem to be aware of the fact and appreciate it.

There were a thousand other inscriptions, all interesting; all had something to say, and all to the point; and they were written by all nationalities, all acquainted with the world. Having finished my soda, I thanked the old fellow and started down again.

I only had a short wait at the station. The car was rapidly filled. I remember having on the same seat with me a Hindoo, a Jap, a Portuguese, and Englishman, and a couple of well-dressed, well-groomed Chinamen. That was cosmopolitan enough for one car seat. Upon arriving at the bottom, I struck out for the California, San Francisco, London and New York Restaurant for something to eat, and found a couple of shipmates already there, one of whom proposed we take a ride to Bayview, a good distance out the road. I believe it is known as the Praya. We accordingly did so. The road is along the bay front and you get a good view of the shipping and the wharves and docks. The Praya is mostly lined with merchants engaged in ship chandlery. One sign struck me forcibly: "A man. Engine clean, hull chip and scrape. Small boy can furnish for boiler." This meant he can furnish small boys to scale and chip the interior of boilers.

The ride takes you past many interesting sights, and everywhere you find hundreds of coolies loading and unloading cargo. All seem contented. There is work for everyone. They can all do an honest bit for their chow. Long lines of them stream across the road carrying coal; the rickshaw men having difficulty in breaking through. Others are ranged around the many numerous stands eating and chattering like monkeys. All are considerate and all sociable. They are a gentle people among themselves. True, they mete out terrible punishment toward criminals, but they are not a fighting people. None are quarrelsome, considering their numbers. There are no people, unless the Japs, that can be so sociable and considerate of each other.

I mention this ride to the Bay View to show what the price of such a common and homely commodity as sauer kraut and frankfurters may be in different localities. We paid our "rickies" off and going into the hostelry, we called for beer. This we got at the usual price, 30 cents Mex for pints, Pabst Beer. A sign on the wall attracted my comrade's attention: "Try our Sauer Kraut and Sausage."

"What do you say we have some?" he questioned.

"Suit yourself," I replied. "I could go a large plate full just about this time."

"Boy! Bring us sauer kraut and dogs for two," and the Chink trotted off.

We indulged in another bottle apiece of beer in the meantime. Finally, the Chinese boy came in with the banquet: five medium sized frankfurters and two tablespoonsful of kraut. This was scrambled over a large platter as a captain of a small company, to make a bold front, stretches his men across a street. We drank our beer and ate the kraut and frankfurters and asked the Chinese boy the price.

"Two dlollar for kloutee and slixty cent for beer."

"What?" we both gasped as soon as we gained our wind to speak.

"Two dlollar, slixty cent," he repeated with the expression of a wooden Indian.

My friend paid. "That was pretty good sauer kraut, wasn't it?" I said with a grin.

"I suppose it depends on where you buy it. Damned if it ain't a dear experiment, tho'."

"I'll tell you what we'll do. Let's see the proprietor. I think that Chinaman is putting it on us. Can't do any harm to ask."

We sought out the proprietor. He was at the bar.

"I say, are you the proprietor?" asked my friend.

"I am," he replied.

"What I wish to see you about is the price of sauer kraut in Hong Kong. We just had four or five small sausages and about a thimbleful of sauer kraut, for which we were charged two dollars, is that the correct price?"

He reddened up a bit. "Yes, I believe that's correct." He produced a bill of fare. "Aw, yes, sauer kraut and sausage, one dollar. You had two, I believe."

"You might call it six, and we wouldn't be any the wiser," I chimed in. "For five cents at home I could get about half a peck of kraut and sausage, with a big high hat of cool lager to wash it down. Of course, I understand we would have to pay a pretty steep tariff for what we got, as no doubt it is imported from Germany, but this seems even beyond our wildest dreams, and we are used to paying extremely high for everything we get. We are American bluejackets, and thus legitimate prey."

"I cannot help it. As you can see, that is the price. This sauer kraut and sausage comes in cans. There are, I think, about four, three or four, sausages, I think," looking very thoughtfully as though in doubt about the correct number of dogs. We had five. "It comes in tins, ye know," this as a clincher. "Well, give us the tins next time, we'll eat the tins," sarcastically said my friend.

"Or at least we can have them as a curio, a souvenir of the price of sauer kraut in Hong Kong."

"I wonder if we draw enough money in a month to get a full feed of kraut," questioned my mate.

"Not at that price. Talk about gold bricks in New York! Say, we are the easiest."[18]

The proprietor felt uncomfortable as we penetrated his thick hide, and there were many others drinking around the bar and at the tables who became interested in the market value of sauer kraut.

"Well, let's have another bottle of Pabst anyhow. I need it," I said.

"I haven't quite recovered from the shock, either. Won't you join us, old man?" to the proprietor. But he politely declined, feeling the prick of conscience, no doubt. So we drank our beer and walked out.

"You can have the tins, old fellow." But he preserved a dignified silence.

Hong Kong

One night Ship Street was in an uproar. It nearly always is in an uproar. The courtesans, tho' Chinese and Japanese, ape the ways of their Western sisters, and when any trouble starts, there are angry screams and mixed curious curses, high pitched, shrill feminine voices, pidgin English, especially among the Chinese *dyo*'s. They are more like the common courtesan as we know them than any other. They wear loose Mother Hubbards, they be-friz their hair, and strive to imitate their tougher Western sisters in every possible manner.

I came up the street one night, salutes on every hand. "Hello, Melican! Clom in. Come here! I know you! Dis house! Come! Dis house, forty five." [There were] English bluejackets, Fusiliers, Americans, merchant sailors, and the whole riff-raff that go to make up this seamy side of the under-world. I stopped and talked [to] a man from the ship. Over on a stone stoop sprawled another, I am sorry to say, American bluejacket. He was most infernally sea-sick, full of sampchoo. He was trying vainly to make the inmates of the house on whose stoop he was, to let him in. They were clamoring from a small portico above, "He no belong dis house. He got no money. To[o] drunkee, belley sick!" came the chorus from the Mongolian bevy of soiled doves.

One of the Hong Kong local police stood looking indifferently on in a very dignified manner.

"I say, friend, that bluejacket over there wants to get [in] that house. He says he belongs there, has paid his money, and that they won't let him in. Can you do anything for him?" I asked his majesty.

"Why, the bloody bleeder doesn't belong in the bleedin' 'ouse, y'know. H'if 'e did, the bloody women would leave 'im in," he deigned to reply.

"I only know what he says. 'Thought' you would investigate," I replied.

"The bleeder is bloody well drunk. You people come ashore and drink bloody well of vat you think is whiskey. Vitriol and water, I bloody well calls it, y'know. Ye gets bleedin' drunk an y' don't know where y' belong. Take my word for it. The bleeder h'only thinks 'e belongs there."

"All right, you know. I think you are right." I tried to soothe him by agreeing with him, as he appeared a little ruffled.

An uproar broke out in one of the houses close by, mingled shouts and curses and screams, heavy thumps, and a Chinese woman came running out shrieking.

"Makee fight! Come! Knifee!"

We forgot the bluejacket on the stoop and a dozen or so of us tore up the steps toward the house, following the "bobby."

"He cuttee my! He cuttee my!!" shrieked one woman, pointing to where an American bluejacket and a couple of merchant sailors, evidently Germans, were struggling.

"He got knifee! Look out! Blad man." Bedlam had broken loose. A Chinese Bedlam with cosmopolitan accompaniment. The man with the knife that the shrieking Chinese woman pointed out was underneath a struggling mass of bluejackets, each trying to get a dig at him. He was a small man, evidently a German.

A bluejacket who was talking with me and the copper, having a little bit of a jag on, rushed into the mix up of legs, arms and curses, and emerged with a large clasp knife of the jack variety such as merchant sailormen carry. This he took from the tightly clenched hand of the knife-using drunk.

"Here you are," he roared triumphantly, holding out the knife to the Bobby.

"Blawst me bloomin bleedin h'eyes. I'll ave to take the bleeder to the lock up, you know."

By this time the little German had surrendered to overwhelming numbers, and was tightly held by a couple of bluejackets. The young fellow he tried to use the knife on [was] standing, glaring at him.

"I haf no knife. I haf no knife," he exclaimed. "Vat I use a knife for?"

"You usee, all right. Look, see," said the Chinese dyo that called us, pulling down the garment she wore, and exposing a red scratch across her back. "I makee charge. I go polis station. You cuttee my."

"That knife wouldn't cut cheese," I exclaimed, looking at it and feeling the edge. It was about the dullest article of this kind yet seen.

"Blow me bleeding h'eyes. Come along me man, and you come, y'know," to the dyo, "h'an wot I sys, don't none of ye attempt to h'interfere with me h'in the discharge of h'me bloody juty," and the "bleeder" looked around at us threateningly. "I knows my juty to the Queen, an' 'tis me juty to take th' bleeder to the station."

"Certainly, certainly, old man. By all means, do your duty. Any man that uses a knife deserves to get soaked for it. Nobody had the least idea of interfering, least of all with a Queen's officer as efficient as you have proved yourself to be," this from me.

This mollified him somewhat, and grasping the little German by the collar and closely followed by the excited Chinese girl, he marched majestically off with his prize, evidently with the single stripe of a lance corporal in view as a reward for his important arrest. That was the last I saw of them, but he was the "bloodiest bleeder" of them all.

The excitement all over, a small bunch of us wandered back to the stoop upon which our sick shipmate lay. With some coaxing, we managed to stand him on his feet, and finding he had blown all his money in, we took up a collection, and putting him on a rickshaw, and one of the fellows volunterring to accompany him, he was packed off to the nearest hotel and hustled into bed.

Ship Street is a lively street at all times. It is practically wide open. Everything goes. Next to Port Said with its brothel in Arab town, it is probably its nearest rival in wickedness. Only the women are more honest in their dealings with drunken sailors of all nations. It is very seldom anyone is robbed, but vice is there in all its nakedness. There is no concealment. The street is set apart for that purpose, as yoshiwaries are in Japan. People that shun such places don't have to go there and haven't any business to complain. It is a necessary evil, and places should be set aside in every town or city of the United States for that purpose, instead of trying to disseminate [dissipate?] it by driving the inmates from certain localities into the flats and tenements and respectable neighborhoods where they can easily obtain fresh recruits and contaminate the young. The sooner people understand the danger of spreading vice, the sooner will they adopt the Yoshiwari system. Isolate it.

~~~

The *Oregon* was going home. That was understood to be the case, at last. No false rumor this. Men were now being transferred to her from the different ships of the Asiatic Fleet. The current rumor was that San Francisco was her destination, there to go out of commission. The *Newark* also was homeward bound, New York the objective point. Draft after draft was sent to both these ships, comprising the "short timers" of both the East and West, the "Snowdiggers" and the "Slopers."[19] As the drafts were sent to the *Oregon,* others of the crew were sent away to other ships. Many of my former shipmates from the *New Orleans* came aboard, their times having expired. Some were doing over-time. Others that I had been with also poured in. Some were thro' their time; others with one, two, and three months to do, according to the rating they held. The majority of water tenders were doing over time. At this time, I had six months yet to finish my cruise, six and a bit, a few days over six months, and I began to smell a "mice." I knew I would soon be drafted to another ship, and I strongly suspected the *New Orleans.* One of the water tenders with less time than I, had to depart on the *Zafiro* with the first draft that left for Manila. He was bound to Cebu to relieve a water tender whose time had expired on the *Don Juan de Austria.*

"At any rate, old man, you have caught a 'home,' for didn't I see the *Austria* endorsed as a 'home' by no less than three of her crew in the book at Vic's Peak?" I said to him.

"That's all right, but I thought having a short time, I would make 'Frisco on the *Oregon,*" he replied, disconsolately. It was a severe blow to him. The *Oregon* had been his only ship for the entire cruise.

"We can't have our way, you know. You have got to do your bit wherever you are sent. Look at me and the ships I have been shifted to. I'll catch another also, I'll bet," I replied.

And I did. Not the *New Orleans* as I expected, but the *Concord.* My name came out on the draft that was posted up on Sunday morning, April 7th [1901], along with nineteen others. There were many other drafts. Some went to the *Isla de Luzon,*[20] *Yorktown, Bennington* and *Kentucky.* Others were reserved for the *Helena, Monadnock* and *New Orleans* at Shanghai. Still another draft was drawn for the *Monterey* at Cavite. Myself, I was well satisfied. I knew I had to go, and having only six months, as well the *Concord* as any other to finish my cruise. What her ultimate destination was, I didn't know. Some said Alaska, but my own idea was the Philippines, as the most possible theory. You never can get away from the Philippines, you know. China, Japan may come and go, but the Philippines, we always have with us. There is no escape.

So, that Sunday evening, the word was passed, "Lay aft on the port side of the quarterdeck all the *Concord*'s draft. And lay aft we did. Something was wrong, I knew, as we hadn't signed accounts clear of the *Oregon*. We had packed up in the morning. I managed to get everything in my bag this time, and didn't have to leave anything behind, as on the *New Orleans* when I so suddenly left her. But beside my regular kit, I had a large tin box covered with canvas filled with clothing and curios. Bag, hammock and [ditty] box and extra box, we were standing by for a call, waiting to sign accounts. So, when called aft we were surprised, but we trundled back with our gear. A tug was alongside the port ladder. They had just disgorged a draft from the *Concord*, and desiring to send us to the *Concord* with this tug, we had been called aft. But finding we hadn't signed accounts, we were sent back and the tug had to wait for over an hour.

Finally, good byes were said and we were off, past Kowloon proper, around to the Cosmopolitan docks where the *Concord* lay. It took the docking company's tug about forty five minutes to make the run. It was raining very hard, and we blessed our lucky star that the tug was well protected with awnings, keeping both us and our gear from getting wet.

The *Concord*[21] was lying tied up to the dock. Ventilators, smoke pipe and deck house had big patches of red lead plentifully scattered here and there. She was evidently being put thro' a complete course of overhauling. Of course, the usual curious crowd was standing by to see the draft, to see if they knew any of the newcomers. And we were just as curious to ascertain if we knew any of the *Concord*'s ship's company.

Wilson spent the final months of his cruise onboard the gunboat *Concord*, which, in addition to steam propulsion, was also rigged as a three-masted schooner. Navy Historical Foundation.

Hong Kong

We were told to bring bags and hammocks, etc., aboard as soon as we were alongside. This we did, and carried them below on the berth deck, temporarily stowing them in one of the locker alcoves until we could stow them permanently in the proper places. I noticed the lockers for the crew's use and sighed as I noted the size of them. "These things won't hold a pea-coat, let alone a complete bag of clothes," I said to one of the draft with a much larger bag of clothing than I. He cursed as he viewed the size of them. The whole ship appeared very small, indeed, after the big battleship.

"From a battleship to a spit kit," remarked someone, and this somewhat vulgar remark aptly described the change. But there was an air of "looseness" aboard the *Concord*. The first thing that attracted us was a young goat, a fine, sturdy, hardy-looking young rascal. At the time, he was busily engaged in trying to swallow an unsuspecting Chinese peddler's queue and it was only when he had it half swallowed and reached for more that the Chink felt the strain, and looking around to find the trouble, let out a wild yawp and proceeded to make Billy disgorge, causing a little inconvenience to his whiskers.

We were finally mustered aft and given the number of our messes by the first luff, upon which we went below and had supper, it being just then "mess gear." Like all changes, everything was very awkward. It always is. Changing ships is much like changing houses. You have got to adapt yourself to them. Everything is changed. You have got to stow away your gear in different places. At first, this is very puzzling. You forget where such and such an article is. You have been accustomed to knowing in the last ship just where to place your hand on any article you want. It has become routine to you. But you soon get used to the new order and soon feel at home, and it was only a few days before we were as thoroughly at home as on the *Oregon*.

One thing aboard the *Concord* that was very pleasant was the entire lack of bolomen. These pests were conspicuous by their absence. You couldn't imagine what a relief that was to men who were accustomed to being dogged around by these imitators of the Chinese *suvang*, or coolie driver. There wasn't any room on the gunboat *Concord* for warrants of any kind, excepting, of course, the pay clerk. No boatswain, no gunner, no carpenter, no warrant machinists or bolos.

Below decks in the [engineering] department, machinery was being overhauled by Chinese workmen. "Small boy for boiler and bilge hab got" were squirming in and out of boilers and bilges full of oil, dirt, red lead, little fellows that could crawl in and out handily in places where an ordinary mortal could hardly get his arm. It is true they didn't work very fast or hard, but then, that's the East. They don't get much pay, either. America is the only place where men work themselves to death to earn a living. The Chinks are philosophers, and from "small boy to large boy," they are all boys. They believe in taking life as easily as possible, even when working, and to this end they consume innumerable cigarettes and hold interminable conversations(?) either in the bilges or the interior of bunkers or boilers. You can't hurry them up. The litter and dirt they make, the ends of burnt candles, with their bamboo punk wicks [and] candle grease [are] everywhere, both in engine rooms and fire-rooms.

A Sailor's Log

The boiler comp[artmen]ts looked as if they had never been cleaned; dirt an inch thick had settled over all. I looked at the four miserable little locomotive kettles [boilers] in despair, and wondered how I could ever start to get my part clean. I had charge of the for'd end, A & B boilers, A being the steaming boiler then. But I was told it wasn't any use to try and clean while the boiler was lit, and with this view I fully coincided after I started in and polished up the steam gauges, for, an hour afterward, an eighth of an inch of coal dust and ashes had resettled. So, I concluded not to waste any more energy, but to take it cool as long as possible, for God wot, I only had six months to do.

But these six months bid fair to be crackerjacks, in a class of their own, most distinctively so. The weather began to get quite warm, very warm in fact, at least we began to think so aboard the *Concord*. It was a slight touch of Manila weather. Go to our lockers on the berth deck and break any article out, and we were bathed in perspiration. At mess gear, we had to break away from our canned William before we had near finished. You must know it was near the later part of April. Just about this time three years ago, this ship, the *Concord*, along with a few others since famous, were fitting out in this very port for the raid on the Spanish warships at Manila.

It was getting warm, and already the ship began to give us an idea of how uncomfortable it could be. Luckily, it hadn't rained any during the nights (I had dropped the hammock and taken to the fo'castle with my caulking gear) and we managed to extract all the comfort we could during the nights. There was always a good breeze blowing up there. The berth deck had been far too warm in a hammock.

On board the *Concord* I had no night watches to stand, and comparatively little work during the day. We had no quarters, either in the morning or afternoon, no "setting up drill"—think of it: no "knee stoop" and "double time" as on the *Oregon* of bad memory. But we had our discomforts to contend with here, and that was lack of room, no space. How heartily sick I was of the whole life! No change of ship would interest me, not even momentarily.

Shortly after we reached the *Concord*, about two weeks, she was towed from alongside the Company's docks and made fast to a buoy in the stream. Here it was a few degrees cooler; the breezes had a more unobstructed sweep. But it was hot, mighty hot. Prickly heat broke out among us, a good forerunner of the "dobie itch" in the Islands. I looked forward with disgust to the future six months still in store for me.

With the advent of warm weather, the landscape around about and in Hong Kong began to change. Lighter clothing of many kinds enlivened the scenes of the streets. Many gorgeous colorings might be observed in a day's ramble. The light, loose-flowing silks of the Chinese, the Hindoo, and other Eastern nationalities became much in evidence. But the neatest, most comfortable and most pleasing to the eye, at least my eye, was the Jap; the Jap and his sensible, picturesque kimono. The girls from Ship Street were especially gorgeous, like the butterflies they were, taking their afternoon airings in rickshaws along the Queen's Road. Soiled doves though they were, yet they were the daintiest of all the sex on show. Not even the English

Hong Kong

young girls or dames, tho' clad in daintiest muslins and laces, could compare with these maids from the Sunland of the Mikado. It may be I am prejudiced. Yet not all these dainty looking girls from Japan were from Ship Street; not all were of the Yoshiwari. Some of them were daughters and wives of many of Hong Kong's prominent Japanese businessmen and officials. These, though, could be detected by the freshness of their looks. Upon the faces of the girls from the Yoshiwaries was the stamp of the pace that kills.

No more could the red coat of the English "coolies" be discerned on street and in bar-room. It had given place to the more sober khaki and white, the jaunty little cap to the unsightly cork helmet. The saloons were studded by groups of khaki, but to the ever flowing shandy, whether in khaki or fuller uniform, the "lod of the ratty-tan cane" can always do justice, and [a] burst of song and laughter and "sup h'up lad, and let yer mate sup h'up, and don't sup it all," could be heard thro' the open door.

Up at the Royal Canteen, the place was not so full. The ships had one by one stolen up north'ard in search of cooler weather and the English sailorman was conspicuous by his absence. So was the American bluejacket. Many were carried to Manila. The *Oregon* had left for Woosung, there to remain until the middle of May. The *Kentucky* had flown to Manila. The *Newark* was the largest of our vessels at this time in the harbor. She was also homeward bound, having aboard a great many Eastern "short-timers" and men whose time had expired.

The *Newark* was flagship, the senior officer being Captain [Bowman H.] McCalla, and from all accounts told me ashore by many of my former shipmates, she was a "mad house," but then, they all are. In the *Newark*'s case, all the officers bore McCalla (whom no finer or more considerate man ever trod the quarterdeck) ill will.[22] They always did, and although he did all in his power, whenever possible, for the men under his command, still despite his efforts, the officers managed to make it pretty lively for the crew. Despite the years that they spend at the Academy, it is impossible to implant the instincts of a gentleman in some of the material that are turned out as officers. At dancing or doing the gallant small talk, and five o'clock teas, the most ruffianly of officers can ape the gentleman, so can a dancing master also. But when it comes to rawhiding a crew, the graduate from the Academy can give your merchant officers cards and spades. They look like gentlemen, act like gentlemen in the glare of the lime-light, but not one half of them have the true instinct of a man. Gentlemen are born, not "turned out" to order.

I often met many shipmates ashore. They were going home to be paid off, and in the shifting around, many came thro' Hong Kong on their way north, there to fill out the ships that were on the North Asiatic Station, or else south to Manila. And during these meetings we would compare notes and ascertain the whereabouts of other friends. The *New Orleans* lay quite a time at Nagasaki after coming down from Chefoo, and from former mates I found out that Kenzo had been treated the same as when we were aboard, and that Moriya had enquired about John and I. They were doing well.

Of Sunawasan, I heard little, but I wished very often that I could be in Nagasaki once more, the port I hold dearest of all in either the Philippines, China, or Japan.

How I longed to be once more in Kenzo's house upon the hill, surrounded by all my Jap acquaintances, sipping hot sake from his small tea cups and otherwise enjoying myself in the house I had always felt so much at home in and being so heartily welcomed. Tender recollections of Osunawa, the daintiest of all the dainty little Nippon *musmees* ran riot in my mind. What wouldn't I have given to be there once again! It had been just a year since I had seen either Osunawa or this old house. It seemed but a short time to look back upon, and the six months before my time was finished seemed interminable. Despite all my visits to different ports and the allurements thereof, I always had the warmest regard and tenderest memory of the house on the hillside and Osunawasan, the prettiest of them all. But—but. Never mind, we shall meet again.

~ ~ ~

One hot night, two companions and myself proposed taking a trip to a Japanese circus that had just arrived in Hong Kong. Being a very warm night, and being on Ship Street, we concluded (having just enough beer in us) to take the girls and to go in kimonos, as the coolest and most comfortable costume we knew of. So, telling the "dyos" we were going to the circus, we asked them if they wanted to go along. Did they? Well, rather. They hailed the suggestion with delight. It doesn't take much to please your Nippon girl; they are as simple and childish in their joys as children. You bet they wanted to go, and they hurried off to their respective rooms to take forth their best silk kimono and *obi* from the fragrant camphor-wood chests, which they all have and keep in such scrupulous order and with such cleanliness.

They also furnished us with a kimono apiece and *obi* and a hat. Mine was a straw hat. From the size, I rather surmised it to be a ladies' straw sailor. It had a most gorgeous band, red and white, the colors of Japan, but I wasn't standing on ceremony. I managed to hold it balanced on the back of my cranium, where it stood undecided whether to stay or not. One of us had a soldier's campaign hat that looked the worse for wear, and the other a larger straw that settled down to his ears, but what of that? Anything went in this land of cosmopolitan costume. It was after dark, at all events, and as the kimono was a good fit and felt comfortable, and the short jag we had on also felt comfortable, we didn't care a picayune whether the elite of the town liked our style or not.

So out we flocked, my little Jap friend Ocheosan and I in the lead, in rickshaws. Clear to the other end of the town was the ride. We attracted no attention, however, as it was dark. We didn't care whether it was dark or not. The only thing that slightly annoyed me was the fit of my hat. It didn't stay on at all, so I had to carry [it] in my hand and use it for a fan as I lolled back luxuriously in my rickshaw and occasionally glanced back to see if the rest of the procession was keeping up, and to smile at Ocheo gracefully smoking a cigarette. Smoking becomes the little Japanese woman.

At the circus we found a motley crowd of Sikhs, Chinese, half-castes, but very few English or Europeans. The circus structure was cleverly built of bamboo poles, the top thatched with dried palms and rice straw, very strong and very neat in appearance, also very large. We paid our dollar Mex apiece to go in, at the ticket office, and we in our kimonos attracted plenty of attention upon our entrance, but that was to be expected. Many smiles greeted us from the Chinese all over the house, and, feeling very good, we smiled also. In fact, we felt at peace with all mankind. Smile, everybody!

In any obscure town in Japan, the mere fact of three Americans in the national dress wouldn't have caused any comment. It would simply have been the proper thing. But Hong Kong was different. It is very seldom you see even the Japanese abroad in anything but European dress, so, of course, the audience smiled. To them, we were three half-tipsy bluejackets with Ship Street *dyo*'s out for a sailor's time. But, as I said, we didn't care. We felt very, very loose and comfortable, and contented, and gazed very benevolently upon the beaming faces around us.

My companion had brought a cushion with her and wasn't content with sitting European-fashion upon the chair, but tucked her little feet under her after kicking off her *zōri* and perched there looking as demure and innocent as the boy caught in the jam closet, at the same time pulling one of the chairs in front around for me to place my feet upon. All these chairs in front each had a card with "Engaged" written upon them. Whether they were or not, I doubt very much. It is simply the Oriental's mode of doing business. However, I smiled at Ocheo sitting there smiling and happy at the prospect of the show before her. It was a holiday occasion for the poor little caged *dyo* of the Yoshiwari. It doesn't take much to please them. They are [alike], are all these little caged birds.

"You very comfortable, Ocheo?"

"I tink so," very gravely.

"You like Japanese circus?"

"Me like ver much. I tink just now no can tell. Bimeby, I see." The curtain was to rise at 8:30.

"Where you come from, Cheo. What city?" Asked I. I am great on the Li Hung Chang act.

"What ceety? Nagasaki."

"Oh, Nagasaki. Yo savvy Idzumo-machi?"

"Idzumo-machi. You savvy Idzumo-machi?" and she laughed and pounded me with her fan. "You savvy girl, Maryanna?" Idzumo-machi bears the same relation to Nagasaki that Ship Street does to Hong Kong.

"I tink you been in Idzumo-machi," she pouted. "You got sweet-heart in Nagasaki, I tink. I no lik you," and she made a feminine motion to move away, almost losing her balance on the chair.

A Sailor's Log

"Yes, Cheo, I have sweetheart in every city. Sailor privilege, you know."

"I no savvy priv-lig, but too man' sweetheart no good you. *Ta ha boku* too much. (*Ta ha boku* means transferring your affections too often, too fickle.) One piecee man alright. You like me, nex week you have oder sweetheart."

"I have one sweetheart in Nagasaki, Cheo. She no. 1. I like her very much. I think I get married next time I go there."

"Marry, al right. What you sweetheart name?"

"Her name Sunawa, Osunawasan. She very nice girl, Cheo. All same you. You very nice girl. I marry and make her work very hard. All right?"

"No all right. I no nicee girl. Sunawasan nicee girl. Cheo no good. My no belong nicee girl. Dis no good, and dis no good," pointing her fingers upon her little, snub nose and eyes.

"Yes! Yes! Cheo, very good. You very pretty girl," which, in fact, she was. I think she was fishing for a little flattery.

"Den why I no Number One? Why I no your sweetheart? I lik you very much," looking at me shyly.

"I also like you very much Ocheosan. More better than any girl in Hong Kong."

"Hong Kong, but not Nagasaki. Sunawa you like," she said jealously.

"I think Sunawa catch another man, then I no like her. Ocheosan my sweetheart then. All right?" She rewarded me with a half-sad little smile, but the curtain was pulled up then, and the stage attracted our attention.

The performance was good, in the main. A half-grown, stout Japanese girl did some neat balancing with her feet, juggling tubs. Also some very good wire walking. A Japanese woman, a very strong, sturdy, young one, also whirled tubs, buckets, in [a] wonderful way. She held a youngster aloft on a perch while he did a very creditable act. The woman, the girl, and four boys were the entire show, the smallest boy a mere baby. Their tumbling wasn't much, but the feats of balancing, or balancing feet, were as good as any I have ever seen. Ocheo enjoyed it immensely. I was getting bored. It was more amusing to me to watch Ocheo's enjoyment than to watch the performance. I piled her lap full of oranges and candies and cigarettes. My two shipmates and their companions soon got tired and left the house, trying to get me to go with them, but Ocheo refused to go and made me remain until the show was finished.

"No go now; bimeby finish, den we go," she begged, and of course I remained as long as it pleased her.

"You like circus very much, Cheo."

"Yes, ver good," enthusiastically. "I like ver much. I like you ver much," shyly squeezing my hand. "Bimeby you be my sweetheart."

"That wouldn't be hard for me." And not to be outdone, and [because I] have a reputation to uphold, I slipped an arm around her waist and gave her a bear-like squeeze without attracting the audience's attention. In truth, she was getting more attractive every time I looked at her, the delicate bloom hadn't been brushed off the flower as yet, but a few months of Ship Street and the attractiveness would be gone.

Hong Kong

She had only been among them a week, sold possibly by her parents in Nagasaki, who had farmed her out for the highest market price, and had found Hong Kong the best market, at least very much in advance of the price to be obtained in Nagasaki, where girls are so plentiful for that purpose.

Ocheo spoke very good English, and was far above the average Nippon girl in point of intelligence. I began to take an interest in her in [a] very small way; this I think she knew. I had told her, in answer to her eager questions, when my time expired, and then I would be finished with the navy, and then I would go back to America, to New York.

"Then my no see you any more. You go home. Ocheo cly very much," and there was a queer little break in her voice. I turned and looked at her quickly with a flippant answer ready enough, thinking she was trying to jolly me, as all girls do, whether Japanese, Esquimo or Fijian or American. But the flippant answer never came. Was it actually a tear that trembled on the long black lashes?

"Holy Moses!" I thought. "What's this? What am I up against this time? This is one on me." Yet it was actually a tear, what [the poet] Byron calls the proof of affection. This caused me no end of astonishment. That a denizen of Ship Street had any affections to throw around indiscriminately was a Chinese puzzle to me. However, the little girl looked so charming in her evident distress at the prospect of never seeing me again (here I swelled with vanity) that if it hadn't been in such a public place, I would have caught up the whole bewitching little dandy bundle of Japanese femininity and chased away the tears and soon restored her smiles again. All I could do was to slip my arm around her and draw her more closely to me without the audience getting next.[23] This was between the acts. Fifteen minutes intermission.

"Never mind, Cheo. I come again, when all finished, to Hong Kong. Then I take you to America." What else could I say?

"I all same European girl den," brightening up. "I wear European dress."

"Yes. All same American girl," I replied. "I think you look very nice in American girl's kimono, eh?"

"I make hair lik dis, look, see," and she made a motion as if fixing her luxuriant perfumed coiffure into a Psyche knot at the back of her head, then successfully imitated doing her tresses up in curl papers, looking at me slyly for approbation. "My savvy everting."

"You must have been there before, Cheo. Somebody show you?" I exclaimed.

"No, no. Nobody show Cheo. Cheo see picture in, wad you speak, book? I savvy dis, see," and she placed both small, plump, pretty hands (all Japanese girls and women have pretty hands and feet) upon her waist (a waist that had never been deformed by a corset), and compress[ed] it. "See, all same Merican girl. Shoes, see? No *zōri,*" kicking one off disdainfully. "Japanese shoe no good," and warming up with her subject, Ocheosan uncurled herself from her perch upon the chair and forgetting in the warmth of her subject where we were at, started to initiate me in the mysteries of a Caucasian girl's toilette, much to my dismay and the amusement of

A Sailor's Log

the audience. In fact, she clearly demonstrated that she was thoroughly conversant with her subject, but I blushed, as a good sailor should, when she made the pantomime of pulling on a pair of long, imaginary silk stockings and slipping the silken band of a garter on. Not to mention other articles of lingerie that I am by far too modest to even think about, let alone write down upon these pages of my log. Suffice to say that Miss Ocheo charmed me by her artlessness, the artlessness of a child. To her, all this was eminently proper and as it should be. There could be no breach of the proprieties where none [was] intended. The charming little girls of Nippon haven't any morals, and not having any, they are decidedly better than those that have 'em and knowing what morals are, decide to be immoral.

"Never mind, Cheo, you show me by and by more better. Too much people see." The show commenced again, and I pulled her down in her seat gently, but she soon grew dissatisfied with that way of sitting and curled up again on the cushion, slipping one hand in the sleeve of my kimono in search of a cigarette, finding which, she fixed her sole attention upon the performers, puffing away daintily.

The wind up was a flying trapeze act by the three boys of the troupe. It wasn't much of a performance either, to my way of thinking, but pleased the Eastern audience immensely, who gave generous applause, clapping and shouting their approbation. As a boy, it brought back recollections of the time my chum and myself would steal off in the woods and do stunts upon an old trapeze, practicing the tricks we witnessed the night before at the theatre, and very good we became at it. We were going to be acrobats in those days long gone. That was the height of our youthful ambition, but we drifted apart and it has been many years since I have lost track of him. Well...

This finished up the show. The boys each swung from a high perch at the top of the structure and were caught by the larger boy, who hung head downward from a small trapeze over the stage. First a straight swing, then half a turn in the air, then a full somersault. No danger; a big net was there to catch them, so a miss would have been only fun to them, but they couldn't miss.

Very well satisfied, Ocheosan, myself and our belongings bundled out after the crowd. Outside was another attraction, a peep-show, "The Capture of Peking." Nothing would have it but my young lady would have a "look, see." So, she bundled in after the last person and I, of course, followed. It was strictly a Japanese affair. It was all Jap. There was the whole panorama spread before us. The lens thro' which we looked [was] pretty powerful and although not anything like our moving pictures, still it was very creditable and show[ed] that our small Japanese friends are fast imbibing our ideas. There [were] the little Japanese soldiers, very spruce and natty, led by very ferocious looking Japanese officers. According to the pictures, they must swell up and grow very terrible, for every officer loomed up at least head and shoulders over the men they led or urged on, and they waved mighty looking swords and wore fierce, bristly mustachios.

Wild charges were being made, shells were bursting everywhere. Here and there was a fallen dead, dying or wounded Jap. Here again, he was being promptly carried

Hong Kong

back to the rear in a litter. In one of the pictures was shown a fully equipped field hospital, surgical cases lying upon the grass stained with the blood of the wounded. A staff of medical officers [was] promptly attending to the wounded. Over in the distance a battery was wheeling into position. Generals and staff were directing the advance from some prominent point of view, scanning the field thro' glasses. An aide de camp could be seen galloping fiercely toward a column of men away off in the distance. The Boxers in their blue and red uniforms were being driven swiftly back. At last the gates of the city are reached, and as everyone knows, blown up. (The story of the Jap who gave his life to accomplish this is history.) The next picture, they are charging thro' the gate. The Japanese slightly in advance and first to enter. On one side are the English. Nearest to us in the picture are the American troops, known anywhere by the campaign hat. The Sun Flag of Japan ever in advance (as, indeed, it was), the Royal Ensign and the Stars and Stripes close behind.

Truly, it was a grand rush, and the Boxers offered but scant resistance. See that big Boxer is rushing so fiercely upon the advancing Allies. See him again in the next picture, a little brown man had put his bayonet clear thro' him, up to the muzzle of his rifle. The blood spurts out and has splashed all over the neat white suit of his slayer. They are bayoneting them right and left. The Allies carry everything before them. The Japs are everywhere, killing, killing, killing, but all in honorable warfare. A Boxer can be seen from the windows of a nearby house, sniping as fast as he can reload his piece. Over all this carnage, this glory of war, can be seen the bursting of the shells bringing Red Ruin everywhere, clouds of flame and smoke over all. And then the next scene all is quiet. The Allies are in full possession. The day has been won and the little brown men and their officers are as neat as if it didn't happen. All honor to you, my Japanese friends. You are all right. You opened the eyes of civilized(?) Europe on that occasion. "Here's to you, you are all right!"

"Come on, Cheo, let's get rickcha. I'm tired. How you like circus?"

"All right, we go. I ver sleepy. Circus all right, but Peking more better."

The ride back along the Praya in the cool of the night was very pleasant. I took off my straw hat and let the cool breezes fan my brow. I had to take it off or it would have [been] carried away by the breeze. As I said before, this particular hat wasn't made for any member of the masculine gender. The bay was full of twinkling lights from shipping and from sampans, thousands of them, and at this hour, all was silent. Few pedestrians were abroad. Perhaps a stray rickshaw would steal swiftly by up some side street, carrying some passengers like ourselves. But Hong Kong at this hour was very quiet. The Peak stood out in bold relief against the clear dark blue of the moonlit sky and far across the harbor shone the lights of Kowloon. From across the water, through the calm hush of the night came the creaking of the cordage and the oars from a junk looming up like a black phantom of the night. The scene was truly Oriental, even to the turbaned Sikh that paced his round in the middle of the road, and the "coolie" who had thrown himself down to sleep in the shadow of a doorway.

A Sailor's Log

Many times I paid Ocheosan a visit while in Hong Kong, and I grew quite attached to her and her quaint and outspoken ways. That her affection was genuine, while it lasted, I have no doubt. She even went so far as to make me two kimonos with her own deft hands. She tried in every way to please me, and she succeeded. On my part, she had nothing to complain of, any more than not taking her to New York. But a man might have done far worse not so far away from home, and when I finally left Hong Kong, I gave her to understand that I would be back at the earliest possible time, that I could never forget her, neither can I. She will always occupy a warm spot in my heart, but then, possibly that don't amount to much. But all I can say is that some ladies of my acquaintance and many more I wot not of would be vastly improved by a page from her book of amiability.

To all intents and purposes, as far as we could hear or conjecture, we were to go back to Manila and around the Islands. But happily, when the actual orders came, it proved to be Amoy, about three hundred miles farther North, where we hoped it would be a bit cooler, as it was most infernally hot in Hong Kong, especially aboard the *Concord*, where in the morning as you awoke, if you slept on the for'd berth deck in hammock or on caulking mat, you would be eaten by red ants, small but ferocious, tantalized into madness by flies, and annoyed by cockroaches of mastodonic proportions. And sleeping in that close space with no ventilation to speak of, the atmosphere was poisonous, and the head one awakened with was vastly worse than one acquired by a long bout with the "booze." But despite these discomforts, there wasn't any "bolomen" to nag and annoy. This was a wondrous blessing. And our chief was as fine a man as the last one was just the opposite, and that is the highest compliment I could pay him. Whenever any work was to be done, he wanted it carried thro. After it was finished, you could play.

Hong Kong

CHAPTER TEN

Amoy, China, & Yokohama

We left Hong Kong the first of May [1901] for Amoy, China, getting under way about eleven A.M., with steam on three of the *Concord*'s dirty, dingy, measly, little kettles [boilers]. As usual, the section, the second, to which I belonged, got her under way. I connected [i.e., to the main engines, and perhaps "cross-connected" to each other] the three boilers and I made it a point to be very, very careful, for I remembered that this particular ship had killed two men and scalded several others in doing the same thing. And if a [valve] gasket and bonnet of a main steam pipe would carry away when the ship was new, from the looks of her, it would be much easier at the present time. I drained the main steam line [of condensation] through [throughout its length], and this occupied some time, for one of the main stops [valves] leaked, the one on the steaming auxiliary boiler, and the steam pipe was full of water owing to the condensation of steam. But happily, I got everything hooked up without accident and we got underway.[1] As usual, the same spirit prevailed among the sections of the engineer's division, trying to beat each other, but 95 was the average revolutions, and we arrived at Amoy about three P.M. the following day, the second of May.

Amoy is a big tea port. It is one of the treaty ports. For miles we were within a stone's throw of the beach, lined with its rows of Chinese shacks and sailing junks, the usual dirty, evil-smelling Chinese hovels. We anchored between Amoy, the Chinese city, and Kulang Su, the island that has the Europeans upon it. Amoy we weren't allowed to go ashore in on account of its foulness and also on account of the bubonic plague which was playing havoc with the coolie population, as high a mortality as two hundred per day was the average during our stay.

We were cautioned about drinking any water ashore (which was entirely unnecessary) and were landed on the island of Kulang Su.[2] At first, the liberty was from four P.M. until seven A.M. But this was changed from all night liberty to sundown. This was quite enough. Of all the dead places, Kulang Su is probably the worst. In fact, it is a graveyard, for it is there that the Chinese bury their dead, and many was the funeral cortège that crossed the stream with its coffin and eatables and weird music. Where a Chinaman was buried during the day, at evening was converted into a golf links by the European inhabitants.

I found the island very dull. The houses, mostly of the Eastern style of architecture, were surrounded by ample parks. There wasn't any streets, just [likely] as not the path you were following would lead into some private park. Only in one place was there anything approaching a street, and that was thro' the Chinese part of the island, lined with its small shops, its horrible smells, its hyena-like mangy curs, pigs that put one in mind of a razor-back, chickens, ducks and geese. Herds of caribao were driven along the narrow streets.

This street also wound along by the side of [a] pond, and this in itself held enough typhoid, miasma, and fever to kill a city, lined as it was with half an inch of green scum. It was a veritable cess-pool. But out in the by paths the air was sweet enough, laden with the perfume of things green: ivy, and creeping vines and blossoms. There are many large, massive boulders scattered throughout the island. Upon one of these some enterprising individual built his eyrie. The face of the rock upon which his house is perched is engraved with Chinese lettering thousands of years old.

The island is filled with many strange freaks of nature, trees growing and pushing stone walls apart. It is more like a curious park than a town. A visit even to the European cemetery is very entertaining to the morbidly curious, but we weren't looking for curious sights. We didn't have any spare time. What we wished, and quickly, was beer, cool, frothy, amber fluid, in which to quench our thirst. We found plenty of it, but it wasn't cool. But this defect was remedied the next time the liberty party came ashore. The most of us patronized the Cosmopolitan Hotel. This place was provided with a bowling alley and [was] comfortabl[y] fitted up. The old German who was the proprietor never had such a run of business before as he netted off these particular American bluejackets. Nevertheless, the crowd treated him badly enough, for one afternoon they engaged in a "free for all" scrap.

At some previous period of their dull life on the farm, these particular six months "seamen?" had been beguiled from the interior of America by fairy tales of seeing the world, etc.; others had been caught in bear traps and with nets from their general uncouthness. These six months seamen, trained and brought to the Chinese Station by the *Hartford*,[3] *Lancaster*,[4] and *Buffalo*,[5] had heard that to be a real sailor, it was eminently fitting and proper that they should start to "mix it up" and they started to do so. I happened to be in the Cosmopolitan that same afternoon and I don't know yet, nor did any one else, how it started. Being full of beer, they wished to use the strong arm, and one of them swung on another of their ilk. This was resented forcibly and one of them getting the worst of it, his friend jumped in. Then they all jumped in. I tried to part them, and came near getting put out with a swinging blow from a chair. This I saw coming in time to wrench it from the poor, weak-chested son of a gun that wielded it. He went down and out with a short arm jolt on the point of the chin, not delivered by me, however. Another peaceably inclined man and myself went and sat on the window sill out of range and viewed the fight with disgust.

"Let 'em kill each other, the poor, ignorant chumps," he growled in deep disgust.

A regular pandemonium prevailed for about two minutes, with wild yowls and howls. Legs, heads, arms and furniture was inextricably mixed. They soon grew tired, however, and disentangled themselves and, lo and behold, not one of the Dixie heroes were hurt. Not one had his skull fractured, but they were far too thick for that. They then settled for a pane of broken glass, that being all the damage that was done. The old German seemed very affable over it all. At first, I could see by his countenance that he expected murder to be committed, but we reassured him during the scrap and he soon tumbled to the whole harmless performance, and after they settled for the broken glass and had a couple of rounds of drinks, he affably informed them that "dey could enjoy demselfs any olt time dot way."

There were only a few Japanese in Amoy, or rather Kulang Su. We had a pretty fair tiffin at one of the Japanese restaurants, waited upon by two very neat Jap girls who entertained us with *koto* and *samisen*, and to whom we made desperate love between courses, being met and encouraged more than half way. How different are the Japanese from the Chinese! Here everything was exquisitely neat and clean, the two maids from Japan well groomed and as neat as their picturesque surroundings. Nothing presents a prettier picture to my eye than Japs and a Japanese setting. Nothing more lovable than a lissome, buxom, gaily kimonoed little Jap maiden, with her beautiful coiffure, her artlessness, her simplicity, and her desire to please, and then her manner. What a royal welcome one receives.

Tho' only ashore in Kulang Su three times, I yet managed to ingratiate myself in the good graces of a Japanese woman from Osaka. She owned and ran a small hotel near the Chinese quarter. Here she provided me with some fine sake and Japanese chow and at my evident relish and appreciation, was well repaid. This excellent Japanese lady, her name Oganisan, made me very sorry to leave Amoy. Thus it is. Whenever you find a friend you are loath to leave, something intervenes.

On account of frequent fights ashore, the plague, etc., all liberty was stopped, and as sailing orders came only a few days afterward, we had to leave. And I didn't even have a chance to bid Oganisan farewell, a goodbye that meant forever, for there wasn't the remotest chance of ever going [back] to Amoy.[6]

The orders came to proceed to Alaska by the most practical route, so on the afternoon of the sixteenth of May, at two P.M., we [upped] anchor and steamed out of Amoy, running with two boilers, enroute for Yokohama, which would probably be our last view of Japanese ports, much to my sorrow and regret, Japan being almost a home to me, and a veritable fairyland, whose charm would never fade.

In Amoy the Chinese came aboard with curiously and elegantly carved nuts and figures cut from soapstone, much the same as in Shanghai, only the nuts, something on the order of peach stones, were the best I had ever seen in China. The carving was wonderfully minute and well executed. We also had several visitors aboard, bent on sightseeing.

These Chinamen up here are on a par with those in Shanghai. The men [are] tall and fine looking, cleaner and better dressed than their brethren in the south at Hong Kong, Canton, and Macao. They had a different method in propelling sampans, standing up and using both oars and facing the stem of the sampan with the oars crossed, the port oar being grasped by the right hand and vice versa. We had found three Japanese cruisers [at anchor,] and a big French tin can[7] came in the harbor shortly after we arrived. We were followed by a German and then an Englishman, but these last only stopped over a day or so.

It was with a sad heart, I say, that I welcomed the news of our departure from the Station. And above all places, to Alaska! Gloomy, rainy, sleety, dismal Alaska. It wasn't so much in leaving China that the shoe pinched, although I had enjoyed myself immensely amid her quaint and strange scenes. Nor the prospects of leaving the Philippines; that, at least, was a relief, to get away from the rainy season and misery of life aboard ship in that hot clime. But to leave Japan, sunny, dazzling, mystic Japan, with all its beautiful coloring, its picturesque setting, the people, and above all, the girls of that wonder land. Aye, that was the rub, to lose all this, perhaps never to see it again for years, if ever. That was the pity of it, the regret.

However, wherever the "powers that be" will it, there must we go, and we left Amoy, China, I with a secret regret at not being able to say "Sayonara" at least to my Japanese lady friend. But life is composed mostly of the savour of parting, and in particular a sailor's life (would that it was as easy to say farewell as it is to meet).

May 16th 1901, steaming with two boilers (the after battery) intending to steam all the way to Yokohama, making about seventy five revolutions, a speed of about eight knots. Of course, I knew that after a few days out another boiler would be added. I never yet saw it fail in this respect. I knew no matter how well we started off and made out on two boilers, that it would be almost impossible to keep up the pace set at the start, and I was right, for after making excellent speed for about seventy-two hours, the sections began to lag, and the revolutions began to drop off, and in spite of everything that could be done, it was impossible to get any more out of the men or [the] boilers. So another one was added, and then we began to "reel 'em off in fine style. This brought our revolutions up to one hundred and as high as one hundred and six. She steamed freer and responded quickly with three boilers, whereas with only two, it was simply a drag.

I had about as easy a run as a man could well have in the service, there being five water-tenders aboard. We stood watches in rotation, at least four of us did, whilst the other stood oiler's watch in the engine room. This gave us four hours on and twelve off, a pretty fair snap. And the run from Amoy to Yokohama was the easiest time I had yet found aboard the *Concord*, for during the stay in Amoy we had cleaned bilges, and fearfully dirty they were—a perfect sewer of filth, what with Chinese candles, "punk" sticks and odds and ends of Chinese rags that the coolies had dropped in them at Hong Kong during the repairs, etc. It made me sick at the stomach. It took us all day to dredge them out and such a "flushing" they hadn't had for a long time. At least, tho' not as clean as one could wish, still they were fresh and clean from the force of water from the fire main and frequent pumping over board. And at any rate, [they] were no longer a menace to health.

Then beside this, we had painted the entire forward fire room after a good scrub down with fresh water. And after cleaning the furnaces and back connections, and scraping tubes and oiling them with greasy waste, then did the compartment look all right, something it had never [done] for a long time. That finished the better part of my work aboard the *Concord*, for as my time was drawing to a close it wouldn't be necessary for me to do the same work over again, although the compartment was nearly as dirty half an hour after they lit the other boilers.

It pleased us well to know that we were going to stop at Yokohama even tho for only a short time. I had much rather it had been Nagasaki, for there I could have seen Kenzo and Osanawasan, who were never very far from my thoughts. But I was glad to touch at Japan once more, even if only to leave after a short stay. It was the skipper's intention to coal ship immediately and leave as soon as possible.

Just six days from Amoy we sighted the harbor of Yokohama, broad enough to accommodate the navies of the world, vast and open as it is. On the starboard beam, away off in the distance just vaguely discernable thro' the haze, could be seen the snowy crest of Fuji, the Pride of Japan, the Sacred Mountain, pictured in all Japanese art, on print, on *kakemono*,[8] and on lacquer and porcelain. Fujiyama: old and hoary, serene and undisturbed by the seismic upheavals of a thousand years, calmly rearing your crested, snowy head above the clouds. What care you for the petty rumblings and disturbances [that] take place so far below? You are calmly indifferent to it all. No wonder the Japanese worship at your shrine and take great pride by you. You are something to be proud of.

We pulled close up by the breakwater and let go the anchor after being boarded by the health officers, three dapper little fellows with plenty of gold bands upon caps and uniform. The breakwater at Yokohama is a fine piece of engineering, built of massive blocks of concrete or cement. It stretches in a vast arc or semi-circle from one end of the city to the other. Inside are mooring buoys and anchorage for all her shipping. Men-o-war are not allowed inside. It sometimes gets very rough outside this breakwater, but inside all is calm. The rise of the tide doesn't amount to much and the breakwater is very low, sufficiently low to allow the waves at high tide to break over the wall, instead of beating against it and wearing it away.

Of course, we were soon surrounded by the usual fleet of sampans containing compradors, peddlers, washer men, shoe makers, and such. And glad enough was I to see them. I like the Japs. It had been a welcome sight to see their small craft outside the harbor, so different from the sights we had been accustomed to. It had been a year since, almost, that I had left Japan, and although I had never been in Yokohama before, still I almost felt as if I were in a home port.

After "pipe down" and at "mess gear" the "perambulating merchants" were allowed aboard, bringing their silks and curios of all descriptions, converting the *Concord* from forecastle to poop into a bazaar much the same as the *New Orleans* in Nagasaki. They did very little business, however, as the crew were short of money. "How long were we going to stay, etc." were eagerly fired at us from all sides. They like

Wilson (second row, seated, center) in a group photo, presumably of an engineering division of a ship on which he served. The presence of three warrant officers, including a commissioned chief warrant machinist (second from right, front row), suggests this probably was a major fleet unit, probably a battleship. Courtesy Muriel Wilson MacFall.

Amoy, China, & Yokohama

to get hold of an American man-o-war. When told only a couple of days, just long enough to coal, their faces fell and they shook their heads dubiously. Business was dull with them, no doubt, for we were the only man-o-war present, excepting one Frenchman, the *Guichen,* a large four funneler.[9] Yokohama was indeed bare of ships.

~ ~ ~

Money was served out to us the next day, to allow us to purchase "sea stores" for the Alaskan trip, and liberty [was] given and I was one of the first to take advantage of it. Yokohama has long been a name to conjure with. The principal sea port of Japan, it is the best known port in Japan and whenever Japan is mentioned, the first question is, "Were you in Yokohama?"

We took a sampan and were landed at the French *hatoba* [wharf] and were assailed by the usual "Rickshaw! Rickshaw!" on every hand. I selected a big, tall intellectual looking fellow for a "ricky" by the name of Yasu, and was soon bowling along thro' the level streets of Yokohama. It was a rainy, drizzly day, but that doesn't damp[en] Jack's spirits by any means, so I was just as contented as tho' the sun shone brightly. I felt at home. The same fragile, low Japanese houses lined the streets on either side. The same signs. The same quaint interiors, open to the passers' gaze. The same shops and, best of all, the dainty, lissome, graceful girls and women tripping along on every side, happy and smiling. Nothing like this in China, thought I. Nothing half so artistic and beautiful to appeal to the senses, conveying entire satisfaction. The landscape [was] only marred by the miserable European structures, business places that occasionally cropped up.

I whirled thro' the Public Garden. It wasn't half as, nay, one thousandth part as cultivated as Central Park. In fact, it couldn't be compared at all. But the trees are oddly shaped, dwarfed. The paths are differently laid out. The houses under the trees are all distinctively Japanese. And there's the charm, infinitely more, greater to my taste than a hundred mathematically, geometrically laid out Central Parks, with all their garish display of money. The Japanese park [was] a perfect setting for the artistic, be-kimonoed figures that flitted here and there along its walks.

There isn't much in these parks, but they are vastly artistic. There isn't much in the furnishing of a Japanese room, with its clean, white mats, springy and soft and elastic to the foot; its polished natural wood hearth and door sills with the sliding paper paneled screens or doors; its chest of camphor wood that occupies one corner; the cunningly devised chest of drawers; the brazier of charcoal that occupies the hearth; the cunning little table, highly lacquered, with the inevitable small tea-pot; the *kakemonos,* or picture[s], upon the wall, in front of which stands upon a small polished stand a vase of curious workmanship with either a dragon or some scene of Japanese life painted upon it, filled with chrysanthemum of all colors, or a spray of cherry blossoms, forming a bright bit of color, the one bright bit, I may say, in the entire room. The soft subdued light falling thru the paper windows bring[s] out the highlights upon table and vase, causing the highly polished surfaces to glow like gem[s], and light up the flowers of the vase, transforming them into a vivid splash of color, a pronounced note in harmony with the rest.

There isn't much, I say, in all this. But not all the infernal hair cloth atrocities and begilded onyx monstrosities and dust catching lace hangings of a modern parlor or drawing room at home can be compared to it. At least I think so, humble indeed tho' my opinion may be. And when, from secret recesses, the cups and tea things, the bowls are brought forth, the highly polished brass and clean white wood of the rice bowl and chopsticks, and all the paraphernalia and material of a meal cooked over the brazier of live charcoal, [it] transform[s] what was and is a most artistic room into a practical living room. Then, I say, the Japs are away ahead of us, for everything they have is designed as much for beauty as for use. But I'll be durned if some of the things purchased at the large department stores are either useful or ornamental, that's wot!

As Yasu whirled me along, many signs greeted my gaze. These signs are very familiar to the bluejacket in Japan. In fact, you find them on every side. They were small public houses, such as "Yokohama House, kept by Charley"; "Vancouver House by Tome, fine beers and wines sold here"; "The Glasgow House"; "The Light House"; and hundreds of others. I visited nearly all of them, taking a glass of beer or lemonade as my thirst desired. In every one, I was greeted effusively by two or three good looking Nippon lassies, who seemed completely overjoyed to see me. In fact, greeted me as if I was an old acquaintance. This suited me to a dot, and I made love indiscriminately and to my heart's content, sitting down with a lovely bunch of Nippon femininity upon each knee, as much as I could comfortably support at any one time.

Beside being so very polite, they are very accommodating and will deny you nothing. This costs lots of money. In fact, with hardly an effort, one can spend his month's pay in two or three liberties ashore. But one roams around in order to take in all the sights and I soon grew tired of small Japanese "pubs," and calling Yasu, I was soon spinning along narrow streets lined with shops of every description.

The day was very unpleasant, a drizzly rain pouring down sufficiently to wet one to the skin before becoming aware of the fact. But from my coign of vantage safely and snugly ensconced in Yasu's jinricksha, covered with oilcloth, I could look out upon the muddy byways and the interesting life teeming all around me. Just ahead of me plodded along "three little maids from school," women of the coolie class, each carrying a pair of buckets filled with water, a load that no other women in the world could carry so sturdily and with so much contentment; buxom, sturdily built *onaga*s, cheerful, and ready to laugh at the slightest provocation. Thro' *Bentou dori*, one of the business streets where you can obtain curios of all kinds from ivory work to silk handkerchiefs and chopsticks, and on out to the Yoshiwara (of course).

There are miles of streets in the Yoshiwara of Yokohama. But the cage houses have their goods shielded from view, having a cloth screen stretching in front of the bars, and unless you go inside the doorway, the inmates are shielded from sight.

Amoy, China, & Yokohama

Perhaps the finest house in Yokohama is No. 9, new No. 9, Nectarine's. This is a most imposing structure, and a glimpse inside shows you the highly polished floor with potted plants arranged artistically thro' out the entire place. The inmates of this house are especially selected for their beauty. If a fine setting can do anything to enhance their liveliness, they surely have it here at Nectarine's. These girls have been repeatedly pictured in photograph and print and Nectarine's is known to all the traveling public in Japan.

To all those that go down to the sea in ships and consider Yokohama one of the best ports in the Far East, men in uniform are debarred from the delights of Nectarine's, but many of us shift in[to] civilians, and go anywhere. For my part, I consider Nectarine's no better than the most of the other houses, the Hana house, or No. 21 or 23. The setting is better, that is all. The girls are the same. Divest them of paint and rice powder and silken kimonos—they are simply on a par with their coolie sisters that toil all day in the rice field. They are all the daughters of poor people who need the money and are not averse to selling their own flesh and blood when the procurer comes along seeking new recruits. One hundred dollars is a fair price. From this, on up to about six hundred, will be paid for a number one girl. Some of the girls like the life; others do not. Perhaps they have a poor lover who is unable to buy them out, and thus sees his loved sweetheart ruthlessly torn from his side. There must be tearful partings, for after all, these girls have their affections that are just as pure, and just as strong, as any that may be entertained by their fortunate Western sisters. Poor girls! Let it be known, however, that all Japanese parents are not the same, no matter how poor some are. They will not part with their daughters under any consideration. There are classes in Japan among the educated where morals attain as high a percentage as anywhere else in the world. But of these, I know little. I am only writing of what I know. A bluejacket can't hobnob with nobility, [but] with the respectable middle classes that I have been thrown in contact with, I know they have morals, and morals stronger perhaps than the same strata have at home.

A married Japanese lady has plenty of latitude, and it isn't one case in a thousand that she will go beyond that latitude. Possibly they are afraid. But no matter what the motive, it is a well known fact. It is so easy for the husband to divorce them that they have a horror of the least breath of suspicion. They haven't any voice at all in that matter. They are not allowed to lodge a complaint of any kind against their "master." Knowing that they have no show, they are "straight" and can be trusted anywhere and under any condition.

I liked Yokohama, but I like Nagasaki better, perhaps from tender recollections of it. Nagasaki seemed like a second home to me; Yokohama only an incident. I always remembered Kenzo, the big rambling house upon the hill, and Sunawasan, the prettiest of them all, and the best. And I wished very often to be back there again. I knew they were my friends in the best sense of the word.

And another thing: I went broke in Yokohama. We were going to get under way for Unalaska immediately, just going to stop in Yoky long enough to coal ship and take on stores, and then away once more on the long three-thousand mile run. I allowed myself to be persuaded, and having some money left over from Amoy, I only drew enough for mess money when we were allowed to put down for monthly money, which we did on the day of our arrival in Yokohama. That will be amply sufficient, thought I. We are only going to stay about three days; no use whatever drawing any large amount of Japanese money and then have difficulty in changing it back into gold. But I reckoned without my host.

The new order changing the commanders revoked the former order, and another thing: I was detailed to tally coal ashore, along with some others, and that completely demoralized me.[10] Thinking that we were going to put to sea as soon as coaled, I started to get rid of my yens very rapidly, with the result that I was soon broke. We had ample time to spell each other, and whilst one would tally, the rest would be away somewhere. This coaling demoralized us all completely.

I went aboard that night and asked to be allowed to go ashore again. Two of us were granted permission, and hailing a sampan, we soon shoved off, both of us being a little befuddled from our deep potations ashore, but completely overjoyed at the prospects of a good old time for the night. Beside, we were told to report at the place of coaling instead of the ship. This was another cause of joy. In fact, we were so overjoyed, what with [the] booze we had aboard and the liberty we were having, that somehow I became overbalanced and fell from the sampan into the cold water. This I didn't enjoy very much, as it took me unawares, and I came to the surface a bit sobered, and soon clambered aboard. However, we had a good laugh over it. That wasn't anything. Clothes would soon dry. We soon jumped in a ricksha and in half an hour I was clothed in a kimono, my own clothes drying, and sitting down enjoying a Japanese "chow" with its accompanying sake, rice as only the Japs can boil it, with delicately browned fish laid over the top, bits of bamboo shoots, onions, and beef diced up in a sort of hash, *koko,* a kind of pickled radish (radishes in Japan are about four feet in length), fresh young cucumbers, and numerous soft boiled eggs, bits of dried fish, etc., all of which I enjoyed heartily after my cold bath.

This was no. 23 Yoshiwari. It was in this house a few days later that I noticed an old Japanese *Okamisan,* evidently from the country, who was waiting for someone. Upon inquiry, I was told that her daughter was going to leave the Yoshiwari, having worked her time out. So I waited around, inviting the old lady to take something, which she did: a glass of port, thanking me with innumerable bobs of the head. Presently, the daughter came down dressed for the street, devoid of paint and all the insignia of her office. Gone was the beautifully flowered and gold embroidered kimono. But she looked immensely better clothed as she was, in street costume. I had seen her often. She was one of the plainer sisters, but with the light of her emancipation shining upon her face she was no longer plain. She was radiant at the prospect of her release, for once released, they cannot be resold into the Yoshiwari again. She was half sorry at leaving her old friends and delighted at the prospect of freedom. In her hand she clutched the bit of paper, her passport from her gilded prison.

Amoy, China, & Yokohama

"What, *dyo*," I said. "All finish here? You make a finish, go home?"

"Yes, *dyo*. Me make a finish. No more Yoshiwari. My go home with Momysan," pointing to the old lady who was all smiles and courtesies.

"I s'pose now you get married, hab old sweetheart. He at house yourself?" said I.

"Yes. I very glad I feenish. I stay in dis house five year to make one hundred dollars. You see, I very plain face. Suppose I have nicee face. I go long go. Clothes, kimono, everyting, plenty money cost. Long time I stay."

"But its all over no[w], *dyo*. You wait long time, but everything comes all right, no matter how long you wait. Now you will be very happy. Plenty other girls have to stay. Look, see."

The other girls were regarding her with mingled feelings of regret at losing their old shipmate, and regret at their inability to go, too.

A couple of salt tears actually rolled down the cheeks of the girl with the plain face as she looked at her companions and responded to their well wishes. In fact, they were all smiling at her with the smile that is akin to tears.

"*Sayonara, dyo*. Just now you no have plain face. Just now you have very handsome face. You very good girl. Bimeby you see your sweetheart at home," I said, feelingly. I thoroughly sympathized with her.

"Momysan live at Kamakura. You savvy Kamakura? *Daibutsu* bid there. I always live there."

"Yes! Yes! I know *Daibutsu*. Kamakura about thirty miles from Yokohama." It is there they have the big bronze statue of Buddha.

I opened up a bottle of wine for the occasion, and wished her good luck. No longer the plain faced girl (or as the Japs call it, the frying pan face), but the poor little Japanese *joro*[11] with the glorified face, glorified at the dawn of the new life.

"Good luck and *Sayonara, dyo*,"[12] I said, shaking her by the hand.

"*Sayonara dyo*," she repeated, bowing to the floor. "Some day you come to Kamakura and see *Daibutsu!* 'Member, I live there."

"I no forget, Takesan," I replied.

And with many "*Sayonaras*" from her girl friends and the household, Otakesan passed out into the new life, out of the Yoshiwari cage, no longer a *joro*, an inmate of the Yoshiwari, but a respectable girl, perhaps soon to be married to some worthy mate. Thro no fault of her own, she was sold to this life, and having no volition of her own in the matter, she was blameless, and thus the world (her world of Japan) holds her. There is no stain of her past attached to her. She can and will take her place in the station of society to which she always belonged, as respected as the best of them.

This was in No. 23 Yoshiwara. It was in this house the same night I fell overboard and just after I had finished the aforesaid Nippon "chow" and had repaired to the bar with that sense of utter satisfaction that comes from duty well performed at the table, and comfortably clothed in kimono and slippers, and just helping myself to a good glass of Port that I heard a terrific uproar and bubbub.

A Sailor's Log

In flew the lady I had for the occasion, and with a great many gestures and Pidgin English, [she] acquainted me with the fact that a sailor had taken possession of my bed (our bed); in fact, was in entire possession of the room and refused to move, arbitrate, or otherwise listen to reason. "What?" I roared. I felt none the worse for my bath, and rather a bit to the good from my libations. "Show me the infernal ——."

Down I dashed, *dyo* a good second. Sure enough, stretched out on the bed, ostensibly taking a good nap, lay French Johnnie Crapeau. "Must be plenty more around," I thought; "however, I'll get this fellow at any rate. One American can lick two Frenchmen any old time."

I pounced upon him and before the sleepy and tired Frenchy knew what [had] happened, he was out of the room, and I was dealing out as many wallops as I could manage upon different parts of his anatomy, he all the time roaring lustily. Thinks I, "This is a cinch. I never had anything quite so much my way before. Holy smoke, but this is easy, just the same as punching a bag." I had him in the air all the time, could land [punches] where and when I pleased. My lady friend all the time egging me on. "This is when you shine, old boy," I thought rapidly to myself. "This is dead——." Just then an earthquake so common in Japan hit me. The enemy had flanked me. There was a dozen reinforcements. I was in it. It put me in mind of association football. I was the ball. I was kicked about a hundred times in about a moment. There was an uproar all about me. The girls of the house ran out screaming. My lady friend called at the top of her lungs for my friends. When they arrived it became a mix up. The police came rushing up. The Japs flocked out of the other houses to get a whack at the Frenchmen, whom they hate. As soon as the police came in, the Frenchmen tried to get out. They were stoned by the mob outside.

In about two minutes, I was alone with the girl, or rather girls, trying to hide me. The room in[to] which they hustled me was devoid of furniture. Someone had thrust a short bar of iron in my hand during the fracas. Just as I reached the room, the panel was raised up and a Frenchman crawled thro. I made for him with the iron bar, thinking that more were coming thro'. I was just about to fetch him a stout thwack across his crown when he held up his hands in token of submission. His face was full of blood. They had put him thro' the mill outside. Just then a policeman came in and took possession of him. He also took my name, but that was all. I wasn't arrested, luckily. Seven of the Frenchmen were arrested. They got much the worst of it. But Great Gertt, how sore I was! They hadn't reached my face, but they had used the *sarate* with pretty good effect upon my body. I was sore for a week after, but I came up smiling. That's the second mix up I had been in without any volition of my own. I hadn't sought either. If I had, I would have been arrested that night.

~~~

An afternoon in Tokio.[13] Tokio is a name to conjure with. What visions of the East it brings before the mind's eye! When anyone mentions Japan, naturally the next question to be asked [is], "have you been in Tokio?" From Yokohama to Tokyo by rail is about [a] fifty minute ride. The fare, second class, for the round trip is exactly 94 *sen*, or forty seven cents, United States coin. "Yokohama to Shinbashi. Shinbashi to Yokohama." Very well indeed do I remember that trip. I had to sell a gold ring I [had] purchased in Kure to make the trip. I was determined to see Tokyo at any price. And I got the chance on the last liberty I made, about two weeks after the time set for leaving Yokohama. We were all broke aboard the little "tin pot," the *Concord*, and money wasn't to be borrowed at fifty per cent. "Fifteen for ten" was offered, but there wasn't actually any money aboard.

Anyway, I sold the ring and I saw Tokyo, the largest city in the Sunland. At the railroad station [in Yokohama] I was regarded curiously by the Japanese, men, women and children who were wondering what was the reason I was traveling by rail. However, I puffed away indifferently at my cigarette. One gets used to this sort of thing in time, and yet as indifferently as I tried to appear, none of the surroundings escaped me. It was as novel a waiting room as one could wish to see in their travels. I noticed that nearly all the Japs purchased third-class tickets. Truly, they are an economical race, no matter how well dressed they were, and they all looked prosperous and well to do. But then, all the race looks that, no matter how poor. From the highest to the lowest, their dress and appearance are nearly always alike. The kimono of Yasu the jinricksha man is as neat and as rich and as well appearing as that of Matsu the banker. There may be more jewelry in sight on the banker, a gold watch and heavy chain, and seals wound in the folds of Matsu's *obi*, and a heavy seal ring of purest gold upon his finger, but that is about all the difference. The purchasers of the third class tickets at the railroad station at Yokohama would compare favorably with the well to do middle classes of any nationality.

However, with a rush and rattle and roar, the miniature train pulled in from Tokyo. The engines (American type) were shunted or switched to the other end of the train, and the passengers for Tokyo rushed aboard as soon as the passengers for Yokohama were all out. I selected an American coach in preference to the English style. Very comfortably arranged it was, with its ample seating accommodation. There were only a few respectable looking Japanese occupying this car, and they looked at me with well-bred curiosity. Evidently it was an unusual sight to see American bluejackets up that way.

All being aboard, the conductor sounded his whistle and the train moved out, slowly at first, but steadily gaining in momentum as we reached the open country. But at any time there wasn't any record breaking speed. We stopped at several stations, one only [of] which I remember, that was called Kawasaki. The road has a good road-bed, good iron bridges of American manufacture. It winds thro' a lovely country, past rice field after rice field with men and women working up to the knees in mud and water, past prosperous looking farm-houses half hidden by clumps of trees, the inhabitants of which rush to the doors and window[s] to watch the train as it glides swiftly by. The picturesque tillers of the soil drop all work until the train glides past. Some parts of this country reminded me very much of Kure and its surrounding scenery. It is a veritable fairyland, one whose charm will never fade.

As the train puffs up a steep little grade, over a bridge and around an abrupt curve, the beautiful bay of Yeddo [Tokyo] bursts in full view. We skirt its borders from there on until the train pulls in at the terminus at Shinbashi. Across the bright expanse of clear water dotted with sail and puffing tugs with their heavy tow of material that is being used in the construction of many forts that are being built, can be distinguished on a clear day white-headed, aged Fujiyama, miles away.

The view across the bay is alone worth the trip. Yeddo bay is a beautiful sheet of water. This is historical country all about. I drank my fill of the panorama spread before me. I won't be able to see it again. It will be dark when I make the return trip. All too soon the train came to a full stop and we jump[ed] out and hurr[ied] up the long train shed that is just like any ordinary station in a medium sized town in the States, out thro' the commodious station. I followed the clattering crowd of Japs, gazed at curiously by the incoming passengers with many a good humored smile and the whispered, "American" to one another in the most friendly way in the world. Handing my ticket to the man at the gate, he tore [off] the Tokyo coupon and handed me back the other half.

Outside, I was besieged by the usual ubiquitous rickshaw men. In justice to Tokyo, I must say they are not as voracious as the average run of them are, but being a bluejacket, I was the target as usual. I selected one who spoke a little English, of which accomplishment he was abnormally proud, and sought every occasion to air his knowledge. I made known to him my wishes, that as I didn't have too much time, I wanted to see the principal points of interest. And by all means, he was to take me as near the Mikado's palace as was permitted, all of which he savvied with many smiles and bobs of the head, and off we started.

The city proper of Tokyo must have been on the other side of the bridge [from] Shinbashi, that side on which the railroad station was situated, for right in front of the railroad station was a large canal. This was spanned by several bridges, all of European construction. Over the bridge nearest to the railroad station we sped, and I found myself in one of Tokyo's main streets. Wide! I have never saw such wide thoroughfares anywhere, and this is not true of one or two streets, but of every street. All along the main thoroughfare are tram-cars like the bob tail car of the cities in the States, drawn by the same identical weary, sprung, and sprained old hat-racks of horses, with their conductors and drivers in uniforms. As I passed by in the rickshaw, the people in the cars looked at me and then called their neighbors' attention. The people looked at me with interest from the dark recesses of their little shops. A whole family would pause and gaze at the stranger, with *hashi*, or chopsticks, poised in air as they were at their evening meal. "Bluejackets very seldom get up here," I thought. Even the women drawing their water in wooden pails and gossiping good-naturedly would stop for an instant and laugh and chatter in the manner of the sex. Passing ricksha men without any fare would exchange a few words with my man and smile, I suppose telling him he had a good thing, and to soak me for at least a yen, large pay for an afternoon's work in the shafts.

A visitor in a Japanese city for the first time no doubt is surprised at the number of shops, the greater majority of them very small, but all well stocked. They are nearly all alike in that there is no counter. The purchaser merely comes in and sits down upon the raised straw matted floor, and goods are reached close to hand for their inspection in the most courteous manner in the world. A good Japanese wife dearly loves to haggle over the price of a bit of silk for sash, *obi* and kimono, or an ornament for the hair, or in the provision stores, over the price of any culinary commodity. The small stores with their big display of fresh vegetables, their grain, fish and meat displays would tempt the appetite of a dyspeptic. The Japanese are very fond of dried fish. I saw these dealers on every hand, with their wares spread to the best advantage. The butchers in the meat stores play a veritable tune with their knives as they chop the beef so as to render it small enough to be eaten by chopsticks.

Here in Tokio everything is distinctly Japanese. The only incongruous sight, the small tram-cars. The streets and shops fairly teem with humanity. There is an utter lack of small pubs as in Yokohama, and other seaport towns. But Tokyo has its beer-halls where nothing else is sold, no other drink of any kind, but simply beer, of a Japanese brew that is very wholesome. I was surprised at the small price asked for a large schooner—cheap for beer in Japan: twelve cents or sen (six cents); for a smaller glass, six sen or (three cents). In America you pay a nickel whether the glass is large or small.

My ricky proposed taking me to see a Shinto temple and we went there, but found the entrance gate to the grounds closed. But from the exterior view, the place was very old. We went past on our way to the palace grounds, a long, low barrack-like building with many windows. This building was a sort of tenement house where many hundred Japanese families lived years ago, but was now used as a barracks by the Mikado's soldiers.

But the wideness of the streets caused more wonderment on my part than anything else. In fact, they looked more like broad driveways such as Riverside drive, and the entrances to Prospect Park, Brooklyn. Especially was this so as one approached the Mikado's palace, broad boulevards converging from all directions. I had an opportunity to ascend the stone steps of a steep hill, an eminence from whose heights I could see the whole of Tokyo stretched out beneath me, so my ricky assured me. But I smilingly objected. The evening was coming on and I told him I had no time. We proceeded on our way. John was beginning to perspire from his run and I thought I was perhaps running him too hard. But I found out he was as hard and tough as a band of wire.

We were on the broad avenues leading up to the palace grounds. John pointed out the naval college, the war college, and in the distance the army building, all of the European style of architecture peculiar to the East: brick with white trimmings. The houses of Parliament are the same. The Prime Minister's house and [those of] all other high officials are of the European style, surrounded by large grounds. The Russian Legation is worthy of the country it represents, as were all the other Legations. But when I asked John to point me out the American Legation, he smiled and shook his head deprecatingly. "Ver small," and I found it to be a fact. It was very small and insignificant compared with the others. But we are an unassuming race, I reflected, and a democratic one, and it isn't for a Republic to have the ostentation and splendor of an empire or a monarchy. But from John's dubious shake of the head (I ascertained afterwards he name was Nomi) the American Legation wasn't considered imposing and of account enough to be classed in his repertoire of Tokyo's sights. So I only contented myself with replying, "Legation very small, John. But America itself very big and very good friends to Japan," at which he nodded his approval very energetically. I didn't get to see the [Matthew Calbraith] Perry Memorial that was to be unveiled, from all accounts, upon the Fourth of July. In fact, at the time it entirely escaped my mind.

We passed a group of Japanese damsels who were out for an afternoon walk. They laughed and giggled and waved their hands as soon as they caught a glimpse of myself in the rickshaw. In fact, this has been my experience all thro' the Empire, not only myself, but any other American. This they kept up until I was out of sight and they derived a great deal of amusement from it. Poor little maids, they don't carry on thus with their own masculine kind, who would quickly rebuff them. Your Japanese never lets anything detract from his sternness and dignity where his women kind are concerned, and he would look with horror upon the very idea of treating the opposite sex with equality. But they, despite the thousands of years of custom, are still women with all the little wiles and coquetries so dear to the feminine heart from Le Grande Dame down to the lowliest Suvash squaw.

We drew up to a short bridge that was originally a drawbridge, crossing as it did, a moat. We were upon the Mikado's grounds. A high, strong wall surrounded a vast park. Over the bridge and thro' the first gate we went, a heavy, arched gateway of the Medieval age. Massive doors studded and bound with iron, mighty hinges and locks. It was almost impregnable to assault by men at arms of a bygone age. But there were two more gates after this in an inner wall, and more moats. Just over the top of the massive wall I could catch a glimpse of the old palace. It wasn't very ostentatious. The buildings were long and rambling, hardly a fit abode for an Emperor, but the massive doors, the moats, and the well regulated grounds gave the impression of royalty. The palace sits well above the surrounding park. A sloping terrace, well sodded, gently inclines down to the level. The whole scene is one that gives the impression of quiet strength. There are more pretentious private palaces in America. But as I gazed, a feeling of reverence come over me, not at being near royalty's abode, but the feeling that comes over one that views the work of a bygone age. Such a feeling I experienced as I viewed Fujiyama. They both belonged to a remote period. I gazed and was satisfied. I had seen the Mikado's palace. And thus was the fairy dream of boyhood's day realized at last.

The day that had hitherto been bright and sparkling, had clouded and a muzzling rain set in. Nomi recalled me from the past by pulling up the hood of the rickshaw and drawing the apron across the front, looking at me enquiringly while he did so. "Go to the Yoshiwari, Nomi." I wanted to take a look at the famous houses of Tokyo, from which the Government derives a good bit of its taxes, a real source of revenue that assists Japan to maintain her vast military and naval establishment.

If I had doubted the size of Tokyo, this long ride thro' the drizzle of that June day would have dispelled it. It was dusk when we started from the palace grounds, about half-past five, and it took Nomi with his ricksha lope nearly three hours to make the distance. From broad lighted thoroughfare to darkened alley and side street he dashed, never slacking speed until he came in thro' the Yoshiwari gates, and I motioned him to stop at a small wine shop where we got hold of a pretty good bottle of Port, and rested until the birds made their appearance in the cages, which took place at eight P.M.[14] Of course, while we were in the shop a crowd of curious Japanese came in, so that the small place was crowded. They sized me up with the most child-like and unabashed curiosity in the world, very good naturedly making remarks about my uniform and nationality, Nomi all the time imparting information about my good qualities, using his knowledge of English with a lordly air. It was all amusing to them, and didn't annoy me.

But the Tokyo people don't seem to savvy English as much as in other parts of Japan. I only heard one express themselves to me in my own language, with the exception of Nomi, and that was a rather homely *joro* thro' the bars of her cage. Nomi and myself finished the bottle of Port and we started out to take in the sights of the great Tokyo yoshiwari, he pulling me slowly along. Yokohama, Nagasaki, Kobe and all other cities in Japan have their Yoshiwaries, but none that rivals in size, splendor and magnificence that of Tokyo. The Yoshiwari set apart in all Japanese towns and cities are the best built and have the most imposing houses, some of them seven or eight stories in height, having as high as a hundred girls. Nomi rolled me along slowly in his ricksha [past] numberless small tea houses. The girls in these small places had served out their time in the Yoshiwari proper and were content to work for their living in this no doubt more congenial occupation, that of serving tea and refreshments to their customers, as well as entertaining them with *samizen* and *koto*. Most of them are geisha girls. Almost the first house we passed was the most imposing of the whole lot. It was the Tokyo rival of Nectarine's in Yokohama. As Nomi explained to me, "Very fine house. All same No. 9 Yokohama."

It was more imposing than Nectarine's, with its wide entrance and hallway. In the cage were grouped about seventy girls clad in sumptuous kimono of the most gorgeous hues. Instead of sitting in a circle at the back of the cage, they were grouped in bevies of three or four, smoking their queer little pipes and touching up their lips with the vermilion to make them more beautiful. The daub they use on the lower lip is of the most uncompromising, glaring red. Some even use black. Others were putting fascinating touches to eyebrows already most artistically penciled. Others used the puff applying rouge and rice powder in the most liberal manner until the faces were almost as brilliant in hue as the kimonos they wore. Among so many rivals, the *joro* has to enhance her charms so as to outshine them, or else her chances of paying her way out are very remote. Behind all these motionless faces, immobile in their thick layer of paint though they seem, their thoughts are perhaps far away from the glitter of their golden cage, to a sweetheart, a father, mother and brother left behind in some remote secluded village. Others, perhaps, are congratulating themselves in escaping the drudgery of the rice field. Where else would they be able to have such lovely silken robes, such a gorgeous *obi* with its arabesques and butterflies worked in with exquisite skill, such attendance, such luxury, and all they have to do is to render themselves agreeable, and have a fair modicum of good looks. Perhaps to some it brings contentment. To others it is a hell. After all, it is a prison, a gilded one, but a prison nevertheless.

Ocheosan being a mercenary, pleasure loving, heartless little Nippon girl with no more feeling as far as the heart is concerned than is depicted in her expressionless, doll-like painted face, likes the life. She can curl up during the day in the most luxurious couch and *meiro*[15] to her heart's content. She is a little animal, that is all. But Ohanasan wears her heart away behind these bars, longing for her freedom. She hates the life with an unutterable loathing for [it] separates her from her own true lover. ("My swee-a heart" she will call him. Perhaps, if you are a lucky man in sympathy with her, she will confide her troubles to you with the most child-like trust. All Nippon *onaga*s are children.) Moto, an humble worker in bronze, who she confides loves her as dearly as she loves him, and is striving with all his might to make enough yen to purchase her freedom and then marry her and make her the mistress of his curious little shop that is also home for them. It may be a matter of a few years, but waiting is made easier by the visits of Moto, who came regularly from a remote village to visit her. Each visit leaves her a little tearful, but the tears are not of sorrow, for each visit brings her nearer the goal. She will not have the luxuries of the Yoshiwari then, but hard work, as all Nippon wives have. But she will be perfectly happy. You see, there are always two sides, at least, to a question.

We passed slowly cage after cage, with its beautiful exhibits, its bewildering array of loveliness, the glitter of gold and brocade, the rich golden lacquer scroll work of Japanese artists, all set forth with a lavish hand to attract the passing crowd. Gorgeous wasn't any word for it. Imagine the pageantry of a three ring circus parade with its golden trappings as a background, with the addition of a spectacular performance, then you have a slight idea of the Tokyo Yoshiwara.[16] One of the most striking cage effects was the costuming of about fifty girls, all clad in black kimono with white sashes, a striking contrast to the red carpet and red silken hangings. The Japanese are masters at grouping and produce brilliant harmonies of color.

Amoy, China, & Yokohama

The houses seemed to be endless. Some were small, with only two or three girls, especially in the side streets. Every house has its crier behind a little wicket, not unlike a ticket office. From this point he will hail you if he knows any English. During intervals, he will cry out the excellence of the particular merchandise of his house, depicting in flowing Japanese the charms of his [number] one or [number] two girl. He is very persistent and very polite. He wants your custom.

Every time I would stop at some window, the girls would chatter and giggle. There would be a great fluttering of fans, many questions would be fired at Nomi, who would interpret. There would be a hundred eyes cast in my direction, the battery of which I was well able to bear up under. I couldn't linger long however, and soon passed by with a "*Sayonara*," which would be repeated by fifty sweet voices with one accord. In one of the poorer houses, a young Nippon maid of about fifteen had great fun with me. She was close up to the bar, her and another older girl somewhat isolated from the rest. Nomi stopped and the young rascal reached out her pipe, giving me a whiff, seeming to derive great amusement when I puffed it two or three times then knocked the contents from the bowl in the most approved Japanese style, returning it with a profound bow. "*O ha ne aragata, musme.*"[17] That's about all the Japanese I knew, at the same time passing her in a pack of cigarettes. She streaked my phisog with a touch of vermilion, at which they all shrieked with laughter. I let her enjoy herself for about five minutes and then had to leave. [She was a] light hearted child, too young to experience anything but the joy of living.

It was getting late. The night was dark and the drizzle had settled into a steady rain. I had done the Yoshiwara pretty thoroughly and was anxious to get back to the railroad station. Nomi started off. Just as we turned the corner in front of one of the most elaborate windows were three European women of middle age, sightseeing, looking at women's conditions in Japan with a disapproving eye; three old tabbies, very severe looking, and no doubt of very severe and stern virtue. "Ugh!" I thought. What a contrast! They were out of place in all this light and glare. A blot. The *joro*s were blinking at them with an air of disdain. One of the old tabbies was gazing thro' a lorgnette at the bevy of loveliness with the air of looking at many insects. Quite superior, no doubt. Hm!

Clear of the Yoshiwarie, Nomi settled down to his work and I threw myself back comfortably with a lighted cigar. Tokyo was almost asleep. It was only about half past nine. A few book shops were open, but there were no saloons. Now and then a sake shop. Business was at a standstill. The ride back seem[ed] very long. Cutting off corners by running thro' narrow, dark side streets to save time tho' Nomi did, yet it was half past ten when he at last reached the station. Having a few moments to spare, I went thro' the bazaar that is just across the bridge from the station. This was on the same plan as the one in Nagasaki, only not quite as large. The owners of the stalls were closing up business for the night. I walked thro' the entire maze and purchased a few small articles: a small ink slab and a few brushes, when glancing at my watch I found it was time to catch the train if I wanted to get back to Yokohama that night. "All finish now, Nomi. Catch train."

And I was just in time, for the few passengers were scurrying thro' the gates. Handing Nomi a yen and fifty *sen*, I hurried after them and was just passing thro' when someone touched me on the shoulder. It was Nomi. Like the usual ricky, he wanted more. Not caring to haggle, which he well knew, I tossed him two ten *sen* silver pieces, at which he bowed and thanked me repeatedly. *"Arigato! Arigato!"*[18] That was enough to keep him for a week.

Only a few passengers occupied the coach on the return trip. An English chief petty officer from the *Glory*,[19] who had made a flying trip to Tokyo, like myself, occupied one corner. A respectable old Japanese gentleman and wife, the latter curled her feet under her and looked out thru the window where she dozed off. A couple of Japs in European clothes and myself were all the occupants. I stretched out at full length on the seat and dozed away until Yokohama was reached. I had seen Tokyo. I had seen the Mikado's palace. I had seen the Yoshiwari, and I had left Tokyo asleep and dreaming. But I found Yokohama awake. The shops were all open as yet. The little pubs were open. And everything looked bright and cheerful within. I went to my particular one, and stayed there for the night, lingering long over a good, warm, substantial repast and a bottle of Port, and entertainment by a couple of strolling tumblers and a woman *Kinno* player.[20] Yokohama is full of these boys, Japanese contortionists, and in every saloon where they catch a glimpse of a bluejacket, they are sure of a few *sen*. So, with the supper, the cold bottle and the laughter of the *okamisan* and the two Japanese bar-maids at my descriptions of Tokyo, or as they had it, Yeddo, I contrived to pass a pleasant evening, my last in Japan.

As I write this log, there stands upon the table at which I am sitting a miniature tree, a good specimen of the Japanese art of dwarfing trees. I think it is a beech. The leaves are green and tender. The trunk and boughs are twisted and gnarled. It has all the appearance of age. It is old. In the same jar is also a young pine putting forth its tiny needles undisturbed by its larger neighbor. It is a constant reminder of Japan. Japan the grotesque; Japan that in its pristine state differs from any other nationality upon the globe. I like to look at it. It is a living reminder of the country and people, a people that do and see things different[ly] from any other. But it needs nothing for remembrance. Even if Fate ordains that I shall not see it any more, the memory of some of the happiest moments of my life will always remain as green as the leaves of the little, old silver beech before me. Some time we will come again. Until then, Land of the Rising Sun, *Sayonara*.

Amoy, China, & Yokohama

CHAPTER ELEVEN

~

Homeward Bound

Having taken aboard the balance of the coal, some in bags on the deck and a load in the fire room, and having gotten our sea-stores all aboard, spuds, onions, flour, poultry, etc., we broke the "Homeward Bound Pennant" the tenth of June [1901]. We were, tho', not exactly homeward bound direct, still [we were] leaving the Asiatic Station for our own waters. The *Guichen*'s band and the English battleship *Glory*'s burst into "Yankee Doodle" as we steamed from the harbor of Yokohama on our three thousand mile run to Unalaska. As usual, I was below on watch. We steamed under two boilers and after a couple of days made sail.[1] This helped us insomuch that it eased the strain upon the propellers.

It grew cooler and cooler, the same monotonous, sullen sea and sky, fogs and rain, with here and there to be seen a spouting porpoise-whale, which are plentiful in these latitudes. We were glad enough to get into heavier clothing, donning sweater and pea-coat, [and] finding them mighty comfortable indeed, after the warm weather we had experienced.

It took us just a few hours over fourteen days to reach Dutch Harbor, a fine run with two boilers. Altogether, it was about the smoothest long run of the cruise. There was no accident of any kind and things went like clockwork. As it grew colder, we worked harder. The coolness of the weather ma[de] us feel very active, and every watch, instead of falling off in revolutions, we gained, running as high as eighty one for an entire watch of four hours; great speed with two boilers in a ship like the *Concord*. We reached the Aleutian group in good time, [and] barren, desolate looking enough we found them. Devoid of all verdure at all times, now in the crevices lay drifts of snow. They were in perfect harmony with the gray monotint of sea and sky. A few gulls were the only signs of animated life. Everywhere gray sky and sullen, gray green sea. Crossing the 180th meridian changed our longitude [from east to west] and thus we lost a day, having two Fridays, the 21st of June, in one week.

Crewmembers of the USS *Olympia* enjoy a meal in their mess. Individual messes comprised of about twenty men were the norm in 1899–1901. Note mess table is suspended from the overhead, where it was stowed when not in use. Sailors' white hats are hung from hammock hooks overhead, as this space was used for berthing as well as messing. Navy Historical Foundation.

We reached Unalaska on the 23rd of June. I was on watch, and coming up thro' the fireroom hatch, I caught my first glimpse of the place. I wanted to ascertain how far we had to go in order to carry fires according[ly]. I was agreeably surprised. In that first glance I caught a glimpse of as beautiful a little land-locked harbor as one would wish to see: high hills everywhere, the apex and ruts of which were filled with snow. The rest was green, but wet and soggy looking from the continual rainfall. The tops of the higher peaks were covered with heavy mists. Just ahead of us nestled the few white painted houses with a church spire looming above all. That composed the town of Unalaska.

We didn't stop here, but continued on past a narrow neck of land and came to an anchor in Dutch Harbor. A few stores, a customs house, and a coaling pier, with here and there a small dwelling, and the North American Commercial Co.'s warehouses and station comprise this place. It is beautiful, but gloomy, with its tall, surrounding mountains rearing rugged skylines. A vast change is this rugged, mountainous country with its murky sky and sea, its continual drizzle and fog, to the Philippines, with its tender tropical sky smiling even when it rains, its strip of dazzling beach with its luxuriant foliage, its fronded palms. The contrast is sharp. But leaving scenic effects apart, I prefer the Alaska weather. It is more comfortable. One can keep warm, but

Homeward Bound

its hard to keep cool in the Philippines. As a happy medium between the two extremes, Alaska and the Philippines, give me Japan with its dazzling sunlight, its dry atmosphere that does not enervate. But . . . I am prejudiced in favor of Japan. There is no country like it. I could well understand how people could worship the Sun if they belonged to Japan.

But Japan and China with all their allurements are temporarily of the past. The bleak mountainous Alaskan peaks and hillsides with the snow drifts are of the present. It is simply another experience, another phase of life in the cruise. It is a most welcome change for the majority of the crew, for with but few exceptions they were all sick and tired of the land of "no savvy" and this is "God's country," they claim, for here it is American soil. At last they are with people of their own tongue, people that "savvy" all right. But, nevertheless, the great American dollar is required to make them savvy all the same, just as much so as it does in uncivilized China and Japan. The universal language is the mighty dollar.

The North American Commercial Co. has a general merchandise store at Dutch Harbor. There you could purchase any article you might wish. The *Concord* was short on small stores, whether accidentally or otherwise I couldn't tell. But the word was passed that anyone who wished to purchase clothing could do so and the paymaster would settle the bills. There wouldn't be any monthly money served out while we were in Alaskan waters, perhaps for four or five months. This was the American sailorman's chance, and the articles that were purchased at fabulous prices and brought aboard would bring tears to the eyes of the most successful slop-chest owner that ever trod the quarter-deck.

Blankets that could be purchased for two dollars anywhere in the States were sold to the credulous Jackie for eight and ten dollars. Sweaters were four and five, and not as good material as the naval sweater at one dollar sixty only. The attraction that attracted Jack's eye [was] the high collar rubber boots stiffened with whale-bone. Great stress was laid on the whalebone. [These] were sold for eight dollars. Heavy shoes for miners' wear cost six and seven dollars per pair. You would wonder how a man could navigate with them on. Wonderful arctic[2] socks, half an inch in thickness, mitts and gloves, underclothing, mostly all shoddy goods, but sold as pure wool, were foisted upon poor Jack, who was in his glory. It didn't cost anything; was just taken off his account, you know. The storekeepers were in their glory. Long will the name of *Concord* be remembered in the annals of Dutch Harbor, and Dutch were the bargains. Some of the bluejackets must have thought they were going on an Arctic expedition. Some staggered aboard with a Klondiker's outfit: heavy boots, rubber, pair of blankets, suits of underwear, socks, oilskins and sou-westers, dungarees. Parts of the ship looked like slop shops from boots (with whale bone) and other articles of gear hanging about.

The temperature was about sixty and quite warm in the protected harbor, and it was a funny sight to see half of the ship's company bundled up in a bag of clothes, wonderful sweaters and boots, for some of them donned their purchases as soon as they got aboard. They were paddling around in boots and shoes so heavy that they could hardly move, while others were running around barefoot and in light underwear. Even the two Filipino boys, washer-men for the officers, shamed some of us. They had never [seen] snow until they caught a glimpse of it on the Aleutian islands. At first they were roaming around like a pair of big monkies, picking out a warm spot to lie down and curl up. But after the chill wore off, they were around in the same clothing they use in the Philippines, and seemed to like it. It looked strange to see the contrast between the tropical garb of the two "Amigos" with their shirt waist floating to the chill Alaskan winds, and the "snowdiggers" from the Middle West in Arctic exploring attire.

But never before did that particular company dispose of such shoddy stock at such fabulous prices, and when any demur was made at the prices quoted, Jack would meet with the retort, "What do you care about the price? You make your money easy. Be nice. Just look at this sweater for nine dollars," etc. Truth to tell, no one was compelled to purchase, unless it was to get rain clothes, and that was compulsory, that is, parts of the outfit for the seaman branch. One young fellow purchased a lap robe of shoddy [a woolen yarn] because it had "Indian Robe" attached to it upon a price card. An Indian never saw it, and if he did, he would take a glass of whisky in preference to it. This cost as much as if it was a genuine Navajo blanket. In the *Concord* Dutch Harbor found quicker returns than Nome.

The waters of Alaska abound in fish. No sooner were we at anchor than lines were over the rail and fish were being hauled in as fast as one could overhaul a line. But the fish caught were poor quality, mostly all sick cod and sculpin, [and] here and there a flounder. Most of the deep sea cod run into the shallow waters of the bay when sick, where feeding is easier. But the fishing parties that were sent from the ship returned laden with heavy catches of cod, a few small halibut, flounder and some salmon trout. Very good eating at first, but it soon pales. Fish has about the [same] staying qualities as canned Willie when it begins to come too regular[ly].

Every other day at least, a fishing party would leave the ship and generally the catch for the day would be good. The deck hands indulged their petty spite against the engineers division by refusing to give them any fish, dividing up the catch among the deck messes and marines. This showed small, petty meanness on their part, but considering the class of cattle they were aboard the *Concord*, nothing else could be expected. When I speak of the deck force of the *Concord*, I mean the rookies. They were in the majority, not the old hand who generally rises superior to all such smallness. But take the "six months sailor" who is recruited from the farm and small inland towns. He is generally young and uncouth and at first sight doesn't seem very promising material, nor is he. In the first place, he can't keep himself clean. He is lazy, terribly so. A boatswain['s] mate, in most cases has to kick them off their caulking mats to make them answer a call. They will stow themselves away in some out of the way place and curl up and go to sleep. Healthy, husky animals with the appetite of a Harlem goat, all they care for is their "chow." That was the principal reason, I judge, that caused them to keep all the catch for themselves.

However, the engineers force sent forth a fishing party one bright day that made the largest catch of the lot. Over a hundred and forty salmon, each one weighing eight or ten lbs., and divided them up among the ship's company, returning good for evil, and showing the "deck" a good example, appealing to gentlemanly instincts, so to speak. But the good action was wasted upon that riff-raff of the farm, for when the other catches afterward were brought aboard, they swiped everything in sight for a rainy day and salted them down, so when at sea, while the engineers were struggling along on canned willie, and canned sausage, and salt port and "horse," the deck messes had salmon and herring and cod, fried and baked.

So, to give them a dose of their own medicine, we refused to let them make coffee in the fireroom during the night watches, the law of Moses being the only way to reach them. This hurt them in a more vital spot than the conscience. It reached their stomachs, the most sensitive portion of their anatomies. After that, it was open war between the two branches.

Fourth of July dawned clear and beautiful, a typical spring day in appearance, and we had the usual sports, boat racing and obstacle racing, mast head race [i.e., mast climbing], etc. A number of the ladies of Unalaska and Dutch Harbor graced the occasion and right here let me say that the ladies of the two places for chic and beauty and "up to dateness" can compare favorably with any city of the Union. There are more bewildering bundles of femininity there in proportion to the population than in any other city or isolated village. Of course, they are not natives of the place, but the wives and daughters of the men engaged in business. We had boxing contests in which the contestants slugged to their heart's content and mauled each other unmercifully, much to everybody's enjoyment. At night a stage was rigged with a few boards and some spare gear and an impromptu performance given in which the participants did their best to add to the evening's fun. What tho one ambitious "rookie" sang "She sleeps by Suwanee River" thro' his nose, and overcome by the pathos of the song, almost broke down and wept, thus getting a large horse laugh from his audience. God wot he did his best. The jests, tho' aged, brought a laugh. The cake walking, tho' not as good as we have seen, was still enjoyed by all. The music, which was good, kept our hearts attuned to its rhythm as it ebbed and flowed, soothing the "savage breast" of coal passer, fireman and marine and ship's cook, [and] they were as if boys again, wafted back to bygone scenes and memories by its sweet strains, far remote from this beautiful, clear Alaskan night.

Our captain was sick and so also was the navigator, and it was decided that the former should be sent home on the first steamer bound that way. But owing to the lack of medical attendance, it was deemed advisable that the *Concord* should perform this service. So, while we were "standing by" at Unalaska, not knowing where we were to proceed, the chief engineer gave orders for three boilers to be gotten ready, that we were to go to Seattle with the captain. This was a "bolt from the blue" indeed. Here we were after a long sojourn on the Asiatic Station, going home, and yet, in a sense, not going home, for we would have to recoal and make the return trip of two thousand miles, getting a glimpse of a home port, and then torn rudely away.

We left Dutch Harbor under three boilers about seven twenty A.M. morning of the eighth of July [1901] and from that time until we arrived at Seattle noon of the 15th, we forced the little ship for all she was worth, making quite a run of it. We stopped at Port Angeles [Washington] to speak the flagship *Iowa*, just at dusk the evening of the 14th; getting the flag officer's permission, we steamed to Port Townsend and came to an anchor about 11:30 that night. The next morning we steamed to Seattle and right here is where the "little tin kettle" distinguished herself. We had four boilers, the full complement, and all fires had been cleaned and all tubes swept and blown during the night. So to speak, the steam was bottled up and the two horizontal engines were "champing" and anxious to be off. After a few attempts, the little gunboat finally got underway and as they gave her her head, the revolutions mounted as high as 124, one hour's average being 120. This is extraordinar[il]y good running for a war-ship, or any ship, after over ten years commission, and the little boat fairly flew. And we were anxious to make her fly. We were bound to an American port—some of us over four years away. But we didn't dare fly the "homeward bound pennant." We were in a queer situation. We were homeward bound and yet not homeward bound. We clearly had no business where we were. We stole in unawares, when we should have been in Alaska.

We didn't know how long we should stay in Seattle, what disposition they would make of the ship, whether we should remain on the Pacific Station or [be] sent back to carry out the orders. What a home-coming for men who had looked forward to this for years, men [who] were very anxious to get back to America, "God's country," as they called it. Unheralded and unsung, the little gunboat *Concord*, the last of Dewey's ships at the battle of Manila Bay except the "tiny battleship" *Petrel*, came steaming swiftly into the harbor of Seattle and let go the anchor, causing no comment and no excitement of any kind. Very few I question[ed] even knew that she had participated in that battle and that there were men aboard yet that was at her guns on that momentous day. Such is Fame, a very fickle Goddess. And such are the American people.

Even I, that hated to leave the Far East, felt a thrill of pleasurable excitement as I gazed upon the steep streets with [their] cable and electric cars, the many manufactures, the high chimneys of which emitted vast volumes of black smoke, the whirr and noise of machinery, of the saw mills along the river front, the puffing, panting tugs, the whistles of the busy steam boats, and the thousand and one noises of the day that characterize an American city. This was home, but what noise and bustle, what a difference from the East! There, no smoke of manufactures, the din and noise of commerce mar the day or night. No noisy whistle proclaims the work hour, but the work is carried on just the same.

Homeward Bound

It was a very good thing for us of the *Concord* that we came down to Seattle, for we were getting down to a diet of "government straight." The ubiquitous "salt horse" was conspicuous by its presence on frequent occasions. Now many old sailor men have exclaimed, as I have often heard, that "it's the finest stuff you can eat; that's the stuff that puts hair on your chest, etc." But even those old war horses could never convince me either by words or by a practical illustration, even when I saw them devour huge chunks of it with gusto. It carries with it an aroma of the days of Paul Jones, of "wooden ships and iron men," when bilge water and weevils and cock roaches were much in vogue, of seamen with long queues done up in rope yarn and tar, who gave and took hard knocks, and who, if all accounts of those days are correct, [were] ninety percent brute; of dimly lit, uncomfortable "forcastles." As for myself and others, I would make a meal from hardtack and coffee any time, in preference.

We had liberty in Seattle. It was good to walk on American soil once more. This town struck me as very wide open. The policemen would lean with kingly air against the mahogany rail of the different bars and take his'n with no one to say him nay. The hotels and furnished room houses were filled to overflowing with soiled doves, regular "man-eaters," every one of mixed nationalities. "Bums and panhandlers" of all descriptions were rife in the saloons and streets. [It was a] typical American city, not yet reached the transition stage, but in a few years Seattle will no doubt arise in its wrath and start house cleaning. The population, a great deal is transitory, miners, prospectors and adventurers of all kinds and sex, make Seattle the Metropolis of the nor-west.

The boys went mad from too much drink, but did no harm to anyone. It doesn't take much to make one drunk, as I have said before, after being a couple of months aboard ship. And it was a noisy throng that gathered in one of the saloons and sang and shouted and drank and drank again until finally having enough we each went our several ways for the night. In the course of our wandering, two of us dropped into the Star theatre, a fierce joint we found it. Cost nothing to go in. Ranging toward the bar, we called for drinks.

"I say, Jack!" exclaimed a voice, "Can't I have a drink?"

The voice came from a soubrette in short skirts, with a "bleached blonde" makeup, who had evidently "seen us first."[3]

"Course you can, Sweetheart. Nominate your bitters," said we, after we had sized this "vision" up.

"I'll take a beer," quoth she.

"It's very good of you," said I. We had expected the worst and this was letting us down reasonably enough.

The price for the three small "beers" was fifty cents. Fifty cents American, not Mexic[an].

"Take another," said my friend, which we did. Then we adjourned to the seats, a highly brazened looking old cat was singing a horrible discord in a husky whiskey voice. I forget what the song was, something about "the Moth and the Flame," or "the Boid in a Gilded Coige." At any rate, she reached such a high note that the paint on her phisog cracked and she broke down amid the wild piping of clarinet and horn and shrieking fiddle, and was so overcome that it took a large tankard of beer to revive her sufficiently to proceed. This she did much to the disgust of the audience. The little "soubrette" had taken the seat between us, and began to talk shop. By shop I mean the language of the stage. She was doing a turn here and would go on by and bye. It wasn't her cue yet. I looked at the poor little painted creature, the hard light about the eyes, the seams caused by dissipation that the make up boy couldn't entirely hide, and a feeling of wonderment crept slowly over me that this article could ever have been a girl or ever knew the tender feeling and sympathy that is part of every true woman. However, she must have been, she wasn't yet twenty-two, and was the best looking girl in the house among a hundred other girls, girls of various ages from sixteen to sixty, slim, slender, fat, bloated, on the lookout like vultures for their prey, ready to swoop down at the first sign of an easy thing.

There was quite a fluttering in our direction. Sailors are probably "easy marks." But the "small un" sat and chatted as long as the drinks were forthcoming, receiving her ticket or check, and telling the story of her life. How many of these stories you hear if you are a frequenter of such places! And how drearily monotonous they all are. The same common place old story. I have listened to so many of them that I get tired and sleepy almost immediately. The poor little thing; no doubt she was doing her best to entertain us conversationally. It was business. Her "stage business." No doubt somewhere in the building the eye of her lover, her "friend," or as they are known in the West, "Macs," her Mac was upon her. And this poor, low caste degenerate off-scouring of humanity, lower even than the poor girl whose shame he subsists upon, a parasite that lives upon a parasite, this microbe's eye was no doubt upon her, seeing that she worked diligently and well so as to acquire the wherewithal that he might "chow" in the morning.

The "sou," seeing a friend in sight, hurried off like the busy bee she was. Evidently there was more in sight and left alone we concentrated our gaze upon the stage. A star feature was about to come on, a strong man. A Strong Man. "Achilles." "Prof. Achilles." "A man whose strength makes Sandow appear as an amateur," said the announcer.[4] Truly he had a fearful paraphernalia. It couldn't be possible that any man living could handle those massive weights and dumbbells. Thousands of pounds. The crazy, half-drunken orchestra strikes up a measured strain, and in solemn majesty of mien, in stalks the Gladiator where, stalking majestically to the front of the stage, he barely deigns to notice the mere worms before him. He had long hair; this he shakes back from his leonine brow with a flick of his big fat head.

We lay back and roared until the tears ran down our cheeks. It was the funniest thing we had seen for a long time. What a big, conceited ass he was, and what airs he took unto himself! And the make up? [He was c]lad in greasy tights, patches in many places, with trunks that were faded, the spangles [of] which had long since lost their luster. His massive, fleshy frame, his mane of yellow rope yarn-like hair, his assumed dignity. His was an appearance calculated to make anyone laugh, but the audience took him seriously. If Achilles had belonged to the *Concord*, they would have had him scrubbed with sand and canvas. Perhaps the most horrible thought of all, at least to "Achilles," he would have been put to work. With what groans and snorts he lifted a dumbbell marked 2000 lbs. What "business" he put on as he dropped this wooden fake, shaking the stage. And then, tossing back the mane that had fallen over his eyes as he kissed his hand to the audience, acknowledging their applause. He knows how to work that head of hair to advantage. We roared at every unconscious break until "Achilles" himself designed to notice us and glared in our direction. Our unseemly mirth hurt his dignity. Finally the greasy apparition vanished, and wiping our streaming eyes, we hailed a passing waiter.

"Two beers, sport."

"Ye can't hav 'em, see," he snapped, "unless de ladies drink wid ye, see?" and he passed on.

We saw, and not caring to treat any more "ladies," we passed out, passing by the sign that readeth, "Any persons occupying these seats are expected to patronize the house." And there ye air: It was a circus. So much for the Star; it is a classic.

And the "bouncer" of this particular resort [was] at once the admiration and criterion of manhood to a few callow and degenerate youths who envy him his position and long to be as he, the admired of all the "girls," Maudye, Maye, and Magye and Blanchye. Short and thick set, with a battered up physiog, like unto that of the "ex-king of Formosa," with only the smallest modicum of brains. Ninety-five percent brute. Presumably a broken down third-rate pug, he is monarch of all he surveys as he leans negligently against the bar, sipping his drink and patronizing in lordly manner the group of admirers that are glad to call him "Chummie" and be known as his intimates and are willing to blow him off for that privilege. All at once a "scuffle" over at the other end of the hall attracts "Chummie's" attention. Loud curses, more noise than fight, mingle with the women's excited screeches. Right here is where "Chummie" shines. This is where he earns his money. With a wild rush the human bull-dog rushes across the floor and digs into the offender, possibly some poor stiff of a "drunk" that is only noisy and only raises a protest when he is getting robbed.

"Chummie" isn't there to discriminate these little niceties. In fact, he is pained not to. He throws a couple of "hot ones" into the already half-beaten wretch, putting him entirely out, much to the admiration of the "goils," Blanchye, Maudye, etc.

"I tell you," in excited tones, "Chummie can handle 'em. He's the boy for my coin. Soak him, Chummie. Bite his ear off." This falling on Chummie's auracular appendages spurs him to renewed efforts, and he grabs the already subdued offender by the slack of his trousers and scruff of the neck and shoots him toward the door, and out, giving him a clip back of the neck as a parting token. Then, if the poor ill-used wretch isn't "copped" by some passing policemen and taken in the "hurry-up wagon," Chummie stands in the door, the centre of attraction (this is meat and drink to him) and looks scornfully at his fallen foe as he leans against a nearby lamp post or telegraph pole and [tries] to quench the "crimson tide" that flows in a copious stream from his battered beak into the gutter.

Finding his victim is entirely subdued, Chummie struts back to the bar, the admired of all, modestly declaiming all praise bestowed on him. "Dat's nuthin. I didn't turn a hair." Then he throws a big beer down the capacious opening in the front part of his face and glares across the hall as if to say, "If der's any more uff youse plugs dat wants any more of me game, why youse kin git it, see?"

~ ~ ~

From Seattle we steamed one morning to Port Orchard, or Bremerton, there to fit out for sea and await our new Commander.[5] We were to go back to Alaska, but when we didn't know. At Bremerton we coaled and received our "sea stores" for the return trip to the North.

We found the *Oregon* there, then after a short time came the Pacific fleet steaming in majestically, the *Iowa*,[6] flagship, in the lead, followed by that very latest addition, the *Wisconsin*,[7] bright work from guns and rails glittered in the sun. Upon the charthouse of the *Wisconsin* crouching upon a shield upon which was emblazoned the word in golden lettering "Forward," was a badger, typical of the state. With flags flying, bands playing, the two big ships came to an anchorage, completely overshadowing the little gun-boat that had been in many seas, and dwarfing even the noble proportions of the old *Oregon*.

And of the *Oregon!* The splendid old ship was almost deserted when a party of us visited her one Sunday afternoon.[8] The decks that had teemed with bluejackets were silent then. Only a very few were left, and of those few, none had but a few more days of service. Many visitors thronged the deck, lending color and gaiety to the scene, but the blue shirt was conspicuous by its absence. Somewhat sadly, I rambled around the big ship. The recollection of many happy hours and many miserable ones wove their spell around me. "These were the pumps that saved the *Oregon* when she was on the rocks in Pechili," I heard a voice say. I looked at the bluejacket, but did not know him. He was showing a group of visitors around. Yes! They were the pumps, but he wasn't [there] at the time. I rambled from deck to deck. The planking seemed more worn than ever by many feet. As I turned down to the orlop deck where the "black gang" held forth, I almost expected to run across the old familiar faces and hear the King's voice in heated debate. But the King had long since gone. His is another story. All were gone. The old faces were absent from their accustomed haunts. Thro' deserted fire rooms and engine rooms I wended my way. All was quiet.

As I stepped into the after pump room, my old station, I heard the light laughter and caught a dim glimpse of a woman's dainty skirt. The faint, almost imperceptible odor of some perfume still lingered upon the air. They were come to pay tribute to you, old warrior of the seas. Well may you rest upon your laurels gained in many climes.

Homeward Bound

From the deck of the *Concord* I have watched the stream of visitors come and go. They come to pay their homage to the splendid old ship whose work is done. As you count the life of a battleship in these very rapid days of improvement, the *Oregon* is old. The *Iowa* has a record also, but not the romance. The *Wisconsin* is very modern. But none of these ships attract but a passing notice. They are alive with men. The old ship seems deserted. The sun as it sinks to rest behind the dark fringe of pines that line the hills far away crowns the grand lines of the old hulk in a purplish mist. There for a space it lingers, as if loath to leave. Over on the western shore of the Sound lies the old *Nipsic*,[9] only survivor of the Samoa disaster. Once this ship was the admiration of the Navy as you were, old *Oregon*. But both have lived your allotted span. Both have contributed their share to history and romance. When darkness grows apace, and golden arrows and spears of light are reflected upon the dark, smooth waters of the Sound, from the many lights that gleam thro' from port and signal lamps, and when "taps" are softly wafted from ship to ship around the fleet, at the sharp boom of the *Iowa*'s six pounder, you alone are silent and dark. As silent and dark as you were when you were somewhere in distant seas on your long run of a few years gone; as silent and dark, and relentless as you were lying off Santiago.

~ ~ ~

"Well! Well! Here we are again," as the clown says when he springs into the ring. Right up alongside the dock at Dutch Harbor, and coaling at that, just as if we hadn't went to Seattle or Port Orchard at all. This time the little harbor presents a most animated appearance. The *Roanoke* is in, and is going to Seattle carrying many passengers from the gold fields of Nome. It is an interesting study of life to watch these people. Some have made their pile and are returning happy. Others have just the fare and are poorer than when they started. These are in the steerage. The others are in the cabin and saloon. Nome must be pretty well cleaned out, as on the *Roanoke* were a number of gamblers, such [is the] sign of a sinking ship when that ilk leaves. Many are old gray beards who should be sitting snugly in some chimney corner, dangling grand children on their knees and drawing consolation from their pipes instead of braving the rigors of the Klondyke. They are a hardy, tough, wiry set of men. The calling seems to make them younger. Some of the young fellows are college men. One young fellow told me he was a graduate of Cornell. He barely pulled out even. "No show there now. Capital has it all taken up," said he. "After the first rush is over and placer mining finished, you may as well quit, unless you want to work for a wage."

Many women with their husbands were returning. Most of these looked contented and well to do. The majority, if disappointed, accepted Fortune's frown with an equanimity of spirit that was willing to try once more when the opportunity offered. What with taking snap shots at us of the *Concord* and rambling along the beach and up the steep hillsides, they whiled away their stay in Dutch Harbor pleasantly enough.

A Sailor's Log

We were over eight days from Seattle and the little tin pot, as we called the *Concord*, behaved badly[;] a rather choppy, cross seaway caus[ed] her to kick up her heels in a disgraceful manner, much to the discomfort of the "rookies" who lay around with the most woe-be-gone case of countenance. You could walk over them, or do anything. All they wanted was to die. At any time you could find one of them hanging over the slop or ash chute with a most dejected and forlorn look. Didn't care a "continental dem" whether school kept or not, being gibed at unmercifully by some of their hardier mates who have no sympathy for a victim suffering with *mal-de-mer*. But when the sea abated and everything became smooth, they were the most hilarious of the crew.

Leaving Dutch Harbor, which we succeeded in doing after two or three ineffectual attempts on account of the fog and mist, we proceeded to Kiska Bay, about three days' run with three boilers. This was the first place that was to be surveyed. This was another of Nature's harbors, completely landlocked by high, bleak hills, at the time of the year more or less covered with a thick green verdure. But despite this green tint of the summer months, [it was] dreary and very bleak. Even here some human beings had tried to settle and wrest a livelihood from the unwilling soil. All that was left of them was [a] deserted, fallen-in dugout and a small black cross that marked the last resting place of one of their number. Whether a man or woman, the cross saith not. But a bleaker, more desolate spot for the eternal sleep could scarce be found this side of the Arctic Circle. In winter all this is covered with deep snow. No sign of animated life, of life of any kind. But at present, wild geese and ducks swarm among these peaks, affording good sport for some of the officers and men.

The "fishing party" succeeded in making a haul of salmon and salmon trout with a few halibut. The salmon at Dutch Harbor we had found unfit to eat, as they were spawning on our second return, and thus a great addition to our rations was lost. The one solitary day's fishing afforded us two or three good meals of fish, which were fit for a king after "canned willie" and "horse."

On one of the surveying trips, one of the boat's crew succeeded in capturing an eagle. Catching him napping, one of them threw a stone with such good aim that it knocked the "King of the Air" into a cocked hat, putting him out in a most ignominious manner. He was easy game. But when brought aboard, he retaliated upon his captors by tearing their clothing and scratching severely before they finally succeeded in getting a piece of stuff bent upon his leg. Even then he made several attempts to break away from the unseen thing that held him in check, only succeeding in flapping around the deck, much to his disgust.

He lay there giving us a gloomy look from his savage eyes, the most of us keeping out of range of the strong, cruel beak and talons. But one of the crew had either an ignorance of or contempt for the prowess of His Eglets, for he came boldly up, while we stood around in uncertainty what to do and grabbed him by the neck as one would grasp a nettle, pushing his bill down on the deck in a most undignified manner, and pulled him around with the same assurance that one would a chicken. Much to our

Homeward Bound

surprise, His Eglets didn't resent it, but cowered down with a subdued hang dog look, letting him take all sorts of liberties with his plumage. He was about six feet from [wing] tip to tip. For one or two days he refused to eat, but at last hunger got the best of him and the way he devoured a couple of ducks and some fish would astonish an epicure. This fellow wasn't half as savage as he looked, for he ate pieces of fish from the men's hands, being very careful not to touch their fingers. He was the most docile wild eagle ever seen. He appeared to be reconciled to his fate, only making a futile attempt to break thro' the bars of the cage that was made for him when he caught a glimpse of the high peaks that were lost to him forever.

There was also excavated in Kiska the bones of a mastodon, or section, rather, of what was probably the frontal bone of a huge skull. The part that was above ground had partly decayed and crumbled away, but that buried was hard as flint, in a good state of preservation. This was brought aboard and cleaned and put away for transportation to the States.

A few days afterward, we were lying in another anchorage a day and a half run from Kiska, known as the Bay of Waterfalls, I suppose from the fact that numerous small streams and rivulets from small lakes among the hills gurgle down into the sea. This bay was very small, about three or four square miles, and entirely open to the sea, with the single exception of an arm of land that formed a small bight.

It was the dawn of a glorious day, the first day of September, when we steamed slowly in and came to anchor at the farther end, right in line with the entrance. A glorious day, I say, for even in Alaska sometimes the sun dispels the mist and fog and renders cheerful and bright what a few moments before was dull, morose and gloomy. But his staying is very uncertain. Perhaps all day. Perhaps an hour. But when he deigns to show his face and irradiate the gloomy, cheerless land and seascape, there is a sky as soft and brightly blue, a sea as smiling as the sky reflected, a verdure and fungus growths on hill and dale as softly green, of many tints, from a bright emerald in the lights to a brownish *terre verte* in the cloud shadows as many a more favorable land can boast. But this weather is the exception, not the rule. The rule means fog, cold winds, driving scriff and flying scud. The sullen water is lashed into furious, white capped, choppy waves against the brown stone cliffs. The sea breaks in a ragged line of white foam that shows as froth against the teeth of jagged, hard, sharp-looking rocks that show as the sea recedes. Everything aboard ship shows the effect of the weather. I know I, for one, felt dull and dispirited and longed for the time to pass when we should leave this dull part of the world.

I have desisted for quite a while in my criticisms of the officers and men of the *Concord*. The ship was run on an entirely different plan from the *Oregon* and the *New Orleans*. Never before in the service at any time did I have so much surplus time to write away, practically no work except sea watches, and no drill worthy of the name. This only applied to a few of us, according to our rating. At general quarters, my station was in the fire room and all I had to do was to go there if I wished. If not, I kept out of the way. No pumps like the *Oregon*'s, thank you. Fire, collision and clear ship for action, practically the same. And right here let me say that the less I had to do, the less I wished to do. The more sleep I had, the more I wanted. It was a dreadful, dull yawning existence, a feeling at times like unto that which animates wild, caged animals, and causes them to dash and tear at the bars of [their] cage possessed me at times.

Then would I hie myself to the fo'castle and pace rapidly up and down for hours at the time, not minding the keen, cutting wind and scriff that wet me through. It grew almost unbearable. I could take no interest in anything. You see, my time was getting short. That was an added strain. The days seemed long, as I would look ahead, but yet short as they passed and were left behind. Even "mess gear" lost its charm. Our food supply was pretty well reduced. We were literally down to the government ration and any bluejacket that knows will tell you it is impossible to live on that. You can subsist. But the paymaster served out flour instead of hard tack and we had bread enough. That was something to be deeply thankful for. And then we had tea and coffee. True, without even a dash of condensed milk, but one can live on that. Another luxury was butter. But the spuds were gone. Of course, we weren't starving, but it was coarse fare and "government straight." Not very appetizing.

"Why, I thought Uncle Sam's Navy was the best fed in the navies of the World?" you ask in surprise. Well, that's not saying much. The whole truth of the matter is you cannot live on Uncle Sam's ration.

"A bold statement," you say.

"Yes! But it's true." Take a mess of twenty men, all hearty eating animals, and serve out nothing to them but their ration. The ration is thirty cents worth of food per diem. Every fifth ration is commuted, i.e., you, the caterer or cook, draw the equivalent in money so as to buy a few extras not specified in your Uncle's menu. That's four rations commuted for twenty men: thirty six dollars. Out of that the cook gets two and a half rations or three, according as you agree to pay him. That's in addition to his regular pay of landsman or coal passer. On the *Concord* our mess paid its cook three rations, twenty-seven dollars. In a mess of twenty, there is then left nine "cold bones" [dollars] for extra chow. That won't buy much extra butter or flour, or canned meat or vegetables from the ship's supply. And you have got to buy or you will go very short.

Many and many a time I have been glad to skirmish up enough hard tack, canned William and coffee. So much for the ration as it is served to you pure and simple. In ports the paymaster serves out fresh provisions. That eases life up a bit. In order to eke out a livelihood and live as an ordinary mortal should, some messes put in the mess from three to five dollars per man, sometimes more, as there may be an "assessment" caused by bad management of the mess affairs by the caterer or cook. That is often the case at sea, or when away from good ports. Then the mess runs in debt in order to live.

Why do all the men desert from the American Navy? Ask any "rookie" that has made a flying visit on the *Buffalo*, the *Dixie*,[10] the *Solace*[11] and other so-called training ships, where they guarantee to turn out full-fledged ordinary seamen in six months. Ask many of the continuous service men that never came back and hear how gloomily and feelingly they will howl about it.

"But, there . . ." you sarcastically remark, "What do you want, a Waldorf Astoria cuisine in the Navy?"

No, no, my friend. Be tolerant. We want good, plain, substantial food of good quality and quantity, food that God almighty intended that every human being should have that earned his living by the "sweat of his brow," whether on the "vasty deep" in one of the big white ships, or whether following the plow upon a farm. And it is only the pig-headed legislation of a lot of sleek, well fed chumps, their indifference, that says, "Damn you, Jack. I'm all right," that makes us have to subsist upon a ration that was obsolete when Decatur captured the *Philadelphia* at Tripoli.[12] I have mentioned about this before. The plan that is pursued now is on the lines of "don't feed 'em too much, as it makes 'em lazy." But you don't gain anything by it, Uncle Sam. Your recruits and your old men don't stay. And there are numerous other causes. You have read them all thro' this log. The most dangerous blow to the efficiency of the naval service is the passing of the "continuous service men," the "old hands," the men that served the guns, the men that handled ammunition and engine, level and slice bar, and shovel and hoe, the old, well-trained crews that knew their duties by rote, knew their duties mechanically and could perform them at the touch of an electric button; the men that won victories at Manila Bay and at Santiago with an ease that appalled the whole civilized world and advanced the country and the flag an hundred fold.

These men are passing. The Navy is too hot for them. Think you that you can win such victories with the crews that are piled aboard ship in these days? No, and the country will find it so. It took years of drill to prepare those men for what they achieved in an hour. You hear some lace-bedecked officer pompously exclaim, "Aw, aw. Yes, the men are not so bad, but then you know *we* supply the brain," forgetting that it is one thing to direct, to tell a man how a thing should be done, and then doing it oneself. And—'nuff said. I grow hot on this subject. Let it pass. Time and the emergency will right all this. But we must wait.

"What? Criticize your commanding officers?"

Yes! I have done so before and I have to do so on this ship. I claim it is my right. A naval officer or man is, I should say, a public character, and as such is not immune. A coal passer can look at an admiral. Altho' a very great man indeed, a naval officer, still there is nothing "like trowing de hooks into dem." Criticism is good for a "swollen head." Since the Spanish-American affair, there is no living with some of them. The first luff of the gunboat *Concord* was, let us say, eccentric. Yes, that's a good word. It aptly describes him. Eccentric, that's it. Known by the sobriquet of "Bugs" by the sailors (this also is a good description word when applied to him) not

A Sailor's Log

"Bugs" from an entomological view, but "bugs" and "eccentric" are anomalous [synonymous?] in the sense that I use them.[13]

There was plenty of excuse for him. Too much learning was a dangerous thing in his case. He wasn't intended by Nature for a naval officer. He was a good "boatswain mate" spoiled. Not a bad hearted old "gentleman" (Congress at least had done its best for him in that respect, and miserably failed). "Jest eccentric, eccentric, that's all." His noodle wasn't intended to be crammed with mathematics and all the science and arts of war, but it was crammed and something had to carry away. He was an engine without a governor, "wery, wery eccentric."

Poor old "Bugs." I have forgiven him and so have all the boys, whose sleep he rudely dispelled, when, with all the "watch" at all times of the day and night, he would chase us with our "mats" when we were snugly snoozin' away on the top and in the vicinity of his chain lockers, in order to bend on the "sheet chain." (The *Concord* required more chain [i.e., paid out when anchoring, to make the anchor less likely to dig itself out under strain] and more anchors to hold her than any battleship I was ever on.) In the first place, we hadn't any business to be caulking off on the deck, and in the second place, we thought he had no business to be "bending" and "unbending" the sheet chain and "monkeying" with the anchor gear as often as he did. So, when the "chain gang" would come, we would pull away, cursing him softly under our breath and damning everything connected with the *Concord*. It was a burlesque and a sideshow rolled into one to watch him, the noise and the roar. He would shout command after command, then fly off at a tangent and swear lustily at some luckless might [mite?] (this was when his boatswain's mate proclivities came in) who happened to blunder, and finally, after pulling and mauling the chain in every conceivable manner, he would finally get things done to his satisfaction and depart.

Then his cohorts would fade away and stow themselves in hole and corner and caulk off through the watch until another idea would strike him. We would crawl back and silently spread our "gear" again, wondering if everything was done to suit him, the Grand Vizier. Aside from the way he demoralized the crew, he had a few favorites that could get anything from him. These he always gave liberty to, but no one else could go while he had the running of the liberty. This caused dissatisfaction and the grumbling was long and loud. A great many men hadn't had liberty for months, unless they "jumped ship." This was always risky.

Queer as this old fellow was, to my idea, he was a much better man than the skipper. The skipper may have been theoretically a much smarter man, but then he was afraid. Somehow or other he couldn't get the weather just to suit him in Alaska, and pompous man that he was, this worried him; it must have been a blow to him to think that he couldn't command the weather, so he could bulldoze it like he did his officers and crew. (A glimpse of a suit of dungarees was as a red flag to a bull with him, this by the way.) He was never more contented than when he had two anchors down. One wasn't enough. He felt more comfortable with two. Three would have added security. Then a good heart-to-heart talk with the "booze" in his cabin and all was well with him until it began to work. Then up he would fly to agitate the "first luff" and thro' him, the crew. Perhaps it was everything he wanted scrubbed, or the bright work didn't suit him. Always some petty trifle like that. How he would bawl "Bugs" out! Poor old Bugs. This was when the weather was mild. When it was rough, there wasn't any word from him.

When the skipper came to the ship, of course he had to read his orders. This he lost no time in doing. It was his first command. But no, he had command of the *Alert* for about eight days, I think, previous to getting his orders for the *Concord*.[14] The word was passed, "All hands to muster," and we trailed aft. After reading his order to command, he hemmed and hawed, cleared his throat, and gazing around the crew with what he considered a knowing and military stern glance, trying to impress us with an "Aha, you might fool some skippers, but not me. I am onto the ropes." He made his grandstand play:

"My men! It is most always customary for a new commander, after reading his orders to take command of the ship, to make a few remarks to the crew." Here he looked over his eyeglasses to see the effect and attention. "So," he continued, "there will be a mutual understanding, I want to say *right here* that I believe in liberty. Plenty of it. Lots of it." Here he glanced over the glasses again. He had hit us in the right spot. That was just what that crew did want, and wanted bad. Seeing the effect, he placed added emphasis on it. "I like to see my men on the beach all the time," he roared, "all the time they can be spared from their duties. Plenty of liberty." He was making a fine impression, doing well. "And let us understand each other thoroughly," he continued. "To do this you must keep away from the mast. You must be first class. A first class man can have every privilege from me," he yowled. "I like to see my men ashore! Ashore all the time. Plenty of it," he howled emphatically, getting redder in the face. "But if you come before me, I shall punish you severely. Severely." He frowned and looked fierce. "And another thing," raising his finger over the palm of his hand and pausing for effect, "don't come before me with a fairy tale about a sick aunt, or dead gran[d]mother, for it won't go," he roared. "Pipe down," he nodded to the navigator.

General approbation and congratulations among the men as they went forward.
"That's the kind of man to be under."
"Now we have got a skipper."
"He is a regular lollopoloosa."
"There's one thing: he means what he says. Anyone can see that," etc., etc.
"Yow! Wow! I tell you, we're all n——."
"That's the stuff."
"Bully boy."
"Damn old Bu[gs]. That's the man for our money. Boo, you, buzz, zip, and all the rest."

Some of the old hands looked wise and dubious as they smoked their pipes.

A Sailor's Log

The next day was a perfect turmoil. The skipper found fault with everything, bawled everybody out, said the ship was filthy, had been neglected, carelessness, etc., hinted at incompetenc[e], ordered everything scrubbed and shined up, from truck to keelson, had all kinds of drills and found fault with everything. Nothing could suit him. Nothing [could] satisfy (unless it was the brand of "dope" he had in his cabin). For the few days before we left for Dutch Harbor, everything [was] topsy-turvy. Things that hadn't been done on the *Concord* for years were done. Everyone was inclined to desert. Then we got under way.

The skipper's popularity had waned considerably, but the crew wouldn't have minded that, hadn't he disgraced himself in their eyes in another way. Underway, the skipper strutted to and fro on the bridge like a flaming turkey cock, with a big, black, fat-looking cigar (he was a chain smoker. Evidently he had heard of Gen. [Ulysses S.] Grant) stuck in his face. He was absolute monarch, king of the rolling deep. Finally, the little pot began to lurch about and kick up her heels, to pirouette, coy little coquette that she was.

Those that were near him watched his changing expressions. Just previous to this he had noticed the queer actions of the quartermaster on watch. Could his eyes deceive him, or was the quartermaster actually in a state of intoxication? Or maybe he, the skipper, had overdone his usual limit and was drunk himself. He rubbed his eyes and looked. Yes, the fellow seemed actually under the influence. Could he believe it? A common sailor drunk, and that, too, on duty, and in the presence of the greatest commander on earth? Wasn't possible. The man seemed loose and careless and evidently had a grievance, was evidently swelling nigh to busting with some pent up emotion. To make sure, the great commander approached him where he stood on the bridge, or reclined in a very careless attitude.

"What point [of land] is that, quartermaster?" he asked.

"Shir?" surlily asked the quartermaster.

"What point is that?" roared the great man.

"Whast point. Whast point!" trying to catch it, and then gloomily, "Liberty Pointsh, sir." Here he clutched the rail and gazed gloomily as became a man that hadn't had any liberty and wanted it badly.

Whereupon the supreme being ordered him relieved from duty and had him consigned to the dungeon for ten days, and then he retired to his room and "stowed away" for the balance of the run, dreadfully, wo[e]fully sick. That's how the great man lost his prestige with the crew.

After that, when everything was fair and smiling and everything snug and secure, when the skipper stirred up the ship's company, the men sought solace by the general reflection: "Oh, never mind, it won't last long. Just as soon as we get to sea, he'll stow himself away."

During the interval of time that elapsed between the departure of our sick commander and the arrival of his Imperial Majesty, the King, "Bugs" assumed the command, as next in rank, of course. The reign of Commander "Bugs" was a very busy

Homeward Bound

one while it lasted. Everybody was continually on the jump, but nothing was ever accomplished. A great cause of discontent, as I mentioned, was that he gave no liberty ashore to the general crew, only to the select few of what he termed "special class men." It was extremely difficult to ascertain Bugs' definition of a special class man. There were smothered growls from the crew and loud denunciations of Commander Bugs' policy, and many cursed the fate that led them to ship in a service that confines men to a ship for months, and many vowed to run away, and a few did.

It was a mean, contemptible trick at any rate. Many had not been ashore for months, not since the ship had left Hong Kong. Many were longer aboard than that. Here they were in a home port, just from a long period of service in the Philippines and China and Japan. In a home port, mind you, where there was no excuse for not giving all hands shore leave, giving liberty to a favored few as he did. There wasn't even the excuse of sailing orders, for then under those circumstances no one could or would expect shore leave. Some few went to the mast and asked permission to go ashore, but asked in vain.

"Well, what is it, my man?"

"I would like permission to go ashore, sir. I have been aboard now three months and am first class, and think I am entitled to a liberty."

"Oh, you think, do you? What business have you to think?" sarcastically. "I think you can't go, so you may as well go forward. There will be no liberty given and that's all there is about it. Go forward."

"But——" expostulated the man.

"Go forward!" yelled Commander Bugs, and he would hear no more.

Another time, a special first class man, at least one who thought he was, and was according to the rules laid down, asked permission, telling him he was a "special first class man," and wanted to know why his name didn't appear on the "liberty list."

"How long have you been in the service?" asked Bugs.

"Two years, sir."

"Two years!" repeated the luff. "Two years. You haven't been in the service long enough even for a liberty. You can't go." And that settled it. Before the man had taken ten steps, the "Commander" called him back.

"Wasn't you ashore in a fishing party at Dutch Harbor?" he asked.

"Yes, sir."

"Well what do you want? That was a liberty. Ain't you satisfied?" And he had to be.

So that's the reason the new skipper's "grand stand play" about liberty warmed every heart.

At Unalaska, after leaving Seattle and after coaling ship, the crew were given the great privilege of an hour's liberty ashore for the purpose of purchasing a few needed articles such as canned fruits and delicacies, clothing, etc., from the company store. The majority availed themselves of this opportunity by putting as much raw, red liquor (Dutch Harbor blend) under their shirts as the time would permit, with the result that they forgot all about the ship and the time of return. The fiery stuff warmed them up, and it didn't take very much of the blend to do it. A couple of drinks will knock any bluejacket out where an officer accustomed to it can drink with impunity.

There was in a few moments a perfect Bedlam of noise and song, yowls, and fighting. Bluejackets swarmed everywhere, and all roaring drunk. Not having any time to spare, they had to spend as much money as they could in the limited time. The time allowance expired and Bugs was in a quandary (he was always in a quandary) what to do, as but a few of the sober, staid sailors showed up. At last he sent forth a call for the marine guard, and with his commando, sallied forth to round up the herd. He had his hands full, for when they caught a glimpse of the enemy, they retreated to another *kopje,* getting away with all their supplies and ammunition. One more befuddled than the rest appeared in the open and "Bugs" charged with a war whoop that echoed and re-echoed thro the surrounding hills.

"Hu! Stop there, you villain! I know you. Come back you scoundrel," he roared, sprinting along at a great gait for a fat man. "I'll string you to the yard arm. I'll court-martial you. You—You—damned scoundrel." Pulling out his gun he fired twice in the air, but the sailor only gave a derisive laugh and flourish[ed] a large quart bottle in the air and took to the bush, leaving the lieut[enant] commander sputtering with rage far in the rear.

The rest of the pursuing party didn't exercise themselves very much, trying hard as they were to keep from exploding in front of the irate Bugs. In despair, he returned to the ship cursing all the way. The gang gradually showed up as they pleased, all gloriously drunk and happy. That night the brig was full.

We left the Bay of Waterfalls, direct for Dutch Harbor, the run being only a short one, and glad enough were we to get back to that dismal hole. At least there was the prospect to receive papers and mail, which is always an event on ship-board. Hardly had the launch returned from its first trip bringing off the mail than a large quart bottle of Dutch Harbor blend was captured by the marine sergeant. With the quart, he captured two drunks. This was the quickest time on record. They were hailed to the mast with the damning evidence of their crime, and "Bugs" fairly frothed at the early beginning. Rushing back to his Imperial Majesty, the faithful Vizier stated the case and produced the bottle. This was sufficient evidence to convict anybody. And the King's eyes glittered when he beheld the large quart that had barely been touched. Whether it was anger or what—at any rate, "I haven't time to attend to them yet, Mr. [Minett]. Place them in the brig in irons until later on."

"Very good, sir. Shall I throw the bottle and its contents over the side?" questioned Bugs delicately.

"Hm. Hm." coughed the King. "Might just as well let it remain. Its not in the way. I'll take very good care of it." And with a stern look, "This drinking has got to be stopped. This cursed drink habit is very, very bad. Mr. M[inett], muster the petty officers aft and give them a good talking to. We have got to stop this business," and righteously and with increasing indignation, "the petty officers have got to take more of an interest in the spiritual welfare of the men. You understand, Mr. M[inett]? Leave the vile stuff here. Hm. That will do, sir. You may go."

The Vizier mustered all the petty officers aft and gave them a characteristic speech.

"The captain wants me to state to the petty officers that they must take more of an interest in the ship, in the moral welfare of the men under them. They must do their utmost to prevent whiskey from being smuggled aboard and drunk, and anyone they catch drinking, they shall immediately report them. There must be no more of this infernal Bedlam ashore or aboard ship as there was when last here. We have only been here half an hour and two of the crew are beastly drunk, and it must be stopped, and you are expected to stop it. The captain will not serve out any monthly money until it is stopped. He is disgusted with the conduct of this crew and the people of Dutch Harbor are also disgusted. It must stop! That will do. Dismissed!"

But it didn't stop. The brig was filled once more during the night. And again, it was filled, for about a week later we went alongside for our deck load of coal, and once again did the bluejackets go on a still hunt for the raw red rum of Alaska[n] distillation. Despite the efforts of the marine, the top soldier, and Jimmy Legs, the gang became gradually warmed up. Not having anything to do with the coaling, I watched some of the manoevres from the fo'castle. A couple of "Dixie Heroes" were the first to succumb to the raw spirit. They rolled and swaggered around in the most approved bluejacket fashion, cussing and using the filthiest language that could emanate from a human being. These representative American boys, the very intelligent classes that are filling the ranks of the navy of today, could give the old shellback pointers when it comes to using foul language.

Wishing to find someone to mix it up with, they sought out the Filipino washerman as one of the easiest marks to get in some good whacks on. Of course, the poor Filipino couldn't resist and they punched him to their heart's content, until he howled and begged in broken English for mercy. Then someone interfered and they desisted, leaving this Filipino more frightened than hurt. At last they were rounded up and taken to the mast. Here they indulged in some more vile language toward Commander Bugs. It is always customary in the service nowadays to give these boys, this very, very excellent material from the middle west and inland towns, all possible leniency. This has been the policy of the [Navy D]epartment. Why, it wouldn't do to treat any of these promising (?) young whelps with the rigid discipline that is accorded the "scum and rakings of seaport cities."

"Why, I am surprised, actually surprised, to see these promising young fellows in this condition. They can't possibly be drunk. It's impossible. Some scoundrel, some vile wretch has poisoned them, poisoned them with this cussed liquor. Take them below, put them under the sentry's charge [i.e., in the brig]. They—they must be poisoned." As another volley of filth was belched forth by one of them, "No doubt, no doubt, some scoundrel has led them astray. Take 'em below." And they were led cursing and swearing and yelling, below. One of them was so noisy and personal in his remarks that finally "Jimmie" lost his temper. Jimmie was a Spaniard, the same fellow that was transferred to a receiving ship during the war. "You wanta come. You wanta come. You Goddamn, goddamn——" he gritted in a rage and gagging the pup with one hand, he choked him into submission with the other, drag[ged] him along the alleyway like a sack of spuds, and dump[ed] him in the brig without any ceremony whatever. This delighted a few of us immensely, for most of the crew suffered for the conduct of these fellows, especially aboard the *Concord,* with officers who either wouldn't or could not discriminate between good men and bad.

Shortly after, another seaman was run up for being drunk. Short shrift for him, an old offender. "Take him below, master-at-arms. He's drunk. Can't keep away from it. Drunk, simply drunk. Well, do it," and he waved him below.

This man was able to do his work, and a good worker around the ship, always willing and quick to answer a call, doing others' work as well as his own. But he was of the old Navy, the Navy before the Spanish-American war. Yes! Short work of him, the scoundrel!

As far as the "Dixie Heroes" are concerned, I have been on three ships that were largely composed of these young fellows recruited from the inland towns and cities, viz, the *New Orleans,* the *Oregon,* and the *Concord.* And I have visited other ships that are manned largely with this "excellent material." If they are a fair sample of budding manhood, then terrible indeed must be the outlook and condition of a country that produces such material and expects to make good citizens [of them]. But I can't believe that these "bums" are representative. Out of all I have come in contact with, not over ten per cent are straight, manly young fellows. The great majority ship simply for the countries they will visit. They do not ship to work. They are shirks. They are dirty in morals and in person. Lazy. Shiftless. [They are o]f no use aboard ship whatever; only fit to give "old guff," degenerate, and with a perverted nature. As an old boatswain's mate said, "I am sick and tired of it all. It takes all my time to round the part of the ship up. They are no use, only fit to give off guff. They won't do any work. If you ask them to do a job, you have got to show 'em how to do it, and you may as well do it yourself. They stow themselves away. If you abuse them, you'll get the worst of it. They won't punish them when you report them. The service is going to h[ell]." And he was right.

Two of these "Heroes" jump[ed] ship, and after having a good old drink ashore, came aboard the next morning. They were taken before the first luff. "Take them men, master-at-arms, and place them under the sentry's charge. But first search them. Keep them from coming in contact with any of the crew. Let them get clean underwear and outside clothing, then have them scrubbed, scrubbed good." Here the two nearly fainted, "then boil their clothing good."

Good for you, old "Bugs." Scrub 'em, scrub 'em good. That was possibly the worst punishment you could put on them. Fear of a court-martial, consequent loss of pay and confinement had not the terror for them that a good bath had. You hit it right that time, old "Bugs." But a number of them got court-martialed, and lost two months' pay and one was sentenced to dismissal, just what he wished for, and had tried for for months.

~~~

I was sick, heartily sick of Dutch Harbor with its ceaseless grey monotone. Sick of Alaska. Sick of the bare hills and the barn-like looking habitations that formed the little port. And many weary hours did I pace up and down the fo'castle awaiting for something to turn up. All days were the same. The same old grind. Nothing to vary the monotony. We had a little target practice, revolver and rifle, and the bare hills reverberated with the sharp crack of small arms, the crackle of Gatling and Colt's Automatic. We were expecting to leave for Sitka at any time, wearily looking forward to an uncertain period of sojourn in that port. At any rate, let us move, do something; this is unbearable. Ah for the patience of a Buddha. Sykya Muni[15] himself with his eighty five thousand doctrines would hardly find any of them adequate to meet the contingency of a winter in Alaska. Anything, any place for a change. But the darkest hour is always before the dawning, and the change was to come unexpected[ly], as changes always come.

Already had the highest peaks taken on their winter dress. Snow capped and bonneted, they stood in severe contrast to their neighbors of a lower altitude, garbed as they were in greenest verdure. Already had the gulls donned winter plumage of a dull brown and flew hither and thither with doleful squeaking [cries] harmonizing with the rest of the doleful surroundings. Even the old ship that lay at anchor not two cables' length away from us added her quota to the desolate scene.

I felt as desolate as the scene. A diet of "canned William" and salt junk, with half-baked bad bread will eventually ruin one's temper and digestive apparatus and cause [one] to take a very pessimistic view of life. A number of us were suffering from disordered stomachs from too much canned goods, and were inclined to curse everything that excited our ire. When you go to a mess table, meal after meal, and find the same old standby, your stomach revolts. "Oh, for a good plain appetizing meal of well cooked fresh meat and vegetables!" you cry. You will never know the value of good, wholesome food until you experience a long siege of ship's food, every day the same, and badly cooked at that: pies made of dried apples with tough leathery crust that would cause a dyspeptic to howl with anguish at the mere sight of them; bread made of bad flour that would tax an ostrich's digestive apparatus. To crown it all, the entire piece or *piece de resistance* of canned William. The mere looks of it is quite enough. Your stomach rebels. You have work to do, hard steaming watches to be stood, and you have to eat. But you suffer for it later on. My stomach became nearly ruined, and I felt like those patent medicine advertisement cuts look, those labeled "before using." I was crabbed and cross; and for the first time in years, found my belly irritated by the slightest trifle, and 'twas all I could do to keep from giving everyone a snappy, disagreeable answer. It was the first time I knew I was the possessor of a stomach. I had been perfectly healthy and able to compete with a goat heretofore.

I was sitting drawn up in the firemen's washroom one night, reading idly the advertisements in a popular magazine at least six months old. I hadn't anything else to read. Every line had been eagerly devoured and I was intently cursing everything that annoyed me, and cursing the fearful prospect of a long sojourn in Sitka, whither we were expected to proceed, and wondering how I was to pass all the dreary time that was to elapse before we got out of Alaska and into a country a little more civilized, when one of the black gang came in. I looked idly from the magazine to see who it was, and I could see [from] the expression on his face he had news to impart; in fact, was bursting to spring it on me. You can always tell when your bluejacket has something to impart, especially when he considers no one else is the possessor of the very important piece of news that he is in receipt of.

"Well, out with it!" I growled. I had had some "canned sausage" ("canned fresh pork sausage," the label on the can read) for supper, and felt like growling. "Let it come. Don't stand there like a big 'chin chin joss' or marine. I know you are achin' to spring the latest on me. What is it?"

"What? Didn't you know?" with a superior air of knowledge. "Didn't hear the latest?"

"I heard lots of latest. Everything is latest. What is it this time? The latest catch of fish? Or is the King under the influence again, or are we going to have canned willie hash for the morning breakfast?" I asked wearily.

"We're going to 'Frisco. Dead sure thing," he said triumphantly and with conviction. "That's no hop dream.[16] Listen . . ."

I heard a muffled yell on deck. The sound of smothered cheers, and could catch the word, "Frisco. Frisco," and I knew 'twas true. The true rumor flies quickly aboard a man-o-war; every blessed soul knows it at the same time.

"Good!" I howled, jumping from my seat on the bucket racks. "Good! Let her go. We can't get there too quickly for me. Any place but this." And I almost forgot the gnawing, sickening pain in the region of my solar plexus in the excitement of the moment.

It was indeed true. We coaled ship, finished putting aboard the deck load in bags, then waited the arrival of the last mail steamer, the *Newport*. This was a three days' wait for she was overdue, and longing eyes many of the crew cast out toward the narrow entrance of the harbor where the Sentinel Rock [stood] in solemn majesty, trying to catch a glimpse of a steamer's smoke upon the faraway horizon. And at last we were rewarded, for a steamer's masthead light was discerned rounding the entrance and it could be none other than the expected packet. This was in the dusk of a foggy September afternoon. There was no mail for us, however, and the next morning at six A.M. the little *Concord*, with long, silken homeward bounder streaming far

Homeward Bound

out on the port beam, got underway for home: the land of the Golden West, of sunshine and of flowers, of native sons and native daughters (who can trace their ancestry back fully half a century and then pause, finding it perhaps convenient to go no farther). We were steaming for California.

Three boilers; would we have whooped the little craft up for all she was worth on the homeward run? You bet, but the King set the speed at ninety turns, easily made and kept up hour after hour. We were all impatient to force matters, to jump in and slice and rake and hoe, and get there. We wanted to get something to eat, and many were going home that hadn't been home since long before the battle of Manila Bay. And quite a few there [were] whose time was up. And quite a few that had just a few days to do. To this category I belonged. And a sailor with only a short time to do to finish the cruise is a very nervous and skittish critter. It is an awful drag the last month. Time flies on leaden wings. Will it never roll around? You lose all interest in the things that formerly made up your life. You mope around from deck to deck, unable to put your mind completely on any one thing. You are full of the time when you are to get your few dollars and are free. Free to blow it in, to go where you please and to stay as long as you please. You haven't time or patience for anything else. If we could only have stoked as we wished! Why, at ninety revolutions, we were only creeping. Crawling along. It seemed a long time to look ahead. Despite that, we were making ten knots on an average. Despite that we used sails to help us along and steady us. The speed seemed very slow.

And another thing: the weather was bad. But the wind was at our stern the whole trip, so we didn't slow down in spite of the heavy seas that made it necessary to place oil bags over the rail to break the angry waves that tried hard to climb aboard. We knights of the caulking mats fared ill for we were unmercifully rolled from side to side on the deck until I thought my hide was as elastic as a rubber man's. It was very uncomfortable. The roll was constant. [It was] impossible to use mess tables, and it was the old game of catching your grub on the fly. But we were homeward bound, and petty discomforts went for naught.

The trip was uneventful. At the last, we made all the speed we could with the three boilers, picking coal from wherever we chose. We managed with right good will to run the revolutions up to one hundred and ten, beating all records with three boilers during the time I was aboard the *Concord*. This was good, considering the condition of the boilers after a ten days' run.

We came to an anchor in Drake's Bay. Stages were gotten over the side for painting the ship's sides. The next morning early, the crew were at work getting everything clean. Decks were scrubbed, gear hauled taut, useless lumber thrown over the side, and everything in readiness for our entrance in 'Frisco Harbor.

Getting under way, the few miles were quickly covered and finally thru the thick haze the Heads were dimly discerned. And soon we were passing through the Golden Gate. This is considered a very portentous moment, that time in your life when first you pass thro' the Golden Gate of California, the Gateway of the West. The Golden

West. It is considered very impressive, but perhaps owing to the haze, much of its impressiveness was wasted. What impressed all of us the most was the cross that marks the spot where the *Rio de Janeiro* went down in sight of the promised land.[17]

But a feeling of relief, of gladness, was upon us all. We felt that we were home. The uncertainty had vanished. Rounding the heads we dropped anchor with the yellow quarantine flag floating to the breeze. The health launch came up as quickly as possible and we were admitted. [We] took up our anchorage farther up the bay opposite Goat Island, or Buena Vista Island, the nautical training station.[18] For many of us, the cruise was nearly over.

Papers were brought aboard. Here we heard of the President's death at the hand of an assassin, the first inkling we received of the dread tragedy—and of a Nation's tears.[19]

Epilogue

Fred Wilson's log ends with his return to the United States and discovery of the assassination of President William McKinley, who on September 14, 1901, succumbed to wounds inflicted by an assassin eight days earlier. William McKinley is little known to twenty-first-century Americans; however, he was much loved and respected in American society of the day. The public reaction to his assassination might easily be compared with that to the death of John F. Kennedy sixty-two years later. As Rear Admiral Charles O'Neil noted in his diary, "I have scarcely ever been more grieved than I am for our beloved president—whose character in public and in private seemed unblemished."[1]

McKinley's untimely death resulted in the elevation of Vice President Theodore Roosevelt to the presidency, "thereby giving," as Harold and Margaret Sprout noted, "the United States a Chief Executive equipped with the knowledge, the initiative, and the driving force which were needed to launch imperial America upon an imperial naval policy."[2] Under his leadership, successive Congresses authorized a long line of battleships and other fleet units that caused the U.S. Navy to grow rapidly among the great fleets of the world. But Theodore Roosevelt more than built the ships; he employed them with great enthusiasm to support American foreign policy around the world, culminating in the world cruise of the U.S. Atlantic Fleet, better known as "the Great White Fleet," December 1907–February 1909.[3]

Wilson served throughout the Theodore Roosevelt years. Though we have no written account of his subsequent naval career, through his surviving service records we can discern some further information. Shortly after the gunboat *Concord* returned to San Francisco in 1901, he was discharged from the service. He made his way east, presumably with his passage paid by the government, as was then the practice. He remained in civilian life for just short of three months and then reenlisted on board the receiving ship *Richmond* at League Island, Philadelphia. This three-month break was a standard aspect of the navy: those who reenlisted within ninety days retained

Wilson served onboard the battleships *Indiana, Oregon* (twice), *Wisconsin,* and *Kansas*. While onboard the USS *Wisconsin,* where these photos were taken ca. 1908–10, Wilson participated in the last half of the world cruise of the Great White Fleet. The other chief petty officers in these photos are unidentified. Courtesy Muriel Wilson MacFall.

their previous ranks and received payment for three months of leave as a reenlistment bonus. Indeed, this procedure was still in place in 1961 when the editor of this work reenlisted after nearly ninety days in the civilian world.

Wilson spent most of this enlistment on board torpedo boats and torpedo boat destroyers. He joined the commissioning crew of USS *Thornton*, a 269-ton-displacement torpedo boat that entered service on June 9, 1902. That ship conducted operations off the U.S. East Coast throughout the summer; in November it moved to the West Indies, where it participated in the combined fleet maneuvers that were conducted in December 1902–January 1903 under the command of Admiral of the Navy George Dewey and against the background of the German-British-Italian naval intervention in Venezuela. The *Thornton* returned to Norfolk on January 28, 1903, and was placed in the Reserve Torpedo Flotilla two weeks later.

The development of the torpedo boat, essentially a coastal defense weapon, and of the "submarine torpedo boat," later more widely known as the "submarine," necessitated the development of a countermeasure. The torpedo boat destroyer, later known as the "destroyer," was the answer. These swift craft were designed to accompany the fleet and, on approach to a hostile coast, provide protection against torpedo boats and submarine torpedo boats. As the principal threat from torpedo boats occurred during the hours of darkness, when they might approach the fleet undetected, the counter-weapon, the destroyer, was painted dark green—an example of the "stealth technology" of the day—to enable it to intercept and destroy them. Life was very difficult aboard these early destroyers, as accommodations were much rougher than those of which Wilson complained during his cruise on Asiatic Station. Nevertheless, early destroyermen, like their much later successors, developed great pride in the nature of their service.

After the *Thornton* went out of commission, Wilson was transferred to the torpedo boat destroyer *Chauncey*, a 426-ton unit assigned to the Coastal Squadron of the newly designated North Atlantic Fleet. This ship was placed in full commission on February 21, 1903, and served with the North Atlantic Fleet until transferred to the Asiatic Fleet. *Chauncey* departed Key West on December 18, 1903, on a cruise that took her via the Mediterranean on a route similar to the one recorded in the prologue of this book. This course was dictated by the fact that torpedo boat destroyers had notoriously short "legs"; their fuel capacity was very limited. Specifically, they were incapable of crossing the Pacific (in that era before underway replenishment). The strategic implications of this shortcoming was nowhere more apparent than the 1907–1909 world cruise of the Great White Fleet, during which sixteen first-class battleships circumnavigated the world without destroyer escorts, with the exception of the fleet's passage through the Straits of Magellan.

While on the Asiatic Station, the *Chauncey* cruised in the Philippines during the winter months and off China during summers. It was in this latter location that Wilson and the *Chauncey* became involved in one of the more bizarre incidents of the Russo-Japanese War of 1904–1905.

Epilogue

The world had followed the fortunes of the Russian Second Pacific Fleet, under the command of Vice Admiral Zinovy Rozhdestvenskiy, as it made its way from the Baltic Sea to the Pacific, dogged by misfortune and delay. On May 27, 1905, it met a Japanese fleet commanded by Admiral Heihichiro Togo off the island of Tsushima and there was totally defeated. A number of the Russian ships fled the scene of the battle and sought shelter in neutral ports: two cruisers reached the Philippines; another sailed to Mare Island, California. All three were interned under U.S. Navy supervision until the end of the war.

On August 12, 1905, the Russian cruiser *Askold* and the torpedo boat *Grosovoi* took refuge in Shanghai, a neutral port, and sought neutral protection long enough to effect repairs. An American force under the command of Rear Admiral Yates Stirling, including the battleships *Wisconsin* and *Oregon*, was then at Woosung, the deep-draft anchorage to seaward of Shanghai; along the Bund in Shanghai were the monitor *Monadnock* and a flotilla of destroyers, including Wilson's *Chauncey*.

At one point in the confrontation that followed, the *New York Tribune* (under the banner headline "U.S. WARSHIPS BLOCK JAPAN") reported that Admiral Stirling had ordered the destroyer *Chauncey* to position herself between the Russian and Japanese warships, and that the American forces were prepared to defend Chinese neutrality.[4] The tense situation was resolved when the Russian commander agreed to intern both ships.

On July 1, 1903, during his service on the *Chauncey*, Wilson received an acting appointment as chief water tender, but he was reduced in rate to water tender the following year for being "insufficient in performance of duty." One is left to wonder about the cause for this demotion: too much time spent with "Cyrus Noble"? perhaps some indiscretion discovered while ashore in Shanghai? overstayed liberty at the Grill Room? A reread of his escapades in Shanghai while on board the USS *Oregon* as recorded in his log suggests many possible causes. It takes little imagination to envision Wilson making his way through his customary haunts in Shanghai: Black Mary's for a good meal; various trips to the tattoo artist for additions to his collection; tours of the old city; nights of heavy drinking in the company of shipmates and probably young Tom Pow Ching; the Grill Room. Being moored along the Bund in downtown Shanghai rather than anchored off Woosung must have made going ashore on liberty a much easier proposition, and thus the temptations probably were considerably greater.

At any rate, on June 20, 1905, Wilson was examined and found qualified for a permanent appointment as chief water tender. In December 1905, nearing the end of his enlistment, Wilson was transferred once again to the battleship *Oregon*, which was then completing another deployment to Asiatic Station. Wilson returned to the United States aboard the *Oregon*, and from that ship he accepted his discharge on April 4, 1906.[5]

Wilson reenlisted in August 1906 and joined the commissioning crew of the cruiser *St. Louis*, which had been built by Neafie and Levy Company of Philadelphia and commissioned on the eighteenth of the same month. Assigned to the Pacific Fleet, the *St. Louis* cruised around South America, calling at Port Castries in St. Lucia; Bahia and Rio de Janeiro in Brazil; Montevideo in Uruguay; Punta Arenas and Valparaiso in Chile; Callao, Peru; and Acapulco in Mexico. The ship arrived at San Diego on August 31, 1907.

On April 4, 1908, Wilson transferred from the *St. Louis* to the *Wisconsin*, an 11,564-ton battleship of the *Illinois* class that had just recommissioned after an extensive overhaul at the Puget Sound Naval Shipyard at Bremerton, Washington. She sailed to San Francisco to take part in the Pacific Fleet rendezvous with the battleships of the U.S. Atlantic Fleet (that is, the Great White Fleet) when the latter reached San Francisco, completing the first half of their circumnavigation of the world, on May 7, 1908. *Wisconsin* subsequently was transferred to the Atlantic Fleet and participated in the remainder of the round-the-world cruise, calling at Hawaii; Auckland, New Zealand; Sydney, Melbourne, and Albany, Australia; Manila; Yokohama; Amoy, China; Colombo, Ceylon; and various Mediterranean ports before returning to the United States on February 22, 1909. There the fleet was reviewed by President Theodore Roosevelt. Wilson also participated in the large fleet review in New York

Wilson poses with four other chief petty officers. Place and time unknown. Courtesy Muriel Wilson MacFall.

Epilogue

City in September 1909 in conjunction with the tercentennial of the discovery of the Hudson River and the centennial of steam navigation of the river. He remained on board *Wisconsin* until the ship decommissioned again in the spring of 1910 at the Portsmouth Navy Yard in New Hampshire.

Unfortunately, there is a gap in Wilson's service record between 1910 and 1914; however, in 1914 Wilson again reenlisted and was transferred from the receiving ship at Philadelphia to the cruiser *Minnesota*, which carried him south to the Gulf of Mexico, where U.S. naval forces were conducting punitive operations against the government of Mexico. On October 16, after *Minnesota*'s arrival on station, Wilson was transferred to the battleship *Kansas*. *Kansas* at this point was engaged in a patrol off Tampico and Vera Cruz, supporting the American expeditionary force that had landed there. She departed from Vera Cruz on October 29, 1914, to investigate reports of unstable conditions at Port au Prince, Haiti, where she arrived on November 3. The battleship departed Port au Prince on December 1 and reached Philadelphia a week later. In 1915 Wilson was assigned to the armored cruiser *Brooklyn*, a Spanish-American War veteran that had been recommissioned "in ordinary" on March 2, 1914, and then fully commissioned at Philadelphia on May 9, 1915, about the time Wilson joined her.

In mid-July 1915, Wilson was transferred to the receiving ship at Norfolk and at the end of the year to the U.S. Naval Hospital in Philadelphia. Wilson never again returned to the sea. From this point onward, his record consists solely of entries indicating his status as a patient—first at Philadelphia; then the naval hospital, Washington; and finally, from the end of 1919 until his death on April 24, 1924, as a patient in St. Elizabeth's Hospital, Washington, D.C. The nature of his illness is unknown.

Most sailors, like the ships on which they serve, leave little discernable trace of their presence. In a sense, a ship's passage across the world's oceans is as fleeting as its wake. It is a reality, yet the trace of its passage is ephemeral. Ships, however, always leave a written record—their deck logs, navigation records, routine reports—all of which document the ship's activities. Normally, sailors leave no such detailed records; Wilson, however, by virtue of his dedication, has provided a unique, articulate record of his experiences. In the process he has ensured the preservation of a memory of his own colorful passage, as well as an important insight into enlisted life in the engine room and on Asiatic Station at the turn of the twentieth century. For this, we might all be thankful.

Notes

PREFACE

1. "Line shot from the quarter or half deck," written from an officer's point of view.

2. Wilson here refers to Rear Adm. Robley D. Evans and his first of two autobiographical volumes, *A Sailor's Log: Recollections of Forty Years of Naval Life* (New York: D. Appleton, 1901). It would have been fresh off the press when this manuscript was completed. Evans, as a captain, commanded the battleship *Indiana*, 1895–96, while Wilson served on board her.

3. Wilson makes frequent use of "wot" throughout his account. In this usage, wot is the second-person singular form of the archaic verb "wit": to exercise the power of comprehending and judging. In essence, it means, "God knows." More frequently, Wilson says, "I wot not." In this first-person usage, it means, "I don't know," or "I cannot comprehend."

INTRODUCTION

1. Wilson's service records claim as next of kin wives of the following names: Mary (1898), May (1902), Anna R. (1906), and finally Nellie E., who married him in 1909 and remained married to him until his death in 1924. Wilson family tradition holds that he was married only three times; therefore, it is possible the name of his first wife was spelled incorrectly either in 1898 or 1902. Further, there is an account—unsubstantiated, but fairly credible based upon conduct recorded in this log—that Wilson once married a Japanese girl while in Japan but had the marriage annulled.

2. K. Jack Bauer and Stephen S. Roberts, *Register of Ships of the U.S. Navy, 1775–1990* (Westport, Conn.: Greenwood, 1991), 2.

3. Rodney G. Tomlinson, ed., *A Rocky Mountain Sailor in Teddy Roosevelt's Navy: The Letters of Petty Officer Charles Fowler from the Asiatic Station, 1905–1910* (Boulder, Colo.: Westview, 1998), 130.

4. Cdr. William G. Miller, Executive Officer, USS *Minnesota*, to Secretary of the Navy [hereafter SecNav], Feb. 7, 1909, National Archives [hereafter NA], Record Group [hereafter RG] 24, entry 88, file 1159–267.

5. Letters, mottoes, and initials were the most popular subjects (26 percent), followed closely by coats of arms and national emblems (25 percent). Female figures appeared in 18 percent, unless one considered tattoos dealing with larger topics that included a woman, in which case the figure rose to 33 percent. "Tattooing in the Navy," *Army and Navy Register* 43 (May 2, 1908): 25.

6. Enlistment record, serial 90, 1906, USS *Lancaster*, at League Island.

7. Louis M. Nulton to Albert Key, Jan. 20, 1907, and Key to Theodore Roosevelt, Jan. 24, 1907, both

in William S. Sims Papers, Naval Historical Foundation [hereafter NHF] Collection, Library of Congress [hereafter LC].

8. George W. Melville, "On Behalf of the Naval Engineers," *Army and Navy Journal* 36 (Sept. 24, 1898): 89.

9. "Navy Line and Staff," *Army and Navy Journal* (Oct. 3, 1896): 69.

10. "Ye Chief Engineer," in Rear Adm. Ammen Farenholt, USN (Ret.), "Singing and Entertainment on Shipboard," NA, RG 45/464, case "NL," box 298.

11. "Our Navy Engineers," *Army and Navy Journal* 37 (Nov. 18, 1899): 273.

12. This term apparently was widely used at the time. It appears in the glossary of Cdr. John D. Alden, USN (Ret.), *The American Steel Navy: A Photographic History of the U.S. Navy from the Introduction of the Steel Hull in 1883 to the Cruise of the Great White Fleet, 1907–1909* (Annapolis, Md.: Naval Institute Press, 1972), 387. According to Wilson, the name derived "from his compatriot of the Philippines. He is likened unto him in that he is a sort of social outcast, a pariah, abhorred by all."

13. Cdr. William G. Miller, commanding officer, USS *Minnesota*, to SecNav, Feb. 7, 1909, NA, RG 24, entry 88, file 1159–267.

14. Fred J. Buenzle, *Bluejacket: An Autobiography* (New York: W. W. Norton, 1939; repr. Annapolis, Md.: Naval Institute Press, 1988), 154. At the time of Wilson's account, virtually all line officers were Academy graduates. There were no procedures at this point for an enlisted man to obtain a line commission.

15. Tomlinson, *Rocky Mountain Sailor*, 23.

16. Buenzle, *Bluejacket*, 54.

17. Ibid., 192–93.

18. Archa A. Adamson Reflections, unpublished typescript, Navy Department Library.

19. Deane C. Hartley Diary, Mar. 5, 1904, Military History Institute, Carlisle Barracks, Pennsylvania.

20. USS *Minneapolis* Annual Report, Sept. 12, 1905, NA, RG 45, entry 464, file "OO," box 473.

21. Commander in Chief [hereafter CinC] Atlantic Fleet [Rear Adm. R. D. Evans] Annual Report, Sept. 12, 1905, NA, RG 45/464, file "OO," box 473.

22. Rear Adm. J. B. Coghlan, "What the Navy Is and What It Needs," *Army and Navy Journal* 42 (Apr. 1, 1905): 826.

23. Capt. John J. Hunker to SecNav Paul Morton, Aug. 25, 1904, NA, RG 24, entry 88/917–107.

24. Rear Adm. H. C. Taylor (Chief of the Bureau of Navigation) to SecNav William H. Moody, July 29, 1902, William H. Moody Papers, LC.

25. This figure is based on a May 1, 2001, navy enlisted personnel strength of 313,051.

26. "The Blue Jacket's Point of View," *Army and Navy Journal* 39 (Mar. 29, 1902): 756–57.

27. A. P. Niblack, in a letter from Lingayen Gulf, May 15, 1899, Sims Papers, NHF, LC.

28. Roosevelt to Taft, Aug. 21, 1907. Elting E. Morison, *The Letters of Theodore Roosevelt*, vol. 5: 761–72. Cited in William R. Braisted, *The United States Navy in the Pacific, 1897–1909* (Austin: Univ. of Texas Press, 1958), 216.

29. There is one short published account of the cruise of the *New Orleans* to Asiatic Station. See Cdr. Frederick L. Sawyer, USN (Ret.), *Sons of Gunboats* (Annapolis, Md.: Naval Institute Press, 1946), 1–14. The announcement of General Lawton's death is contained in there.

PROLOGUE: TO ASIATIC STATION

1. Here Wilson is referring to the protected cruiser USS *New Orleans*. Protected cruisers possessed a "protective," or armored, deck from two inches to four inches thick. They differed from the heavier "armored" cruisers in that the latter carried side armor as well as a protective deck. "Lemon Peelers' gold brick" in this context meant the British fraud, or shoddy British product. It had been designed and built for the Brazilian navy at Armstrong, Mitchell, Newcastle-on-Tyne, England. The United States purchased the ship just before completion, when the government was augmenting the fleet prior to the war with Spain. She displaced 3,769 tons, was 354 feet 5 inches long overall, and had two vertical, inverted,

triple-expansion engines. She carried a crew of 375 officers and men. Unfortunately the design of the ship was inadequate for the U.S. Navy. It had very poor crew accommodations, a fact to which Wilson frequently refers. Her Brazilian name was *Amazonas*, a name Wilson uses in a derogatory manner in some entries. For details, see, K. Jack Bauer and Stephen S. Roberts, *Register of Ships of the U.S. Navy, 1775–1990: Major Combatants* (Westport, Conn.: Greenwood, 1991), 145. She had a sister ship, USS *Albany*. This short dialog originally was attached to the preface.

2. *Prairie* was a 6,620-ton merchant ship acquired in 1898 and converted to an auxiliary cruiser. After the war with Spain, it was redesignated a training ship, in which category it served until 1917.

3. A ship was said to be "a home" if it had good morale and officers who enforced discipline fairly.

4. Throughout the original text, Wilson used "their" and "there" interchangeably. For ease of reading, the text has been altered to reflect current usage.

5. In addition to ratings such as Wilson's [first class petty officer], all enlisted men had liberty "class" assignments based upon their behavior. Standards differed from ship to ship; however, fourth class generally was the lowest class, entitling a man to liberty once every three months.

6. Wilson misspelled Philippines throughout, opting for "Phillipines." The correct spelling has been used for ease of reading.

7. *Chicago*, a protected cruiser, displaced 4,083 tons and was commissioned in 1891.

8. Tompkinsville, on Staten Island, was a popular naval anchorage. In the preceding month, Adm. George Dewey's flagship *Olympia* had anchored there before his official welcome to the city on his return from the Orient.

9. William Clark Russell (1840–1913) produced fifty-three volumes of sea fiction; biographies of the British buccaneer and explorer William Dampier (1899), Adm. Horatio Nelson (1890), and Adm. Cuthbert Collingswood (1891); and a volume of ballads. Stanley J. Kunitz, *British Authors of the Nineteenth Century* (New York: H. W. Wilson, 1936), 539.

10. Frederick Marryat (1792–1848), Royal Navy captain and popular novelist about life at sea. His works included *The Naval Officer* and *Mr. Midshipman Easy*.

11. "Rookie" was this generation's slang equivalent of "boot," a raw recruit. Unlike today's recruits, Wilson's "rookies" lacked the benefit of formal recruit training ("boot camp") before being assigned to sea duty.

12. Living on "government straight," or "paymaster's [or "pusser's", corruption of "purser's] straight" meant subsisting in a mess exclusively with government-issue rations, with no mess fund to augment rations from the local market.

13. *Minneapolis*, a 7,375-ton protected cruiser, was built at Cramp's in Philadelphia and commissioned on Dec. 13, 1894.

14. "Eaganized" beef, poor-quality canned beef so named in "honor" of army Commissary General Charles P. Eagan, who was responsible for the purchase of this canned meat, some of which contained maggots, gristle, and pieces of rope. An investigation exonerated Eagan of wrongdoing. The navy purchased about five hundred thousand pounds of this meat annually. For details, see Graham A. Cosmos, *An Army for Empire: The United States Army in the Spanish-American War* (Columbia: Univ. of Missouri Press, 1971), 162–63, 170, 173, 287–91.

15. It is clear that Wilson is using the word "home" here and in the Nov. 1 entry to imply exactly the opposite. In the slang of the day, Wilson considered the *New Orleans* to be a "madhouse," a ship poorly regulated by her officers and therefore uncomfortable for her enlisted crew.

16. "Canned Willy" was canned beef; "canned Teddy" was canned ham.

17. The League Island Navy Yard was in Philadelphia.

18. Presumably, Wilson is referring to Punta Delgado.

19. "Hooker," generally derogatory slang term for a ship.

20. Presumably, *she* is Mary Wilson, whom he listed as his wife when he reenlisted for three years on board the receiving ship *Richmond* at the League Island Navy Yard, Philadelphia, on Oct. 30, 1898.

21. The Battle of Trafalgar occurred on Oct. 21, 1805.

22. This is a reference to the Personnel Bill of 1899, to which Wilson refers as the Personnel Bill of 1898. For further discussion, see the introduction.

23. To "toe the seam" means to stay in formation in straight lines along the tarred seams of a wooden deck. The term stems from sailing ship days.

24. "Portuguese" refers to the language in which all the valves and other fittings on the *New Orleans* were marked, as it had originally been destined for service in the Brazilian navy.

25. "The old Nick," the devil.

26. Duff was a kind of pudding very much favored by the men. Generally it was made with raisins in it.

27. Enlisted men's clothing was then—and at least into the late 1950s—stowed by being rolled and tied with clothing stops, pieces of white cord eighteen to twenty-four inches. Each piece of clothing had a prescribed method of "stopping" and all stops were required to be tied with square knots. This arcane practice caused the editor of this manuscript considerable anguish as a seaman recruit in 1958.

28. The 4 P.M.-to-8 P.M. watch is often "dogged," or divided, generally from 4 P.M. to 6 P.M. and from 6 P.M. to 8 P.M. The effect is to cause the sequence of watches for a three-section watch to change (and also to allow the evening watch section to have dinner without being temporarily relieved on station). Without dogging watches, each section would be permanently assigned to the watches it stood on leaving port. On the *New Orleans,* dog watches were instituted once a week. In the modern navy, there are dog watches every day.

29. A bum-boat, as Wilson implies, was a small boat from which a peddler offered a wide range of merchandise for sale to sailors. The term originally developed from the fact that these boats tied to a ship's boom—thus "boom-boats."

30. Wilson consistently spelled auxiliary as "auxillary"; this has been corrected throughout.

31. "Dog," slang for a bottle of alcoholic beverage.

32. Wilson later reveals that at some time before he enlisted he was part of a tumbling act in a small circus.

33. James J. Jeffries, who earlier in 1899 knocked out world heavyweight champion Robert Fitzsimmons at Coney Island, broke several of Tom Sharkey's ribs during a twenty-five-round fight that ended in a decision in favor of Jeffries. Jeffries held the world heavyweight title until 1905.

34. Filibustering: engaging in an illicit arms trade.

35. *Nashville* was a 1,371-ton gunboat built specifically for service on Asiatic Station. She commissioned on Aug. 19, 1897.

36. *Marietta* was a nine-hundred-ton gunboat of the *Wheeling* class, commissioned on Sept. 1, 1897.

37. The yellow flag is an international symbol for medical quarantine.

38. These are remarkable temperatures and probably are somewhat exaggerated. However, there are numerous reports of poor ventilation in ships of the period; one surgeon reported that in the engineers' workshop of the battleship *Illinois* the average temperature "obtained by careful observations" was 120°F "and often reached 124°." *Army and Navy Register* 36 (Dec. 10, 1904): 11.

39. Salt horse is corned beef stored in barrels of brine.

40. *Brooklyn* was a 9,215-ton armored cruiser mounting eight eight-inch guns. She commissioned on Dec. 1, 1896.

41. Capt. Theodore F. Jewell. His executive officer was Lt. Cdr. Dennis H. Mahan, brother of Alfred Thayer Mahan. Unlike his famous brother, Dennis Mahan had a major drinking problem.

42. By way of comparison, an ensign during his first five years of service on sea duty earned a hundred dollars per month. "Navy Pay Tables, Table 1: Rates of Pay of Officers of the Line, Medical and Pay Corps, in effect prior to July 1, 1899," *Register of the Commissioned and Warrant Officers of the United States Navy and Marine Corps, January 1, 1909* (Washington, D.C.: Government Printing Office, 1909), 250.

43. Emilio Aguinaldo, leader of the Philippine nationalists (or insurrectionists, depending upon one's point of view) in their struggle first against the Spanish and then against the United States.

44. Old salts believed that a pig tattooed on a foot protected them from death by drowning. See "Tattoos in the Navy," *Army and Navy Register* 43 (May 2, 1908): 25.

45. This was Chaplain William T. Helms, a Methodist. One of his fellow chaplains later wrote that he "was a good preacher and a man of good appearance. He might have made a very useful man in the navy but for the fact that he lost his faith in his own religion." NA, RG 24, entry 378, box 6.

46. The *New Orleans* was assigned to the Flying Squadron in May 1898 and patrolled off Santiago. At the time of the Battle of Santiago, she was in Key West. Thereafter, she helped maintain the blockade of Cuba and Puerto Rico. She deployed to Asiatic Station in Oct. 1899.

47. HMS *Centurion*, eleven-thousand-ton battleship completed in 1892. Her main battery consisted of four ten-inch guns.

48. HMS *Hermione*, 4,360-ton protected cruiser, completed in 1895, mounted two six-inch guns as its main battery.

49. Wilson actually was closer to the Equator than he thought. Singapore lies at one degree, seventeen minutes north, roughly seventy-seven miles north of the Equator.

50. "Roulade," a flourish on the drums.

51. "Square heads," slang for individuals from northern European nations: Germans, Norwegians, Swedes, Russian Finns, etc.

52. "Fly," slang for "sharp, wide awake."

53. "First Luff," first lieutenant, or executive officer of the ship, the officer second in command after the captain.

54. "Hobson's choice" refers to Thomas Hobson (1544–1631), an English liveryman who required each customer to take the horse nearest the door. The identity of Wilson's "Hobson of oscillatory fame" is not entirely clear; it may be an indirect reference to Naval Constructor Richmond Pearson Hobson, USN, of Spanish-American War fame, who appears later in this account. "Osculation" is the art of kissing.

55. Russell had published biographies of Dampier, Nelson, and Collingwood. His 1898 publication, *The Romance of a Midshipman*, might have further convinced Wilson of Russell's bias.

56. Windsails, funnel-shaped canvas devices arranged to direct natural circulation from the main deck to the lower decks, principally berthing areas. These cheap devices can be very effective.

57. Binnacle list: sick list. In the olden days, the list of sick crewmen was posted by the binnacle on the bridge of the ship.

58. Sheol, in the Old Testament, was a place under the earth where the departed spirits were believed to go. In this context, it means he "got hell."

59. Salt junk: could refer to "salt horse," salted pork, or any other salted meat.

CHAPTER 1: MANILA

1. The *Brooklyn* served as Commodore Winfield S. Schley's flagship at the Battle of Santiago in 1898 and was at this point the flagship of Rear Adm. John C. Watson, Commander in Chief, Asiatic Station. The *Newark* was a protected cruiser of 4,083 tons displacement and had entered service in 1891.

2. The 333-foot collier *Merrimac* was intentionally sunk on June 3, 1898, in an effort to block the channel and trap the Spanish squadron in Santiago Harbor. The *Merrimac*, however, despite the heroism of its all-volunteer crew, sank outside the channel and caused only a minor obstruction. Naval Constructor Richmond P. Hobson became a national hero and subsequently served as a U.S. congressman.

3. "Mex" refers to Mexican dollar, the currency most widely used at the time. The exchange rate varied between forty and fifty cents U.S. to a Mexican dollar.

4. *Casco*, Spanish for hull or hulk. In Manila, the word described a kind of boat used in loading and unloading ships.

5. Banca, or *bangka*, a small, open boat with a narrow beam.

6. Named after John Raines (1840–1909), Republican politician and lawyer. The Raines Excise Act of 1896 was his most lasting claim to fame. The act continued an existing ban on Sunday liquor sales

but added an exemption for hotels with ten or more beds. "Raines Law hotels" soon figured prominently as houses of prostitution.

7. Gambrinus (1251–94), duke of Brabant, was reputed to have been the inventor of lager beer.

8. *Glacier* was a 4,154-tons-displacement refrigerated stores ship.

9. The *Reina Christina* was a 3,520-ton cruiser built in 1887. She served as flagship for Adm. Patricio Montojo at the Battle of Manila Bay. *Castilla* was a wooden-hulled cruiser of 3,260 tons displacement completed in 1881. John D. Long, *The New American Navy*, 2 vols. (New York: Outlook, 1903), 1: 169.

10. The reference here, of course, is to USS *Maine*, sunk Feb. 15, 1898, with the loss of 268 American lives. At the time, it was thought to have been blown up by Spanish saboteurs, but now it is most widely recognized to have been the victim of an internal explosion. The hulk of the *Maine*, its masts above water in Havana Harbor, was not raised and removed until 1912. In the intervening years, ceremonies were held at the wreck annually on the anniversary of the sinking.

11. Presumably Wilson meant the shell casings, not the shells.

12. *Oregon*, a first-class battleship displacing 10,288 tons, was commissioned in 1895. *Monterey* was a 4,084-ton monitor that mounted two twelve-inch and two ten-inch guns and was commissioned in 1893; *Helena* was a 1,392-ton gunboat commissioned in 1897.

13. "Dobie dollars," also known as "dungaree dollars": local currency, specifically Mexican dollars.

14. The reference here is to William Jennings Bryan, the Democratic Party's unsuccessful 1896 and 1900 presidential candidate, famous for his opposition to the imposition of a gold currency standard and his espousal of the free and unlimited coining of silver. Bryan served as colonel of the Third Nebraska Volunteer Regiment, which never deployed overseas. After the war, he sought the rapid demobilization of his regiment, even though the other Nebraska regiments had served longer and had seen combat. Thwarted in this, he resigned his commission. This provided fodder in the 1900 presidential campaign, in which war hero and vice presidential candidate Col. Theodore Roosevelt flaunted his military achievements while other Republicans highlighted Emilio Aguinaldo's endorsement of the Democratic Party. See Margaret Leech, *In the Days of McKinley* (New York: Harper and Brothers, 1959), 337–38, for regimental service, and Stuart Creighton Miller, *"Benevolent Assimilation": The American Conquest of the Philippines, 1899–1903* (New Haven, Conn.: Yale Univ. Press, 1982), 140–44, for implications for the 1900 presidential campaign.

15. Note that Wilson regularly uses the now-infamous "N word" solely to describe the Filipino insurrectionists, not African Americans.

16. Presumably, this was Acting Warrant Machinist Oscar Berentson, USN, who was a native of Norway.

17. Ecru lambrequins: brown whiskers.

18. In this context, "words" means "orders."

CHAPTER 2: NAGASAKI

1. Presumably, Lt. Cdr. Martin E. Hall, USN, who was listed in the Jan. 1, 1900, edition of the *Register of the Commissioned and Warrant Officers of the United States Navy and Marine Corps*. At that time, officers of the rank of commander served only as commanding officers; therefore, all executive officers on major combatants were of the rank of lieutenant commander.

2. This was Acting Boatswain Hugh J. Duffy.

3. *Columbia* and *Minneapolis* were sister ships. They commissioned in 1894 and displaced 7,375 tons. Their three vertical, inverted, triple-expansion engines and three screws drove them to remarkable trial speeds of 22.8 and 23.07 knots, respectively. Wilson served on board *Minneapolis* from Jan. 12 to Oct. 29, 1898, and took part in the West Indian campaign on board her.

4. "Dream sacks," slang for hammocks.

5. Presumably, this was Lt. Harold K. Hines, the only officer with a name beginning with "H" listed in the *Register* as being on board the *New Orleans*.

6. By this time, the controversy over which of the two admirals, Sampson or Schley, should receive credit for the victory off Santiago, Cuba, was receiving wide publicity. Rear Adm. A. Schuyler Crowninshield added to the controversy in his annual report as chief of the Bureau of Navigation by seeming to demean the importance of Adm. George Dewey's victory at Manila Bay. See "What Admiral Crowninshield Said," *Army and Navy Journal* 37 (Nov. 18, 1899): 266, and "Dwelling Together in Unity," *Army and Navy Journal* 37 (Nov. 18, 1899): 273.

7. Although relations between Russia and Japan were tense, the anticipated war did not break out until 1904.

8. At this time, the Japanese yen was valued at approximately fifty cents U.S. One hundred *sen* equaled one yen; therefore, five sen were worth two and a half cents.

9. "Hully gee" is not a Japanese term. It is possible this was a nickname given to him by someone in Japan; perhaps it derived from an expression he used frequently. Perhaps he used the phrase "Holy Jesus" or "Holy Jeez," which then was adopted by one of his Japanese acquaintances. Wilson later used the term "*O-ji-ji*" for his friend. *Ojiisan* is the Japanese word for "old man"; O-ji-ji is a somewhat less formal way of saying *Ojiisan*. It can also be used when referring to someone with whom the speaker is very well acquainted.

10. *Charleston* was a 3,730-ton protected cruiser commissioned in 1889 and wrecked on Camiguin Island, the Philippines, Nov. 2, 1899.

11. "Make love," in this context, means, "to flirt with."

12. "Wheel," slang for a bicycle.

13. "Oura" is a common street name. Contemporary maps of Nagasaki show the Oura skirting a portion of the waterfront of the city.

14. The actual word is *jinrickishaw*, "human powered wheeled vehicle."

15. As with many of the general comments in this account, this observation may well be autobiographical in nature. Wilson himself was married three times.

16. At this point, the U.S. Army had more than fifty transports in service, most of them carrying troops to and from the Philippines.

17. Wilson spelled Japanese terms as he heard them. They have been corrected to reflect current spellings: *tabi*, Japanese-style socks; *zōri*, Japanese sandals; *geta*, Japanese wooden sandals.

18. *Sou*, a former French coin, a hundredth of a franc—now generally signifying a trivial amount. "Without a *sou*" means penniless.

19. A wallah means a person employed in a particular job; in this case, "Russian gin mill wallahs" probably would be correct.

20. Presumably, *Okamisan*, wife, or probably in this context a "steady" girlfriend, somewhat like a "wife in every port."

21. Wilson rendered this name "Qenzo." "Kenzo" would be a more appropriate spelling, and thus it has been changed in this text.

22. *Kasa*, an umbrella. The original text says *cazar*.

23. The protected cruiser *Irene* was one of the ships involved in the German buildup in Manila Bay after Dewey's victory there in 1898. *Jaguar* was a nine-hundred-ton displacement gunboat, built in Schichau, Danzig, completed in 1899. *Taschenbuch der Kriegsflotten*, VI. *Jahrgang, 1905* (Munich, 1905), 14–15, 125. My thanks to Lt. Cdr. Krzysztof Kubiak, Polish Navy, for this information.

24. *Chishi*, an old Japanese term, no longer in use, to describe a suckling infant. Later Wilson employs the term as a general word to describe small children.

25. *Bennington*, a seagoing gunboat, displaced 1,700 tons. She was commissioned in 1891.

26. "Bobbery," a disturbance, squabble.

27. "Ni" here is a misspelling of *ne*, which is the Japanese equivalent of saying "right?" at the end of a sentence, as in the United States, or "eh?" in English-speaking Canada.

28. The "old" captain was Capt. Edwin Longnecker. He had been appointed to the Naval Academy in 1861. *New Orleans* was his last sea command. He subsequently commanded navy yards at Boston, Port Royal and Charleston (South Carolina), Norfolk (Virginia), and League Island (in Philadelphia).

He was promoted to rear admiral on July 8, 1905, and retired on Feb. 19, 1906 (William B. Cogar, *Dictionary of Admirals of the US Navy*, vol. 2, 1901–1918 (Annapolis, Md.: Naval Institute Press, 1991), 167–68. The new commanding officer, Capt. George E. Ide, also entered the naval academy in 1861. He commanded the *New Orleans* for little more than a month before being ordered home to the United States. He retired with the rank of rear admiral in Sept. 1901 (Cogar, 142–43). He in turn was succeeded by Capt. James G. Green, who commanded from June to Dec. 1900. He also retired with the rank of rear admiral, May 11, 1901 (Cogar, 116–17).

29. *Dixie* was a 6,114-ton ex-merchant ship designated auxiliary cruiser and commissioned in 1898.

30. *Culgoa* was a stores ship, or "supply steamer," as she was then described, of 3,612 tons.

31. *Petrel* was a gunboat of 890 tons, commissioned in 1889.

32. *Glacier*, along with refrigerated stores ships *Celtic* and *Culgoa*, had just instituted a supply service between Australia and Manila. *Army and Navy Journal* 37 (Dec. 2, 1899): 312.

33. Presumably Wilson is referring to Lt. Cdr. Martin E. Hall; however, the Naval Academy Register of Alumni indicates that Commander Hall retired on June 30, 1900, and died on Feb. 21, 1904. The 1901 *Register of Officers of the US Navy* lists Lt. Cdr. James T. Smith as executive officer.

34. Punkah wallah: a person who operated a fan.

35. Presumably *nicht*, German for "nothing."

36. To "go aft" in this context means to request assistance or advice from the officers. Generally in that period the officers' quarters were located aft on a ship, while the enlisted quarters were forward.

37. It was common practice to offer bounties for enlisted men who overstayed leave in a foreign port, as an incentive for local police to locate and return them. The bounty generally was ten dollars, a huge sum, which was then deducted from the enlisted man's pay.

38. There is no earlier mention in the original manuscript of a need to replace a casting, presumably for the starboard engine that had failed en route to Manila from Nagasaki.

39. Reference here is to the Boxer Rebellion and the siege of the legations in Peking (Beijing).

40. Twelve hundred British troops died in the initial assault on Cronjé's *laager* near Paardeberg on the Modder River, Feb. 18, 1900. His *laager* surrounded and besieged, Cronjé surrendered with four thousand combatants on Feb. 27, 1900, the most humiliating Boer defeat in the war. See Peter Warwick, ed., *The South African War: The Anglo-Boer War, 1899–1902* (Harlow, U.K.: Longman, 1980), 92–93.

41. Wilson's skepticism was warranted. Neither Daet nor Monyagaray appear in any of the published accounts of the Philippine Insurrection.

CHAPTER 3: AGROUND IN THE YELLOW SEA

1. The *Oregon* was the most widely known battleship of the U.S. Navy at this time, having completed a remarkable voyage from Seattle to Key West, Florida, on the eve of the war with Spain, thus being in position to take part in the critical Battle of Santiago, July 3, 1898. She was the third unit of the *Indiana* class, displacing 10,288 tons, and was commissioned on June 10, 1896. She had two vertical, triple-expansion engines and a rated speed of fifteen knots. For a detailed history of the USS *Oregon*, see Sanford Sternlicht, *McKinley's Bulldog: The Battleship* Oregon (Chicago: Nelson-Hall, 1977).

2. At this point, the United States and other naval powers were assembling ships off the Taku forts, preparing to take action to relieve the legations in Peking, during the Boxer Rebellion.

3. Nickname for the *New Orleans*.

4. *Zafiro* was a two-thousand-ton supply ship that had originally been a British-flag merchant ship and had been purchased by Commodore George Dewey in Hong Kong on the eve of war with Spain.

5. *Monadnock* was an *Amphitrite*-class monitor with a unique background. Laid down in Brooklyn in 1875, she was shipped in pieces to Vallejo, California, for assembly but was not commissioned until Feb. 20, 1896. She mounted two ten-inch guns. K. Jack Baer and Stephen S. Roberts, *Register of Ships of the U.S. Navy, 1775–1990: Major Combatants* (Westport, Conn.: Greenwood, 1991), 99.

6. Probably a corruption of "gazob," a silly fool, a foolish blunderer. Eric Partridge, *A Dictionary of Slang and Unconventional English*, 7th ed. (New York: Macmillan, 1970), 319.

7. CPO, chief petty officer.

8. More commonly known as Subic Bay, north of Manila Bay on the west coast of Luzon. At the time of Wilson's visit, the naval base there was very small. It later became the principal American base in the western Pacific, particularly after World War II, until it was vacated in compliance with the demands of the Philippine Senate at the end of 1992. James M. Morris and Patricia M. Kearns, *Historical Dictionary of the United States Navy* (Lanham, Md.: Scarecrow, 1998), 303.

9. A ship "laid up in ordinary" was, in essence, in temporary reserve—more modern technical term, "restricted availability." The crew was generally reduced to a caretaker force, too small to get the ship under way. That *Oregon* was placed "in ordinary" for a six-week repair period suggests that the Asiatic Station was very short of enlisted personnel.

10. The war referred to was the Boxer Rebellion. The "powers" were assembling forces to relieve the Boxer siege of the legations in Peking (Beijing). Wilson failed to mention one of the principal participating powers, Japan.

11. Father Damien, Joseph Damien de Veuster (1840–89), Belgian missionary who devoted his life to care of the lepers in Hawaii.

12. "Celestial," slang for a Chinese person.

13. "To get good shipmates with" in this context means to become intimately familiar with (the pumps).

14. *Oregon*'s "first luff," or executive officer at that time was Lt. Cdr. Charles A. Adams. Although Wilson often expressed pity for him, the fact is that an executive officer with a temperament such as this could totally demoralize the ship's crew. A member of the Naval Academy class of 1868, Adams retired from the navy in 1903 with the rank of commander and died in 1929.

15. *Oregon*'s commanding officer, in his haste to reach Taku, had taken the shortest, though clearly not the safest, route. He had anchored three miles south of the How-ki Island light, in the Chang-Shan Channel, not far from the Shantung Peninsula and the Gulf of Pechili. When they got under way, they struck Pinnacle Rock. Sternlicht, *McKinley's Bulldog*, 121–22.

16. Handy billy, a portable hand-powered pump.

17. *Maru* is a common Japanese term for "ship."

18. For a detailed account of Captain McCalla's role in lifting the siege of the legations during the Boxer Rebellion, see Paolo E. Coletta, *Bowman Hendry McCalla: A Fighting Sailor* (Washington, D.C.: Univ. Press of America, 1979), particularly chap. 7, 103–32.

19. *Yorktown* was a 1,700-ton-displacement seagoing gunboat commissioned in 1889.

20. This was the cruiser *Hai Chi*. She had been on duty at nearby Tengchow, protecting foreigners there. She was the first ship to reach the *Oregon*. William R. Braisted, *The United States Navy in the Pacific, 1897–1909* (Austin: Univ. of Texas Press, 1958), 108.

21. At this time, a person successfully completing an enlistment under honorable conditions received, upon the recommendation of his commanding officer, a "testimonial for fidelity, obedience and ability during his term of service." The other types of discharge then available were an "ordinary discharge" and a "bad-conduct discharge." See *The Bluejacket's Manual, United States Navy (1902)* (repr. Annapolis, Md.: Naval Institute Press, 1978), 284–85.

22. Marline spike, or marlinspike, a pointed metal spike used to separate strands of rope in splicing.

23. The Battle of Santiago occurred on July 3, 1898.

24. For an excellent account of the *Oregon*'s wartime performance, see Sanford Sternlicht, *McKinley's Bulldog: The Battleship* Oregon (Chicago: Nelson-Hall, 1977).

25. The Japanese ship was the *Akitisushima*. Sternlicht, 122.

26. In Wilson's manuscript, there are two versions of these events. The following passage has been excluded in favor of the passage that follows in the text. "The *Endymion* had given us a tow before and parted [a] hawser and steel cable without budging us in the least. The *Kwongchang* and *Nanchang*, the former on our port bow and the latter on our [starboard], each backed as the *Endymion* pulled, but [to] no avail. Finally, haste was given up and all hands started to clear out everything forward thoroughly

before undertaking to get off again, the awful strains doing no good to the ship, only seesawing her from side to side. We [were] using our own engines in conjunction with the others."

27. This rumor was incorrect. The gunboat *Concord,* commissioned in 1891, continued in service and was not sold until 1929. Indeed, Wilson was later transferred to this ship and spent several months in Alaskan waters on board her.

28. The *Charleston* had been wrecked on Camiguin Island, the Philippines, Nov. 2, 1899, while Wilson was en route to the Philippines.

29. This sentence appeared originally at the end of the second paragraph before its current location; it has been moved to improve the flow of Wilson's prose.

30. Mr. Peterson, of Calender, Peterson and Curtis, salvors, was paid five hundred pounds for his services. Correspondence between Fred J. Curtis and J. Fowler, U.S. consul, Chefoo, Sept. 17, 1900, NA, RG 45, Subject File, box 180.

31. "To lose the number of one's mess"—slang, to die.

32. *Iris* was a 6,100-ton supply ship.

33. The threat of such treatment by the crew of unusually dirty shipmates continued at least through the 1950s and early 1960s.

34. Presumably, "Clarence/Flying Jib" was Acting Warrant Machinist Clarence E. Wood, USN, who was then assigned to the *Oregon.*

35. By this point Wilson was referring to the *Nanchang* as the *Nanchane.* However, the former name is correct; therefore his original spelling has been retained.

36. "Classed" means that they were assigned the lowest liberty status, generally fourth class, which permitted liberty only once every three months.

37. "To be brought up with a round turn" means to be stopped.

38. Now a drinking fountain, the scuttlebutt in 1900 was a barrel of drinking water equipped with communal cups.

39. Unfortunately for enlisted men, officers such as this were not uncommon in the navy of the day.

CHAPTER 4: KURE, JAPAN

1. On July 13, 1863, Cdr. David McDougal, commanding the steam sloop USS *Wyoming,* attacked the forts and three naval vessels protecting the Shimonoseki Straits, in response to an earlier, unprovoked Japanese attack against the American merchant steamer *Pembroke.* For a detailed account, see Dudley W. Knox, *A History of the United States Navy* (New York: Putnam, 1938), 293–94.

2. Wilson is correct in this assertion. For an account of the *Oregon*'s chase, see G. J. A. O'Toole, *The Spanish War: An American Epic 1898* (New York: Norton, 1984), 337.

3. Wilson enjoyed painting and indulged in it in later years.

4. Many of these old brick buildings survived World War II and are still in use on the Kure waterfront. In fact, Kure is famous for its old red-brick buildings.

5. That is, en route to participate in the campaign to relieve the legations in Peking.

6. At this point in its development, the Imperial Japanese Navy was strongly influenced by Great Britain's Royal Navy.

7. Wilson is incorrect here. The only U.S. Navy docks capable of accommodating *Oregon* were in New York and Bellingham, Washington.

8. Presumably, this was the IJNS *Shikishima,* completed in 1899, displacing 14,850 tons. She mounted four twelve-inch guns.

9. The Sino-Japanese War (1894–95) ended in a major Japanese victory and concluded with the Treaty of Shimonoseki. The subsequent intervention of Germany, France, and Russia (the "*Driebund* Intervention") compelled Japan to relinquish territory it had taken from China in the terms of the treaty. This caused Japan to embark upon a major buildup of its army and navy, and led to the Russo-Japanese War of 1904–1905. Wilson was observing the early results of the Japanese buildup.

10. It is possible some of the "rookies" Wilson described were actually midshipmen from the Imperial Naval Academy, which had been established across the bay from Kure, at Eta Jima, in 1888. Rowing the cutters used for this drill was a very strenuous undertaking.

11. This was a continuous complaint regarding the U.S. Navy of the day. Records indicate that in 1900, only 67 percent of the enlisted force were native-born Americans. An additional 12.6 percent were naturalized citizens, while a whopping 20.4 percent—one in five—were noncitizens. Figures cited in Frederick S. Harrod, *Manning the New Navy: The Development of a Modern Naval Enlisted Force, 1899–1940* (Westport, Conn.: Greenwood, 1978), 181. This nevertheless represented considerable progress over the preceding decade. In 1890, the Navy Department reported that only 58 percent of the enlisted force were citizens and that 47 percent native born. Harrod, 17.

12. The only reference to granting liberty in the *Laws of the Navy and Marine Corps, 1898*, is in article 1431, which charges commanding officers "to exercise carefully a discrimination in favor of the faithful and obedient." From this regulation stemmed the practice of "liberty classing." Many commanding officers granted liberty only when all excuses for keeping the men on board had been used.

13. Due largely to practices such as those Wilson describes, the U.S. Navy in the decade following the war with Spain suffered a remarkable average of 14 percent desertions of the enlisted force each year.

14. *Ladrones* was a name then in common use for the Marianas Islands, of which Guam was the principal island. In this context, *Ladrones* means the people of the Marianas, now properly Chamorros.

15. "Having a pull," having influence. At this time, political influence was an important factor in the appointment of most staff and warrant officers, and it also played a significant part in determining line-officer duty assignments.

16. The careful description here of Mr. Rollo's enormous breakfast is actually a commentary on the poor quality and quantity of navy food.

17. "Turn to," to begin work.

18. Coasters Harbor Island, then the site of a training station for naval apprentices and the Naval War College.

19. "Guy," to make fun of.

20. Spring tide is an exceptionally high tide; presumably a spring tide was necessary to float the *Oregon*, in its current state, over the sill of the dry dock.

21. "Bootleg," coffee.

22. On May 1, 1897, Adolph L. Luetgert murdered his wife in his large sausage factory and destroyed her body, allegedly with acids and chemicals in a vat used at his factory. He was convicted and sentenced to life in prison. The implication here, though, and possibly the perception of the population at large, was that Mrs. Luetgert ended up in the sausages. See *New York Times*, Feb. 10, 1898.

23. The oldest large stone dock still in use in Kure is the one that was used to build the battleship *Mikasa*, Admiral Heihichiro Togo's flagship at the Battle of Tsushima, the climactic battle of the Russo-Japanese War of 1904–1905.

24. Naval Constructor Richmond P. Hobson, then prominent as a hero of the Spanish-American War, was a graduate of the Naval Academy class of 1889.

25. Acting Warrant Machinist Rush C. Steele, USN.

26. The USS *Franklin* began life as a sailing ship of the line. Authorized in 1853, she was laid down in 1854 but was not completed until 1867. She had served as a stationary receiving ship since 1877 and ultimately would be sold for scrap in 1916. Baer and Roberts, *Register*, 54.

27. Wilson is here implying that before enlisting, this warrant officer had been a hobo.

28. "His Imperial Jiblets" in this case was Carpenter John P. Yates, USN.

29. The *Regulations for the Government of the Navy* (1898) were bound in navy blue covers—hence, "the blue book."

30. Hiroshima actually is north of (or above) Kure.

31. The Yoshiwara was the "red-light" district of Tokyo. Sailors therefore used the term to describe all red-light districts in Japan. Presumably, "Yoshiwaries" referred to the denizens of the Yoshiwara (i.e., prostitutes).

32. *Chishi* is actually a term for an infant; Wilson used it to describe all young children.

33. *Okamison* means "wife"; however, Wilson used it quite loosely to describe his girlfriends in various ports.

34. Wilson identified his liberty partner simply as "K——" until much later in the account, when he began using the name "Ken." For ease of reading, "Ken" has been inserted where "K——" originally appeared.

35. Japanese women did not use betel nut to blacken their teeth. Married women soaked iron in either sake or green tea to make a mixture that turned their teeth black. Wilson might have seen women with betel-blackened teeth in the Philippines or elsewhere and assumed the same process was used in Japan.

36. Laura Jean Libby (1862–1925) was an author of "working girl novels" in which, generally, the working-class heroine struggled to keep her virtue intact in face of unwanted advances of an upper-class villain.

37. "Komshir," more commonly spelled "cumshaw," is a slang term referring to petty graft, secret commissions, or, as in this case, tips.

38. It is possible that Wilson and his friends were traveling along the road toward the summit of Mount Yasumiyama. The view from a particular point along that road is still considered the finest of the Inland Sea in the Kure area, and it is probably the view Wilson described.

39. *Combawa* (Konbonwa) is correctly translated here. *Onaga* is not a common Japanese word. Wilson may have been trying to say, "Good evening, girls." If so, the proper word would have been *onna*, and not *onaga*.

40. "Push," slang, crowd or gang.

41. More probably "Morimoto's."

42. The closest probable word to Wilson's *musmee* is *musume*, which translates to "daughter," or sometimes, more loosely, to "young girl."

43. The reference here is to Philip Dorner Stanhope (1694–1773), fourth earl of Chesterfield, known for his urbanity, from which "Chesterfieldian," meaning suave, polished, or elegant, derives.

44. "Fly," slang for sharp, wide awake.

45. "Water" in this context means the transparency or luster of a precious stone, thus its excellence.

46. Jean Louis Ernest Messonier (1815–91), French painter.

47. Presumably, William-Adolphe Bouguereau (1825–1905), whose work was widely collected by Americans during his lifetime.

48. Jean Baptiste Camille Corot (1796–83), French painter.

49. Presumably, one of the Sabatinis. Lorenzo Sabatini (1530–76) had an alternate spelling, "Sabadini."

50. Theodore Rousseau (1812–67), French landscape painter, and Henri ("Le Douanier") Rousseau (1844–1910), French painter. It is unclear whether Wilson is referring to one of them or both.

51. Edward Gay (1837–1928), prolific landscape painter. He spent much of his life painting scenes of open farmland with sunny meadows and orchards, such as the painting Wilson describes.

52. *Kohi* actually refers to coffee. Tea is *kocha*. However, it is not difficult to understand Wilson's confusion.

53. *Koto*, a thirteen-stringed musical instrument.

54. *Samisen*, a three-stringed instrument.

55. "Running a 'muck," "running amok [or amuck]," comes from a Malay term, *amok*, which means to be in a frenzy to do violence or kill, such as in "rioters running amok."

56. *Katana*, sword.

57. This doubtless was Wilson's attempt to spell phonetically something a group of Japanese was singing; however, its meaning is not apparent to the Japanese speakers consulted in the preparation of this text.

58. "O.T.," on time.

59. The reference here is to Secretary of the Navy John D. Long, in office 1897–1902, who, not unlike a successor, Josephus Daniels, showed considerable concern for the "welfare" of the enlisted men. After

leaving office he was active in the Sabbath Protective League and sought to have the navy forbid sailors from playing sports on the Sabbath, the only day they routinely had off.

60. This vow notwithstanding, Wilson reenlisted several more times and was promoted to chief petty officer.

61. In this context, "graft" is slang for "work."

62. Wilson refrained from using names; however, the only acting warrant machinist on board *Oregon* whose name began with an "H" was Charles Hammond.

63. Wilson here implies that he has done everything ordered, strictly according to regulations (i.e., like a marine).

CHAPTER 5: WOOSUNG, CHINA

1. This procedure is called "swinging ship." Its purpose is to calculate the amount of deviation being registered in the ship's magnetic compasses. As this deviation varied with the ship's heading as well as changes in latitude, and as gyroscopic compasses had not yet been introduced, calculation of deviation was an important and frequent function on board ship.

2. A court of inquiry that convened while the *Oregon* was in Kure found Capt. George Francis Faxon Wilde guilty of "error[s] of judgment" in the groundings and recommended a court-martial. The commander in chief of the Asiatic Station concurred and recommended a general court-martial; however, due to a shortage of senior officers on the Station, a court was not convened. In this situation it behooved Capt. Wilde to stay on the Asiatic Station as long as possible. This tactic paid off. The secretary of the navy ultimately decided not to proceed against Capt. Wilde, who subsequently was promoted to rear admiral. The records relating to the court of inquiry are in NA, RG 125, Records of the Office of Judge Advocate General, Entry 30, box 71, "Records of Proceedings of Courts of Inquiry, Boards of Investigation and Boards of Inquest," May 1880–Dec. 1940, vol. 691, no. 4933. Correspondence relating to the recommendation of general court-martial, Rear Adm. George Remey to Secretary of the Navy John D. Long, Aug. 19, 1900, and Long to CinC Asiatic Station, Oct. 3, 1900, NA, RG 45, Subject file, box 180.

3. "Went ashore," went aground.

4. A "mustang" officer had worked his way up through the enlisted ranks and gained a commission. They are generally well regarded by the enlisted men, but in the class-conscious officer corps of this period, Academy graduates definitely affected an air of social superiority over them.

5. Wilson probably was incorrect on this point. The captain doubtless was waiting for a spring tide, when the range of high tide would be greatest and the level of water over the bar therefore greatest, rather than a neap tide, when the conditions would be reversed.

6. Li Hung-Chang (1823–1902), Chinese statesman and general. As viceroy of Zhili (1870–95), he controlled Chinese foreign affairs for the dowager empress Tz'u Hsi. Li was the chief negotiator of the Treaty of Shimonoseki (1895), which ended the Sino-Japanese War. He protected foreigners when he was viceroy of Guangzhou during the Boxer Uprising (1900), and he was able to reduce the demands of the foreign powers for reparations. The implication of Wilson's comment here is unclear.

7. Reference here is to the acquisition of overseas territories in Puerto Rico, the Philippines, and Guam. The inclusion of New Jersey possibly is a reference to the change in corporate laws that permitted the creation of huge and sprawling monopolies like Standard Oil of New Jersey, which was established as a holding company in New Jersey in 1899.

8. Pseudonym of Linn Boyd Porter (1851–1916), who wrote romantic novels. Her most recent publications at the time Wilson wrote were, *A New Sensation* (1898), *The Naked Truth* (1899), *Thou Shalt Not* (1899), and *Stranger Than Fiction* (1900). Presumably, Porter wrote under a male pseudonym to avoid the difficulties of nineteenth century gender stereotyping.

9. Cumshaw.

10. This unusual title stemmed from the fact that in sailing days the paymaster's assistant worked from the bread room, where was stored the ship's flour.

11. "Shell back," or "shellback," a sailor who had already crossed the Equator—thus, an "old salt."

12. "Guardo," slang for receiving ship.

13. The League Island Navy Yard is now more commonly known as the Philadelphia Naval Shipyard, which was closed in 1996.

14. PRR: Pennsylvania Railroad.

15. The Cob dock was the main dock at the New York Navy Yard in Brooklyn, where the "guardo" was moored.

16. William Cramp and Sons Ship and Engine Building Company, Philadelphia, the builders of the *Indiana*.

17. Bitt: short, vertical steel posts on a ship's deck, generally in pairs, used to secure mooring lines. They are convenient for sitting on, a practice even today generally discouraged by boatswain's mates.

18. The "top bolo" at this time was Acting Warrant Machinist John F. Green, USN, who was fifth in seniority among the hundred acting warrant machinists in the navy. *Oregon*'s other acting warrant machinists, in order of seniority, were Clarence E. Wood (twenty-three), Charles Hammond (twenty-seven), Angus C. Bates (fifty-six), and Lemuel T. Cooper (sixty-one).

19. "Government-educated asses," Naval Academy graduates.

20. Presumably this is another reference to the grounding of June 1900.

21. Unlike present practices, sailors' general-quarters stations then varied, depending whether they were in the section on watch that had just been relieved, or was preparing to relieve; therefore, if general quarters was called away in the middle of the night, a sailor had to know what time it was in order to determine where to go.

22. The koodoo (or kudu) is a large striped African antelope with spiraling horns.

23. To "take the shilling" means to be in the service of the queen.

24. "Dart"—dirt, "the old sod," Ireland.

25. A territorial dispute over the border between British Guiana and Venezuela in 1895.

26. A Turk's head is an elaborate knot.

27. "Sheeney" was a common term for any sailor who owned a small sewing machine and earned additional income by making uniforms. The term, heavily anti-Semitic to twenty-first-century American ears, did not carry pejorative connotations a hundred years ago. Indeed, the position of "sheeney," like that of barber, was much sought after by industrious crewmembers because of the additional income it afforded, and the term was applied to any shipboard tailor, regardless of religious affiliation or cultural background. That is not to say that anti-Semitism did not exist in Wilson's navy. However, such feelings were far more pronounced within the officer corps than among enlisted men.

28. The same complaint was loudly made concerning "issue" uniforms when the editor enlisted in 1958, more than half a century later. I suspect a new recruit of today would sympathize with Wilson, even though a century has passed since he penned these lines.

29. Reference here is to the blue flat hat, which remained in service until around 1960. The editor last stood inspection wearing a blue flat hat on board USS *Atka* (AGB 3) in Port Lyttleton, New Zealand, at the end of 1959.

30. The "ship's writer" rating had officially been changed to "yeoman" in 1896; however, the nature of shipboard duties dictated a continuance of specialized names within the rating: "captain's writer," "executive officer's writer" [the latter more commonly called the "ship's writer"], "navigator's writer." Other shipboard areas used the "yeoman" title: "engineer yeoman," "pay yeoman," "equipment yeoman," etc. The "ship's writer" was responsible for the ship's executive correspondence, enlisted service records (except Marines), muster rolls, conduct books, etc. For more detailed discussion, see Tomlinson, *A Rocky Mountain Sailor in Teddy Roosevelt's Navy*, 137. Harrod, *Manning the New Navy*, 192, cites date.

374

CHAPTER 6: SHANGHAI

1. The cross of St. George implies the white ensign of the Royal Navy.
2. Whereas British and French ships were painted gray, U.S. Navy ships' hulls were white—a practice discontinued in 1909.
3. "Gentlemen aft," officers.
4. Cesare Lombroso (1836–1909), Italian physician and criminologist. He held that the criminal is a distinct anthropological type, and that criminality is the product of heredity, atavism, and degeneracy.
5. Here Wilson most probably is describing the Hu Xin Ting (Heart of the Lake Pavilion), still a popular tourist attraction in the old Chinese city of Shanghai.
6. "Joss house" was a term then used to describe a Chinese temple or place for idols.
7. "Jim-jams," slang for delirium tremens.
8. Presumably Wilson intended an other-than-normal interpretation of "panhandling" here.
9. Presumably a shortened form of "biddy," which in the usage of the time meant Irish servant girl or, alternatively, a young wench. I suspect Wilson meant the latter.
10. "Cash" was the smallest Chinese denomination of coin. It often had a hole in the middle, enabling it to be carried on strings. The value fluctuated somewhat, but one could get as many as two thousand cash for an American dollar.
11. The Krag-Jörgensen rifle was a five-shot military weapon developed in 1889 and adopted by Denmark and Norway. A modified .30-caliber version was adopted by the United States and was the standard arm from 1892 to 1903. The rifle was named after the inventors, Capt. O. Krag and E. Jörgensen of Norway. John Quick, *Dictionary of Weapons and Military Terms* (New York: McGraw-Hill, 1973), 263.

CHAPTER 7: AFLOAT AND ASHORE IN SHANGHAI

1. "Run to the stick," send to Captain's Mast for punishment.
2. A passage of 513 words relating to the election of a mess caterer for Wilson's mess has been omitted.
3. "Port lamp," left eye.
4. "Smokers" were common in the navy at this time, with matches normally conducted in a ring constructed on a ship's forecastle specifically for the event. Large sums of money normally were subscribed from each ship in the form of bets, and this practice generally was sanctioned. It is unclear why this particular event was organized ashore or why so much difficulty ensued.
5. Presumably Acting Warrant Machinist Cooper, who at that time was the fifth-senior acting warrant machinist on board the *Oregon*.
6. Presumably, Wilson intended to use "umbra," an uninvited guest.
7. "Gazabo": an eccentric or quaint fellow; a queer fellow.
8. *Brandenberg*, a 9,784-ton German battleship completed in 1893. She mounted six eleven-inch guns.
9. A passage of 593 words of the original text relating to Wilson's unsuccessful search for the Grill Room has been omitted.
10. Halidom, something considered holy, a sanctuary. Presumably, Wilson was referring to his own intellect.
11. This discussion refers to the chief engineer.
12. Note that at this point, around 7 A.M., and after a night of considerable drinking, Wilson has already had two gin and lime, a large measure of whiskey, and at least two bottles of ale, and this before breakfast!
13. *Valet de chambre*.
14. Presumably on some earlier voyage. According to his own account, Wilson had no liberty when the *New Orleans* visited Port Said.
15. Brian Boru (Brían mac Cennéidigh) of Munster, King of Ireland, decisively defeated the Vikings at Clontarf in 1014.

16. St. Patrick (389?–461?), patron saint of Ireland.

17. It is possible this is a description of the Yu Yüan (Jade Garden), a classical Chinese garden with pools, walkways, bridges, and rockeries built in the sixteenth century by a high official of the imperial court to honor his father. It remains a popular tourist attraction in Shanghai today.

18. This probably was the Hu Xin Ting (Heart of Lake) Pavilion that Wilson had first visited on an earlier liberty.

19. Amyas Leigh was a fictional character in Charles Kingsley's *Westward Ho!* (1855). He was a Devonshire seaman of Elizabethan times who helped defend the south coast of England against the Armada. Rosemary Goring, ed., *Larousse Dictionary of Literary Characters* (Edinburgh: Larousse, 1994), 424.

20. A passage of 663 words, a dialogue between Wilson and a barmaid at the Grill Room, has been omitted here.

21. "Cratur," Irish whiskey.

22. "Dog," bottle of liquor.

23. "Stag dancing" was a not uncommon practice at the time. It involved two sailors, generally with one designated the female by a ribbon tied around one arm. The practice was common before a crew-sponsored party, when dancing practice was in order before the arrival of female guests.

24. *Solace*, a 4,700-ton hospital ship engaged in transport service between San Francisco and Manila.

CHAPTER 8: BOLO-MEN, ROUTINE, AND DISCIPLINE

1. HMS *Goliath*, a 12,950-ton displacement battleship, commissioned in 1900.

2. "Beno," according to the *Army and Navy Journal*'s Philippine correspondent, was "a very rank wine made from the cocoanut. It is nearly pure alcohol of a poor but strong quality. The effect upon an American of this stuff is to cause him to become temporarily insane. He imagines his friends are insurgents and his one desire is to fight and kill everyone he sees." "From Our Philippine Correspondent, Los Baños, Dec. 9, 1899," *Army and Navy Journal* 37 (Jan. 27, 1900): 499.

3. "Steerage," on warships: quarters generally for midshipmen and warrant officers.

4. Hell.

5. A *cadi* is a Moslem chief magistrate or justice. Presumably the fellow in question was brought before the executive officer and then sent to the brig.

6. *Yosemite* (ex–*El Sud*) was built in 1892. It was purchased by the Navy on Apr. 6, 1898, and commissioned as an auxiliary cruiser, but it was actually used as a transport. She was scuttled off Guam Nov. 13, 1900, after being damaged in a typhoon. Bauer and Roberts, *Register*, 298.

7. "Punk": a no-good, a waster, a person of no importance.

8. *Kopje*, a word of Afrikaans origin meaning "hillock."

9. When a sailor was reduced in liberty class, a prescribed percentage of his pay—as much as two-thirds—was withheld from him and not paid out until the end of his enlistment.

10. Presumably *Daibutsu*, "Great Buddha," a reference to the huge Buddha in Kamakura, Japan.

11. "Hitting hop," smoking opium.

12. "Bindle stiff," a tramp who seldom rode trains, and then only the slowest trains, but was content to walk from town to town. This name came from the roll of blankets he carried, known as a "bindle" or a "turkey."

13. Pathans are Pashto-speaking people inhabiting parts of southeastern Afghanistan and northwestern Pakistan.

14. *Subedar* and *jemadar* were ranks only used in the Sepoy regiments of the British Indian Army. *Subedar* was equivalent to lieutenant and *jemadar* to second lieutenant. Officers holding these commissions ranked below their British counterparts of the same grade. Many thanks to Dr. Peter Stanley of the Australian War Museum for this information.

15. Wilson is unfamiliar with cavalry sabers and their scabbards; when the cavalryman is mounted, as he would be in battle, the long straps put the saber in convenient position for drawing. Christiaan

Rudolf de Wet (1854–1922) succeeded Cronjé as commander in chief of Orange Free State forces (1900). He became legendary as a guerrilla leader against the British.

16. "Sot" in this context presumably means "stubborn."

17. Capt. [later Rear Admiral] Charles M. Thomas took command. Thomas was promoted to rear admiral in 1905 and commanded a squadron of battleships, the Atlantic Fleet, from Jan. 1907 to May 1908, including the first half of the "Great White Fleet" world cruise.

18. Lieutenant Commander Adams, the first lieutenant.

19. Carpenter Yates.

20. *Hobo:* an itinerant who works odd jobs as he travels, usually traveling by hitching rides on trains. *Tramp:* a hobo that does not take odd jobs and generally walks between towns. *Gaycat:* a tramp that hangs about looking for women. *Blanket stiff:* a western tramp who generally carried a blanket with him and walked, or "drilled" as they said, between Salt Lake City and San Francisco. *Prushun:* originally this term meant an older tramp who had a young boy to beg for him. This man often acted like a Prussian bully toward the youth; hence the name. By 1900, the term often applied just to the boy.

21. "Lump," a handout of food; something to eat; a donation of victuals to a bum, intended for consumption away from the house of the donor.

22. "Snipe": in this context, slang for cigarette or cigar butt.

23. Presumably Lemuel T. Cooper.

24. "Shark," railway policeman.

25. "Stew bum," an habitually drunken hobo, tramp, or beggar.

26. "Can house," a brothel or house of prostitution.

27. The reference here is probably to Acting Warrant Machinist Angus G. Bates, also then stationed on board USS *Oregon*.

28. "To take the beans for it": to go through hell for it.

29. "Dogs," bottles of alcoholic beverage.

30. "Hit the grit": to jump, voluntarily, from a moving train.

31. "Con," conductor.

32. Acting Warrant Machinist Cooper.

33. "Fetch them" in this context means, "fetch them up with a round turn," or stop them. Wilson's account seems correct. When in 1903 Captain Thomas took command of the receiving ship *Franklin*, he immediately had every sailor's bag inspected. All nonregulation items of clothing were confiscated and immediately destroyed, without regard to the property rights of the individual.

34. It actually was Captain Thomas's third command. He had commanded the cruiser *Baltimore*, Feb.–Apr. 1900; the armored cruiser *Brooklyn*, Apr. 1900–Apr. 1901; and he assumed command of *Oregon* in Apr. 1901. However, in the five years 1895–99, he spent only eight months at sea, and the five years after his command of *Oregon* were also spent ashore. His "pull" might have been that he was married to the daughter of Rear Admiral Simpson. His own daughter later married a future four-star admiral, Harry E. Yarnell. Cogar, *Admirals*, vol. 2, 281.

35. Acting Warrant Machinist Cooper, again.

36. Czar, *Oregon*'s chief engineer.

37. Eleven thousand tons displacement, completed in 1893.

38. Harp, an Irishman.

39. A "striker" is a junior enlisted man who is, essentially, an apprentice in a particular specialized job.

40. Harveyized steel—nickel steel hardened by a process developed by Augustus Harvey in the 1880s and adopted for U.S. warship armor plating.

41. "The Peak," Victoria Peak, the most prominent landmark in Hong Kong.

42. Unfortunately, Wilson left no clues to this intriguing officer's identity.

43. Fireman and coal passers wore red piping where their sleeves joined the body of their jumpers. Piping on the left side identified the wearer as a member of the port watch; right side, starboard watch. Deck seaman's watch marks were white (on blue uniforms) and dark blue (on whites). This color arrangement has since been transferred to the fireman/seaman rating stripes on modern uniforms.

44. The "Jack" here referred to is the Union Jack, the starry field of the national ensign, which until 2002 was flown at the bow of every commissioned ship of the Navy when not under way; today (as in the bicentennial year, 1976), the "Don't Tread on Me" flag is flown as a jack.

CHAPTER 9: HONG KONG

1. *Kentucky*, the second unit of the *Kearsarge*-class 11,500-ton displacement battleships, had been commissioned on May 15, 1900, and was on its first overseas deployment. These ships were highly acclaimed at the time; however, even as Wilson wrote his log, one of the officers on board *Kentucky*, Lt. William S. Sims, was writing a highly critical assessment of the ship, noting serious shortcomings in turret design, ammunition handling, and location of the armor belt, among other things. See Elting E. Morrison, *Admiral Sims and the Modern American Navy* (Boston: Houghton-Mifflin, 1942), 78–80.

2. *Oregon* and the armored cruiser *Brooklyn* had participated in the Battle of Santiago, July 3, 1898.

3. *Concord*, a gunboat, had been part of Commodore George Dewey's squadron at the battle of Manila Bay, May 1, 1898.

4. A slipper boat is a light boat with low freeboard.

5. At this point a short dialogue of eighty words between the sailors and the bird seller has been omitted.

6. These activities were still the norm for U.S. Navy ships calling at Hong Kong in the early 1960s.

7. "Big foot" girl—girl without bound feet.

8. *Buffalo* (ex-*Nitcheroy*), was a 6,114-ton auxiliary cruiser purchased from Brazil in 1898. At this point she was assigned to training service and was used as a personnel transport; Baer and Roberts, *Register*, 297. The U.S. Navy's official *List and Station, 1901* lists her displacement as 9,888 tons.

9. The material that follows is from a separate essay entitled "The King of the Orlop Deck," included with, but separate from, the original manuscript.

10. "Compass and square," the symbol of the master-at-arms rating.

11. The King was of Irish origin.

12. A fusilier is a soldier attached to one of the British army fusilier regiments, which originally carried fusils, or flintlock muskets.

13. "Provo" [provost] duty, the equivalent of "shore patrol" in the modern navy.

14. The Rock, Gibraltar.

15. Queen Victoria died on Jan. 22, 1901, ending a reign of more than sixty years. Her son Edward succeeded her and became the king emperor. These events occurred just a few weeks before *Oregon* [and Wilson] arrived in Hong Kong.

16. The reference here is to the tenement district in New York City.

17. USS *Don Juan de Austria*, an 1,130-ton gunboat, began its service life in the Spanish navy, as a light cruiser. Built in Cartagena, Spain, in 1887, she was sunk at Manila Bay in 1898 and was later raised and reconditioned at the Hong Kong and Whampoa Dock Company under a navy contract. From 1907 she served as a training ship. She was stricken from the navy list in 1919, became the merchant ship *Dewey* in 1921, and was scrapped in 1932. Bauer and Roberts, *Register*, 159.

18. "Gold brick" in this context indicates a "rube," or a gullible person from the country likely to be overcharged for goods purchased.

19. "Sloper" was a common slang term for people from the West Coast—more properly, west of the Continental Divide, the Pacific "slope."

20. The gunboat *Isla de Luzon*, formerly a small Spanish cruiser, was built in Britain in 1886 and displaced 1,030 tons. She sank at Manila Bay, May 1, 1898, and was subsequently raised and reconditioned by the Hong Kong and Whampoa Dock Company. She was used as a training vessel, 1903–1907 and stricken in 1919, after which she became a civilian salvage ship and was scrapped in 1940.

21. The gunboat *Concord*, 1,700 tons, was authorized in 1888 and commissioned in 1891. This class "represented an attempt to produce the smallest possible cruising ship with good seakeeping qualities and a heavy battery" (six six-inch/thirty-caliber guns). Bauer and Roberts, *Register*, 155.

22. These assertions are borne out in Rear Admiral McCalla's unpublished memoirs, in chapter 29, "The Aftermath of My Oriental Service, and the Return of the *Newark* to the United States, 1900–1901." McCalla Papers, NHF, LC.

23. "Getting next," becoming aware.

CHAPTER 10: AMOY, CHINA, AND YOKOHAMA

1. Wilson's concerns were warranted. Four years later, on July 21, 1905, a sister ship, USS *Bennington*, suffered a catastrophic boiler explosion in which sixty-five men died, thirty-eight were injured, and the ship sank. President Theodore Roosevelt was "inexpressibly shocked" by the disaster. NA, RG 24, file 88, case 1703 contains correspondence relevant to the disaster.

2. Wilson incorrectly rendered this name "Kulang Sue" throughout. The more commonly accepted spelling has been substituted.

3. USS *Hartford*, a 2,250-ton steam sloop originally commissioned in 1859, had served as Admiral Farragut's flagship at the Battle of Mobile Bay during the Civil War. She was completely rebuilt in 1894–99, served as a training ship until 1912, a receiving ship 1912–26, and foundered at Norfolk in 1956 after nearly a century of service. Bauer and Roberts, *Register*, 67.

4. USS *Lancaster*, a 3,290-ton steam sloop, was originally commissioned in 1859. She was completely rebuilt in 1879–80. She served as a training ship 1900–1904, receiving ship 1904–13, and then with the Public Health Service until 1930. Bauer and Roberts, *Register*, 62.

5. USS *Buffalo*, 6,114 tons, was built in 1891 as a Brazilian merchant ship and was purchased in 1898 and fitted out as an auxiliary cruiser. She was used as a training ship and transport until 1916, then a destroyer tender until 1920. Bauer and Roberts, *Register*, 297.

6. Wilson, in fact, returned to Amoy on board the battleship *Wisconsin*, Oct. 30–Nov. 5, 1908, as part of the Great White Fleet's cruise around the world. At that time, no liberty was permitted to Kulang Su, so it is unlikely he ever again saw Oganisan. Unfortunately, Wilson left no account of his experiences on this cruise. For a brief account of the fleet visit to Amoy in 1908, see James R. Reckner, *Teddy Roosevelt's Great White Fleet* (Annapolis, Md.: Naval Institute Press, 1989), 119–22.

7. "Tin can," a familiar term for a torpedo boat destroyer, later more commonly known as a destroyer. The term "tin can" remains in use to describe modern destroyers.

8. *Kakemona*, a painting (either a picture or calligraphy) in the form of a hanging scroll.

9. *Guichen*, a French protected cruiser of 8,151 tons displacement.

10. Cdr. Harrison G. O. Colby was relieved by Cdr. Harry Knox in May 1901. Knox's command would be short. He was relieved by Cdr. Gottfried Blocklinger in July 1901. All three officers ultimately attained flag rank.

11. *Joro*, prostitute.

12. It is possible that here Wilson was attempting to spell phonetically the Japanese word *jo*, as in *josan* or *ojosan*, meaning girl or woman. At any rate, it is clear he is referring to his female companion.

13. Wilson spells Tokyo in a number of ways. At the turn of the century, "Tokio" was a common spelling. Before that name was adopted, the city was known as Edo, which name also had several spellings, including Yedo and Yeddo.

14. Wilson's math is faulty here. Presumably, he left the palace earlier or the trip took less time, as a three hour trip beginning at 5:30 would have him arrive at the Yoshiwara thirty minutes after the 8 P.M. appearance of the "birds."

15. *Meiro*, to "bitch," or complain.

16. A 1907 tour guide to Japan describes the Yoshiwara of Tokyo as follows: The "world-famed Yoshiwara [is] the principal quarter inhabited by the licensed hetairae of the metropolis. Many of the houses within this district are almost palatial in appearance, and in the evening present a spectacle probably unparalleled in any other country, but [is] reproduced on a smaller scale in the provincial Japanese cities. The unfortunate inmates, decked out in gorgeous raiment, sit in rows with gold screens

behind, and protected from the outside by iron bars. As the whole quarter is under special municipal surveillance, perfect order prevails, enabling the stranger to study, while walking along the streets, the manner in which the Japanese have solved one of the vexed questions of all ages." Basil Hall Chamberlain, F.R.G.S., and W. B. Mason, *A Handbook for Travellers in Japan, including the whole Empire from Saghalien to Formosa*, 7th ed. (London: John Murray, 1907), 233.

17. *Ohane* translates to "hussy" or "tomboy." Apparently it is no longer part of the Japanese daily vernacular.

18. *Arigato*, thank you.

19. HMS *Glory*, a new, 12,950-ton battleship.

20. *Kinno*, presumably *kinnokoto*, a seven-stringed Japanese harp.

CHAPTER 11: HOMEWARD BOUND

1. *Concord* and sister ships *Yorktown* and *Bennington* were specifically designed for cruising on distant stations. For this purpose, all three were rigged as three-masted schooners. Alden, *The American Steel Navy*, 376.

2. Wilson uniformly misspelled "Arctic." The correct spelling has been inserted.

3. "Soubrette," a theatrical term for a maidservant or lady's maid as a character in a play or opera, usually one of a pert, coquettish, or intriguing character, or an actress playing such a part.

4. Eugen Sandow (1867–1925), physical culturist, born Friedrich Wilhelm Müller in Königsberg, East Prusisia. He had an awesome physique. Promoted with Florenz Siegfield's assistance, he became a symbol of strength, masculinity, and sexual potency. He toured throughout the United States for several years at the end of the nineteenth century.

5. During this period, the *Concord* had a rapid-fire series of commanding officers:

Cdr. Harrison G. O. Colby, June 1900–Apr. 1901
Cdr. Harry Knox, May–July 1901
Cdr. Gottfried Blocklinger, July–Dec. 1901
Cdr. William W. Kimball, Jan.–Feb. 1902.

All of these officers eventually achieved flag rank.

6. The battleship *Iowa*, built in Cramps, Philadelphia, was commissioned in 1897. She displaced 11,410 tons and mounted four twelve-inch guns.

7. *Wisconsin* was an *Illinois*-class battleship. She displaced 11,565 tons, mounted four thirteen-inch guns, and was commissioned in Feb. 1901. Wilson subsequently served on this ship from Apr. 1908 to Aug. 1910, and participated in the last half of the famous world cruise of the Great White Fleet on board her.

8. The *Oregon* was at this point "in ordinary," with crew strength reduced. She was not decommissioned until 1906 and recommissioned in 1911. She finally decommissioned in 1919. John C. Reilly and Robert L. Scheina, *American Battleships, 1886–1923: Predreadnought Design and Construction* (Annapolis, Md.: Naval Institute Press, 1980), 51.

9. The gunboat *Nipsic* was originally designed for general overseas cruising; however, she was badly damaged in a Mar. 16, 1889, hurricane at Apia, Samoa, and never again cruised. From 1901 to 1903 she served as a receiving ship at Bellingham, and then as a prison hulk. Bauer and Roberts, *Register*, 77.

10. *Dixie* (ex–*El Rio*), 6,114 tons, was built as a merchant ship in 1893, purchased in 1898, and rated as an auxiliary cruiser. She was used as a transport until 1909 and a destroyer tender after 1911. Her sister ships were *Yankee*, *Yosemite*, and *Buffalo*. Bauer and Roberts, *Register*, 297.

11. *Solace*, 5,700 tons, was used at this time as a transport. She later served as a hospital ship.

12. In 1804 Stephen Decatur led a group that stormed the captured frigate *Philadelphia* in Tripoli and set fire to her, causing her total destruction. It was an action that Horatio, Lord Nelson called "the most bold and daring act of the age."

13. "Bugs" was Lt. Cdr. Henry Minett, USN, who served as executive officer, or first lieutenant ("fist luff"), throughout Wilson's service on board *Concord*. He retired as a captain in 1905 and lived until the end of 1952.

14. Sources indicate that Blocklinger had in fact commanded the training ship *Alert* for a portion of July 1901 before assuming command of *Concord* later that same month. Cogar, *Dictionary of Admirals*, vol. 2, 29.

15. Presumably this is a corruption of Sakyamūni, "the sage of the Republic of Sakka," a title given to the Buddha.

16. "Hop dream": opium dream.

17. The *Rio de Janeiro* sank in the Golden Gate on Feb. 22, 1901, with the loss of at least 128 of the 210 people on board. She sank within shouting distance of the Presidio of San Francisco.

18. Buena Vista Island: Yerba Buena Island.

19. William McKinley, the twenty-fifth president of the United States, died on Sept. 14, 1901, as a result of wounds inflicted by an assassin eight days earlier. Theodore Roosevelt succeeded him.

EPILOGUE

1. Charles O'Neil diary, entry for Saturday, Sept. 7, 1901, Charles O'Neil Papers, NHF, LC. O'Neil subsequently served as a guard of honor for the presidential funeral.

2. Harold and Margaret Sprout, *The Rise of American Naval Power, 1776–1918* (Princeton, N.J.: Princeton Univ. Press, 1939), 249.

3. For details of that cruise, consult, James R. Reckner, *Teddy Roosevelt's Great White Fleet* (Annapolis, Md.: Naval Institute Press, 2001).

4. *New York Tribune*, Aug. 24, 1905, cited in William R. Braisted, *The United States Navy in the Pacific, 1897–1909* (Austin: Univ. of Texas Press, 1958), 162.

5. Interestingly, Charlie Fowler and Wilson served together on *Oregon*, Dec. 1905 to Feb. 1906, when Fowler, who was just beginning his cruise, was transferred to the monitor *Monadnock* in the routine reshuffling of crews as the *Oregon* prepared to return home.

Bibliography

ENLISTED ACCOUNTS

Beunzle, Fred J. *Bluejacket: An Autobiography.* Norton, 1939. Repr. Annapolis, Md.: Naval Institute Press, 1986. Principally Asiatic Station, 1880s.

Bolster, W. Jeffrey. *Black Jacks: African American Seamen in the Age of Sail.* Cambridge: Harvard Univ. Press, 1998.

Calhoun, C. Raymond. *Tin Can Sailor: Life Aboard the USS Sterett, 1939–1945.* Annapolis, Md.: Naval Institute Press, 2000.

Cooper, James Fenimore, ed. *Ned Myers; or, A Life Before the Mast.* Lea and Blanchard, 1843. Repr. Annapolis, Md.: Naval Institute Press, 1989. Period of War of 1812.

Kelly, Mary Pat. *Proudly We Served: The Men of the USS Mason.* Annapolis, Md.: Naval Institute Press, 1995. African Americans in World War II.

Kernin, Alvin. *Crossing the Line: A Bluejacket's World War II Odyssey.* Annapolis, Md.: Naval Institute, 1997.

Marvel, William, ed. *The Monitor Chronicles.* New York: Simon and Schuster, 2000. Civil War.

Mason, Theodore C. *Battleship Sailor.* Annapolis, Md.: Naval Institute Press, 1982. Enlisted life on board USS *California*, 1940–1941.

———. *Rendezvous with Destiny: A Sailor's War.* Annapolis, Md.: Naval Institute Press, 1997. WW II.

———. *"We Will Stand By You": Serving in the Pawnee, 1942–1945.* Annapolis, Md.: Naval Institute, 1996.

McBride, William M. *Good Night Officially: The Pacific War Letters of a Destroyer Sailor.* Boulder, Colo.: Westview, 1995. World War II in the Pacific.

McKenna, Richard. *The Left-Handed Monkey Wrench.* Annapolis, Md.: Naval Institute Press, 1986. Short stories of interwar years in Pacific and Orient.

———. *Sand Pebbles.* Annapolis, Md.: Naval Institute Press, 2000. Autobiographical fiction. Pre-WW II Asiatic Station, Yangtze River Patrols.

Newton, Adolph W. *Better than Good: A Black Sailor's War, 1943–1945.* Annapolis, Md.: Naval Institute, 1999.

Nordhoff, Charles. *Man-of-War Life: A Boy's Experience in the United States Navy During a Voyage Around the World in a Ship-of-the-Line.* Dodd, Meade, and Co., 1855. Repr. Annapolis, Md.: Naval Institute Press, 1985. Experiences in mid-1840s.

Paynter, Jon. H. *Joining the Navy, or, Abroad with Uncle Sam.* Hartford, Conn.: American, 1895. African American sailor in mid-1880s cruise to Asiatic Station.

Purdon, Eric. *Black Company: The Story of Subchaser 1264.* Annapolis, Md.: Naval Institute, 2000. African American experiences in WW II.

Ringle, Dennis J. *Life in Mr. Lincoln's Navy.* Annapolis, Md.: Naval Institute Press, 1998.

Stark, Suzanne J. *Female Tars: Women aboard Ship in the Age of Sail.* Annapolis, Md.: Naval Institute, 1996.

Swift, John R. *An Iowa Boy around the World with the Navy, 1898–1902: A True Story of Our Navy.* Des Moines, Iowa: Kenyon, 1902. From landsman to chief yeoman for C-in-C Asiatic Fleet in one year.

Tisdale, L. G. *Three Years behind the Guns.* New York: Century, 1908. Enlisted service from 1895 to 1898, including the Battle of Manila Bay.

Tomlinson, Rodney G., ed. *A Rocky Mountain Sailor in Teddy Roosevelt's Navy: The Letters of Petty Officer Charles Fowler from the Asiatic Station, 1905–1910.* Boulder, Colo.: Westview, 1998.

Warren, H. V. *Afloat with Old Glory, by a Bluejacket of the Old Navy.* New York: Abey, 1901.

GENERAL STUDIES

Alden, Cdr. John D. *The American Steel Navy: A Photographic History of the U.S. Navy from the Introduction of the Steel Hull in 1883 to the Cruise of the Great White Fleet, 1907–1909.* Annapolis, Md.: Naval Institute Press, 1972. Rev. 1989.

Baer, George W. *One Hundred Years of Sea Power: The U. S. Navy, 1890–1910.* Stanford, Calif.: Stanford Univ. Press, 1994.

Bauer, K. Jack, and Stephen S. Roberts. *Register of Ships of the U.S. Navy, 1775–1990: Major Combatants.* Westport, Conn.: Greenwood, 1991.

Braisted, William R. *The United States Navy in the Pacific, 1897–1909.* Austin: Univ. of Texas Press, 1958.

Chamberlain, Basil Hall, and W. B. Mason, *A Handbook for Travellers in Japan, including the whole Empire from Saghalien to Formosa.* 7th ed. London: John Murray, 1907.

Clark, Charles E. *My Fifty Years in the Navy.* Boston: Little, Brown and Co., 1917. Commanding officer of the battleship *Oregon* during war with Spain.

Cogar, William B. *Dictionary of Admirals of the U.S. Navy: Vol. 2, 1901–1918.* Annapolis, Md.: Naval Institute Press, 1991.

Coletta, Paolo E. *Bowman Hendry McCalla: A Fighting Sailor.* Washington, D.C.: Univ. Press of America, 1979.

Cosmos, Graham A. *An Army for Empire: The United States Army in the Spanish-American War.* Columbia: Univ. of Missouri Press, 1971.

Evans, Robley D. *An Admiral's Log: Being Continued Recollections of Naval Life.* New York: D. Appleton, 1911.

———. *A Sailor's Log: Recollections of Forty Years of Naval Service.* New York: D. Appleton, 1901.

Harrod, Frederick S. *Manning the New Navy: The Development of a Modern Naval Enlisted Force, 1899–1940.* Westport, Conn.: Greenwood, 1978.
Knox, Dudley W. *A History of the United States Navy.* New York: Putnam, 1948.
Langley, Harold D. *Social Reform in the United States Navy, 1798–1862.* Urbana: Univ. of Illinois Press, 1967.
Leech, Margaret. *In the Days of McKinley.* New York: Harper and Brothers, 1959.
Long, John D. *The New American Navy.* 2 vols. New York: Outlook, 1903. Memoirs of secretary of the navy, 1897–1902.
McLean, Ridley H. *The Bluejacket's Manual: United States Navy.* Annapolis, Md.: Naval Institute Press, 1902. Repr. 1978.
Melville, George W. "On Behalf of the Naval Engineers," *Army and Navy Journal* 36 (Sept. 24, 1898): 89.
Miller, Stuart Creighton. *"Benevolent Assimilation": The American Conquest of the Philippines, 1899–1903.* New Haven, Conn.: Yale Univ. Press, 1982.
Morison, Elting E. *Admiral Sims and the Modern American Navy.* Boston: Houghton-Mifflin, 1942.
———. (ed) *The Letters of Theodore Roosevelt.* 8 vols. Cambridge: Harvard Univ. Press, 1951–54.
Morris, James M., and Patricia M. Kearns. *Historical Dictionary of the United States Navy.* Lanham, Md.: Scarecrow, 1998.
Niblack, Albert P. *The Enlistment, Training, and Organization of Crews of Our New Ships.* Washington: Naval Historical Foundation, 1972. Reprint of 1891 Naval Institute *Proceedings* article.
O'Toole, G. J. A. *The Spanish-American War: An American Epic, 1898.* New York: Norton, 1984.
Quick, John. *Dictionary of Weapons and Military Terms.* New York: McGraw-Hill, 1973.
Reckner, James R. "'The Men Behind the Guns': The Impact of the War with Spain on the Navy Enlisted Force." *Theodore Roosevelt, the U. S. Navy, and the Spanish-American War.* Ed. Edward R. Marolda. New York: Palgrave, 2001. 95–107.
———. *Teddy Roosevelt's Great White Fleet.* Annapolis, Md.: Naval Institute Press, 1989, repr. 2001.
Reilly, John C., Jr., and Robert L. Scheina. *American Battleships, 1886–1923: Predreadnought Design and Construction.* Annapolis, Md.: Naval Institute Press, 1980.
Sawyer, Frederick L. *Sons of Gunboats.* Annapolis, Md.: Naval Institute Press, 1946.
Sprout, Harold, and Margaret Sprout. *The Rise of American Naval Power, 1776–1918.* Princeton, N.J.: Princeton Univ. Press, 1939.
Sternlich, Sanford. *McKinley's Bulldog: The Battleship* Oregon. Chicago: Nelson-Hall, 1977.
United States Navy. Bureau of Navigation. *Register of the Commissioned and Warrant Officers of the United States Navy and Marine Corps.* Washington, D.C.: Government Printing Office, 1899–1902.
———. *Laws Relating to the Navy, Marine Corps, Etc., 1898.* Washington, D.C.: Government Printing Office, 1898
———. *Regulations for the Government of the Navy of the United States.* Washington, D.C.: Government Printing Office, 1909.
Warwick, Peter, ed. *The South African War: The Anglo-Boer War, 1899–1902.* Harlow, U.K.: Longman, 1980.

Index

acting warrant machinists: and black gang, 114; and bolo-men, xxiii, 118, 130–32; and coal, 218–19; competence of, xxiii, 114, 123, 141; creation, xxiii, 115; criticism, xxiii; drunkenness, 66; in Kure, 139; relationship with crew, xxiv, 115, 118, 119, 123, 132, 175; seniority of, 373n18; Wilson and, 123, 127, 141, 161–62

Adams, Lt. Cdr. Charles A., 102, 138, 164–65, 187, 219, 259–60, 275, 368n14; abusive, 112, 119, 120–22, 138, 166–67, 273; attitudes, 142; and bag inspections, 180; as "Jack the Ripper," xxv

Adamson, Archa A., 361n18

Aden (gulf), 19, 20

Admiral Chips (warrant carpenter), 139

African Americans, xiv–xv, 17, 59

Aguinaldo, Emilio, xxx, 21, 43, 94,

air bedding, 29

Akitsushima (Japanese cruiser), 368n25

Alaska, 330

Albany (protected cruiser), 361–62n1

alcohol: at sea, 88, 250–51; availability of, 23, 107, 220; shellac cocktail, 23; and Wilson, 88, 109

American businessmen (Philippines), 92

American (Manila newspaper), 85

American petty officers, 129

Amoy, China, 308

apprentices, 34

Arcadia bar-hotel (Shanghai), 209

Askold (Russian cruiser), 357

bad conduct discharge, 107

bag inspection, 11, 180

Baltimore (cruiser), 68

Barfleur, HMS, 270

barmaids, xiv, xix, xx, 23, 72–73, 75–76, 247, 288

bars: in Hong Kong, 283, 288; in Kulang Su, 309–10; in Kure, 143; in Manila, 90; in Nagasaki, xix, 68, 73, 76; in Seattle, 334; in Shanghai, 209, 226, 283; in Yokohama, 315

Bates, Angus G., 262–65, 376

battalion drills, 102

Bay of Waterfalls, 340

beach combers, 252; in Hong Kong, 285–86

beer ration, 22

Bennington (gunboat), 79, 83, 296, 366n25, 378n1

Berentson, Oscar, 59–60

black gang, iv, 9–10, 114, 161

Black Mary's Restaurant (Shanghai), xx, 195–96, 254, 357

Blocklinger, Cdr. Gottfried, 344, 345, 378n10, 380n14

boat racing, 220

Boer War, 62, 93, 120

bolo-men, xxiii, 118, 130–32
Boru, Brian (king of Ireland), 235, 374n15
bound feet, 214, 245
Boxer Rebellion, 106, 130
boxing, 221
Brandenberg (German battleship), 228, 250, 374n8
Bremerton, Wash., 337
British: accent, 94; arrogance of, 212; soldiers as panhandlers, 288
British Indian Army, 375n14
Brooklyn (armored cruiser), 20, 31–33, 48, 84–85, 206, 276, 364n1
Bryan, William Jennings, 56, 365n14
bubonic plague. *See* Amoy, China
Buenzle, F. J, xxv, 361n14
Buffalo (training ship), 342, 377n5
bumboat girl, 92, 277
bumboatmen, 26–27, 30–31, 92, 113, 128, 180–81, 276–77, 312–13, 363n29
Bund, the (Shanghai roadway), 191, 208

canned willie, xvii–xviii, 17, 134–47
captain's mast, 86–87
Castilla (wooden cruiser), 55, 365n9
Centennial House and Happy Home Saloon (Nagasaki), 68
Centurion, HMS (battleship), 32, 364n47
Cervera, Adm. Pascual, xv
chaplains, xxvii
Charleston (protected cruiser), 69, 107, 366n10, 369n28
Chauncey (torpedo boat destroyer), xii, 356–57
Chicago (cruiser), 3
chief engineers, 101, 117, 138, 160, 176, 224
China: division of, 99; and imperialism, 178
Chinese, 311; girls, 199, 245; life in Hong Kong, 289; navy uniforms, 109–10; as pirates, 114. *See also* bound feet
City of Peking (ship at Woosung), 169
cleaning station assignments, 133, 161
climate: impact on sailors, 82, 85
clothing issue, 170
coal, 20, 24, 38, 206, 217–18, 219

coal passers, vii, xxii, 16
coaling, 6–7, 12–13, 19, 36
cockroaches, 85, 307
Coghlan, Radm. J. B., xxviii, 361n22
Colby, Cdr. Harrison G. O., 378n10, 379n5
collier crew, 221–22
Columbia (protected cruiser), 365n3
Columbia Bar (Nagasaki), 73
Concord (gunboat), 276, 298, 333, 377n3; to Alaska, xxi; in Amoy, 310; boilers, 308; cleaning bilges, 312; discipline, 298; in Drake's bay, 352; in Dutch Harbor, 333; in Hong Kong, 307–8; living space, 298–99, 307; in Port Angeles, 333; in Port Townsend, 333; red ants (cockroaches), 307; reported lost, 111; in San Francisco, 351, 353; in Seattle, 333; under sail, 328, 379n1; Wilson ordered to, 296; in Yokohama, 312, 328
Cooper, Lemuel T., 262–65, 376
Corunna (Army transport), 164
Cosmopolitan Hotel (Kulang Su), 309–10
court-martials, 10–11, 22, 41
CPOS, 97–98, 109, 216
crew quarters, 30, 41, 43, 65, 83, 84
crickets, 201
Cristobal Colón (Spanish cruiser), 126, 151
Cronjé, Gen. P.A., 93
Crowninshield, Radm. A. S., 366n6
Culgoa (stores ship), 82, 367n32
curios, 181
currency, 164

De Wet, Christian (Boer general), 256
desertion: causes of, 342; impact on recruiting, xxix; officer attitude toward, xxviii
Dewey, the (Nagasaki bar), 73
discipline: frequency, xxviii; impact on reenlistment, xxviii; for minor infractions, 130; statistics for, xxviii
Dixie (auxiliary cruiser), 82, 342, 367n29, 379n10
dog-watch, 363n28
Don Juan de Austria (gunboat), 296, 377n17
Drake's Bay. *See Concord*

Dreadnought, HMS, xii
drills: battalion, 41–42; infantry, 24, 29, 33
drunkenness, 14, 22, 346–48; public perception of sailors and, 39; Wilson on, 92, 229
dry docks (U.S. Navy), 128
duff, 363n26
Duffy, Hugh J., 64
Dutch Harbor, 328–29, 338

eaganized beef, 362n14
Endymion, HMS, 106
engine room, 41
engineer officers, xxii–xxiii, 39
engineering: competition, 165–66, 270–75; vs. deck work, 275; watches, 10, 45, 65
enlisted men: changes in, 178–80; education of, xxiv; in Kure, 143; qualities of, 23; quality of, xxiv, 29; relations with officers, xxv
enlistment experience, 170–72
entertainment, 25; boxing, 221–22; minstrel, 220, 221, 249; music, 35; obstacle races, 220; pie-eating contests, 220; sack races, 220; stag dancing, 249; Thanksgiving, 220; tug-of-war, 220
Evans, Radm. Robley D., vii; 360n2

Farenholt, A., xxi, 361n10
Father Damien (Joseph Damien de Veuster), 99, 368n11
field day, 11, 21, 39
fighting, 13, 18–19, 46, 78
Filipinas, 51, 91
Filipino (civilian ferry), 49
Filipinos: boat dwellers, 49; insurgents, 52
Flags of All Nations (Nagasaki), 76
fleet review (New York), 359
foreigners: deck petty officers, 60; in navy, 370n11
Fowler, Charles, 360n3, 380n5
fragging, xxxi, 179
Franklin (receiving ship), 370n26
Fujiyama, 312, 321
fusiliers, 283–87

Gay, Edward (artist), 154, 371n51
general muster, 8
Glacier, 55, 83, 365n8
Glasgow House (Yokohama), 315
Globe (Hong Kong), 283, 288
Glory, HMS (battleship), 327, 379n19
Goliath, HMS (battleship), 250, 375n1
government straight, 362n12
Great White Fleet, 354
Grill, the (Hong Kong), 283
Grill Room (Shanghai), 226, 230, 357
Grosovoi (Russian torpedo boat), 357
Guichen (French protected cruiser), 314, 378n9
Gurkhas, 188–89

haggling, 91, 180
Hai Chi (Chinese cruiser), 368n20
half-caste boy (Shanghai), 193–94
Hall, Lt. Cdr. Martin E., 64, 365n1
hammocks, 8, 18, 44, 103
Hammond, Charles (warrant machinist), 161–62
Hana House (Yokohama brothel), 316
Hartford (training ship), 378n3
Hartley, Deane C., 361n19
Helena, 55, 296
Helms, Chaplain W. T., xxvi, 364n45
Hermione, HMS (protected cruiser), 32, 364n48
Hines, Lt. Harold K., 66–67, 365n5
Hobson, Richmond P., 48, 139–40
home, ship as, 362n3
homesickness, 82
Hong Kong (harbor), 276–78
How ki Island, 133
Hu Xin Ting Pavilion, 375n18

ice machines, 44, 168
Idzumo-machi (red light district), 302
imperialism, xi-xii; and China, 178, 181; by England (Transvaal), 178
Independence (receiving ship), xxi
inspections, 34, 39, 41, 179, 185; admiral's, 205
insurgency (Cavite), 58–59

Index

Iowa (battleship), 333, 337, 379n6
Iris (supply ship), 114, 369n32
Irishmen, 182–84
Isla de Luzon (U.S. gunboat), 296, 377n20
Italia (Nagasaki bar), 73

Jack the Ripper. *See* Adams, Lt. Cdr. Charles A.
Jaguar (German gunboat), 366n23
Japan: furnishings in, 314–15; Japanese cruisers, 128, 369; Japanese divers, 137; Japanese navy, 128, 129; ports, 129; taxation in, 164; and Western ways, 74, 238
Japanese women, 65, 76, 78, 300, 310, 315–16; coal ship, 78; Japanese Mary (Nagasaki barmaid), xiv, 72–73, 78; Moriya (Nagasaki), 69–71, 73, 75, 77, 81; Ohana (Nagasaki), 65, 78–79; saloon, xix, xx, 72, 78
Jewell, Capt. Theodore F., 363n41

Kamakura, 318
Kentucky (battleship), 276, 296, 300, 377n1
Kenzo (washerman), 163–64, 301, 312, 316; Wilson and, 76, 80–81
Key, Lt. Cdr. Albert, xxii
Kimball, Cdr. William W., 379n5
Kiska Bay (Arctic), 339–40
Knox, Cdr. Harry, 378n10, 379n5
Krag-Jörgensen rifle, 374n11 (chap. 6)
Kulang Su (China), 308–9
Kure (Japan), 128

Lambroso, Cesare, 197, 374n4 (chap. 6)
Lancaster (training ship), 378n4
Land We Live In, The (Hong Kong), 288
landsmen, 82
Lawton, Maj. Gen. H. W., xxxi
League Island Navy Yard, 362n17
Li Hung Chang (Chinese general), 169, 372n6
Libby, Laura Jean (author), 147, 371n36
liberty: call, 143; classing, xviii, 140, 186, 362n5; in Cavite, 49; in Colombo, xix, 28; drunkenness during, 23, 145, 178, 226, 334; end of, 91, 204; in Hong Kong, xix, 129; infrequency or lack of, xviii–xix, 21, 23, 28, 55, 60, 82–85, 88–92, 129, 133, 205, 229; in Kulang Su, 308; in Kure, 159–60; in Manila, xxvii, 49, 85, 88–92; murder during, 50; in Nagasaki, 70; one hour liberty, 346–47; in Seattle, 334–37; in Shanghai, 186–88; 195, 204–6, 226, 255–56; in Singapore, 32; Wilson and, xix, 86, 133, 142, 145, 159, 164, 206, 226; in Woosung, xix, 185; in Yokohama, 314–19
libertymen, special first class, xviii
Light House, the (Yokohama), 315
line officer, vs. engineers, xxiii
line vs. staff controversy, 9
liquor, illicit, 12–13
Logan (Army transport), 93
Long, John D. (secretary of the navy), 371–72n59
Longnecker, Capt. Edwin, 366n28
lucky bag, 11
Luetgert, A. L., ix, 137, 370n22

Mahan, Dennis H., 363n41
Maine, 365n10
Maintop Saloon (Nagasaki), xix, 73, 78
Malacca Straits, 27
Manila, 22, 47–49, 50–54, 81, 90, 92
Manila Freedom (newspaper), 85, 93
March, Maj. Peyton C., 94
Marietta (gunboat), 49, 55, 363n36
Marimoudo's House (Kure), 151
Marryat, Frederick, 362n10
mastodon bones, 340
McCalla, Capt. B. H., 106, 300
McDougal, Cdr. David, 126, 369
McGurk's Saloon (Bowery), xix, 2, 23
McKinley, William, xii, 353–54
meals (Kure), 155–57, 196
Melville, Radm George, xxii, 361n8
Merrimac (collier), 364n2
mess: assessment of, 341; breakfast, 18, 45; commuted rations, 42; cooks, xvii, 42, 114; general system, xvi; in Hong Kong, 277; in Kure, 133; lunch, 46; on *New*

Orleans, 3; officers and, 168; on *Oregon*, xvii; quality of food, 30, 44, 124; scarcity of food, 17; supper, 46; Thanksgiving dinner, 26; Wilson and, 66, 114, 123; at Woosung, 177
Metropolitan Museum of Art, 154
Mexican dollars, 56
midshipmen, 177
Miller, Cdr. William G., 360n4, 361n13
Minett, Lt. Cdr. Henry, 342–43, 380n13
Minneapolis (protected cruiser), xi, xv, xvi, 42, 123, 180, 362n13
Minnesota, 359
missionaries, 99, 191–92
Monadnock (monitor), 96, 296, 357, 367n5
monkeys, 36
Monterey (monitor), 55, 296, 365n12
Mrs. Dale's Restaurant (Shanghai), 200, 204
Mustang officers, 168

Nagasaki, 68, 164, 301–3, 312
Nanchang (salvage ship), 105, 107, 119, 120, 123, 126, 129, 132
Nashville (gunboat), 48, 55, 114, 119, 123, 126, 129, 132, 191, 363n35; in Kure, 129; at Port Said, 14; in Shanghai, 176
Navy Personnel Act, 1899, xxii, 9, 115, 177
Navy regulations, 34
New Orleans (protected cruiser), xi, xii, 1, 4, 84, 296, 301, 340, 361–62n1; accommodations aboard, 5, 7, 9, 18; and the Azores, 5; in Bab El Mandeb, 18; and British army, 20; census aboard, 95; engine repaired, 91; in Gulf of Aden, 19; instability, 57–58; in Manila, xxvii; minstrel troupe, 85–86; in Nagasaki, 64, 67; passes Corregidor, 47; in Philippines, 2; in Port Said, 12, 15; speed of, 93; and Straits of Gibraltar, 8; and Suez Canal, 15; ventilation on, 84; in Woosung, 175, 181
new sailors, 331–32, 348–49
Newark (protected cruiser), 48, 55, 296, 300, 364n1
Niblack, Lt. A. P., xxx, 361n27

Nipsic (gunboat), 338, 379n9
Nomi (Tokyo rickshawman), 321, 326–27
North American Commercial Co., 329, 330

officers: and alcohol, 23; education, xxxii, 176; failed leadership of, xxvi; and gambling, 184; lack of manners, 300; mustang, 168; points of view, 40; relationships with crew, xxix, 29, 342; transfer of, 84
oiler, 160
Ojisan (saloon keeper Hully-gee), 68–69, 72–73, 75–76, 81
O'Neil, Radm. Charles, 354
opium smoking, 198, 238, 256–58
Oregon (battleship), xii, 55, 100–101, 109, 117, 126, 163, 177, 206, 300, 337–38, 340, 357, 365n12, 367n1; and crew, 175, 185; damages to, 113, 117, 140, 159–60; grounding of, 103, 104, 105–7, 109–10, 111–12, 124, 133, 372n2; gunnery practice, 167–68; homeward bound, 296; at How-ki Island, 103; to Japan, 117, 119; in Kure, 128, 138, 163; liberty, 99, 129, 140; and minstrels, 215–16, 221; in Nagasaki, 163–65; reported sinking of, 133; in Taku, 99; in Woosung, 167–68, 174–75, 270
Oregon House (Kure bar), 143, 150–51
Orlop Deck Debating Society, 182
Orlop Deck, King of, 220, 221, 278–83

Paardeberg, battle at, 367n40
panhandlers, 255
Pasig River, 49
pay allotments, 21; and gambling, 56
paymaster, 96, 97, 185, 205–6
Petrel (gunboat), 96, 163, 367n31
Philadelphia (frigate), 379n12
Pinnacle Rock, 103, 368
Port Orchard, Wash., 337
Port Said, 11, 12, 16–17
Portsmouth Arms (Nagasaki bar), 76
Prairie (training ship) xvi, 1, 164, 362n2
Prince of Wales (Nagasaki bar), 76
Princeton (gunboat), 191

prisoners, 166
Puget Sound Navy Yard, xii
Punta Delgado (Azores), 362n18

Queen's Road (Hong Kong), 283

rank, 67
rations, xviii, 46, 84, 96, 113, 124, 185, 334, 341, 342, 350
recruits, xvi–xviii, 24, 84, 130
reenlistment, 33
Reina Christina (cruiser), 55, 365n9
restaurants, xx, 287
rickshaw men, 38, 189–90, 192–93, 195, 197, 203–4, 206–9, 215; in Shanghai, 226; trouble with, 258–59; Wilson and, 68; in Yokohama, 314–15
Rio de Janeiro (ship), 353, 380n17
Roanoke, ss, 338
Roosevelt, Theodore, xii, xxx, 354, 358
Ross, Albert, 170, 372
routine: boredom, 55, 84, 87, 205, 226, 261; daily, 10
Rozhdestvenskiy, Vadm. Zinovy, 357
Russell, William Clark, 362n9
Russian wrecking tug, 115

sailors, xiv, 178–80
salt horse, 334, 363n39
salvage crew, 105
Sampson, Radm. W. T., xi
San Miguel Saloon (Manila), 51, 90
Santiago, battle at, xi, 48
Schley, Radm. W. S., xi
sea bag, 21
seamen, xxiii, 10, 21, 92
Seattle, Wash., 333
Seymour, Vadm. Sir Edward H., 106
Shanghai, 177, 191–92, 193, 205–7, 209, 212, 241, 255–56; German army camp at, 242–43; Hu Xin Ting Pavilion, 201; Mrs. Dale's Restaurant, 200, 204; police station, 202–3; tea houses, 197; Whangpoo riverfront, 207–8
sheeneys, 373n27
Shikishima (Japanese battleship), 369n8

Shimonoseki, Straights of, 126
Ship Street (Hong Kong), xx, 294–96, 300–302
ship's writers, 373n30
shirkers, 107, 108, 120–21
short-timers, 84, 252, 278, 341, 352
sick bay, 25, 26, 29–30
Sikhs, 188
Singapore Harbor, 30–32, 37
sleep, 84–85, 114
small stores, 133
smoke-stack drunk, 24
snake charmers, 27
Solace (transport), 249, 252, 342, 379n11
souvenirs, 91
Spanish paroled soldiers, 53
square heads, 9, 34
St. Louis (cruiser), xiii, 357
St. Patrick, 235, 375
Stag, the (Hong Kong bar), 283
Star House (Kure), 143
Star Theater (Seattle), 334
Steele, Rush "Dopey," 139, 370n25
Stirling, Radm. Yates, 357
stops, 363n27
Subic Bay, 368n8
swimming (Kure), 148–50, 153

Taaleño (government ferry), 49
tattooers, 27; Chyo (Yokohama), 196; in Hong Kong, 284–85; Horishaw (Shanghai), 196–97, 204, 206; Inouye (Kobe), 151; Ohashi (Shanghai), 227
tattoos, xxi, 27, 247, 360n5; as art, 24, 227–28; associations with, 27; in Kure, 151–52; and the navy, xxi; popularity of, 27; prejudice against, 196–97; Wilson and, xxi, 197, 228; on women, 228
Taylor, H. C., xi, xxviii–xxix, 361n24
technology, 178
temperatures, 363n38
theft, 115–16
Thomas, Capt. Charles M., 259, 266–69, 376n17
Tientsin (China), 106
Togo, Adm. Heihichiro, 357

Index

Tokyo (Tokio; Yeddo), 319–27
Tom Pow Ching, 190–91, 193–94, 219, 224, 247, 253–54, 357
Tom, C. H. (Shanghai tailor), 208
Tom, C. H. (Young Tom), 209–15
torpedo boat destroyers, 356
Townsend, Nellie E., xiv
Transvaal, 178
Tungsha (light-ship), 175

U.S. Army: 35th Infantry, 94; 45th Infantry, 94
U.S. Navy Club (Nagasaki), 73
Unalaska, 329
uniforms, xvii–xviii, 21, 184–86

Vancouver House (Yokohama), 315
Vermont (receiving ship), xv–xvi

warrant officers, 43, 175, 185
watch marks, 376n43
water: shortage of fresh, 65–66
wheelbarrow transport, 208
white mice (informers), 261
Wilson, Anna R., 360n1
Wilson, Frederick T.: as 2d class libertyman, 28; as 3d class libertyman, 13; as 4th class libertyman, 2; and alcohol, 14, 92, 109, 195, 226, 229, 248; anti-imperialist sentiment, xxx–xxxii, 93, 99, 111, 169, 181, 212; attitudes and observations, xiv, xxi, xxvii, xxix, xxxi, 39, 58–59, 124, 129, 204, 224, 260, 270, 298, 311, 315, 329–30, 341; buys food, 31–32, 44; and the Caribbean, xii, 356; and Chinese culture, xiv, 100, 111, 198, 199–200, 202, 243–44; and Chinese women, 204; death of, xii, 359; discharge, 354; and discipline, xxii, xxvii, 107, 269; early life, xiii, xiv; enlistment, xi, xv, 85, 170, 355; fight with French sailor, 319; and a half-caste boy, 194; and home, 12, 124; and Hong Kong, 96, 284, 290–92; illness and injuries, xi, xvi, 25, 28, 30;
and Japan, xii, xiii, xiv, xx, 311; and Japanese women, 76, 145, 260–61, 284, 315; liberty, 32, 86, 143, 204–5; on the log, vii, xii, 261, 229; marriages, xiv, 360n1; meets friends overseas, 51–52, 54–55; and missionaries, 99, 100, 169–70, 192; and Nagasaki, 70, 74, 301–3, 316; and navy life, xx, xxi–xxii, 6, 17–18, 29, 39, 44, 99, 101–2, 124, 160, 167, 174, 299, 331–32, 350; and officers, xxv–xxvii, 25–26, 28–29, 67, 119, 132, 160–62, 167, 223; and opium, 198, 256–58; and *Oregon*, 337–38; personal qualities, xiii, 44, 359; in Port Said, 13–14; service, xii, xiv–xv, 172, 296, 341, 356–57, 358–59; and Shanghai, 177, 195, 200–203, 204, 206, 232–40; sights Trafalgar Bay, 8; and tattoos, xxi, 204, 228, 284; and tea houses, 197; transfers, xx, 1, 25, 95, 99, 172, 297, 356, 358; tries water pipe, 198; views Emperor's palace, 323–24; visits German army base, 242–43; visits Tokyo, 319–27
Wilson, Mary, 360n1
Wilson, May, 360n1
Wilson, Nellie E., 360n1
Wisconsin (battleship), xii, 337, 357, 379n7
Wood, Clarence E., 117–18
Woosung, 168, 176–77, 188
Wyoming, 126, 369n1

Yasu (Yokohama rickshawman), 314–15
Yates, John P., 139–40
Yokohama Hotel (Kure), 143, 150–51
Yokohama House (Yokohama), 315
Yorktown (gunboat), 296, 368n19
Yosemite (auxiliary cruiser), 252, 375n6
Yoshiwara (prostitutes), 144, 145, 157–58, 315–16, 324–25, 370n31, 378–79n16
Yu Yüan (Jade Garden), Shanghai, 234–36, 375n17

Zafiro (supply ship), 96–98, 186, 296, 367n4